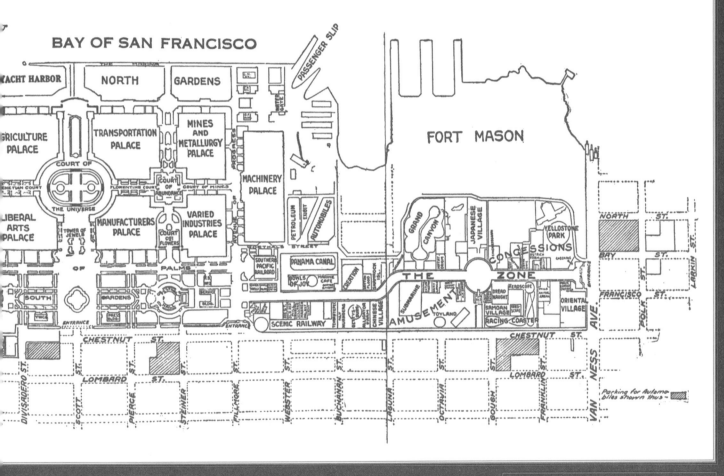

A plan of the Panama-Pacific International Exposition from the Official Guide. (Laura Ackley)

SAN FRANCISCO'S
JEWEL CITY

TO MY FAVORITE SAILOR AND BELOVED STAR TO STEER BY,
SANDER C. TEMME

SAN FRANCISCO'S

JEWEL CITY

THE PANAMA-PACIFIC
INTERNATIONAL EXPOSITION
OF 1915

LAURA A. ACKLEY

HEYDAY, BERKELEY, CALIFORNIA

CALIFORNIA HISTORICAL SOCIETY,
SAN FRANCISCO, CALIFORNIA

Library of Congress Cataloging-in-Publication Data

Ackley, Laura A.
San Francisco's Jewel City : the Panama Pacific International Exposition of 1915 / Laura A. Ackley.
    pages cm
Includes bibliographical references and index.
ISBN 978-1-59714-292-2 (hardcover : alk. paper)
1. Panama-Pacific International Exposition (1915 : San Francisco, Calif.) I. Title.
  TC781.B1A29 2014
  907.4'79461--dc23
                            2014031314

Cover Photo: The Tower of Jewels and palaces of the Panama-Pacific International Exposition are
    illuminated by the rays of the Great Scintillator. (Branson DeCou Digital Archive, University of
    California, Santa Cruz, Special Collections)
Back Cover Photo: The north façade of the Exposition viewed from the fighting top of the
    battleship Oregon. (The Bancroft Library, University of California, Berkeley)
Cover and Interior Design/Typesetting: Ashley Ingram
Floral Border: www.freevectors.net

    Orders, inquiries, and correspondence should be addressed to:
        Heyday
        P.O. Box 9145, Berkeley, CA 94709
        (510) 549-3564, Fax (510) 549-1889
        www.heydaybooks.com

    Printed in California

    10 9 8 7 6 5 4 3 2 1

Major support for the 2015 Centennial Celebration of the Panama Pacific International
Exposition, of which this glorious book is a part, was provided by AT&T.

CONTENTS

ACKNOWLEDGMENTS

Although I did not realize it at the time, in a sense this book began a little more than a quarter of a century ago at the University of California at Berkeley. "Environmental Design 169B: History of the US Cultural Environment, 1900–1980," taught by Professor Paul Groth, was a perennial favorite among students, and I was among the many enthralled by his lectures on the myriad factors shaping the built environment.

At the time, I believed that, as a California native, I was reasonably knowledgeable of the significant events that had influenced my region. Then a series of astonishing images shone on the screen of the lecture hall. They depicted a continuous line of building façades formed into angels and elephants, ships and soldiers; medieval castles packed cheek by jowl with pagodas, mosques, and Aztec temples. And, of course, there was the beautiful Palace of Fine Arts. Amazingly, all these had existed in 1915 within sight of my university at a world's fair about which I had never known. Instantly, I was captivated by the Panama-Pacific International Exposition.

Years later Professor Groth was kind enough to serve on my degree committee when I wrote my master's thesis on the Fair's spectacular illuminations. And so it is with Paul Groth that I begin this list of thanks.

Despite my best intentions, I inevitably will omit some of those who have assisted me in researching and preparing this book, but here is my sincere effort:

At the Bancroft Library: I discovered that one of the most superb archives in the world was also one of the most accessible. The Bancroft's friendly and encouraging staff of top-notch professionals includes David Kessler, Crystal Miles, Susan Snyder, Baiba Strads, David de Lorenzo, Jack von Euw, James Eason, Peter E. Hanff, and Theresa Salazar.

At Heyday: Malcolm Margolin, founder and publisher, is a personification of the true gold of California. His incisive comments regarding the Exposition inspired me to think about the event in new ways. It has been a special pleasure working with editor Gayle Wattawa, who strikes a perfect balance of editorial skill, larger vision, and the unique ability to calm an author's nerves. Heyday's talented staff, including designer Ashley Ingram, art director Diane Lee, copyeditor Lisa K. Marietta, marketing director Mariko Conner, education and outreach director Lillian Fleer, development director Marilee Enge, and publicist Mary Bisbee-Beek, along with many others, have worked uncountable hours to assure the best possible book is before you.

Archivists and librarians: These professionals are a rare breed, sharing the very treasures they guard. The time I've spent in archives and libraries has been one of the most enjoyable parts of the process. Although I do not know all their names, I wish to thank all the reference desk personnel at all of the following institutions for their patience and assistance. At each location, one or more individuals went above and beyond to provide special help.

California Historical Society: Eileen Keremitsis, Alison Moore, and Executive Director Anthea Hartig and her staff supplied primary source materials collected from some of the leaders of the Fair.

Marin County Free Library: Laurie Thompson, head librarian at the Anne T. Kent California Room, and Carol Acquaviva, digital archivist, furnished stunning, rare images and been staunch champions of this project.

Henry Madden Library, California State University, Fresno: Jean Coffey, Adam Wallace, and Tammy Lau facilitated my examination of rare souvenirs, informative documents, and beautiful prints from large glass negatives found in the Donald G. Larson Collection on International Expositions and Fairs, held in the Special Collections Research Center.

San Francisco Main Library: City archivist Susan Goldstein, photo curator Christina Moretta, and the staff on the sixth floor of the library guided me through the Daniel E. Koshland San Francisco History Center, a cache of wonderful material.

California State Library, Sacramento: To use another appropriate gold rush metaphor, the California History Room revealed a vein of contemporary PPIE material. Mike Dolgushkin went out of his way to help me uncover hidden riches, and his colleagues also were cordial and informative.

Environmental Design Archives, University of California, Berkeley: Waverly B. Lowell and Miranda Hambro aided my exploration of the Bernard Maybeck Collection.

San Diego History Center: Jane Kenealy and the History Center staff contributed invaluable background on the San Diego Panama-California Exposition.

Fine Arts Museums of San Francisco: Curators Emma Acker and James Ganz shared astute insights into the immense 1915 Fine Arts exhibit.

Finding information about the most interesting people involved with the Fair was often challenging, but many kind individuals gave of their time and resources:

Diana Serra Cary (a.k.a. "Baby Peggy"), Virginia Ryan Durrant, and Catherine Hurtado Wood gave interviews about their personal connections to the Fair.

Carolyn and Norman Bailey were especially kind in granting access to material regarding Carolyn's grandfather, Walter D'Arcy Ryan.

Patricia Keats of the California Society of Pioneers and the staff of the Schenectady Museum assisted my research into the illumination of the Exposition.

The personnel of Chesterwood, the studio museum of sculptor Daniel Chester French, were very helpful in uncovering the sculptor's role at the Fair. I am grateful to Donna Hassler, Dana Pilson, and Anne Cathcart there. Wayne Hammond, assistant librarian at the Chapin Library at Williams College, Massachusetts, also helped me with research on French. Verification of Jack and Charmian London's visits to the PPIE was discovered by Natalie Russell, Assistant Curator of Literary Manuscripts at the Huntington Library in San Marino, California. Laura Sorvetti delved into the Julia Morgan Collection in the Special Collections and University Archives at Cal Poly San Luis Obispo on my behalf.

The life's work of architect Louis Christian Mullgart was illuminated by Nancy Clark, wife of the late Robert Judson Clark, who graciously opened her home and her husband's collection, and by Edward R. Bosley, the James N. Gamble Director of the Gamble House.

Other experts have been unfailingly responsive and willing to share their knowledge. These generous individuals and their areas of expertise include Nelson Barden (Edwin Lemare), Sue Boardman (Gettysburg), Gray Brechin (Bay Area), Michael Dobkins (Seal Beach), Lynn Downey (Levi Strauss & Co.), David P. Eyler (marimbas), Stephen Haller (Crissy Field), Woody LaBounty (earthquake shacks), Pascal Lecocq (Arnold Böcklin), Efraín Figueroa Lemus (marimbas), Richard Longstreth (Willis Polk), Michael Meloy (Asian Americans in California), Michael Pisani (Native American music), George Harwood Phillips (Native Americans), James Tranquada (ukuleles and Hawaiian music), and Dion West (Maori).

Stacey Laumann and Steve Moran-Cassese charitably printed a large-format map of the Joy Zone for me, and Robert G. Pimm provided solid legal advice.

Friends have offered support, followed up leads, lent equipment, and occasionally read troublesome text. These benevolent people include, but are by no means limited to, Linda Danner; Miguel Farias; Jesica, Henry, and Emma Garrou; Barry Goldblatt; Gary and Aileen Kelly; Lisa Sardegna; Hella Sziklai; Chris Williams; and my Cal alumni community. The late Aaron Joseph Katzman (BA Architecture, UC Berkeley, 1989) continues to inspire me with the desire to do my best work in hope of achieving the same incredible quality that characterized his projects.

Writing this book generated the happy side effect that I've had the pleasure of interacting with many of the finest intellects and nicest members of the Bay Area history and collector communities, including Merry Alberigi, Tim Amyx, Kathryn Ayres, Lew Baer, Jan Berckefeldt, John Bosko, Bob Bowen, Teri Brunner, Urso Chappell, Jeff Craemer, Robert J. Chandler, Meli Cook, Bob Elvin, William French, Jr., René de Guzman, Arlene Halligan, Kit Haskell, Ed Herny, Jim Horner, Carol Jensen, Bill Kostura, Donald G. Larson, Robert Lawhon, Dewey Livingston, John Martini, Marcie Miller, Barbro and Mike Moran, Robert Paine, Therese Poletti, Thomas Rogers, Ron Ross, Fred Runner, Judy and Bob Van Austen, Roger Weed, Gary Widman, and Bruce Williamson.

Chuck Banneck, Glenn Koch, Donna Ewald Huggins, Scott Seligman, Edward A. Rogers, Mary Mitchell, Lynn Wilkinson, Tim Vos, Jim Caddick, John Freeman, Dr. William Lipsky, Paul Robertson, Richard Torney, Zoë Heimdal, and Jay Stevens have been astoundingly munificent in sharing artifacts and images from their personal collections.

Donna Ewald Huggins and Chuck Huggins warmed my heart by becoming the first donors to this tome. Donna, whom many regard as the reigning queen of the PPIE, has been a special advocate of this project, which has meant the world to me.

My loving extended family, who has indulged and encouraged my fascination with the Fair, includes the Beards, Boomers, Fulmers, Hayeks, Petersens, and Tavsses.

Jonathan, Casey, Madeleine, and Charlotte (Chip) Ackley; Mark, Janet, Katie, and Sarah Petersen; Nico and Gré Temme; Szilvia Sziklai; Jeroen, Ambrus, Fabian, and Nimrod Temme; and Murphy Danlowe Ackley all lent willing ears and moral support.

I was blessed with two other gifted editors, Nancy and Michael Ackley, who coincidentally happen to be my parents. It is a literal and literary truth that without their countless hours of painstaking and loving work, this book would not have come to fruition. Beyond these labors, any writing skill I possess can be traced to their nature and nurture.

My husband, Sander C. Temme, entered the fray in 1999 and has since provided everything I have needed, including roadie service, proofreading, airline miles, IT support, and other items critical to my survival—especially himself.

INTRODUCTION

One afternoon in mid-July of 1915, several thousand people standing on San Francisco's blustery Marina Green collectively craned their necks to watch aviator Art Smith pilot his hand-built craft through a series of aerobatic stunts overhead. For many, this was the first time they'd ever seen an airplane fly. Some held their breath as Smith's machine rolled and looped above the stately complex of ivory palaces accented with luminous colors and cut-glass jewels that stood at the verge of the sparkling silver-blue bay: the Panama-Pacific International Exposition (PPIE).

In the crowd, a child might be standing shoulder to shoulder with an actual gold rush forty-niner, a Civil War veteran, or a survivor of the Donner Party. And that same child would be transfixed by the images on her home television set sixty-four years later as she watched a man walk on the moon. The span of history witnessed by visitors to the 1915 Exposition reveals an era of astounding change. An examination of this event—perhaps the last in the original era of great world's fairs—offers a kaleidoscope of culture and progress. The Exposition's highs and lows echo into the twenty-first century.

The story of the PPIE, officially nicknamed the "Jewel City," began more than two decades before it opened, and surprisingly gained momentum following the Great Earthquake and Fire of 1906. San Francisco leaders' first thought, as they surveyed the nearly four square miles of shattered masonry and charred wood left by the disaster, was to rebuild. Their second thought was to throw a giant celebration and invite the world to come. Perhaps a judicious course would have been to delay or cancel the world's fair the city had contemplated since 1891, but San Francisco—steep, brash, wayward San Francisco—was never known for its prudence.

In name, the celebration would commemorate the United States' completion of the Panama Canal. More importantly to the city, and to California, it was intended to replace in the eyes of the world the image of a destroyed San Francisco. Organizers hoped the international exposition would increase tourism, settlement, and investment, and spur development and cement the Golden State as a trade gateway between Europe and Asia through the newly opened waterway.

The city's audacity was rewarded when the subsequent years of intense labor culminated in the triumphant 1915 opening of the Panama-Pacific International Exposition. "Just think of what they have done!" said *Current Opinion* magazine. "San Francisco nine years ago was in ruins. To-day it is rebuilt; and…they have brought into being at the same time this superb International Exposition…."[1]

The PPIE aspired to present no less than "a microcosm so nearly complete that if all the world were destroyed except the 635 acres of land within the Exposition gates, the material basis of the life of today could have been reproduced from the exemplifications of the arts, inventions and industries there exhibited," stated the Fair's official history. Essentially, the Exposition attempted to "curate the planet," a concept that seems grandiose and naïve by modern standards, yet was magnificent in its aspiration.[2]

---

1   "The European War and the Panama-Pacific Exposition—A Monumental Contrast," *Current Opinion* (May 1915): 318.
2   Frank Morton Todd, *The Story of the Exposition*, vol. 1 (New York: G. P. Putnam's Sons, 1921), xv.

This Fair provides a lens through which to view the discoveries, celebrities, politics, arts, and zeitgeist of the era. Visitors could watch the assembly of a pair of Levi's jeans or a brand new Ford, take in an avant-garde art display or listen to a speech by Teddy Roosevelt. They could see a temple molded entirely from soap or a tiny rosebush made of gems—or butter. When tired of riding around a six-acre replica Grand Canyon or a five-acre model of the Panama Canal, attendees could ascend nearly three hundred feet into the sky in a "house" attached to a steel arm. If the midway did not attract, they could enjoy a daily rotation of bands, parades, pageants, and headlining entertainers, including bandmaster John Philip Sousa, renowned composer Camille Saint-Saëns, and flamboyant dancer La Loïe Fuller.

Even as the PPIE strove to present the finest of mankind's products and achievements—a "comprehensive and representative contemporary record of the progress and condition of the human race," according to its director of exhibits—the Exposition also unintentionally exposed the evils of the era. Prurient shows and racist material were on display adjacent to booths offering delicacies, handicrafts, or the latest technologies. Radium, touted during the Fair as a source of bountiful clean power, eventually was proven lethal. The Palace of Education and Social Economy presented public health programs designed to improve quality of life around the world, but at least one ideology— eugenics—promoted what are now widely considered human rights abuses. And overshadowing every aspect of the PPIE was the Great War then engulfing half the globe.[3]

With its moments of sublimity and iniquity, the PPIE also represented a tremendous enterprise, the collaboration of tens of thousands of individuals, many of whom were otherwise foes, who worked in concert toward a greater goal.

As US vice president Thomas Marshall said during his dedicatory visit to the Fair: "A people dies when it loses its vision, when it ceases to dream its dream, and when from its loins there come forth no more pioneers or pathfinders."[4] Exploring the wonders of the Panama-Pacific International Exposition allows us to celebrate the dreamers, pioneers, and pathfinders of that era, and to draw parallels with the visionaries of our own epoch.

3   Asher C. Baker, "Division of Exhibits: Official Report," PPIE Exhibits: Director's Report, p. 1, Daniel E. Koshland San Francisco History Center, San Francisco Public Library.
4   Frank Morton Todd, *The Story of the Exposition, vol. 3* (New York: G. P. Putnam's Sons, 1921), 35.

FAIR FIGHT
The Battle for the 1915 Exposition

ooking east from San Francisco's Presidio in 1915, visitors saw ivory-walled, red-roofed palaces topped with golden statues and pale green domes, all surrounding a jeweled tower. What they saw was not a mirage. What they saw was the Panama-Pacific International Exposition.

Only nine years earlier, refugees camped in the same spot would have thought such grandeur impossible. Peering from their flimsy, rain-soaked tents, they would have viewed a muddy plain with scattered buildings, an ironworks, a seventy-acre tidal lagoon, and an isolation camp for those seriously ill in the wake of the Great Earthquake and Fire of 1906.

Indeed, in the days following the dual calamities, the idea of building a dream city and inviting the world to see it would have seemed preposterous. San Franciscans, faced with the reality of 2,600 acres of ruined metropolis, had more immediate needs.

Five days after the disaster began, sheets of rain hissed down on the smoking ruins, a sight especially cruel to those who had watched their homes and businesses go up in flames after the April 18 earthquake had shattered gas and water mains, causing vast fires and depriving firemen of the water to fight them. When an embattled bucket brigade on Telegraph Hill ran out of well water, the firefighters breached barrels of red wine to save a few homes.

Immediately following the catastrophe, more than half of the city's population of about 400,000 was homeless. More-fortunate survivors found shelter with family or in less-damaged cities, but tens of thousands of refugees huddled in misery as a heavy downpour drenched the tents they had set up in city parks and the Presidio. Those who dared venture onto Market Street did so at their peril. The walls of partially ruined buildings visibly swayed in the stiff winds blowing toward the bay, and stronger gusts sent some crashing dramatically to the ground.

In the midst of this squalor and terror, however, local leaders, who had conceived the idea for a world's fair years before, saw the Panama-Pacific International Exposition (PPIE) as a possible linchpin of recovery. As the wreckage was cleared away and reconstruction commenced, they revived the idea less than nine months after the cataclysm.

To succeed, San Francisco had to surmount multiple additional obstacles—a battle with New Orleans over the right to host the celebration, a contentious site-selection process, and the special challenge of construction on land deeply submerged beneath San Francisco Bay at high tide.

FAIR PORTENT

The first public inkling of the PPIE came on Christmas Day 1891, when the *San Francisco Examiner* published an article entitled "1900: Let the Next Great World's Fair Be Held in San Francisco." The newspaper suggested the exposition might commemorate the achievements of the past century, and it further claimed, "Visitors from every nation under the sun will find delight in this climate. To those from the frozen countries, it will be an inexpressible luxury; to those from the tropics, it will be like rich wine. The Wild Man of Borneo will learn the luxury of clothes and the fur-wrapped people of Kamchatka will revel in comparative nakedness."[1]

The proposed site was on the northern edge of San Francisco between the Presidio and Black Point, on a marshy area called Harbor View Beach. The *Examiner* story provided sketches by local architect Willis Polk depicting a large, elliptical, colonnaded court with a central tower and triumphal arch. Echoes of that design would appear on that very site twenty-four years later. Although the *Examiner*'s proposal for a San Francisco world's fair in 1900 was not realized, the city did host a major exposition in 1894— the Midwinter Fair in Golden Gate Park.

Around the turn of the twentieth century, the United States was on a world's fair roll, hosting

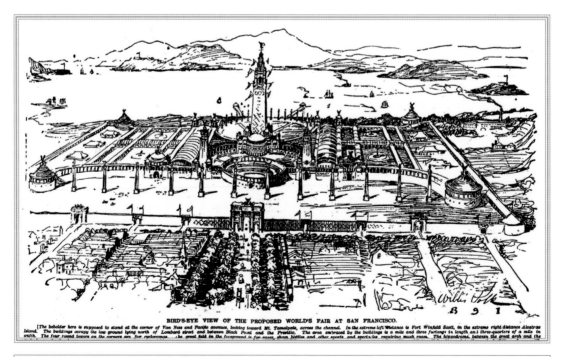

BIRD'S-EYE VIEW OF THE PROPOSED WORLD'S FAIR AT SAN FRANCISCO.

[The beholder here is supposed to stand at the corner of Van Ness and Pacific avenues, looking toward Mt. Tamalpais, across the channel. In the extreme left distance is Fort Winfield Scott, in the extreme right distance Alcatraz Island. The buildings occupy the low ground lying north of Lombard street and between Black Point and the Presidio. The area embraced by the buildings is a mile and three furlongs in length and three-quarters of a mile in width. The four round towers on the corners are for restaurants. The great field in the foreground is for races, shows, battles and other sports and spectacles requiring much room. The hippodrome, between the great arch and the

A speculative rendering of a San Francisco world's fair, drawn by then-twenty-four-year-old architect Willis Polk, ran in William Randolph Hearst's *San Francisco Examiner* on Christmas Day 1891. Twenty years later Polk became chairman of the Executive Architectural Council for the PPIE. (*San Francisco Examiner*, December 25, 1891)

Men stroll past burning ruins near Howard and East Streets (now the Embarcadero), April 18, 1906. The photo is by Ned Torney, whose father was commander of the US Army General Hospital at the Presidio. (Torney Family)

international expositions in 1893 in Chicago and 1901 in Buffalo, New York. By January 1904, the cry of "Meet Me in St. Louis" was sweeping the nation in advance of the Louisiana Purchase Exposition, set to open April 30.

Twelve years after the *Examiner*'s feature story, Reuben Brooks Hale, founder of the Hale Brothers Department Stores, reintroduced the concept of a fair in California's leading city. In a January 1904 letter to the Merchants' Association (later the Chamber of Commerce) he suggested San Francisco host a world's fair in 1915. He wrote, "The occasion could be advertised as the opening of San Francisco as the center of trade for the Pacific Ocean, or in commemoration of the completion of the Panama Canal."[2]

Hale's confidence in America's ability to complete the canal so swiftly was remarkable given the project's history. France had recently failed in its final attempt to construct the waterway—a process it had begun twenty-three years earlier—and the United States had signed a treaty to assume construction of the canal on November 18, 1903, just two months before Hale's proposal. And it was not until May 1904, five months *after* Hale's letter, that the US took over the French equipment and works.

Once San Francisco decided to campaign for a world's fair, planning proceeded at a desultory pace, the consensus being that there was plenty of time. Hale proposed in January 1906 that the exposition be ready by 1913, to coincide with the four hundredth anniversary of the discovery of the Pacific Ocean by Vasco Núñez de Balboa. That same month, San Francisco congressman Julius Kahn introduced a bill in the House of Representatives to "claim precedence" for a 1913 exposition.[3]

Then, on April 18, 1906, fate introduced a nearly apocalyptic obstacle. Today's seismologists calculate the Great Quake at about magnitude 7.8, and the subsequent fires raged for three days. It is estimated that 3,000 people died and $500 million of property was lost, about $27.3 billion in 2012 dollars.

Louis Levy of the PPIE's publicity department wrote of the national skepticism regarding San Francisco's ability to recover fully: "The prophecy was freely made that it would be decades, if ever, before San Francisco would rebuild to her former strength. Those who came to look upon these miles of twisted steel and broken brick could see little hope for the city...." But a mere eight months after the quake, on December 10, San Francisco's "Pacific Ocean Exposition Company" filed for incorporation.[4]

One year after the calamity, refugee camps still dotted the city, but most of the rubble had been cleared away, and San Francisco's rebuilding was progressing at a blistering pace. But other troubles loomed. In early 1907 a state bill to appropriate $1 million for the exposition suffered a gubernatorial pocket veto. That October, the "Panic of 1907" brought a nationwide depression and effectively stymied all work on the fair. As official Fair historian Frank Morton Todd wrote, "Nobody could quite see an International Exposition built with clearing house certificates." Further, New Orleans mayor Martin Behrman had called a meeting to discuss a Panama Canal Exposition in *his* city.[5]

Meanwhile, San Francisco was enduring a protracted political upheaval that began in late 1906, when it was revealed that Mayor Eugene Schmitz and the entire Board of Supervisors were under the control of political puppeteer Abe Ruef. In exchange for political favors, Ruef, a local lawyer and Union Labor Party boss who was instrumental in Mayor Schmitz's campaign and election, had been taking bribes from prize-fight organizers, liquor interests, real estate speculators, and telephone, power, and railroad companies.

Ruef was arraigned in December 1906 and pled guilty in May 1907 at a circus-like trial during which prosecutor Francis Heney was shot and badly wounded in court. Mayor Schmitz and the supervisors were removed from office, leaving San Francisco's government in a shambles.

A STATE DIVIDED

By 1909 nearly a dozen cities had expressed interest in hosting a fair in 1915, including Baltimore, Tampa, Boston, Charleston, Galveston, Mobile, Denver, and Washington, DC. As the race heated up, only San Francisco, San Diego, and New Orleans were regarded as serious contenders, and San Francisco felt a need to test its ability to host a major fete.

To this end, the City by the Bay paused in its rebuilding efforts and on October 19, 1909, kicked off the five-day Portola Festival, which marked the 140th anniversary of Don Gaspar de Portolá's discovery of San Francisco Bay.

More pertinently, the festival served as "a celebration of such a victory of man over loss and discouragement and vast disaster as had never been exhibited to the world before," according to the PPIE's official history. The Portola Festival was attended by 480,000 people and featured outdoor tableaux vivants, auto races, open houses at hotels and cafés, and nighttime parades under festoons of electric lights. Local businessman Charles C. Moore arranged for the presence of an international armada of warships from the United States, Italy, the Netherlands, Japan, Germany, and Britain.[6]

The Portola was so successful that many of those previously doubtful of San Francisco's ability to host a world's fair became convinced it was possible. Three days after the festival's triumphant close, Reuben Hale gave a dinner for some of its sponsors at the Bohemian Club, and these men—including Charles C. Moore, future

This cartoon depicts Charles C. Moore, who successfully invited a fleet of international ships to visit San Francisco during the 1909 Portola Festival. (The Bancroft Library, University of California, Berkeley)

mayor James Rolph, and Hale himself—became members of the Board of Directors for the PPIE. On December 6, Congressman Kahn submitted a bill that would declare San Francisco the site of the exposition and appropriate $5 million to help pay for it. The bill was subsequently referred to the Committee on Industrial Arts and Expositions, and at the end of December, President William Howard Taft declared his support, saying, "The magnificent recovery of San Francisco was not only an inspiration to the whole world, but an assurance that an exposition held there would be splendidly successful."[7]

Yet competition to host the fair was intensifying. In March of 1910, New Orleans sent a delegation to Washington, DC, to "lay the matter before President Taft."[8]

Before entering the national fray, California needed to decide whether San Francisco or San Diego stood the best chance of defeating the New Orleans bid. The Santa Barbara Chamber of Commerce called a March 22 convention of commercial interests from "every city with a population 3,000 or more" to choose which city would be California's best candidate.[9]

San Diego immediately cried foul, saying the convention was rigged for San Francisco. Indeed, in 1910 San Francisco was the "first city of California." According to that year's census, its population was nearly 417,000, whereas the entire population of San Diego County was only about 61,500, and the city of Los Angeles was also smaller, home to about 319,000. The majority of the state's residents lived in Northern California as well. Thus, by calling a vote of larger cities, the deck apparently was being stacked in San Francisco's favor.

Fifty-eight municipalities were represented at the convention, but only nine were in counties south of Monterey. D. C. Collier, president of the San Diego exposition, said, "[W]e will not go into any convention framed or programmed to confer this exposition on San Francisco as a free gift...." The Los Angeles Chamber of Commerce joined this boycott, but the Santa Barbara meeting went ahead as planned. With San Diego absent, San Francisco was endorsed unanimously.[10]

The "Logical Point" campaign hoped to convince Congress that New Orleans was the best site for a 1915 world's fair. (Laura Ackley)

TAKING ON NEW ORLEANS

Although San Francisco had been anointed as California's choice in the fight against New Orleans, San Diego declared it would go ahead with its plans for a smaller fair, intimating, however, that it was willing to negotiate with San Francisco. In May the two cities reached a compact that stipulated San Diego would waive all demands for federal help for its fair and would assist San Francisco in preparation for 1915. In exchange, San Diego would receive a portion of "any appropriation made by the state legislature for the San Francisco and San Diego expositions," and assistance in obtaining a permanent agricultural experiment station and in securing federal invitations to Mexico and Central and South America to exhibit at the Southern California fair.[11]

San Francisco raised $4,089,000 in subscriptions for Exposition stock in only two hours on April 28, 1910, at a mass meeting held in the main hall of the Merchants' Exchange. (Donna Ewald Huggins)

During the tussle between San Francisco and San Diego, New Orleans had been busy mounting a spirited campaign called "The Logical Point." Its delegates had returned from the nation's capital in a jubilant mood. They had met with President Taft as well as "Uncle Joe" Cannon, the powerful Speaker of the House, and William Rodenberg, chairman of the Committee on Industrial Arts and Expositions.

The *New Orleans Times-Picayune* announced the "conquering committee" had "won the personal indorsement [sic] of President Taft." However, a closer reading of the article shows Taft said only that "the matter must ultimately… rest with the Congress.…[If] Congress selects New Orleans, there will be no doubt that I will sign the bill."[12]

After the New Orleans Panama Exposition had incorporated and raised nearly $200,000 in subscriptions, San Francisco countered by holding a "Mass Meeting" on April 28, 1910, at the Merchants' Exchange, where subscription books for its fair were opened. This auction-style event was held on the floor of the exchange, hosted by "auctioneer" Larry Harris, well known for writing the popular poem "The Damn'dest Finest Ruins" shortly after the quake.

In just two hours, $4,089,000 was pledged, with major subscribers including railroad magnate Charles Crocker, newspaper publishers William Randolph Hearst and M. H. de Young,

bankers Isaias W. Hellman and William Crocker, sugar barons Adolph Spreckels and W. G. Irwin, companies such as the D. Ghirardelli Company, Levi Strauss & Co., Hale Brothers, Wells Fargo Nevada National Bank, A. P. Hotaling & Co., Matson Navigation Company, Shreve & Co., and various local banks and industrial associations.

In contrast with San Francisco's impressive fund-raising, New Orleans did not surpass the $1 million mark until mid-May. By June San Francisco's subscriptions were up to $7.5 million, and two exposition bills, for an additional $10 million, were also in the works. Both legislative measures passed in November, bringing the total guaranteed by San Francisco to a colossal $17.5 million.

A delegation left for Washington on May 1 to plead San Francisco's case. M. H. de Young, addressing the House Committee on Foreign Affairs, implored, "Permit us to conduct…a fitting celebration of the opening of the Panama Canal—*at our own expense* [author's emphasis]. We do not come here to ask for an appropriation. We do not come here to ask the nation for a dollar to aid us in this exposition."[13]

Louisiana governor Jared Sanders responded with a number of arguments in favor of New Orleans but would not go so far as to guarantee his city would not seek financial assistance for its exposition. Sanders was quizzed about $1.35 million the US government had extended to New Orleans in 1884 and another $300,000 in 1885 for the World's Industrial and Cotton Centennial Exposition. When it was noted that New Orleans had never repaid the money, Sanders declared the federal funds had not been loans but rather money to be returned out of any profits, of which there were none.

The Foreign Affairs Committee amended two exposition bills to require that at least $7.5 million be raised by either city before the president would invite the nations of the world. Amusingly, the press in both cities reacted as though this all but guaranteed their site would host the Panama Canal fair.

PROS AND CONS

As the legislative campaign was being waged, so, too, were the public crusades. A variety of promotional items including postcards, pamphlets, trunk labels, and pins were produced for both cities' efforts. Politicians and businesspeople lobbied hard for their locations, and ordinary citizens were urged to get involved.

New Orleans argued it was in the perfect location for a 1915 celebration. The population within 900 miles was twenty million, while the population within 900 miles of San Francisco was only one million. Further, the average distance from US cities to New Orleans was 792 miles—compared to 2,400 miles for San Francisco—making the point that it would be easier to transport fairgoers and exhibit materials to the Big Easy.

Supporters also noted that New Orleans was only four days' travel from the Panama Canal, as opposed to three weeks for San Francisco. New Orleans considered itself the "Gateway City" to South American trade. It boasted of twenty-three miles of wharf space, excellent hotels, and experience hosting Carnival crowds at Mardi Gras. The nation's north-south railroad lines also added their support to the New Orleans campaign, while those running east-west predictably lobbied for San Francisco.

The Logical Point campaign also set forth a financial argument: It was less expensive to travel to New Orleans, so the "everyman," not just the wealthy, could afford to attend. New Orleans claimed it would cost only about $25

for "the most remote of 50 million to reach New Orleans and would cost ten times that to visit San Francisco."[14]

San Francisco countered that the City by the Bay was the commercial and industrial center of the Pacific Coast, midway between Europe and Asia, and the gateway to the Asia trade. In addition, there were many other points of interest in California, and a long journey cross-country would be an advantage rather than a detriment. On the way to San Francisco, fair visitors could, according to a popular slogan, "See America First," stopping at Yellowstone, the Grand Canyon, Yosemite, or other scenic wonders, or even pass through the very canal the exposition celebrated. Navies could anchor and display within the bay, and visitors could easily disembark from passenger ships. And, of course, the climate was the finest.

Last but not least, San Francisco had been planning the fair since 1904, and as part of its remarkable renaissance since the 1906 disaster, the city had been rebuilt with the fair in mind. By December 1910, $300 million had been spent on reconstruction, and there were hotel rooms for 100,000 guests, many more than New Orleans could accommodate.

But San Francisco's financial argument was perhaps its strongest. Citizens and legislators were reminded that New Orleans still owed money from 1884 and now wanted more funds from the government. San Francisco asked for no federal money and assured $17.5 million for the creation of the exposition.

Both cities claimed they would fight fair, and they did—until the conflict became heated. Then, off came the gloves. A *New York Times* article reported, "New Orleans assures all inquirers that there is no mud to be flung in the fight. She knows, of course, that there has been bubonic plague in San Francisco for years, but she would not say anything about it for the world."[15]

San Francisco answered by mocking the southern city's infamous sewers: "The plumbing in the streets is open, there are practically no bathtubs in the city, and in the few buildings that have bathtubs—namely the largest hotels—the water comes out of the tap almost black. Of course, one is informed that this is the finest kind of water....As for the drinking water, even the most patriotic citizen of the old city would hardly describe it as a beverage."[16]

New Orleans riposted that her ordinary soil "might be used with profit to fertilize the arid sands of California," and that the Golden State might "boast of beautiful flowers, of luscious fruit, of minerals in her massive mountains, and...of the alkali deserts, and of Abe Reuff's [sic] crowd."[17]

San Francisco also played upon the nation's heartstrings, using its remarkable recovery from the earthquake and fire to elicit sympathy. However, some of its advertising was deplorable. One brochure said of New Orleans that "during the past decade the tendency of negroes to live in town has increased. Here is an immense showing of poor people in addition to poor whites. If there are 100,000 negroes in New Orleans today they must be practically counted out of the population as supporters of the fair."[18]

As reprehensible as the mudslinging and racism were, the contest seems to have boiled down to location versus money.

In November 1910, in advance of the winter congressional session, San Francisco opened a full-time campaign headquarters in Washington, DC, at the New Willard Hotel. Just across the street, the New Orleans headquarters operated from the New Ebbitt House Hotel. At the New Willard, a visitor could partake of California fruit, flowers, and wine; at the Ebbitt House, New Orleans had a Creole chef serving jambalaya and pralines, and a bar dispensing Sazeracs and orange flower gin fizzes.

When Congress opened in December, New Orleans led by a margin of thirty-three votes in the House. Of even more concern to the California contingent was the astonishing discovery that Julius Kahn's 1909 bill requesting a $5 million appropriation for a San Francisco fair had never been officially withdrawn. When Kahn attempted to withdraw the bill on December 20, Louisiana congressman Robert Wickliffe blocked the request. Kahn tried to turn this to California's advantage, taking the opportunity to say on the record that California would not ask for or accept congressional funding. Nonetheless, the

Committee on Industrial Arts and Expositions, composed of mostly Southerners, voted 9-6 in favor of New Orleans on January 20.

A final vote of the full House was scheduled for January 31, 1911, and with only ten days left, New Orleans was still in the lead. Then, the tide began to turn. About this time New Orleans began to realize that rather than supporting its effort, President Taft was actively working against it. Taft stepped in and swung Pennsylvania to the side of San Francisco. William Randolph Hearst and California politician Theodore Bell were instrumental in converting New York's votes, and de Young was credited with personally getting eight votes for San Francisco.

On January 23, 1911, San Francisco placed broadside ads in every major newspaper west of the Mississippi, asking residents to send telegrams to Taft expressing support for a San Francisco exposition. The San Francisco Chronicle reported, "Portland leased a wire for the day and for 24 hours kept it hot with telegrams...." In Canyon County, Idaho, one intrepid horseman spent thirty-six consecutive hours in the saddle battling a snowstorm to add 110 names to a petition given to Taft.[19]

Historian Frank Morton Todd wrote, "Thirty-four extra telegraphers worked five days and

Uncle Sam rejects New Orleans, saying, "I danced with you in '84 and it was too expensive," a reference to the southern city's unpaid debt from the 1884 World's Industrial and Cotton Centennial Exposition. (Laura Ackley)

San Francisco   1915

We've got the time—1915.
We've got the place—San Francisco.
We've got the money—$17,500,000
And now we want the Fair.

We ask your help.
Be sure your Congressman votes right.

PRINTED IN SAN FRANCISCO BY WALE PRINTING CO., 555 MARKET   COPYRIGHT APPLIED FOR

Dozens of postcard designs urged the public to lobby Congress to vote for San Francisco as the site of the 1915 world's fair. (Laura Ackley)

nights receiving the dispatches....It has been said there were 40,000 messages." Even as New Orleans denounced the telegram crusade as "despicable trickery," it admitted the tactic was "helping in doubtful districts," and it encouraged Southerners to mount a similar effort.[20, 21]

At the final hearing on January 31, each faction was given thirty minutes to speak. California's delegation chose a rapid-fire barrage of two-minute speeches by influential men from across the nation. Louisiana opted for a single speech by Rodenberg. Said de Young, "He took twenty-one minutes in demanding the House favor the recommendation, and with rivers of perspiration running down his face, he talked all about his bill and not about New Orleans."[22]

VICTORY

When a preliminary vote was called, San Francisco led 188 to 159. Recognizing the inevitable, many representatives changed their final votes, making the ultimate tally 259 to 43. As the news reached San Francisco, sirens shrieked, firecrackers popped, and cheers rang in the streets. At the New Willard Hotel, champagne was poured for the California delegation, all of whom sported fancy dress.

Delegation Chairman A. W. Scott said, "Every factor we won was indispensable to our victory. In the last ten days we swung at least twenty votes into the San Francisco column." De Young confirmed, "It had been bad—oh, bad...but by the jumping crickets of Tuolumne, we won!"[23, 24]

It appears that two things turned the tide: Taft and money. California delegate Thornwell Mullally said, "California owes a great debt of gratitude to President Taft, which we ought never to forget." Aside from a few grumbles, New Orleans was gracious in defeat. After the Senate affirmed the House vote on February 11, 1911, the heads of the New Orleans exposition effort sent a polite telegram of congratulations to San Francisco mayor P. H. McCarthy.[25]

SITE SELECTION

The dust stirred up in the conflict with New Orleans had not yet settled when the next great battle for the PPIE began. Immediately following the House vote, and even before the Senate affirmed San Francisco's victory, wrangling began over the site of San Francisco's Panama-Pacific International Exposition.

As early as November 1910, de Young's *Chronicle* published elaborate renderings of how the Fair might look in Golden Gate Park, which was the site specified in that month's successful city bond issue. The *San Francisco Call*, on February 2, 1911, published a list of potential sites, including Golden Gate Park; the waterfront from Rincon Hill to Telegraph Hill; Lake Merced; Harbor View, which included parts of the Presidio and land from the James Fair estate; and farther flung areas like the city's Bay View District, the Tanforan District in San Mateo County, and the Oakland shoreline.

Everyone in the city had a favorite site, and all the local fraternal organizations, clubs, and "improvement districts" weighed in. As official historian Todd wrote, "The curious fact developed that each organization seemed in favor of the site nearest it." During the second quarter of 1911, a newspaper would often feature several articles on competing sites on the same page. One editorial cartoon suggested building the Exposition on a gigantic truck and moving it around the city to each site on a different day of the week. City engineer Marsden Manson set to work preparing descriptions and cost estimates for the likely alternatives.[26]

Many of the men who had been instrumental

in the effort to win the Fair were installed as directors, including Reuben Hale, M. H. de Young, James Rolph, A. W. Scott, and James McNab. The entire board, totaling twenty-eight men, elected Charles C. Moore president of the Exposition. Before he accepted the appointment, he required the board to sign a compact of business rules for the Fair, including one stating directors "would not be prejudiced proponents of sites."[27]

Lake Merced, Golden Gate Park, and Harbor View quickly emerged as strong favorites. The proposed Lake Merced site was between 1,200 and 1,500 acres, by far the largest of the locations under consideration. Most of this land belonged to the heirs of Adolph Sutro, tunnel builder of the Comstock Lode and former mayor of San Francisco. The lion's share of the remaining acreage was owned by the Spring Valley Water Company.

The site was attractive and its sloping character afforded beautiful views. Local springs provided plentiful freshwater, and Lake Merced itself offered "a protected body...for recreation, exhibition and ornamental purposes." The location could be reached by the Southern Pacific and Ocean Shore Railroads and by north and east trolley lines, and the Twin Peaks Tunnel would hopefully be completed prior to the

Exposition. A number of influential men were in favor of Lake Merced, including famed urban planner Daniel Burnham, painter F. D. Millet, architect Cass Gilbert, sculptor Daniel Chester French, and Exposition president Moore.[28]

Despite these positive attributes, building the Fair at Lake Merced could be pricey. The cost to grade the area, also called Sutro Forest, made it the most expensive of the locations—more than double the cost of the next most expensive, Golden Gate Park. And because the site was about six miles from the center of population of San Francisco, transporting people to Lake Merced would require swift completion of the Twin Peaks Tunnel (which ultimately opened in 1918).

A strong contingent supported holding the Fair in Golden Gate Park. The portion of the park suggested for the Exposition was about six hundred acres west of 20th Avenue, which over time expanded to include two hundred additional acres in Lincoln Park and a connecting strip between the two parks through the Richmond District.

Boosters argued that several streetcar lines served Golden Gate Park and the city bond passed by voters had specified the park as the location for the Exposition. Perhaps most importantly, they said, the park land was already city owned. Because

Jubilation reigned in the streets of San Francisco when the final House of Representatives vote was tallied, favoring the city 259–43 over New Orleans. (Glenn D. Koch)

The proposed Golden Gate Park site for the Exposition, as shown in M. H. de Young's *Chronicle*, included permanent buildings in the park, a pier extending into the Pacific Ocean, and a concessions avenue connecting to Lincoln Park to the north. (*San Francisco Chronicle,* July 23, 1911)

the land would not be leased, any improvements could become permanent assets to the city. Advocates envisioned features like an art gallery, an aquarium, a permanent exhibition building, statuary, fountains, waterways, and an observatory.

However, the park plan also had its detractors. While many cherished the structures remaining from the 1894 Midwinter Fair, including the Music Stand, museum, and Japanese Tea Garden, many others remembered that celebration's devastation of the park and the years it took to restore the area. Constructing the Exposition in the park, opponents noted, would require the destruction of many existing improvements and mature trees.

William Hammond Hall, the first superintendent of Golden Gate Park, decried use of the park for the Exposition in a sixteen-page letter to the Board of Directors. He felt the cost in site preparation before the Fair and site restoration after the Fair would represent a huge financial loss to the citizens of San Francisco. Hall and others pointed out that while streetcars could reach the park, no heavy rail or water access was available.

The appealing illustrations of the park site showed a pier extending from Ocean Beach into the Pacific for cargo and passenger ships,

conveniently ignoring the fact that a pier with water deep enough to dock ships would need to extend half a mile into the sea, where tides and waves would make it dangerous much of the time. Additionally, the city engineer reported the cost of grading the park would be more than three times that of the landfill needed at Harbor View, and restoration costs also would be much higher.

The final popular site contender was Harbor View, a natural amphitheater of a little more than six hundred acres on the north shore of the city, bounded by Lombard Street on the south and by Van Ness and the Presidio on the east and west. Backers of Harbor View pointed out that its 8,000 feet of unobstructed, nearly level shoreline would provide not only easy access for pleasure craft and ferries but also a convenient landing for building and exhibit materials. The site provided superb views of the bay, its islands, and Marin County, and it was protected by the hills and forests of the Presidio, which together provided a climate advertised as "the best that San Francisco has to offer."[29, 30]

Harbor View also was the closest to the city's center of population. "Twenty-five thousand people can walk to Harbor View," proclaimed one pamphlet, which further pointed out the

"San Francisco's Great Exposition on Wheels!" suggested mounting the Fair on a truck and driving it around the city to a different site each day of the week. (*San Francisco Call,* March 6, 1911)

large pool of potential employees near the site. Three streetcar companies already served the neighborhood, and the city engineer's report said a Fair there would be the least costly to construct. Perhaps most persuasive to a city a mere five years removed from the 1906 disaster was the fact that Harbor View's waterfront location offered the best fire protection.[31]

But Harbor View's foes seemed particularly vitriolic, suggesting that placing the Exposition there would be embezzling from the public. Historian Frank Morton Todd cited one letter received by the directors that declared, "We are not going to vote or tax ourselves to raise money…to fill in mudholes…to make land valuable for a few millionaires who spend their money in New York City."[32]

Other arguments against the site were compelling. Acquiring rights to the land, owned by a large number of individuals, might be complicated. While there were several

streetcar lines nearby, transportation was seen as inadequate for the volume of visitors expected at an international exposition. Harbor View's adversaries were especially fond of mentioning that a large portion of the proposed site was marshy or fully submerged. Filling the underwater portions of the site could be costly, and the resultant land might not be stable enough for foundations.

The area already had been partitioned into "water lots" under the assumption that it would someday be filled, and many of these lots belonged to the estate of the late silver tycoon James G. Fair. Seven blocks (sixteen acres) were owned by his daughter Theresa Oelrichs, and the other twenty-two blocks (fifty-five acres) by her sister, Virginia Vanderbilt. Oelrichs offered her land to the Exposition rent-free. It was hoped Vanderbilt would do the same.

PARTISAN PROMOTERS

The directors had signed off on Moore's stipulation that they not be "selfish or prejudiced proponents" of any particular site, but it soon became obvious which site each director preferred, and these preferences were often publicly expressed. Hale wrote an editorial supporting Harbor View, while A. W. Scott favored Golden Gate Park, also the choice of *Chronicle* owner M. H. de Young.

Each site had its hearing before the Board of Directors. The first vote, on June 22, 1911, resulted in a stalemate: eleven votes for Harbor View, eight for Golden Gate Park, and four for Lake Merced. Finally the board members directed a three-member subcommittee made up of directors Isaias W. Hellman, Jr., Captain John Barneson, and Andrew M. Davis—each known to favor a different one of the top three sites—to come up with a unified site proposal.

On July 25 they submitted the Whole City Plan, featuring a series of connected sites circling the north and west portions of the city. Under this scheme, Telegraph Hill would receive a huge telegraph tower, and Fort Mason would house the US government building. The amusement concessions (or midway), yacht harbor, and heavy exhibits would be at Harbor View. A tower or statue would surmount Lincoln Park, which would be linked by a grand boulevard through the Richmond District, lined with the state and foreign pavilions and leading to the permanent buildings in Golden Gate Park. An "intramural railroad" would connect all the locations. In addition, a new auditorium would be built near the Civic Center.

This scheme, totaling 1,800 acres, mollified advocates of every site but Lake Merced. The directors voted unanimously in favor of the Whole City Plan, although "unanimous" turned out to be a flexible term, as several men groused to the press that their original choices were better. Publicly, this plan was in place for the remainder of 1911.

President Taft broke ground for the Exposition in Golden Gate Park on October 14, and all appeared to be proceeding smoothly. However, behind the scenes, the Architectural Commission and Building and Grounds Committee were in a quandary. They had been allotted a mere $13 million to construct the entire Fair. This included land acquisition, site preparation, and construction. And the Whole City Plan was a budget-buster.

Calculations showed that only about 437 acres was needed for the Exposition, including space for palaces, livestock areas, storage, the midway, national pavilions, and federal, city, and state buildings, as well as roads and open space. Architect William Faville put it best: "We have ten times too much ground for the money."[33]

Construction costs were estimated at $2.50 per square foot just for the buildings, and when the cost of obtaining, preparing, and later restoring the land was factored in, the budget allowed for only twenty-eight acres of interior space to be constructed across the sites of the Whole City Plan. If Golden Gate Park alone were used, 36.5 acres could be built, and at Harbor View, the acreage went up to 45.4.

The Executive Architectural Council, consisting of Faville, Willis Polk, and Clarence Ward, recommended on December 5 that, pending the acquisition of the privately held lands, "all the temporary buildings, State,

County and National Buildings, as well as the Concessions be located at Harbor View, and that an architectural feature be constructed in Lincoln Park." On December 12 this vote was affirmed by a Site Committee vote of 4-1, with one abstention. The dissenting vote was de Young, who owned much valuable real estate near Golden Gate Park.[34]

Thus, the Jewel City finally and irrevocably came to reside at Harbor View alone. Once again it looked like full speed ahead for the Exposition.

Then, on December 28, 1911, a one-sentence telegram from Virginia Vanderbilt's lawyers arrived regarding her twenty-two blocks of land. It read, "Mrs. Vanderbilt does not consider she would be safe in making proposed Exposition lease and therefore declines to enter into it."[35]

Despite the telegram's firm tone, Vanderbilt let it be known she might be convinced…for $60,000 per block. As the Fair was only able to pay $35,000 to $40,000 per block, her price was out of the question. Fortunately, the Exposition Company had a trump card to play.

The previous March, Governor Hiram Johnson had approved an amendment to the law of eminent domain, allowing condemnation of property for Exposition purposes. Wouldn't it be better, reasoned the PPIE's lawyers, for Mrs. Vanderbilt to accept a reduced lease price and benefit from the increased value of the land after the Exposition's improvements? This was stated obliquely and cordially, but the subtext was clear: accept a lower price or have the land seized. A lease was signed on January 13, 1912.

Three years and one month later, the finished Panama-Pacific International Exposition opened on time and to tremendous fanfare. It became one of the most successful American fairs, both popularly and financially. Looking at the challenges that had to be overcome just to reach the point of construction, it is easy to see how any one of them—the earthquake, the battles with San Diego and New Orleans, and the site selection and acquisition—might have changed the PPIE fundamentally or even entirely erased it from San Francisco's history. ⚹

ENVISIONING THE EPHEMERAL CITY

When Jules Guérin, the PPIE's Director of Color, first beheld the site of the Jewel City from the half-encircling hills, he was struck by its resemblance to European rivieras, in both topography and coloration. Here, according to *Scribner's Magazine*, was a "natural, even if not yet classical amphitheatre between the tawny Grecian hills and the blue Italian seas which are California's." "It reminded me much of the French Rivieri," said Guérin, who saw an opportunity to set the San Francisco Exposition apart from its predecessors with luminous color.[1, 2]

Chicago's Columbian Exposition of 1893 was popularly termed "The White City" because of its chalky, whitewashed surfaces of "staff," a mixture of plaster, cement, and fiber. The Pan-American Exposition of 1901 in Buffalo, New York, had attempted a uniform color program under the direction of muralist C. Y. Turner. However, Turner's concept of expressing human progress through a gradation of colors from vivid to delicate from one end of the fair to the other proved too oblique for many viewers to understand. At St. Louis in 1904, color in architecture was not emphasized, and the buildings were uniformly off-white with domes and steeples in shades from gray to orange.

San Francisco's own geography inspired the coloration of the Fair. Guérin felt the local light was much the same as in Spain, which dictated the PPIE be a city of ivory and warm "Oriental" hues, not "garish as dead white would be, in the strong California sunshine." California itself suggested much of the palette: "the gold of California's orangeries and poppy fields, the blue of her skies on fair days, the browns of the summer hills, the deep red of the setting sun as it sank into the rim of the Pacific Ocean, the lighter pinks fringing the clouds at eventide." He called his inspiration "Latin with a touch of the Oriental," with "Oriental" denoting the Near East.[3, 4]

15

Always he kept in mind how the Exposition would appear from the hills above. "Imagine a gigantic Persian rug of soft melting tones," he said, "with brilliant splashes here and there, spread along the waterside for a mile or more, and you may get some idea of what the 'City of Color' will look like when viewed from the heights about the bay."[5]

The director of color's work was emblematic of the myriad complex design problems that were addressed simultaneously as the planning of the Fair and preparation of the site proceeded on multiple fronts. The Exposition Company began sometimes contentious lease negotiations and started clearing existing structures from the land. Meanwhile, architects, artists, engineers, and landscape designers bent over their drafting tables to create plans for the palaces, sculptures, murals, and gardens of what was effectively a complete city in miniature.

DREDGING AND FILLING

A brisk, salty wind blew through the Golden Gate as a motor launch bearing PPIE president Charles C. Moore and three Exposition directors came alongside the dredger *John McMullin*. The dredger was moored about a quarter mile toward Alcatraz Island from the swampy section of Harbor View, called East Lake. This was the artificial basin separated from San Francisco Bay by a sea wall of riprap and rubble from the 1906 quake.

The officials clambered onto the dredger and made their way to the pilothouse, where each grasped one of the control levers that would

In the foreground of this 1912 aerial view of the site looking east from the Presidio is the "mudhole" that would become the Palace of Fine Arts Lagoon. The large enclosed body of water on the left is the seventy-plus-acre tidal lake that lay where the main Exposition palaces were to stand. (Laura Ackley)

On April 13, 1912, the first fill material gushed into the site from dredgers offshore. Standing atop the pipe were Official Herald Billy Hooper (left, with trumpet and banner), PPIE president Charles C. Moore (center, in creased hat), and other Exposition dignitaries. (The Bancroft Library, University of California, Berkeley)

activate the first Exposition site work. It was April 13, 1912, and on a signal from the president of the San Francisco Bridge Company, which won the contract to fill seventy-one acres of the PPIE site, the men pulled the levers. Pumps roared, the *John McMullin's* whistle piped three times, and the crowd watching eagerly from shore cheered.

Material sucked from the sea floor thirty to fifty feet below began to flow through a twenty-two-inch-diameter pipe laid across pontoons on the surface toward the tidal lagoon at the foot of Webster Street. The officials came ashore to pose for a photo standing atop the pipe as it spewed sand into the future fairgrounds.

This first portion of dredging was the trickiest. The "water lots" that needed to be filled were under as much as twenty feet of water at high tide. The dredger alternated pumping sand, mud, and silt with seawater to blast ooze from the site. With an additional dredger in service, it was possible to fill about 20,000 cubic yards daily. Eventually, the area of the water lots was filled with 1.3 million cubic yards of material. Additional fill required in the Presidio added 400,000 cubic yards, bringing the total cost of fill to $302,000—about $7.4 million in 2012.

When engineering tests showed that the fill material was unable to support the planned structures, and actually produced a downward

drag as it settled, foundation piles were driven deep beneath the fill. The structural frameworks of all but one of the major buildings were constructed on pile foundations. The Festival Hall, which lay on more stable soil, received spread-concrete footings, as did the structures on Presidio lands, which were smaller and lighter. The rest of the palaces and courts were built on piles driven into a layer of "green sand and clay" overlying the hardpan beneath the site.[6]

CLEARING THE SITE

While Harbor View was not densely populated, it was by no means empty. The property on which the Exposition would be built was the site of more than four hundred buildings—many with murky titles—on two hundred parcels held by 175 different owners. The structures varied in size and function—from a fifty-unit apartment building to the Fulton Engineering and Shipbuilding Works—and all would need to be cleared. Owners of the land could either arrange to have their structures moved, demolished, or sold to the Exposition Company, which was authorized to pay as much as $500 above the assessed value (about an extra $12,000 in 2012).

Most owners were cooperative, but some sued, claiming the Exposition's offer was lower than the value of their property. After one lawsuit in which the owner received a verdict of $900 on a property for which the Fair had offered $1,500, the number of suits dropped dramatically. On April 20, 1912, the Exposition Company began auctioning off the buildings it had purchased. Teardown of structures that were not moved began April 25.

For most of the site, the Exposition bought the buildings but merely leased the land. Only 12.26 acres of the 635 total were purchased by the Exposition. Forty structures were moved, the rest wrecked and salvaged piecemeal.

EARTHQUAKE SHACKS

The Exposition Company was not above collusion in its efforts to secure the PPIE site at a reduced cost.

While the Exposition Company mostly seems to have dealt squarely with owners of Harbor View properties, it is clear that both sides sought the advantage. Owners placed the highest possible value on their improvements, and the Exposition tried to pay as little as possible. The Exposition leased almost all the land and paid the property taxes, and it also compensated owners for structures that would be torn down. However, if buildings were condemned by civic authorities, the Exposition not only avoided paying for them, but the owners were also responsible for demolition costs.

Some structures on the site were "earthquake shacks," moved there after the 1906 refugee camps were dissolved. The largest camp and the last to close in 1908 included about 1,500 cottages at Lobos Square, which lay on the site of the upcoming Fair. As with the other camps, many Lobos Square cottages were moved either by tenants or investors, often to nearby lots.

After the camps closed, the shacks were offered for sale to their refugee tenants, but not all were purchased. The Earthquake Relief Corporation discouraged real estate developers from buying cottages en masse and reestablishing collections of shacks on privately owned land, as the practice would perpetuate camp life, and, "lacking superintendence and control, such camp life would be worse than that which then existed [following the earthquake]." Ultimately, the agency was not entirely successful, and neighborhoods of rental cottages sprang up near the parks they had previously occupied.[7]

Though the Associated Charities of San Francisco believed the little homes provided pride of ownership, healthful living with plenty of fresh air, and were "infinitely better than the best tenement," the Department of Health did not agree. Between 1908 and 1915, the department's board conducted a campaign to remove properties it considered substandard and unhygienic, and the surviving earthquake shacks constituted nearly 70 percent of the structures condemned during that period. The Department of Health's 1911–1912 Annual Report rated as its most important goal the "stupendous task of eliminating the refugee shack with its attendant insanitary conditions, and in the majority of instances extreme poverty of its occupants, that remain as a legacy of the catastrophe of 1906." Neighbors often complained that the tiny houses lowered adjacent property values and created a type of slum. The Chamber of Commerce vowed to eliminate the shacks from the Exposition city, along with everything else it considered "unsightly and unclean."[8, 9, 10]

Thus, the goals of the Department of Health conveniently matched those of the Exposition regarding the earthquake cottages remaining at Harbor View. Dozens of the structures lay scattered across the PPIE site, the largest enclave of which was on a block bounded by Bay, Octavia, Francisco, and Laguna Streets. Landlord Horace Woolley had moved 119 cottages onto the land, owned by Mrs. Kate Austin.

The Buildings and Grounds Committee of the Fair, tasked with securing the land and constructing the Jewel City, enlisted the sympathetic Department of Health to condemn the shacks. Dr. T. G. Howe, an inspector for the board, wrote that "every effort will be made in having the shacks removed from this district."[11]

Most of the cooperative efforts of the health department and the PPIE prevailed, but Austin and Woolley fought back. The cottages on the Austin property were condemned as unsanitary on November 28, 1911, along with about forty other Harbor View refugee shacks. Two weeks later the owners were given forty-five days to vacate and clear the land. Austin and Woolley went to court to preserve their property, saying their shacks were "equipped with modern sanitary conveniences," and claiming they should be compensated for the $72 yearly rent they earned from each building. Further, Woolley protested that evicting his indigent tenants would cause them severe hardship, since most of the families' breadwinners worked in the Alaskan canneries and were paid only once a year. The owners were granted an injunction against demolition at the end of January 1912.[12]

As late as September of that year, the Exposition still was attempting to have the shacks on Austin's land condemned, but Health Officer R. G. Brodrick reminded Director of Works Harris Connick of the injunction, saying it prevented his department from "taking further action in this matter." After filing suit against Austin, the Exposition negotiated a settlement in January 1913 and paid her $23,333—about $1.08 million in 2012—for the earthquake shacks.[13]

Although the PPIE was required to purchase some of the shacks, its conspiracy with the Department of Health succeeded. Excepting those on the Austin property, many shacks were condemned to facilitate the Fair's construction. In the end, the Fair got its land and Mrs. Austin got her money. This was likely of little comfort to the hundred or more impoverished families who lost their homes as a result.

These earthquake cottages lined the south side of Bay Street. The PPIE tried to have them condemned to avoid paying owners Horace Woolley and Kate Austin for the structures. The Exposition lost in court and had to pay $23,333 for 119 buildings. (San Francisco History Center, San Francisco Public Library)

PRESIDIO AGREEMENT

Though San Francisco had stipulated it would ask for no federal assistance in creating the Exposition, the Harbor View site depended on gaining permission from the US government to use portions of the Presidio and eighteen acres of Fort Mason. After obtaining congressional approval in February 1912, Secretary of War Henry L. Stimson empowered the Exposition to use 287 acres of the Presidio, which constituted a little over 45 percent of the entire 635 acres of the Fair. As with much of the PPIE, a portion of the Presidio shoreline had to be filled to support many structures, including part of the Palace of Fine Arts, most of the state buildings and national pavilions, the stadium, the livestock exhibits, the racetrack, and the athletic fields.[14]

LEGACY OF THE BURNHAM PLAN FOR SAN FRANCISCO

The novel site plan for the Panama-Pacific International Exposition grew from seeds sown a decade earlier in a visionary design for the improvement of San Francisco. In 1905 the Association for the Improvement and Adornment of San Francisco tasked famed planner Daniel H. Burnham with developing a plan to beautify the City by the Bay. Burnham, called "the architect of the Chicago World's Fair and the maker of cities," offered a scheme built on old-world precedents used by cities like Paris and Vienna.[15]

Burnham advocated the principles of the "City Beautiful" movement, which sought social reform through urban improvements. City Beautiful exponents favored Beaux-Arts style, which was, in part, a codification of urban renewals implemented in Paris from 1853 to 1870 by Georges-Eugène Haussmann on behalf of Napoleon III. The style featured long, straight boulevards that emphasized focal points with architecture and monuments.

The "Report on a Plan for San Francisco," completed by Burnham in September 1905, featured a series of concentric rings radiating from the new Civic Center and sliced by axial boulevards, a design that provided at least

This rendering shows a small portion of the 287 acres of Presidio lands used for the Fair. The Presidio was the site of the racetrack (left), the livestock complex (center), and the state and foreign buildings (right). (Seligman Family Foundation)

a partial remedy for the existing orthogonal grid unfeelingly draped across the city's steep topography. On the drawings, the diagonal roads were clearly visible, but the planned "rings" succumbed to hilly geographic reality and became almost indiscernible.

The hills of San Francisco would be accessed via contour roadways, garnished with terraced parks and crowned with special monuments— an observatory on Telegraph Hill, a casino on Sutro Heights, and an "Athenæum" on Twin Peaks. A grand artery studded with parks and glades would girdle the waterfront all the way to the Presidio, while the panhandle of Golden Gate Park would be extended east to Van Ness Avenue. Mission Street would be widened and connected to El Camino Real, running down the peninsula in a fashion echoing the designs of not only Haussmann but also Pierre Charles L'Enfant, who had prepared a conceptual plan for Washington, DC, in the late eighteenth century.

Historian Robert Cherny writes, "All in all, [Burnham's] master plan was not economically feasible, not practical, not even very original. Monumental in its assumptions and objectives, however, it may be best understood as a lesson in both beauty and order."[16]

Then the earthquake and fire offered a unique opportunity. The devastation wrought by the 1906 disaster seemed to have a silver lining—rebuilding San Francisco according to Burnham's plans could place it on par with Paris in loveliness. But the idealized layout failed to consider legal realities such as the existing lot lines and real estate ownership. James D. Phelan, the former mayor of San Francisco who had been chairman of the Association for the Adornment of San Francisco, wrote in 1918, "[The people] dropped the ideal plan in order to house themselves and rehabilitate their affairs. It was the worst time to talk about beautification. The people were thrown back to a consideration as to how again they would live and thrive."[17]

As it turned out, the very businessmen who had promoted the Burnham Plan in 1905 were in such a rush to reconstruct the city that only a few of the "Burnhamesque" artifacts materialized in the wake of the catastrophe. These included the Beaux-Arts grouping around the Civic Center plaza, the widening of 19th Avenue and Geary Boulevard, and the new Romanesque wharves along the Embarcadero.

THE BLOCK PLAN

While Burnham's grandiose plan was fading, its legacy was waxing in a different "dream city" on the northern shore of San Francisco. Many of the men who had promoted the Burnham Plan were now in positions of power in the hierarchy of the Exposition.

When the Whole City Plan for the PPIE was introduced in July 1911, directors John Barneson, I. W. Hellman, Jr., and Andrew M. Davis credited Burnham's ideas as a partial inspiration. Willis Polk, chairman of the Executive Architectural Council, immediately suggested that Edward Bennett, who had assisted Burnham with the 1905 report, be retained to prepare an overall plan for the Jewel City, which came to be known as the Block Plan, or sometimes the Court Plan. The central portion of the Block Plan was strongly Beaux-Arts, featuring defined axes, symmetry, uniform cornice heights, and a neoclassical planning vocabulary including fountains, reflecting pools, parterre gardens, colonnades, and monumental statuary.

A system of "palaces and courts" was devised in which the eight central palaces were similar in plan but differed in façade detail and were separated by grand courts. Each was to be designed by a different architect. Three main avenues split the block north and south, and one east-west. In the formal gardens south of these palaces and courts, two domed structures faced each other across fountains and neatly patterned flowerbeds.

This layout of the exhibit palaces differed significantly from the three previous American fairs. While the expositions at Chicago, Buffalo, and St. Louis had striven for a unified appearance, they still consisted of buildings of individual character set within a plan. Thus

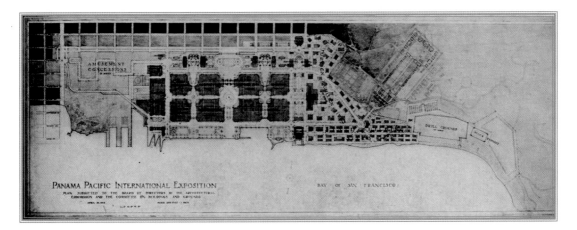

Edward H. Bennett, who had worked with Daniel Burnham on a 1905 plan for San Francisco, collaborated with the PPIE's architects to prepare the novel, Beaux Arts–influenced Block Plan for the Exposition. (*San Francisco Architectural Club Yearbook*, 1913)

the walled citadel conceived for San Francisco was a distinctive departure. At the Columbian Exposition of 1893, unity was achieved via uniform white color, cornice heights, and neoclassical forms. The 1901 and 1904 fairs used more color but otherwise largely conformed to Chicago's design precedents.

In San Francisco, where widely spaced palaces might have been better from a fire-protection standpoint, the designers decided on a different plan. Taking note that at the 1904 Louisiana Purchase Exposition visitors had become exhausted by the great distances between buildings—as much as 400 feet—the PPIE implemented special fire protection precautions to allow the palaces to be placed about 150 feet apart.

Beyond its adherence to Beaux-Arts ideals, the compact system of courts had notable advantages, one of which was that the famously mild California climate can become not-so-mild, and the walled citadel would provide shelter from wind and fog. The architects even consulted meteorology professor Alexander McAdie about the direction in which to orient the main axes of the Block Plan to take advantage of local weather patterns.

Since the courts, rather than the buildings, would define the space; the voids carved by the five major courts dictated the volumes of the exhibit palaces rather than vice-versa. This "inside-out" approach harkened to Mediterranean and Middle Eastern precedents in which the courtyards were designed to shield inhabitants from hot winds and scorching sun. Polk joked that the PPIE would be the first example of courts designed to "shut out the cold, piercing windy fogs that sweep in through the Golden Gate and keep our city so healthful and clean."[18]

There was one other feature of the Harbor View site that made a coherent, formal plan desirable. It was the first American world's fair that could be easily viewed from above, specifically from the hills of San Francisco that rose abruptly along its southern edge.

THE ARCHITECTS

The PPIE directors naturally wanted to retain the very best architects, not only to create a beautiful Fair but also to attract the interest of the nation. Their top choice, however, was a man whose polarizing personality jeopardized the design of San Francisco's beloved Palace of Fine Arts and spurred the resignation of several colleagues.

The San Francisco chapter of the American Institute of Architects (AIA) was solicited for a list of men to advise on the selection of architects for the Fair. The chapter's 129 members nominated a list of twelve, from which they finally recommended William Curlett, John Galen Howard, Albert Pissis, Willis Polk, and Clarence R. Ward. The PPIE Board of Directors promptly appointed all five on August 5, 1911, to be the Architectural Advisory Council, under the stipulation that the council would be allowed to select its own chair.

Less than four weeks later, on August 30, Exposition president Charles C. Moore was asked to make this committee permanent and to appoint Willis Polk as its chairman, contradicting the earlier stipulation of self-governance. Members of the resultant Executive Architectural Council would not themselves design Exposition structures but would preside over an eventual roster of twelve designers.

Polk had executed commissions for several PPIE officials and investors and had designed homes for both William Crocker and his nephew Charles T. Crocker. But though Polk was popular in some circles, he could be abrasive. Stories of his drinking and brawling misadventures were often featured in the society pages. As historian Richard Longstreth notes, Polk "had a great gift for insulting people." *Architect and Engineer of California* called him "the stormy petrel."[19, 20]

The Exposition's management had not reckoned with Polk's tempestuous professional relationships, and architects Curlett, Howard, and Pissis declared they would not serve if Polk was put in charge. Howard said his decision to quit was "irrevocable" if Polk was chair, and all three "respectfully suggested" the Exposition reconsider Polk's appointment. When the

The planning team of the PPIE included: (back row, l. to r.) Clarence Ward, Karl Bitter, Alexander "Stirling" Calder, Robert Farquhar, Henry Bacon, Louis Christian Mullgardt, and Jules Guérin; (front row, l. to r.) Harris D. H. Connick, William S. Richardson, William R. Mead, George W. Kelham, Theodore Blake (of Carrère & Hastings), Willis Polk, Arthur Brown, Jr., Clarence E. Howard (an associate of Edward Bennett), Edward H. Bennett, John McLaren, and William B. Faville. (Donna Ewald Huggins)

Exposition Company would not change its stance, the three declined their appointments on September 11. After this contretemps, Polk vowed he would not seek to design any part of the Exposition, though eventually he was assigned the Palace of Fine Arts.[21, 22]

Neither Curlett nor Pissis was actively involved in the PPIE, but apparently Howard had burned no bridges by resigning. In collaboration with John Reid, Jr., and Frederick H. Meyer, he received the commission for the Exposition Auditorium, located at the downtown Civic Center, where many conferences were held in conjunction with the Fair. Now known as the Bill Graham Civic Auditorium, this building was the only structure built for the Exposition that was intended as a permanent improvement.

In the wake of the resignations, the Buildings and Grounds Committee added another local architect, William Faville of Bliss & Faville, who

had tied for thirteenth place in the AIA voting, and thus the Executive Architectural Council became a three-man body, with each one assigned the design of a major structure at the Exposition. Ward was given the Palace of Machinery and Faville the overall design of the eight-building central block. This group recommended on December 11, 1911, that the Whole City Plan be abandoned in favor of the much smaller and more cost-effective Harbor View site.

The Department of Architecture was placed under the auspices of the Department of Works, headed by engineer Harris D. H. Connick, described as a "human dynamo" by Exposition director John Britton. Connick's right-hand man was Arthur H. Markwart, chief of construction, who was likewise respected. William Faville later said that if Connick and Markwart had not been sympathetic to the architects' goals, "the result might have been disastrous...." Instead,

Faville praised the engineers for lightening the load on the architects by removing responsibility for construction details, thus freeing them to concentrate on architecture and aesthetics.[23, 24]

Thereafter, Polk's status as head of the Executive Architectural Council was somewhat "defanged." *Architect and Engineer of California* said that Faville, Ward, and Connick "outvote Polk whenever they please—which is most of the time." Though relations on the Executive Architectural Council and the eventual Architectural Commission were cordial, Polk was not finished creating drama for the Exposition.[25]

Those invited by President Moore in January 1912 to serve on the Architectural Commission would attend three conferences in San Francisco, originally scheduled for February, May, and August 1912. Drawings were to be completed by the first of November, to leave as much time as possible for construction. The first conference of the Architectural Commission began on February 19. From New York came Henry Bacon, Thomas Hastings of the firm Carrère & Hastings, and William Symmes Richardson of McKim, Mead & White. Southern California was represented by Robert Farquhar of Los Angeles and by Polk, Ward, Faville, Louis Christian Mullgardt, Arthur Brown, Jr., and George W. Kelham from the San Francisco Bay Area.

With this roster of architects, it was clear that Beaux-Arts would influence the layout of the Jewel City. Though the buildings themselves would be more eclectic, virtually every man had a Beaux-Arts or City Beautiful pedigree. Bay Area architect Vernon DeMars, who was seven years old during the PPIE, said of his predecessors, "[A]ll of the architects talked the same language at that time. It was done in the Beaux Arts, and they would never get a chance to build anything as big and stupendous as all this."[26]

Once the Fair opened, University of California art professor Eugen Neuhaus wrote, "The Burnham Plan for San Francisco was such an unrealized dream, but here the dream has achieved concrete form."[27]

THE DESIGNS COALESCE

At the February 1912 meeting, the architects toured the site and pored over Bennett's many options for the Block Plan, then each sketched his own ideas. Draftsmen worked around the clock making revisions until finally the best of each was incorporated and a draft plan accepted. From its inception to completion, about 150 versions of the plan were explored.

On the last day of the meeting, the men chose who would design which buildings. Architects are not generally famed for their humility, and those selected to design world's fairs were at the top of the profession, with egos to match. These architects, however, did not aggressively vie for the most desirable buildings but actually took pains to allow their confrères the choicest commissions.

Polk said later, "The assignment of the work to the various architects was interesting. Each stood back and refused to take the pick. Mr. Hastings gave Mr. Ward the Machinery Palace; Mr. Mullgardt gave Mr. Bacon the Court of the Four Seasons...." After the meeting, the Eastern architects boarded trains for New York, and from there they worked with those who had adjacent commissions via mail and telegram.[28]

The second Architectural Commission conference, originally slated for May, still had not taken place by mid-June, and PPIE president Moore was growing concerned. As the head of such a vast enterprise, he could not afford to allow the architects to expend extra months on design that would shorten an already tight construction schedule. The filling of Harbor View was nearly complete, permission for the PPIE to use the Presidio had been granted, and he wanted construction begun. When William Faville explained that the next meeting would be convened in about two months, Moore railed against "this everlasting 60 days."[29]

Another month passed, and Moore's anxiety escalated. On July 19 he sent a letter to each architect asking for an update and guarantees that the drawings would be complete by the next meeting of the Architectural Commission, scheduled for the second week of August. While most of the men responded that their drawings would be ready, Polk's letter was vague about his design for the Palace of Fine Arts. Moore was annoyed by Polk's evasiveness and sent several more requests for commitment and even met with him in person. Finally he sent his secretary, Joseph Cumming, to lean on the architect for assurance that the blueprints would be ready.

While Polk was known for his fractious personality, his reluctance to produce his plans was likely because he was covering up his struggles with the assignment. The site for the Palace of Fine Arts was a swampy tarn, and Polk was stymied. Finally, Polk called upon his friend Bernard Maybeck, whom he'd known since the 1880s, to come work on the Exposition. Maybeck was a respected architect who had completed many residential commissions in addition to larger projects, including a grand residence for Phoebe Apperson Hearst, the Bohemian Club's Grove Clubhouse, the Faculty Club and the first Hearst Women's Gymnasium at the University of California, and most recently the tour-de-force 1913 Church of Christ, Scientist, in Berkeley. Further, he had studied for five years at the École des Beaux-Arts in France. Maybeck was regarded as rather eccentric, and although he was well known in the East Bay, he was less so in San Francisco and was not even mentioned on the list of 129 men considered for the original Executive Architectural Council.

Maybeck was hired the first week of August, not as an architect but rather a "designer in the drafting room," at a rate of $400 per month. The timing certainly was not coincidental. Polk, in desperation, asked Maybeck to see what he could do with the project. Over a weekend, Maybeck executed a romantic rendering. According to fellow Bay Area architect Walter Steilberg, Maybeck rolled out his drawings on Polk's desk and said, "[T]his thing you call a mudhole, that's your opportunity: you can make a reflecting mirror of that."[30]

When the Architectural Commission met again beginning August 13, the men presented their most recent design sketches for approval and made any minor revisions necessary to the Block Plan. Among five designs presented for the Palace of Fine Arts, one outshone the others—a haunting gray-and-black charcoal sketch depicting an open rotunda embraced by graceful, arcing colonnades. While loosely executed, the composition exuded melancholy grandeur. Several decades later, Maybeck recalled the power of his original drawing: "How important spirit is in architecture. There were many drawings and some fine designs, but when Henry Bacon saw this charcoal rendering, he was immediately impressed. So I received the commission, because the drawing reflected the spirit of the building. That is the essence of architecture…."[31]

Architect Bernard Maybeck's evocative, moody sketch for the Palace of Fine Arts won him the commission and became his most famous design. (*Universal Exposition[;] San Francisco 1915* (viewbook))

The architects congratulated Polk on his singular vision, but Polk had a surprise for them. The design was not his, he told them, but Maybeck's, and he felt Maybeck ought to be engaged to finish the design. The commission agreed wholeheartedly.

The president, however, was irked by Polk's high-handed reassignment of the Palace of Fine Arts to Maybeck. Moore wrote several scathing letters to William H. Crocker, chair of the Buildings and Grounds Committee, condemning Polk's appointment of Maybeck as an "impropriety" and "not a gift for him to confer."[32, 33]

While it seems the primary cause of Moore's indignation was that he had not been consulted or notified, he also was concerned that the Exposition would have to pay Maybeck's fee in addition to that of Polk. He wrote, "The fee to be paid to Mr. Polk under the agreement included his services for preparing the design for one of the exhibit palaces. In the present state of our finances it is more than essential that we must get value received...." And though he acknowledged Maybeck's "skill and standing" within architectural circles, he said the Exposition architects had also been selected for their publicity value, which suggests that Moore did not believe Maybeck's renown was as great as Polk's.[34, 35]

At the Buildings and Grounds Committee's next meeting, Polk tried to assuage Moore's concerns. He explained that of the five designs submitted for the Palace of Fine Arts, only Maybeck's "met with universal approval" from the Architectural Commission. Further, Polk said that he, as the architect originally assigned to the project, would pay Maybeck's fee. Moore was placated and the creation of San Francisco's most beloved Panama-Pacific International Exposition building was launched.[36]

Polk, however, was suddenly left without a PPIE commission. Maybeck thanked him in a letter that said, "You have put up a monument to your ideals and made a sacrifice for them—there is in you a yearning for the highest ideal." This episode marked another diminution of Polk's role in the Fair. George Kelham was appointed chief of the Department of Architecture and took over day-to-day management of the design process, and while Polk continued to work for the Exposition, his responsibilities were minimal. Polk himself alluded to this marginalization in 1914, when he told the *Santa Barbara Morning Press*, "I am 'out of it' up there. I wanted to run everything my own way and they wouldn't let me do it!"[37, 38]

When Designers' Day was celebrated exactly one week after the Exposition opened, neither Polk nor Edward Bennett (creator of the Block Plan) received the bronze plaques awarded the other architects and the chiefs of sculpture, landscape, and color. When the other architects complained of the omission, President Moore said the honor recognized only those who had created "various elements of the architectural picture." Buildings and Grounds Committee chairman William Crocker responded, asking why "those who conceived the entire picture" were not among the painters of Moore's "architectural picture." Then, on behalf of the Buildings and Grounds Committee, he gave Moore two choices: recognize Polk's and Bennett's contributions or expressly deny they'd made any.

In June, Moore sent silver medallions to the two men with a letter that read in part, "I feel it proper on behalf of the Exposition to give you this recognition, and I take much pleasure in sending to you a medal, which I trust will give you the same pleasure in receiving it as it affords us in giving it to you."[39, 40]

After their second conference in 1912, the architects gained momentum. Their designs were nearly complete, but still there were obstacles. The architects were asked to curtail their budgets as much as possible, which was a difficult task. Robert Farquhar was asked to reduce the cost of the Festival Hall to $200,000, which he was unable to do while retaining its 3,000-person seating capacity. The cost of the building eventually came in at $270,000.

Within the constraints of time and budget, the work was progressing well. Architect Mullgardt said that he wanted to "get all the life, color and animation and suggestiveness of the joy of living" within his Court of Abundance, which he preferred to call the Court of Ages. Henry Bacon wrote from New York that if his Court of the Four Seasons was not successful, he'd "kick himself to China."[41, 42]

After drawings were presented at the final conference of the Architectural Commission, during the first week of December, it was but four short weeks until the gala groundbreaking for the Palace of Machinery, held on New Year's Day 1913.

Other design appointments came thick and fast through 1912. Chief of Architecture George Kelham was sent to New York in July to parlay with illustrator Jules Guérin and sculptors Karl Bitter and Alexander "Stirling" Calder. Guérin was engaged as director of color, and Bitter and Calder would run the sculpture department.

COLOR

Jules Guérin already was a celebrated illustrator when he was appointed director of color for the PPIE. He had studied painting in Paris, where his ability as a colorist became evident. His early career was as a scenic artist for the theater, from which he gradually ascended the ranks to become a noted set designer for spectacular productions like Shakespeare's *Antony and Cleopatra*. As he moved into illustration, magazines clamored for his work.

As an architectural renderer, he had been hired by Charles McKim of McKim, Mead & White to illustrate the McMillan Plan for Washington, DC, in 1902, after which Daniel Burnham retained him to paint perspectives for the 1907 plan of Chicago. He'd also executed views of the 1893, 1901, and 1904 American world's fairs, as well as the smaller 1905 Lewis and Clark Exposition in Portland, Oregon. By 1912 he was creating murals for Exposition architect Henry Bacon's planned Lincoln Memorial. With this résumé, it is no wonder the designers of the Jewel City wanted him to color their Exposition.

The *Century Magazine* had sponsored Guérin's trips to continental Europe, Egypt, Syria, Italy, and Greece in the first decade of the twentieth century as research for a series of illustrated articles that subsequently were made into books. The resultant plates were resplendent in tones of glowing gold, complemented with azure skies, vermilion accents, and violet shadows. On these trips he also absorbed the fact that ancient civilizations had used brilliant polychrome in their architecture, not the bleached white of their ruins.

Guérin's color schema for the Fair, inspired by these journeys, ultimately comprised ivory, gray, golden orange, oxidized copper green, cerulean blue, three variations of "Pompeian Red," and several other tints. Every area of the Exposition was required to conform to the palette, right down to the guards' uniforms. The bottoms of

Director of Color Jules Guérin likened his color plan for the Fair to "a Persian rug of soft melting tones," an inspiration evident in this aerial view taken at 1,500 feet from aviator Silas Christofferson's airplane. (*Natural Color Views of the Panama-Pacific International Exposition* (viewbook))

The great South Gardens are viewed from the top of the Festival Hall. Directly opposite, beyond the central Fountain of Energy, is the domed Palace of Horticulture. On the left are the twin Press (near) and YWCA (far) Buildings. To the right of the lawns is the stately Avenue of Palms and the sixty-five-foot-tall wall of the palace block, at the center of which is the forty-three-story Tower of Jewels. (Donna Ewald Huggins)

pools were painted blue; the murals, electric light standards, and floral plantings reflected the director of color's choices; and the road surfaces were treated with roasted Monterey beach sand to create a pinkish hue. Even the trash cans were given a coat of faux travertine. Critic William Woollett said, "You feel that you are looking at one of Jules Guérin's prints...."[43]

Creamy façades were accented by columns mimicking the rarest red and green marbles. The great domes at the intersections of the palace aisles were weathered turquoise, while those capping each corner were burnt orange. The back walls of the stately alabaster colonnades were washed in light vermilion, while the ceilings of the ambulatories were celestial blue studded with an orderly line of golden stars. An asbestos and asphaltum fabric embedded with crushed brick was rolled onto the roofs of the palaces, and the parapets of the high walls were

topped with terra-cotta tiles. The flagpoles were painted an orange-pink. When local flag makers told Guérin they could not create his desired shades, he said, "Very well, we'll start up a dye works of our own."[44]

The color plan helped resolve a number of design challenges, foremost among them providing additional unity among the disparate styles of the courts. "The great problem," Guérin explained, "was to 'pull together' structures of different designs by means of the color...."[45]

The specific pigments selected for the finishes and murals were calculated to look good under Walter D'Arcy Ryan's new lighting scheme. At a conference of the muralists, artist Edward Simmons noted "cobalt disappears under any artificial light; cerulean blue stays." Lastly, "fiscal appeal" was considered: "Colors affect the spirits," Guérin remarked. "To make the dominant colors purple or blue—it would ruin [the Exposition] financially. Such colors make even the worst spendthrift close-fisted."[46, 47]

Reception of Guérin's color plan was generally rhapsodic, but, as with any artistic undertaking, there were naysayers. William Woollett thought the coloration of the Tower of Jewels destroyed its architectural unity, but he praised the Courts of the Four Seasons and of Ages for their more restrained tints. Even the pundits at the satirical magazine the *Wasp* conceded that the color plan was nearly universally acclaimed, and "it is just the proper thing to rave about the color scheme of the Exposition," though it also said that some artists admitted, "I loathe it, but I wouldn't wish to be quoted as saying so."[48]

TRAVERTINE

Guérin's subtle colors required a neutral canvas. He envisioned a background tone like the monuments of ancient Rome, and thought of the warm, light-honey-colored travertine quarried near Tivoli. Because it is deposited by precipitation of mineral springs, travertine is durable, yet lighter than marble. Its surface is not smooth but striated and features gaps, inclusions, and bubbles; the makers of the Exposition wanted to capture the weathered character lent by travertine to Italian edifices.

William Symmes Richardson of McKim, Mead & White recalled the treatment of the firm's recently completed Pennsylvania Station, which had a Roman baths architectural motif. The wainscoting of the station was of genuine travertine, but using actual stone to finish the walls and vaulted ceilings of the grand waiting hall would have been far too costly. They hired Paul Denivelle, described as "a happy combination of the artist and artisan," to create a finish that would simulate real limestone. The substitute developed by Denivelle was so convincing that Guérin himself had been fooled while he worked on murals for the station. Richardson recommended Denivelle formulate a version especially for the Jewel City.[49]

The entire color plan hinged on the success of the imitation stone, but there was a huge difference between the few tons of colored plaster

used inside Penn Station and the twenty-five to thirty tons needed for the PPIE. Not only would the faux travertine be applied to exterior surfaces, which had to withstand at least two years of weather, but the sculpture department needed a version capable of being molded into the most intricate of architectural ornaments and statuary.

Among the problems to be surmounted was creating a uniform color across hundreds of train carloads of material. Denivelle wanted the pigment mixed at the source, but gypsum suppliers resisted. They worried that producing a colored amalgam in the same factory would ruin their standard offerings, or that they would "go broke" creating an experimental product made to perform as needed on the great palaces. Finally, Denivelle convinced the president of the Nephi Plaster and Manufacturing Company in Utah of the feasibility of the process.[50]

This proved an effective partnership, as the Nephi gypsum was dense, pure, and non-crystalline. Before leaving Utah, the gypsum was mixed with asbestos fiber, wood pulp, and silicate of alumina, which limited expansion and added plasticity and weather-fastness. This concoction was called "hardwall," and it formed the base material for seven different formulas for various uses at the Fair.

The versatile faux travertine developed by Paul Denivelle was formed into everything from architectural sculpture, such as Albert Laessle's dignified lions, to striated wall surfaces, varicolored "marble" columns, and the fancy ornaments adorning the portals. (Laura Ackley)

Between thirty and eighty pounds of pigment—raw sienna, French ochre, burnt sienna, and raw umber—were added at the mills to each ton of hardwall to create the standard travertine shade. There were also special admixtures to simulate Numidian yellow, Sienna red, brown, black, and green marbles. Compounds created at each plant were checked against those from other facilities to ensure consistent coloration.

When the hardwall reached the Exposition site, contractors created several formulae for different uses around the Fair. For the high walls of the palaces, a "scratch coat" of uncolored hardwall embedded with hemp fiber was applied, then finished with a coat of colored material mixed with sand, hydrated lime, and water. This topcoat was stippled using special brushes to simulate stratifications, then troweled over to create a smooth, hard finish with natural-looking irregularities. Variations in the scale of texture were based on the scale of the objects. The grandeur of the Palace of Fine Arts called for a large, deeply modeled texture, whereas in smaller, more detailed objects and ornaments, the travertine pattern was correspondingly more delicate.

A little faith was required for molded ornaments like cornices, medallions, and fluted column drums. Denivelle taught the workmen a complex casting process, which they had to follow exactly, all the while unable to see the result until each piece was unmolded. Negative molds were built, into which were sprayed dark and light veins of liquid hardwall from cans with multiple-veining nozzles. Care was taken that the veining ran horizontally on every finished piece, no matter how elaborate.

Chief of Construction Arthur Markwart said each unmolded cast showed "stratifications, color veinings and variegated indentations. The indentations occurred at all points where the semi-dry mixture was placed on the mould, the whole giving the general effect of the chemically precipitated stone it was intended to imitate."[51]

In a ceremony held after the Fair opened between the softly radiant walls he helped create, Denivelle was awarded a commemorative bronze plaque for his contributions.

SCULPTURE

The moment they entered the grounds, visitors encountered not only lovely gardens and impressive buildings but also giant sculptures of heroic figures and whimsical animals. For the great architectural sculptures adorning the structures or placed artfully about the courts, a version of the travertine was concocted that was nearly as malleable as modeling clay.

Artists also had formed the mock travertine into supple balustrades, elegant bas-reliefs, and exuberant finials. Such details appeared throughout the palaces and courts. The colonnades of the Palace of Horticulture were borne upon the heads of solemn caryatids surmounted by deep, scrolled pediments draped in flower garlands of faux stone. Graceful ovoid urns with sinuous handles stood on walls bordered with deeply incised Greek motifs under the rotunda of the Palace of Fine Arts. An Exposition worthy of being called "International" also needed minarets and medallions, friezes and fountains, consoles and cartouches, and the Department of Sculpture provided them all. Beyond such architectural encrustation, about 820 large figurative statues bedecked the grounds.

Chief of Sculpture Karl Bitter, anointed at the architects' conference in August 1912, planned the integration of sculpture into the design of the PPIE. Bitter had begun his world's fair career as a sculptor for the 1893 Columbian Exposition in Chicago, and he had served as director of sculpture for the 1901 Pan-American Exposition in Buffalo and as chief of the Department of Sculpture for the 1904 Louisiana Purchase Exposition in St. Louis.

The lean, dark-haired man, with an opulent mustache and pointed beard, had developed several themes for the sculptural program and they were quickly adopted. He suggested that figures of explorers would provide an engaging historical background; this was realized in the equestrian statues *Pizarro*, by Charles Niehaus, and *Cortez*, by Charles Carey Rumsey, at the base of the Tower of Jewels. For the central Court of the Universe, he sought more tranquil features, including figures atop columns within the court representing sunrise and sunset, and groups representing the East and the West on the triumphal arches on either side. These eventually became the Columns of the Rising and Setting Sun, by Adolph Weinman, and the great ensembles *Nations of the East* and *Nations of the West*, collaborations by Stirling Calder, Frederick Roth, and Leo Lentelli.

Bitter also wanted to solve several problems of earlier fairs: inflated demand for artists, overcrowding of sculpture, viewer fatigue, and the logistical challenges of assembling such behemoth statuary. His experience told him to employ the best sculptors as soon as possible, because as the Exposition's opening drew near, exhibitors and concessionaires would want to hire these same artists for their booths and pavilions. By starting early, he said, "we will get the best men and at reasonable wages."[52]

One of Bitter's guiding principles was that sculpture needed to be given breathing space. He said Frederick MacMonnies' *Columbian Fountain* at the 1893 Chicago exposition was acclaimed because of its isolation on a barge in the lagoon, while at other expositions, "for instance St. Louis, where a great deal of sculpture was heaped together, the effect desired was lost."[53]

The chief of sculpture also wished to highlight the theme of the PPIE: the opening of the Panama Canal. He decided to place a prominent sculptural feature just inside the main gates. His initial suggestion of two large groups of equestrian figures "tearing the continents asunder" to form the Panama Canal was not implemented, but in their place stood the Fountain of Energy by Stirling Calder. Water splashed from the top of a large globe into a basin in which figures representing the oceans of the world gamboled. Atop the globe on a prancing steed rode the Lord of the Isthmian Way, his outstretched arms pushing the continents apart.

For the Buffalo and St. Louis expositions, most of the large sculptures were created in New York, then shipped to the sites. Many of the planned PPIE sculptures were immense—the top of the canopied seat on the elephant of the *Nations of the East* was forty-two feet above the pachyderm's soles, and the humans in the group stood more

than thirteen feet tall—and it was clear that such massive, fragile pieces could not be moved safely across the continent to San Francisco.

Bitter had another solution for this problem. He was so busy with commissions in New York, he felt unable to assume full responsibility for the Exposition's sculpture, so he suggested his friend Stirling Calder be named acting chief of sculpture. In practice, this meant that Calder directed operations in San Francisco while from New York Bitter supervised the selection of top sculptors, solicited creation of the smaller models of the statuary, called "maquettes," and oversaw their shipment to California. The leading artists selected by Bitter included Isidore Konti, Robert Aitken, Haig Patigian, Daniel Chester French, Charles Niehaus, Bruno Zimm, Adolph Weinman, and James Earle Fraser. They were paid between a few hundred dollars for a small model from a lesser-known sculptor to more than $2,000 for a major work from a more established artist.

Maquettes between three and four feet tall were enlarged into massive architectural sculptures for the Fair, including these figures ready for hoisting onto the Tower of Jewels. (Jim Caddick)

The small partial maquette of a bull, left, is being enlarged by a sculptor onto the framework in the foreground. The bent metal rails form the armature for the animal's hind legs. (Edward A. Rogers)

Calder moved to San Francisco for two years, where he supervised the cadre of artisans in the three "staff shops" on the grounds of the Fair. These men enlarged the reference maquettes into full-sized versions. In San Francisco Calder retained Leo Lentelli and Frederick H. G. Roth as his assistants. Many young artists also came from the East Coast to work on the statuary, including Marius Azzi, Max Kalish, and Beniamino Bufano. Bufano eventually settled permanently in California and his works became Bay Area favorites.

Once the maquettes, which averaged about three to four feet tall, reached San Francisco, they were usually sliced into smaller pieces for enlargement using a three-dimensional pointing machine called a pantograph. Robert Treat Paine, sculptor and inventor of the "Sculpto-point" pantograph, directed sculptors in use of his device. Previously limited to about 50 points, a sculptor could reproduce up to 1,000 points a day using the Sculpto-point.

For each sculptural fragment, the artists built a crude armature of lumber, pipe, or bent steel rail covered in wire mesh, which was filled in with plaster to create the basic form, not exceeding the boundaries of the final object. Next, a grid of nails was pounded into the structure, leaving the nail heads above the surface. The sculptors placed one end of the Sculpto-point on the surface of the maquette piece, and its corresponding arm would indicate the correct location on the finished sculpture. If the nail head was too high, it was hammered in; if it was too short, a longer nail was substituted. The slender iron arm of the Sculpto-point caressed the surface of the smaller model until the nail heads of the larger model correctly mirrored its contours.

The resultant partial sculptures were distinctly unbeautiful—their rough, tawny surfaces bristling with exposed nails. But their coverall-clad attendants toiled diligently as the creations grew ever larger and smoother as they were coated with faux travertine.

The creators were dwarfed by a Brobding-nagian body shop of limbs, faces, and wings as elephants, bulls, walruses, lions, eagles, and all manner of gods and goddesses took shape beneath their hands. Finally the men ascended plaster-spattered ladders to assemble the finished components and smooth the seams between the pieces. Most of the statuary was finished in the same ivory shade as the palaces, but those works that were near the viewer were a simulated bronze likened to "the color of blue eucalyptus," while those that were "far away and free standing" were golden in hue.[54]

A twenty-ton crane with a thirty-five-foot boom and an additional extension pole lifted statuary destined for heights under eighty feet. For higher elements, a special hoisting tackle was used. The Tower of Jewels sported sculpture all the way to its 435-foot apex, where it was crowned by four Atlas figures supporting an armillary sphere.

Sunset magazine said, "Now, above creamy colonnades and frescoed cornices, angels are flying to proud perches by domes and minarets. Painting derricks are hoisting the Exposition sculpture into place—angels and goddesses and fairies, artisans, explorers and pioneers are taking their places on pedestals and in niches, overlooking roof and garden and spreading green lawn beside the greater spread of the blue bay."[55]

A commemorative booklet distributed by the Owl Drug Company bragged, "No conquest ever brought to Rome such statuary as the $300,000 collection…at the Panama-Pacific International Exposition. Every work tells a tale—discovery, event, accomplishment, aspiration."[56]

On Designers' Day in February 1915, Bitter and Calder were honored along with colorist Guérin and the Exposition's architects. Bitter then returned to New York, where in April he and his wife attended a performance at the Metropolitan Opera House. As they stepped onto Broadway to catch an uptown streetcar, a taxi pulled away, and another car swerved around it, striking and killing Bitter, who, according to a report in the *New York Times*, pushed his wife clear of the oncoming vehicle.

Calder and writer Stella Perry dedicated their book *The Sculpture and Mural Decorations of the Exposition* to Bitter's memory.

MURALS

In addition to his development of the overall color plan and his creation of renderings for the Architectural Commission, Guérin became the "conductor of a pictorial orchestra," its players the nine prominent artists selected to paint large murals for the Exposition. These were Robert Reid, Edward Simmons, Frank DuMond, William de Leftwich Dodge, Charles Holloway, Childe Hassam, Arthur Mathews, Milton Herbert Bancroft, and Frank Brangwyn.

The men agreed that Guérin would dictate a palette of five colors, plus dark and light values, to which all the tones of their murals would be subordinate. Simmons endorsed this idea wholeheartedly and, recalling his experience as a young muralist for the 1893 Chicago Exposition, said, "I felt in Chicago…that everybody was going off on his own tack….It was a Tower of Babel…."[57]

In addition to the cohesive color scheme, the PPIE murals would feature another departure from previous fairs. Rather than being painted directly on the temporary Exposition buildings, the works were on canvas, which could be taken down and preserved. "Their life is not limited to the brief period of the Exposition, but will be lasting," wrote publicity man Hamilton Wright. "This has resulted in the very best efforts on the part of the artists…."[58]

While Holloway, Hassam, and Mathews were assigned only a single simple lunette apiece, several painters had mammoth works to prepare, for which they were well compensated. Robert Reid was assigned eight octagonal 23-by-27-foot panels for the raked coffers beneath the Palace of Fine Arts rotunda. Simmons and DuMond each prepared two 47-by-12-foot murals for inside the Arches of the Rising and Setting Sun. Bancroft painted eight 14-by-9-foot and two 14-by-18-foot canvases for the Court of the Four Seasons, and Frank Brangwyn eight for the Court of Ages, each 12 by 27 feet. William de Leftwich Dodge had the most gargantuan task: two great triptychs to line the arch under the Tower of Jewels, each set of three murals totaling 96 by 12 feet. The men assigned the largest murals were paid more than

$20,000, double the design fees of the highest paid members of the Architectural Commission.

As most of the men, including Guérin, were based on the East Coast, the director of color scheduled two planning meetings for April and July 1913, which he hoped all would attend. At the first meeting, only Brangwyn, who lived in England, and San Franciscan Mathews were absent. The others brought studies of their planned murals and discussed the details that would unify them. Hassam voiced his opinion that the color palette should be "joyful," while Simmons simply said he'd accept whatever Guérin chose, because "I think he ought to have control in driving a team of unruly cattle."[59]

The artists also talked over the performance properties of various pigments and how factors like weather and height above the ground would affect the appearance of their murals, and they all agreed to a range of tones.

By July many of the finished studies were completed, and the muralists were able to set desired sizes for the figures and borders of their works. They also made suggestions for each others' compositions. DuMond's peers suggested he simplify his horizon line, establish a uniform tone for the earth in each mural, and remove some extraneous details, changes he graciously implemented. As discussion of the color values continued, the group admired William de Leftwich Dodge's sea and sky colors, so they asked him to paint large samples of each, then cut up the samples and send pieces to the other artists. Likewise, Guérin prepared swatches of the darkest and lightest values he wanted to see in the paintings.

Some of the "unruly cattle" required more herding than others. It was discovered that Hassam's colors were much lighter than all his peers', and he was absent from the July meeting. Guérin lamented, "[Hassam] is a man I wanted here above all and he is not here. That is the purpose of these meetings." Later in 1913, the chief was pleased to report that Bancroft's ten panels were coming along well, that Hassam "will be practically finished with his work on arrival in San Francisco," and that Dodge's progress was "perfectly bully." But Guérin was

The vividly hued *Water,* by Frank Brangwyn, was one of the eight 12-by-27-foot murals he designed for the corners of the arcades around Louis Christian Mullgardt's Court of Ages. (Laura Ackley)

worried about Robert Reid. "In four months… he has accomplished about as much as I could do in two weeks," he wrote in exasperation.[60, 61]

All the men save local Arthur Mathews and Londoner Brangwyn met in California in January 1914, where an airy studio was set up under the lofty vaults of an aisle in the Palace of Machinery. Even though he was local, Mathews again abstained, preferring to paint in his San Francisco studio because "the concert method did not appeal to him." As the paintings neared completion, Jessie Williams wrote in *Scribner's Magazine,* "Each man's work is related by color to every other man's work, to the advantage of all concerned...."[62, 63]

INSCRIPTIONS

Porter Garnett, literary editor of the *Call*, was paid $200 to create a proposal for inscriptions to complement the courts and the sculptural program. Most inscriptions were labels for the attendant statuary, but some were purely evocative. Garnett considered several factors when choosing inscriptions, including their "cosmical, elemental or epical qualities." But most crucial was that the engravings be appreciated by "all classes of persons—the man in the crowd as well as the scholar." Garnett drew from many classical texts, but a few Greek gods were too salacious; director-in-chief of foreign and domestic participation Frederick Skiff objected to Priapus "on lines of delicacy."[64, 65]

Garnett keyed his inscriptions to the themes of each court and to the nearby architectural or sculptural features. On the Arch of the Rising Sun, which supported the great statuary group *The Nations of the East*, he chose quotations from the Persian poet Firdausi, the Arabian poet Zuhayr, the Classical Sanskrit writer Kālidāsa, Chinese philosopher Confucius, and Japanese poet Hitomaro, as well as a proverb from the Siamese (Thai) Phra Ruang dynasty. For the Arch of the Setting Sun, he chose selections from England's Shakespeare, the United States' Whitman, Spain's Cervantes, Italy's Dante, Germany's Goethe, and France's Pascal. Inscribed in the Court of the Four Seasons were excerpts from Spenser's *Faerie Queen*, reading:

> So forth issew'd the seasons of the yeare. First lusty Spring all dight in leaves and flowres. Then came the jolly Sommer being dight in a thin silken cassock coloured greene. Then came the Autumne all in yellow clad. Lastly came Winter, cloathed all in frize chattering his teeth, for cold that did him chill.[66]

The quotations selected were not always the most obvious choices. For instance, Garnett said that for a representative Persian inscription he might have simply selected something from poets better known in America, like Omar Khayyám or Hafiz, but he instead chose Firdausi, whom he asserted "was to Persian literature as Homer is to the literature of Greece." Further nuance was added by choosing poems that also suggested aspects of California or the PPIE. The Persian stanza read, "The balmy air diffuses health and fragrance. So tempered is the genial glow that we know neither heat nor cold. Tulips and hyacinths abound. Fostered by a delicious clime the earth blooms like a garden," which Garnett felt evoked the climate of California. Hitomaro's poem inscribed in the Court of the Universe called to mind the Fair's illuminations: "Our eyes and hearts uplifted seem to rest on heaven's radiance."[67]

With help from Director of Works Connick and travertine expert Denivelle, Garnett tested several different lettering sizes on partially completed structures to determine which would be most legible to passersby. For instance, the optimal font size for the great Arches of the Rising and Setting Sun was determined to be eighteen inches tall with ten inches of space between lines.

LANDSCAPE ARCHITECTURE

As the merrymakers in funicular streetcars tipped over the vertigo-inducing grade of the Fillmore Street hill, they saw below the grand entrance to the Fair, a seemingly solid wall of dark green more than two stories high and running four city blocks along Chestnut Street. Over the main gates at Scott Street, the barrier leapt upward into nine undulating, thirty-six-foot-high arches. Closer still, this portal was revealed to be an impossibly vertical hedge of *Mesembryanthemum spectabilis*—a small variety of ice plant—across which spread a blush of starlike pinkish-purple flowers in season.

This "hedge fence" was the brainchild of John McLaren, chief of landscape gardening, who had been the superintendent of Golden Gate

Park since 1886. The transplanted Scot was as "uncommunicative as an oyster" about himself but would happily discuss his work for hours. He was enlisted early in the planning process and worked closely with the architects to achieve stunning landscape effects. In managing Golden Gate Park, McLaren had overseen the transformation of thousands of acres of dunes into a verdant playground for San Francisco's citizens, and few men in the world were better suited to adapting the enormous plot of sandy bayfill into elegant Exposition gardens. He felt his work was "as much a part of the general plan as were the architecture, the color, the sculpture, and the lighting."[68, 69]

Shortly after McLaren's appointment, he started a temporary nursery in Golden Gate Park. Later in 1912 he built six greenhouses, a huge "lath house," potting sheds, and a heating plant at the Presidio, all for the cultivation of the plants that would embellish the Fair's grounds. Gardeners planted vast numbers of flowers, including 3,000 azaleas, 5,000 junipers, 8,000

rhododendrons, 60,000 veronicas, 75,000 violas, 100,000 geraniums, 400,000 pansies, and more than three-quarters of a million bulbs. He directed that 50,000 cubic yards of loam be spread over the inhospitable PPIE site for future lawns and flowerbeds.

Over the course of the Exposition, the flowers in the parterres were changed several times, and were coordinated with Jules Guérin's color scheme. The number of changes depended on the locations and the lifespans of the various blossoms. In the South Gardens, spring pansies and daffodils were succeeded by red and yellow tulips, then finally begonias of ethereal cotton-candy pink. The rotation of just these beds required more than 250,000 plants. The gardens bloomed continuously, as if by magic; one journalist wrote, "To John McLaren, nothing is impossible."[70]

Viewers were often skeptical that the many mature trees on the grounds had not stood there for decades. McLaren grew tall eucalypti and acacias from seedlings especially for the Fair. He

Some of the largest trees transplanted onto the site weighed sixteen tons. Here, a crew of men and horses moves a thirty-foot-tall palm into place at the southwest corner of the Palace of Varied Industries. (Edward A. Rogers)

also sent "scouts" throughout the region to find and acquire venerable cypress, orange, and palm trees to adorn the grounds. Many owners agreed to donate or sell the chosen plants, which were side-boxed in place and carefully tended for up to a year in advance of transplantation to the Exposition site.

Official Fair historian Frank Morton Todd said of these skeptics, "Visitors who could not believe that the great palms and eucalyptus trees surrounding the Exposition palaces were transplanted had to be told gently and firmly that the Bay had covered the whole central portion of the site when construction began; especially where some of the largest trees stood. Some believed, but many lacked faith."[71]

To build the hedge fence, McLaren had the ice plant grown flat in boxes, each measuring six by two feet and two inches deep, filled with soil, and covered with a fine wire mesh. These panels were then affixed to a vertical framework. The hedge's walls were placed eight feet apart to increase its apparent mass, and fairgoers were often startled when water sprayed from its surface, sprinkled by gardeners watering from within.

Even the guests' sense of smell was considered. The Court of Palms featured a selection of fragrant shrubs like myrtle, lavender, and verbena, while violets sprinkled on the margins of the Palace of Fine Arts Lagoon breathed their sweet, velvet fragrance into its shadowy glades.

When the first work of dredging and filling began on the PPIE site, its design team had less than three years to turn a mudflat into a spectacular world's fair. It was a task of vast and detailed scope. It required gaining permission to use land owned by the government and 175 private citizens, filling hundreds of thousands of cubic feet of waterlogged bay front, and agreeing on the best configuration of buildings. Though architect Willis Polk provided some early drama, the cooperation between some of the top architects, artists, and sculptors of the era was one of remarkable amity considering the stature of the men representing professions that demand strong opinions. From those creating the sculptures on the topmost towers to those determining the smallest blossoms in the

To construct the imposing thirty-six-foot-tall arches of the living "hedge fence," Chief of Landscape John McLaren had ice plant grown in shallow six-foot-long boxes covered in fine wire mesh, which were mounted as vertical panels on a wooden framework. (Seligman Family Foundation)

flowerbeds, they worked together to prepare a visual feast that would be served to the world starting on February 20, 1915.

BUILDING THE DREAM

"For the love of Mike—Start something and give some of the city's unemployed something to do!" [1]

So wrote a frustrated San Franciscan to the Exposition Company in March 1912, but as months flew past, visible progress remained scant. Mud and sand poured into the fill area, underground conduits were laid, and the ground was cleared, surveyed, and graded. Unfortunately, none of these kindled public ardor as had the campaign to win the Fair or the battle over which site to use. Nevertheless, these humble signs represented thousands of efforts happening in parallel in the race to complete the PPIE before Opening Day.

The recipe for the fully functioning miniature city was inscribed on 2 million square feet of blueprints. Its ingredients were 635 acres of land, much of which lay under water at high tide, mixed with 109 million linear feet of timber and 800,000 tons of other materials. These were leavened with an advanced infrastructure and kneaded together with a budget of $14,847,607 for site, administration, architecture, engineering, and construction—the equivalent of $1.54 billion in 2012.

From these components, the Division of Works hoped to concoct exquisite palaces set among sumptuous gardens and garnished with colorful plasterwork, glorious mural paintings, and finely molded architectural details. And all of this needed to rise in what was arguably the strongest construction union town in the United States. A few grandiose plans did not come to fruition, but those that did were enough to satisfy the most finicky world's fair gourmet.

THE FIRST STEPS

The year 1912 was frustrating for San Franciscans. Already they had spent several years taxing themselves and paying stock subscriptions, yet in the year since they beat New Orleans to become the world's fair site, they had seen few physical changes along the bay. Not until February was the Harbor View site formally selected, and only in April did filling of the underwater portion begin. The balance of the year was spent laying more groundwork, literally and figuratively.

The minutes of the Buildings and Grounds Committee give a sense of the flow of tasks, which must have seemed glacial to the uninitiated. First were hundreds of lease negotiations, along with a handful of land purchases and a few condemnation lawsuits to dislodge recalcitrant owners. Next, the Exposition sold as many existing structures as it could (about forty) and demolished the rest. Swift construction of a sea wall was critical to enable the landing of tons of lumber at the site.

On the planning side, the lead architects settled on the final Block Plan before preparing schematic designs that would allow contractors to bid accurately on constructing the Jewel City's palaces. Finally, bids were taken and contracts awarded. Meanwhile, the Division of Works was hiring surveyors, engineers, architectural designers, draftsmen, and Chief of Construction Arthur Markwart. The chiefs of sculpture, color, and texture were appointed, as well as directors of the various exhibit departments. Landscape architect John McLaren, assisted by his son Donald, established a nursery at the Presidio and planted the twelve- to eighteen-inch-high acacia and eucalyptus seedlings that would grow to twenty and thirty feet tall by the time they were transplanted onto the Exposition grounds. The senior McLaren acquired plants from near and far, including one hundred Italian cypresses from the Oak Hill cemetery in nearby San Jose, magnolias shipped from Tennessee, and rhododendrons from West Virginia. Royal palms from Cuba, giant tree ferns from Australia, banana and olive trees from Central America to add a taste of the tropics, and 800,000 bulbs

and hyacinths from Holland would to paint the grounds with vivid color.

Several key political acts also were executed in 1912. San Francisco passed a promised $5 million city bond, augmenting private subscriptions, and the state levied a $5 million tax to pay for the Fair. The US government granted use of the necessary Presidio and Fort Mason lands and allowed a right-of-way through Fort Mason. The Exposition accelerated expansion of San Francisco's sewer system by purchasing city bonds for sewer lines that were planned for future streets across the Exposition site. New local measures were required to close streets, allow the use of Lobos Square, and create special building and utility regulations within the grounds.

Groups of frock-coated men scurried over the muddy, barren tableau, hoping to convince august representatives of nations and states that it would soon be a wondrous fairyland in which their governments would be proud to exhibit.

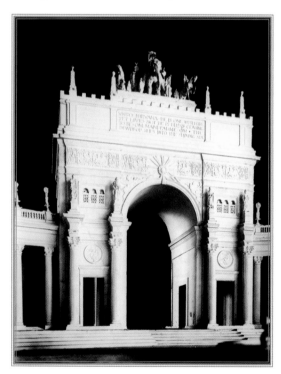

Architectural models such as this one of the Arch of the Rising Sun were displayed in the Exposition Office Building in May 1912. (Laura Ackley)

The PPIE dodged potential difficulties with construction unions by negotiating an informal compact with the most powerful building trades associations in the city. (Jim Caddick)

PPIE managers did the best they could to keep interest high. Plans and models were displayed, first in January 1912 at 334 California Street, then in May at the new Exposition offices at Pine and Battery Streets. A brass band played merrily from atop a wagonload of rough lumber as it trundled through the streets on October 17, followed by a parade of ten trucks laden with hardware, millwork, and plumbing. The materials were slated for the Service Building, the first edifice of the Jewel City, which would serve as the new headquarters for Exposition planners.

At the close of 1912, much headway had been made, although little of it was visually impressive. In addition to design development, site acquisition, and clearing, the fill was nearly complete. One could at last walk across the site with dry feet. The grounds were being graded and fenced, the Yacht Harbor deepened, the roadway through Fort Mason laid, the Service Building constructed, and the sewers fabricated.

But, as the Fair's historian, Frank Morton Todd, later wrote, "A pipe-line on pontoons, a tube discharging mud, however gratifying to the engineer...can never be depended upon to

inflame public enthusiasm and make the blood of a people boil with joy."[2]

BUILDING IN A UNION TOWN

Opponents of San Francisco during the congressional battle with New Orleans argued that the City by the Bay was such a strong union town that it would be difficult, if not impossible, to build the Exposition there. Strikes, delays, and high costs were predicted.

At the congressional hearings to decide which city would host the Fair, former mayor P. H. McCarthy testified that San Francisco labor would cooperate. He was reminded later of his testimony by PPIE president Charles C. Moore. McCarthy, an Exposition director as well as president of the Building Trades Council, suggested in 1912 that the Exposition enter into a contract with organized labor. Moore refused, asserting that the Exposition represented the US government, so it would not discriminate between union and non-union shops. McCarthy's union and the San Francisco

Labor Council, which together represented most of San Francisco's construction trades, offered a covenant, without any reciprocity from the Exposition. The covenant had several interesting features, including:

- The two unions would not change established laws and rules regarding hours, wages, and trade during the construction and operation of the Exposition.

- The unions would cooperate with foreign and state exhibitors and construction crews.

- No new unions would be organized with a view toward controlling Exposition wages or working hours.

- All materials and exhibits would be handled without discrimination as to their origins.

While the Exposition never ratified this labor agreement, which was a concession from the labor side alone, the PPIE somewhat miraculously sidestepped union difficulties.

QUENCHING THE THIRST

Feeding the appetite of the Jewel City for water, power, light, communication, and transportation was no simple undertaking. The tale of the Exposition's freshwater supply exemplifies the many dramas enacted out of public view, any one of which might have crippled the massive yet delicate enterprise. Originally, arrangements were made to obtain all of the Fair's water from the Spring Valley Water Company, San Francisco's monopoly supplier. The PPIE constructed a distribution system stemming from the Spring Valley lines at Van Ness Avenue on the east side of the Fair.

Then, just a few months before Opening Day, Spring Valley, locked in conflict with the city over its rates and a possible condemnation suit, informed the Exposition that it could supply only about 10 percent of the water required on an average day. A new supply of drinkable water was needed—and quickly.

Attention turned to Fort Mason, to the east of the Fair, which obtained water from Lobos Creek in the Presidio. While Spring Valley claimed half of the Lobos Creek supply, the water company was not using it, so Frank S. Brittain, attorney general of the PPIE, was dispatched to Washington, DC, to request this water for the Exposition. This brought the total available supply to about two-thirds of what was needed on an average day, but woefully only about 40 percent of the 2.5 million gallons per day forecast as peak demand during the Fair.

The Exposition's engineers knew the groundwater in the Richmond District, along the northern margin of Golden Gate Park, was underutilized, but they were also aware that wells there were prone to failure because the area lay atop sand dunes. They were delighted when a test well they bored in the area worked perfectly, and they promptly drilled four more.

Their elation turned to desperation when the new wells silted in within hours. The team tested a number of different well configurations, finally arriving at an arrangement of two concentric, perforated pipes, with a "naturally graded" beach gravel between them. This natural filter stopped sand but allowed the water through, resulting in more than a million additional gallons of freshwater daily. The water was then filtered, chlorinated, and piped to a shared reservoir in the Presidio and then onto the PPIE grounds. For the duration of the Fair, patrons enjoyed the amply irrigated gardens, bubbling fountains, and potable water without an inkling of the creative engineering behind it.[3]

COMFORT STATIONS

If salvaging the drinking water supply was a melodrama, the restrooms were a tragedy. It was decided the toilet facilities would operate as a concession to recoup some of their cost. Western Sanitary Company was to install and maintain all the toilets within the palaces and keep them supplied. In exchange, they would charge patrons at two-thirds of the facilities, also providing shoe shines, barbering, manicures, and toiletries. This proved to be a terrible idea.

The arrangement meant it was not in the interest of the concessionaire to keep the *free* toilets accessible or well stocked. There were problems from the start. Pay toilet attendants demanded tips and insulted those they deemed ungenerous. There were rumors they vandalized the free toilets, removed the toilet paper, and even locked the doors. When the free restrooms were open, they often were filthy, and exhibitors frequently had to search for working facilities.

Eventually the Exposition had to fix and clean many of the restrooms at an unanticipated cost. Repeated reprimands and letters escalated into an ongoing dispute as to whether Western Sanitary or the Exposition was owed money, and neither entity profited from the ill-considered scheme.

ENERGIZING THE FAIR

Though almost all existing structures on the PPIE site were leveled to build the Fair, one notable survivor was the 1893 Romanesque Revival–style administration building of the San Francisco Gas Light Company (which, after a series of mergers and acquisitions, became Pacific Gas and Electric). Located near the Palace of Machinery, today it is a restored office building and San Francisco Landmark #58, at 3640 Buchanan Street.

Pacific Gas and Electric won the contract to supply all Exposition power—gas, electricity, and steam. Gas was brought across the city from the Potrero District to an eight-inch main encircling the palaces, while four-inch loops ran around the state and foreign pavilions and the Joy Zone midway. During its run, the Fair consumed nearly 123 million cubic feet of gas.

Electricity was delivered from a PG&E substation east of the Palace of Machinery, using hydro- and steam-generated power from throughout California. (An additional steam plant, kept under continuous operation in case of interruption of regular power, was never needed.) Once the Exposition was complete, only the lines on the Joy Zone remained overhead. The rest of the cables for power, illumination, and telephones were hidden underground in wood-fiber conduits. Power for lighting the buildings was supplied at 115 volts, and there were also provisions for 230-volt and direct current.

During the Exposition period, almost 16 million kilowatt hours of electricity were consumed.

In the week before the Fair opened, nearly 50,000 telephone calls flooded the eighteen-seat switchboard in the Palace of Food Products. Calls from frantic exhibitors, season ticket holders, and others were answered without a technical hitch. This main switchboard and several branch exchanges connected to the Pacific Telephone and Telegraph system and served more than 2,000 dedicated Exposition lines. In some buildings phone lines ran through rings hung from the roof trusses or under the floors. On the Zone, subscribers connected to a weatherproof cable fastened to the fence behind the concessions. In addition to telephones used by the administrative offices, concessionaires, palaces, and state and foreign pavilions, there

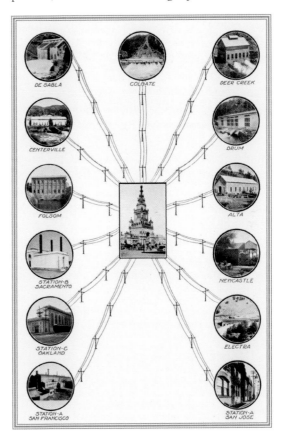

Electricity was brought to the Jewel City from hydropower and steam plants all across California. (*Pacific Service Magazine*, January 1916)

were one hundred manned pay stations and fifty-three coin-operated stations scattered throughout the grounds.

For trash collection, a "dual-sort" system was used to reduce refuse at the PPIE. Organics were separated from "ordinary waste," and, where feasible, the regular trash was used to fuel the Cobwell Garbage Reduction Process, which treated the organic waste. Solids were crushed to create stock feed, and all other refuse—about thirty tons of street sweepings and stable litter per day—was hauled to an outside dump.

To keep the Fair's "plant" running smoothly necessitated a collection of specialized services to maintain plants, machines, and animals. In addition to a sawmill, shops were built for groundskeeping, automotive repair, machining, and blacksmithing.

The Exposition even had its own standard-gauge railway, with eleven and a half miles of track, rolling stock leased from Southern Pacific, and a terminal on the eastern bay front of the Fair. The terminal also featured several spurs connecting to the freight harbor in the cove between Fort Mason and the North Gardens. Train cars could be unloaded from barges directly onto the tracks, then brought to the Exposition on one of three parallel lines that ran the length of the site. Three and a half miles of track actually ran inside the palaces so exhibits could be delivered with ease. A tunnel under Fort Mason connecting the Exposition Railway with the Belt Line along the waterfront was completed in November 1914. The tunnel provided convenient delivery of materials and exhibits from the main piers along the Embarcadero, so the spurs to the freight harbor were paved over and the slip converted to a landing for passenger ferries.

SAFEGUARDING A $50 MILLION EXPOSITION FROM FIRE

Winds buffeted an Exposition guard, stationed more than four hundred feet above the ground on the highest parapet of the Tower of Jewels. His lonely job, to look out over the Exposition for signs of fire, represented a tiny fraction of the elaborate and modern fire-protection scheme for the Fair. Fire protection was a paramount concern, since the Exposition was located close to a residential district physically and to 1906 temporally. In the wake of several blazes at domestic and European expositions, many exhibitors said they'd only send their wares if the Jewel City was utterly fire safe.

With these concerns in mind, a comprehensive system was devised to protect the Fair and its contents. The walls of the palaces adjacent to the courts had concrete wells to serve as firewalls. Three firehouses were erected within the grounds, and a sophisticated system of 102 electrical alarms was supplemented by seventy-six miles of Aero Alarm wire tubing. The alarm would trip automatically if fire caused the air within the tubes to expand. The system was so sensitive that just before the Fair opened, an alarm was triggered by heat from an incandescent lamp placed too close to one of the wire tubes.

A high-pressure water system ran as far west as the Livestock Stadium, and hydrants on the grounds, spaced about 300 feet apart, were concealed beneath manholes so they would not disrupt the landscape design. Inside the palaces, hydrants were placed to reach any part of the structures using, at most, 150 feet of hose. Should a fire break out, sprinklers on the outer cornices would send curtains of water down the sides of the buildings. Each of the palaces had an automatic sprinkler system, and two municipal fireboats were available to pump saltwater directly from the bay into the Exposition system. The total cost for fire protection was about $900,000, roughly $21.5 million in 2012.

During the Exposition, the internal fire department quenched a few dozen small blazes, keeping the losses to about $250. By comparison, fires at the 1893 exposition in Chicago caused $478,000 in damage and killed seventeen, and fire loss at the 1904 St. Louis fair was estimated at $100,000.

TRANSPORTATION

Some infrastructure vital to the Exposition's success was outside its grounds, including transportation lines needed to bring customers to the gates. San Francisco's effort to move tens of thousands of patrons to the Fair daily laid the foundation for its next four decades of transit improvements, but it also thwarted a transportation plan to bypass some of the steepest hills in the city.

After completion of the Geary Street railway in 1913, San Francisco turned its attention to rail lines to serve the Fair. As development of the PPIE was ramping up, San Francisco was transitioning from a tangled network of privately owned street railways into its first system of publicly owned mass transit—the San Francisco Municipal Railway, or Muni—created under a 1909 bond measure.

One main objection to the Harbor View site had been inadequate public transit. The city commissioned a 1912 study by consulting engineer Bion J. Arnold to assess the transportation facilities for the PPIE, then implemented several, though not all, of his suggestions. United Railroads (URR) and the California Street Cable Railroad, rivals to the city's new system, had been unwilling to build extensions for Jewel City traffic, although eventually the URR extended its 19-Polk line to offer service to a loop near the Exposition's east entrance.

For access to the central and western portions of the Fair, the nascent Muni built three new lines and took over a fourth. A loop on Chestnut Street brought streetcars directly to the main gates. When the franchise of the Presidio and Ferries Railroads' Union Street line expired in 1913, the city bought the line and rebuilt it to service the western Baker and Presidio entrances to the PPIE. Transport to the Exposition was further aided by the city's first municipal tunnel, dug beneath Stockton Street, connecting the Chinatown and North Beach neighborhoods with downtown. Muni also ordered 125 new fifty-person streetcars, more than quadrupling the number operating in 1913.[4]

United Railroads also beefed up its somewhat terrifying Fillmore Counterbalance, a funicular line that traveled the steepest blocks of Fillmore Street, overlooking the Fair. Portions of the grade in this stretch exceeded 25 percent and could not be traversed by a normal electric streetcar. The Counterbalance used an uphill car connected by an underground cable to a downhill car; as the upper car descended under power, it helped pull the lower car up the grade, and the lower car helped brake the top car's descent.

A trip on the Counterbalance was hair-raising. Helen Eells, who was eleven years old in 1915, recounted a ride: "[T]he people would be all standing straight, and they started over the hill. And then everybody was smashed to the bottom of the streetcar, of course, going down, with all on top of each other....[T]hen we straightened out again, and everybody straightened themselves up...trying to pretend they'd never been off balance and lost their dignity. But that's how we got to the Fair."[5]

On June 7, 1915, a fully loaded uphill car was mistakenly given the go-ahead to descend before the lower car was hooked to the cable. Passengers in the top car could not escape as the runaway train careened down Fillmore and smashed into the car at the bottom. Miraculously no one died, although a dozen were injured, including James O'Neil, the PPIE's chief of concessions.

The Fair impelled the purchase of rolling stock and creation of the route structure San Francisco used well into the 1940s, but it also thwarted a major transportation project: the building of the

Fillmore Street Tunnel. In the second half of 1911, the Fillmore Street Improvement Association crystallized plans for the ambitious dig, which would burrow a 3,816-foot tunnel with a mere 2.5 percent grade beneath eleven of the steepest blocks in the city. The project would be financed by special assessments on about four hundred city blocks north and south of the tunnel. Therein lay the problem.

Exposition directors realized several of its largest leases stated that in addition to property taxes, the PPIE would pay any extra assessments within its lease period—including those for tunnels. The directorate calculated that the Fair would be responsible for about 10 percent of the cost of the tunnel, which added up to roughly 8 percent of the money raised to build the Fair. Exposition management vehemently lobbied against the tunnel, and in September 1913 the idea was dropped.

Naysayers predicted rail lines to the PPIE would be overwhelmed on peak attendance days and during morning and evening rushes, but in reality the system performed quite well. On Opening Day about 44 percent of the quarter of a million people who attended arrived using the Muni lines. Surprisingly, traffic was not as concentrated in rush hours as anticipated but more or less evenly spread throughout the day.

Street railways were not the only options for Fair guests. Chartered ferries from all counties bordering the sixty-mile-long bay tied up at the Exposition slips, their passengers then entering the Fair through a dignified Grecian-style terminal building. And in the days before bridges spanned the bay, a twenty-minute ferry ride from the Oakland mole was often the final leg of the long journey for transcontinental rail passengers.

On land, streetcars were supplemented by private cars; taxis; double-deck omnibuses; open-topped, multi-row "rubberneck wagons"; smaller five- or ten-cent jitneys; and even horse-drawn hacks. Together, these various modes of transport could deliver as many as 50,000 people per hour to the gates of the Exposition.

This editorial cartoon from 1913 illustrates the city's concern over public transportation to the PPIE. In an accompanying article, Mayor James Rolph, Jr., warned that without more trolleys, the "Fair would fail." (*San Francisco Call*, February 6, 1913)

THE PALACES RISE

New Year's Day 1913 dawned with the kind of brilliant, crystalline winter sunshine that can trick the visitor into believing San Francisco's fickle weather is eternally benevolent. That day an estimated 100,000 citizens assembled for a parade down Van Ness to Lombard, then onto the grounds at Fillmore Street to witness the first spadeful of earth turned for the first and largest hall of the PPIE, the Palace of Machinery.

Several bands marched. Three hundred schoolchildren warbled "Columbia, Gem of the Ocean" and other patriotic tunes. Hot air balloons ascended and several stunt planes showered confetti over the site. In the bay, a submarine mysteriously surfaced and submerged, and the US cruiser *Marblehead* fired a booming salute.

As he stood before a backdrop of blue waters and amethyst hills beyond, Exposition president Charles C. Moore reminded the crowd that it was "a mistake to say that work begins on the Exposition today. It began three years ago…and has been vigorously prosecuted ever since." He looked out over the barren site, littered with equipment and the first loads of wood, and painted a word picture of the Fair. For the first time, the celebrants could see in their imaginations the beauty of the palaces and courtyards to come. Architect Clarence Ward spoke about his Palace of Machinery: "It will contain 8,000,000 cubic feet of lumber, which if converted into flooring, would cover 200 acres. It will be a mile's walk around the building—and a little more."[6, 7]

When Moore plunged an ordinary shovel into the earth and tossed the soil over his shoulder, the crowd threw hats into the air and roared in approval, their cries joined by those of startled seagulls.

With a mere twenty-six months until the Fair's gates would be thrown open to the world, the palaces were rising at last.

The balance of 1913 was uniquely satisfying to those who had worried about the Exposition's progress. By April, two giant, giraffe-like derricks were craning their long necks to lift into place the skeletal, hundred-foot-high arched trusses of the Palace of Machinery.

As the massive palaces rose, their aisles were used as studios and staging areas for the sculptures and murals. This view shows one of the three great naves inside the Palace of Machinery, each 75 feet wide, 101 feet high, and 968 feet long. (Laura Ackley)

ENGINEERING THE DREAM

While the Exposition's star architects occupied the public spotlight, they were governed by a benevolent dictatorship of engineers. The ornamental façades, portals, towers, and domes were designed by the architects, but engineers controlled the utilitarian frameworks within.

The Division of Works, presided over by the sometimes-prickly Harris D. H. Connick, was divided into departments of construction, architecture, electrical and mechanical engineering, color and decoration, landscape engineering, sculpture, and civil engineering, with each employing dozens of technical staff.[8]

As the pace of building accelerated, Exposition payrolls grew commensurately. More than half the $14,847,607 spent on site design and construction went toward labor costs. Thousands of teamsters, carpenters, masons, steel workers, gardeners, painters, and plasterers swarmed over the site daily.

While designers were freed from some technical concerns, they were subjected to budgetary tyranny. As historian Frank Morton Todd said, the engineering team "ruthlessly sacrificed to the Moloch of economy some of the fairest-looking architectural babies ever born." As the design phase continued, a back-and-forth "dance of drawings" commenced. The architects provided structural engineers with general drawings that included the locations of wall lines, columns, and openings so that contract drawings could be expedited. All these specifications, plus the bid and contractor bond, were made part of each streamlined contract.[9]

Hopeful builders had to prove they held fire and workmen's compensation insurance, and once plans were approved by the mechanical, electrical, or structural department, contractors had to file a bond and purchase an Exposition builder's permit, to a maximum permit fee of $50. While modest, these fees were enough to keep most contractors honest. As Opening Day loomed, contractors received a bonus of $100 for each day they finished ahead of schedule, or were fined the same amount for every day late.

On the West Coast, timber was abundant and inexpensive, so steel frames were used in only three of the thirteen main structures—the Tower of Jewels, the dome of the Palace of Horticulture, and the curved gallery portion of the Palace of Fine Arts. The other palaces were framed in wood, with two-by-six studs on eighteen-inch centers, and horizontal girders every thirteen vertical feet. The lion's share of wood was Douglas fir, delivered by a fleet of about thirty schooners from ports from Puget Sound, Washington, to Mendocino, in Northern California.[10]

Once onshore, most wood was moved using actual horsepower. Teamsters hand-guided "hoop-horses" over plank roads to the building sites. Moving lumber required as many as 200 trucks, 68 horses, and 140 men a day. The PPIE was also the first world's fair for which motor trucks proved especially useful, as builders seized upon the truck as a flexible, powerful alternative to rail lines or horses.

One wooden construction element proved better than steel. When even the old-growth timber, then available, was not long enough for the lofty columns in the palaces, splices were required. Tests showed that Hawaiian 'ōhi a lehua (*Metrosideros polymorpha*, a member of the myrtle family) outperformed all other woods and even solid steel pins for this purpose. So the Exposition sent to the islands for bars of the remarkable spiral-grained hardwood and used them throughout the palaces. The resultant joints proved so strong that after the Fair, "when the structures were wrecked with dynamite, the joints held together like solid blocks."[11]

Many of the construction details were predicated on the temporary nature of the Exposition. Because the buildings would be open for just 288 fleeting days, the wooden piles that supported the structures were not treated with creosote. Concrete foundations were unnecessary when timber sills would do. Many temporary sewers were built of wood staves because the newly filled areas of the site were still settling and needed more flexibility than vitrified pipe would allow.

SPECIAL PALACE FEATURES

Though the palaces' interior layouts were similar, a few design details were specific to certain locations. The Palace of Transportation had a huge "transfer table" for moving the largest locomotives displayed at the fair. All rolling stock to be displayed came in on a single track and then was distributed throughout the palace using fourteen subsidiary tracks. In the Palace of Machinery, the great central nave was spanned by two giant traveling cranes that ran along tracks underneath the roof trusses fifty feet above the floor. Each crane could lift exhibits weighing thirty tons, and two smaller cranes in the side aisles could carry twenty tons each.

Refrigeration was available for exhibits in the Palace of Food Products, also known as the Palace of Nibbling Arts, and in parts of the Palace of Horticulture. Heat was provided in just a few locations, including the dome of the Palace of Horticulture, to protect its tropical plantings, and in the Festival Hall, for the comfort of its late-night audiences.

This glass lantern slide taken from atop the Festival Hall shows the construction of its dome ribs. Beyond, the Court of Flowers and one of the four Italian Towers are taking form, along with the sculpture-topped Arch of the Rising Sun. (Laura Ackley)

As 1913 wore on and the lacy frames of the palaces rose, small locomotives emblazoned with the names of contractors puffed along the Exposition Railway tracks, delivering their loads. The tang of tar and coal tinged air already laden with the scent of freshly sawed fir. In June 1913, the first large trees, their roots neatly boxed, were unloaded from horse-drawn wagons and tilted into place in their specified locations. As summer gave way to autumn, seven hundred cypresses and eucalypti, each between thirty and thirty-five feet tall, were planted into soil that lay where the waters of the bay recently had lapped.

Hundreds of horse and mule teams plodded about, pulling graders across the site and dragging dredgers through the water of the emerging lagoon of the Palace of Fine Arts. Pile drivers thunked rhythmically, pounding the supports of the palaces that lay on fill land. Steamers docked at the newly deepened Yacht Harbor and disgorged millions of board feet of lumber.

Historian Todd wrote, "What riveted the eye and awed the soul was a vast scatteration of material all over the place, as though some giant's children had just been called away from a game of jack-straws with the débris of a forest.... That order, symmetry, and beauty could arise from this picture of old Chaos was a bit beyond the average understanding."[12]

INCIDENTS AND ACCIDENTS

During construction, untethered workmen shinnied up the wooden ribs of the unfinished palace domes and perilously balanced 160 feet above the ground. While construction safety precautions were weaker than today's, the Exposition was actually at the forefront of worker safety regulations, and California law

Although the PPIE took worker safety seriously, rules were far more lax in the days before OSHA. Here two men casually risk their lives driving a bolt on the Tower of Jewels, four hundred feet above the earth. (Edward A. Rogers)

as a whole was changing to provide stronger protection for workers.

Injuries were reported on bright yellow forms bearing the admonition, "Accidents, however slight, must be reported immediately." Many mishaps were minor and to be expected on a huge construction site—punctures, scratches, bruises, fingers and toes mashed by hammers or dropped loads of wood or pinched in machinery. More serious accidents, such as fractures, were corroborated by the treating physician and reported to the state's Industrial Accident Commission. A surprisingly high number of cuts, bruises, and broken bones were caused by fractious horses or mules.[13]

Several mishaps delayed progress, including a windstorm that sent the partially finished dome of the Palace of Manufactures crashing sixteen stories to the ground. An August 1914 blaze in the blueprint room of the Service Building was quickly doused by the Exposition's own three firefighting companies, and damage was limited to about $500.

Although accidents were comparatively rare given the pace of construction and gargantuan size of the operation, there were a number of fatalities. Two 25-ton steel trusses for the gallery of the Palace of Fine Arts crushed a foreman, and several men perished in falls from the towering heights of the palaces.

THE ICING ON THE CAKE

As the capacious palaces were put under roof, their aisles became studios for the artists who would decorate them. Part of the Palace of Machinery was fitted up as a grand atelier for the mural painters in January 1914. Even William de Leftwich Dodge's ninety-six-by-twelve-foot triptychs that would adorn the arch under the Tower of Jewels fit easily in the soaring aisle, where they were illuminated by shafts of light filtering through the clerestories. The mammoth panels hung side by side with works by all the other painters.

As many as one hundred workmen bustled about the staff shop in the empty Palace of Transportation, where thousands of architectural embellishments were modeled. An orderly forest of completed spiral-twist columns in one corner contrasted with the working side of the studio. There, the floor was littered with stacks of scrap wood and metal used to build armatures, fluffy piles of hemp fiber, buckets, ladders, and the myriad tools employed to form the ornaments.

Ropes and pulleys slung through the latticed trusses overhead lifted the molds for huge architectural details—some cornices were twelve feet tall and would trim hundreds of feet of roofline. Below, modelers in white overalls mixed a gypsum concoction in vats and barrels and poured it into the molds, which had been treated with the special veining technique that made the finished products resemble real limestone. Once unmolded, hundreds of friezes,

decorative panels, niches, medallions, and pilasters were assembled.

Meanwhile, sculptors were engaged in enlarging the main figural statuary of the Exposition in less impressive quarters: two corrugated metal buildings near the Exposition's railway terminal. There, fifty artisans, many of whom moved to San Francisco to work on the sculpture for the Fair, used Sculpto-point machines to magnify pieces of small original models. Often, the men had to climb ladders or scaffolds to reach the figures on which they worked. Subordinate pieces were assembled into whole statues—a head here, a leg or arm there—and until the seams were plastered over, the figures looked like three-dimensional jigsaw puzzles. More than 1,500 figures were constructed, at a cost of more than $300,000, about $7.1 million in 2012.

ONE YEAR BEFORE

Exactly one year prior to Opening Day, the tremendous jumble of lumber, pipe, and hardware was beginning to resolve into the semblance of a world's fair.

A great deal of the structure of the main palace block had been erected by February 1914, but only the Palace of Machinery was nearing completion. Once its framing was in place, sheathing and flooring were added and then the plumbing, electrical, and sprinkler systems. Windows and skylights were framed in and glazed. Sub-roofing was covered with crushed brick laid onto asbestos-asphalt fabric. The palace was frosted with a coat of alabaster-toned faux travertine mimicking the porous stone used in ancient Roman monuments. Next, the carefully modeled ornaments and sculptures were applied. The Palace of Machinery alone required more than a mile of cornices.

A year out from the fair, the eight central palaces designed by William Faville were mostly framed, and some were receiving the domes that marked the intersections of their cross-shaped roofs. Scaffolding still covered the façades, only some of which were ready for their travertine surfaces. As the months wore on, they followed

A workman mounts hundreds of sparkling cut-glass Novagems along the cornice line just below the knees of four Atlas figures atop the Tower of Jewels. (Seligman Family Foundation)

the same sequence of completion as the Palace of Machinery.

Across town in the new Civic Center, the million-dollar Exposition Auditorium designed by John Galen Howard, Frederick H. Meyer, and John Reid, Jr., was being constructed of stone and steel, as it was designed as a permanent gift to the City of San Francisco from the PPIE. Its foundation had been finished late in 1913, and its cornerstone was laid in April 1914. Less than nine months later, on January 9, 1915, masked dancers whirled eighty feet below the dome of the 10,000-person hall in celebration of the auditorium's completion. The auditorium and its ten subsidiary halls, each of which could hold several hundred people, were used extensively throughout 1915 for the hundreds of conventions held in conjunction with the Fair.

Notably absent from the fairgrounds early in 1914 were the steel-framed structures: the Column of Progress, the central Tower of Jewels, and the arcing gallery of the Palace of Fine Arts. The only steel in evidence was the nascent framework for the glass dome of the Palace of Horticulture.

Landscape engineer John McLaren had noted the sandy fill material was unsuited to planting, so he had shipped in tons of rich loam from the Sacramento River Delta and had it spread over the new land. Smooth lawns now surrounded the rising buildings. A team of eight sturdy horses pulled wagons bearing thirty-foot-tall California fan palms to the road along the sheltered southern façade of the palaces. Here they were planted—alternating every twenty feet with date palms—on either side of the Avenue of Palms. Meanwhile, the eucalypti and cypresses planted the previous year against the palace walls were attaining their full heights. Within the courts, gardeners were adding distinctive treatments.

Gradually, brown wooden palace walls were covered in faux travertine plasterwork, and acres of scaffolding came down. A battalion of painters added color to the surfaces of the palaces following Jules Guérin's meticulous renderings. The house painters recruited for this job had a distressing tendency toward improvisation and had to be carefully monitored lest they "improve" the color scheme with their own interpretations.

As months passed, the three largest domes finally arose: the Festival Hall and the Palace of Horticulture in the South Gardens, and the rotunda of the Palace of Fine Arts west across the lagoon from the central block of eight exhibit palaces. The Column of Progress was the last steel structure begun, in October 1914.

Most dramatic was the rapid growth of the forty-three-story Tower of Jewels. The first steel was laid on March 27, 1914, and the structure reached its full 435-foot height in just 270 days. By December, especially intrepid workmen braved the wind-lashed parapets to hang the two-inch-diameter cut-glass gems that gave the tower its name.

As the heart of the Exposition sped toward completion, work commenced on the amenities that would enrich the guests' experiences. The Inside Inn hotel; postal, telephone, and telegraph stations; a bank; cafés; souvenir kiosks; and several bandstands sprang up, and an emergency hospital was fitted up inside the Service Building. At the westernmost end of the Fair, an 18,000-seat grandstand faced the automotive and horse racing oval that surrounded a state-of-the-art, one-third-mile cinder running track and athletic field. All these were built on what later became the Crissy Field airstrip, now part of the Golden Gate National Recreation Area. Nearby, feed silos rose next to the Livestock Stadium, which was surrounded by an elongated octagon of tiered bleachers from which spectators would watch animal judging.

PRE-FAIR VISITING

Starting in September 1913, the PPIE took advantage of the public's natural fascination with the construction process and opened the gates to pre-fair visiting. At twenty-five cents for adults and ten cents for children, visitors could walk on the plank roads between the partially complete palaces. The well-dressed visitors stepping carefully on the boardwalks contrasted sharply with nearby workmen in shirtsleeves, loose-fitting dungarees, and caps. As the natty spectators strolled, music played by Lo Forti's Band echoed from the scaffolded walls of the courtyards.

Starting in September 1913, the public could tour the nascent Exposition. Here sightseers stroll along a temporary boardwalk next to the almost-complete Palace of Machinery (left). (The Bancroft Library, University of California, Berkeley)

The boardwalks solved a problem of past fairs, where the weight of construction traffic had reduced newly laid roadways to dust by opening day. Once underground utilities were put in place at the PPIE, sixteen-foot-long planks were laid down over a base made of crushed brick, concrete, and stone salvaged from the demolished structures on the site. The base had been laid over the sandy fill, then rolled. At intervals, traffic was barred from portions of the roads and the boards were removed so the roads could be finished with either sheet asphalt or asphalt and sand mastic. The planks were then replaced over the final surface, allowing the remaining construction materials and heavy exhibits to be hauled over the roadways without damaging them. The planks were discarded shortly before Opening Day, leaving pristine paths wending throughout the grounds.

Those Joy Zone concessions that opened during the pre-Fair period did a brisk business. L. A. Thompson's Scenic Railway coaster recouped nearly half its cost before the Fair officially opened. Prior to its grand opening on February 20, pre-fair attendance had topped 2.5 million and raked in $679,383.[14]

CHANGES AND CUTBACKS

As they perambulated the temporary rough-plank walkways between the walls of the stately palaces, visitors would not have guessed how drastically some of the original plans differed from what they saw. In truth, the Fair underwent continuous metamorphosis from inception to completion.

Over the course of construction, the Division of Works' budget was slashed several times, forcing cutbacks or the outright sacrifice of some features. In September 1914, the construction budget suffered a final reduction, bringing the total belt-tightening to about 10 percent of the division's original budget.

Among the elements excised from the Fair were two towers dedicated to the explorers Balboa and Columbus, and a dedicated five-

By June 20, 1914, the central palaces were nearly finished. The steel skeleton of the Tower of Jewels was rising, and the Palace of Fine Arts (left)

acre Automobile Building to have cost a quarter of a million dollars. Though already designed by G. Albert Lansburgh under the auspices of the National Association of Automobile Manufacturers, the building was cancelled when the group failed to find the needed financial backing. The automotive exhibits subsequently were relegated to the Palace of Transportation.

Louis Christian Mullgardt's Court of Ages was especially affected by budgetary strictures. First cut was his ambitious outdoor organ and its planned "echo towers," smaller organs electrically connected to the large instrument to create an echoing effect. Then the dual curving staircases and parapet promenade were eliminated in favor of two water cascades, although these, too, evaporated from the final plans.

The Palace of Fine Arts also was modified to save money, and architect Maybeck lamented that his design for a "Peace Palace," pendant to the Palace of Fine Arts on the south side of the grounds, was sacrificed in favor of the potentially profitable Inside Inn.

In a few cases the architects fought to retain designs threatened by cutbacks. Director of Works Connick asked the architects to erase the "sunken gardens" from the designs for the Court of Ages and Court of the Universe, as raising the site to accommodate them would cost an additional $71,000. However, the architects successfully argued that without the recessed gardens the views across the courts would be spoiled, and thus the necessary 400,000 cubic yards of fill was approved.

Banker Ignatz Steinhart offered to donate $40,000 in memory of his late brother Sigmund toward an aquarium in Golden Gate Park, to operate in conjunction with the Fair. PPIE management worried about potential conflicts with the exhibit of the US Bureau of Fisheries and about the possible loss of revenue to an outside attraction. Steinhart's aquarium was ultimately delayed. Upon his death in 1917, his bequest of $250,000 went to the Academy of Sciences to build what would become the Steinhart Aquarium, which opened in 1923.

A number of the major sculptures were shuffled from their original spots, including the *Beauty and the Beast* fountain by Edgar Walter. It was intended for the Court of Palms but moved to the Court of Flowers after the latter's *Arabian Nights* fountain was cancelled. Since both courts were initially designed with fairy tale themes, the substitution made sense.

Visitors entering the immense Palace of Machinery were to have been greeted by sculptor Douglas Tilden's *Modern Civilization*, a group of seventeen-foot-tall figures representing Valor, Imagination, Truth, Morality, and Industry. However, after a dispute between Tilden and Stirling Calder, the local chief of sculpture, *Modern Civilization* was not constructed and, just weeks prior to Opening Day, Daniel Chester French's powerful *Genius of Creation* was

and the Festival Hall (right center, behind two scaffolded towers) were being assembled. (Library of Congress, Prints and Photographs Division)

relocated from the center of the Court of the Universe to replace it.

Genius of Creation was an ambiguous sculpture of a hooded, hermaphroditic, winged figure perched atop a rough rock. Its arms extended over a smaller man and woman whose hands were clasped around the back of the group. French was regarded as the dean of American sculptors and had designed the statue for the Lincoln Memorial. He was concerned to learn his work would be moved from its position of honor at the center of the Fair. However, Chief of Sculpture Karl Bitter assured him the new location was desirable. French wrote to Calder, "It was a great relief to my mind to learn... that my group is to be carried out as originally intended. I am so glad that it is to be executed that I should not demur even if the site given it were not a very good one...."[15]

In reality, French may not have been as pleased as he claimed. His daughter Margaret wrote in his biography, "The Exposition gave him the Medal of Honor and wined and dined him, and did everything for him but feed him peanuts, but it remained a disappointment none the less."[16]

KINGDOMS REAL AND IMAGINED

Construction of the Joy Zone and the state and foreign pavilions lagged about a year behind that of the palaces. Through the autumn of 1913, Frederic Thompson's fanciful Noah's Ark–shaped office building for the Toyland Grown Up concession stood alone near what had been the corner of Laguna and Francisco Streets. Eventually it was joined by the Santa Fe Railroad system's replica Grand Canyon of Arizona, but beyond that was nothing but bare earth and a long line of power poles stretching toward Van Ness Avenue. At the other end of the fairgrounds, Honduras was pioneering construction within the state and national area by August 1913, but the large swath of land reserved for these buildings remained mostly blank until the following January, when Idaho launched work on its pavilion.

Long negotiations with many participants, all with their own needs and goals, caused the delay in building the Zone and government areas of the Fair. For the Division of Works, corralling the planning needs for all the external entities was especially time-consuming. Concessionaire contracts needed to be finalized and connections to the PPIE water, natural gas, and electrical systems designed and laid down, all prior to building construction. Worse yet, more than two dozen states and countries and a number of concessions selected sites only to abandon them, leaving the Exposition with empty lots to fill.

Governments and concessions were allowed to use outside architects, but their designers were required to submit their drawings and specifications to the Division of Works for approval. Once they received plans, the Exposition's architects and engineers carefully reviewed them to verify they met rigorous standards. Many flaws were easily correctable: adjusting the size of a structural member here, or moving a façade line there. Other issues, however, had Exposition officials throwing up their hands in frustration.

Chief structural engineer H. D. Dewell wrote of a proposed concession, "The plans and specifications are in very poor shape, the construction in general being faulty....It is useless to suggest changes to make these plans satisfactory. In my opinion they should be returned to the concessionaire and he should be required to furnish structural plans drawn up by a competent engineer." The fire protection engineer chimed in, "[T]he whole structure is a huge pile which has been arranged in the best possible manner for burning up in the shortest space of time."[17, 18]

Overseeing growth of the Joy Zone was especially difficult as the Exposition dealt with the sometimes-overblown ambitions of dozens of show promoters. While concessionaires paid a nonrefundable deposit and provided a surety bond to guarantee they'd complete their attractions, some Zone features that received early fanfare failed to materialize. Some simply did not have sufficient financial backing. Neither Roadtown (a skyscraper turned on its side) nor a replica of the Grand Trianon of Versailles was built, and plans for an ice rink melted away.

Other attractions were poorly managed. When Charles A. de Lisle Holland announced Mahomet's Mountain, his investors were confident. The showman and painter had more than thirty years' experience creating "amusement illusions" and had already painted a popular illustration for the PPIE, the allegorical "Kiss of the Oceans." His concept sketch for

the mountain showed patrons ascending the 150-foot-tall peak on an escalator through several mystical caverns. Fantastic electrical illusions would include a "dry waterfall," statues that came to life, strange Martians, and stalactites that would play exquisite music. After enjoying a view from the Smoking Pagoda at the summit, visitors could either slip down the Devil's Slide through the Caves of Mystery or enjoy a more conventional descent via stairway.

But as 1914 wore on, the site for Mahomet's Mountain remained empty and Exposition officials became concerned. Gently cajoling memos gave way to an ultimatum: if construction were not commenced, the concession would be revoked. After Mahomet's Mountain was cancelled as threatened, investors discovered that the $30,000 bank account they'd funded was as dry as the mysterious waterfall.

MAHOMET'S MOUNTAIN WITH ITS CAVES OF MYSTERY & MOVABLE STAIRWAY.

Mahomet's Mountain was one of several ambitious midway attractions that failed before construction even began, leaving the Exposition scrambling to fill its space. (The Bancroft Library, University of California, Berkeley)

THE TEMPLE OF CHILDHOOD

The Exposition was bound to attract some schemers, and the Temple of Childhood was an outright scam, designed to profit by leveraging the allure of the Exposition together with natural parental vanity.

Photographers across the country were contracted to be "official" local snappers for the Temple of Childhood. In exchange for this title, they paid a flat fee, plus a 25 percent commission of any photo sales made to parents. Further, they had to agree to supply 1,000 names (preferably 10,000) of potential kiddie subjects.

Parents were phoned or sent official-looking correspondence claiming their especially beautiful child had been chosen for the honor of appearing in the Temple, to be gazed upon with delight by millions of Jewel City visitors, with prizes awarded to the prettiest children. After the likeness was taken, parents received a lustrous certificate with a foil seal, silk ribbon, and elegant rendering of architect Louis Christian Mullgardt's neoclassical design for the building. The missives sported a PPIE return address and were signed by Richard M. Sayers, who styled himself "Director of Exhibits," when in reality he was simply head of the concession. These blandishments implied that the Temple of Childhood was part of the official exhibits, not merely an attraction.

The scheme started to unravel when articles congratulating local tykes on this "honor" began appearing in newspapers and people realized that the accolade was hardly exclusive. Further, the PPIE repeatedly issued warnings to the Temple's operators to stop claiming it was an official PPIE entity.

Eventually, photographers began to run ads disclaiming connection with the Temple, but by then the damage was done and Mullgardt's elegant design was never built. The day after the Exposition opened, the remaining assets of the Temple of Childhood's San Francisco office were sold at bankruptcy auction.

The Temple of Childhood proved to be a scam designed to separate proud parents from their money by informing them their tot had been selected for the exhibit, then selling them a photo session. (Laura Ackley)

BUNTING AND BLOSSOMS

As the palaces neared completion, 1913 and 1914 were punctuated with dozens of groundbreaking ceremonies as construction of state and foreign pavilions and Joy Zone concessions finally got under way. Early celebrations usually followed a standard form, with colorful national costumes where applicable, speechifying from a bunting-hung platform, and the requisite tossing of a shovelful of dirt.

As time passed, however, planners created more extravagant and imaginative events to attract crowds. At Denmark's groundbreaking, 20,000 attendees watched an aviator drop the Danish flag onto the site from his airplane. This was a modern homage to the fable that the country's flag originated when it miraculously fell from the sky after a victory in battle with Estonia in 1219. For Hawaii's dedication, maidens placed leis upon the ground to spell "Watch Hawaii Grow," showered the crowd with blossoms, and christened the earth with pineapple juice. At the outdoor luncheon on the Zone to launch the Orange Blossom Candy concession, a huge decorative orange burst open and four little girls popped out carrying baskets of fruit and candy.[19]

ELEMENTS OF FANTASY

World's fairs are occasions for grand schemes that often leave landmarks for posterity. Legacies of these expositions include the Eiffel Tower, the original Field Museum in Chicago, the *Atomium* in Brussels, and the *Trylon, Perisphere,* and *Unisphere* in New York. For the PPIE, both planners and ordinary citizens submitted a variety of elaborate ideas. Most were not constructed and faded into obscurity.

One of the best-publicized ideas for the PPIE that never materialized was a monumental feature to be placed in Lincoln Park. This proposal was often labeled a "memorial tower," though what it was to memorialize was never explained. It was to be 850 feet tall atop a "great memorial hall," with four express elevators to speed visitors to its roof deck. To take advantage of its great height, a weather observatory, wireless station, and lighthouse would be installed at the top. Another idea was to create a gigantic statue, an allegorical female "San Francisco," shading her eyes and gazing out over the western ocean. Others suggested that Father Junípero Serra, founder of the California mission system, be commemorated.

One frequently mentioned proposal was to place a colossal telegraph tower atop Telegraph Hill, but as the telephone was supplanting the telegraph, perhaps this was seen as outmoded. The Greek community in San Francisco looked further into antiquity and planned a reproduction of the Parthenon for the summit, however it, too, remained but a fantasy. Instead, the State of Oregon constructed a sylvan replica of the ancient temple as its state pavilion, with huge Douglas fir logs, complete with bark, in place of the original marble exterior columns.

An 850-foot Memorial Tower was one of several monumental features suggested for the PPIE. (Laura Ackley)

Having lifted the figure to its lofty perch, proud workmen stand atop a colossal elephant, part of the *Nations of the East* sculptural group crowning the Arch of the Rising Sun. (Edward A. Rogers)

THE FINAL PUSH

With the dawn of 1915, the Exposition was rushing toward completion. Finishing touches were being added to the grounds. General Electric crane trucks hoisted heavy sculpted urns and figures into place atop decorative plinths. Bright banners were hung around the tops of some of the gorgeously modeled lamp standards, while others received glass globes specially tinted to match the ivory of the faux travertine. Balustrades and benches were set along walkways of roseate roasted beach sand. Crews tested the spectacular illuminations, the wiring throughout the palaces and concessions, and the pumping systems for the pools and fountains.

When the first mighty tones of the great pipe organ drifted out over the grounds during its trial run, hundreds stopped their work and clambered over the lumber littering the entrance of the Festival Hall to listen, even though the instrument was not yet complete.

The number of workers on the site in 1914 had regularly exceeded 5,000 men a day, but that tally soared, culminating the day before the Fair opened, when more than 15,000 workers scurried over the site. In the frenetic rush to finish, the Exposition called upon an unusual source of labor—"earthquake carpenters." These were men who had become skilled woodworkers out of necessity following the 1906 disaster.

While the gardeners had placed hardier plants much earlier, the most delicate flowers were transplanted in the final weeks before Opening Day. Chief of Landscape McLaren had decided to begin the Fair in a blaze of California gold, so the first rotation of blooms in the South Gardens created a carpet of 600,000 yellow pansies, daffodils, and tulips, while the Court of Palms received 27,000 golden Spanish irises and the Court of Flowers a like number of pansies.

Dozens of boxcars filled with plants arrived to fill in nine acres of gardens south of the Palace of Horticulture. Eleven countries and twenty-three states exhibited their floral treasures, including two acres of Dutch gardens, considered the most important ever displayed outside of Holland. Gardens by East Coast states showcased irises, peonies, and vivid heliotoropes. The growers for the competition rose garden remained anonymous so judges would not be swayed. A perfect yellow bud from Ireland took the $1,000 prize and was christened the "Lillian Moore Rose" after the wife of PPIE president Charles Moore.

Builders slogged through the last, rainy month, during which there were only three dry days. The tracks of the miniature Overfair Railway, a concession designed to carry fairgoers along the northern waterfront, were washed out and rebuilt with a sturdy trestle. Inside the palaces, a "rain squad" located wet spots on the floors, then found the corresponding roof leaks by shooting a 22-caliber rifle straight up from the puddles, as bullet holes were easier to pinpoint than tiny flaws.

On the Zone, which had been an almost blank canvas just twelve months earlier, two long rows of imaginative, sculpted façades in varying states of completion faced each other. More than six hundred men scrambled to finish

the huge Buddha atop Japan Beautiful, the imperious King Neptune beckoning from the Submarines concession, and the three-masted ship terminally trapped in burlap ice floes on the front of "London to the South Pole." After all its struggles, when the Fair opened, only about 50 feet of the Zone's 6,000-foot frontage was empty, a fact cleverly disguised by building false fronts that matched adjacent structures.

With less than a week to go before the February 20 opening, continuous day and night shifts labored toward the finish. Pools were drained and cleaned and their bottoms repainted a pale turquoise so they sparkled like tiny fragments of the Mediterranean. A score of men donned foul-weather gear before they clambered into the wide basins to test the Fountains of the Rising and Setting Sun in the Court of the Universe, but they were still drenched by thousands of gallons before the task of tuning the waterworks was accomplished.

Starting on the morning of February 19, and continuing for twenty-six hours without sleep, a detachment of eight hundred men swept through the grounds, on horseback and in trucks, cleaning up evidence of construction. Although the site had been kept relatively tidy,

A replica of the Grand Canyon, constructed by the Atchison, Topeka & Santa Fe Railroad, was one of the first concessions built on the Joy Zone, the midway of the Fair. (Laura Ackley)

This photo, taken in the second half of 1914, shows the partially constructed Festival Hall, beyond which a largely empty Joy Zone stretches to Van Ness Avenue. The building with the striped minaret near the head of the Zone housed the Fair's carousel. (Edward A. Rogers)

they collected 262,000 cubic feet of debris, including leftover building materials, scaffolding, and exhibit packing material.

Around midnight, President Moore took a tour of the grounds. At about the same time, Chief of Construction Markwart called a halt to construction for the night. He declared that henceforth building on the Zone and delivery of materials and exhibits would be allowed only at night, though daytime construction among the state and foreign pavilions still was permitted. In the last hours of darkness, a gas-powered street sweeper and battalion of men with brooms set to work cleaning the paths muddied by delivery of exhibits after the protective planks had been removed.

What greeted the quarter million attendees the next day was stunning. Long stretches of creamy travertine were relieved by exquisitely detailed spires, colonnades, and portals. The majestic sculptures were in place, as were luminous jewel-toned murals affixed to buildings as integral architectural elements. Overnight rains had diminished, and as the Opening Day procession reached the gates, the sun broke through and set the unspoiled miniature city aglow. The 102,000 gems suspended from the Tower of Jewels danced and sparkled.

Locals who had watched the Exposition evolve from a ragtag assortment of structures and a seventy-one-acre tidal lagoon were justifiably proud. They had witnessed every stage, from the unromantic pumping of sludgy fill material to the application of the last speck of gold leaf on the Tower of Jewels. Now they were able to wander among colorful palaces decorated with grand murals and set amongst gorgeous verdure and embracing elegant courtyards made musical with the splash of fountains. No matter that some of the foreign pavilions were still under scaffolding—the main block of palaces was inarguably a splendidly realized architectural achievement. The PPIE was as complete upon opening as any exposition in history.

Tower of Jewels architect Thomas Hastings, writing to Director of Works Harris Connick, summed up the public's amazement: "It was a tremendous undertaking....[T]he execution is as good as the design, and the whole thing is going to be a wonderful success. You are certainly to be congratulated more than any...and I take my hat, and shoes, and stockings off to you!"[20]

A GLOBAL COURTSHIP

On a cloudless autumn day in 1913, San Francisco served as bridesmaid for a "wedding" 3,300 miles away. October 10 marked the "Wedding of the Oceans," when President Wilson pressed a key in Washington, DC, that detonated 1,600 pounds of dynamite. The resulting blast destroyed the Gamboa Dike in Panama, the last artificial impediment to a continuous waterway between the locks on the Atlantic and Pacific ends of the Panama Canal. The earthen dike had been thrown up to keep the water of Gatun Lake out of the nine-mile Culebra Cut while that deepest, most slide-prone section of the canal was excavated.

At 2:01 p.m. on the East Coast, Wilson's signal flashed by telegraph to Galveston, Texas, through a cable resting upon the seafloor of the Gulf of Mexico, across the Isthmus of Tehuantepec, under water again down the Pacific Coast, surfacing at Nicaragua, and finally reaching its destination at Gamboa, Panama. The hour for the explosion had been changed to accommodate San Francisco's celebration of the event, and Western Union rigged a branch connection so that the presidential signal was transmitted simultaneously to California.

As a curtain of rock, mud, and water blasted into the Panamanian sky to the cheers of thousands of rapt spectators, an aerial bomb burst in the air above Union Square in San Francisco. Whistles shrilled, bells pealed, and the twelve-year-old daughter of Mayor James Rolph, Jr., hoisted the American flag while Aldanita Wolfskill sang "The Star-Spangled Banner." Back in Washington, Wilson exclaimed, "Gamboa is busted!"[1]

Reuben Brooks Hale, the man who had first suggested holding a San Francisco exposition to commemorate the canal, proposed a toast in California, even as turbid water rushed from Gatun Lake through the new 125-foot-wide gap in the dike and into the Culebra Cut. He

News of the detonation of the Gamboa Dike in Panama was relayed live to San Francisco to a Western Union telegraph stand in Union Square. Twelve-year-old Annette Rolph, the mayor's daughter, raised the American flag as Aldanita Wolfskill sang "The Star-Spangled Banner." (Glenn D. Koch)

said, "Here's to the Panama Canal, to those who conceived it, to those who achieved it, and to the event that celebrates it, in San Francisco, 1915."[2]

Later in the day, the "wedding reception" moved to the Fair site, where Señor José E. Lefevre, Secretary of the Legation of Panama, dedicated the site for the Panama Pavilion. Newspapers across the country covered the dual celebrations.

This symbolic linking of the canal to the event commemorating it was part of the massive effort to interest potential exhibitors and attendees in the upcoming PPIE. The *San Francisco Chronicle* summarized the Exposition organizers' goals in associating the two: "The mighty blast at Gamboa has already echoed around the world and it will be as the trumpet call to the nations to…prepare for the new era in commercial activities. It is also the signal

to all peoples to arrange for the shipping of their exhibits to the Panama-Pacific Exposition and to devise their plans for attendance at the festival, the grandeur of which will be a fitting celebration of the great undertaking."[3]

The Jewel City's planners realized they could not simply throw open the gates and expect millions of people to stream into halls magically filled with exhibits. Thus, as the sumptuous palaces and courts rose on land reclaimed from the tidal mire, the next terrifying challenge emerged: How would the Exposition Company fill sixty-five acres of exhibit space and draw the millions of visitors needed for the Fair to break even?

At risk was the $50 million invested by the City of San Francisco, the State of California, and the concessionaires, companies, and individuals who had put their money and faith into the endeavor.

The potential reward was a profitable Fair that would bring glory, residents, and, perhaps most importantly, more gold to the Golden State. Beyond financial perils, if the PPIE did not attract enough visitors, its backers would fail in their attempt to declare San Francisco, largely ruined in 1906, restored and open for business. Coming up short could set back the city's perceived recovery by years or even decades.

The goals of filling the Jewel City with exhibits and attendees were far from trivial. Though the Exposition offered space within the palaces free to exhibitors, substantial outlays by nations, states, and purveyors of goods would be required to create displays, ship them to San Francisco, and build the spectacular booths in which they'd be presented. A truly "international" exposition required foreign participation, and Europe in particular was weary from the dozens of fairs held in preceding decades.

Even though railroads and the State of California advertised the opportunity to "See America First" as a bonus to those traveling to the PPIE, there was no denying that San Francisco was a remote destination for much of the nation's population. Fairgoers would have to travel days or weeks to be able to spend their hard-earned money within the Exposition and at the city's hotels and restaurants.

ORGANIZING THE EARTH

For all its parades, pageants, and fireworks shows, exhibits are the true heart of any fair, and one

San Francisco promoted the PPIE's connection with the completion of the Panama Canal using postcards like this one. (Glenn D. Koch)

of international scope required a monumental classification system to organize its displays. For this work, the PPIE turned to Dr. Frederick James Volney Skiff, a journalist and doctor of laws. Since 1894, the former Colorado legislator had served as director of the Field Museum in Chicago, and he had worked on every major exposition since the 1893 Chicago Columbian Exposition, where he was deputy director-general. He had also been in charge of the US exhibits at the Paris Exposition Universelle in 1900 and was the director of exhibits for the 1904 St. Louis Louisiana Purchase Exposition.

Skiff was hired by the PPIE in late 1911 as director-in-chief of foreign and domestic participation and quickly set about assembling a team of directors for the exhibit departments. He also developed a taxonomy that would define the space needed for each palace and also designate award categories. Awards were critical in attracting exhibitors, who could use the honors for years in their advertising.

Exposition taxonomy was an evolving discipline that had changed appreciably since the inception of world's fairs. For instance, electricity so permeated life by 1915 that it no longer had its own exhibit hall, as it had at previous fairs—it was simply everywhere. Exhibit classification was difficult, as an installation might fit into several categories, so Skiff, assisted by Director of Exhibits Asher Carter Baker, consulted with universities, governmental authorities, and industry and international experts to make sure classifications were up to date.

Skiff organized the sequence of palaces according to perceived patron interest, finishing his work in April 1913. He said, "The general theory is that Art is first, because it is through Art that we find our oldest history. Education comes second because it is through education that a man enters life. Then the Liberal Arts, because it is through invention, as man has developed, that he has met his necessities. Then come the natural resources of Mines, and Agriculture, and Horticulture. And then man goes to Manufacturing, and Transportation, and so you follow it along down." This outline helped determine the layout of the Jewel City.[4]

Of course, any endeavor of such magnitude entails some conflict, and the Exposition's hierarchy of directors, managers, and appointed officials provided it. Men resigned, men were fired, and a few passed away. San Joaquin County's commissioner to the PPIE was dismissed because of his alleged laziness in promoting the Exposition. Harris D. H. Connick, director of works, incurred the wrath of the press when he did not provide sufficient access to his staff.

Director M. H. de Young had a supremely bad year in 1913. While serving as chairman of the Division of Concessions and Admissions, he argued with PPIE president Charles C. Moore. De Young wanted authority to approve concessions, but Moore insisted on final say, and de Young ended up resigning his chairmanship, though he remained an active vice president and director of the Fair. In September he experienced a far greater loss. His only son, thirty-two-year-old Charles de Young, himself an Exposition director, died from typhoid fever.

Nevertheless, the Exposition apparatus adapted. Replacements for the departed were found, and feuding parties set aside their disagreements for the good of the overall effort. Momentum built toward Opening Day.

Chiefs for the various exhibit divisions were hired between 1912 and 1914. The departments included Fine Arts, Education and Social Economy, Food Products, Agriculture, Liberal Arts, Horticulture, Manufactures and Varied Industries, Mining and Metallurgy, and Transportation and Machinery. These were divided into 156 exhibit groups and 800 classes. Most of the chiefs had prior exposition experience, and all were experts in their fields.

COURTING EXHIBITORS

While the advantages of showing at the Fair were many, space in the palaces still had to be "sold." The national economy was in recession in 1913, and mounting an exhibit was costly. The

"Bear in Mind: 1915," as seen on this postcard, was one of many visual puns used to advertise the upcoming Exposition. (Laura Ackley)

Exposition mailed circulars to industry, trade, and scientific organizations proclaiming the benefits of exhibiting. These included full police and fire protection and the aforementioned awards, which not only could increase the visibility and value of their wares but also could demonstrate them to an immense and international audience.

Traditionally, fairs exhibited the finest examples of products and processes, but the PPIE sought items that "exemplified the research and productive skill of the decade just passed." Further, the Exposition encouraged "working exhibits" whenever practical. Some disciplines, such as Education and Social Economy, recommended that exhibitors collaborate with each other to create well-rounded presentations that avoided duplication between booths.[5]

Once they decided to show at San Francisco, exhibitors had to abide by a strict code. They were required to erect booths conforming to published Exposition-defined standards, including the prescribed heights for platforms, railings, tabletops, display cases, and cornices. Rules dictated that display labels be printed or typed and that signage be "moderate in size and neat in design." Electricity, steam, or natural gas was provided by the PPIE at special rates for those who wanted to show machinery in motion, and manufacturers of musical devices had to build soundproof demonstration rooms.[6]

While the Exposition was under way, behavior within the booths also was regulated. Employees could not eat in display spaces. Advertising handouts had to be preapproved by the chief of the pertinent department. Goods could be sold from booths, but exhibitors needed to apply for and purchase a concessionaire license. Only duplicate items kept outside the Exposition grounds could be sold; actual display items could not be sold until the end of the Fair.

The first exhibitor application, from the Standard Gas Engine Company of San Francisco, was submitted January 31, 1911, the same day the House of Representatives voted to endorse San Francisco as the Exposition site. A flood of additional applications followed. Despite such an enthusiastic early response, Skiff knew from experience that about one-third of planned exhibits would not materialize, so the PPIE purposely overbooked them, reportedly by as much as double the available space. Yet in spite of this precaution, the outbreak of World War I was an unanticipated catastrophe that left the Fair scrambling to fill the palaces.

Director of Exhibits Asher Carter Baker later wrote, "In order that an exposition should become the center of civilization two things are necessary—universal peace and universal prosperity. The prospects of foreign participation looked very bright when, on February 3, 1912, President William Howard Taft issued a proclamation inviting the nations of the world to participate in the Exposition….[But] international complications began to present themselves early….The Alien Land Bill nearly lost Japan's participation; the Mexican complications made difficult Mexico's active interest in our national government; and the European conflict, with the business complications following, had such a serious influence on foreign and domestic exhibitors that…disaster faced the Exhibits Division."[7]

DIPLOMATIC PERILS

Merely announcing a "world's fair" did not guarantee the world would exhibit, yet by 1915 official national pavilions showcasing the natural resources, handicrafts, and industries of civilization were considered essential to achieving a "universal" character at any international exposition.

The near loss of Japan's participation was a good example of the tangle of political intrigues Exposition boosters encountered. Japan had been an enthusiastic contributor to world's fairs since 1867, and the nation's presence at the PPIE, along with that of China, was considered critically important to strengthening the image of San Francisco as an entrepôt to Asia for goods traveling through the Panama Canal. But Japan's relations with California had chilled dramatically in the decade before the Exposition, first because of San Francisco's attempts to segregate Japanese schoolchildren beginning in 1905, and then due to a series of proposed bills designed to bar Japanese residents from owning land in the state.

Japanese and Chinese participation was considered essential from the earliest days of planning the Fair. Despite diplomatic relations being jeopardized by passage of the Alien Land Act, the two countries were major participants. Here a throng in the Festival Hall listens to Commissioner-General Haruki Yamawaki's address celebrating the opening of the Japanese Pavilion. (Edward A. Rogers)

Even in the earliest planning stages San Francisco considered strong Japanese and Chinese participation not just desirable but vital to the success of the PPIE. In May 1910 Governor James Gillett asked for congressional recognition of the Fair in part to help "interest the people of China and Japan in coming to San Francisco and putting in an exhibit bigger than they have put in anywhere…." Shortly after San Francisco was confirmed as the host city, the Exposition directorate began courting Japanese leaders to secure that nation's presence.[8]

Although Japan accepted early, in May of 1912, its participation was in grave doubt just a few months later. In the first months of 1913, the California legislature began considering the Webb-Haney Alien Land Act, which would prohibit land ownership by aliens ineligible for citizenship. PPIE officials worried Japan would withdraw from the Fair if the act passed. The legislation was aimed squarely at the Japanese, as federal law at the time permitted only Caucasians and persons of African descent to be naturalized. The Chinese were already effectively barred because the 1882 Chinese Exclusion Act prohibited most immigration from their country.

Labor and farming interests backed the Alien Land Act. They said they felt threatened by Japanese immigrants who, they argued, were usurping the state's agricultural acerage and driving up land prices. Exclusionists cited Hawaii, where they claimed the 41.5 percent ethnic Japanese population was "a curse." Further, they justified the bill by arguing Americans were barred from owning land in Japan.[9]

The chiefs of the Fair opposed the measure and argued against it several times in the state legislature. While the personal opinions of all Exposition executives are not known, their public objections were not on the grounds that the statute was morally repugnant but that it would imperil the PPIE. Enact anti-Asian legislation if you must, they said, but please wait until the Exposition is over.

In a concerted effort to stop the bill, Exposition directors Reuben Brooks Hale, Frederick Skiff, Leon Sloss, James McNab, and two of the three official state commissioners to the Fair went to Sacramento on April 2 with a polished presentation that included motion pictures. They were upstaged by the dramatic laments of a group of farmers, who claimed their livelihoods were jeopardized by the influx of "Asiatic standards" and mixed-race children. Was a "little fair," they asked, more important than the welfare of California?[10, 11]

The Tokyo newspaper *Asahi* said that if the Alien Land Act passed, "Japan must immediately withdraw her support from the Panama-Pacific Exposition…." Washington, too, was concerned, as the California law could damage the national relationship with Japan. President Wilson first asked Secretary of State William Jennings Bryan to send a sternly worded telegram asking that the "ineligible for citizenship" verbiage be stricken from the bill, then dispatched Bryan himself to persuade California legislators to reword the law. Nevertheless, the measure, offending language included, carried on May 3 to the chagrin of Exposition proponents.[12]

Some factions in Japan protested heartily, so there was much relief at the Exposition offices when on May 21 Japan appropriated $1.2 million yen ($600,000) for its PPIE displays and national pavilion. Thus one disaster was averted, but another threatened.

Although Mexico had been suffering through ongoing revolutionary upheaval since 1910, it accepted the invitation to participate in the Exposition. Henry Lane Wilson, the American ambassador to Mexico, received an official letter of acceptance from Mexico's minister of foreign relations on March 31, 1912. The difficulty was that the United States refused to recognize the new regime of Victoriano Huerta following the assassination of Mexican president Francisco Madero in February. In *Mexico at the World's Fairs: Crafting a Modern Nation*, Mauricio Tenorio-Trillo writes that Huerta still advocated Mexican participation in the Exposition, perhaps in an effort to secure US recognition of his government. US-Mexican relations continued to be tense, with multiple border skirmishes and the 1914 US bombardment and occupation of Veracruz. In the ensuing period of political unrest and financial depression, plans for an official Mexican display at the PPIE were dropped, leaving only the Tehuantepec Village concession

on the Joy Zone to represent America's neighbor to the south.[13]

With national and international political and economic conditions precarious, teams were dispatched to states and nations to extend President Wilson's personal invitation to participate in San Francisco.

THE EXPOSITION LEGIONS

From San Francisco and New York, men ascended the gangways of steamships and stepped up into train cars to evangelize about the Exposition. Starting in 1912, all continents except Antarctica were visited by representatives of the Fair. While they sought acceptances, even refusals were useful. If a state or country was not sending an official exhibit, the PPIE could then solicit unofficial and commercial representation. International missions targeted Europe, the Mediterranean and North Africa, Australia and New Zealand, Thailand and China, Central and South America, the Caribbean, Indonesia, and South Africa, while a "Flying Legion" visited North American cities.

This Flying Legion developed after members of San Francisco's Chamber of Commerce, Rotary, Down Town Association, and Merchants' Exchange decided to travel to the centennial celebration of Astoria, Oregon, in August 1911, "boosting" the PPIE along the way. This trip was so successful they suggested to the Fair's Division of Exploitation that an official recruiting body of several hundred prominent men be enlisted. Special trains chugged to Arizona and up and down the West Coast from Los Angeles to Victoria, British Columbia, carrying businessmen and luminaries including Mayor James Rolph, publisher Paul Elder, Bank of America founder A. P. Giannini, University of California president Benjamin Ide Wheeler, and scientist Luther Burbank, who was considered the star attraction.

In addition to these promotional trips, legion members kept track of California county exhibitors and used their own automobiles to chauffeur visiting delegations, which saved hundreds of dollars a month in car rentals. Some members coordinated the special events

US president William Howard Taft (on right side of platform), PPIE president Charles C. Moore (at right with shovel), and the attending crowd listen as Lillian Nordica sings at the Exposition's official groundbreaking on October 14, 1911. (John Freeman)

and exhibits, such as the polo tournament and livestock show. Others worked with fraternal and national orders—societies like the Danish American, Greek American, and Swiss American auxiliaries were asked to send letters inviting their home countries to the Fair.

When four Flying Legion members boarded the steamer *Tasman,* bound for the Antipodes in September 1913, they did not expect high-seas danger. The *Tasman* struck Bramble Cay Reef between Queensland, Australia, and Papua New Guinea, and lodged there on December 27. Pumps kept the water gushing into the hold at bay, but the passengers endured an ordeal of several days before they could be taken off the ship safely. Coincidentally, opera diva Lillian Nordica, who sang at the PPIE groundbreaking ceremony, also was on board. Nordica suffered from exposure, which developed into pneumonia. She died in Batavia, Java (now Jakarta, Indonesia), on May 10, 1914.

COMMISSION EXTRAORDINARY

The largest and most important delegation of Exposition boosters, the "Commission Extraordinary," set sail for London in April 1912, less than two weeks after the *Titanic* sank. Little did they realize their efforts were jeopardized by a different sort of hidden menace—the invisible network of diplomatic agreements prevalent in Europe.

For fifty-five days, by sea and rail, the deputation traveled 25,000 miles, visiting fifteen European capitals and attending forty-five official banquets. Along the way, they were received by an emperor, an archduke, a crown prince, three presidents, and six kings as they traced a path through England, Germany, Russia, Austria, Hungary, Italy, France, Belgium, Portugal, Spain, Switzerland, Sweden, Norway, Denmark, and the Netherlands. At each stop, American ambassadors secured audiences with national leaders and hosted lavish events where they met representatives of government, the military, and commerce. The Commission Extraordinary presented each monarch or president with a portfolio of sketches of the proposed Exposition and an album of photographs of the reconstructed City of San Francisco. Daily wires, sent to thirteen news agencies, tracked the group's progress.

The commissioners diplomatically specified they were not seeking an immediate, definitive response but simply conveying the presidential invitation to the event, which would promote the "peace, tranquility, and commercial development and opportunity enabled by the Panama Canal."[14]

The worst risk of dozens of banquets, receptions, and parties was not indigestion, though commission member William Sesnon wrote to Moore that if he "returned with a worn out disordered liver," he'd hold the Exposition's president responsible. There were more serious stakes.[15]

The European nations raised some surprising concerns and objections to exhibiting abroad. Russia complained that time was too short to mount an adequate display. For other countries, the expense of preparing an overseas exhibit or a national pavilion was a major factor. Many were concerned about high tariffs that might be imposed on exhibit goods, as well as the protection of their patents and trademarks. A disastrous fire at the 1910 Exposition Universelle et Internationale in Brussels, Belgium, made nations wary of fire and worried about protection for their priceless artifacts.

Though the American delegation was fully credentialed by the State Department and armed with an official letter of invitation signed by President Taft, some European leaders thought that because the US government was not paying for the Fair, the Jewel City was not officially sanctioned. This concern was uniquely galling, as San Francisco's insistence that it would not accept federal funds was critical in its winning the right to host the Exposition.

Lastly, the Commission Extraordinary found to its dismay that Europe was somewhat "exposition-tired" after sixty years of world's fairs. They "were inclined to think that there have been too many great expositions in our time and generation," said one dispatch.[16]

To some objections there was no easy remedy, but the commission quickly dispensed with others. They recommended that the PPIE establish bonded warehouses, assure protection for international intellectual property, and allow entry for foreign nationals so they could create exhibits. In September 1913, Congress passed the Kahn Copyright and Patent Act, which allowed items intended for exhibit to be admitted duty free and also protected foreign patents for the Exposition period plus three years. Passage of the bill persuaded France to exhibit.

THE PLOT THICKENS

The Commission Extraordinary's sojourn produced mixed results. About half of the countries visited decided to build pavilions at the PPIE, but three of the biggest fish wriggled through the net. First Russia declined, but this was not a major shock, as that nation had not been a regular participant in previous world's fairs. Moreover, relations were frosty after the United States' 1911 abrogation of the 1832 Russian-American Commercial Treaty, which had

The Commission Extraordinary departs San Francisco for Europe on its quest for international participation. (Panama-Pacific International Exposition Photograph Album (SFP17), San Francisco History Center, San Francisco Public Library)

allowed free commerce between the two nations.

More worrisome was that major industrial powers England and Germany, mainstays at world's fairs, were waffling. Britain cited the high cost of exhibiting at ever-multiplying expositions, and Germany complained about tariffs, despite the fact that the legislation to dismiss tariffs on exhibits had been introduced. *Sunset* magazine called England's and Germany's reticence "sulking."[17]

Both countries were lobbied aggressively. Newspapers and magazines counseled that the PPIE would be a form of "international advertising" and create new opportunities for trade. Prominent English writers, led by *Sherlock Holmes* author Sir Arthur Conan Doyle, urged British participation, and businessmen in both nations formed coalitions to encourage their countries to exhibit.

For a time there was reason for optimism. Albert Ballin, the powerful director-general of the Hamburg-American shipping line, threw his weight behind official German cooperation. The British Board of Trade favored the Fair. San Francisco's former mayor James D. Phelan wired from London that he thought both countries eventually would come around. Then came a revelation: reports circulated that England and Germany had a secret pact that neither would exhibit at the PPIE. This accord was characteristic of the labyrinth of covert ententes rife within Europe before World War I.

A young mining engineer and future president of the United States, Herbert C. Hoover, was the Exposition's official European representative, and he intimated that the Anglo-German conspiracy was in reaction to America's new toll structure for the Panama Canal. Hoover warned that if the European nations were forming backroom agreements regarding the PPIE, they also might be doing so on more vital diplomatic issues. Both Germany and England hotly denied any collusion.

In the end, while both British and German art and commercial wares were shown on a small scale at the PPIE, neither country had an official presence. Two German concessions were under construction when World War I erupted. The Parseval Airship Company planned to

Pennsylvania Railroad System cars are maneuvered into position as exhibits in the Palace of Transportation, using the special transfer table designed to move huge rolling stock. (Seligman Family Foundation)

give dirigible rides, and the Kali Syndicate to showcase the nation's potash industry. But once hostilities commenced, the dirigible mooring remained empty and the Kali Syndicate building was repurposed as the Greek Pavilion.

THE WORLD'S WARES COME TO SAN FRANCISCO

As state and national pavilions were readied, around the globe costly and wondrous artifacts were packed carefully into crates and hoisted into freight cars or gingerly swung from docks onto ships bound for San Francisco. The Customs and Deliveries and Traffic departments of the Exposition, responsible for managing the flow of goods in and out of the grounds, commenced a logistical minuet. At the end of May 1914 the Palace of Machinery became the first hall ready to receive shipments, and the rest followed. Scant months remained to build the exhibit booths and load approximately 80,000 displays.

Inside the palaces, light filtered down from the long rows of arched clerestory windows onto floors swept clean of construction debris. White-coated men had sprayed a neutral coat of creamy paint onto the wooden column assemblies, trusses, walls, and the undersides of the domes sixteen stories above the ground. Now the huge, echoing spaces waited to fill with the wares of the world.

A. M. Mortensen, the PPIE's traffic manager, made a special trip to the East Coast to negotiate discounted shipping for exhibits to the Fair. Virtually all domestic railroads agreed on standard reduced rates. More than a dozen steamship lines, including American-Hawaiian, Pacific-Alaska, Luckenbach, Pacific Mail, and Matson lowered their rates to San Francisco by 25 to 50 percent and offered still cheaper— even free—return freight. Several international shipping lines, including New Zealand's Union Steamship Company and Germany's Hamburg-American and Kosmos lines, patriotically offered to carry exhibits from their nations free of charge both to and from San Francisco.

To qualify for the favorable rates granted by the rail and shipping lines, packages had to contain "certified exhibits," all shipping charges

and Exposition terminal fees had to be prepaid, and an advance notice of shipment sent to the traffic manager. The PPIE's charge for handling exhibits arriving in San Francisco by rail was ten cents per hundred pounds with a $1 minimum charge. Terminal charges on water shipments were twelve and a half cents per hundred pounds. For goods not likely to make the return trip, such as items to be sold at the Fair or materials to construct the exhibits, a one-way rate was available. Loads that did not make up an entire railroad car could be routed to New York, Chicago, or St. Louis, where an Exposition representative would consolidate them into complete carloads to qualify them for further rate reductions. For the most fragile or expensive items, exhibitors were instructed to use one of a few express companies authorized for pickup and delivery on the grounds.

Ships emblazoned with exotic names like *Maitai, Yaroslavl, Tenyo Maru, Vega, Manchuria,* and *Marama* weighed anchor, their holds packed with crates full of exhibits. They embarked from such ports as Yokohama, Tegucigalpa, Manila, Copenhagen, Bangkok, Auckland, and Lisbon, their journeys ranging from the pedestrian to the perilous. Some ships were racked by vicious storms while others faced manmade dangers. The *Jultandra,* entrusted with part of the Norwegian art collection, steered an Arctic course north of the Orkney Islands to avoid the war zone. Carrying five hundred tons of Scandinavian exhibits, the Danish freighter *Rhodesia* also picked her way north, dodging underwater mines in the North Sea.

Trainloads and boatloads and truckloads of goods flowed into the grounds, tracked by Customs and Deliveries and routed into the correct locations by the Traffic Department. The total volume of goods pouring into the Exposition was staggering: there were nearly fifty-seven million pounds of material in more than 202,000 separate packages, most arriving in the ninety days before the Jewel City's opening. Once a package arrived, it was delivered to the palace, aisle address, and space number on its label. If the exhibitor was not present to take delivery "within a reasonable time," the Traffic Department stored the goods at the exhibitor's expense.[18]

The Exposition's Department of Customs and Deliveries oversaw the relations between exhibitors, the Fair, and United States Customs. It kept track of all shipping documents and administered the patent and copyright protections extended to foreign exhibitors under the Kahn Act. One provision of the legislation allowed exhibitors the option to send their goods home at the end of the Fair or to sell them in the United States, at which point they became subject to regular duty, less any depreciation from damage while on display.

Even with such detailed supervision, disorder struck in the weeks before and immediately following opening. Too late the PPIE realized it could have reduced the number of last-minute arrivals by raising its terminal fees. Once the Fair opened, moving the exhibits was costly and inconvenient, and these late deliveries, only allowed between 11:00 p.m. and 9:00 a.m., cost at least one-third more than they would have prior to opening. Traffic Manager Mortensen estimated that had the Exposition simply raised the rates by 50 percent in the weeks leading up to the Fair, fewer exhibits would have arrived late.

ASSEMBLING THE EXHIBITS

As exhibits arrived, workmen putting the finishing touches on palace roofs could peer through the skylights into the hives of activity beneath. Beyond the wired glass and X-braced trusses supporting the ceilings, they could see clearly the grid of streets and avenues that organized the mammoth display floors five stories below. Along these aisles, a lone man could maneuver heavy or unwieldy loads using a powerful electric truck. Within the blocks created by the street grid, tiny figures built either low railings or fifteen-foot-tall, free-standing colonnades to separate exhibit areas. In some booths men on ladders or scaffolds added elegant cornices and pediments, arches or domes to mark the entrances to the spaces.

Down on the floor, the noise of hammers, saws, and machinery was incessant and the air moted with plaster and sawdust. The area was strewn with the tools, sawhorses, paint cans,

drop cloths, brushes, and hardware needed to transform waiting stacks of rough lumber into sumptuous settings for the treasures en route. Small, sturdy, black-painted Ohio Locomotive cranes puffed about the standard-gauge tracks laid along the floors of the palaces.

The biggest machines to be shown at the PPIE had been moved in on these same tracks before the perimeters of the booths were constructed, and now they waited midst the chaos for the more puny elements to be positioned around them. For instance, giant embroidery looms inhabited an otherwise empty enclosure in the Palace of Varied Industries, awaiting the smaller showcases that would complete the exhibit. In the Palace of Transportation, locomotives and rail cars had been distributed across the hall on a network of rails connected to a huge "transfer table," while automobiles, motorcycles, and model ships would arrive later.

THE DIVISION OF EXPLOITATION

With the palaces nearly filled, all that was needed were guests, and promoting the Fair was the task of the Division of Exploitation. In exposition parlance, "exploitation" meant "publicity," and in an era a few years prior to the start of broadcast radio and decades before television, the exploitation division used some surprising avenues to promulgate the Fair's appeal. From early 1912 until Closing Day, the PPIE's team garnered miles of print coverage one column-inch at a time, employed innovative marketing strategies, and found itself embroiled in one bona fide media scandal.

John Brisben Walker, the original director of exploitation, had the bright idea in August 1912 to ask the Trans-Mississippi Commercial Congress to solicit $5 million from the United States Congress for the PPIE, a request that violated the Fair's pledge neither to ask for nor to accept federal aid. Walker's resignation was tendered and accepted. He was swiftly replaced by the competent and less controversial George Hough Perry, the founder of *Everybody's Magazine* and a former advertising manager for the Siegel-Cooper, Wanamaker, and

Theater impresarios, industrial magnates, and railroads donated space on large signs from Broadway to Chicago to tout the Fair. San Francisco's Ferry Building announced "California Invites the World" in huge letters. (Laura Ackley)

Gimbel Brothers department stores. Perry said he viewed his PPIE department not as a "promotion bureau, but a thoroughly first-class news and literary service...."[19]

Yet the efforts of the Division of Exploitation were jeopardized when a group of advertising executives threatened the PPIE. They said that without $1 million spent on advertising, the Fair would fail, and that "the papers of importance would print nothing concerning the Exposition unless it was paid for...." Still the Fair refused to buy ad space, calling upon the press to report on the Exposition as a national event celebrating a national achievement—the completion of the Panama Canal. William Randolph Hearst pledged his nine newspapers, two weeklies, six magazines, and his wire service in support of the Fair, and others followed suit. Eventually, Perry's department secured the equivalent of about $50 million in newspaper and magazine space at no cost. He claimed proudly, "Seventy-one percent of what we send out is printed, and one hundred percent of the seventy-one percent is printed free."[20]

Although the PPIE would not pay for advertising, it did erect a well-appointed Press Building on the grounds to house the Division of Exploitation and visiting journalists. All the San Francisco dailies maintained branch offices there, and traveling correspondents were supplied with desks, typewriters, telephones, stenographers, messengers, and bulletin boards. Western Union provided telegraph service, and United Press a wire office.

Perry oversaw a permanent staff of thirty-five, which comprised editorial, art, information, printing and engraving, publications, and records bureaus. A stable of talented writers was organized into four newspaper-like beats, which covered the Fair's executive departments, construction, concessions, and exhibits.

As the division's editor-in-chief, journalist Hamilton Wright gathered information from those in charge of the departments and penned many of the most detailed stories on the Jewel City, with effusive titles like "A World Epitome," "Oh, the Zone, the Zone, the Dizzy Zone," "The Mecca of the Nation," and "The Panama Exposition in Its Glorious Prime." The newsroom-like atmosphere of the Press Building was one of the few environments on the grounds where women contributed as near-equals. Writers Lucy G. White, Genevieve Yoell Parkhurst, and Jessie Niles Burness composed stories on the grandeur of California and the Exposition, while Marie Hicks Davidson covered the activities of the Fair's Woman's Board.

The team of writers and artists produced

general articles and boilerplate pictorial layouts for distribution by the syndicated wire services, as well as specialized articles for elite periodicals. The department solicited detailed descriptions of exhibits, then crafted articles for relevant industry journals. When well-known figures visited San Francisco, they were interviewed and the resultant stories sent to their home newspapers.

By 1913 more than 21,000 newspapers in the US and Canada were covering Exposition news, and the Division of Exploitation's staff was "keeping publications in China, Japan, Australia, Sweden, Norway, Denmark, Great Britain, the Netherlands, France, Germany, Spain, Italy, India, Egypt, and even far-away South Africa in touch with the development of the 1915 celebration." By 1914 an average of 60,000 column-inches a week were devoted to the PPIE, but as news of the escalating European conflict required more and more space, the Exposition news was increasingly squeezed.[21]

Innovative campaigns were required to secure public attention, and the exploitation division produced far more than just newspaper and magazine articles. It also created collateral material in eighteen languages, including fact booklets, railway "rack folders," color

supplements, literature for exhibitors, calendars, and even what would be considered "multimedia" presentations today. One of the most recognizable pieces was the "Hercules Booklet," with a striking cover by artist Perham Nahl titled *The Thirteenth Labor of Hercules*. The image showed the muscular hero forcing apart the rock walls of the Culebra Cut to form the Panama Canal, with an ethereal Exposition shining in the background, visually linking the Fair to American imperialism through classical allusion. *The Thirteenth Labor of Hercules* also was lithographed on 10,000 posters distributed by the American Poster Association.

Nolan Davis was in charge of publications for the Division of Exploitation, and in addition to printed matter, his group prepared sets of colorful "lantern slides" for use by lecturers. A department headed by Dr. Frederick Vining Fisher dispatched speakers on tours across the country, where they presented 2,715 talks to chambers of commerce, Chautauquas, church groups, and the like, reaching an audience just shy of one million. Brilliant images projected through the three-by-four-inch glass slides illustrated each speaker's words. Davis' department published nearly ten million pieces of literature prior to the

The Division of Exploitation, the PPIE's marketing department, sent a cadre of lecturers across the nation equipped with colorful lantern slides to illustrate their talks on the Fair. The slides featured scenes like this view of the tranquil Court of the Four Seasons, designed by Henry Bacon. (Laura Ackley)

Fair, leading one magazine to declare, "After two years' service he has succeeded in covering the earth with the knowledge of the Exposition...."[22]

The PPIE also leveraged the allure of show business. All the interesting pre-Exposition events were filmed, including groundbreaking ceremonies, parades, flag-raisings, and construction progress. These films were shown in newsreels at theaters across the country. Harry Lauder, a Scottish comedian and singer of sentimental songs, even touted the PPIE on his 1914 tour of Australia and New Zealand.

PHILATELY

Although the PPIE stipulated it would accept no federal funds for the Exposition, it did receive some publicity courtesy of the US Post Office Department, which issued new stamps and a cancellation in honor of the Fair. "The Whole Country Will Lick Us Now" trumpeted the *San Francisco Call*. One-, two-, five- and ten-cent stamps were produced, with "San Francisco, 1915" appearing on each denomination. The five-cent stamp pictured the Golden Gate viewed from Alcatraz, and the ten-cent stamp depicted the discovery of the San Francisco Bay. Assistant Postmaster William Burke suggested creating a postal cancellation for the Exposition, but a 1901 order preventing cancels advertising any undertaking for which Congress had not appropriated money seemed to preclude this. After a flurry of correspondence among various postmasters, however, the San Francisco post office was permitted to use the cancellation beginning in May 1911. Requests from other Pacific cities eventually saw the cancellation in use in municipalities from Seattle to Los Angeles.

CLEVER CO-PROMOTIONS

Many commercial and public organizations stood to profit from a successful Exposition. San Francisco–area publishers printed sheet music, postcards, and serialized folios. Local manufacturers and merchants produced maps to help visitors navigate the city, each marked with the PPIE grounds and, of course, the location of the relevant business.

The Fair worked with banks nationwide to promote Exposition Accounts that allowed investors to save for a journey to the Jewel City. Three hundred and seventy-eight American newspapers ran contests in which readers sold subscriptions in hopes of being a top seller, each of whom would receive a free trip to the Fair. Thus for the price of a single vacation, the PPIE received multiple large display ads in each paper, eventually totaling the equivalent of $400,000 of advertising space. In exchange, newspapers increased their readerships; one paper reported $25,000 in new subscriptions.

In exchange for the title "Official Typewriter of the Panama-Pacific International Exposition," the Remington Typewriter Company lent and maintained all the machines the PPIE needed. The Division of Exploitation published a colorful brochure featuring the explorer Balboa on the cover, which was offered in all 658 Remington sales offices countrywide. Since most businesses used typewriters by 1910, this was an effective avenue for publicity, and Remington distributed one million copies of the Balboa booklet.

"California Invites the World" read huge letters mounted atop the Ferry Building at the foot of San Francisco's Market Street, but this was not the only giant advertisement for the Exposition. "Public spirit and generosity" prompted the Billboard Advertising Association to donate 10,000 outdoor advertising spaces. Five large signs in New York and Chicago advertised the Fair in flashing electric lights. In New York, theater proprietors Marcus Loew, Cohan and Harris, and William Morris contributed their signs along the Hudson River, on the Astor Theater in Times Square, and atop the New York Roof Garden, respectively. The Candler Building on West 42nd Street, owned by the founder of Coca-Cola, was likewise adorned. Chicago's Rush Street Bridge issued an invitation to San Francisco on a fifty-foot-square sign gleaming with 3,860 animated lights, courtesy of the Chicago & Northwestern Railroad.[23]

Travel-related businesses hoped to profit during the Exposition year, so travel clubs, resorts, regional tourist associations, passenger ship lines, and especially railroads produced an abundance of marketing materials. Hotels added the PPIE logo to their stationery. "Travel Without Trouble," advertised the firm of Thomas Cook, which, like other tour agencies, put together customized tour packages advertised in detailed brochures.

East-west rail lines were zealous in promoting the PPIE. Several had a vested interest in the Fair beyond the tourist dollars it might bring them, having subscribed to stock in the Exposition. Southern Pacific bought $150,000 in stock, its sister company Central Pacific $100,000, and the Atchison, Topeka & Santa Fe $125,000.

These lines—along with feeder rail lines that expected a corresponding surge in passengers, and rolling stock manufacturers such as Westinghouse Electric—endorsed the Fair energetically. They used newspaper and magazine ads, special rates and itineraries, and "uncountable millions" of pamphlets, flyers, and viewbooks describing the wonders of the PPIE, California, and the scenery en route. *Sunset*, the Southern Pacific Railroad's magazine mouthpiece until 1914, devoted scores of articles and at least half a dozen colorful covers to the Exposition.[24]

BOOSTING FOR AND BY CALIFORNIA

The PPIE recognized its symbiotic relationship with the State of California: tourists attending the Fair would bring money to the state's coffers, and the state's diverse attractions would bring more tourists to the Jewel City. The *Call* newspaper quoted one Division of Exploitation source: "This Fair is for California….We are not interested in where people go after they get to California, but we are interested in getting them here." The Division of Exploitation promoted California even as towns up and down the state boosted the Exposition.[25]

Beyond commemorating the Panama Canal, the not-particularly-subtle secondary goal of the PPIE was to replace the image of San Francisco as a smoking ruin with one of a cultural rather than seismic epicenter. The Fair circulated photos featuring side-by-side views of destroyed areas just after the 1906 disaster next to their

splendid rebuilt forms, showing off the fine new buildings. It also repurposed a post-quake image popularized by the California Insurance Company to advertise its liberal payouts: the dramatic illustration of a California grizzly standing atop the smoldering city, the bear pierced by an arrow yet snarling and "Undaunted." The Exposition brightened the design and replaced the burning buildings with a colorful imaginary version of the Jewel City.

Local companies and individuals championed the Exposition on postcards featuring clever drawings, poems, rebuses, song lyrics, and optical illusions. Many cards featured puns, including "San Francisco weather forecast for 1915: FAIR" and "A fair deal: fair time, fair weather, fair treatment, fair girls, fair hotels." Cartoonist T. E. Powers created a series of cards featuring his impish "Joys and Glooms" characters convening

The "Undaunted" bear, originally used in advertising for the California Insurance Company following the 1906 earthquake, was repurposed to promote the Exposition. (Laura Ackley)

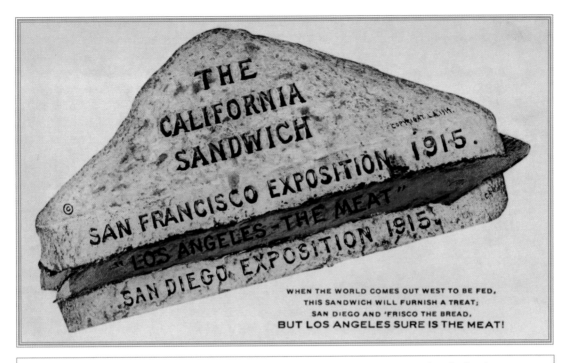

THE
CALIFORNIA
SANDWICH

SAN FRANCISCO EXPOSITION 1915.

LOS ANGELES THE MEAT"

SAN DIEGO EXPOSITION 1915.

WHEN THE WORLD COMES OUT WEST TO BE FED,
THIS SANDWICH WILL FURNISH A TREAT;
SAN DIEGO AND 'FRISCO THE BREAD,
BUT LOS ANGELES SURE IS THE MEAT!

Cities all over California saw the PPIE, along with San Diego's Panama-California Exposition, as beneficial to the entire state, as illustrated by this Los Angeles postcard entitled "The California Sandwich." (Laura Ackley)

in San Francisco. The PPIE's publications bureau sent to any interested party free brochures that included not only details of the Exposition but also descriptions of side trips within the Golden State. A full quarter of the *Exposition Fact-Book* was devoted to such trips.

Cities reciprocated by advertising the Jewel City. Los Angeles positioned itself as the way station between the San Francisco and San Diego fairs. The city printed a postcard depicting "The California Sandwich" that read, "When the world comes out West to be fed, this sandwich will furnish a treat; San Diego and 'Frisco the bread, but Los Angeles sure is the meat!"

The American West had helped San Francisco to victory in its fierce contest with New Orleans to host the fair, and the region continued its support as Opening Day drew nigh. A special train left St. Paul, Minnesota, on November 27, 1911, laden with Western governors and exhibits of their states' bounties. This "Western Governors' Special" canvassed thirty major cities from Chicago to Washington, DC, in twenty days, funneling 90,000 visitors through its

California car and distributing PPIE literature.

In addition to "making the Exposition known throughout the world," the Division of Exploitation's other main charter was to secure participation from thirty-seven of the forty-eight states (the other eleven being handled from a New York office). Perry said, "It was early found to be difficult to impress the legislatures with the desirability of appropriating large sums of money for participation in an Exposition which was still two years distant, and which was considered at the outset as merely an advertisement for California."[26]

Their efforts were hindered further by natural and manmade disasters, including devastating cyclones in Nebraska, floods in Ohio and Louisiana, drought in Missouri, Iowa, and Kansas, labor troubles in Colorado, and tussles over sugar and cotton in the southern states. The group reached out to state legislatures, boards of trade, and other commercial bodies to endorse Exposition appropriation bills. Where such bills failed in state legislatures, the PPIE advocated participation by popular subscription. Eventually, the West Coast exploitation office succeeded in attracting twenty-four of the states that eventually built pavilions or mounted exhibits in the palaces, while the East Coast office secured six.

PREPARING FOR THE CROWDS

The PPIE also needed to arrange special events to boost attendance and add interest. For these, much planning was required, so again experts were retained. Fabled amateur athletics expert James E. Sullivan was appointed to take charge of sporting events early in 1913. He prepared an ambitious schedule that included championships in track and field, swimming, tennis, cycling, and a score of other sports. Meanwhile, Director of Music George Stewart was laboring to assemble an impressive slate of entertainers from the realms of opera, classical and popular music, and dance.

Professional conferences, congresses, and fraternal or other group meetings were seen as the largest potential draws. Beginning in 1912, more than 250,000 four-page folders and 300,000 *Exposition Fact-Books* were distributed, encouraging organizations to hold conventions at the Fair during 1915. Reservations began to pour in.

"NO GOUGING OF EXPOSITION VISITORS!"

"San Francisco Hotel Men Prepare for a Killing" warned the ominous headline of a newspaper article predicting extortionate rates for 1915.[27]

In fact, representatives from four hundred local hotels met at the end of 1913 and adopted a resolution to keep rates low during the Exposition. However, these hotels represented only about one-third of the area's hostelries and, magnanimous language aside, not a single hotel had actually published its 1915 rates. The PPIE refuted claims of inflated rates, but newspapers sarcastically noted that similar denials had been issued for previous fairs in Chicago and St. Louis, where excessive hotel prices "had been the rule." As San Francisco hoteliers remained cagey about their rates, it seemed

as though they, too, planned to overcharge.[28]

The rumors were particularly worrisome as just then the PPIE's planners were attempting to attract conventions and professional congresses to the city for 1915, and organizers of these events were trying to book accommodations. The Bureau of Conventions was embarrassed that it could not promise hotel reservations or even guarantee fair pricing. For millions of potential visitors, lodging costs were a major factor in deciding whether to attend the Fair.

Charles C. Moore grew more and more incensed, finally declaring at a luncheon that the Exposition would protect its visitors from exorbitant prices, even if it meant setting up a tent city. Eventually, the PPIE went considerably beyond a tent city, approving an 1,800-room hotel within the grounds—appropriately called the Inside Inn—on a prominence south of the Palace of Fine Arts Lagoon. It was operated as a concession, but the Exposition controlled the Inside Inn's rates, set between $2 a day for a single room without a bath to $7 a day for a deluxe double room with bath, and $15 a day for a suite with a view.

Outraged proprietors of local hotels, rooming houses, and apartments tried to kill the scheme, declaring they were among the earliest and most generous supporters of the Fair, and now the PPIE was taking food from their mouths. Also, they said the Inside Inn should be subject to the same building codes as typical hotels, not the special regulations in place for temporary Exposition structures. The Board of Supervisors referred the matter to the city attorney, who declined to interfere.

While the Inside Inn, eventually reduced to 638 rooms, represented a tiny fraction of San Francisco inventory, the threat it represented was heard, and most local hoteliers finally fell into line. The newly galvanized hotel men created the Official Exposition Hotel Bureau in November 1914, under the supervision of Director of Exploitation George Hough Perry, and adopted the slogan "Protect Our Guests." Further, they branded any hotel, taxi, or café that raised prices astronomically "a menace to the interests and a danger to the reputation and credit of San Francisco."[29]

The Hotel Bureau was funded by dues of $1 for each room advertised under the program. The 212 member hotels in San Francisco, Oakland, and Berkeley submitted desired rates for each room and number of occupants. The rates were reviewed and approved or adjusted by a committee of hotel men, then published in an *Official Exposition Hotel Guide*, hundreds of thousands of which were distributed free. Uniformed guides on every train or steamboat approaching San Francisco during the Exposition informed travelers about the Hotel Bureau, assuring them that the system was the first "to protect visitors against extortion by hotels and from other forms of petty graft and abuse."[30]

Arrivals still without lodging were directed to information booths at several terminals, including the San Francisco Ferry Building, which were staffed by attendants kept informed on an hourly basis of current hotel room vacancies. Any hotel found guilty of overcharging was stricken permanently from the list of approved hotels.

Many San Franciscans who were accustomed to living full-time in hotels and apartments saw their expenses rise significantly when their monthly "American Plan" rate, which included meals, was converted to a daily "European Plan" tourist rate without meals for 1915. The Exposition contended this might seem unfair, but pointed out that many new hotels had been built in anticipation of the PPIE, so in recent years their rates had been artificially low.

Overall the Hotel Bureau served its purpose. While not every hotel joined and some were dropped for nonpayment of dues or violations, participation still was sufficient so that rooms were to be had at reasonable rates. Most critically, the bureau served to thoroughly quash reports of price gouging by Bay Area hotels during the Fair.

THE APPARATUS OF ADMISSIONS

Once visitors had been lured to San Francisco and adequately housed, the Exposition needed to control their admission to the Jewel City. Pedestrians passed through eighty-four turnstiles at eight entrances, an adequate capacity for even the busiest days. The turnstiles themselves were complicated new machines with a self-checking system that correlated the number of tokens or coins inserted against the number of times the stile revolved. They were connected electronically with the Department of Admissions, which could track attendance hourly if necessary. The busiest single turnstile, Number 31, at the Fillmore Gate, admitted more than 1.4 million guests. The new design worked well, though a slight alteration in the guardrail was required when it was discovered that slim individuals could squeeze through without turning the cloverleaf arms.

The 638-room Inside Inn, an official concession located within the Jewel City, was advertised in a brochure as a "modern, up-to-date hotel" with "all modern conveniences" for "the comfort of a discriminating public." (Edward A. Rogers)

In 1914, Virginia resident Major Algar M. Wheeler wrote to President Moore suggesting that season ticket books be sold. Some directors objected to the idea, saying it was tantamount to giving away gate receipts before the Jewel City even opened. But the PPIE was badly in need of funds, projecting a shortfall even after slashing the construction budget several times, and season ticket sales would provide an immediate cash infusion.

President Moore endorsed the idea, feeling that the nontransferable tickets would promote "educational uplift" and stimulate attendance because their holders would also bring friends. Also, he pointed out, every attendee was likely to spend money on concessions whether or not they had paid for daily admission. Moore also favored a relatively low price for the ticket books, which had sold poorly when priced at $25 at previous Expositions. He averred a lower price would improve sales and make the Fair accessible to "the average wage-earner."[31]

Demand for the slender little books was overwhelming. They were priced at $10, and an initial run of 10,000 was offered starting the first week of November 1914. Only holders of Exposition stock were allowed to apply, but within three weeks 25,000 requests were made. The print run was raised to 30,000, then a few weeks later to 50,000 books, and still the public clamored for more. Management eventually approved an additional 5,000 "late season" tickets, with coupons good from October 1 until the Fair closed.

A book was not usable until the owner had his image taken by an official photographer and affixed inside the cover, had the picture perforated with the letters "PPIE," and then signed the cover. Each book came with three sheaves of coupons that could be inserted into the cover one at a time to keep the book from becoming too bulky to fit in a vest pocket. Each of the 288 small, undated coupons—one for each day of the Exposition— was stamped in red ink with the same number as that of the ticket book cover. If every coupon was used, the price of admission would have averaged about three and a half cents, but in reality the average number of visits per book was seventy,

A young woman drops her coin into one of the new turnstiles designed especially for the PPIE to track admissions automatically and prevent gate fraud. (Edward A. Rogers)

yielding a fourteen-cent average price instead of the fifty-cent regular admission.

A season ticket book became a popular holiday employee gift for many businesses, and later the director of admissions reported that 80 percent of all books were used by "salaried persons." In fact, some snobbier San Franciscans eschewed their use. One woman, characterized by the *Wasp* as a social climber, was quoted, "Indeed I would not buy a season ticket. They are only for chauffeurs and maids."[32]

In addition to the season ticket books, San Franciscans were urged to purchase a pinback badge on a brightly colored ribbon to wear on Opening Day, which admitted the wearer through the gates in lieu of a ticket. One hundred thousand of the bright emblems were sold at fifty cents each. As a show of Exposition fealty, many chose to buy an Opening Day badge rather than use a season ticket coupon that day.

FILLING THE FAIR

Those outside the Exposition organization likely thought the biggest challenges—winning the right to host the Fair, choosing the site, and raising the buildings—had been overcome. But enticing exhibitors and patrons was perhaps equally challenging and beset by unexpected complications. Yet the planners and staff did a magnificent job of promoting the San Francisco World's Fair.

Their efforts to attract world patronage exposed rents in the international fabric that hinted at the inherent instability of the whole cloth. In Europe, the invisible mesh of clandestine agreements was ready to erupt into a war that, unfortunately, would not "end all wars."

Across the United States, disparate groups banded together to encourage participation in San Francisco's Fair. Laws were enacted to protect exhibitors, shipping companies created special rate packages for exhibits, and travel-related businesses ramped up advertising in support of the Exposition. Meanwhile, an experienced Division of Exploitation embraced novel ways to get the word out, shunning paid advertising in favor of a grassroots campaign of legitimate news

articles, traveling lecturers, donated billboard space, and co-promotions with businesses that would benefit from a profitable international exposition.

While there were missteps along the way, the PPIE's directorate leveraged knowledge gleaned from several prior international expositions to avoid some of the larger pitfalls the earlier events encountered. Guests of the Jewel City would not be disappointed with either the international participation (its thirty-one nations was on par with or exceeded previous world's fairs) or the lavishly filled palaces. Yet the successes the Exposition had so painstakingly earned since 1911 would yet be jeopardized by the global calamity that arrived just six months before the PPIE opened. ⁂

Ten-dollar season ticket books for the Exposition sold out quickly. Each contained 288 coupons, one for each day of the Fair. (Donna Ewald Huggins and Laura Ackley)

THE EXPOSITION WILL NOT BE POSTPONED

Charles C. Moore, PPIE president, was entertaining the Argentine Exposition Commission at his summer home among the cool evergreens of the Santa Cruz Mountains when the evening was interrupted by a phone call. It was August 1914 and with a full-scale war engulfing Europe, the Associated Press and local newspapers wanted to know if the PPIE would be postponed or even cancelled.

With no time to consult his board of directors, Moore issued a swift and unequivocal statement: "The Exposition will not be postponed." A few years later, the Fair's official historian called this moment "the quick turn of the helm that prevented shipwreck."[1]

The cataclysm that was World War I sent shock waves over the entire globe, and San Francisco had to work quickly to stave off a collateral disaster.

THE BALL OF ALL NATIONS

Just a few months earlier there had been much to celebrate. On the first weekend in May, a "Phoenix Fete" was held to commemorate the recovery made in the eight years since the disaster of '06. On May Day children danced around a maypole on the plaza of the incomplete Zone. The next night, 18,000 guests attended the grand Ball of All Nations in the newly finished Palace of Machinery. Three different bands played, so far apart in the immense nave that they did not interfere with one another.

Perhaps the most ingenious feature of the Ball of All Nations was the "Human Telephone." The wife of a Pacific Telephone and Telegraph official, wearing a costume topped off with a bell-shaped hat, sashayed 'round the floor carrying a telephone set. She would approach

Mrs. George Van Buren, the wife of a Pacific Telephone and Telegraph official, attended the Ball of All Nations dressed as a "Human Telephone." She was able to connect calls from amazed attendees via a clever system hidden within her costume and beneath the dance floor. (*Popular Mechanics,* September 1914)

attendees and ask if there was anyone with whom they wished to speak. When she handed them the earpiece they'd find themselves connected to the person they mentioned. The secret lay in the soles of her slippers, which were fitted with thin copper plates connected to the telephone by hidden wires. She would stand upon pairs of bolts strategically set into the floor and connected to phone lines. Calls were completed as if by magic.

Celebrants danced under the watchful gaze of the forty-two-foot-tall faux-travertine elephant and other gigantic figures of the *Nations of the East* sculptural group that was soon to be installed atop one of two triumphal arches bracketing the Court of the Universe. As morning light crept through the long row of skylights above the arched trusses, none of the tired crowd below realized this would be the last gala before the Great War began. The war would call into question not only foreign participation in the PPIE but whether the Fair would even open.

GLOBAL CATACLYSM

Summer brought a familiar weather pattern to the City by the Bay. Morning fog was pulled through the Golden Gate by the heat of the state's interior valleys, but it burned off by noon, leaving near-perfect conditions for building the Exposition. Political obstacles were past, all the contracts had been let, construction was proceeding smoothly, and exhibitors clamored for more space within the palaces than was available. Events in Europe were disquieting but not yet alarming.

Then, on June 28, 1914, Archduke Franz Ferdinand of Austria was assassinated. A month later the Austro-Hungarian invasion of Serbia began. Exposition leaders believed skirmishes would be isolated and quickly resolved, but soon Germany marched through neutral Belgium to invade France, and Russia invaded the German province of East Prussia. By the first week of August the intertwined diplomatic agreements between European nations had dragged nine "belligerents" into war. The number of combatant countries and their colonies eventually would swell to more than thirty.

RADICAL COUNTERMEASURES

In addition to Moore's August message to the press, the Exposition sent an official statement in September to the commissioners of all states, territories, and foreign nations that had declared they would attend. It read: "There have been reports that the exposition, because of the war in Europe, would be postponed. It will not be postponed. There have been published statements that the war in Europe would seriously affect the commercial or educational importance or the financial success of the exposition. They will not be so affected. The exposition will open on its schedule date—February 20, 1915. It will be completely ready when open. It is more than 90 per cent completed today. Nothing will be permitted to interfere with the consummation of the plans originally laid down." The communique further asserted that the Exposition would succeed "whatever the situation in Europe may be."[2]

Despite all assurances that the Exposition would go on as scheduled, exhibitors started to cancel in large numbers. Reservations for nearly 100,000 square feet in the Palace of Liberal Arts evaporated. It was estimated that nearly 20 percent of the palaces would be empty unless something was done. This was despite deliberate overbooking by Frederick J. V. Skiff, director-in-chief of foreign and domestic participation.

Historian Frank Morton Todd recounted the stress of those days: "The war affected foreign exhibitors to a larger extent than domestic, but the cancellations from both classes were heart-breaking. To put things on their feet after this reverse, was like starting all over again, with Opening Day but a few months off and the opinion widespread and persistent that the Exposition would be postponed."[3]

To counter this impression, the Exposition management had to be aggressive. A first Letter-Writing Day, on September 22, was so successful,

Eighteen thousand merrymakers attended the grand Ball of All Nations within the just-completed Palace of Machinery, where multiple bands played, a military dress parade was reviewed, queens of the ball were enthroned, and international dances were performed. (Edward A. Rogers)

with about two million letters sent, that two more were held. On these days, every Californian was urged to write three letters to friends in the East assuring them the Exposition was to go on and asking them to spread the news. Stationery stores were given a stock of letter paper with halftones of the palaces. Six hundred thousand postcards with images of PPIE buildings were issued free to hotels, and another 250,000 cards advertised the Exposition in conjunction with specific hotels.

The Southern Pacific Railroad published display ads that read "Write to your Friends in the East and tell them that California's two great 1915 expositions…will open on schedule time. There will be no postponement on account of the European War or for any other reason."[4]

Prominent men, including Secretary of State William Jennings Bryan, were asked to write articles denying any delay. Bryan declared, "There will be no postponement of the Panama-

Pacific International Exposition."[5]

Other entreaties ranged from hortatory to patriotic to outright shaming. Some echoed the railroads' "See America First" campaigns: "The trip across the country to the Pacific coast is interesting and instructive; it will familiarize many of our countrymen with a great portion of their country which is but little known to them," said former US vice president Charles W. Fairbanks.[6]

David Starr Jordan, the influential president of Stanford University, said, "Europe is closed for repairs and will remain so for some time….The cure for war is the extension of patriotism. The Exposition stands for 'planetary patriotism.'"[7]

Some warned that the opportunity offered by the fair was fleeting. Seth Low, former mayor of New York, earnestly urged a 1915 visit to California, suggesting, "The events through which the world is now passing make it probable that this will be the last international exposition for many years to come."[8]

University of California president Benjamin Ide Wheeler said, "An American who does not attend the Exposition will have to explain why, all the rest of his life."[9]

The Division of Exploitation kicked into overdrive, peppering newspapers across the world with reassuring intelligence about the Fair. These articles pointed out that no nations had cancelled their attendance, many had recommitted to exhibiting, and several, including the Netherlands, Japan, and Argentina, had actually increased their appropriations and requested more space. "Not one of the nations at war has notified us of an intention to withdraw her participation. France and Italy have, in fact, notified us that their plans have remained unchanged, but even if we should lose the others, the interest and importance of the exposition will still, as a whole, surpass all precedent," said a story in the *San Francisco Chronicle*.[10]

COLLATERAL DAMAGE

Beyond the missing exhibits, the war affected dozens of special events planned in conjunction with the PPIE. Not surprisingly, the idea of

PPIE president Charles C. Moore's assurance of an "Exposition That Will Be Ready" was printed in the October 1914 edition of *Sunset* magazine.

celebrating "One Hundred Years of Peace Among the English Speaking Peoples" was abandoned.

A grand reprise of the 1909 Portola Festival's pageant of international ships was to dedicate the Panama Canal, and at the moment war broke out, 160 great warships from twelve nations had already accepted a congressional invitation to assemble their vessels at Hampton Roads in Virginia. The ships were to parade through the locks at Panama and reconvene in the San Francisco Bay within sight of the Fair. Instead, in 1915 the US Navy performed some saber-rattling drills in the canal. The battleships *Missouri* and *Ohio* were towed from the Pacific to the Atlantic, with the *Wisconsin* following, to prove the US could move its main fleet through the canal in a single day.

Fifty thousand troops were expected at the PPIE for "international military games," but mock hostilities were shelved in the face of the real carnage in the trenches of Europe. A "mounted military competition" was held in conjunction with the Fair's autumnal horse show, but it included only domestic entrants.

Beyond the impact on military-influenced events, several other ambitious projects were hobbled by the war. Fourteen international polo teams had signed up for a tournament of the sport of "princes, kings, and rajahs," on the fields encircled by the Exposition racetrack and on sites on the San Francisco peninsula. But many of Europe's best players were called to arms, and the other international teams dropped out, transforming the Universal Polo Tournament into a wholly American contest.[11]

From its headquarters in Brussels, the Union of International Associations called upon the leading thinkers of four hundred international organizations to gather for a World's Congress of Congresses at the Exposition. Again, the war precluded this proposed gathering of intellectuals.

The "Pageant of Peace," staged in Mullgardt's Court of Ages on June 5, 1915, featured a cast of five hundred, including scenes with children singing national songs. (Edward A. Rogers)

DARING AVIATORS TO ENCIRCLE THE GLOBE

The most audacious Exposition event was to be the Around-the-World Air Race. When the race was planned in 1914, only eleven years had elapsed since the first successful powered flight at Kitty Hawk. Contestants were to have ninety days in which to fly a staggering 28,000 miles. The monumental scope of the challenge befitted an age when "explorer" was still a viable profession and large cash prizes for new achievements were common.

The intrepid birdmen would take to the skies from San Francisco in May 1915 and fly east across the country. The most frightening part of their journey would be three long jumps across the waters of the Atlantic, first over 610 nautical miles of open ocean from Newfoundland to Greenland, then 670 miles to Reykjavik, Iceland, and concluding with a 570-mile leg to the Hebrides. After stops at London, Paris, Berlin, Warsaw, St. Petersburg, and Moscow, the daring flyers would trace the route of the Trans-Siberian Railway across Russia. Upon reaching Japan, they would head north to Kamchatka, then either follow the Aleutian Islands or cross the Bering Strait to North America. The last segments of the daunting course ran down the Pacific Coast to the Fair.

The PPIE's management deposited $150,000 in an account to cover the main prizes—$100,000 for the first finisher (approximately $2.37 million in 2012), $30,000 for second place, and $20,000 for third. Any plane that could finish the portion of the trek between North America and Great Britain by air in less than seventy-two hours would also win the $50,000 prize offered in 1913 by Lord Northcliffe, owner of the *London Daily Mail*.

Logistical problems were myriad. Caches of fuel and oil would be required at approximately one-hundred-mile intervals. Armies and navies along the way were asked to provide safety patrols for the most remote mountain, desert, and water portions of the course. Race organizers arranged for four hundred "aero clubs" around the globe to provision the supply stations and provide local maps to the airmen. Some experts said the feat simply couldn't be done—existing machines were not advanced enough to finish the race within the prescribed ninety days.

Glenn H. Curtiss, who was at the time building a hydroplane, believed the transatlantic legs could be conquered, but he felt the world-encircling route was still too challenging for the current planes. "To cross the barren Alaskan and Siberian wastes would be more dangerous for an aviator in case of accident than flying across the Atlantic," he asserted.[12]

But the pilots of the era were by nature indomitable, and many expressed interest. Bay Area favorites Lincoln Beachey and Bob Fowler signed on, and soon fifty entrants representing fifteen countries said they'd undertake the contest. But with the first shots of the Great War, plans for the air race swiftly disintegrated as much of the route traversed war-torn territories.

For the next four years, advances in aviation were largely driven by the war. It was not until June 1919 that the Atlantic was finally conquered by a team flying a British "Vickers Vimy" bomber. The first aerial circumnavigation was accomplished by a United States Army Air Service team, which finished in September 1924 after a trip lasting nearly five months. A full decade after the Exposition's Around-the-World Air Race had been cancelled, man had finally, as the *London Daily Mail* had prophesied, put "a girdle around the world."[13]

"WAR OR NO WAR, THE EXPOSITION!"

The PPIE's publicity department claimed that not one of as many as forty-two countries that planned to exhibit had cancelled. While this might have been true in letter, it was untrue in fact. Many simply did not show up, lowering the tally to thirty-one participating nations. Some reduced the number of exhibits they sent, and many international exhibits were delayed because of wartime transportation conditions. As the conflagration swept Europe, many of her nations insisted they would still exhibit. But the reality was that bringing valuable goods across a mine-strewn, warship-filled Atlantic was a dicey proposition.

Neutral Belgium was being martyred on the pyre of war. In the conflict's first six months, the German army laid waste to wide swaths of that country as it pushed toward France. Belgian poet Emile Verhaeren described in *Belgium's Agony* how German soldiers carried naphtha grenades

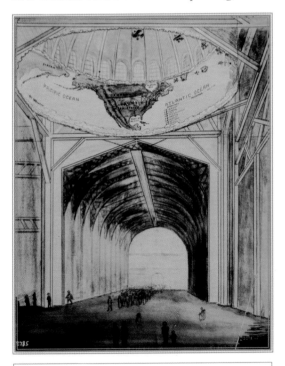

Prior to cancellation of the event, a display commemorating the Around-the-World Air Race was designed to line the dome of the Palace of Transportation. (Edward A. Rogers)

and packets of pitch to facilitate the large-scale arson of Belgian towns.

The German advance toward Paris was halted only at the cost of hundreds of thousands of French lives. The resultant stalemate lasted through four years of deadly trench warfare. In the face of the burgeoning tragedy, it seemed impossible that any of the combatants would fulfill their Exposition aspirations. Belgium had regretfully cancelled the space she had reserved in the palaces, and France, the first European nation to accept America's Exposition invitation, seemed poised to follow suit.

In San Francisco, as autumn 1914 gave way to winter and the other foreign pavilions rose, the French site remained forlorn and empty. Even while they hoped France would still manage to exhibit, the directors of the Exposition decided that if she could not, they would leave the site vacant and marked with a tablet dedicated to the French people.

JASON PURSUES THE GOLDEN FLEECE

Though the Exposition's managers and publicity department were putting on a brave face, the European exhibits required rescue. Salvation came in the unlikely form of a US Navy coal ship bearing the name of the classical hero Jason.

The saga began when the *Chicago Herald* mustered more than two hundred newspapers, forty-four railroads, and six express companies to gather Christmas gifts from the children of the United States to be given to the children of the stricken nations of Europe. One hundred railroad cars full of food, clothing, shoes, and toys were collected. Secretary of the Navy Josephus Daniels and Secretary of State William Jennings Bryan negotiated with the belligerent countries for safe passage of the goods. The Fair's representative in New York, Thomas Moore, asked whether the same ship might carry European exhibits back from the war zone on its return trip. The warring nations agreed, and the US Navy collier *Jason* was chosen.

Much as her fabled namesake had pursued the Golden Fleece, the *Jason* quested after treasure in the form of the art and industry of Europe. The "Christmas Ship" steamed out of New York Harbor on November 14 on a course for England, bearing about five million gifts valued at $2 million, plus hospital supplies and coal.

Meanwhile, two PPIE men were already on the continent working to save European participation. Asher Carter Baker, director of exhibits, was respected in France and had been created a Chevalier of the Legion of Honor for his services as a jurist at the 1900 Exposition Universelle in Paris. J. Nilsen Laurvik, special representative of the Department of Fine Arts, originally was sent to Norway in the summer of 1914 to encourage his native country to send an art collection to the Fair. Through diligent coaxing and negotiation, he obtained more than two hundred works by Norwegian artists. Then Laurvik had traveled to Sweden, Denmark, Germany, Austria, and Hungary to "test the sentiment" for the Exposition in their artistic communities.[14]

Both men were dismayed to find the streets of the nations at war nearly devoid of fighting-age men, and their cafés dark and shops boarded up. In Paris, Baker sought out members of the French Exposition Commission, who had so heartily endorsed the Fair months before. Now he found the men consumed with their country's travails. Baker tactfully suggested a renewed French exhibit would hearten her citizens, fairgoers would be more appreciative of French exhibits in light of the war, and the gesture would show gratitude for US monetary aid. France responded positively to his entreaties, and as the *Jason* churned through the Atlantic, the French cabinet voted to reaffirm Gallic participation in the PPIE.

Laurvik later said that if he had known the obstacles that faced him, he "would not have undertaken the task" of securing art from the belligerent nations. He found that the artists of Germany and Austria-Hungary were indeed interested in the Fair but feared it would be impossible to finance their exhibits or get the art safely to the US. On a second trip he appealed to Hungary to "show that it can do something else than fight." He eventually secured 460 Hungarian objects for display at the Fair, as well as irreplaceable works from collectors and artists in Italy and Austria.[15]

The Exposition envoy also capitalized on the havoc war was wreaking upon the art world, securing some of the works intended for Italy's 1914 Biennale di Venezia exhibition, which the war had cancelled after its artworks had been assembled. He also gathered art from the recent International Urban Exposition at Lyon, France,

The US Navy collier *Jason* sailed from New York Harbor on November 14, 1914, her hold stuffed with Christmas presents for the children of the embattled European nations. (Library of Congress, Prints and Photographs Division [LC-DIG-ggbain-17768])

that could not be returned to its owners because of the strife. Lastly, he collected pieces that had been sent back to Europe from the cancelled 1915 Carnegie Museum exhibit in Pittsburgh and likewise had been marooned.

Both Baker and Laurvik also discovered an unexpected inducement to sending valuables on the *Jason*. Many museums, artists, and collectors, having witnessed the devastation in Belgium, wanted to ensure the preservation of their finest paintings, tapestries, ceramics, and furniture by moving them far away from the war zone. Treasures that otherwise never would have been removed from the great galleries of Europe were placed on the *Jason* in order to protect them. "Owing to the eagerness of European countries to get their artistic masterpieces into safer regions, it has been possible to collect from those countries the most valuable and largest collections of art ever shown at an exposition," noted *Travel* magazine.[16]

In the meantime, the *Jason* was carrying out her humanitarian mission. The ship reached Plymouth, England, on November 25, where the gifts bound for Britain and Belgium were taken off. She continued to Marseilles, where she unloaded the French consignment. In Genoa, the gifts for Austrian and German children were discharged. The final cargo, for the children of Serbia and Montenegro, was delivered at Salonika, Greece. Upon reaching the Mediterranean, the *Jason* loaded the US cruisers *Tennessee* and *North Carolina* with coal and supplies.

Having completed the first half of her lengthy journey, she retraced her route, picking up the exhibits secured by Baker and Laurvik. Some private individuals, keen on safe passage for their wares, leapt at the opportunity to put them on the *Jason*. This caused no little confusion for the Exposition's customs department, as some of the cargo was poorly documented. "It is said that some of [the items] are private property," said the *San Francisco Chronicle*, "consisting of rare heirlooms, relics and valuable collections of paintings and books which individuals desired to get out of the country on account of the war."[17]

Although at the moment Italy was nominally allied with Germany and Austria-Hungary,

actual Italian sentiment ran strongly against the alliance. Plenty of time had been budgeted for Hungarian art to be transported by rail to Genoa, but somehow the train arrived three days after the *Jason* was scheduled to leave. Laurvik believed the "intense feeling among Italians against anything Austro-Hungarian was in some way responsible for the hold-up of the car." Luckily, the *Jason* also was delayed, the art arrived in time, and the ship departed for France.[18]

The *Jason's* return voyage was more exciting than her captain, H. T. Meriwether, would have preferred. As she approached Marseilles, a French torpedo boat emerged from the fog and stopped the *Jason* to determine her errand. Captain Meriwether said his ship was "treated courteously" and allowed to proceed. At Marseilles the *Jason* took on the French and Belgian consignments, and at Barcelona those from Spain and Portugal.[19]

Meriwether was confident the *Jason* was safe from torpedoes, as her distinctive profile could never be mistaken for anything other than an American collier, but floating mines were not so discerning. When the ship entered the mine-filled English Channel on February 18, 1915, he had the lifeboats swung out on their davits and life preservers at the ready. After a stop at Plymouth for many of the Scandinavian, Dutch, and Russian exhibits and those mounted by British merchants, she headed for San Francisco via the Panama Canal. Though a landslide in the Culebra Cut meant the *Jason* had to reduce her draft by pumping all the water from her bilges, the captain described the passage through the canal and the rest of the sojourn as "practically without incident."[20]

The *Jason's* capacious hold was a neutral country in which 3,500 tons of treasures from embattled nations lay peacefully. Although an insurance appraisal of her cargo was an estimated $3.5 million ($165 million in 2012), in reality the value of the works of art, historic artifacts, rare books, and heirlooms was incalculable.

As the ship was collecting the European exhibits in January 1915, ground was finally broken for the French Pavilion in San Francisco.

At a luncheon for its architect, Henri Guillaume, S. J. Brun of the French Auxiliary to the Exposition said, "In these days, when death is stalking the land and sorrow is in every home, the French nation is not inspired by any material motives in going ahead with its plans for participation here. It is the expression of true sympathy and friendship of the French for the American Nation...."[21]

The pavilion was completed in just nine weeks, with most of the days rainy. It opened April 9, 1915, with a solemn ceremony. The eyes of many a French American in the throng within the courtyard grew misty as the French band, led by Gabriel Parés, rendered a stirring "La Marseillaise" and the tri-colored flag was lifted above the building. A spontaneous cry of "Vive la France!" burst from their throats. After the crowd quieted came the speech making. Chester Rowell, California's commissioner to the Exposition, declared France's participation "a supreme act of courage...."[22]

Two days later, after a voyage lasting five months, the *Jason* swung triumphantly through the Golden Gate and anchored off the Exposition, where lighters began to transfer her priceless cargo to shore to the accompaniment of the PPIE's official band. For their efforts in bringing the European exhibits, the *Jason's* crew was honored at a ceremony in the Court of the Universe at which each sailor received a bronze button, and her Captain Meriwether was awarded a bronze medal.

France had financed the shipping of many of Belgium's exhibits on the *Jason* and set aside space for them in her pavilion. In the catalogue of the Belgian exhibits, Verhaeren, the poet who had so movingly described his country's suffering, said his nation would recover from her desolation: "The marvelous Cloth-Halls of Ypres and the wonderful Church of St. Peter at Louvain are but depressing and mournful heaps of ruins; the frescoes, paintings, altar-pieces and triptychs they contained are now but ashes; nevertheless, the unconquerable resolution and tenacity of our race is such that nothing shall or can prevent us from renewing our endeavors and efforts and rising again from our fall."[23]

AN EXPOSITION RESCUED

On Opening Day only a fraction of the foreign installations in the pavilions and palaces were complete. Though 96 percent of the international displays in the Palace of Transportation had arrived, most of the other palaces reported that 60 to 70 percent of the foreign goods were still absent. Signs in empty booths bravely declared, "This space reserved for the Kingdom of Italy, whose exhibits are now on the way on board the SS *Vega*," or the equivalent for Greece, England, and other countries.[24]

Even as they marveled at the Exposition as a whole, visitors during the early months noted these gaps. In April the official hostess of Idaho's pavilion advised her fellow Idahoans that "the real time to visit the fair, in my estimation, will be during September, October and November, when everything will be complete. At present Italy, Switzerland, Siam and Turkey, and some state buildings, are incomplete...." Her comment indicates that even two months into the Fair, the PPIE still hoped the pavilions would be finished. While Italy, Siam (Thailand), Turkey, and many of the states did construct and open their buildings, Switzerland and several states that had selected sites did not.[25]

In hindsight 1915 was a remarkably bad year in which to host a world's fair. The global economy had been suffering for several years, and the onset of war on an unprecedented worldwide scale nearly destroyed the PPIE. Even though it recovered from the initial shock of mass cancellations, the impact of World War I on the Exposition was profound. Participation by many nations was compromised or extinguished, and travel was disrupted around the globe. The Fair's huge domestic attendance was largely offset by the obstacles to foreign visitation.

Further, as parts of Prussia, Austria-Hungary, Russia, Turkey, Mesopotamia, France, and Belgium were bombed and burned, so plans for many international events at the Exposition went up in smoke. Many of Europe's talented artists, musicians, athletes, engineers, and philosophers, who otherwise would have enriched the PPIE's intellectual gatherings, lost their lives to bayonet,

The French Pavilion at the PPIE, a replica of the Parisian Palais de la Légion d'Honneur, was completed in a mere nine weeks, opening officially on April 9, 1915. Inside were displays of historical artifacts and some of the finest French and Belgian art, all brought on the ship *Jason*. (Laura Ackley)

bullet, or poison gas on European battlefields. In its planning stages the PPIE promoted itself as a monument to an era of relative peace; after World War I began, it recast itself as a bastion of peaceful ideals on a globe sundered by war.

An article in *Current Opinion* asked, "Did the world ever show a more massive and monumental contrast than this—the greatest war of history on one side, on the other the greatest exhibition ever seen of the triumphs of peace and international intercourse?"[26]

On June 5, the Christian Women's Peace Movement mounted a "Pageant of Peace" with a cast of five hundred, which included local children portraying the nationalities from which they descended. The *New York Times* noted that some of the American-born children resisted wearing traditional ethnic costumes, but the spectacle of seven scenes and fourteen tableaux was otherwise successful. The pageant's planners hoped the event at the PPIE would "lay the foundations of a love of peace and a horror of war."[27]

For a veritable instant, the PPIE's directorate had considered postponing the Fair but quickly decided that its readiness was too far advanced and a year's delay might not find the world any more peaceful. Ultimately, their decision was vindicated. The world was certainly worse off in 1916 than in the year of the Fair, and the United States itself entered the conflict in 1917. Each of the war-related difficulties endured by the Exposition would have been magnified by a delay.

The Panama-Pacific International Exposition finished its run as one of the few American world's fairs to tally a profit. Of all the domestic expositions until 1915, only the 1893 Columbian Exposition was more profitable, exceeding the San Francisco Fair's receipts by only about $500,000. Had the PPIE not contended with the wartime privations that reduced attendance and resulted in the cancellation of many special events, one can surmise that this very successful Exposition easily might have exceeded that of the famous 1893 "White City" in both attendance and profit. However, every world's fair is the product of its era, and the history of the PPIE is irrevocably colored by the hues of conflict.

AN ARCHITECTURAL TOUR OF THE PALACES AND COURTS

tiquette expert Emily Post attempted what few others had in 1915: she tried to cross the country in an automobile. She was chauffeured by her son Ned and accompanied by her cousin Alice, and their car was alternately buffeted by dust storms and steeped to the axles in mud as they followed "a road [that] was as yet not a road" on their expedition to the Jewel City. When they reached Arizona, they put their "seriously crippled" car on a train and shipped it, along with themselves, to California, where they finished their drive on the gentler roads between Los Angeles and San Francisco.

Now Post stood atop a hill to the south of the fairgrounds and saw spread before her "a biscuit-colored city with terra-cotta roofs, green domes and blue." Beyond it, to the north, were the waters of the Bay, then a fringe of gray-green mountains.[1]

This was the first time an international exposition could be viewed from a commanding height. From above, it was possible to comprehend the cohesive plan of the panorama, spreading two and a half miles along the bay. No ensemble of this scale had ever been built on the West Coast, and locals and visitors alike were awestruck by the expertly interwoven palaces, gardens, and courtyards spread over the stage of Harbor View. While the whole fair landscape was harmonious, the four most memorable structures were conceived by designers who embraced the fleeting nature of Exposition architecture and were not afraid to play with the canons of the discipline.

THE VIEW FROM ABOVE

From her lofty vantage, Post saw a masterpiece of collaborative architecture that architect Bernard Maybeck said resembled an intricate cloisonné brooch. The Exposition was separated from the hodgepodge San Francisco neighborhood to the south by eight blocks of the high green wall of the remarkable hedge fence. Beyond this barrier were the magnificent South Gardens, showcasing a great quatrefoil fountain centered between two wide rectangular pools set within flowerbeds enameled with the colors of the season. Set within this plain, like smooth-polished gems, were the translucent beryl dome of the Palace of Horticulture on the western side and the soft, opaque jade dome of the Festival Hall on the east end. To her far right, Post could see the entrance to the Joy Zone, and left beyond the Palace of Horticulture, the international pavilions.

Behind the South Gardens ran a broad thoroughfare lined with palm trees in alternating sizes, and beyond that were the alabaster-toned walls of the complex of exhibit palaces, sixty-five feet high, topped with red tiles and punctuated by four slender minarets. Centered upon these lengthy ramparts was a Roman triumphal arch topped with a bejeweled, stepped tower that stretched more than forty stories into the sky.

When architect William Faville designed the eight palaces, he placed them four wide by two deep back toward the bay, along half a mile of shoreline. Triangular pediments marked the four ends of a cross-shaped clerestory gable atop each otherwise flat palace roof. Miniature domed pavilions stood at the corners of each of the eight halls.

From above, spectators could see that the interior corners of the exhibition buildings had been carved away to form three elaborate courtyards along the east-west axis of the

The wide Avenue of Palms ran along the southern face of the ivory walls of the main palace complex. William Faville added interest to the six-story-high façade with pilasters and Spanish-influenced portals. The entrance to the Palace of Varied Industries, near right, interpreted the doorway of the Hospital de Santa Cruz in Toledo, Spain. (*Views of the Panama-Pacific International Exposition in Natural Colors* (viewbook))

Exposition. North of the courtyards, colonnades reached toward the glinting San Francisco Bay. Past the northernmost palaces, toward the water, was a generous flat greensward from which daring aviators took flight and where a demonstration encampment of teepees stood.

The walled citadel was bookended on the east by a massive Roman-inspired building and on the west by a naturalistic lagoon embraced by an arcing colonnade centered on a rotunda.

The overall effect was one of astounding harmony, especially since the neighborhood immediately south of the Fair was a jumble of homes and businesses sometimes known as "Dumptown," as people would move unwanted structures there. Just beyond the fence of this mishmash the latest ideas in exposition planning were on exhibit. A cadre of renowned architects had developed a group of buildings that synthesized styles from southern Europe to the Near East geographically and from the classical period to the Beaux-Arts temporally.[2]

BALANCE AND RHYTHM

Post wrote that while the sheer size of the Fair was dizzying, "…its architectural balance was one of the most noteworthy things about it."[3]

The designers had conspired to thoroughly curate the visitors' experiences, and in this city, designed to live only ten months, they could control the space more rigorously than in any enduring metropolis. Though the structures themselves were eclectic, each major element was balanced by another, and every wide expanse was first entered through a compressed portal, amplifying the impact of the open spaces.

If the Exposition were a galaxy, its gravitational center was the grand, oval Court of the Universe. The central Tower of Jewels provided a fulcrum between the Column of Progress to the north and the Fountain of Energy to the south. The grandeur of the Palace of Fine Arts to the west of William Baker Faville's palaces was counterbalanced by the severe bulk of the Palace of Machinery to the east. The galaxy's arms spiraled away to the northwest in an orderly spray of state and foreign pavilions, the livestock area, and the racetrack,

and to the southeast along the undulating length of the Joy Zone midway, which ran from Fillmore Street to Van Ness Avenue.

In manipulating the rhythms of tight and open spaces, architects had fairgoers enter each court through a proportionately scaled opening. From Chief of Architecture George Kelham's southern courts, spectators passed through sober doorways that opened into the large Courts of Ages and of the Four Seasons. Fittingly, the dignified Court of Palms led into the restrained Court of the Four Seasons by Henry Bacon, while the more embellished Court of Flowers accessed the sumptuous Court of Ages by Louis Christian Mullgardt. While the triumphal arch beneath the Tower of Jewels was imposing in size, the plain into which it opened was commensurately enormous. Likewise the three straight colonnades to the north widened onto the grandest court of all, the hill-fringed, island-studded waters of the San Francisco Bay.

MEDITERRANEAN SYNCRETISM

Art critic Christian Brinton compared the architecture of San Diego's concurrent fair, the Panama-California Exposition, to that of the PPIE, writing, "While San Diego keeps modestly within the confines of a concise and characterful local tradition, San Francisco boldly proclaims herself a world creation."[4]

Brinton was accurate if by "world" he meant the sunny climes of the Mediterranean and Near East, for these were the only regions from which the PPIE's architects drew inspiration. The planners selected from a variety of more southerly traditions and achieved a harmonious ensemble. Official historian Frank Morton Todd wrote of the Fair's syncretic architecture: "It suggested Damascus and Stamboul, it was Oriental, south European, Mediterranean, Greek, Italian, and Spanish."[5]

A CALIFORNIA ÁLCAZAR

The main palaces were offered a mix of architectural styles set within the walls of a

Moorish royal compound. The rooflines and domes were Byzantine, the façades recalled Rome, Athens, Paris, and Seville, and individual details started in pre-Christian antiquity, touched on the Middle Ages and Renaissance, and finished in the Industrial Age.

Willis Polk, chairman of the PPIE's Executive Architectural Council, said of the Fair's composition, "In general outline…façades and roofs are to blend together; it is to be one grand palace, as the Orientals build them, spreading over the area at Harbor View—colonnade after colonnade, dome after dome, arch after arch, penetrated by avenues, flanked by gardens—an Aladdin's palace, facing the azure harbor and the mountains beyond." By "Oriental," Polk betokened the Near East and Islamic-influenced architecture. The courts especially bore the imprint of Moorish Andalusia in southern Spain, where elaborate,

Long, narrow pools, manicured trees, and a Moorish-styled bandstand added Andalusian flavor to the Court of the Universe. (Laura Ackley)

courtyard-focused complexes were built between the eighth and fifteenth centuries.[6]

Visitors promenading through the series of connecting courts were soothed by the scent of sun-warmed herbs and the melodious plash of fountains. Not only did the internally focused plan of elegant buildings around sublime courts suit the programmatic and climatic requirements for the PPIE, it was utterly appropriate geographically, as San Francisco lies at precisely the same latitude as southern Spain.

Other cultures have created courtyard complexes, but the interconnected courts of the PPIE were most evocative of the grand Spanish compounds. Architect Louis Christian Mullgardt said of the Exposition, "The eight centrally grouped palaces…including the main tower, the courts and the connecting longitudinal and lateral avenues, together form a homogeneous unit as compact and correlated as are the various departments of a residential palace." The courts were outdoor "rooms" within fortress-like perimeter walls, and each was lined with colonnades or arcades, some overhung by ornamental galleries.[7]

To assist in the illusion of Islamic-Iberian grandeur, the planners used a combination of water features, landscaping, and color. Every court or colonnade included a water feature, many of them Moorish in execution. Long, slender channels with burbling jets lined the central axis of the Court of the Universe. Many fountains included shallow bowls that overflowed into larger basins, a design often seen in the palaces of Andalusia.

San Francisco's climate facilitated the use of Mediterranean plants, and Chief of Landscape John McLaren's implementation also was distinctly Moorish in flavor. Two of the courts featured sunken gardens, and all were formally planted. Orange trees, their neatly trimmed branches heavy with golden fruit, were arrayed in orderly rows about Mullgardt's opulent Court of Ages, after the fashion of the Aljafería, the forecourt of the Great Mosque of Córdoba, and the Patio de los Naranjos of Seville Cathedral, a remnant of an earlier mosque complex. Carefully pruned cypresses lent a resinous bite to the

The Giralda Tower in Spain, originally an Islamic minaret, inspired the four so-called Italian Towers at the PPIE. The two here, flanking the Court of Flowers, were mirrored by those near the Court of Palms. (Seligman Family Foundation)

heady fragrance of citrus in the Court of Ages. All over the grounds, McLaren employed flowering plants and herbs common to the Mediterranean.

Where the Moors used faience and glazed, colored brick to enliven their architecture, Director of Color Jules Guérin employed versatile faux travertine. His official palette, informed by his travels to the Near East and Mediterranean, included French Green, Yellow-Golden-Orange, Pinkish-Red-Gold, Cerulean Blue, Mud Pink, Oxidized Copper-Green, Wall Red, and the blue-green he called Oriental Blue, all of which could have been seen in the dazzling mosaics of the Alhambra.

The fairgrounds were sprinkled with a few smaller buildings that were also clad in the robes of the Moors. Though he was not an official member of the Architectural Commission, architect Edwin J. Symmes was appointed "supervising architect of concessions." He was put in charge of these buildings and many of the fanciful structures along the Joy Zone midway and among the state and foreign pavilions, many of which expressed Moorish influences. Several pavilions he designed along the south wall of the palace block were expressly Moorish and featured stylized vegetal column capitals, slender pillars, and intricate multifoil "cusped" arches. Octagonal concession kiosks that dotted the broad avenues of the Fair were fenestrated with pointed or horseshoe arches, and some were garnished with Moorish domes.[8]

The largest exemplars of Moorish style at the PPIE were the misnamed "Italian Towers." Chief of Architecture George W. Kelham guarded the opening of each of the courts he designed with a pair of these towers, each 204 feet tall and 38 feet on each side. Each set differed slightly from the other, but all four were based loosely on the Giralda Tower, a former Islamic minaret constructed in the late twelfth century in Seville, Spain. The sides of the towers were decorated in pink tones with a diamond pattern called an "arabesque," a colorful surface treatment common to Moorish architecture.

Southern California architect Octavius Morgan summed up the Moorish ambience at the PPIE when he said the Fair most reminded him of his "late run through Spain, of Salamanca, Toledo, Cordova—truly they have caught the medieval spirit."[9]

THE DOMES OF BYZANTIUM

Explorer and military officer John C. Frémont wrote in 1846, "To this Gate I gave the name of *Chrysopylae*, or Golden Gate; for the same reasons that the harbor of Byzantium was called Chrysoceras, or Golden Horn."[10]

Frémont felt that the San Francisco Bay's narrow strait resembled the entrance to Constantinople, seat of the Eastern Roman Empire, not only topographically with its impressive, island-adorned harbor, but also because of its advantages as a trade center. Architect William Baker Faville brought to mind the splendors of Byzantium in the Greek cross configuration of the roofs and domes of the PPIE.

Faville had been educated at MIT, where he met his future architectural partner, Walter Danforth Bliss. His was the largest commission at the PPIE, encompassing the palaces of Education, Food Products, Agriculture, Liberal Arts, Manufactures, Transportation, Mines and Metallurgy, and Varied Industries, in addition to the surrounding walls. The footprint of the group covered more than three million square feet, and Faville's salary—$22,500—was commensurate, equivalent to about $538,000 in 2012.

While he chose Spanish Renaissance and Greco-Roman ornament for the exterior palace walls, the configuration of the exhibit halls within owed most to Byzantium. Once the volumes of the courtyards had been subtracted from their edges, the palaces basically were rectangular, with very slightly pitched roofs

broken by skylights. Each roofline was bisected by cross-shaped clerestories finished with triangular gables. This arrangement resembled the Greek cross-in-square plan common in Byzantine churches. An angelic figure sculpted by Louis Ulrich balanced gracefully on the peak of each gable end and proffered a wreath with outstretched arm. The gables terminated in open pediments framing large arched windows. At night these windows were lit by rosy lanterns, giving what Chief of Illumination Walter D'Arcy Ryan called "the life within."

Low, blue-green domes on short, salmon-colored drums capped the buildings at the intersections of the clerestories. Faville introduced this idea at the August 1912 meeting of the Architectural Commission. He said the skyline of the palaces was of paramount importance, thus he had introduced "at the crossing of these great naves, domes of rather simple form...."[11]

Inside the palaces, the achievement of the engineer was clear in the fretwork of cross-braced Howe trusses, the martial lines of dimensional-lumber columns, and the finishes that were purely utilitarian. Millions of board feet of lumber framed vast industrial spaces using two-by-fours on eighteen-inch centers. But here, too, an aura of Byzantine solemnity pervaded. At the intersection of each pair of cross-aisles, the interior of the dome soared sixteen stories above the floor. Each dome floated above a lambent halo cast by a ring of small windows around the drum below, evoking the basilicas of the vanished empire.

THE IMPACT OF THE ÉCOLE

The architects of the PPIE sought to differentiate their designs from the architecturally momentous 1893 World's Columbian Exposition in Chicago and from those that would follow. But the Columbian Exposition's Beaux-Arts repercussions were still detectable in the formal attributes and circulation of the PPIE. In some ways, as historian Gray Brechin says, the PPIE "had opened beyond its rightful era."[12]

As noted, every member of the Architectural

Commission had trained in the Beaux-Arts tradition. Bernard Maybeck, George Kelham, Robert Farquhar, Thomas Hastings, and Arthur Brown, Jr., all had studied at the École des Beaux-Arts in Paris, for which the movement is named. Further, the balance of the commission had worked under major practitioners of the style— Willis Polk and Clarence Ward for Burnham & Root, William Faville and Henry Bacon for McKim, Mead & White, and Louis Christian Mullgardt for Henry Ives Cobb.

The dictums of Beaux-Arts included formal, symmetrical circulation and neoclassical elements. At the PPIE, Beaux-Arts was manifested in the rigorous design of its circulation and landscaping as well as the prevalence of French, Greco-Roman, and Spanish-inspired details.

THE AVENUES

Four wide, straight thoroughfares circumscribed the central block of eight palaces. The Esplanade and the Avenue of Palms ran alongside the north and south façades, while Administration Avenue separated the lagoon of the Palace of Fine Arts from the semi-domes of the west wall enclosing the palaces, and the Avenue of Progress made its decorous way between the east wall and the Palace of Machinery.

The Exposition's planners concurred that the lawn area north of the Esplanade, eventually part of the Marina Green, should be left open not only for varied activities but also to capitalize on the matchless view of the San Francisco Bay. It was here that spectators watched troupes of dancing children, a range of sporting competitions, and drills by the US Life-Saving Service. On the south side of the roadway, next to the walls, McLaren selected hardy plants that could withstand the maritime climate, including tall Monterey cypresses, acacias, and evergreen shrubs.

On the city side of the palaces, north of the Palace of Horticulture and the Festival Hall, a

Bears holding shields topped the pilasters (left) along the Avenue of Progress, which ran north-south between the block of eight central palaces and the massive Palace of Machinery (right). (*Natural Color Studies of the Panama-Pacific International Exposition* (viewbook))

In the South Gardens, the Festival Hall, a thoroughly Francophile edifice, was set within fifteen acres of Beaux-Arts architectural embellishments, gardens, fountains, pools, and paths. (Lynn Wilkinson)

broad, straight avenue ran parallel to the south wall. The Avenue of Palms was lined with opulent sprays of Canary Island date palm trees, alternating every thirty feet with more slender California fan palms. McLaren had planted ferns, geraniums, and nasturtiums in the serrated trunks of the trees to suggest even more tropical richness. Passion vines planted at the bases of the trees climbed up and out onto the fronds, dropping tendrils bearing exotic purple flowers. The Avenue of Palms provided an ideal venue for the many parades and military drills held during the Fair, and also left an open boulevard from which to appreciate the majestic façade to the north.

The Avenue of Progress, running north-south between the Faville palaces and the Palace of Machinery, was the most sedate main boulevard. On its western side, the Palaces of Varied Industries and of Mines and Metallurgy featured arched Italian Renaissance portals. Whimsical standing grizzly bears atop the pilasters clutched shields bearing the seal of California. On the opposite side of the roadway, the entrances of

the Palace of Machinery were guarded by a series of paired Corinthian columns under discreet entablatures along its nearly 1,000-foot frontage. The avenue itself was enlivened by a row of vermilion flagpoles topped with stars and light standards bearing shields decorated with coats of arms.

McLaren's first plants went in alongside the broad Avenue of Progress. He banked the travertine walls on both sides with tall cypresses, firs, and spruces, and lined the lawns with twenty-foot-tall, spiky-leaved dracaenas. To add color, he devised a seasonal rotation of flowers in the beds, starting with cherry-red Japanese Hinode-giri azalea, followed by banks of hybrid European rhododendrons and Japanese lilies, and finishing with pink hydrangea hortensia. This lane provided the only clear view north from the South Gardens to the bay, and many were lured along its windswept length to view the changeable waters beyond.

Pedestrians along Administration Avenue had a choice of fine views. On the east side, Faville's high wall was penetrated by a number of small niches featuring sculptures by Charles Harley, and visitors also could see the large coffered half-domes over the palace entrances. To the west, the Palace of Fine Arts was reflected in the picturesque lagoon. The interconnecting aisles and small courts between the palaces were simpler but still conformed to the Beaux-Arts style in details such as patterned walls, medallions, and Renaissance arcading.

THE FRENCH INFLUENCE

THE SOUTH GARDENS

After paying and pushing through the turnstile, a visitor passed under the verdant arcade of McLaren's hedge fence and emerged into the open expanse of the thoroughly Francophile South Gardens. Immediately inside the main gate the guest might pause between the matching Beaux-Arts YWCA and Press Buildings, whose trellises were borne on the heads of pairs of caryatids by sculptor John Bateman. These delicate, flower-adorned mademoiselles were repeated on the porches of the Palace of Horticulture and even on the small boiler house in the gardens. From here the fairgoer gazed upon a wide vista of pools, flowerbeds, lawns, and carefully arranged trees and sculpture that recollected the glories of Versailles.

Directly in front of the Tower of Jewels lay a bizarre fountain of mammoth proportions that some likened to a giant sugar bowl. This Fountain of Energy, by Alexander Stirling Calder, the local chief of sculpture, commanded attention as jets of water sprayed from a colossal globe crowned with a prancing steed. Astride the horse, a youthful Energy figure stretched out his arms, symbolically splitting the continents to form the Panama Canal. Two angelic trumpeters stood upon his shoulders, their arms linked as they leaned away from each other. Below, sea creatures representing the oceans of the world cavorted in a quatrefoil basin. More figures supported and embellished the globe, resulting in a hodgepodge of symbolism that was arguably the weakest of Calder's many contributions to the PPIE. Nevertheless, the Fountain of Energy served as an imposing introduction to the largely allegorical nature of the Exposition's entire sculptural program.

Flanking the Fountain of Energy two 300-foot-long rectangular pools of still water mirrored the sumptuous buildings and gardens. Matching *Mermaid* fountains by Arthur Putnam adorned the ends of each pool before the entrances of the Palace of Horticulture and the Festival Hall. In the surrounding beds, McLaren planted a tapestry of low blooming flowers that he changed with the seasons. When one planting began to wilt, he'd have gardeners swiftly cut the plants and pitch them onto trucks for removal.

The flowerbeds were bordered by ornate light standards, graceful balustrades, and large plant-filled urns. Comfortable benches invited the footsore to rest and take in the grandeur of the nearly fifteen acres of formal gardens.

THE FESTIVAL HALL

The Festival Hall appeared to be sinking into the ground under the weight of its own dome. Architect Robert Farquhar, the Exposition's lone designer from Southern California, had the best of intentions with this most definitively French building of the Fair. He'd studied at Harvard and MIT, but his Festival Hall reflected his education at the École des Beaux-Arts. Its 221-foot-tall celadon-green central dome was crested with a lantern and surrounded by four corner cupolas. Unfortunately, the hefty dome seemed to crush the proportionately short base story.

Many of the Festival Hall's details were lovely when considered independently from the entire composition. Enormous arching windows pierced the east and west sides of the dome, recalling the apertures on the late-nineteenth-century train stations of Paris and creating an interesting engineering challenge in a wood-framed building. The pilasters, balustrades, garlands, and other details were inspired by the French Renaissance–style Grand and Petit Trianons of Versailles. Sweeping, inward-curving porticos welcomed visitors at the east and west entrances, and convex arcades undulated outward on the north and south sides of the building, creating a satisfying sense of motion around the edifice.

The sculptural program around the Festival Hall was the output of another École des Beaux-Arts man, Sherry Edmundson Fry. His lithe *Torch Bearers* posed at the apex of each cupola. A mischievous *Pan* below on one side of the entry and a pensive *Dreaming Nymph* on the other were guarded by two *Flower Girls* stationed upon pedestals behind them. On the cornice above, *Bacchus* and a *Listening Nymph* reclined on sarcophagi and pondered the programs offered within the auditorium.

ECHOES OF ANTIQUITY

As a natural outgrowth of its Beaux-Arts lineage, many of the PPIE's elements were inspired by classical Greek and Roman prototypes. Scattered throughout the Exposition were temple fronts, colonnades, arcades, and their Renaissance descendants.

In the South Gardens, the porch of the U-shaped Service Building was faced by an elegant Renaissance arcade supported on paired columns. Across the lagoon from the Palace of Fine Arts, William Faville planned the stately concave half-domes of Plenty and Philosophy, which enclosed the western entrances to the Palaces of Food Products and Education. The 112-foot-high coffered domes sheltered cast concrete fountains, also designed by Faville, allegedly from examples in the Italian cities of Siena and Ravenna. In each, water cascaded over the rim of the upper bowls in silvery sheets into a wellhead receptacle, then through multiple openings into a round lower basin.

THE PALACE OF MACHINERY

When designing the Palace of Machinery, architect Clarence Ward never considered whether it was large enough in which to fly an airplane. Nevertheless, the Roman-inspired pile was so immense that Lincoln Beachey flew his biplane through its 968-foot length as construction of the building was nearing completion in December 1913. Beachey attempted to land inside the palace, but his plane skidded on the wet floor and crunched into the wall nearest the bay. He walked away unscathed and with the title of

"world's first indoor aviator."

The architect, assisted by his partner J. Harry Blohme, had made the palace even more colossal than necessary for displaying the largest machines. It loomed over the eastern end of the Faville walls, its vast proportions making it the largest wood-framed building in the world at the time. Nearly three football fields long, it enclosed more than thirty-eight million cubic feet of space and required a mile of cornice and the support of nine miles of pilings.

The three long north-south aisles were 101 feet tall inside and were bisected by even

Haig Patigian's sculptures of "The Powers," sixteen-foot-tall nude males standing atop the columns in front of the Palace of Machinery, represented Electricity, Invention, Steam, and Imagination. (*The Sculpture and Mural Decorations of the Exposition*, by Stella G. S. Perry)

Local flyer Lincoln Beachey earned the title of "world's first indoor aviator" on December 30, 1913, when he flew through the long aisle of the Palace of Machinery before the exhibits were installed. (Lynn Wilkinson)

taller naves 136 feet high and 368 feet long, a vault configuration reminiscent of the Imperial Roman baths of Diocletian and Caracalla. When asked why he made the palace so towering and severely classical, Ward said that he wanted to demonstrate the beauty of wood-frame construction on a grand scale, and "to form a contrast with the poetically designed fine arts palace at the westerly end of the main group."[13]

Ward revealed that the exteriors of the palaces were designed to present a "gradation of period and refinement" from east to west in parallel with their contents. The "grosser arts and crafts," including machinery on the east, gave way to more refined disciplines, culminating in the fine arts, whose Maybeck-designed abode Ward clearly regarded as the pinnacle of loveliness at the PPIE.[14]

Some of the sculpture on the Palace of Machinery was considered the most scandalous on the grounds. Armenian-born California sculptor Haig Patigian's four male nudes poised atop the freestanding pillars in front of the palace's main entry caused consternation among defenders of "purity." The sixteen-foot-tall figures symbolizing Steam, Invention, Electricity, and Imagination posed in a state of splendid undress, and the scale of this full-frontal nudity offended some. Ironically, Patigian's smaller high-relief friezes depicting several equally unclothed Genii of Machinery around the bases of the vestibule columns were well received.

THE COURT OF THE UNIVERSE

On a sunny day, the Court of the Universe seemed like a radiant Roman piazza. Here architect William Rutherford Mead and William Symmes Richardson, one of his younger partners, had assembled a pastiche of Roman elements into a monumental plaza on the shore of San Francisco Bay. Bernard Maybeck said it suggested a Rome "inhabited by some unknown placid people."[15]

The oval shape and colonnades of this court echoed the celebrated seventeenth-century

The axis of the Court of the Universe was punctuated by Adolph Weinman's figures *Descending Night* and *Rising Sun*, which stood ninety-five feet above the court's floor on fluted glass columns that rose from majestic fountains. (Laura Ackley)

from the curved cornices at measured intervals were ninety *Star Maiden* sculptures by Stirling Calder, reminders of one of the court's earlier names, the Court of Sun and Stars. While petite in appearance, each maiden was actually six feet tall, with sixty small Novagem jewels adorning her crown.

The curved colonnades terminated in small pavilions, each finished with an orange dome, and around the perimeter of these pavilions ran a cameo frieze by Hermon A. MacNeil of the *Signs of the Zodiac*, yet another astronomical reference.

Though Polk had been squeezed out of the main commissions for the Fair, as the head of the Executive Architectural Council he likely influenced the design of the Court of the Universe. Though Piazza San Pietro provided a recognizable precedent, the incorporation of triumphal arches into the curving arms of the court bears a strong resemblance to Polk's unbuilt 1897 design for a peristyle-enclosed oval plaza in front of the San Francisco Ferry Building. And the Tower of Jewels centered on the Court of the Universe looks suspiciously like the proposed world's fair spire he had drawn twenty-four years earlier for publisher William Randolph Hearst's *San Francisco Examiner.*

Encompassing more than ten acres, the Court of the Universe was so huge that while it was rich with sculptural elements, it still felt somewhat empty. John McLaren understood that no landscape treatment could make the space seem lush, so he wisely kept plantings minimal. The slopes of the sunken garden were first carpeted with masses of rhododendrons, which were replaced with hydrangeas when their blooms faded. Alternating male and female figures served as lampposts along the balustrade that encircled the flowerbeds. Two dotted lines of neatly trimmed, boxed trees ran down the north-south line of the court.

Along this same axis, the steps down to the floor of the garden were guarded by four titanic reclining figures by Robert Aitken: *Fire, Water, Earth,* and *Air.* Somewhat incongruously, figures of *Music* and *Dance* by Paul Manship gamboled above the eastern and western staircases.

piazza of St. Peter's Basilica. In place of Bernini's radiating travertine paving, the architects created a sunken garden. To amplify the idea of the twin fountains by Maderno and Bernini at St. Peter's, they added lofty sixty-five-foot sculpture-crowned columns. Two triumphal arches spanned the passages to the courts by Louis Christian Mullgardt and Henry Bacon. In Rome, a red granite Egyptian obelisk more than 4,000 years old stands in the center of St. Peter's Square, while in San Francisco a victory column was offset, placed instead at the juncture of the palace block and the Marina Green.

In June 1912 Mead sent Willis Polk a sketch of the proposed court. He explained its sweeping colonnades would form a pleasing contrast to the polygonal plans of the two other interior courts. The fluted Corinthian columns were two deep, instead of the four at St. Peter's, and set against a coral-tinted back wall. Looking down

THE FOUNTAINS OF THE
RISING AND SETTING SUN

The lower portions of the Fountains of the Rising and Setting Sun were similar to those in Rome, with large bowls atop polygonal bases. But in place of the mushroom-like top of the Italian antecedents, fluted columns of opalescent glass rose to a height of ninety-five feet above the garden floor, and each was topped by a winged figure by Adolph Weinman. *Rising Sun* was a heroic male poised for flight, while *Descending Night* depicted a languorous maiden with wings half-furled and her face delicately shielded by her hands.

The Arches of the Rising Sun and Setting Sun also were loaded with ornament. Both arches were incised with inscriptions, crowned with great sculptural groups, adorned by friezes, medallions, and obelisks, then crenellated for good measure. It is a testament to the size of the Court of the Universe—which was seven hundred feet wide—that these triumphal arches, each almost identical in size to the Arc de Triomphe in Paris, were in perfect scale with their surroundings.

One detail was uniquely and accidentally unclassical—a series of three windows on either side of each arch. Stirling Calder admitted he'd doodled the windows onto a copy of the original McKim, Mead & White plans, and the builders had used the altered drawings by mistake. Writer John D. Barry enthused, "In similar ways many a new idea must have been introduced into art and permanently established. Those windows, with their green lattices, when lighted from within, provide a lovely color effect at night."[16]

Just below the spring of each stately arch, a pair of murals illustrated themes of exploration. Each mural was twelve feet tall and ran forty-seven feet through the depth of the arch. In the Arch of the Rising Sun, Edward Simmons

The classically inspired Court of Palms featured a long, still reflecting pool leading to a circular basin, sloping lawns, and, over the portals, arched murals by Childe Hassam, Charles Holloway, and Arthur F. Mathews. (Seligman Family Foundation)

illustrated ships and adventurers on the Atlantic Ocean, beginning with an explorer from the lost city of Atlantis and continuing with the voyages of Latin and Anglo-Saxon sailors, a missionary priest, an artist, and a "modern immigrant." Frank Vincent DuMond interpreted the march of pioneers across the American continent in his two murals beneath the western arch, depicting various types of immigrants on their way to California.[17]

THE *NATIONS OF THE EAST* AND *WEST*

From a perch 160 feet above the ground, a four-story-tall elephant stared down a covered wagon across the court. These were the centerpieces of the *Nations of the East* and *Nations of the West*, the great sculptural groups that topped the Arches of the Rising and Setting Sun, respectively. Stirling Calder and his chief assistants Leo Lentelli and Frederick Roth created statues to replace the traditional quadriga, or four-horse chariot, seen on Roman monuments. In San Francisco, the Occident and Orient faced each other across the court, expressing the Fair's theme of nations brought closer through the Panama Canal.

The decoratively caparisoned elephant of the *Nations of the East* was surrounded by figures of "all Oriental civilization—China, Persia, Oriental Africa, Mongolia," according to *Travel* magazine. The ensemble was roughly symmetrical and evoked the exotic and mystical. The elephant was flanked by camels ridden by an Egyptian and an Assyrian by Roth, and Mongolian and Arab horsemen by Lentelli. Striding in front were a Bedouin falconer and a brooding Buddhist lama, while two servants by Calder, each thirteen feet tall, carried baskets of fruit upon their heads.[18]

The *Nations of the West* struck a note of racial integration unusual for its time. When Calder was puzzling over a western motif to balance Roth's resplendent elephant, he struck upon the idea of the all-American prairie schooner drawn by two oxen. On either side were pioneer types—Alaskan, Latin, Italian, German, English, Native American, and French Canadian, their simple garments contrasting with the finery of their eastern counterparts. The central figures

in this group were the most metaphorical of either arch: an undaunted young Mother of Tomorrow stood on the tongue of the wagon, while two boys, one Caucasian and one African American, perched atop its bonnet, holding hands. According to Calder they represented the "Hopes of the Future." Above them all loomed the slightly bizarre, bare-breasted, winged figure of Enterprise, whose open mouth "summoned initiative, encouragement and perseverance to the brave and adventurous who advance our progress."[19]

THE COLUMN OF PROGRESS

The view toward the blue bay waters from the Tower of Jewels was a prospect between two straight colonnades bordering a long pool. The liquid mirror reflected a 185-foot-tall freestanding column like those of Rome, and marked the northern edge of the palaces. This reimagining of a classical device was considered daring and successful. As in its prototypes, a bas-relief frieze spiraled up the shaft, but rather than illustrating martial victories, it showed the Ship of Life ascending. The culmination of the column was *The Adventurous Bowman* by Hermon A. MacNeil, in which a virile young hero launched his arrow toward new enterprise, while on his left he was supported by his fellow man and on his right a woman knelt behind him holding a palm frond and laurel wreath to celebrate his victories.

While the bowman himself was vigorous, the silhouette formed in combination with his helpmeets was frankly lumpy. In addition, the positioning of the woman in the group was unintentionally emblematic of the role of female artisans at the PPIE. John D. Barry wrote, "His wife is not his equal, a circumstance that serves as a reminder of the lack among the artistic features of the exposition of notes expressing the new social and economic ideas and the changing relation between women and men."[20]

Although women had executed some of the artworks within the foreign and state pavilions and the exhibit halls, of the more than one hundred commissioned structures, murals, and sculptures for the main palaces, only three pieces

The view from the Tower of Jewels revealed the grandeur of the Court of the Universe, with its matching Fountains of the Rising Sun (left) and Setting Sun (right). A bandstand marked its northern edge, where a colonnade and reflecting pool led to the triumphal Column of Progress. Beyond, the San Francisco Bay was the grandest court of all. (Donna Ewald Huggins)

were by women: Evelyn Beatrice Longman's *Fountain of Ceres* in the Court of the Four Seasons, and two fountains secluded within the colonnaded wings of the Tower of Jewels.

These fountains, of *El Dorado* and *Youth*, continued the theme of New World discovery introduced by sculptures in front of and on the tiers of the tower, and their concealed placement paid homage to the mysterious locations of their fabled inspirations. *El Dorado*, by Gertrude Vanderbilt Whitney, a member of the famed Vanderbilt banking family, and the woman who went on to found New York's Whitney Museum of Art, interpreted the traditional New World myth. In the central niche, supplicants reached in vain as a door guarded by somber attendants closed. On the other side of the great arch, Edith Woodman Burroughs' *Fountain of Youth* was identical in plan, but the naiveté of its subject was more charming: a young girl standing amongst primroses while on either side elders were rowed toward destiny by children.

THE COURTS OF PALMS AND FLOWERS

"Here summer first unfolds her robes, and here she longest tarries," wrote Ben Macomber of the twin Court of Palms and Court of Flowers, both by George Kelham, who also designed San Francisco's Bohemian Club and Palace Hotel. Each half-oval court opened onto the South Gardens between a pair of Italian Towers and penetrated about three hundred feet deep beyond the ivory walls. Though both were similar in size and Italian Renaissance style, the Court of Palms was held to be more Grecian and the Court of Flowers more Florentine.[21]

Both courts were encircled by a colonnade with attic sculptures by Stirling Calder. The closed upper story of the Court of Palms was supported on gracious Ionic columns with scrolled capitals. Winged caryatids by Calder and John Bateman above each column were separated by floral garland plaques. In the Court of Flowers, acanthus leaf–coiffed Corinthian columns upheld an airy, open loggia. Here the balcony openings

JAMES EARLE FRASER'S *END OF THE TRAIL*
AND SOLON BORGLUM'S *PIONEER*

Whether intentional or accidental, the two heroically sized statues at the entrance of Kelham's courts sent a lamentable message. *The Pioneer*, by Solon Borglum, brother of Mount Rushmore sculptor Gutzon Borglum, stood before the Court of Flowers to the east, while *The End of the Trail* by James Earle Fraser was positioned in front of the Court of Palms to the west. This was an unfortunate juxtaposition. Fraser's powerful image of an exhausted, dispirited Indian brave on his drooping steed could only be interpreted as a requiem to Native Americans when seen alongside the sinewy, upright *Pioneer*. Author Ben Macomber said, "As representative of the conquering and the conquered race, the two must be studied together."[22]

Had the planners chosen differently, the arrangement might have been stripped of this condescending subtext. Near the Palace of Fine Arts stood another equestrian statue of a Native American warrior, *The Scout* by Cyrus E. Dallin. The youthful bronze warrior sat proudly atop his alert mount, hand held to his brow to shade his penetrating gaze. Had Dallin's sculpture been put in *The Pioneer*'s place, perhaps *The Scout* and *The End of the Trail* together might have been seen as episodes in an individual's life. As it was, in context of the prior one hundred years of American history and the nation's treatment of her native peoples, a reading of vanquishment was likely unavoidable. Perhaps pairing *The End of the Trail* with *The Scout* instead of *The Pioneer* might have evoked a sense of tribute rather than one of white man's victory over the Indians.

The End of the Trail, by James Earle Fraser, and *The Pioneer*, by Solon Borglum, stood before the entrances to the Court of Palms and Court of Flowers. (*Views of the Panama-Pacific International Exposition in Natural Colors* (viewbook) and The Bancroft Library, University of California, Berkeley)

were divided by copies of Calder's *Flower Girl* statues in shell-shaped niches.

The Court of Palms was the more serene of the two. Simple lampposts studded a balustrade around a sunken garden, and smooth lawns sloped down to the row of palm trees that gave the court its name, which were interspersed with marble benches facing a long rectangular pool. At the curved end of the court, water splashed gently into a plain raised bowl. The main décor here comprised three lunette murals over the portals: *Fruits and Flowers* by Childe Hassam, *The Pursuit of Pleasure* by Charles Holloway, and *Triumph of Culture* by local painter Arthur F. Mathews.

As might be expected in a court kept brilliant with a changing profusion of vibrant blooms, Kelham was freer with ornament and color in the Court of Flowers, and a selection of exquisite sculpture was used in place of murals.

Visitors to the court felt unusually tall as they promenaded between long, narrow lawns spaced with small Australian *Albizia lophantha* trees only four feet tall, their crowns trimmed into flat, mushroom-like heads five feet across. As they approached the back of the court, they found themselves shrinking in stature in comparison to the fountain of *Beauty and the Beast* by local sculptor Edgar Walter. Golden in hue and rising thirty feet above its circular basin, the playful composition depicted a lissome beauty, clad only in sandals and an attractive, if impractical, pointed hat, seated atop a writhing serpent.

Elaborate spiral-twist lampposts dotted the edge of the walkway encircling the fountain. These were topped with sculpted baskets of fruits and flowers that concealed the lamps and provided a diffuse glow, so at night the court was a veritable fairy garden. A frieze of griffins decorated the band above the columns, and each portal was guarded by a pair of stalwart seated lions by Albert Laessle.

Each of Kelham's courts covered about one and half acres, and though they differed in style, both were, according to Macomber, "calm, peaceful spots to rest and dream in the sun."[23]

THE COURT OF THE FOUR SEASONS

The sober Court of the Four Seasons, by eminent architect Henry Bacon, harbored secrets. In plan, the court was 340 feet square, but Bacon had designed double rows of columns that chamfered the four corners at 45-degree angles, making the court appear octagonal, with one open side connecting to a columned corridor reaching 470 feet toward the bay.

At the angled junctures, columns concealed niches with sculptural groups by Furio Piccirilli representing *Spring*, *Summer*, *Autumn*, and *Winter*, each group surmounting an identical semicircular fountain that splashed gently down three steps into a pool. Milton Herbert Bancroft painted ten murals for Bacon's piazza, all themed around the abundance of the seasons and the fruits of human labor.

Bacon, whose luminous Lincoln Memorial was then under construction in Washington, DC, said that in the Court of the Four Seasons he hoped to "remind one as far as possible of the old Roman villas." To this end he created a huge half-dome on the south end of the court and a long colonnade extending to the north, reminiscent of the large piazzas with exedrae at Hadrian's Villa near Tivoli. The coffers of the dome were arranged in a diamond pattern and brightly colored according to Jules Guérin's wishes. The brilliant pigments provided a welcome contrast to the dignified classical themes of the court.[24]

Art professor Eugen Neuhaus suggested the court would be better named for Albert Jaegers' sprightly figures of *Sunshine* and *Rain* on the lofty composite columns framing the dome, because "The Court of Two Seasons" would more accurately reflect California weather. Jaegers' *Harvest* presided from the roof of the dome, and on the open side of the court, his paired statues of *The Feast of the Sacrifice* surmounted the corners of the colonnade. These depicted a youth and a maiden, each leading a bull leashed by a floral garland.[25]

The landscape was understated in this court. In its center, no fountain sprayed and no effigy abided. Serene lilies floated on the surface of a simple round pool rimmed with evergreen shrubs, while acacia, eucalyptus, cypress, laurel, and olive trees stood sentry along the surrounding walls.

Beyond Renaissance triple-archways, smaller connecting courts led to the Court of the Universe to the east and the Palace of Fine Arts Lagoon to the west. Albert Jaegers' younger brother August designed spandrels for these archways, as well as small figures that were repeated along their upper margins.

Between the long rows of columns that extended northward, the goddess Ceres, envisioned by Evelyn Beatrice Longman as bearing a wreath and a scepter of corn, seemed to dance atop a twenty-foot-tall drum-shaped pedestal. At night, Ceres' capers were silhouetted against the brilliant rays of the Great Scintillator, forty-eight beams of polychrome light that swept the sky in a spectacular drill that was part of the elaborate illumination program.

The Court of the Four Seasons received virtually unanimous acclaim for its lovely proportions and restful quality, yet today it is not especially well-remembered alongside its flashier peers: the behemoth Court of the Universe and the riotously detailed Court of Ages.

THE FLAVOR OF SPAIN

Details borrowed from Mudéjar and Renaissance Spanish monuments added Iberian spice to the mostly French and neoclassical Beaux-Arts palace block.

One of William Faville's main challenges was to avoid monotony in the outer palace walls, which, though broken by the entrances to the various courts, stretched an imposing mile and a half in length and rose sixty-five feet tall. While the pale, plainly finished walls topped with fired red clay tiles also gave a nod to the adobe walls of California missions, their details and portals were distinctly Spanish.

Faville left the north faces of the palaces free from ornament save identical rich portals on the four edifices facing the bay. Author John D. Barry thought the architect "showed remarkable skill in varying the surface by means of his richly ornamental doorways, his niches, and his half domes." The doorways were executed in the Spanish style known as "plateresque," after the manner of the elaborate designs used by gold- and silversmiths. In three niches above each entry, two raffish, bandy-legged *Pirates* flanked a helmeted *Conquistador* leaning somberly on his sword, perhaps mortified to be seen in such mirth-inducing company. Around these figures, sculpted by Allen Newman, the intricately modeled surfaces might have been of chased metal.[26]

The southern façade behind the Avenue of Palms was saved from austerity by careful, symmetrical variation. Pilasters and colorful portals marched down its length. The sculpture over the Spanish Renaissance door of the Palace of Education by Gustave Gerlach depicted a mother reading with her children, a teacher and pupils, and a young man continuing his study independently.

For the main entrance to the Palace of Varied Industries, Gerlach reinterpreted the sixteenth-century doorway of the Hospital de Santa Cruz in Toledo, Spain. The original featured a Spanish cardinal and saints in the tympanum above and on either side. On the Palace of Varied Industries, Faville substituted figures by Ralph Stackpole representing Spinning, Building, Agriculture, Manual Labor, and Commerce in the arch above the door, with four copies of his *Man with a Pick* in vertical pairs on the right and left sides. In a niche above these was *Age Transferring His Burden to Youth*.

Bliss & Faville's most recent structure prior to the Fair, the Masonic Temple on Van Ness, directly influenced Faville's portals at the PPIE. Traces of the Renaissance were visible in several of the firm's earlier San Francisco commissions, including the Columbia Theater (now the American Conservatory Theater), the Eastman Kodak Building, and the Children's Hospital, but Faville borrowed most heavily from his latest work. Inspiration for the conquistadors on the Fair's north doorways could be traced to the canopied King Solomon on the Masonic building, which was executed by Adolph Weinman. Weinman and another Exposition sculptor, Ralph Stackpole, also molded figures for the Masonic Temple's elaborate door and

With its seven ascending sculpture-garnished, gem-lined tiers, Thomas Hastings' confection-like Tower of Jewels was often compared to a bejeweled wedding cake. (Anne T. Kent California Room, Marin County Free Library)

tympanum, echoes of which were felt in the doorways to the Palaces of Education and of Varied Industries. Even the lions on the scroll corbels of the Masonic edifice reminded one of the grizzlies Faville placed on scrolled pilasters on the Exposition's walls.

EMBRACING THE EPHEMERAL

"An Exposition allows some poetic license to the architect, some departure from pure logic, some playful fancy, or even extravagance," said architect B. J. S. Cahill. At the PPIE, the four architects who embraced the ephemeral, festal nature of Exposition architecture created the most memorable buildings, whether they were considered good or bad. Thomas Hastings, Louis Christian Mullgardt, Arthur Brown, Jr., and Bernard Maybeck each brought to bear his deep understanding of historical precedents, then used the opportunity of the Fair to approach his commission playfully.[27]

THE TOWER OF JEWELS

Writers struggled to describe the Exposition's skyline-dominating, 435-foot-tall Tower of Jewels. Critics

were ambivalent, offering muddled descriptions like "developed from Italian Renaissance architecture, with Byzantine modifications, designed to suggest an Aztec Tower." Some loved it, while others found it too squat, too busy, or too frivolous.[28]

The spire was designed by Thomas Hastings, then chairman of the American Institute of Architects, and he asserted that exposition architecture should be joyous and amusing while avoiding overly fanciful ideas. He said, "I believe that it is perfectly legitimate, architecturally, to design temporary buildings of an exposition in a character that one would not contemplate for a permanent building…because the exposition motive is made up not only of the educational aspect, but also has purposes of diversion and amusement, and it is therefore proper to relax our seriousness to some extent. Nevertheless, I think there is always the danger that we may go too far in this direction and make our work over fantastic."[29]

Whether Hastings succeeded in avoiding "the fantastic" in the Tower of Jewels is debatable, but it is certain that the architect faced difficult design challenges. Not only did he need to incorporate the tower as a gateway through William Faville's austere palace walls, he had to coordinate its treatment with the ostentatiously classical Court of the Universe within. The tower originally was slated to be even taller, and at one point Exposition management had considered deleting it entirely. It was ultimately retained, albeit at a truncated height, and this, along with the variety of colors used on the tiers, contributed to the criticism that the tower was ungraceful. Nevertheless, in an era when the next-tallest structure in San Francisco was the not-quite-three-hundred-foot Central Tower on Market Street, the Tower of Jewels was audacious. Even today, a forty-three-story building dropped onto the Marina District would dwarf its modest neighbors.

To span the Faville walls, Hastings chose a mammoth triumphal arch after the fashion of the Arch of Constantine in Rome, topped with a series of drum-like layers of decreasing diameters, each bedecked with statuary. One critic said these suggested a pile of column-encircled hatboxes. The confection of a building stepped up in seven tiers, culminating in a jewel-studded armillary sphere seventeen feet in diameter and borne upon the backs of four Atlas figures.

Fourteen hundred tons of structural steel and a million board feet of lumber framed the tower. The triumphal arch portion was supported on six 152-foot-tall "two-hinged" steel arches supported on spherical cast-steel bearings to counteract uneven settlement. The steel framework was invisible beneath a wood exoskeleton coated with the lath and plaster faux travertine that frosted all the palaces. Director of Color Jules Guérin decreed that the columns on the tower be plastered in light green and the walls behind them salmon pink, while the ornamental corner pavilions and statuary were golden.

Early in planning the Exposition, the tower had been slated to serve as the Administration Building, but these functions were moved to the Service Building and the California Building, rendering the tower strictly decorative. It would have been impractical and dangerous to allow the masses to ascend the tower, but occasionally a special guest was allowed up on the thin planking that floored the tiers, and from this windy vantage the views of the city, bay, and Exposition were breathtaking. Photographs hint that mildly larcenous visitors divested the tower

of some of the Novagem jewels hanging within arm's reach of the parapets.

The tower's base was 120 feet square and rose fifteen stories astride the 110-foot-tall coffered arch that was lined with murals of gigantic scale by William de Leftwich Dodge of New York. The murals were twelve feet high and ninety-six feet long and depicted allegorical interpretations of the creation of the Panama Canal.

The sculptural program ascending the levels comprised conqueror, cavalier, adventurer, priest, philosopher, warrior, and eagle, by John Flanagan and F. M. L. Tonetti. Many of the sculptures were admired individually, especially the equestrian statues standing before the tower: *Pizarro* by Charles Rumsey and *Cortez* by Charles Niehaus. The skyscraper was so loaded with sculpture that the resulting agglomeration took on the character of a statuary yard sale.

Over all of this opulence were strewn 102,000 cut-glass Novagems—two-inch-diameter colored-glass jewels prescribed by Chief of Illumination Walter D'Arcy Ryan. The Novagems were suspended from the tower on hooks, where they swung in the bay breezes and sparkled like a thorough dusting of rainbow-hued sanding sugar.

Indeed, various giant desserts were the most common metaphors cooked up by perplexed chroniclers of the tower. Emily Post wrote, "The scintillating…Tower of Jewels looked like a diamond and turquoise wedding-cake…." Artist Joseph Pennell, who'd drawn some early renderings of the Fair, said, "The Tower of Jewels might be made of ice cream."[30, 31]

Had the Tower of Jewels endured, perhaps it might have garnered the eventual affection of San Francisco, as did its successor, the Transamerica Pyramid. The 1972 Pyramid sparked considerable controversy when first constructed but is now heralded as a loveable oddity; the Tower of Jewels was granted no stay of execution.

While the tower had many detractors, it had defenders as well. An editor for the *San Francisco Call* wrote, "Our opinion is that Mr. Pennell is right in saying that the Tower of Jewels has an ice cream connotation. His error lies in assuming that the dominating architectural feature of the

Exposition should not be of holiday, festal design, fitted to arouse in the soul of the beholder joyous exultation….There is joyous force and sprightly power in the Tower of Jewels, and holiday beauty in the structure, and whether it could be duplicated in ice cream is a matter of small concern."[32]

THE COURT OF ABUNDANCE/COURT OF AGES

Passing under the arches into the Court of Ages at night was like entering the cloister of a mystical religion. Star-shaped lamps like huge snowflakes softly illuminated the extravagant sculptural details on the surrounding arcades. Around the dark mirror of the central pool, serpents with tongues of flame gathered around glowing cauldrons. In the middle of the lagoon, the figures around Robert Aitken's *Fountain of Earth* encircled a radiant glass globe that seemed to roil with molten, nascent life. The two-hundred-foot tower on the north end of the court resembled a high altar, with electric candles in place of flickering votives. Plumes of steam suggested the smoke of a sacred pyre rising before a reliquary.

Exposition management changed the official name of the court to the Court of Abundance, but architect Louis Christian Mullgardt preferred the original moniker, the Court of Ages. He'd envisioned its sculptural program as an allegorical development of life through the epochs, as suggested by Shakespeare's "seven ages of man" monologue from *As You Like It*.

Within its 340-foot-square footprint, the details of this court were unconventional and inventive. *Architect and Engineer of California* said of Mullgardt, "He tramples time-worn rules and obsolete precedents; he possesses imagination and originality, and his architecture is a great step in the progress of the art."[33]

Because of the expense, Mullgardt altered his original design, which had featured dual curved staircases and a pipe organ in the main tower. He then proposed a double cascade of water in front of the tower, emerging from unseen sources from behind a curtain of vines and enriched with sculptures of sea life symbolizing the "Mystery

Louis Christian Mullgardt's effervescent Court of Ages, officially named the Court of Abundance, underwent several design revisions. Its final form featured restrained plantings, Robert Aitken's *Fountain of Earth*, and an allegorical sculptural program representing the "seven ages of man." (*Official Publication[;] Panama-Pacific International Exposition: Hand-Colored* (viewbook))

of Water." The cascades were also jettisoned due to cost, but the marine theme remained in the finished court, though several aquatic denizens were left high and dry.

The arcades of the court remained encrusted with sculpted lobsters, crabs, and tortoises, while *Water Sprites* by Leo Lentelli supported freestanding pillars of Earth and Air in front of the tower, with "water spirit" archers as finials. Shells shielded the light standards in the side approaches, and Sherry Fry's *Daughter of Neptune* guarded the bayside forecourt with a trident while resting one foot delicately upon a dolphin and holding a shell to her ear.

Mullgardt said the floor of the court, with its sunken gardens, pool, and fountain, represented the development of a nebulous world with innate human passions. The sea life and bubble motifs on the piers and columns symbolized the "second stratum," what he called the Crustacean Period. For this display of "seafood gothic," Mullgardt drew upon his previous exposition experience as chief designer for Henry Ives Cobbs' Fisheries Building at the 1893 Columbian Exposition in Chicago, where he also had designed flamboyantly fishy details.

Subsequent strata in the Court of Ages showed plants, animals, and humans in a series of progressively more "civilized" eras, starting in the Stone Age with statues of *Primitive Man and Woman* by Albert Weinert on the tops of the piers of the arcade. The next layer showed the struggle to overcome the ignorance and superstition that Mullgardt audaciously claimed arose from religion and war. Higher still, medieval figures on the tower represented the "dawn of understanding," prefiguring the next level, the Christian era. The topmost figure on the tower symbolized Intelligence, with youthful Learning and Industry at her feet. All the sculpture on the two-hundred-foot tower, from slimy saurian through groups denoting the Stone and Middle Ages to wise goddess, was by Chester A. Beach.[34]

Rather than weighing down the structure, the lavish sculptural treatment of the surfaces created a lace-like effect. In addition to the molded elements on the surfaces of the arcades and figural statuary, Mullgardt placed hundreds of ornamental finials around the perimeter of the seventy-five-foot-high walls enclosing the court. Mullgardt's whimsical "crockets" looked like a legion of genii-inhabited bottles of varying heights lining the upper gallery. Mullgardt used a similar forest of turned ornaments on the cornices of the new de Young Museum (1919–1925) in Golden Gate Park, and a similar allegory in its frieze. At the museum he portrayed the development of California starting with plants and animals, then continued through aboriginal peoples, explorers, missionaries, and forty-niners before culminating in "a figure of Superior Intelligence."[35]

Perhaps because of its abundant three-dimensional ornament, the color scheme in the Court of Ages was kept more subtle than in any other area of the Fair. B. J. S. Cahill said, "In daylight… it is rather cold and colorless, but at nighttime this court is a veritable dream of loveliness."[36]

Frank Brangwyn's eight richly pigmented murals depicting two each of the elements of *Earth, Air, Fire,* and *Water* in the corners of the surrounding arcade matched Mullgardt's theme nicely and were commended by critics and visitors alike. However, some complained they could not be adequately appreciated beneath the ambulatories. "They need space about them," wrote Ben Macomber. "When they were first unpacked and hung up on the vast walls of Machinery Hall, they were ten times more effective. As they hang now, they are as incongruously placed as a lion crammed into a dry goods box." As with all of the commissioned murals, Brangwyn's *Elements* were painted on canvas so they could be moved, and today they are given a place of pride on the walls of the Herbst Theater in San Francisco's War Memorial Veterans Building on Van Ness Avenue.[37]

The exuberant details of the Court of Ages served as a striking contrast to the sober elegance of the Court of the Four Seasons, and Mullgardt's creation was acclaimed. If the Exposition was an ephemeral city, the Court of Ages was its chapel, where the air was perfumed with citrus blossoms and hyacinth instead of incense. Even Mullgardt said it was "designed as a sermon in stone." Many described its glamour reverently, including writer Beatrice Wright, who one evening sat enjoying the twilight in the Court of Ages as the lanterns in the arcades winked on. She wrote, "Eventide had come and the dim mysterious gloaming found me sitting there alone, in this old temple cloister."[38, 39]

Pacific Coast Architect critic Cahill thought it was the cleverest architectural moment of the entire PPIE. He said, "Here one finds that the departure from the conventional, while unfamiliar, is not fantastic, nor is it disturbing. It is wholly peaceful, yet wholly novel." The architecture of this court was characterized by various scribes as Portuguese Gothic, Hindu, Romanesque, Moorish, Oriental, or French in influence; but Macomber had it right when he suggested the style simply be termed "Mullgardt."[40, 41]

The architect "must have had in mind the transitional character of an exposition," wrote John Barry. "He knew that he could afford to try an experiment that might have been impracticable if the court had been intended for permanency."[42]

The glass celestial globe of Aitken's *Fountain of Earth* arose from the waters of a 150-by-65-foot basin on the floor of the court. Surrounding the sphere, four clusters of figures were separated by iterations of the god Hermes standing tall on each corner, while serpents around the rim spat water onto the globe. Ten crouching characters representing Destiny extended away from the main grouping. Finally, on the parapet of the pool sixty feet away, the god Helios grappled with the setting sun while enmeshed in the coils of a snake. Aitken's fountain netted him a medal for sculpture from the Architectural League of New York.

THE PALACE OF HORTICULTURE

The Palace of Horticulture was like an Ottoman mosque cast in iridescent turquoise glass, then dipped into a fondue of French architectural ornament. Realizing the life of the building would be fleeting, architect Arthur Brown, Jr., gave himself over to architectural excess, producing an oddly successful mélange of

The Palace of Horticulture was a flamboyant interpretation of the Blue Mosque in Istanbul. Executed in glass and steel by architect Arthur Brown, Jr., it was embellished with French-style ornament by his associate, Jean Louis Bourgeois. (Laura Ackley; gift of Bruce Ahlgren)

Islamic and French splendor, even as his firm was constructing a more sedate monument a mile and a half away from the Fair on Van Ness Avenue, the new San Francisco City Hall.

The arrangement of the palace's glass domes and semi-domes mirrored that of the circa 1616 masterwork Sultanahmet Camii, or "Blue Mosque," in Istanbul. While the domes of the Turkish monument built to a gentle crescendo, at the PPIE the 152-foot-diameter central dome dominated, floating 185 feet above the earth like a great iridescent bubble or fire opal. The airy, magnificent steel-and-glass dome was larger than those of both the Pantheon and St. Peter's Basilica in Rome, making it, temporarily, the largest dome in the world.

Below the relatively unadorned Ottoman sequence of domes atop the building, the structure was replete with French-style ornament, as one might expect of an École des Beaux-Arts–educated architect. (Arthur Brown, Jr., had attended the French academy after graduating from UC Berkeley.) The plenitude of the earth exhibited inside the Palace of Horticulture was expressed on its exterior by lushly modeled garlands of fruit- and flower-framed plaques. Scarcely a surface was left bare of acanthus-leaf molding, scroll, or shell, or unfinished by a latticed mansard or urn.

The French accent of this opulent embellishment was authentic, coming from the drafting board of French expatriate Jean Louis Bourgeois, a talented designer employed by Bakewell & Brown. Bourgeois never saw his fantastic festoons in place at the PPIE, as he volunteered for the French army shortly after the outbreak of hostilities and died fighting for his native country in February 1915.

The Palace of Horticulture resembled traditional mosque form but did not replicate it. An authentic mosque would have been "aniconic," as depiction of people or animals is discouraged in Islamic religious art and architecture. In Brown's horticultural fantasia, however, the human figure was conspicuous in the sylphs dancing about the bases of the spires. Also, in place of the "sahn" or courtyard of the Blue Mosque, a low rectangular building extended to the west, with skylights protecting the fragile plants of the demonstration gardens within.

Although the Palace of Horticulture's dome was naturally balanced by that of the Festival Hall across the South Gardens, the latter was only a cousin to the ebullient structure, not a sibling. The Palace of Horticulture's true brother was under construction at the new Civic Center, across town. There, a vastly more restrained dome—one standing more than 100 feet taller than its lighthearted horticultural predecessor at 307 feet—was nearing completion in the new City Hall, by Brown and his partner, John Bakewell, Jr. The gleaming government building was of more explicit Beaux-Arts extraction than the Palace of Horticulture, and its dome is a facsimile of the seventeenth-century French Renaissance Parisian Church of the Val-de-Grâce by Mansart.

THE PALACE OF FINE ARTS

Few realized the domed temple dreaming over its reflection in the placid, tree-lined lagoon west of the main palace block was inspired by a funeral barque and a murderous eastern European noblewoman. While conforming to no historical precedent, the rotunda with its rhythmic lines of columns curving gently toward the pool and palaces beyond seemed as inevitable and eternal as a Roman ruin.

In the Palace of Fine Arts, Bernard Maybeck's mastery of the canons of classical architecture enabled him to subvert them and conceive something entirely new and profoundly satisfying. The combination of romantic invention and technical virtuosity embodied in the arcing colonnades was quintessential Maybeck. As a rule, Maybeck did not write extensively about his designs, preferring to let the buildings speak for themselves. But for this, his most famous creation, he left two documents that explicate his deft handling of both the artistic and prosaic challenges of the Palace of Fine Arts.

Maybeck dedicated his *Palace of Fine Arts and Lagoon*, published by Paul Elder in 1915, to Director of Works Harris D. H. Connick and to fellow architect Willis Polk. Polk had relinquished his commission for the building after he saw

Bernard Maybeck's melancholy Palace of Fine Arts appears deceptively simple as it dreams over its placid lagoon, but it remains a tour de force that shows the architect's mastery of the canons of classical architecture. (Donna Ewald Huggins)

Maybeck's superlative conceptual sketch. In the slender volume, Maybeck discussed his artistic inspirations for the rotunda and colonnades in front of the main gallery building.

He recounted a trip through an art gallery in Munich where he saw "a picture which portrayed a Polish princess sitting on a throne in a courtyard in midwinter, who, in a mad fit, ordered freezing water to be thrown over nude maidens, amid snow and icicles….[A]nd farther on we saw Boecklin's 'Island of Death,' and on we wandered." He then left the gallery and glimpsed a bust of a mischievous boy labeled "Dear God, make me pious," which broke the spell cast by the bleak paintings within. Maybeck concluded that "an art gallery was a sad and serious matter," and he designed his Palace of Fine Arts to capture that ambience.[43]

The depiction of the "Polish princess" that so horrified Maybeck was almost certainly István Csók's 1893 painting of the notorious Erzsébet Báthory. Báthory was actually a Hungarian countess convicted of murdering girls and young women in the late sixteenth and early seventeenth centuries, many in exactly the manner portrayed. Only photographs of Csók's powerful work remain, as the painting was destroyed during World War II.

Swiss-born Arnold Böcklin painted a number of variations on the "Isle of the Dead" in the 1880s, thus it makes sense that one could have hung alongside the Hungarian artwork in Munich. Each version of Böcklin's image shows a white-robed figure escorting a coffin via rowboat to an atoll mausoleum embracing a grove of dark cypresses. The sweeping plan of the Palace of Fine Arts alludes to the semicircular form of the island, as does its mood, which Maybeck said he intended as "sentiment in a minor key."[44]

The architect also hoped to elicit the same spirit as the engravings of eighteenth-century artist Giovanni Battista Piranesi, whose elegiac renderings of overgrown Roman ruins struck a note of beauty tempered by sadness. Maybeck said, "There seems to be no other works of the builder, neither Gothic, nor

Moorish, nor Egyptian, that give us just this note of vanished grandeur." He also wished to establish a transitional space between the "exciting influences of the Fair" and the more contemplative art galleries.[45]

Imbuing the Palace of Fine Arts with such subtle emotional connotations took superb technical prowess. Maybeck said the coffers inside the 165-foot-high dome were constructed with their steps skewed to correct for perspective distortion in the same way as those of the Pantheon in Rome. He carefully proportioned the arches so they'd appear to advantage from across the lagoon. A truly classical structure would have required denser structural elements, but the architect took advantage of modern construction techniques and made his work more airy, filling the voids with more of John McLaren's hedges and other plants.

Ulric Ellerhusen's mysterious "Weeping Women" atop the Palace of Fine Arts colonnade were designed "for sentimental reasons and to strike the minor key of sadness," according to architect Maybeck. (Laura Ackley)

Neither was Maybeck above conflating and adjusting prescribed orders to suit his needs. Above the doubled Corinthian columns around the rotunda he echoed a cornice from the 2,000-year-old Roman Temple of the Sun because it reflected "Greek simplicity." The colonnades, which described an 1,100-foot-long arc, featured a novel combination of shorter Corinthian columns supporting the entablature and taller, paired Corinthian columns that held unusual sarcophagus-like boxes. Today the colonnades are a uniform warm ivory, but in 1915 the shorter columns were a pale green and the taller columns a ruddy terra-cotta tone.

Female figures draped over the corners of the boxes atop the colonnade were among the most talked-about features of the Fair. Unlike her outward-facing Grecian predecessors, each of Maybeck's supple goddesses, modeled by Ulric Ellerhusen, turned away from the viewers and appeared to weep into caskets, which were to have held plants. The conceit that the women were watering the verdure with their tears would have been wonderful, but the plants were eliminated to reduce expense, and many wondered why the maidens were crying.

Author John D. Barry related a humorous episode in which a woman asked an Exposition guard, "What are those women doing up there?"

> The guard looked at the urns, surmounting the columns. "They're supposed to be crying."
>
> "What are they crying about?"
>
> The guard looked a little embarrassed. "They are crying over the sadness of art," he said. Then added somewhat apologetically, "Anyway, that's what the lecturer told us to say."[46]

The guard's explanation was not far off. Maybeck himself said the enigmatic figures were "done for sentimental reasons and to strike the minor key of sadness." Emily Post thought they looked like nothing so much as "the coffin of a very fat Mormon and his four wives weeping for him."[47, 48]

The architect also integrated the work of a greater number of sculptors in a smaller area than on any other structure at the Fair. Ellerhusen also modeled elaborately gowned women bearing garlands for the receptacles at the base of the rotunda, and large figures for its attic. The *Struggle for the Beautiful,* by Bruno L. Zimm, appeared on the panels around the top of the rotunda. Underneath the dome, eight copies of Herbert Adams' angelic *Priestess of Culture* looked down solemnly from the interior columns. Leo Lentelli's *Aspiration* seemed to hang rather precariously over the door to the main gallery building.

Robert Reid's eight murals, which Director of Color Jules Guérin had despaired of completion, finally hung finished underneath the dome. Four panels illustrating the Progress of Art alternated with four Golds of California. The Progress of Art consisted of *The Birth of European Art, Inspiration in Art, The Birth of Oriental Art,* and *Ideals in Art.* The Golds were Reid's conception of the riches of California: wheat, oranges, poppies, and the precious metal itself.

Many of the artists whose maquettes had been enlarged by the sculpture shop to decorate the palaces were invited to display their works in bronze and stone on the grounds of the Palace of Fine Arts. These included Frederick Roth, Robert Aitken, Isidore Konti, Herbert Adams, Daniel Chester French, and Chief of Sculpture Karl Bitter.

When Emily Post and her party first arrived at the Exposition, the statuary was still being installed around the Palace of Fine Arts, and she particularly liked the figure of *Art, Tending the Fires of Inspiration,* by Ralph Stackpole. She wrote, "When we first came, the little kneeling figure on her peninsular front of the Fine Arts Temple and her reflection…gave an impression of a dream." But during their stay, so much sculpture was added that it eventually looked "merely like a museum." In fact, this sculpture garden was meant as an outdoor annex to the

Ideals in Art, by Robert Reid, was one of eight murals, each approximately twenty-three by twenty-seven feet, that the artist painted for the coffers underneath the Palace of Fine Arts rotunda. (*Scribner's,* September 1914)

statuary within the palace.[49]

Not every critic agreed Maybeck's subversion of the rules of classical architecture was warranted. B. J. S. Cahill, who'd so admired Mullgardt's Court of Ages, found the alternating column heights in the Fine Arts pergolas "restless" and said Maybeck had "gone a little over the border line of logic. The perilous step from the sublime to the ridiculous is often taken when two or three steps might carry one over to a safer region." But such objections were barely a whisper amongst the vociferous accolades for the Palace of Fine Arts. "Ancient Greece or Rome boasted nothing so exquisitely beautiful," said the *Morning Oregonian.*[50, 51]

According to Charles G. Odd, a Southern California architect, Maybeck "dared to originate," with "motives individual and artistic in daring profusion." Odd continued, "Let us pray that the citizens of San Francisco may not lay hands upon this Great Temple, but that they may preserve it and leave it there, so that also those who were not able to visit San Francisco during the year of 1915 may be able to enjoy the

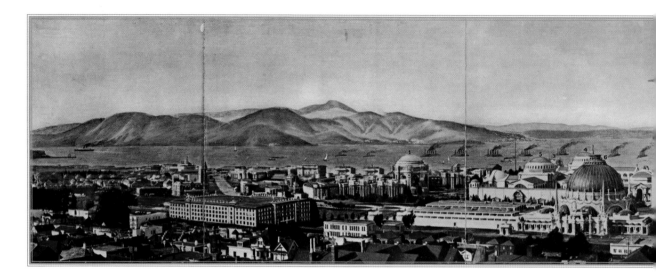

The palaces of the Jewel City were the most harmonious grouping ever designed for an international exposition. Its designers wrapped a carefully sculpture and color, comprehensive landscape planning, and colorful murals to form a cohesive whole. (Laura Ackley)

most impressive feature of the entire Fair."[52]

San Franciscans were in accord. The haunting, magnificent ruin so quickly became beloved that October 16, 1915, was christened Palace of Fine Arts Preservation Day. The Exposition promised to donate 75 percent of all receipts above the average to help save the building. That day 92,865 people crowded into the Exposition to see a panoply of entertainments, including a replication of the siege of Troy on the Marina Green, band and vocal concerts, one hundred children dancing under the direction of La Loïe Fuller, athletic contests, auto races, and a speech by Maybeck. By 11:00 p.m., $8,000 had been added to the fund, about $189,000 in 2012 dollars. Phoebe Apperson Hearst, honorary president of the Woman's Board of the PPIE, threw her considerable clout, and that of her son, William Randolph Hearst, behind the effort to save the palace. A campaign led by Hearst's *Examiner* newspaper garnered an additional $30,000 to cover operating expenses for Maybeck's masterpiece.

In contrast, preserving the Tower of Jewels was never seriously considered. There was simply no use for a huge structure not designed for occupancy. Retention of the Court of Ages depended on keeping the walls around it, so it was sacrificed as well. The Palace of Horticulture

lay on leased land that by contract had to be returned to its owners before January 1, 1917, and although M. H. de Young proposed rebuilding its dome portion as a conservatory in Golden Gate Park, his plan did not come to fruition.

The Palace of Fine Arts, however, was put under the care of the Art Association of San Francisco, for whom the Regents of the University of California were trustees. The building was still imperiled because the land under it was owned by the government. Former mayor and then-senator James D. Phelan and Representative Julius Kahn, who both had been instrumental in winning the Exposition for California, stepped up once more to support this cause. They successfully amended the 1917 army appropriations bills to include a provision to transfer Presidio lands underneath the palace to the Regents of the University of California in exchange for donated lands of equal value.

A few years later, the building began to weather and the plantings about it matured. In 1919, *Architectural Review* said, "Mr. Maybeck's splendid Fine Arts Building on the Exposition grounds, grows even more beautiful as weather and plant life give it added interest. There is a poetic beauty and almost sadness of charm about it now, which does not detract from its grandeur,

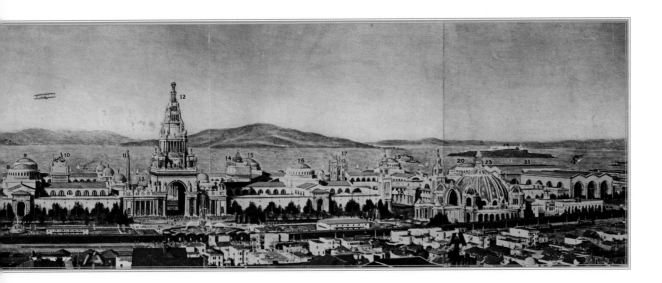

considered selection of Near Eastern and Mediterranean styles in an elegant Beaux-Arts package, augmented with water features, architectural

but rouses hope that it will be kept in enduring form for the years to come."[53]

AN EVANESCENT ARCHITECTURE

The sunset of the PPIE was also the sunset of the great Beaux-Arts world's fairs. The next international exposition held in the United States was almost two decades later, after the dust of World War I had settled. By then, two European expositions had changed architectural fashion radically, and the US was struggling through the privations of the Great Depression.

Chicago's 1933 Centennial of Progress Exposition replaced the PPIE's ostensible mission of education, which included a hearty side of sales, with overt commercial sponsorship. Where industry had largely been contained within San Francisco's palaces, businesses like *Time* and *Fortune* magazines, Armour and Co. Foods, Sears Roebuck, Johns-Manville, General Motors, Chrysler, and Firestone each sponsored a building at Chicago. Architect Almus Pratt Evans admitted that the 1933 Fair was "a glorification of our commercial development. More than that, it is a commercial enterprise." He also lamented

the loss of the type of cohesive plan reified at the PPIE.[54]

The Jewel City's cultured courtyards and gardens of a Moorish caliphate, its temples of Athens and Rome, the hallowed domes of Byzantium, and Frenchified ornaments were replaced by the industrial curves of the Streamline Moderne. A meticulously ornamented Mediterranean palace among the sparely detailed industrial buildings of the 1933 fair would have seemed like a courtly old gentleman in fine but antiquated garb amongst a crowd of young hepcats in tapered trousers.

In 1915, however, the architects of the Tower of Jewels, the Palace of Horticulture, the Court of Ages, and the Palace of Fine Arts all adopted a more imaginative, festive approach to their commissions than their peers, knowing the buildings were slated for demolition in just a few short months. In so doing, they created the most memorable structures at the PPIE, and, in the case of Maybeck, the most enduring. Ironically, the unfettered innovation enabled by the evanescence of the Exposition resulted in the only building made permanent on the site: the Palace of Fine Arts. ⚶

A MASTERPIECE OF ILLUMINATION

"Mr. Polk, I am going to illuminate your Exposition!"

illis Polk, chairman of the PPIE's Architectural Commission, stared in amazement as the dapper, dark-haired gentleman from General Electric described dozens of new lighting effects—none of which had been tried before.

Polk knew that Walter D'Arcy Ryan was a skilled engineer. He had authored important papers on measuring light, lit Niagara Falls in myriad colors, and illuminated the Buffalo Electric and Singer buildings. Ryan even possessed exposition experience, having created spectacular lighting for the 1909 Hudson-Fulton Celebration in New York. What Polk had yet to learn was that Ryan was one of the most persuasive men he would ever meet.

The architect was taken aback by Ryan's presumption. No one had solicited the man's advice or his elaborate concepts. It was August 1912, and the Fair's planners knew what they wanted: an updated version of the lighting used at previous expositions. Polk decided to "fix this fellow" by allowing him to speak to the architects' board, allocating Ryan exactly thirty minutes, after which the chairman was sure the proposal would be rejected.[1]

Four and a half hours after he began speaking, Ryan was the first to leave the meeting, taking with him the Architectural Commission's tentative approval to implement his ambitious designs.

It appears the architects hedged their bets, however. Documents in General Electric's historical files indicate a backup lighting designer also was hired, described as "a local man who promised to illuminate the whole Exposition in outlining lighting with small incandescent lamps." One of Ryan's assistants at the PPIE, A. F. Dickerson, wrote, "While encouraging Mr. Ryan to go ahead, and giving him every facility for making his demonstration of the lighting, the management at the same time had another illumination specialist lay out an alternate plan, even down to the smallest detail....[T]hey were simply taking no chances, merely thought it best to be prepared for all possible eventualities."[2, 3]

WALTER D'ARCY RYAN AND OUTLINE LIGHTING

Ryan was an unusual combination of creative artist, engineer, showman, and self-promoter. Born in 1870, he studied engineering at a military college in Canada and at MIT. In 1892 he joined the Thomson-Houston Electric Company, which that year merged with Edison General Electric to become the General Electric Company, where he eventually became the first director of the firm's new Illuminating Engineering Laboratory in Schenectady, New York.

After this, he completed several important lighting commissions, including illuminating Niagara Falls in 1907, for which three batteries of searchlights were projected through colored celluloid, and the first floodlighting of a skyscraper, the forty-seven-story Singer Building, in 1908.

Virginia Ryan Durrant, Ryan's daughter, characterized her father as outgoing and polite, though he traveled much of the time. Virginia said her father was very generous. "He never went away without bringing us back gifts, sometimes unusual," she explained. "Once it was marmoset monkeys; another, waltzing white mice. They didn't last very long. The cat got them, which made Mom very happy."[4]

Ryan also was known for meticulous planning and mathematical analysis. He recalled, "As soon as any particular phase of the lighting was fully decided upon, the illumination and luminous flux values were calculated in all their minute details, so that long before the Exposition opened there were on hand complete sets of illumination diagrams for all the various courts, buildings and towers."[5]

Chief of Illumination Walter D'Arcy Ryan was an unusual mix of engineer and showman. (Laura Ackley)

Prior to 1915, standard practice for architectural illumination was a technique called "outline lighting," in which rows of tiny lights traced cornice lines, windows, and other architectural elements. Unfortunately, this yielded a "skeletal" delineation, the gaps from burned-out bulbs were distracting, and often the glare from so many exposed bulbs caused eye fatigue.

With his designs for the PPIE, Ryan sought to change lighting art decisively. "Contrary to general expectation, there will be no outlining of the Panama-Pacific Exposition buildings with incandescent lamps," he announced.[6]

Fortunately for the engineer, world's fairs typically were showcases for new technologies, including illumination. Although lighting infrastructure did not exist in many parts of the country, the new construction of fairs allowed for the installation of the latest technology. After Thomas Edison's development of the first practical electric lightbulb in 1877, every fair since had featured the newest in illumination technologies, all variations on outline lighting. Illumination was considered critical because fair organizers wanted to maximize attendance by allowing patrons to remain after dark.

Also, because expositions were not permanent,

there was more room for experimentation and even failure; and since fairs and exhibitions were a good way for the industry to introduce the public to new products, corporations often donated money, equipment, and the work of their best engineers and designers. Ryan later estimated that General Electric spent $52,000 (about $1.23 million in 2012) creating and supporting the PPIE's illumination department.

Yet Ryan was after more than pure utility. He admitted that his designs had inefficiencies from an engineering standpoint, but he was aiming for artistry, not merely adequate engineering.

THE FINAL LIGHTING TEST

Four nights prior to the opening of the PPIE, thousands of expectant citizens stood in buffeting rain and wind on the streets above Harbor View and gazed down on the dark Exposition grounds to witness the final test of the lighting scheme. At 10:00 p.m. a select group of dignitaries, including poet Edwin Markham, left an organ concert in the Exposition's Festival Hall to brave the elements on the exposed Esplanade fronting the bay. Suddenly, 2.6 billion candlepower burst forth from the miniature Morro Castle just off the Marina, and a great fan of colored light, called "The Great Scintillator," filled the sky. For two hours the tenacious spectators witnessed the most enduring innovation of the PPIE, its spectacular illuminations.

A battalion of specially trained marines rotated and dipped the forty-eight giant spotlights of the Scintillator in a precision drill, interweaving and circling the beams into a prismatic aurora that touched the Marin hills and Alcatraz Island. Comets and planets spun as if captive inside the gigantic glass dome of the Palace of Horticulture. As colored spotlights centered on the Tower of Jewels, the spire was draped in a lambent veil. Tens of thousands of varicolored gems limning its cornices sparkled like giant versions of falling raindrops. In the courts of the Exposition, fountains gleamed, two giant "candles of glass" glowed, and sculpted serpents spat plumes of fire toward an eighteen-foot-diameter glass sphere that appeared to writhe with life from within. The

Palace of Fine Arts was bathed in emerald light.

Poets, as a rule, are not noted for verbal restraint, so Markham took especial care to note he was not exaggerating the splendor of the effects. He wrote: "I have to-night seen the greatest revelation of beauty that was ever seen on the earth. I may say this meaning it literally and with full regard for all that is known of ancient art and architecture, and all that the modern world has heretofore seen of glory and grandeur. I have seen beauty that will give the world new standards of art, and a joy in loveliness never before reached."[7]

THE EFFECTS

Ryan was vindicated. All the effects he had laid out so minutely on paper were successful. The combination of purely spectacular effects, as well as practical architectural lighting, set a new standard. One viewer said, "There was no more skepticism after that, nor were any further slighting remarks heard as to the

Prior to 1915, "outline lighting," seen here on the tower of San Francisco's Ferry Building, was the standard for architectural illumination. (Laura Ackley)

'art of illumination,' or regarding Mr. Ryan's qualifications as a creative artist." A close look at each of Ryan's effects reveals how the illuminating engineer was able to blend technology and art.[8]

THE GREAT SCINTILLATOR

Three nights a week, wide spokes of chromatic light swept the skies above the Marina, weaving and dancing through hundreds of vivid patterns. The Great Scintillator was the PPIE's splashiest illumination effect, culminating Ryan's long fascination with light transmitted through vapor.

Legend held that he had been inspired while watching a train pulling up a grade one night. The Pan-Pacific Press Association's history of the Exposition stated, "The fireman opened the firebox door to throw in a shovelful of coal, then shut the door while he was filling his shovel.... This gave a weird effect; the smoke curling up over the engine cab, then the flash of light illuminating the black smoke for an instant, then darkness, then another flash and again darkness."[9]

In 1907 Ryan lit Niagara Falls using three batteries of searchlights located between one-half and three-quarters of a mile from the falls. He installed a smaller, one-million-candlepower prototype of the Scintillator at the Hudson-Fulton Celebration of 1909 in New York.

The Great Scintillator at the PPIE was his ultimate achievement in this medium. The miniature Morro Castle, patterned after Caribbean prototypes and complete with a tiny lighthouse, extended into San Francisco Bay on a spit of land near the Yacht Harbor. Here, forty-eight three-foot-diameter projector spotlights were arranged in two tiers. The weatherproof pier supporting the lights sheltered colored screens, filters, resistors, distribution circuits, and motors for machines that generated various effects.

Each searchlight was installed so it could swing both horizontally and vertically. New programs were created daily, and four section sergeants megaphoned instructions to the company of marines who moved their lights as though under a symphony conductor's baton. Color screens of "gelatine were mounted in wooden frames, and supported by chicken netting," and the colors projected were changed on the fly. *Pacific Service*

A special detachment of marines was trained to weave brilliantly colored beams of light into the gorgeous patterns of the Great Scintillator by maneuvering forty-eight spotlights. (Jim Caddick)

Ryan obtained a 224-ton locomotive from Southern Pacific to create steam and smoke for the Great Scintillator on nights when the San Francisco fog did not appear. He had the engine painted to match the faux travertine finish of the palaces. (Laura Ackley)

Magazine recounted the drill: "On receiving a color command, an apparently wild scramble ensues, but in five seconds the screens are in place, the lamps trained to position and, behold! The Aurora."[10]

The famed San Francisco fog was a distinct asset to the Scintillator, creating a wonderful canvas for the plumes of colored light. Ryan, however, prepared for those occasions when the fog failed to appear. Flagpoles nearby were actually perforated steam tubes, and, when needed, a 224-ton Southern Pacific locomotive, mounted above the ground and running at the equivalent of a mile a minute, provided copious smoke and steam. Ryan even had the engine painted to match the cream-colored faux-travertine of the palaces so the train would not "make an inharmonious blot adjacent to the Exposition buildings."[11]

The Scintillator beams became a medium for "fireless fireworks," as pyrotechnic bombs exploded and loosened hoses sent plumes of steam writhing into the shafts of light. The fanciful names of these effects included "Fighting

Serpents and Octopus," "Birds of Paradise," and "Aladdin's Lamp." The show usually ended with an American flag of colored mortar smoke hundreds of feet long drifting slowly toward the bay through the Scintillator's rays.

Ryan described the experience:

You take up a position anywhere on the Marina or North Gardens and wait for the signal gun.... [A]n Aurora Borealis will reach from the Golden Gate to Sausalito and will extend for miles in every direction. Wonderful Scotch plaids appear in the sky and one is sure to be impressed by the weird 'Ghost Dance' or the 'Spook's Parade' of the beams. The north façades of the Exposition are illuminated in ever-changing colors....Fireless fireworks, mammoth steam effects, some rising to a height of over 100 feet, including the 'Devil's Fan,' 'Plume of Paradise,' 'Fairy Feathers,' 'Sunburst,' and 'Chromatic Wheels,' are novel features. Explosions of mines produce great banks of smoke giving forth radiations of every known tint and shade. Sunset clouds burst forth in the night, strange and grotesque figures move across the sky illuminated by the concentrated rays of the searchlights. Flags of all nations float through the air. Artillery thunders, driving belching smoke into the blaze of artificial glory.[12]

THE ELECTRIC KALEIDOSCOPE

As twilight fell each night, those promenading through the grounds saw the fifteen-story steel-and-glass dome of the Palace of Horticulture glowing like an immense iridescent bubble, half-submerged amid the dark minarets of a grand Ottoman mosque. Among the planting beds and reflecting pools, the glass globes of pathway lights began to wink on. Then, the bubble began to change color. A virtual sunset in gradients from crimson to sapphire rotated smoothly across its surface. Next, twelve ribbons of colored light chased each other around the dome, followed by comets and planets changing color while revolving in swinging orbits, and finally dissolving into fluttering spots of light that evoked birds and butterflies.

The Electric Kaleidoscope, centered below the great dome, produced these and other astounding effects. The glass of the dome was airbrushed with opalescent paint that allowed the colossal hemisphere to serve as a translucent "canvas" for effects projected from the inside. Those outside saw "revolving bars, rings,

A device called the Electric Kaleidoscope projected vivid moving comets and planets against a luminous virtual sunset inside the iridescent glass dome of the Palace of Horticulture. (*The Literary Digest*, February 20, 1915)

and spots in astronomical movements, or the dissolving of colors from one shade to another without a sharp line of demarcation."[13]

The apparatus, screened from view by coconut palms, consisted of a dozen projector spotlights throwing their beams through three layers of mechanisms, allowing patterns to be evenly dispersed over the interior of the dome. The light passed first through what were called "shadow bars," then color screens, and finally onto one of five five-foot-diameter composite lenses atop a fifteen-foot tower. Each of the three elements—shadow bars, color screens, and lenses—was mounted on a vertical shaft and rotated slowly at slightly different speeds, enabling operators to produce a tremendous variety of effects. As the layers rotated around their central shaft, colors dissolved smoothly into one another and bright highlights appeared on the glass of the dome, giving the illusion of a majestic, glimmering opal.

NOVAGEMS ON THE TOWER OF JEWELS

The 435-foot-tall Tower of Jewels took its moniker from the 102,000 glittering Novagems that adorned its cornices. These cut-glass jewels in several colors swung in the winds swirling around the spire, making it appear to radiate its own flashing, sparkling light, an effect Ryan called "augmented daylight." The author of a novel set at the PPIE had one character poetically relate that the tower "seemed as if a million fireflies had lighted on it."[14]

The Novagems on the tower were about two inches in diameter and came in the colors emerald, ruby, canary, diamond, and aquamarine. Ryan chose a top-grade flint glass that had very high refractive indices. General Electric's Illuminating Engineering Laboratory in Schenectady tested a variety of facet configurations, then had ten tons of jewels fabricated in Austria according to its scientific findings. To make the gems, artisans poured a molten glass called Sumatra Stone into molds the approximate size and shape of each Novagem. After the glass cooled, the jewels were hand-cut and polished.

To increase the Novagems' brilliance, Ryan

mounted them in brass holders with small mirrors placed at their pointed apexes. This increased the number of spectra, or tiny rainbows, the jewels emitted by 40 percent. Finally, each gem was suspended on a loop held away from the tower by an arch of wire bolted into the structure, enabling the jewel to oscillate with every breeze. Courage was required of the jewel hangers who ascended the tower to install the gems. Writer John Barry observed, "The wind up there is very strong. Some of the men came near being blown off."[15]

The Novagems were not scattered randomly across the tower but were clustered in colored designs. The twenty-foot-diameter armillary sphere crowning the tower was covered in green jewels and striped with diagonal bands of white. Columns were encrusted with white brilliants with horizontal bands of red, and the horizontal moldings were lined with yellow gems. During testing, the finial sphere was seen from a ship seventy miles out to sea. About 4,000 Novagems in smaller sizes spangled the headpieces of sculptor Stirling Calder's ninety elegant *Star Maidens*, who gazed serenely from the entablatures above the Court of the Universe.

Today, the idea of bedecking a building with 100,000 mirror-backed hanging crystals seems fantastic, even though we regularly see signs with wind-oscillated mirrored disks advertising bottled water, casinos, and shopping malls. In 1915 the Tower of Jewels was unprecedented. General Electric historian John Winthrop Hammond chronicled an episode in which a few jewels were hung on the tower while Ryan was visiting the East Coast. They cast shadows on the building, and Hammond wrote, "The architects' commission wanted to throw all the jewels bodily into San Francisco Bay."[16]

Upon his return, Ryan demonstrated that when mounted according to his specifications, the jewels would not cast shadows, and the Novagems were saved from a watery demise. In fact, the jewels were so unobtrusive, they are largely invisible in photographs. Postcard manufacturers resorted to adding glitter or drawing in the jewels to highlight them. In films and in person, though, they flashed and sparkled both day and night.

More than 100,000 Novagems—two-inch-diameter cut-glass jewels in several colors—were hung in patterns to highlight the architectural features of the forty-three-story Tower of Jewels. (Donna Ewald Huggins and Laura Ackley)

While the public adored the Novagems and the effect was praised by critics, some thought the building they adorned was less successful. John Strong Newberry, a noted intellectual, found the only tolerable view of the Tower of Jewels to be at night. He described the building as "banal" in daylight, stating, "It is the fair's one glaring error. And San Francisco spent $70,000 for those bits of colored glass, a glittering disguise for an artistic blunder."[17]

THE TOTAL ILLUMINATION PLAN

In addition to the spectacular Scintillator, Electric Kaleidoscope, and Tower of Jewels, the courts of the PPIE were a fairyland of novel lighting effects. Ryan's Total Illumination Plan marked the first occasion when lighting was part of an international exposition's early design process. Ryan's plans included avant-garde proposals for lighting each court, the Joy Zone, building interiors, and pathways. He and his team of assistants, also imported from General Electric, created individual lighting designs to match the mood of each of the great courts by harmonizing with their architectural themes. Ryan conferred with Chief of Color Jules Guérin so that even the wiring would not clash with the architectural colors. He also devised non-glare lighting for the galleries of the Palace of Fine Arts and a method for evenly illuminating the interiors of the large exhibit palaces.

THE COURT OF THE UNIVERSE

The two stately, fluted pillars of the vast Court of the Universe were changelings. By day, the freestanding columns in the Fountains of the Rising Sun and Setting Sun, each supporting a finely modeled winged figure by sculptor Adolph Weinman, gave the illusion of warm marble. But by night, they were great incandescent candles.

A thirty-one-foot section of each sixty-five-foot column was made of heavy opalescent, fluted glass lined with a layer of sandblasted glass to eliminate shadows. Each of these glass sections was lit from within by ninety-six 1,500-watt lamps. A large glass sphere, also lit

from within, topped each glowing column. The heat from these lamps was so great that fans were placed at the base of each shaft to direct heat upward to vent at the base of the sphere supporting each statue. If the air supply to the fans was compromised, the column lights automatically switched off.

The glow from the fountains was the principal illumination of this court at night, augmented by lighted glass amphorae on the heads of atlantes and caryatids spaced evenly along the balustrades around the sunken garden. Friezes above the colonnades surrounding the court were lit from below by concealed lights in waterproof metal reflectors submerged in the pools. The space was roofed in a bright lace of beams from 180 spotlights—two positioned behind each of the ninety *Star Maiden* statues who overlooked the court. Each pair focused on the *Star Maiden* on the court's opposite side. Many sculptures at the PPIE were similarly lit, with rays from two different angles and in varied colors to emphasize the depth of the statues.

In addition to its spectacular effects, the Total Illumination Plan for the PPIE comprised specially tailored lighting designs for each court and cunningly devised "indirect lighting," using colorful banner standards, as seen here along the Avenue of Palms. (Laura Ackley)

By day the Columns of the Rising and the Setting Sun appeared to be classic marble, but by night the frosted glass columns became glowing shafts of light. (Laura Ackley)

THE COURT OF AGES/
COURT OF ABUNDANCE

Louis Christian Mullgardt's Court of Ages, officially the Court of Abundance, was the architectural fantasy of the Exposition. Its illuminations helped give the illusion of an outdoor cathedral dedicated to a mysterious religion, complete with incense urns burning all around with colorful flickering flames. On the perimeter of its central lagoon, quartets of coiled snakes spat tongues of live flame into wide, steaming braziers.

At one end of the basin, a submerged disc of lighted glass simulated sunset at the water's edge. At the other end, Robert Aitken's muscular figures of the *Fountain of Earth* embraced a great eighteen-foot sphere of opalescent glass. This glass ball was too heavy to rotate, but Ryan wanted to imbue it with life. A seven-inch-diameter globe covered with two hundred multicolored 150-watt bulbs in reflectors was placed inside the larger sphere, and when the smaller interior globe spun, it gave the illusion of rotation to the larger outer sphere. Steam

completed the effect of a shimmering world-in-the-making turning on its axis.

Author Ben Macomber was impressed by the scene: "[The fountains] are red, with clouds of rosy steam rising around them. Writhing serpents spout leaping gas flames on the altars set around the Pool of the Ages, and from other altars set by the entrances of the Court rise clouds of steam given the semblance of flame by concealed red lights. By the high altar on the Tower of Ages the same device is used to make the lights flame like huge torches."[18]

THE COURT OF THE
FOUR SEASONS

Lighting in the classical Court of the Four Seasons reinforced its theme of peaceful contemplation. Within the colonnaded niches in each of its four corners, Ryan added a vivid dimension to the stepped fountains beneath Furio Piccirilli's allegorical statuary representing the seasons. In *The City of Domes*, John Barry wrote, "In the Court of the Four Seasons we watched the Emerald Pool turning the architecture into a mermaids' palace. The water flowing under the four groups of the seasons shone from an invisible light beneath, coloring it a rich green. When Ryan promised to illuminate the water here without letting the source of the light be seen, it was thought by the people that it couldn't be done." But the illuminating engineer succeeded, achieving an iridescent effect by lighting the rear of the cascades in green and the front in orange and red.[19]

THE FESTIVAL HALL

Ryan's lighting finesse was also evident within the Exposition's halls. As the audience gave a standing ovation to Clarence Eddy's spirited rendition of "The Star-Spangled Banner" on the great organ in the Festival Hall, they were unaware that the dome soaring above them was suffused with light from an invisible source located below their feet. The novel lighting system for the dome was almost as innovative as the grand new musical instrument.

Lighting for the lofty vault was completely concealed in the floor in a twelve-foot-deep

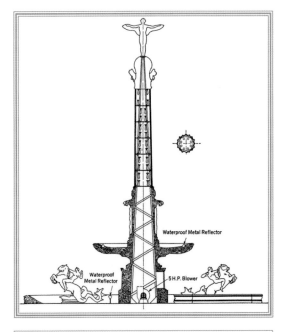

Ninety-six 1,500-watt lamps, concealed within each glass column, created a warm, soft glow that provided the principal illumination for the immense Court of the Universe. (Laura Ackley)

"ornamental well." Its top extended to about the level of the backs of the auditorium seats. Inside the well the beams of eight searchlights shone up through a sandblasted glass diffusing disc, encircled by an inverted, mirror-lined cone. Since a storm sewer ran directly through the center of the well, four more lights had to be mounted higher than the others; the light from these was first reflected onto mirrors before hitting the diffusing plate. The lights created a soft, even glow over the entire dome. The twelve six-million-candlepower searchlights were extremely hot, and to cool them a stream of water continually ran over the lenses.

THE LIFE WITHIN

"The Life Within" was Ryan's name for the night illumination inside the main palaces. Since the exhibit halls were usually closed in the evenings, he suspended tungsten lamps in tin reflectors behind the windows of the buildings and then filled them with a soft orange light so that they did not present cold, black voids to the nighttime revelers. Where the clerestories were glazed with frosted glass, the backs of the windows were painted orange, and where the glazing was clear, bulbs were dipped in orange lacquer.[20]

THE JOY ZONE

At regular intervals, merrymakers on the Zone strolled beneath slender arches festooned with knots of colored incandescent bulbs hung with red streamers that danced gaily in the zephyrs from the bay. Ryan wanted to demonstrate a nostalgic approach on the Zone so that fairgoers could "contrast the illumination of the future with the light of the past."[21]

Every seventy-five feet along the Zone's mile length stood a thirty-nine-foot-tall lamppost, its cross-arms carried by whimsical molded seahorses. From each arm depended a delicate ornamental lantern containing five low-pressure gas mantles. Various "Oriental" designs decorated the translucent canvas panels of each nine-hundred-candlepower wood-framed lamp. Outline lighting was permitted on some façades, completing the retrograde strategy.

GAS LIGHTING

Ryan declared that "all modern sources of intrinsic merit," including gas, should be used. In 1915 there was still plenty of gas available for lighting, and gaslights had enjoyed renewed popularity because of new gas mantle technology. Approximately four miles of pathways at the fair, including all of the state and national pavilion areas, were illuminated by high-pressure gas mantle lamps surrounded by twenty-inch globes of frosted glass. Unfortunately, the glass globes around the high-pressure emergency lights were not as reliable as the gas itself. Early in the Exposition about 40 percent of the globes burst due to uneven glass thickness and had to be replaced. [22]

A backup system of gas lighting was also installed in the colonnades of all the courts, so that if the electrical system failed, crowds could find their way out of the grounds. After the Exposition closed each evening, gaslight provided patrol lighting, being deemed "far more dependable and less liable to be affected by the elements" than electric illumination.[23]

PAINTING WITH LIGHT

Special days occasioned special lighting effects. Nine years to the day after the great earthquake and fire swept through San Francisco, onlookers gasped as smoke and flame wreathed the ornate Tower of Jewels, as if the tragedy were being repeated. Fortunately, the blaze was just a luminous simulation on Nine Years After Day, which celebrated the city's remarkable recovery.

Even days not designated as "special" presented their own spectacles. As dusk fell, the six towers punctuating the skyline of the Panama-Pacific International Exposition seemed to glow like molten metal in a forge, red gradually giving way to a warm, mellow, clear light with no visible source. This was Ryan's crowning achievement—the definitive change of the architectural illumination standard from outline lighting to "indirect illumination," an effect now known as floodlighting. Ryan declared the theme for the PPIE's illuminations was "light, not lamps," and he observed that, unlike at previous

Gas lighting, then being supplanted by electricity, was used on the Zone to provide a nostalgic effect, as exemplified by these lanterns borne by whimsical seahorses. (Laura Ackley)

world's expositions, "you will not spend your time at this fair counting lamps." He mused, "The light will be so perfectly and unobtrusively distributed that nine-tenths of the people will not know that it is night but for the fact that they have had dinner." The indirect illumination scheme was multifaceted, constituting an entire palette for architectural illumination.[24]

THE "MOSQUITO FLEET"

Ryan asserted the best illumination would mimic the natural effect of bright, directional sunlight complemented by the diffuse light from clouds or reflection. This combination would reveal details without harsh shadows. Architecture at the PPIE was to be "washed with light" so that Guérin's colors, and the foliage and flowers, would retain all their natural, delicate hues. To achieve this, each exterior was lit by remote spotlights mounted discreetly atop other Exposition structures, some as much as a quarter of a mile distant. These alone would have created deep, sharp shadows, so red lamps were concealed in the shadowed areas to lightly tint and soften the effect. Thus, the contrast between fully illumined areas and adjacent shadows approximated the tonal relationship of direct and ambient illumination in daylight.

Fifty eighteen-inch and four thirty-inch spotlights were required to light just the Tower of Jewels. These fifty-four lights were part of what Ryan nicknamed "the mosquito fleet" of more than 370 arc and 450 tungsten filament "searchlamps" hidden throughout the palace block. The number of searchlights used at the Exposition was greater than all those owned by the US Army and Navy combined in 1915. Since the Illuminating Engineering Department strove for a soft, diffused light, as distinguished from the sharply focused beams of typical searchlights, Ryan planned, tested, and perfected new lights with parabolic mirrors.

Each light in the mosquito fleet was aimed at an individual pennant or sculpture. When the switch was closed to turn them on, the three hundred flags along the parapets appeared to "burst into flame." "Dispersion doors" on each lamp controlled the spread of its beam to between 10 and 40 degrees horizontally and vertically.[25]

Colored screens were kept near each light so that the color theme of the lighting could be changed easily for special occasions. On St. Patrick's Day, buildings were clothed in Kelly green, while on Orange Day, of course, orange prevailed.

COLUMN CUPS

Inside the grand colonnades, golden drops of light appeared to roll down the central flute of each column. Here Ryan had needed to solve the problem of deep shadows in a manner disguised from pedestrians. Unlike on the towers, he could not simply place red lights in areas on which the floodlighting would cast strong shadows. Instead, "column cups" were embedded at heights of ten, twenty-four, and thirty-four feet. These opalescent glass fixtures were set in recesses that focused the light onto the rear walls of the colonnades.

Ryan said, "This brings out the Pompeian red walls and the cerulean blue ceilings with their golden stars…at the same time the sources are so thoroughly concealed that their location cannot be detected from any point in the court."[26]

Pressed opalescent glass cups embedded in the columns cast even illumination on the roseate interior walls of the palatial colonnades and resembled golden droplets of light rolling down the flutes. (Laura Ackley)

ORNAMENTAL STANDARDS

The final and most cunning mode of source camouflage was accomplished by building special light standards throughout most of the grounds. Ryan wanted the façades of the buildings to be lit from a height, as if by natural sunlight. However, he also wished to avoid cluttering the grounds of the Exposition with unattractive lampposts, so he had James Gosling, his "artistic assistant," design special cartouche and banner standards.

These tall standards served as bright spots of color, contrasting with the pale travertine façades. The cartouche standards were sculpted plaster fixtures molded around three canvas-covered openings. Banner standards were three-sided "boxes" of heavy canvas, decorated with the heraldic shields of early Pacific explorers and weighted to prevent them from whipping about in the wind. The fronts of the banners were thematically matched to the architectural style of each court or garden, while the open backs were covered in a reflective white material. Each masked a group of between two and nine arc lights and stood on twenty-five- to fifty-five-foot shafts. Both types of standards allowed light to filter through the translucent canvas for a stained glass effect, but most of the radiance was thrown upon adjacent façades. Lampposts with glass globes and electroliers with between one and twenty-one glass shades were supported on ornamental posts along walkways or on the shoulders of sculpted figures to supplement the banner standards.

The indirect treatment allowed a nuance and theatricality never before seen. As fairgoers walked through the courts at night, they seemed to be strolling through a vast stage set. The palaces were "dressed in their evening clothes," and the Palace of Fine Arts was steeped in "triple moonlight" reflected in the lagoon.[27]

A LEGACY IN LIGHTS

World's fairs have given civilization many notable monuments and popularized countless new products. The Eiffel Tower, the Brussels Atomium, New York's *Trylon* and *Perisphere*, and Seattle's Space Needle all were constructed for world's fairs. The Ferris Wheel made its debut at Chicago's Columbian Exposition in 1893, the ice cream cone gained fame at the 1904 Louisiana Purchase Exposition in St. Louis, and Walt Disney presented the "It's a Small World" ride in 1964 at

New York's fair. The PPIE's legacy is less concrete but perhaps more important: it changed the standards of architectural illumination indelibly.

The lighting program of the PPIE was an immense undertaking. The energy load for illumination was about 5,000 kilowatts, enough to light a contemporary city of about 200,000 people for one night. It consumed $830 in electrical power nightly, the equivalent of about $19,600 in 2012. Ryan was willing to use not only the most cutting-edge technologies but also what was most appropriate for each situation, including both gas and electric—each in several forms.

The night of the final test of the PPIE's illuminations, when viewers were "swept off their feet by the beauty and artistry of the lighting itself," not only proved the lighting scheme would work but it marked a decisive moment of change in illuminating engineering, the moment when man was finally able to "paint with light."[28]

Ryan's efforts were rewarded by the Exposition's International Jury of Awards, which for the first time classed illumination as a "decorative art" and presented Ryan with a Grand Award for Illumination and several other medals for individual effects. What before had been mainly theory became a realized art.

The spectacular lighting at the PPIE marked a new epoch in the science and art of illumination, allowing the designer to "paint with light" for the first time. (Laura Ackley)

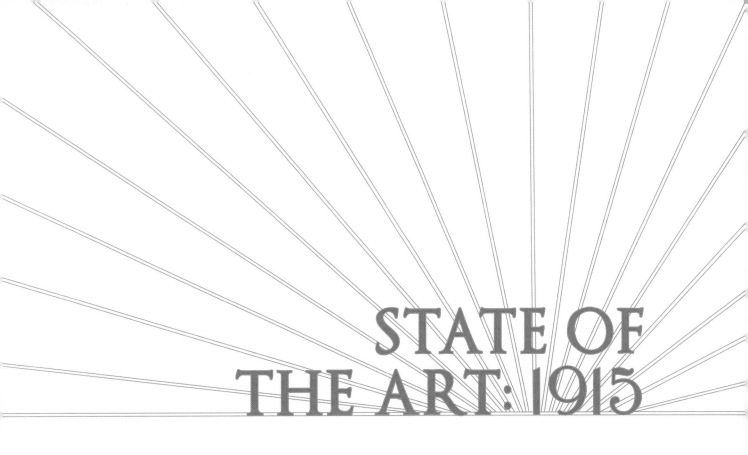

STATE OF THE ART: 1915

NEW TECHNOLOGIES AT THE PPIE

It was still dark when the trolley bells pealed and the sirens shrilled at 6:00 a.m. on February 20, but thousands of San Franciscans already had awakened in anticipation of Opening Day. Rain fell intermittently, but the crowd was eager to see what awaited them on the far side of the twenty-foot-tall ice-plant hedge that had magically sprung up along Chestnut Street. For two and one-half miles down Van Ness Avenue a solid throng waited in the winter drizzle, speculating on the new technologies to be viewed after two years of construction.

While many already had toured the site on plank walkways before the Fair opened, the contents of the grand exhibit palaces remained mysterious, reportedly containing the latest advances and portents of the future. *World's Work* magazine declared that at San Francisco, the young twentieth century had "paused to take stock of itself" with "an inventory of progress."[1]

Some had heard whispers about a turbine that could "swallow two rivers whole." Boys clamored to ride in an imitation submarine, and one daring young lady begged her mother to let her go aloft in a tiny seaplane. Society women, accustomed to riding in limousines, looked forward to driving little wicker electric carts along the paths of the great Fair. Farmers and industrialists hoped to see the newfangled machines that might bring them increased profits. Many who skipped breakfast merely craved a bite of the largest cheese in the world.

Even the most ardent fairgoers could not hope to absorb the complexities of the more

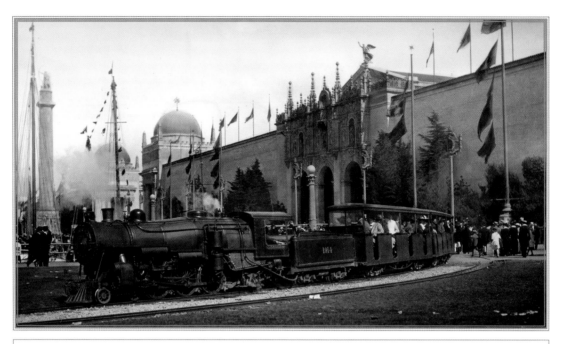

The miniature steam Overfair Railway carried guests along the bay side of the Fair. (Branson DeCou Digital Archive, University of California, Santa Cruz, Special Collections)

than 80,000 exhibits, even if they purchased season ticket books and attended every one of the Exposition's 288 days.

Some displays reflected the tastes and interests of a bygone era, others hinted at what was to come, and a few turned out to be missteps along the path of progress. The most successful and memorable exhibits created something, imparted facts about new processes, or gave a virtual experience of a far-off place or event. Fair officials weren't dispensing blue ribbons for grandma's blackberry jam; here awards were reserved for things developed since the previous American world's fair, the 1904 Louisiana Purchase Exposition at St. Louis.

On that winter morning in San Francisco, signs of this progress were evident in the gala opening ceremonies. As the sun finally broke through and more than 250,000 attendees jostled for the best view, aviator Lincoln Beachey circled the glittering Tower of Jewels in a biplane. Precisely at noon a wireless signal from President Woodrow Wilson in Washington, DC, activated the huge Busch-Sulzer diesel engine in the Palace of Machinery, and all across the Fair the

machines it powered thrummed to life. These advances—aviation, wireless communication, and diesel power—had all occurred since 1904.

FAIR SKIES

Stunt flyer Beachey's loops and dives on Opening Day manifested one of the foremost modern technologies at the Fair, the "aeroplane." The Wright Brothers' first successful flight at Kitty Hawk was in 1903, so aviation was simply not part of any previous world's fair. The PPIE was the first international exposition with airplanes as a major component. Even after Beachey's death in a March crash at the Exposition, organizers concluded that aviation was critical to drawing crowds. Aerobatics continued for the run of the Fair with pilots Art Smith, Charles Niles, and Silvio Pettirossi.

Adventurous citizens could take airplane rides themselves at the Exposition, as brothers Malcolm and Allan Loughead ran a charter hydro-aeroplane service, offering ten-minute flights for $10. After signing a waiver that assumed "all risk of every nature," customers

Fairgoers could pay the Loughead brothers $10 for a ten-minute ride in their Model G hydroplane—the first flight most had ever experienced. (Laura Ackley)

boarded a Model G hydroplane at the Yacht Harbor. Each flight passed over the Presidio to Fort Point, up the Marin Headlands, and back over Sausalito and Alcatraz before landing in the water and taxiing up a wooden ramp. This was the first airplane ride for nearly every customer, made all the more hair-raising because the blue of the bay could be seen through the floorboards of the homemade craft.

The PPIE marked a turning point for the Loughead brothers. The plane had been built in 1913 with financial help from Max Mamlock of the Alco Cab Company, but its early charter flights failed to make money. Mamlock had seized the plane, and the brothers had to borrow money from investor Paul Meyer to redeem it. The PPIE charters, which began in September, took in $4,705, in just a few weeks of service. After paying Exposition concession fees of $705, the brothers made a $4,000 profit, money they used to found what would become—after a spelling change—the Lockheed Aircraft Corporation.

ON THE GROUNDS

Patrons searching for technological breakthroughs had only to look as far as the grounds to discover up-to-date modes of transit. Although the PPIE was more compact than its predecessor, it still encompassed 635 acres and was more than two and a half miles long. Footsore visitors were offered several choices in Fair transportation, including pedal rickshaws, push-chairs, or one of three powered options.

The miniature steam Overfair Railway moved passengers along the breezy Marina Esplanade on the bay side of the Exposition, making six stops between the eastern end of the Exposition and the line's terminus at the racetrack in the Presidio. The one-third-scale, nineteen-inch-gauge trains were created by Oakland entrepreneur Louis MacDermot. But a ride on an ordinary railroad, however petite, did not capture public interest, and the Overfair Railway only brought in about $22,000, a pittance compared to the approximately $150,000 invested in the line's creation. Today, some of the engines from the Overfair Railway are still running as the Swanton Pacific Line in the Santa Cruz Mountains.

A much more successful and ingenious "train" was the Fadgl Auto Train, named for its creator, whose last name actually was spelled Fageol. It took in over $377,000 in nickel and dime fares, most of that pure profit as its cost of operation was only one cent per mile. These "trains" were actually little white tractors that pulled three or four trailers. Passengers sat facing outward, with a central passage running the length of the car between the two rows of seats, which allowed the conductor to collect fares without treading on toes.

The Auto Trains had several advantages: they were unfettered by rails, tired people could

J. Paulding Edwards (closest to camera), demonstrates the two-seat model of his battery-powered "Electriquette" vehicles, available for rent at the PPIE. (Anne T. Kent California Room, Marin County Free Library)

board easily since the running boards were just a few inches from the ground, and cars could be either uncovered to provide unobstructed views or covered to provide shelter from sun and rain. More than four million visitors rode the Fadgl trains, which were shipped to Chicago and used in Lincoln Park after the Fair. The fleet presaged the "people movers" at modern amusement parks.

Automobiles—of a sort—also were available to fairgoers. Customers could rent a little electrically powered wicker basket chair called an Electriquette to drive around the grounds. They cost $1 an hour and early guidebooks have them priced at $5 per day, but as their popularity grew, that figure rose to $7.50 or more. The Fair's official historian, Frank Morton Todd, said of the Electriquettes, "There were two models, one that ran on three wheels and carried two people, and one on four wheels that was supposed to carry four people and sometimes was seen wandering about with seven." Local engineer J. Paulding Edwards took in more than $112,000 from his Miniature Motor Vehicle concession.[2]

THE PALACE OF HORTICULTURE

One of the most striking buildings at the PPIE was the extravagant Palace of Horticulture, the first structure at an international exposition devoted entirely to the science of plants. The edifice itself was state of the art, starting with the heating system. Even on the chilliest San Francisco days visitors could revel in the tropical warmth of the conservatory beneath its enormous opalescent glass-and-steel dome, heated by a new circulating hot water system. This warmth enabled the Republic of Cuba to show off living palms, mangos, breadfruit, and bananas as dulcet tones of ukuleles and the scent of Kona coffee wafted in from the nearby Hawaiian Pineapple Packers Association's booth.

The exhibits within also showed off modern technologies. Near the exotic specimen plants, delicately tinted peaches rolled gently along the Anderson-Barngrover "single line," one of several model canneries housed in the palace.

The Palace of Food Products was dubbed the "Palace of Nibbling Arts" because so many free samples were available. Sperry Flour presented the Booths of All Nations, where visitors could enjoy tastes of various international baked delicacies. (Edward A. Rogers)

The Heinz Pure Food Products Company assembled an impressive tower of stepped tiers, each representing one of the company's "57 Varieties," with a column of numbers that lit in ascending sequence. The Heinz exhibit, like many others, also incorporated a small movie theater. (Edward A. Rogers)

One particularly florid writer said, "The tin can is the emblem of civilization. Its absence defines the savage: its use sets apart from barbarians the modern, forehanded, sanitary man."[3]

The big news in canning included the new technique of crimping, rather than soldering, the tops on cans, which prevented corrosion. Prior to this innovation, it was common to find bits of solder inside a can, a contaminant that could cause dangerous chemical reactions. Also, cans now were sealed in a vacuum and evenly heated to sterilize their contents.

These model canneries were illustrative of major changes in food safety set in motion by the Pure Food and Drug Act of 1906, the first federal law to seek comprehensive regulation of food quality and labeling of patent medicines. A 1911 article in *World's Work* magazine described the impetus for the law:

Such a law was necessary to meet the changed conditions regarding foods....To preserve foods, all manner of ingredients were used, and to increase the profits every known device of adulteration and misrepresentation was adopted.... The strong arm of the National Government with the power it possessed under the interstate commerce clause of the Constitution was needed effectively to throttle the thoroughly organized and equipped manufacturers of impure drugs and adulterated and misbranded foods.[4]

Eight years after the law's 1907 enactment, the theme of "Pure Foods" rippled throughout the Palace of Food Products.

THE PALACE OF FOOD PRODUCTS

Described as the "temple of the tin can and the food package," the Palace of Food Products truly could have been nicknamed the "Castle of Cuisine," the "Stronghold of Sustenance," or, as a local humorist dubbed it, the "Palace of Nibbling Arts." Patrons crowded the booths where they could fill up on a variety of free samples, many produced on-site. One young lady wrote to her grandmother, "There are all sorts of demonstrations of jello, shredded wheat, canned fish, crackers, and so on, so that if you had patience enough to wait for the talk and then nibble a thimbleful of food, you really could get quite a meal in time."[5, 6]

Those in search of edible innovations were assailed by an international array of ambrosial aromas. A *San Francisco Chronicle* reporter claimed that by "picking and choosing, a sort of gastronomic Esperanto" might be achieved. One could make a meal of Alaskan salmon or Italian tagliarini, followed by a dessert of Lowney's chocolates or a Scottish scone, washed down with Japanese tea, Portuguese Madeira, Guatemalan coffee, or California wine, and finished with a postprandial Cuban cigar rolled on the spot.[7]

In competition with the munching were serious demonstrations of the latest techniques in food production. For the first time, the previously secretive American Chicle Company allowed the public to view the mysteries of its chewing gum manufacturing operations. Another display featured an imposing conical tower of circular shelves packed with jars with lighted numbers that traveled upward in sequence, each highlighting one of the "57 Varieties" of the Heinz Pure Food Products Company. Alongside, a small auditorium screened moving pictures of Heinz items making their way from field to table.

Also ensconced within the lofty palace was a monumental four-story, colonnaded neoclassical structure disguising a $100,000 flour mill built by California's Sperry Flour Company. Viewers could watch raw grain, untouched by human hands, being processed into fifty large bags of flour a day. An on-site quality control laboratory calculated exact percentages of fiber, protein, and carbohydrates.

However, it was Sperry's Booths of All Nations that most tempted the hungry crowds. The milled flour was delivered directly to tiny kitchens between the structure's columns, each booth staffed by a costumed baker who transformed the flour into baked goods from his or her native region, including Chinese almond cakes, Russian piroshkis, Polish matzos, and Alaskan sourdough. The *Pacific Rural Press* enthused over a forty-niner cooking flapjacks over a campfire, a Southern cook baking johnnycakes and corn pone, a señorita assembling tamales, and "other chefs making their national wafers and cakes and giving samples!"[8]

Four large Kewpie dolls poured cream into bowls of porridge made by Albers Brothers Milling, signaling another recent development in food production. In the early twentieth

New York State sent the largest cheese ever made, which weighed in at 11,000 pounds. (Laura Ackley)

The Keen Kutter exhibit by the Simmons Hardware Company featured animated scenes executed entirely in pieces of hardware, including moving fountains that used chains to mimic flowing water. (*The Blue Book* (viewbook))

century, the typical American breakfast was evolving away from heavy foods like pancakes, biscuits, sausage, and bacon toward lighter fare. A breakfast of fruit, eggs, and cereal was now popular, and cereal was front and center at the PPIE. Oatmeal and shredded wheat were proffered, and the Quaker Oats Company shot puffed rice out of "cannons," then distributed morsels to peckish guests.

Many exhibits were concerned with the sanitary preparation of milk products and safe ways to transport them without spoilage. An array of "sterile" milk products was presented, including malted, evaporated, and condensed varieties from companies including Libby, Pacific Coast, and Borden, with its venerable Eagle Brand. The Pacific Coast Condensed Milk Company kept a herd of 125 "contented" Holstein cows in the Fair's livestock area. Milk from these cows was sent to a condensery near the Palace of Fine Arts, where Carnation produced 6,000 cans of evaporated milk daily.

THE PALACE OF AGRICULTURE

A cow mannequin drew a surprising amount of interest in the Palace of Agriculture, where more processes for "pure" milk products were displayed. The manufacturer of the Calf-Way Milker wisely considered bovine behavior and instead of live specimens used plaster cows in the display of its motorized milker.

Another lactose-intensive exhibit was the largest cheese ever created—New York State's "Giant Cheese." At four feet, seven inches high and seventy-eight and a half inches in diameter, it weighed 11,000 pounds and succumbed to its own popularity. As Todd colorfully related:

This hill of nutriment...contained the casein from 150,000 pounds of milk, the yield of 10,000 cows....Speeches were made from the top of it. It was a rendezvous, of popularity. When the crowd couldn't stand it any more but stood hungrily glaring at it and wondering why it was made, and with watering mouths looked ready to mob it, the people in charge of the booth started to cut it up with piano wire and sell it to the cheese-hungry at 25 cents a pound, and in a few brief days it was not.[9]

The Palace of Agriculture was "arranged to show the most up-to-date methods in all things incidental to modern intensive agriculture…not only in the United States of America, but in all the leading agricultural countries of the world," said one Fair guidebook. The seven-and-one-half-acre building was not large enough to host all the desired examples, so many were dispersed into the state and national pavilions.[10]

Objects within the palace ranged from the whimsical to the ominous, and most of the machines on display were in motion. A cream separator skimmed away while a twine mill spun, twisted, and balled twine, then tied it into small bands distributed as souvenirs. Beyond a low balustrade, ninety-three different electrically actuated farming machines rotated, sliced, or swung with unusual quiet—part of the 26,700-square-foot area occupied by the International Harvester Corporation. Engines that usually ran on oil instead used compressed air to reduce noise and fumes, and the manure spreader, out of olfactory consideration, laid bits of leather onto a conveyor that returned them to the machine.

The centerpiece of the exhibit was an animated diorama of the four seasons on a model farm. In its "winter" panel, a small gasoline engine attached to a line shaft provided power for the farm's lights, milk house, and machinery. At that time, most farms using electrical equipment would have had to supply their own power using such an arrangement, because as of 1910, only 2 percent of United States farms were electrified. It was not until 1935 that the Rural Electrification

Administration was charged with making funds available to finance electrification in remote locations. As late as 1942, less than 40 percent of America's farms were electrified.

In addition to such luminous harbingers of the future, a grim portent of the Great War was on display in this most rural of palaces. The Holt Manufacturing Company of California displayed a train of Holt Caterpillar trucks drawn by a Caterpillar tractor featuring the first commercially successful continuous track, the forerunner of modern tank treads. In 1915 six European armies were using these vehicles for military transportation, and by the following year Holt machines were being sold to the Allied Forces and refitted as true armored tanks.

THE PALACES OF MANUFACTURES AND OF VARIED INDUSTRIES

At first, it might have been difficult to ascertain what was innovative within the Palaces of Manufactures and of Varied Industries. With their long aisles of luxurious tapestries, elegant sculptures, and delicate porcelains, they may have seemed more in keeping with the great exhibitions of the nineteenth century, which often presented the finest examples of goods rather than the most groundbreaking. But even in these buildings, the goal was to exhibit "only such products of the inventive trades as mark a decisive and original step forward."[11]

Thus, a technology-seeker rounding the corner from a booth featuring ornately carved furniture might be surprised to find himself in front of a full-sized house, its red-tiled roof terminating just below the industrial beams of the palace. Inside the tidy Mission-style bungalow, General Electric presented the latest in home conveniences operated by electricity. Even though only approximately 10 percent of American homes were electrified, GE promoted its wares with a view to the future. The company took care to state that the purpose of this Home Electrical was not to amaze or astonish but to present practical applications to "reduce the drudgery of

Levi Strauss & Co. brought an entire scaled-down factory to the Palace of Manufactures, where children's "Koveralls" were cut, sewed, and finished. (Levi Strauss & Co.)

housework" for anyone of "moderate means."[12]

Appliances in the Home Electrical included an electric fireplace, an intercom, a player piano, fans, a toaster, a coffee maker, a sewing machine, a clothes washer, and ironing machines. The electric stove was a breakthrough to those accustomed to cooking on a "dirty, insufferably hot heat-wasting coal range." Many of the electric appliances are still common, but their 1915 versions were immense compared to current compact models. The refrigerator was predictably located in the kitchen, but its attendant plumbing and "motor-driven ammonia compression tanks" were in an adjoining room, and the "stationary vacuum unit" took up most of one wall in the utility shed.[13]

Some appliances in the Home Electrical would be comfortably familiar. According to the *General Electric Review*, "In the bathroom was a drying apparatus that made the exertion of toweling your hair unnecessary; a blast of hot air did the work, and perhaps saved you a cold in the head." One

amenity showcased in the garage of the Home Electrical would still be considered forward-thinking: the electric car charging station.[14]

In addition to the visionary, there was also the downright odd. On the walls of one bizarre booth, the blades of an eleven-foot-long pocketknife, animated by unseen forces, snapped open and shut while fountains made of moving chain flowed, a windmill of butcher's cleavers revolved, and on each quarter hour, robotic blacksmiths played a tune on anvils using sledgehammers. This forty-eight-foot-long, thirty-two-foot-high display of the Simmons Hardware Company, makers of the Keen Kutter brand of tools and cutlery, was decorated entirely in more than 10,000 pieces of whirling hardware. *The Story of the Exposition* reported, "The hair of the angels was made of brass chain, their armlets were of brass butts and furniture nails, the draperies were limned in flowing lines of jack-chain, the trumpets were made of bit extensions and spoke pointers, and the wings were feathered with case knives, butcher knives, and soup spoons."[15]

A number of small-scale factories created wares on site. A visitor to the Palace of Varied Industries wrote, "We saw silk being spun by silk worms and silk being woven into handkerchiefs; and in a Switzerland exhibit, how Swiss embroidery is done by machinery. We saw Alaskan garnets extracted from rock and polished, and heard a beautifully toned organ with chimes....One very instructive exhibit is that of the Crane Co. stationers, where you can see the whole process of making note paper, from rags before they are ground up to putting your monogram on."[16]

In the Palace of Manufactures, electric knives buzzed, each cutting a stack of ninety-six thicknesses of cloth at once. These were part of the Levi Strauss & Co. demonstration of large-scale production of children's "Koveralls." Once the fabric patterns were cut, about thirty young men and women assembled the garments using electric sewing machines and buttonhole-makers, then sorted the Koveralls by size to be sent to stores.

THE PALACE OF EDUCATION AND SOCIAL ECONOMY

On the bright, breezy afternoon of August 30, forty-three students received special diplomas in the Court of Abundance, also known as the Court of Ages. While a graduation ceremony might not seem exceptional, in this case it represented the progressive educational theories introduced in the Palace of Education and Social Economy, where, for the first time, prototype schools were conducted at a world's fair. At the Standard Commercial School, high school–aged pupils, selected by competitive exam, gave up vacations and holidays to participate in rigorous business training. Beginning in February, these students studied stenography, the Palmer method of penmanship, Gregg shorthand, typing, bookkeeping, business English, commercial arithmetic, office practice, public speaking, and commercial law in a 3,000-square-foot glass-enclosed space featuring a balcony for observers. Its commencement at the PPIE was a world's fair milestone.

Elsewhere in the palace, spectators peered through the glass walls of the Casa dei Bambini, "like tourists at an aquarium, watching to see whether any visible effects would break out." This demonstration school, for children aged three to six, featured the new Montessori Method. According to an article in the *San Francisco Chronicle*, the system molded students "not by the hammering out of a product on the anvil of a teacher's command, but rather by permitting to develop themselves through 'indirection,'" in which they selected their own tasks and worked at them for as long as they liked.[17]

Today there are more than 3,000 private Montessori schools in the United States, as well as several hundred public schools with Montessori programs. Worldwide, there are over 8,000 Montessori schools.

Other exhibits in the Palace of Education and Social Economy covered public health, hygiene, economics, child welfare, medicine, and a number of state and international educational systems. Each display was required to be of a new sort and to impart a lesson in education, rather than just displaying the work of outstanding students.

THE PALACE OF LIBERAL ARTS

Movements of colorfully draped dancers and the sounds of music lured patrons into the Palace of Liberal Arts, which contained some of the most fascinating inventions of the era. Parisian dancer Louise La Gai was retained by the Victor Talking Machine Company to dance with her *corps de ballet* to the accompaniment of the "latest and most elaborate Victor Machines." Once inside the palace, visitors could relax in a small, opulently decorated temple-like pavilion while listening to music from Victrolas.[18]

The phonograph had matured greatly in the years preceding the PPIE. *World's Work* magazine claimed it had "grown from a raspy, tin-panny, wire-edged, mechanical sound-reproducer into a responsive instrument for the most accurate and beautiful interpretation of the most difficult music." The Edison, Columbia, Sonora, Wurlitzer, and Victor companies all exhibited their versions.[19]

Decades before the malt shop and the sock hop, the first multiple-record jukeboxes in the world captivated audiences in this palace. "Gabel's Automatic Entertainers," unveiled in 1915, were the latest models of a device for which the patent was first filed in 1906 by John Gabel. The machines held twenty-four phonograph records from which the user could select, and each time a new record played, the steel playing needle was exchanged for a fresh one. The Automatic Entertainers won the gold medal over all other "talking machine" exhibits at the Fair.

The Palace of Liberal Arts also housed displays relating to printing, photography, coins and medals, medical implements, musical instruments, moving picture and theatrical equipment, "electric methods of communication," public works, architecture, and engineering. Precision instruments included a ten-ton telescope with a twenty-inch refracting lens later moved across the bay to the Chabot Observatory in Oakland.

Under an elaborate arched tympanum, a curtained portal beckoned passersby to discover the mysteries of the Eastman Kodak pavilion. Inside the darkened gallery, beautifully

illuminated transparent color photographs glowed with gem-like hues. These comprised the first exhibit of samples of actual color photography, according to the *Photographic Times*. While this early version of Kodachrome technology was never marketed, it won a gold medal at the Fair.

"Hoy! Hoy! Mr. Watson! Are you there? Do you hear me?" called Alexander Graham Bell to his former assistant, Thomas Watson. As he had thirty-eight years earlier when they'd tested the first telephone, Watson answered in the affirmative. But in 1915 Watson was conversing with his old boss across 3,400 miles, not merely two. On January 25, 1915, Bell was in New York and Watson in San Francisco, and they were participating in the first official transcontinental telephone call.[20]

Prior to 1915, it was simply impossible to make a telephone call to the East Coast from San Francisco. But after Bell and Watson's successful test, which took place between telephone company offices on each coast, transcontinental telephony became one of the most popular exhibits at the entire Fair. The Bell System had first exhibited an early telephone at the Centennial Exposition at Philadelphia in 1876,

Patrons in the Transcontinental Telephone Call Theater listen intently to headlines and music over a live connection from New York. Prior to 1915, cross-country calls were not possible. (Seligman Family Foundation)

and less than forty years later, telephony was a cross-country affair.

In the Palace of Liberal Arts the American Telephone and Telegraph Company erected the Transcontinental Telephone Call Theater, and it was a sensation. *World's Work* magazine described the attraction:

> Here you enter a little theatre and sit for half an hour. For the first ten minutes of that period you hear a lecture on the development of the telephone. For the next fifteen minutes you watch motion pictures of the building of the transcontinental telephone line. Then you take a pair of receivers from the back of the seat in front of you and put them to your ears, the lecturer presses a button, and New York is switched on the wire. A boy in the New York office of the telephone company reads the headlines from the afternoon papers, describes the weather conditions at the moment, and then switches on a phonograph and you hear 'canned music' by telephone over a wire 3,400 miles long. It is a thrilling sensation, especially to anyone who has just traveled from the Atlantic Coast, to be carried back in an instant to a place from which he has traveled five days and nights by train to San Francisco.[21]

By September 1915 wireless technology extended telephony so that calls from the East Coast to Hawaii were possible.

When then Secretary of State William Jennings Bryan called via the Transcontinental Telephone Line to congratulate the PPIE's Press Club on its April 3 inauguration, his voice was recorded using the Poulsen Telegraphone, another futuristic invention that appeared in the Palace of Liberal Arts. The Telegraphone was an extremely early incarnation of magnetic media (the technology used in tape recorders and computer disks) and could be used to archive telephone calls, serve as a dictating machine, or record music. Journalist Hamilton Wright described the apparatus: "As one talks into the receiver a thin steel wire is magnetized at the actual point of contact with the needle. The wire…runs between two small revolving drums, which will take down 75 minutes of continuous conversation." Danish inventor Valdemar Poulsen had won a gold medal with an early Telegraphone at the Paris Exposition in 1900, and an updated model was shown at the PPIE.[22]

Legend implicates a German-built Telegraphone in a precipitating moment in the United States' eventual involvement in World War I, the sinking of the *Lusitania*. An amateur radio operator named Charles Apgar was experimenting at his wireless station in Westfield, New Jersey, when he was asked by the Secret Service to record unusual transmissions from the wireless station of German company Telefunken in Sayville, New York—transmissions that were likely sent by a Telegraphone. When these signals were decrypted, they were found to be military instructions, including the alleged order to a German U-boat to sink the *Lusitania*. The supposed order, never confirmed or denied, was "Get Lucy." The US government seized the Telefunken station on July 6, 1915, on the strength of Apgar's evidence.

While viewing the Telegraphone exhibit in the Palace of Liberal Arts, audiences might have been distracted by a ponderous *thud-thud-thud* from just down the aisle. This noise was caused by the huge type bars of a twenty-one-foot-wide, fourteen-ton Underwood Typewriter striking a nine-foot-wide sheet of paper. The giant typewriter's ink ribbon was six inches wide and printed letters three inches tall. Its slow-motion typing enthralled onlookers, even though it was actually driven by a normal-sized Underwood connected to the behemoth via three one-horsepower motors.

The giant Underwood Typewriter stood fifteen feet tall and twenty-one feet wide and printed news bulletins in letters three inches tall. (Donna Ewald Huggins)

The mammoth typewriter delineated daily news reports, including a bulletin that read, *Liverpool, May 7—The Cunard Liner Lusitania with a heavy passenger list of Americans, was torpedoed and sunk off the Irish coast this afternoon.*

THE PALACE OF TRANSPORTATION

A merrymaker trying to escape the worst crowds on Opening Day might have discovered another portent of the future on the quieter side of the great World's Fair. Just four minutes after the official opening, a Model T rolled out of the Palace of Transportation—the first car to be built on the Exposition's Ford assembly line. That little Model T represented the worldwide sea change occurring in personal transportation. This transition from literal horse power to mechanical horsepower was also illustrated May 21, when several horses were driven through the grounds on a truck emblazoned with the sign "Our First Joy Ride!" The *Story of the Exposition* said, "An exhibit of horse-drawn vehicles at San Francisco would have looked like a hangover from the days of Rip Van Winkle. Instead we had the automobile in its glory and almost in its ultimate designs...."[23]

The Palace of Transportation *did* have a display of mules, however—Electric Mules. General Electric offered a half-inch-to-one-foot scale model of the Panama Electric Towing Locomotive, forty of which pulled vessels through the locks of the Fair's namesake, the Panama Canal. The model Electric Mule was sixteen inches long, while the full-sized engines were thirty-two feet long and weighed 86,000 pounds.

An array of automobile marques, some familiar today and others now extinct, were also on display in the Palace of Transportation, including Jeffery, Pathfinder, Maxwell, Haynes, King, Oakland Motorcar, Kissel Kar, Paige-Detroit

Eighteen Model T Fords, representing a single day's production of the operational onsite factory, sat proudly in front of the Palace of Transportation, where each was assembled from bare chassis to completion in about ten minutes. (*Ford Times,* July 1915)

Motorcar, Saxon, Willys-Overland, Western Motor Car, Chalmers, Beardsley Electric, Isotta Fraschini, White, Pierce-Arrow, Studebaker, Packard, Olds Motor Works, Cadillac, Buick, the Dodge Brothers, and Rolls Royce.

But the star attraction of the palace was the operational Ford factory. The assembly line concept was developing rapidly along with the automobile, and spectators were spellbound. Twenty-eight mechanics worked the fifty-foot line from 2:00 until 5:00 p.m., completing about eighteen cars daily, or one about every ten minutes. The Model Ts moved down the line at about fifteen inches a minute. Each car started as an empty chassis, pulled along by a chain. Everything was attached on the line, including axles, wheels, engine, transmission, interior, windshield, and soft top, then gas was added, and "promptly on the 10-minute limit the little Ford left the platform and rolled easily out

through the door to one of the courts where it stood in line ready to be driven to the company's offices a mile or so away." From there, the cars were shipped all over the country.[24]

Henry Ford himself took Thomas Edison on a tour of the assembly line, where he pointed out that due to improvements in the process, cars were made more quickly at the Exposition than at his Detroit factory. Edison quipped, "I dare say they will begin to spawn before long."[25]

Also in this palace a 156-ton Westinghouse electric locomotive rotated majestically on a turntable twelve feet above the floor under the central dome. Its driving wheels were six feet in diameter, it could produce 4,000 horsepower, and its normal speed with a full train behind it was sixty miles an hour.

THE PALACE OF MINES AND METALLURGY

Tourists in search of cutting-edge exhibits in the Palace of Mines and Metallurgy would have been well advised to wear lead vests. The palace illustrated progress in "utilization of the products taken from beneath the surface of the earth," and one popular display was even located beneath the palace. The Demonstration Mine attracted more than four million visitors during the Exposition season, all of whom may have been unintentionally exposed to a health hazard.

To access the mine, passengers stepped into an elevator cage and were told they would descend a few hundred feet. The cage would shake, air would rush upward, and the rock walls would pass by—an illusion created by reeling a painted panoramic canvas vertically outside the cage. In actuality passengers exited at the same level they entered. They were handed miners' lamps before descending a short staircase to a timbered "mine" with ore-encrusted walls six feet below the level of the bay and kept dry by sump pumps.

First, guests visited stopes, drifts, and shafts replicating various anthracite, coal, iron, and gold mines around the world with state-of-the-art features, including drills, hoists, pumps, and mechanisms to bring fresh air and sanitary water to miners.

After visiting an underground movie theater, patrons came up through a darkened room to view "real specimens of radium, through a microscope, and see the palpitating rays of this most marvelous of recent physical discoveries, the infinitely energetic element that perpetually emanates power without loss of its capacity to throw out more." The magazine *The World's Advance* described the crystals as "outlined by a white scintillating light which in appearance resembles an electric brush discharge, while the circumambient region glows with a phosphorescent and aurora borealis effect."[26, 27]

In 1915 radium was thought to be a "wonder material" with tremendous potential curative powers. We now know this element to be incredibly dangerous. During the 1930s it was found that workers exposed to radium through handling luminous paints experienced serious side effects, including sores, anemia, and bone cancer. Use of radium was stopped soon afterward.

Twice daily, at 11:00 a.m. and 2:00 p.m., visitors on the floor of the Palace of Mines and Metallurgy were startled by the sharp boom of an explosion. As smoke billowed from the mouth of the Model Mine and into the dome above, a rescue truck rushed around the corner of the Marina Esplanade to the north entrance. After donning safety gear and self-contained breathing masks, a ten-man crew "rescued" an "asphyxiated" miner, resuscitating him using "artificial respiration methods and a lung motor," and treating his simulated wounds in the nearby prototype mine hospital.[28]

While most of the exhibits in the palace dealt with mining technologies, its immense square footage also housed some other large exhibits, including those of the US Mint, the US Steel Corporation, and the Model US Post Office.

Even the simple act of mailing a letter at the PPIE was an adventure. Visitors standing on an elevated gallery above the 11,000-square-foot post office could drop a piece of mail into a chute and observe its travels all the way to the outbound mail pouch or the general delivery window. A card mailed at this station was ready at the general delivery window within three minutes, so that appointments to meet friends could be made with facility. One could mail himself a picnic lunch by parcel post in the evening and receive it at the Exposition by noon the next day.

Tired sightseers also could send home empty lunch baskets, baby carriages, and unneeded overcoats from the Fair. There were at least seventy-five mailboxes on the grounds, and during the ten months it was open, more than 86,000 packages and three million letters were mailed from the Exposition, each receiving a special cancellation.

THE PALACE OF MACHINERY

"Really mahvellous," murmured one East Coast woman as she stood in the Palace of

Machinery, mesmerized before the colossal Hoe Printing Press as it printed, folded, inserted, and counted four-color Sunday supplements for the *San Francisco Examiner*, cornerstone of William Randolph Hearst's publishing empire. The printing press had traveled from New York to San Francisco through the Panama Canal, no doubt towed by the General Electric Mules. Color inserts reeled hypnotically through the press at a rate of 15,000 copies an hour.[29]

Passing the portals of the vast palace, the visitor encountered the din of stamping, thumping, rumbling machines in action. In its three great naves and cross-aisles were nine acres of displays of interest to the "scientist, the practical engineer, the mechanic, the electrician, the manufacturer, the student, the farmer and last, but not least, the housewife." There were machines of precision and power for transportation, construction, agriculture, mining, and home use. Wherever possible, machines were shown in operation, and often in cross-section or cutaway views.[30]

A glass tank containing a model of a harbor studded with mines enabled schoolboys to indulge their bloodthirsty tendencies. As part of the US government's exhibits at the Fair, the School of Submarine Defense in Monroe, Virginia, offered an animated simulation of a fortified harbor intended to be "inhospitable to undesirable guests." It was yet another example of the specter of war that haunted the Exposition. Miniature ships plied waters thickly laid with tiny mines while the attraction's operator explained that mines could be rendered inert to friendly vessels and deadly to foes. When an enemy ship struck a mine, an electric light simulated an explosion, and the boat would turn over and sink, delighting children, who gleefully watched the mayhem again and again.[31]

Another of California's growing empires, the hydroelectric power industry, appeared as what looked like a twenty-six-foot-tall donut standing on edge. The "river-swallowing" turbine that had been whispered about on Opening Day was completed just in time to be installed in the Palace of Machinery. Eventually, it would be used in a huge Pacific Gas and Electric project on the Yuba River. The Pelton-Francis Turbine was the most powerful such waterwheel in existence in 1915, capable of generating 20,000 horsepower.

One electrical marvel was just east of the Palace of Machinery. At night, passersby saw a glowing corona above a small building and caught a whiff of ozone emanating from this High Tension Research Pavilion, built by C. H. Thordarson of Chicago. The structure contained a million-volt transformer used for scientific research, and just outside, visitors could interact with its mysterious powers. The public could walk under a charged wire screen connected to the transformer and suspended thirty feet above the ground (with a safety net beneath). According to Todd, "One was curiously affected. The ends of the fingers glowed. If a hat were held up, angry little sparks would jump from the hat band to the fingers. A metal ball tossed in the air became a shooting star. Ladies' hat pins were highly charged."[32]

THE ZONE

After viewing so many educational and improving exhibits in the great palaces, fairgoers were tempted into the Joy Zone by its carefree amusements. But even on the PPIE midway were technological marvels erected in the name of fun and games.

Forty-four years before Disneyland opened its Submarine Voyage in Tomorrowland, the Zone harbored its own virtual underwater ride. Passengers seated in the $250,000 ride, called simply "The Submarines," saw water rush past the portholes while the depth gauge indicated they were descending. For fifteen minutes the craft appeared to navigate past "hulks of wrecked ships, treasures scattered about on the floor of the 'ocean,' coral formations and Davy Jones' Locker." The illusion was created simply, through a sheet of water over each window.[33]

The Safety Racer on the Zone could trace its ancestry directly back to America's first roller coaster. Industry pioneer L. A. Thompson, who had built the first American coaster, the Gravity Switchback Railway, at Coney Island in 1884, offered the "fastest, safest and longest coaster ever built in the United States" at the PPIE. This was

The Jewel City's Joy Zone midway, seen here from the Aeroscope ride, was the site of many innovative attractions. (San Francisco History Center, San Francisco Public Library; and Laura Ackley)

essentially a pair of gravity-driven roller coasters that raced against each other for the duration of a ride. Since the winner was "determined by difference of momentum due to inequality in load, fat girls were of great assistance to victory," according to the Fair's official history. The Safety Racer was among the ten top-grossing attractions on the Zone, pulling in almost $134,000.[34, 35]

Several spectacles on the Zone were based around functioning scale models of places or historical events, including the Battle of Gettysburg and Captain Robert Scott's ill-fated South Pole expedition. Another such attraction recreated the Dayton Flood of 1913. Over the door a Herculean figure held great floodgates closed, and inside, a disaster in four acts unfolded over an elaborate mechanical model. The first scene depicted the peaceful city the night before the flood, the second used real water and fire to re-enact the calamity, the next act showed the stricken metropolis snow-shrouded and strewn with debris, and an epilogue illustrated the city's recovery.

Panama-Pacific attendees were not impressed. Todd says, "Perhaps after having lived through earthquake and fire, a flood seemed a comparatively comfortable experience to the inhabitants of San Francisco. At any rate, the Dayton Flood closed after a few months of slim patronage, and the benignant giant disappeared, having nothing more to do."[36]

For fifty cents, revelers could actually visit the

Panama Canal—in miniature. The most amazing panoramic model of the Fair was the Zone's five-acre, accurate model of the canal. The attraction, which could accommodate 1,200 visitors at time, consisted of 144 cars that circled a 1,440-foot track.

World's Advance magazine described it:

> Miniature ships travel through the locks, trains run along the tracks bordering the Canal, the illuminated buoys marking the channel flash in various colored lights, sparks leap about the miniature aerials of the radio-telegraph stations; and all this occurs without the aid of visible mechanism. The secret of this lies in the application of electromagnets, which are moved about on tracks placed beneath the model and directly underneath the route to be taken by the working model above. At the locks the steamers drop their hawsers, tow lines are magically attached to them and miniature electric locomotives tow them through the locks.[37]

137. THE PANAMA CANAL, WORLDS FAIR 1915 SAN FRANCISCO CAL.

Workmen are dwarfed by the huge five-acre model of the Panama Canal. Patrons could watch miniature ships traverse the locks while trains ran along tracks nearby, all powered by magnets moving beneath the replica. (Chuck Banneck)

Panoramic paintings replicating the area surrounding the canal covered the walls around the model, simulating a 5,000-square-mile portion of the Isthmus of Panama. The trip took about twenty-three minutes. The audio program was delivered by forty-five phonographs, and the records were played so many times that each one lasted only about six weeks. The Panama Canal Model was a tremendous success, taking in more than $338,000 (about $7.9 million in 2012). Unfortunately, the attraction had been so expensive to build that despite its spectacular drawing power, it lost at least $100,000.

After traipsing the length of the Zone, weary walkers could duck into the cool darkness of one of more than two dozen small movie theaters, which represented another shift typified at the PPIE—the new ubiquity of cinema. The *Independent* magazine said, "[T]his is the first great exposition since the popularization of moving pictures, and you often find a dozen little cinema theaters in a single building."[38]

It was estimated that more than one million feet of film were expended Exposition-wide

for what Ben Macomber called "the fastest and most vivid method of displaying human activities and scenery."[39]

Pre-Exposition events—including ground-breaking ceremonies, parades, flag-raisings, and construction—had been filmed and were shown in newsreels at theaters across the country to promote the Fair. Once the PPIE opened, states and nations showed films extolling their unique virtues, beauty, and prosperity in small theaters located in their pavilions. All through the main palaces, displays were augmented with movies, though in this pre-talkie era, most of the instructive films were accompanied by live narrators. Writer French Strother said, "Motion pictures—they have become the servant of industry no less than they are the handmaid of drama. There are nearly a hundred little picture shows in the various buildings at the Exposition…."[40]

As the main Exposition grounds had the Tower of Jewels, the Zone had its own soaring structure. Laura Ingalls Wilder wrote of the Zone's most visible attraction, "It looks like some giant with a square head, craning his long neck up and up." She was describing the Aeroscope, the PPIE's answer to the Eiffel Tower and the Ferris Wheel, wonders introduced at the 1889 and 1893 world's fairs. More than twenty years prior to his even greater triumph, engineer Joseph B. Strauss created this ingenious device, whose long steel arm rose and fell over the Exposition.[41]

This ride operated like a counterweighted bascule bridge, and at the end of its two-hundred-plus-foot arm was a passenger car that could carry 120 people, including two operators, on two levels. Its huge concrete counterweight weighed 380 tons, and the whole apparatus 700 tons. When loaded with passengers, weight differences between carloads were balanced by water ballast tanks on the underside of the car that equalized with a tank on the ground. The Aeroscope was so perfectly balanced that it took only two 11-horsepower motors to lift the arm into the air.

Each trip took about ten minutes, about three and a half of which were spent in the ascent. The entire machine was mounted on a turntable, enabling the car to describe a great helix as it soared. Riders were carried to a height of about 265 feet above the ground and were provided with field glasses through which they could see parts of seven counties.

The Aeroscope was not only a marvel of engineering but also a popular success. More than 65,000 people rode in the first four weeks of the Fair, and on May 27, one couple chose to marry on

The Aeroscope, designed by Joseph B. Strauss, lifted passengers 265 feet above the ground aboard a car attached to a steel arm, which was balanced by a 380-ton concrete counterweight. Mounted on a turntable, the device provided panoramic views. (*Scientific American*, April 10, 1915)

the ride. The novel concession earned $67,489—about $1.59 million in 2012—but it had cost almost as much to build, so its profit was minimal. It was, however, an unequivocal engineering triumph, and Joseph B. Strauss went on to become chief engineer of the Golden Gate Bridge.

A visitor soaring high over the Fair in the Aeroscope might have contemplated not only the gorgeous views of bay and city but also the marvelous new products and ideas displayed across the 635 acres of palaces and courts below. Perhaps he would be motivated to buy a Model T Ford for $490, a better typewriter or talking machine, a refrigerator for his newly electrified home, or a Calf-Way Milker for his farm. Maybe he would look to the future, when hydroelectric power would energize homes and factories, and the mysteries of radium would be unlocked. In hindsight some of the advances exhibited at the PPIE may seem innocent, amusing, or even frightening. But pondered from the vantage of the Aeroscope in 1915, they must have been inspiring.

Patrons rode around the oval Panama Canal Model on a moving platform while overlooking the scenery and listening to a phonographic description of the canal's workings played through a telephone receiver. (*Popular Mechanics*, September 1915)

THE UNIVERSITY OF THE WORLD AND SHOP-WINDOW OF CIVILIZATION

A booth draped in dinosaurs, a temple carved out of soap, and an on-premises factory populated with live silk worms producing shimmering fibers—all were intriguing features of the 1915 Fair. The exhibit palaces of the Panama-Pacific International Exposition presented serene façades to the strolling multitudes, but once fairgoers stepped inside the grand portals, a rich hodgepodge of displays vied for their notice. "It is a sharp shift from the exquisite unity of plan and color outside to the vast spaces within, where heterogeneous ideals clash with each other and metaphorically (or even actually) clamor for your attention with more or less dignity," said Jessica Peixotto, an assistant professor at UC Berkeley.[1]

The exhibits reflected the Fair's dual goals: to serve as a "University of the World" and "Shop-Window of Civilization." Asher Carter Baker, director of exhibits, summed up the twin purposes—intellectual and mercantile—of the displays. The first aim of the exhibits department, said Baker, was to bring the best the world had to offer to San Francisco for study as a "practical and popular university where [everyone] can obtain an idea of the world's progress to date and where every student can find the subject of his interest...." Additionally, the exhibits would allow nations to see where their areas of excellence and deficit were complemented by those of other countries, thus stimulating trade, advancing technology, and raising production standards. Baker said without the PPIE this knowledge would "take many years and untold capital to acquire."[2]

The exhibit areas were called "booths," but that was something of a misnomer. Some displays were tiny nooks, while those of some behemoth corporations covered tens of thousands of square feet. Many featured full-sized buildings by big-name architects,

Iowa's forty-foot-high mountain of corn poured from a cornucopia labeled "The Land of Plenty." (Seligman Family Foundation)

resting in perfect comfort under the lofty trusses of the palaces. Westinghouse's gargantuan 25,000-square-foot display beneath the dome of the Palace of Transportation was edged out in size by International Harvester's 26,700-square-foot array of whirring farm implements in the Palace of Agriculture. But both of these were dwarfed by the 44,000-square-foot US Steel Corporation exhibit in the Palace of Mines and Metallurgy.

"Including exhibits, no man will ever see all the fair," said John Heaton of the *New York World*. Analogously, no single volume could cover adequately all of the important advances shown among the 80,000 individual exhibits. To make room for just the highlights of the items presented still requires omission of the lion's share of exhibits, including improvements in engines, agriculture, medicine, batteries, and medical technology, among so many others.[3]

The total value of the millions of objects in the palaces and pavilions was at estimated at $450 million (about $21.2 billion in 2012). Showmen built wondrous displays and devised clever marketing ploys to lure fairgoers to their booths.

THE UNIVERSITY OF THE WORLD

"The Panama-Pacific International Exposition may be considered a world university for 1915," said James Barr, the PPIE's director of congresses. "The Director-in-Chief, the Chiefs of Departments, the officers of the many Congresses might be considered members of the faculty: the Exposition, in fact, all California, a working laboratory; the world at large the student body."[4]

The palaces, it was suggested, operated much as the colleges within a university. Students strode purposefully through the palaces as they used the Exposition as a monumental academy. Teachers in San Francisco developed a "Course of Study at the Panama-Pacific International Exposition" for elementary schoolchildren. Each plan consisted of eight visits, organized in a building-by-building format, tailored for either third through fifth grades or sixth through eighth. The text described a desired route along which the students would examine specific exhibits. In many spots, teachers were advised to phone ahead to receive a special demonstration or lecture by the exhibit manager.

Samples from the younger students' curriculum in the Palace of Mines and Metallurgy included:

> Across B St. to Fifth St. to The Mine. (a) Mine Rescue Work, 2 P.M. (b) May descend into the mine and its formation. (c) Machines, cars, lamps, explosives, etc. used in mine work.
>
> Proceed along Fourth St. to Ave. B to U.S. Post Office. (a) Observe from platform. (b) Have children bring postals and mail them. Thus they may see the manner of post-marking, assorting of mail, etc.
>
> Exit from Post office Ave. A and Fourth St....along Ave. B to First St. to U.S. Mint. (a) Making of coins from beginning.[5]

In other areas of the Fair, the Smithsonian Institution, with its charter to foster the "increase and diffusion of knowledge," provided a selection of paintings, photos, and artifacts representing its natural history and industrial collections. It mounted photos of astronomical phenomena and set up dioramas depicting the world's indigenous peoples. Other showcases focused on the history of fire-making, illumination, the jackknife, the saw, and weaving tools. The

Smithsonian also brought a model of the 1896 Langley experimental "aerodrome," an early unmanned flying machine.[6]

Along with encouraging scholars, the Department of Congresses promoted attendance as a route to professional advancement. A week at the Exposition "will give you a view of the World's Progress that could not be obtained in a Year of Travel," proclaimed a pamphlet asking organizations to hold their meetings at the Fair.[7]

Professionals could study at the PPIE to improve practices, and conferences capitalized on the educational opportunities of the Fair. Organizations holding meetings in conjunction with the Fair typically developed study guides to the exhibits, then distributed programs to attendees with a selection of recommended exhibits relating to their disciplines. Thus, a physician might attend the American Academy of Medicine Conference in June at the Exposition Auditorium, then investigate the latest medical and surgical equipment in the Palace of Liberal Arts.

The "grouping plan" scheduled conferences and conventions covering related topics in calendar

Parents could have their children examined at one of several booths. This youngster seems less than thrilled to be assessed by the Mouth-Hygiene Association of America. (Edward A. Rogers)

blocks, so that interested persons could pay for a single trip yet attend more than one meeting. Some of the grouped topics included agriculture, economics, social service, history, pharmacy, nursing, and livestock. Insurance and engineering organizations held massive gatherings.

Teachers' institutes met during the first week of April, and forty-one educational organizations held conferences in conjunction with the Fair during the second half of August. Teachers burnished their skills at these meetings and listened to inspiring addresses from the likes of Dr. Maria Montessori and Helen Keller.

And so they came to the great university: bankers and grocers, humorists and telegraphers, fraternal groups and expatriates, adherents of movements from Esperanto to Spiritualism, all descended on San Francisco in 1915. More than nine hundred congresses and conferences were held during the year, and were credited with boosting daily attendance from about 25,000 per day to more than 60,000 per day.

THE KEYNOTE IS SERVICE

Each modern world's fair offered a theme. The keynote of the 1893 Columbian Exposition had been religion, the 1904 Louisiana Purchase Exposition focused on "abstract learning," and the PPIE emphasized "Service: economic, educative, social." The Fair hosted many exhibits fostering "human uplift," and most of these displays were in the Palace of Education and Social Economy, including a diorama in which mannequins costumed as Japanese Red Cross doctors and nurses earnestly tended to waxwork patients using the latest battlefield first aid techniques. [8]

Worldwide public health efforts were underscored with charts and models chronicling the struggle to eradicate terrifying scourges including leprosy, tuberculosis, trachoma, typhoid, and hookworm. These diseases are still difficult to treat and were typically fatal in 1915. Folk remedies were ruthlessly debunked.

Some of the aisles of the Palace of Manufactures, such as this Italian sculpture section, looked like a grand bazaar tucked inside an industrial train station. (Seligman Family Foundation)

The Rodman Wanamaker exhibit in the Palace of Education displayed photographs and movies of Native Americans taken on several expeditions the department store magnate had sponsored. (Paul Robertson)

Improving the lives of children was a special concern. Alvin Pope, chief of the Department of Education and Social Economy, cited an alarming statistic: "The death rate for hogs in the United States during the first year is five per cent, for sheep three, for calves one. For babies it is 12." In June, Child Welfare Week featured a calendar of useful lectures, and during the entire run of the Fair, parents were invited to bring their children for examinations at several booths. Babies were weighed, measured, and "scored" against standard American Medical Association guidelines. If "defects" were discovered, tips on how to correct them were dispensed. The quality of this advice was sometimes questionable. Humorist Rube Goldberg mocked the service in a cartoon showing a professor intoning to spellbound mothers, "Scientific investigation shows us that the nourishment from one condensed shoe is equivalent to 55 veal cutlets."[9, 10]

At previous world's fairs, scholastic exhibits had relied heavily on specimens of outstanding student work, but PPIE exhibitors were directed instead to illustrate specific lessons in developing a child "into the highest type of citizenship." Argentina, Guatemala, Uruguay, and the Philippines all presented extensive depictions of their national school systems. Demonstration classrooms were also popular. The model Montessori school, the Standard Commercial School, the Palmer Penmanship classroom, and a school for the blind were all set up like fishbowls inhabited by learning humans. Alice Trask, wife of the director of the Department of Fine Arts, was deaf and gave lip reading classes on behalf of the New York School for the Hard of Hearing.[11]

Other booths decried exploitation of children in the workplace. Nearly two million Americans under age sixteen were held in the "thralldom of labor," according to the National Child Labor Committee, which sent an exhibit of more than 5,000 photographs, taken over the previous decade by Lewis W. Hine, which showed children as young as six "dragging their wan little bodies to work eleven or more hours a day...out in the bitter cold of the winter's morning, ill clad, hopeless...oftentimes crippled and maimed for life." The booth was intended to spark discussion of standardizing child labor laws at the federal level. An early version of such a law was passed in 1916 but was struck down by the courts. It was not until 1938 that a comprehensive act was passed, although child labor continues to be exploited widely in the United States agriculture industry today.[12]

Nor was spiritual life neglected. Local churches printed welcoming messages in the Fair's daily *Official Program*, and a variety of religious organizations exhibited in the palaces. Mormons and Methodists, Catholics and Christian Scientists, even the Vedanta Society, a faith founded in 1894 that reveres the great teachers from all religions, distributed literature at the Fair. The Federal Council of the Churches of Christ formed the Committee of One Hundred to coordinate Christian religious work in connection with the PPIE. But when baseball player-turned-evangelist Billy Sunday came to town the first week of August and preached a fiery oration, the vice president of the committee, prominent local clergyman Charles Aked, resigned in protest, saying, "[T]here is no such Christ, no such heaven, and no such hell as Dr. Billy Sunday pretends...."[13]

Various other organizations used the PPIE as a stage to fight for their causes as well. The

Congressional Union for Women's Suffrage pleaded for nationwide voting rights for women from their position in the Palace of Education. The Anti-Saloon League, the Prohibition National Committee, and the World's Woman's Christian Temperance Union all clamored for Prohibition, while the perils of the "dry movement" were preached by United California Industries, an association of liquor interests. They distributed an article entitled "Bleeding Kansas" that blamed Prohibition for the woes of that state, including increased pauperism, insanity, and—counterintuitively—divorce due to drunkenness.

In the realm of social rights for minority populations, a beautiful yet highly romanticized display of photographs and movies of Native Americans in the Palace of Education betokened the increasingly complex and ambivalent relationship between the federal government and the nation's native peoples. To collect the footage on more than eighty-nine reservations, Joseph K. Dixon had led three expeditions bankrolled by department store magnate Rodman Wanamaker. Dixon's involvement with native tribes was problematic, however. While on its face the goals of the final expedition, in 1913, were progressive, its real intent was more ambiguous. The trip sought to improve health care and education for Native Americans, to abolish the reservation system and paternal control of tribes by the US government, and to promote full citizenship for Indians. It also was an exercise in jingoism designed to indoctrinate "this great original race of people, to the principles of the Government of the United States," as Dixon wrote to Wanamaker.[14]

Dixon came to the PPIE to give a lecture titled "Indian Life and Customs" and participate in two conferences. The first meeting addressed such matters as poverty, illness, and widespread homelessness among California Indians. A second conclave, the Congress on Indian Progress, was mainly attended by Indian Service employees. Topics ranged from contagious disease at federal Indian schools, to the railroads' disruption of hunting and fishing, to liquor trafficking, prejudice in public schools, agricultural and

vocational education, and "Improvement of Primitive Homes." Ultimately the conferences, however well-intentioned, had little substantive impact. Native Americans were not granted full citizenship nationwide until 1924.

At least one con man leveraged the wave of arcane beliefs and philosophical systems that flourished in the late nineteenth and early twentieth centuries. Many of these, including metaphysics, Spiritualism, and Theosophy, were represented at the PPIE, as was the "Newthot" movement. Newthot's leader, John Fair New, styled himself "Dr. Newo Newi New" and put one over on the Exposition. In the *Official Program*, he grandiosely yet vaguely promised that a visit to his "Newthot Science Temple" in the Palace of Education would illuminate "every subject which rounds out a man's life upon earth and prepares him to enter the Kingdom of Heaven without going by way of the grave." Joseph Cumming, secretary of PPIE president Charles C. Moore, was frankly puzzled when he handed Dr. New his bronze medal on "Newthot Day," September 11. "I am not familiar with its philosophy," said Cumming, "but I assume it has something to do with thinking." "Amen, brother," intoned Dr. New, who was planning a World's Newthot Congress for December at the Fair. The Exposition was saved from further embarrassment when Dr. New was arrested in October and indicted on federal mail fraud charges. He was convicted and sentenced to two years in jail.[15, 16]

Japan displayed its wares in a dedicated national pavilion, on the Zone, and in every exhibit department save the Palace of Machinery. Shown here are some of the country's goods in the Palace of Manufactures. (Laura Ackley)

RACE BETTERMENT

One popular Education and Social Economy exhibit, repugnant from a modern perspective, was the Race Betterment booth, which featured the latest theories on eugenics. Although "race betterment" as shown at the PPIE aimed to improve the *human* race, not a particular ethnic ancestry (it might have been more accurately titled "human betterment"), it nonetheless demonstrated racial biases. Race betterment was seen as a means to ameliorate social woes such as poverty, crime, disease, and mental illness. The sign above the entrance to the booth pronounced the campaign a "popular non-sectarian movement to advance life-saving knowledge."[17]

Eugenics sought freedom from disease and longer, healthier, happier lives—all laudable goals. But as with most utopian ideas, the reality was far darker. Actual implementation of eugenics has been elitist at its best, racist most commonly, and abusive at its worst. At the time of the PPIE, eugenics was a relatively new discipline and could be seen as a natural analog to contemporary breakthroughs in plant science by Luther Burbank, who spoke at the Fair's Conference on Race Betterment. During a question-and-answer period, he claimed a "perfect specimen of manhood" could be achieved in just six generations of selective breeding.[18]

Nor were most proponents of eugenics part of a crackpot fringe element. They included top scientists, thinkers, and successful businesspeople, like Dr. John H. Kellogg of cornflakes fame. Stanford University's chancellor, David Starr Jordan, and Charles W. Eliot, president emeritus of Harvard, were two of eugenics' most visible supporters, and the list of Race Betterment conference officers was studded with judges, physicians, professors, and clergymen.

Modern scholars of ethnology at world's fairs have concentrated on the racist implications of the movement but neglected mention of its vocal opponents. The *San Francisco Chronicle* reported that at one of the Conference on Race Betterment sessions the speaker asserted, "Eugenics should hesitate to assume too much authority, since...we only have to go back 5,000 years to find that we all have the same ancestors." And an expert representing Prudential Insurance declared, "It is a wicked attitude of mind to carry the idea of eugenic marriages too far. When people of well-meaning sort think to regulate the flow of human multiplication, it is the height of infamy." He did concede, however, that eugenic law ought be applied to the insane or "morally delinquent."[19, 20]

It was generally acknowledged that eugenics was still in its infancy, and most eugenic recommendations in 1915 were comparatively mild. "Eugenic registries" were proposed to establish an "aristocracy of health" and to discourage breeding of "undesirable" individuals. Many believed that the will of the individual would always outweigh so-called hygienic ideals of "eugenic mating," a scheme to produce racial perfection. But already California had "eugenical sterilization" laws on the books and was performing hundreds of forced sterilizations each year on sex offenders, mental patients, addicts, epileptics, and the learning impaired.

While in subsequent decades eugenics was used as a justification for white-supremacist pogroms, not all participants in 1915 were promoting a white agenda. One expert at the conference contended the "perfect woman of the future...will be ruddy or brown, not white."[21]

The overall message of the Race Betterment booth, however, was one of white racial superiority. Even the Course of Study provided to San Francisco teachers cautioned that the exhibit was "not for mixed classes," meaning classes of students from differing ethnicities. Later in the twentieth century, implementation of eugenics became even more coercive, and at the greatest height of the movement, thirty-three US states had eugenics programs.[22]

The atrocities committed in the name of race betterment culminated in Nazi extermination programs during World War II. After the war, most US eugenics programs were abolished, but forced sterilization lingered in several states through the 1960s. North Carolina was the final state to abolish these practices in 1974, but until then surgeries continued to be performed on people with "undesirable traits," including mental health patients, prisoners, the poor, or people the state deemed promiscuous. In 2011 a North Carolina task force finally recommended compensation for survivors of eugenic policies.

Even without foreknowledge of the later abuses of race betterment, many in 1915 thought eugenics ought be confined to agriculture. An editor of the *Pacific Rural Press* wrote, "[Eugenics] is a perfectly rational and practicable scheme of improvement in the reproduction of organisms which are under control of man. If mankind were under the control of man its improvement would also work...but man has never gained control of mankind...." Therefore, "the art of the plant and animal breeder does not apply to the breeding of mankind, for the enforcement of it would be a resurrection of slavery...." The editor also deplored the use of Luther Burbank's celebrity status to promote eugenics: "Naturally our race-betterment reformers try to get something concrete to put in the foundation of their propaganda, and so they call upon Mr. Burbank to pour his experience into the trenches they have dug."[23]

While recognition of the evils of eugenics is widespread today, with apologies and monuments common in states where it was practiced, it is nonetheless important to acknowledge that the PPIE lay at the top of a slippery slope of good intentions that ended disastrously. Yet even with nearly a century of understanding of its perils, new forms of eugenics are on the rise. As historians Chloe Burke and Christopher Castaneda wrote in their article "The Public and Private History of Eugenics: An Introduction," "Recent developments in reproductive technologies...have raised concerns that we are witnessing a new age of eugenics, as consumers with the resources and access to health services can seek out perfection through biological manipulation."[24]

The Race Betterment booth espoused the eugenics movement, which sought to improve societal ills through techniques including sterilization and selective breeding. (Edward A. Rogers)

China assembled an exquisitely carved gate as the entrance to its exhibits in the Palace of Education and Social Economy. (Paul Robertson)

THE SHOP-WINDOW OF CIVILIZATION

"Around the corner they are selling carved ivory souvenirs and floor oil and neckties and popcorn and chewing gum. You begin to wonder if after all an exposition is anything more than a department store in costume....[B]ehind the whole enterprise there is one purpose—to make money," said Geddes Smith, a writer for the *Independent* magazine.

He called the PPIE a "Shop-Window of Civilization."[25]

It was true. Beyond its educational mission, the Fair was unabashedly mercantile. Exhibitors from all over the world were attracted by the prospect of "an immense audience, drawn from the four quarters of the globe...."[26]

The aisles of the palaces resembled the greatest bazaar ever seen. Though exhibitors were not allowed to sell the items actually displayed until the end of the Fair, they were at liberty to sell duplicate stock they stored in the Exposition warehouses, as long as they purchased a concession license. The "more refined and luxurious" commodities, such as jewelry, porcelain, marble, glass, and laces were housed in the Palace of Varied Industries, while bulkier and more utilitarian products like furniture, carpets, and hardware were arranged in the Palace of Manufactures.

Charles Green, chief of the two palaces, said the wares represented "not only the goods one would find in the principal retail shops of a large city, but also everything that goes into the interior

A peek inside the bite taken from a gigantic apple in the Palace of Horticulture revealed a diorama of Oregon's Hood River Valley. (Edward A. Rogers)

finish and decoration of public and private dwellings, including the plumbing, heating and ventilating, lighting, [and] art wares...."[27]

Many of the nations that did not mount their own pavilions placed their commodities in these two palaces. Here fairgoers could browse incised Austrian glassware, colored photos from Peru, Uruguayan leather, Henckels cutlery from Germany, Indian brassware, and Royal Doulton pottery from England. Switzerland proffered watches, wood carvings, and chocolates served from a mimic chalet. The "Shah's Room" in the Persian display glittered with a profusion of gemstones, including a ten-carat ruby, a massive turquoise, and a tiny rosebush fashioned of diamonds.

Countries with pavilions often supplemented their presence with exhibits within the Varied Industries and Manufacturing palaces. Contributions from Japan and China were especially notable. A visitor from Chicago exclaimed, "The Japanese have outdone themselves....The Japanese exhibit is...so large that it has overflowed into other departments. The machinery, the fine arts, the agricultural and all the other exhibits are very fine, but you will find that the Japanese exhibit is always perfect...."

Japan spent $1.6 million to fill more than 86,000 square feet throughout the palaces, comprising more than 5 percent of all the available exhibit space. The nation garnered 1,513 Exposition medals and concluded its PPIE participation by generously donating many of its exhibits to the University of California and various museums. While its main aim was to foster "a better understanding of the life, ideals and attainments of her people by the world," Japan also sold about $100,000 worth of goods from her exhibits (about $2.36 million in 2012).[28, 29]

A veritable forest of miniature Chinese pagodas, some standing taller than a man, occupied the northwest corner of the Palace of Education and Social Economy. These accurately detailed scale replicas of the most famous pagodas in every Chinese province were carved by students from the Jesuit missionary school at Zi-ka-wei near Shanghai, and they represented the remarkable display of student work sent from China. More than one hundred tons of wares by vocational institutions were shipped to the Fair, part of China's abundant offerings. The country reserved nearly 69,000 square feet of space in the palaces. Like Japan, China sent a wide selection of artisanal food and exquisite manufactures, but the little pagodas and a map showing a proposed new rail line across the nation drew the most interest from visitors.

WAYS OF DISPLAY

With the opportunity to showcase one's goods came a quandary: how to draw the public to an individual booth within forty-seven miles of aisles filled with 80,000 exhibits and millions of individual objects. Imaginative booth designs and merchandising techniques set the best exhibits apart.

Cornices had to conform to a maximum fifteen-foot height for visual unity, but "ornamental features and special fixtures" could be taller, and materials and profiles varied widely. Many were classically inspired, with molded profiles, pediments, or arches marking their entrances. Others were finished in elegant dark wood with carved appliques, while some

BRAND IDENTITIES

Though many have ceased to exist, scores of products shown at the PPIE are still household names. In a typical day, a twenty-first-century consumer might use many of the brands exhibited a hundred years ago. For example, our fictional customer might breakfast on Quaker Oats, Shredded Wheat, or Aunt Jemima pancakes topped with Log Cabin syrup, then cut fabric to a Butterick pattern and stitch it up on a Singer sewing machine. While she is taking care of chores, she could run a Bissell vacuum over the carpet.

Next, she might slap some Champion spark plugs into her International Harvester tractor and tighten them down with an Ingersoll-Rand compressed-air wrench. This farmer could then don her Levi's, clap a Stetson hat on her head, and plow the back forty while chewing a tasty stick of Wrigley's Doublemint gum.

After work, today's consumer might get in her Buick, with its Goodyear tires, drive to an ATM built by National Cash Register, and withdraw some cash in order to buy a *San Francisco Chronicle* or *Sunset* magazine. While in town, she could window-shop for baubles at Shreve & Co. jewelers or purchase a new scent from the California Perfume Company (now known as Avon). Although most of her travel bookings are now made on the Internet, she can still use Thomas Cook to help plan her next trip.

Upon returning home after her long day, she may relax with three fingers of Dewar's whiskey or a sip of Korbel sparkling wine from a Gorham crystal glass. If she doesn't imbibe alcohol she might choose Welch's Grape Juice instead. A round of billiards on her Brunswick table helps her wind down, and she can blame her missed shots on the outdated prescription for her Bausch & Lomb lenses. Though the medium is now digital, she might still listen to the latest songs released by Columbia Records or watch an RCA television.

Dinner might consist of Libby's corned beef hash seasoned with Morton salt, salad with McCormick dressing, and a side of Heinz pickles. She might conclude her meal with a Del Monte pineapple upside-down cake or a Baker's chocolate torte, using just the right amount of milk from Borden's, and baked in a General Electric oven. After enjoying the dessert along with either Hills Brothers coffee with a bit of rich Carnation condensed milk or Lipton tea served in a delicate Sèvres cup, our consumer well might resort to a dose of Bromo-Selzer.

Modern brands displayed at the PPIE included Log Cabin Syrup, Wrigley's gum, Libby's, Butterick patterns, the Victor Talking Machine Company, and Bromo-Selzer. (Edward A. Rogers, Donna Ewald Huggins, and Laura Ackley)

used white latticework and pergolas to evoke outdoor trellises. Within some enclosures rose whole buildings resembling temples, mosques, cottages, and even multistory French Renaissance palaces. Many booths draped fabric from their ceilings to create a luminous, tent-like effect, while others were furnished like comfortable living rooms.

Some exhibitors employed playful railings, like the miniature oil derricks that defined the boundaries of the Marine Gas Engines display and the small electrical poles that cordoned off the space reserved for the *Journal of Electricity, Power and Gas*. The Guatemala Coffee Parlor in the Palace of Food Products captured a tropical air with palm trees studding its perimeter and a red-roofed gateway set with glazed tiles.

MANUFACTORIES IN MINIATURE

"The exhibits that draw are those that show real machinery doing real work—looms that weave, pumps that pump, talking machines that talk," wrote journalist Geddes Smith. Some of the many working production lines inside the palaces churned out gold leaf, grass rugs, gloves, brooms, fire hoses, and coins. According to an article in the *Gas Institute News*, plants in the Palace of Food Products "daily turn out immense stores of flour, mush, bread, chocolate, tea, candies, wines, and the entire range of household commodities." Humorist Rube Goldberg said that after viewing the Levi Strauss & Co. Koverall

Stepping into the colossal Globe constructed by a consortium of railroads, patrons found themselves under a star-sprinkled night sky and surrounded by twenty-four illuminated dioramas depicting the most beautiful scenery along the rail lines' routes. The scenes were enlivened by animated sunrise, sunset, and storm effects. (Donna Ewald Huggins)

In the Palace of Horticulture and throughout the Exposition, exhibitors expressed prosperity and opportunity through displays of abundance. (Laura Ackley)

EXHIBITS GREAT AND SMALL

Rivers of corn, Lilliputian locomotives, and immense pieces of faux fruit were all in the world's fair display vocabulary. As Burton Benedict described in his 1983 *Anthropology of World's Fairs,* abundance, miniaturization, and gigantism all compelled the public's attention at international expositions.

Exhibitors projected prosperity and opportunity through extravagant collections of goods. No sign of drought, famine, or pestilence was admitted. A thousand apples artfully arranged made a much stronger case than a single piece of fruit. Iowa was not subtle in its

factory in the Palace of Manufactures, one would "class the inventor of overalls with Edison and Marconi."[30, 31, 32]

Palace of Agriculture exhibit. Inside a railing with gateposts capped by sheaves of grain, ears of corn formed a forty-foot-tall mountain pouring from a cornucopia labeled "The Land of Plenty." "Iowa" was spelled out in darker ears across the middle of the hill.

California Fruit News borrowed Sir Francis Drake's prose when describing the bounty within the California Building. "The 'many blessings' of that 'fruitfull soyle' are shown by the exhibits to have been showered in lavish abundance," it said. Glass cases filled with hundreds of iridescent abalone shells testified to Monterey County's opulence, Siskiyou offered a wall of wine, and the Sacramento Valley mounted a tower of processed foods, a room of olives, and a block-long rampart of 1,500 boxes of dried fruits.[33]

"If the real machinery or real ranch is too big, a model that goes is almost as good," wrote Geddes Smith. Tiny trains, ships, and cars moved across

Butter art at expositions dated back at least to the 1893 Columbian fair, and the tradition continued at the PPIE with these butter roses sculpted for the California Central Creameries by Alice Cooksley. (Edward A. Rogers)

dioramas in dozens of pavilions as miniaturization enabled exhibitors to bring renditions of buildings, towns, and sometimes entire regions to the Fair. Japan sent its shrines at Nikko, Belgium displayed the Port of Antwerp, and a relief map of New York State in the Palace of Education was made entirely of pulped currency.[34]

Some models enabled a look back, some a forward vision. Dolls in exquisite antique court costumes took to the tiny stages of detailed theaters in the French Pavilion, while other dioramas showed soldiers fighting in the trenches of the ongoing war. Industrial models demonstrated modern processes. One half of a model factory presented by Aetna Life Insurance was dangerously bereft of industrial safeguards, while the other was equipped with up-to-date safety features for comparison. Sweden used a replica of its Trolhättan Falls to demonstrate its hydropower system.

One model proved a disappointment to young visitor Helen Eells. She expected the miniature "mules" that pulled ships through the locks of the Panama Canal would be animal, not electric.

Gargantuan replicas of everyday objects also drew crowds. The most famous of all was the fifteen-foot-tall, $100,000 Underwood

Typewriter in the Palace of Liberal Arts, but there were other oversized appliances attracting admiration, including a two-story telephone in the center of Western Electric's booth.

To many it looked as though Paul Bunyan had dropped his shopping basket inside the Palace of Horticulture. The California Fruit Canners' Association office appeared to be carved out of a huge peach and pear. Elsewhere in the palace, both Walla Walla, Washington, and Hood River, Oregon, constructed apples more than ten feet tall, the latter of which was covered with realistic "bites" containing cunning dioramas depicting scenery of the Columbia River Valley.

"The Globe" in the Palace of Transportation combined the enticements of both gigantism and miniaturization. A consortium of railways built this forty-four-foot-tall model, touted as "the largest spherical relief map in the world." The routes of the participating railways—the Western Pacific, the Denver & Rio Grande, the Missouri Pacific, and the St. Louis, Iron Mountain & Southern railways—were picked out in moving lights on the map of the United States sculpted upon the sphere's surface. The entire model earth rested like an egg in a cup on a pedestal with arched openings through which visitors could enter. Within the darkened interior, electric stars twinkled on the vaulted sky, and the walls were lined with a series of illuminated dioramas of the most beautiful scenery along the rail lines.[35]

Four colossal sinuous plaster dinosaurs leaned against the front of the Union Oil Company pavilion inside the Palace of Mines and Metallurgy. Their petulant, gape-mouthed heads on long, supple necks, argued above its roof, their front legs braced against the façade and their tails undulated along the floor. This structure, encircled by a frieze of other ancient reptiles, was the work of architect Louis Christian Mullgardt, who also authored the sumptuous Court of Ages. According to the *Mining and Scientific Press*, the saurian theme was intended to "testify that the officials of the company believe in the organic origin of oil—a theory that has the support of most scientists."[36]

OBJECTS OF REVERENCE

Temple forms were another popular trope of exhibit design, and architect Louis Christian Mullgardt produced yet another outstanding composition, this one for the W. P. Fuller Company, a paint manufacturer. His Moorish-flavored "temple of paint" within the Palace of Mines and Metallurgy rose in four faceted tiers to a gracious dome. Inside, a small mill produced the "Pioneer White" lead paint for which Fuller was noted. In the California Building, the Los Angeles Soap Company erected a circular, pure-white temple carved from seven tons of soap and featuring a central fountain from which soap bubbles drifted continuously. The Ceresit concrete company demonstrated that its product was waterproof in another petite temple in the Palace of Machinery. Water poured from a fountain at the peak of the temple's dome down to its cornice, then through eight supporting pillars. Each channel was faced with glass and illuminated, allowing visitors to view water flowing down the cement tubes.

CROP ART AND BUTTER ROSES

Another entertaining display technique was a kind of "agricultural illustration," in which images were assembled from the goods on display. This technique had been in use at least since the 1893 Columbian Exposition, but it reached new levels of complexity at the PPIE.

California counties expressed their plenitude with "a bear modeled in beeswax, shown in connection with the honey display," and "idealistic and practical transparencies, wonderful pictures, resembling oil paintings at a short distance, but worked cleverly in vari-colored seeds...." The Sacramento Valley represented its riches with a mountain lion made of nuts and a horse covered in hops.[37]

Spectacular butter sculpture was a fair phenomenon that began in the late nineteenth century and continues today. At the PPIE, lilies, daisies, and roses, all molded from butter,

were gathered into creamy bouquets by the California Central Creameries for their display in the Palace of Food Products. Alice Cooksley of Idaho sculpted these delectable blooms. In the California Building, golden coins of butter poured from a butter cornucopia in Tulare County's booth.

ARTIFACTS ADVANCED AND ANTIQUATED

"An enormous locomotive clanks and rattles its half hundred wheels and snorts its contempt of an old-fashioned, leather springed Wells Fargo mail coach on a stand nearby," wrote Herman Whitaker in the *Rotarian* magazine about contrasting

Among the many examples of agricultural art were these seed portraits displayed in the San Joaquin County booth. Clockwise from upper left: San Joaquin County official George Roeding, PPIE president Charles C. Moore, California building commissioner W. D. Egilbert, and exhibits director Frederick J. V. Skiff. California governor Hiram Johnson is in the center. (*The Blue Book* (viewbook))

A temple carved from seven tons of soap was presented by the Los Angeles Soap Company. (Edward A. Rogers)

Other antediluvian items were also placed next to their current counterparts. Contrasting vividly with the gigantic, elaborate harvesters and tractors in the International Harvester's enclosure in the Palace of Agriculture was the first reaper, built by Cyrus McCormick in 1841, and winner of a gold medal at the 1851 Great Exhibition in London. In the Palace of Liberal Arts, the original Remington typewriter that had been shown at the 1876 Centennial Exposition in Philadelphia was presented atop an old-fashioned table with curly cast-iron legs and attended by a comely young lady in period costume.

Some antiques exhibited were truly ancient. Five hundred examples of historical shoes— one pair ostensibly 1,600 years old—were on loan by the United Shoe Machinery Company, which showed its manufacturing equipment in the Palace of Varied Industries. The "oldest set of golf clubs in the world" and early "featherie" golf balls also were shown in this palace alongside an exhibit of modern clubs.[39]

INGENIOUS EXHIBITORS

Having the most fascinating display in the world was of no use if no one saw it. How to entice fairgoers to an individual booth hidden among the 68.3 acres of displays inside the palaces, excluding the state and foreign pavilions, was a baffling task that many exhibitors sought to solve via clever marketing. Some took out ads in the *Official Program*, suggesting visitors use their concessions as convenient meeting places, taking care to note their "address" by street and avenue. Other incentives were more creative.

displays in the Palace of Transportation. Here and there among the modern wares, a variety of relics were scattered. The older artifacts combined the appeal of the museum with the smug satisfaction inherent in comparing the latest products to their earlier forms.[38]

The Palace of Transportation was a natural place for this type of display. The mammoth Southern Pacific Railroad "4943 Mallet," a steam locomotive weighing 435,800 pounds and capable of hauling 17,000 tons, loomed over the old congress coach, its heaviest challenge having been the ascent of the Sierra Nevada foothills' Hangtown Grade. Also diminutive in the shadow of its younger brethren was the *Collis P. Huntington*, one of the original Central Pacific Railroad locomotives in service over the Sierra Nevada in the 1860s. The *C. P. Huntington* had its cab and signature "sunflower" smokestack painted maroon and its brass and steel trim brightly polished. The little locomotive is still on display today, at the California State Railroad Museum in Sacramento.

Siskiyou County was one of many exhibitors that offered giveaways to lure visitors. In this case, a genuine gold nugget was the prize. (Donna Ewald Huggins)

Versatile architect Louis Christian Mullgardt designed the Moorish-influenced Temple of Paint, within the Palace of Mines and Metallurgy, for the W. P. Fuller Company. (Donald G. Larson Collection on International Expositions and Fairs, California State University, Fresno)

Giveaways were the easiest and most popular inducements. Canny vendors gave away free PPIE maps, always thoughtfully marked with the location of their concessions. Others doled out postcards, stationery, calendars, notebooks, or dance cards. For children there were coloring books or storybooks featuring the manufacturer's products and characters. Ghirardelli Chocolate offered a small cookbook titled *Delicious Desserts*.

Some premiums were more elaborate. Libby suggested its foods would "sharpen and satisfy your appetite," and to that end distributed a scissors sharpener. Fatima Cigarettes gave out "flip books," which, when the pages were turned, created instructional animations of the latest dance steps, including the One Step, the Argentine Tango, the Hesitation Step and Butterfly, and the Maxixe. Singer presented a folded paper flyer reading "Pin your faith to the Singer sewing machine," through which fifteen straight pins were stuck. Siskiyou County gave

away genuine gold nuggets through a "novel and fair system of distribution" that they claimed afforded "equal opportunity to each visitor."[40]

Prize contests were a surefire method of generating enthusiasm. The Fischbeck Soap Co. held a raffle for "valuable merchandise" every afternoon and evening but required contestants not only to drop their tickets into a ballot box but also to be present at the drawing, thus ensuring at least two visits per person. The Tehuantepec Village on the Zone offered an impressive $1,000 in gold to the first person who could decipher a set of faux-Mesoamerican glyphs. No record has been found indicating anyone collected this fortune.

"Sleuthing contests" featured searches for human quarry. During Mining Week, a so-called Mysterious Visitor lurked about the Palace of Mines and Metallurgy, popping up at various locations and times published in the program given to conventioneers: "2:00 P.M. Mysterious visitor appears in the vicinity of Straub Stamp

Another of Mullgardt's commissions was the irreverent dinosaur-draped pavilion for the Union Oil Company, in the Palace of Mines and Metallurgy. (Chuck Banneck)

Mill." Competitors had to locate the Mysterious Visitor and identify him, whereupon he would hand out raffle tickets. Each evening, the Mysterious Visitor made himself known in the center of the palace, drew a ticket, and awarded a $20 gold piece.

Similarly, the Wahlgreen Company, publishers of the daily *Official Program*, sponsored a month-long hunt for the "Elusive Miss Maud." Rules for winning the $10 gold piece offered daily were stringent. Contestants were required to "capture" Maud in one of the booths or amusement concessions listed in the program each day and produce a receipt proving they'd purchased something from the concession. In addition, they had to have a daily program visibly in their possession, and they had to greet Maude with the exact salutation, "Pardon me, you are the Elusive Miss Maud of the Daily Official Programme of the Panama-Pacific International Exposition, the greatest Exposition ever held in the world."[41]

REWARDING EXCELLENCE

Gold, silver, and bronze medals were nearly as plentiful as butter coins and ears of corn at the PPIE. The awards given by the Exposition for outstanding goods and exhibits were so numerous they required administration by an entire department. Since the Fair celebrated a contemporaneous event—the opening of the Panama Canal—its management reasoned awards should be given only to "products or processes of the last ten years." According to *World's Work* magazine, "What have you done since the World's Fair at St. Louis?" was the challenge each exhibitor had to answer.[42]

In addition to the immense audience they would gain by simply being part of the Fair, the most alluring advantage to prospective exhibitors was the "opportunity to secure valuable awards by the International Jury," and the attendant publicity. The awards would help "bring their products to the attention of the buyers of all nations, in a quicker, more economical and more effective manner than in any other way at their command."[43]

The Exposition's International Jury, comprising experts in the relevant fields, bestowed awards profligately, conferring 20,344 heavy, three-inch-diameter medals designed by John Flanagan. Each medal winner, plus an additional 5,183 awardees, also received a "diploma." A further 22,500 ribbons were given to winners in the livestock department, which had its own jury system. All of the Medals of Award were distributed in bronze, but if the winner had received a gold, silver, or grand prize, the recipient could have the award plated in the correct metal at his own expense.

As predicted, Exposition prizes were leveraged by their recipients. An image of the award was likely to grace a product's packaging and advertising for years to come, and some companies minted small versions of the awards to give out as promotional tokens, featuring a facsimile of the Flanagan medal on one side and a slogan on the other. Labels around the necks of bottles of Greece's Metaxa brandy continue to advertise a PPIE grand prize a century after the Fair.

The International Jury of Awards bestowed these elegant medals, designed by John Flanagan, upon the winners of each exhibit category. (Laura Ackley)

A WORLD EPITOME

Chief of Exhibits Asher Carter Baker said the contents of the palaces represented "the highest achievements in the arts and sciences of the nations of the earth brought together for comparison and study." *National Magazine* called it "A World Epitome."[44, 45]

The Department of Exhibits did not, however, succeed perfectly in cataloging the achievements of the entire world. Many nations were absent from the Fair, and on an illuminated map of the planet representing countries at the PPIE, there would be many dark patches, including Russia, large swaths of Asia and the Middle East, and almost the entire African continent. Further, the decisions on what constituted "the highest achievements in the arts and sciences" reflected the biases and desired messages of the empowered cultures, religions, and gender. Lastly, the governments and concessions mounting displays were interested in portraying their regions and industries in the best possible light. No poverty, revolution, or oppression need apply to be shown, even if they were commonplace in the real world beyond the Fair's high hedge wall.

Yet to a great extent, fairgoers could indeed learn from the world and shop in a global market at the PPIE. For many whose access to media and travel was limited, the Panama-Pacific International Exposition transcended mere amusement or even awe-inspiring spectacle. It was a revelation. Here a visitor could be exposed to new ideas, technologies, and philosophies. One could see, hear, touch, and taste works of art, music, industry, and foods from all over the world displayed in clever, beautiful, even astonishing ways. Perhaps he or she could even carry examples home.

Edith Stellmann, a writer for *Overland Monthly*, described her encounter with a schoolteacher from a small South Dakota town who had left her state for the first time to visit the PPIE. Stellmann said, "She sketched in graphic words all that the Exposition had meant to her, the new outlook[,]...the knowledge of people and places that had come to her, and what a sweeping vision it had opened."[46]

Italian

A WORLD TOUR WITHIN THE GOLDEN GATE

n San Francisco, the jaunty stroller could travel from a lacy Portuguese Gothic porch, pass the arcades of a Renaissance Italian streetscape, and finish at a many-roofed Thai temple next to an Ottoman mosque—all in just a few yards along the PPIE's gravel paths. The Fair's twenty-one national pavilions were laid out somewhat haphazardly along a diagonal avenue on lots tucked between the eastern edge of the Presidio and the Palace of Fine Arts, offering, as one magazine put it, "scenes and color plucked from the odd corners of the world and punched into the area of States and Nations."[1]

By 1915 there was already a tradition of free-standing international buildings at world's fairs. In his *Recollections of the Paris Exhibition of 1867*, Eugene Rimmel wrote:

> Without undertaking long and perilous journeys, without running the risk of being frozen in the North, or melted in the South; we have seen the Russian drive his troïka drawn by Tartar steeds, the Arab smoke the *narghilé* or play the *darbouka* under his gilt cupolas, the fair daughters of the Celestial Empire sip their tea in their quaint painted houses....[2]

Actual world travel was becoming more common, but the "Grand Tour," popularized beginning in the sixteenth century, was still available primarily to the very wealthy. At an international exposition, however, pavilions gave the everyman a taste of many cultures, albeit highly curated in flavor.

Clockwise from upper left: The pavilions of Denmark, the Netherlands, Norway, and Sweden reflected the countries' choices of how to present themselves, whether with the modern architectural ideas expressed in the Dutch building or with the regional historical styles seen in the Nordic pavilions. (Laura Ackley)

Each country chose how it would present itself at the PPIE. Some were illustrative of the imperial era. Many of the Central and South American countries, including Argentina, Guatemala, Cuba, Panama, and Honduras, chose a Spanish-Renaissance idiom reflecting their colonial past. The Bolivian Pavilion recalled not only the era of conquistadors but also its pre-Incan heritage. Its mammoth, highly decorated Churrigueresque doorway reproduced the sixteenth-century portal of the Church of San Lorenzo de Carangas in Potosí. Two carved pylons, copied from a monolith found at the ancient Andean site of Tiahuanacu, bracketed the walkway in front of the building.

The United States was at the height of its imperial reach, and this was detectable among the national pavilions. Not only was the Fair a commemoration of its completion of the Panama Canal, America also controlled the Philippines and part of Panama as protectorates, as well as the Hawaii and Alaska territories. While writers were usually comfortable categorizing Hawaii's pavilion among the state buildings, they often had trouble pigeonholing the Filipino offering, perhaps a reflection of its uneasy state of governance. In 1916 the US declared it would withdraw sovereignty over the Philippines, though several decades elapsed before Philippine self-governance was a reality. Panama's building was more easily classified as a foreign pavilion, as the nation asserted "qualified independence." The United States held full dominion over the Canal Zone, the strip of land through which the canal passed, but had only unofficial influence elsewhere within Panama.

Many countries invoked historical precedents. Italy created a small complex of seven arcade-connected buildings, each reflecting a different phase of the Renaissance. The Turkish building took the form of an Ottoman palace, complete with a small adjacent mosque with domes and minarets. France's contribution was a replica of the low, colonnaded Palais de la Légion d'Honneur in Paris. Portugal's pavilion sported gossamer Gothic arches, round hanging corner turrets, and filigree parapet decorations typical of "Manueline" architecture and derived from the Belém Tower in Lisbon and the Convent of Christ and the Monastery of Batalha, both in Tomar.

The pavilions of Norway, Sweden, and Denmark all expressed regional architecture, with square towers capped by pyramidal roofs. All three were funded and built by Scandinavian

American societies and filled with displays sent from the Nordic lands. Designed as a meeting-place for Danish Americans, Denmark's pavilion proffered a mélange of historical references, borrowing features from several castles, including Kronborg in Elsinore, the setting for Shakespeare's *Hamlet*. A pair of two-story-tall plaster trumpeters stood on a platform above its arched portal, each blowing into a *lur* horn that curled above his head. These figures were copies of those on the Lurblæserne column that still stands next to Copenhagen's Rådhus. Atop a smaller tower, an iron wind harp in the form of a traditional *tidskugle,* or "time ball," chimed on breezy days.

China, Japan, and Siam (Thailand) first constructed their buildings in their home countries, then disassembled them and sent them to the Fair, where they were painstakingly rebuilt by native artisans. Within the elaborate Chinese and Japanese complexes, the visitor could imagine himself transported across the Pacific Ocean in an instant. The Chinese compound featured eight palaces and an extravagant entrance gate, a pagoda, and a tower

Visitors could stroll from Turkey (left) to Thailand in just a few steps in the Exposition's international section. (Anne T. Kent California Room, Marin County Free Library)

set about a serene formal garden. Solid ebony pillars supported the miniaturized Tai-ho Tien (Hall of Supreme Harmony) at Beijing, which was flanked by two audience halls. All three edifices were based on actual structures in the Imperial Quarter of the Forbidden City.

At the dedication of the Japanese Pavilion, Exposition president Charles C. Moore's daughter, Josephine, pulled a silken cord and released water into a stream running through the country's site. The winding waterway coursed under delicate arched bridges before tumbling down a cataract and into a miniature lake. Japan's buildings, with latticed windows and curving eaves, were set within nearly four acres of manicured gardens and meandering paths. The Kinkaku-ji Temple, or Golden Pavilion of Kyoto, was the model for the largest structure in the compound, which included stone pagodas, two public teahouses, and a small structure for the tea ceremony.

In contrast with the symmetrical layout of the Chinese landscaping, the garden on the Japanese site was irregular and naturalistic although still meticulously designed. Its builders imported from Japan not only native dwarf trees and shrubs but also 250 boulders, several weighing three tons apiece. Even the unique fine grass for the lawns was brought by ship to the Fair. Each month the plantings highlighted a signature flower or plant, including plum, peach, cherry, wisteria, iris, lotus, and chrysanthemum.

Originally, Siam declined its invitation to the PPIE, but after a visit from one of the intrepid official legations from the United States, it reconsidered and sent a jewel-like, temple-form pavilion. The building was an enlarged replica of the Phra Thinang Aphorn Phimok Prasat on the grounds of the Grand Palace in Bangkok. While the original was open on all sides, at San Francisco the teak, lacquer, ivory, and hammered metal traditional structure was enclosed by hundreds of panes of delicately tinted glass. Each of its heavily carved roof ridges terminated in a snakelike, upward-curving finial called a "chofa."

The clean, swooping lines of the Netherlands Pavilion contrasted starkly with the historicized or Beaux-Arts pavilions nearby. Designed by W. Kromhout of Rotterdam, it was not meant to evoke historical Dutch buildings but rather modern architectural concepts. Relatively unornamented openings were surmounted by an effervescent series of ascending domes, culminating in a lofty rounded tower surrounded by dozens of flagpoles. The entire streamlined structure prefigured the Art Deco movement still a decade in the future.

THE MISSING UNITED STATES BUILDING

Conspicuous in its absence was a dedicated United States pavilion. Once again the PPIE's vow to decline federal funding became a bone of contention between the lawmakers who had supported and those who had opposed San Francisco's 1911 campaign for the Fair. Some congressmen who had worked against San Francisco objected to raising a United States building. They said the city had won on the

The lack of a US national pavilion was a sore subject among many of the Fair's promoters. (*San Francisco Call*, February 13, 1913)

Neoclassical design was favored by many nations and states, making portions of the Esplanade and Avenue of States resemble a line of bank buildings. (*Official Publication[;] Panama-Pacific International Exposition: Hand-Colored* (viewbook))

grounds that it would not ask for aid in building the PPIE, and financing a government pavilion constituted "aid." Meanwhile, President Taft urged Congress to appropriate $2 million for an edifice to house US government exhibits at the Fair. He said, "The United States cannot with good grace invite foreign governments to erect buildings and make extensive exhibits while itself refusing to participate."[3]

The August 1914 Sundry Civil Bill included $500,000 to fund the US government exhibits, including a building on Presidio land that would be retained for military use after the Exposition. Only one month later it was clear that the proposed structure could not be completed in time for the opening of the Exposition, and the projected exhibit space was woefully short of the 157,000 square feet of displays planned by the Government Exhibit Board. Also, the secretary of war insisted on a structure more martial than festal, entirely out of character for a world's fair.

The solution was facilitated by cataclysm. When the advent of World War I caused massive cancellations of exhibits, suddenly a great deal of space was available within the palaces.

Thus, the United States' extensive departmental exhibits were distributed among them. Though scattered throughout several buildings, the official US exhibits were easily identifiable. Each was enclosed by a heavy ornamental balustrade divided by pillars bearing gilt eagles and hung with patriotic bunting. In all, nearly four and a half acres were allotted for governmental exhibits, including one-quarter of the entire Palace of Liberal Arts.

THE STATE BUILDINGS

North of the international pavilions lay the Avenue of States, which in some places looked like nothing more than a line of banks. The architecture of the state and national buildings reflected the messages the civic entities wanted to send, and the majority went with the solidity of neoclassical design, featuring balustrades, pediments, and be-columned porticoes. But between these sedate monuments, others among the twenty-eight state and territory pavilions demonstrated different architectural personalities.

The Oregon State building was designed by Foulkes and Hogue to resemble a rustic log version of the Parthenon in Athens, Greece. (*The Panama-Pacific International Exposition Illustrated in Color* (viewbook))

A few states chose to use general historical styles that invoked continuity and tradition. The Missouri Building was Georgian, Illinois built a Tudor-style mansion, and the host state's entry was a monumental variant of California Mission style. The façade of the Texas Building was a clear reference to the Alamo.

"Greetings, ye gentle reminders of the Colonial age!" said architecture critic William Woollett of pavilions that borrowed elements from specific early-American buildings. Pennsylvania took Independence Hall's proportions and gable outline but sheared off its signature tower and hollowed out its center. The resultant loggia created a roofed, open-sided reliquary for the Liberty Bell, which traveled from Philadelphia to the PPIE. The pavilion also featured a fireproof vault from which the bell was wheeled out by an armed guard for daily display. Maryland's entry was a replica of Homewood, a Palladian mansion built by the son of a signer of the Declaration of Independence. A copy of the Trenton Barracks served as New Jersey's pavilion, while Virginia offered a faithful reproduction of George Washington's home, Mount Vernon. Massachusetts and Ohio built imposing versions of their historic capitols, though Ohio's was sans-cupola.[4]

The oddest state pavilion was a huge version of the Parthenon with columns made of logs, complete with bark. The popular "Oregon Parthenon" was designed by architects Foulkes and Hogue of Portland. While early

drawings showed a more literal rendition of the classical Greek structure, the final version was considerably more rustic. The outer colonnade consisted of forty-eight huge Douglas fir columns, the same number as on the outer colonnade of the Parthenon and the number of US states in 1915.

To supplement or replace governmental funding for pavilions and palace exhibits, some states sold special bronze medals, albeit with mixed success. These tokens, known as "so-called dollars," typically cost $1 and featured versions of the state seal and an Exposition slogan or scene. Louisiana, Mississippi, Montana, and Oregon mounted successful campaigns using the collectibles, but those sold by Alabama, Georgia, Florida, Kentucky, North Carolina, South Carolina, and Tennessee did not raise funds sufficient to finance dedicated displays at the Fair. Arkansas and Maryland also minted medals that were given away as keepsakes during the Fair. While states had medals, Denmark had a special plate, made by the Royal Copenhagen factory. In 1913 the *Chronicle* reported, "Only 1000 copies of the plate have been made, so it will soon become rare....It will be retailed here at $5. Of the 1000 plates made, 200 will be disposed of in Denmark, 400 will be reserved for sale in the Eastern States, and the balance will be put on sale here." In 2013 the plates sold to collectors for about $150 each.[5]

Delicate Sèvres porcelain and richly hued Gobelins tapestries were among the treasures brought to the French Pavilion on the American ship *Jason*. (Laura Ackley)

TROVES OF THE
NATIONS AND STATES

Generally, the collections in the state and foreign pavilions were classed as "displays" rather than "exhibits," and thus were ineligible for the coveted medals of award. In almost all cases, governments also mounted official exhibits in one or more palaces so they could win prizes. A few countries, such as China and Japan, exhibited in *all* of the palaces. One state exception was North Dakota, which had no displays outside its pavilion. In its foyer, amidst specimens of the state's abundant agricultural, mineral, and fuel resources, stood a whimsical thirty-foot tower executed in varicolored ears of corn. Sweden had a showing in the Palace of Fine Arts but otherwise abstained from exhibiting in the palaces. In her pavilion, new industries like hydropower and steel contrasted with *slöjd*, or domestic crafts, including furniture, ceramics,

lace, and a collection of half-life-sized dolls dressed in folk costumes of various regions.

Some pavilions contained few displays and served mostly as community centers. This was particularly true among the states, which naturally could expect a larger number of their citizens to visit the Exposition than those from foreign nations. These pavilions emphasized social spaces, such as ballrooms; meeting, smoking, and writing rooms; and even theaters showing promotional films. Official hostesses welcomed callers, who could sign the guestbook or make appointments to meet friends. Comfortable lounges with leather club chairs and crackling fireplaces invited tired visitors to rest and perhaps find refuge in a newspaper from home.

Most pavilions, however, showed examples of their industries, products, natural resources, and attractions. Although the displays could not receive awards, they were designed to attract tourists, investors, settlers, or all of these in varying proportions.

Filipino artisans demonstrated traditional crafts within the Philippines Pavilion, which was detailed with beautiful native hardwoods and windows glazed with capiz shells in place of glass. (Edward A. Rogers)

Native materials often were highlighted in the furnishings and finishes of the buildings themselves. Curving staircases of Argentine gray marble ascended from the soaring ivory-and-gold lobby of that republic's pavilion. Wisconsin, home to plentiful hardwood forests, expressed these riches in its floors and walls. Unshaped *palma brava* trunks supported the portico of the Philippines Pavilion, and its interior was appointed with the euphoniously named *narra, yacal, tindalo,* and *lauan* woods. Light filtered onto these gorgeous surfaces through windows glazed with pearly, translucent capiz shells instead of glass. Some took the trend of indigenous materials to extremes—every stick of construction material for the Indiana Building was freighted in from the Hoosier State.

Naturally, the buildings were decorated with handicrafts, furniture, artwork, murals, and stained glass from the lands of origin. Turkish carpets and Greek statuary enhanced their home pavilions. The French Pavilion was almost overwhelmingly replete with treasure, including crystal by Lalique, tapestries by the Gobelins factory, sculpture by Rodin, and paintings by Monet, Manet, Cézanne, Renoir, Pissarro, Gauguin, Tissot, Toulouse-Lautrec, and Degas. Its rooms featured fine perfumes and mannequins dressed in the latest couture. Humorist Rube Goldberg warned, "The exhibit of expensive Parisian gowns in the French Building has brought sorrow into the lives of many honest men."[6]

Many governments also touted their intellectual, historical, and cultural attainments. Argentina, Honduras, the Philippines, Indiana, Massachusetts, and Missouri brought libraries either describing their realms or featuring native authors. Italy highlighted exploration and scientific discovery with displays of items owned by Galileo, Galvani, Volta, Marconi, and Columbus. France countered by presenting artifacts of military and literary lions. Furniture, portraits, and swords owned by American Revolutionary heroes Lafayette and Rochambeau were juxtaposed with items from the romantic authors, including the inkstand, armchair, and candleholder of Honoré de Balzac, a

reproduction of the hand of Alexandre Dumas, and a pen and clock that once belonged to Victor Hugo. Presidential relics of George Washington and Abraham Lincoln were proudly displayed in the Virginia and Illinois buildings.

Relatively young nations like Cuba and New Zealand sought new citizens, and they distributed thick handbooks extolling their opportunities for settlers.

Eventually, the standard exhibits could begin to pall. After dutifully absorbing a dozen or more edifying motion pictures, after gazing at renderings of famous beauty spots, after perusing charts describing outstanding infrastructure, agriculture, and school systems, after inspecting detailed models of local industries, and after filing past seemingly endless glass display cases of mineral specimens, straw hats, lacework, or pottery, a fairgoer became understandably satiated with these wonders.

The most popular pavilions, therefore, were ones that had found novel ways to appeal to visitors' senses of sight, sound, and taste. In the Washington Building, a helix of apples was mounted on a wire around a rotating tapered column, which made the fruit appear to spiral skyward toward the amber glass of the rotunda. The "3D panoramas" in Canada's pavilion were so widely acclaimed they merited an article in *Scientific American,* and many deemed Canada's the "best foreign exhibit." In its long aisles, guests peered between columns onto skillfully built dioramas in front of painted backdrops that gave the illusion of vistas encompassing hundreds of miles. Transitions were so skillfully blended, it was difficult to tell where the model left off and the background began. Miniature trains moved to and fro from diminutive grain elevators as tiny steamers plied lakes of actual water in the scenes depicting Canadian agriculture and industry. Thousands of children were delighted when they found live beavers disporting themselves at the front of one tableau, taking dips in a pond and working desultorily on a pre-made beaver dam.

Living animals were a sure draw. Swift flashes of yellow, pink, red, and green lured the curious into a primeval landscape of exotic specimen tree ferns adjacent to the Australian building. There they discovered an enclosure in which a variety of rare birds—green and yellow bowerbirds, cockatoos with flaring crown plumes, and brilliantly hued parakeets—darted amidst the greenery, accompanied by the chortles of the "laughing" kookaburras. Kangaroos and wallabies loped with elastic grace across nearby paddocks. Inside the Hawaiian Building, the islands' famous "painted" fishes swam in aquariums filled with seawater imported from Waikiki.

ISLAND AIRS

Hawaii's central atrium was already appealing, with luxuriant ferns and palms under its glass rotunda and colorful lunette friezes depicting island legends over its portals. But Hawaii's organizers added to the allure and, in the process, spawned the biggest musical craze at the PPIE by adding a quintet of musicians who strummed the plaintive airs of the islands on ukuleles. Historian Frank Morton Todd wrote, "People were about ready for a new sensation in popular music at the time of the Exposition, and the sweet voices of the Hawaiians raised in

those haunting minor melodies you heard at the Hawaiian Building and the Palace of Horticulture were enough to start another musical vogue."[7]

Ukuleles were first brought to Hawaii in the late 1870s by Portuguese immigrants from the island of Madeira. They were called "machetes," and the larger version "rajãoes." The instrument quickly became a Hawaiian mainstay. After Hawaii's annexation by the United States in 1893, Hawaiian music was known on the mainland but was not widespread, remaining somewhat of a novelty nationally into the nineteen-teens.

In San Francisco, Hawaiian music became a huge hit and was performed from one end of the Exposition to the other. The gentle call of ukuleles and guitars lured as many as 34,000 people per day to the modest Hawaiian pavilion. Visitors could purchase their own koa-wood ukuleles and five-stringed rajãoes made by Jonah Kumalae from a booth in the Palace of Liberal Arts with a hula dancer depicted in relief above the entrance.

In the Pineapple Packers' Association's café in the Palace of Horticulture, weary fairgoers felt transported as they relaxed in the warm, humid

Fairgoers packed into the Guatemala Pavilion to hear the talented Hurtado Brothers Royal Marimba Band. (Edward A. Rogers)

Eight Southern California counties mounted a collective exhibit amid the four acres of controlled chaos in the California Building's exhibit wing. (Seligman Family Foundation)

air, again among palms and ferns. There they were serenaded by singers as Hawaiian women served Pineapple Melba à la Mode and other tropical treats. Other notable Hawaiian performers at the PPIE included George "Keoki" Awai, Henry Kailimai, and the Hawaiian Glee Club.

On the balmy night of June 11, Kamehameha Day, Hawaiian music at the Fair reached its zenith. Two thousand Hawaiians and an additional 25,000 attendees succumbed to the enchantment of the "Paradise of the Pacific" as honorary "queen" and Hawaiian mezzo-soprano Marion Dowsett sang "Aloha 'Oe," "Ona Ona," "Ihole Manu," and other island ballads from a jewel-studded, shell-shaped float pulled by outrigger canoes across the lagoon of the Palace of Fine Arts. Colored lights glowed, the paddlers chanted, and the sweet strains from five separate Hawaiian string quintets floated out over the placid water. This pageant was so gorgeous it was repeated the following morning so that it could be filmed for a newsreel.

Other factors, including promotional efforts by Hawaii to position itself as a vacation destination, undoubtedly helped spread awareness of Hawaiian music in general and ukuleles in particular. But the PPIE was the flashpoint for the infatuation with Hawaiian music that spread across the nation.

"The ukulele has forged to the front and has become a fad from the Pacific coast to Portland, Maine," said the *Duluth News-Tribune*. Even though Honolulu makers of ukuleles increased their production by about 300 percent between August 1915 and October 1916, they were still unable to keep up with demand from the continental US. Publishers from Honolulu to Tin Pan Alley churned out scores of Hawaii-inspired songs in the next few years. The trade winds had wafted through San Francisco, permanently dispersing enthusiasm for Hawaiian music throughout the mainland.[8]

MARIMBA ROYALTY

To supplement the official musical program offered by the Exposition, music was available in many state and foreign pavilions. One could sample a variety of international music in a single day, perhaps listening to clarion tones of ancient *lurs* in the Danish Pavilion, then an operatic soprano in Italy's courtyard, the strumming of harp-like *kotos* in the Japanese gardens, and finally a concert by the Young Australian League Band in the Australian building.

In the Guatemalan Pavilion, the Hurtado Brothers caused a sensation as their mallets flew over the keys of two large marimbas.

Guests crowded onto the staircases and into any available standing room to hear the dulcet, plinking melodies of the Royal Marimba Band, which consisted of three fraternal Hurtados, the two sons of elder brother Vicente, and three other musicians. The adaptable band, led by brother Celso Hurtado, could render everything from patriotic marches to Strauss waltzes to ragtime.

The instruments had been constructed for the brothers by their father, Sebastian, of blocks of native Guatemalan hardwoods—*granadillo, chico zapote, campeche, hormigo,* and *clohón*—which chimed with tones evoking their home forests of South America. These purveyors of the "music of the forest" were so popular they also were engaged for parades, society teas, dances, and weddings at the Exposition. The band's popularity earned a medal of honor from the PPIE, and the musicians eventually recorded more than eighty songs for the Columbia and Victor Talking Machine companies. The group played again at the 1939 Golden Gate International Exposition on Treasure Island, but Celso Hurtado's daughter, Catherine Hurtado Wood, says he preferred the PPIE, calling it the "Forever Fair."[9, 10]

DRINKABLE, EDIBLE, AND VISIBLE DELIGHTS

San Francisco has ever loved its coffee, and the scent wafting from several of the international pavilions delighted local gourmets. They could savor the smooth version in the Honduran building or dare to imbibe in the sludgy concoction served in tiny cups at the Turkish Pavilion. A huge tent was set up next to the Guatemalan Pavilion to celebrate that country's "special day" at the Fair on November 20. Inside, women in pale dresses poured free samples and gave away 50,000 bags of Guatemalan beans. Lovely young women in traditional costumes also served typical national delicacies in the pavilions of Norway, Turkey, Japan, and the Netherlands.

Those state buildings along the bay's shore commanded a magnificent vista of the Golden Gate, and the view from Marin County's exhibit in the California Building offered a tongue-in-cheek jest. While the state's other counties relied on paintings and photos to convey their beauty, Marin simply cut a large picture window in the northern wall and framed the gorgeous view toward the county. The panorama of Mt. Tamalpais' tawny, oak-flecked ridges beyond the azure bay rivaled the canvas of a master.

SHOWCASING THE GOLDEN STATE

Marin and the state's other counties were lucky to *have* a place to display. Despite the vast amount of money and effort California poured into securing and building the PPIE, the state almost did not have a building of its own. Most states made appropriations to pay for their pavilions, but Californians were weary of funding all things Exposition from their own pockets, whether through individual stock subscriptions or the four-year tax that raised $5 million under a 1910 state constitutional amendment. But, of course, the home state's citizens wanted to put on a good show of California's bounty.

Many thought that a state display ought to be funded out of the existing tax, but the State Exposition Commission, which controlled the money, firmly rejected taking money out of general PPIE coffers to fund a California Building. Many counties began to set aside appropriations, and a few initiated plans to erect individual county pavilions. But on May 20, 1913, all agreed instead to pay for exhibit space within a single large building constructed by the Exposition. Under this plan, the Exposition would construct the pavilion, and counties would pay $2.50 per square foot for exhibit space to defray its cost. Some grumbled about paying for space when territory in the palaces was free for exhibitors, but far northern Humboldt County signed on the very next day, and eventually all fifty-eight counties reserved space.

The $1.25 million California Building, designed by Thomas Burditt, was a dignified pastiche of the state's Spanish Missions fabricated on a grand scale. At five acres, it was the largest state pavilion ever built for an exposition. Four domed belfries adorned the central tower, which stood well back from the façade and overlooked the central garden patio between the two main wings. From a niche in the courtyard wall, a statue of Father Junípero Serra presided over a tranquil replica of the Forbidden Garden at Mission Santa Barbara, from which women had been excluded. At San Francisco, the fair sex was welcome to stroll the peaceful paths defined by forty-year-old cypress hedges—cleverly repurposed remnants of the old Harbor View Baths pleasure grounds that had stood on the site.

Its west wing held administrative offices for the Exposition and reception suites governed by the Woman's Board of the Fair. In these gracious rooms the loftiest VIPs were entertained. Every afternoon but Sunday, thousands of fashionably dressed ladies and gentlemen danced in the California Building's 120-by-55-foot ballroom. These "tea dances," instituted three weeks into the Fair, were instantly popular.

A riotous sensory overload of county showcases, loosely grouped by region, cluttered the open industrial expanse of the eastern wing. Striped bunting and hundreds of banners, flags, and festoons were draped from the roof trusses under the long skylights. On the floor several stories below, the fifty-eight counties partitioned the four-acre space into collective exhibits via balustrades, open-topped arcades, and ornate gateways. According to the *California Blue Book*, within these fanciful enclosures lay an attempt to present "an industrial, agricultural and horticultural fair, a treasury of artistic work, a condensation of the State's varied scenic splendors, as well as her flora and fauna, a review of California's accomplishments, and an index of the breadth of her future possibilities." Here was "California in epitome."[11]

The chaos of the county exhibits conveyed the state's abundance and variety. Wherever the eye rested, ranks of apples, plums, oranges, lemons, and olives were arranged into sumptuous rainbow-hued patterns. Sheaves of grain were affixed to the walls in geometric motifs, and every horizontal surface was crammed with baskets or curved glass apothecary jars holding fruit, beans, honey, nuts, sugar, or rice. Processed foods including olive oil, tobacco, jams, canned goods, and bottles of wine lined the walls. The mineral-rich counties presented case upon case of valuable ores, while the coastal regions highlighted their timber riches. Native American baskets took their place near furniture made in the state's vocational schools. Hundreds of mounted native animals inhabited imaginative dioramas. In Mendocino's space, stuffed mountain lions stalked the oblivious deer that stood casually next to a bobcat, while raccoons, bears, and birds looked on unconcernedly.

Amid the bewildering assortment, some regional exhibits were standouts. Monterey created mimic reefs under glass, including crabs, fish, and a helmeted deep-sea diver searching for the area's famous abalone. The eight counties of the San Joaquin Valley styled their area the "Palace of Plenty," decorating the sinuous cornice surrounding their display with plaster heads of sheep, cows, and pigs beneath overflowing baskets of molded fruits. A hollow, snow-crested mountain in the middle of the exhibit contained a movie theater, one of seven scattered throughout the building, with aggregate seating for 2,000. A four-hundred-square-foot sculpted model of Yosemite Valley was cleverly lit to replicate sunrise, sunset, and moonlight.

Eight Southern California counties created a collective display after the Mission style, with a silvery façade capped with red tiles. Inside, ivory-colored kiosks were touched with green and gold leaf and enhanced with painted glass. San Mateo offered a relief map of the county surrounded by banks of flowers under an opulent glass-domed Moorish pavilion.

The Sacramento and foothill counties section, home of the original gold discovery site at Coloma, featured models of a hydraulic mine and a gold dredger, along with eight safes displaying $100,000 in "virgin gold." A 1:20 scale quartz mill crushed one hundred pounds of ore a day and turned out real gold. Sacramento expressed

MODELING DOMESTIC LIFE

A number of full-scale model homes were scattered across the PPIE grounds, each exemplifying recent developments in single-family housing. The "White and Sugar Pine" and "Home of Redwood" bungalows in the South Gardens advertised California's plentiful timber resources. Each was constructed by a consortium of lumber companies, but the Home of Redwood had a distinct advantage, as its architect was Louis Christian Mullgardt.

Mullgardt's Court of Ages, between the eastern quartet of PPIE palaces, was an exotic open-air fantasia and anything but domestic, but prior to the Fair, the architect had been best known in the Bay Area for his residential designs. It was estimated that three million people visited the dignified, low-slung Home of Redwood, which won a gold medal for its tour-de-force use of the ruddy lumber. Its structural elements, casements, decorative paneling, and roof shingles were all of the California wood. Of the timber elements, only the floors, which required a harder surface, were not of redwood.

The Home of Redwood also embodied the tensions between the nascent conservation movement and the lumber industry. At its dedication, the president of the Northwestern Railway noted a "multiplicity of reasons for leaving the redwood forests as monuments to the infinite power and also a corresponding number of reasons why they should be cut down and utilized by man."[12]

The Brick Home, sponsored by the Panama-Pacific Clay Products House Association, came late to the game. Due to fund-raising difficulties, it opened five months into the Fair on the northern fringe of the bay on a site abandoned by the State of Colorado. Its handsome, Prairie-influenced design was a welcome contrast to the mélange of historical replica and neoclassical state and national pavilions in the vicinity. The Brick Home was an explicit attempt to defend one building technology against others. To its planners, it was a bastion of the "burnt clay" industry on the Pacific coast, an inoculation against the "insidious" spread of wood-framed California-style bungalows and stucco homes through the infection of susceptible fairgoers.[13]

Each exhibitor extolled its product's physical and its building's alleged scientific properties. The California Redwood Association's brochure drew attention to the wood's stability and fire- and weather-resistant properties. It also reminded the reader that "modern medical science recommends out-door sleeping for sturdy bodies," so a redwood sleeping porch would actually reduce doctor bills. In a city lately burned, the Brick Home's non-flammability and its corresponding lower fire insurance rates were greatly admired.[14]

In addition to the pine, redwood, and brick homes, several prefabricated cottages were stashed at the far western end of the fairgrounds near the livestock area, evidence of yet another emerging homebuilding trend.

The Home of Redwood, by Louis Christian Mullgardt, was one of several demonstration homes built on the grounds. (Glenn D. Koch)

its "River City" nickname with a working model of the Sacramento River on which traveled a miniature steamboat, complete with lights and turning paddlewheel. A lounge and information bureau was sheltered beneath a replica of the state capitol's dome.[15]

Two sections of a twenty-foot-diameter giant redwood, one upright and one lying on its side, formed the centerpiece of the North Bay Counties section. Inside this "log and stump house" a chandelier suspended from the polished redwood ceiling illumined a gallery of paintings of Humboldt County framed in burl. After the Fair, the two massive sections of redwood were moved to Des Moines, Washington, where they became the Big Tree Inn.

A WORLD TOUR WITHIN THE GOLDEN GATE

One girl wrote in her diary that her tour of the world among the 130 acres of state and foreign pavilions at the PPIE was "simply grand." She and millions of others regarded a visit to the

The four belfries of the California Building overlooked the "Forbidden Garden" in its central courtyard, which repurposed hedges from the Harbor View Baths that had previously occupied the site. (Seligman Family Foundation)

spray of buildings west of the Palace of Fine Arts as essential to the World's Fair experience.[16]

The pavilions were exercises in selection, inside and out. Some chose current neoclassical architectural fashion, while others invoked their imperial progenitors or recalled high points in their regional histories by replicating specific buildings. Whether to attract investment, immigrants, tourism, or a bit of each, the collections inside the structures were designed to catch the eye and tell a story of local industries, products, resources, or cultural achievements.

While most state and national displays were impressive, a few were half-hearted. The Pan-Pacific Press Association lauded the coffee and cordial attendants at "Porto Rico's" booth in the Palace of Food Products but also said the territory's exhibit was "not a creditable one and the United States Government can have no feeling of pride when the display from this truly beautiful island is mentioned." Neither was the territory of Alaska properly represented, they said.[17]

The absence of some nations from the global showcase reflected the international political climate. A few British, Russian, and even German arts and manufactures were shown in the palaces, but that these world powers were largely missing was obvious. Further, not a single African nation mounted a pavilion; the entire continent was represented only by a few exhibits by Morocco and South Africa within the palaces.

As former New York mayor Seth Low said, when war broke out in the first week of August 1914, "[T]he financial heart of the world almost ceased to beat." Thirty states and countries that had selected or requested sites at the PPIE abandoned the idea of building dedicated pavilions. Though not all of the withdrawals were due to the conflict, many nations were profoundly affected by the wartime disruption of trade routes, credit, and insurance markets, heaped on top of an already recessed worldwide economy. Nations that decided not to build included Austria, Brazil, Chile, the Dominican Republic, Haiti, Mexico, Monaco, Persia (Iran), Peru, Puerto Rico, Spain, and Switzerland. Many others reduced their displays within the palaces. Ironically, Panama, for which the Fair was named,

The layout of the Chinese Pavilion was orderly and formal in contrast to the Japanese Pavilion's naturalistic landscaping. Visible beyond the complex of teahouses, audience halls, and pavilions are the Turkish, Italian, and Siamese sites. (Edward A. Rogers)

left her pavilion at the PPIE empty and shuttered after holding a July dedication ceremony. Instead, the country decided to concentrate on its already much-delayed Exposición Nacional, scheduled for Panama City in 1916.[18]

Empty lots along the Avenues of States and Nations were undesirable from the PPIE's point of view, but some parties benefitted from pavilion cancellations. When Colorado abandoned its site, the brick manufacturers were given a place to erect their handsome demonstration home. When at the last minute Greece was able to send an impressive collection of casts of ancient statuary onboard the US naval ship *Jason*, the evaporation of the German Kali Syndicate's plans gave the figures a roof over their plaster heads.

The Pan-American presence remained strong, especially with Argentina's huge $1.7 million investment in the Fair. However, the reduction in Latin American and European exhibits resulted in tilting the balance of the Fair distinctly toward the Asia-Pacific region. Stanford University president David Starr Jordan said, "California is the door to incomparable Japan, to marvelous Hawaii. 'The second turn to the left after leaving San Francisco' and you come to Stevenson's place at Samoa. Then there is Tahiti, Fiji, New Zealand, Australia and China, all likewise 'Out West.'"[19]

With strong contributions from Australia, China, Hawaii, Japan, New Zealand, the Philippines, and Thailand, it was clear that as far as San Francisco was concerned, at least, "the hub of civilization" had moved and was now centered on the Pacific Ocean.[20]

However, claims that "more nations are represented as exhibitors [at the PPIE] than at any previous world's fair" were exaggerated. Chicago's Columbian Exposition garnered forty-six international contributors, the 1915 Exposition only thirty-one. The 1900 Paris Exposition Universelle featured twenty-four country pavilions to San Francisco's twenty-one. Nevertheless, considering the precarious political and economic circumstances in 1915, the Panama-Pacific International Exposition was able to attract an impressive number of international exhibits of high quality.[21]

That the PPIE "faced the Orient" more than any prior Exposition suited San Francisco's aspirations just fine. The Panama Canal had opened a new avenue for trade, and as Mayor Rolph said in a telegraphed speech, "We in San Francisco are in the very center of that new avenue. We are situated where all must pass our doors, midway between the East and the Far East—the Orient."[22]

FAMOUS AND INFAMOUS VISITORS

There never was anything like it in the world's history," said Secretary of the Interior Franklin K. Lane as he first glimpsed the Exposition. Lane, a Californian, was President Woodrow Wilson's official representative at the opening of the Fair. "The people will come. They can't be kept away when they know what is ready for them here."[1]

Come they did—nearly nineteen million revelers over the 288-day life of the PPIE. By any measure, the Fair was successful, despite World War I, already raging in Europe, severely hampering foreign attendance. A daily average of more than 65,000 visitors passed through her gates. And what visitors they were—cowboys and inventors, entertainers and captains of industry, foreign dignitaries and daredevils. Rubbing shoulders with the hoi polloi were magnates, ministers, envoys, commissioners, consuls, and governors. Some were already famous, others dreamed of fame, and still others wished they were less notorious.

Like an image frozen by a tourist's camera, the PPIE represents a quintessential moment in cultural history. The eager amateur photographer could purchase a twenty-five-cent camera license and take all the pictures he wanted within the Exposition (as long as his negative size did not exceed four by five inches and he did not use a tripod). If he were lucky, his lens might capture the likes of Helen Keller, Buffalo Bill Cody, or Luther Burbank. It might catch an impassioned political orator he admired, a stage idol of his youth, or one of the new movie stars he'd seen projected on the screen of his local nickelodeon. He probably tried to photograph the fantastic loops and dives of a stunt pilot, but the fixed lens of his device meant the resulting picture was most likely of a crowd of people gazing at a dot in the sky. Perchance that laughing urchin who ran through the frame as he was trying to get a shot of his wife at the Fountain of Energy would, in time, become an eminent author.

Former secretary of state William Jennings Bryan's July 5 speech was a plea for peace. The pacifist diplomat had resigned from his post in June because he felt President Wilson's letter to Germany protesting the sinking of the *Lusitania* violated American neutrality. (Edward A. Rogers)

These grainy prints are a modern amber that preserves the personalities that defined an era. At the time, the images were mementoes of a once-in-a-lifetime vacation, but today they reveal the epochal transitions occurring in politics, technology, economics, civil rights, and entertainment manifested by the notable personalities who attended the PPIE.

PRESIDENTS, PACIFISM, AND PREPAREDNESS

While President Woodrow Wilson was unable to visit the PPIE because of the demands of wartime politics (and perhaps his upcoming December wedding), his office was represented by one chief executive of the future and two of the past.

Franklin Delano Roosevelt, then a hale thirty-three-year-old assistant secretary of the navy, was given a seventeen-gun salute as he embarked from the Marina on a barge with Vice President Thomas Marshall, who received nineteen guns. Their party reviewed the fleet at anchor off the Exposition as part of the Fair's official dedication in March. They were piped aboard the USS *Colorado,* where Roosevelt chatted genially with his wife, Eleanor, as the vice president's flag was hoisted aloft. Marshall joked, "[T]his is the first time in the history of the country that a vice-president has ever been recognized and appreciated."[2]

The PPIE was the scene of a rhetorical battle familiar today. The United States was understandably unnerved by the war in Europe, but the reaction of its citizenry was divided. The "hawks" of the preparedness movement advocated building military might while the "doves" of pacifism advocated "peace at any price." These two birds circled warily over the Court of the Universe while a series of fiery orations took place below.

At the start of 1915, William Jennings Bryan, a renowned orator and pacifist, was secretary of state. According to the 2013 State Department website, "When World War I broke out, Bryan made it very clear to Wilson that he favored strict neutrality and strongly opposed any US involvement." When a German U-boat sank the *Lusitania* in May with 128 Americans on board, President Wilson sent a letter of protest to Germany. Bryan felt the letter violated American neutrality and he resigned in June. Bryan, however, remained the keynote speaker for the PPIE's Independence Day celebration on July 5, an event attended by more than 121,000 people. The Fair's official historian gave the context of Bryan's speech: "He had resigned from President Wilson's cabinet a little while before, and occupied the position of a sort of itinerant political clergyman, preaching peace in the midst of war and war's alarms, and bravely holding aloft the ensign of human brotherhood when close to fifteen million men in Europe were trying to starve, blast, bayonet, and gas one another to death...."[3, 4]

In his address, Bryan declared, "Threaten your neighbor and he will threaten you. Force begets force, and love begets love. Across the seas our brothers' hands are stained in brothers' blood.... They need a flag that speaks the sentiment of the human heart, a flag that looks towards better things than war."[5]

Former president Theodore Roosevelt, whose foreign policy motto was "speak softly and carry a big stick," spoke at the PPIE later that month on the topic "Peace and War." His disdain for Bryan's opinions was clear. Upon his arrival, he said of his upcoming speech, "I think I might call it, 'Damn the Mollycoddles!'...I'm heartily sick of this bleating, wheedling, simpering cry of peace at any price. Standing pat in pink tights, like an angel of peace, and beseeching that no one say anything to offend those men over there is all very pretty, but what if they come from over there to offend us with guns?"[6, 7]

The next day, he referred to Bryan's speech with contempt, speaking scornfully of "your Fourth of July orator," saying that "no good can come from telling us on the Fourth of July how great a nation we are unless we are prepared to prove it the other 364 days of the year."[8]

Another July orator was House Speaker Champ Clark, who welcomed the Liberty Bell on July 17. He waffled, saying, "I differ...with the proponents of 'peace at any price.' That is...a demoralizing, a degrading doctrine. On the other hand, I am utterly opposed to those who advocate a large standing army, and to those who advocate a navy equal to the two biggest navies in the world."[9]

In contrast was William Howard Taft, the final US president to pay a visit to the PPIE. On Taft Day, September 2, to an audience of 40,000, the former chief executive called the existing 100,000-man army "ridiculously small...in a country of the expanse of the United States." He suggested that the expiring war tax and sugar tax be renewed to finance increased military equipment and manpower.[10]

The next night, as the flames of a tall bonfire in the Court of the Universe warmed his face, Taft's thoughts turned to his own history with the Exposition. His political heft while president had been instrumental in winning the campaign

On July 21, former president Theodore Roosevelt preached in opposition to Bryan in a fiery speech the "preparedness" advocate called "Peace and War." (Edward A. Rogers)

Thomas Edison (inset, upper left, to the right of Henry Ford and Western Union manager J. G. Decatur) was honored by Telegraph Operators at an October 19 banquet at which all the evening's speeches were delivered in Morse code via telegraph lines strung between the tables. (Laura Ackley)

to host the Fair—it was he who in 1909 declared that "San Francisco knows how"—and he had turned the first spadeful of earth at the Fair's groundbreaking in 1911. On the night of September 3, 1915, he was to drop the deed of trust and the mortgage for the Exposition into the fire on Out of Debt Day.

One hundred thousand spectators watched avidly from the other side of the pyre as Exposition president Charles C. Moore exchanged a check for the balance owed for the mortgage papers. Moore handed the sheaf to Taft, who used a long pair of tongs to toss it onto the flames. A great cheer went up as the papers flared and burned. After the ashes had cooled, aviator Charles Niles bore them aloft and scattered them, a fitting finish to Taft's PPIE involvement.

INVENTORS AND INNOVATORS

Two other influential pacifists came to the Fair in October. For pioneering inventors and personal

friends Henry Ford and Thomas Edison, 1915 followed radically different trajectories. Edison's year began in sadness. When the Exposition opened, he was rebuilding his company and his research after a fire the previous December had destroyed his laboratory in West Orange, New Jersey. Meanwhile, Ford's "model assembly line" in the Palace of Transportation and his employee profit-sharing exhibit in the Palace of Mines were drawing rave reviews.

Edison's year was about to improve. The two friends traveled west with their families in Ford's private rail car to enjoy the Exposition's Edison Day, on October 21. Upon arrival, they were swept up in a series of events celebrating Edison's achievements. General Electric had promoted the event, celebrating the thirty-sixth anniversary of the incandescent electric light with an illustration titled "Edison's Dream Come True." It depicted Edison gazing through a window onto a cityscape made brilliant by his invention. On the night after he arrived, San Franciscans were asked to turn on all their electric lights in honor of the "Wizard of Menlo

Park." A photograph of Edison taken that night, while no doubt partially staged, was a remarkable match to the illustration.

At a banquet of telegraph operators honoring Edison, wires strung between miniature telegraph poles connected the tables, and the "speeches" were made via Morse code. M. H. de Young, a "key man" in his youth, clicked out a description of installing the first electric lights in San Francisco—at his newspaper, the *Chronicle*—in 1878. Edison passed over all the food that evening except apple pie and milk, of which he was famously fond.

Before his public appearance on Edison Day, he and Ford attended a luncheon at which each guest received a full-sized model of the first successful incandescent bulb. At the Inside Inn, Ford and Edison "were the center of throngs that crowded about and shook the hands of the distinguished guests in a thoroughly American, democratic manner." That night Edison attended a dinner cooked entirely by electricity in the Home Electrical exhibit and watched illuminations that featured his likeness executed in fireworks.[11]

Mutual friend and industrialist Harvey Firestone joined the two men in San Francisco. Mr. and Mrs. Edison took a jaunt through the city with Firestone in an open, chauffeur-driven touring car. After their visit to the Fair, Ford and Edison went north to visit agricultural scientist Luther Burbank, the "plant wizard," at his home

Edison and Ford flank Luther Burbank during an October 22 visit to Burbank's farm in Santa Rosa. There the famed plant scientist explained his work and toured the industrialists through his experimental gardens. (*Edison Sales Builder,* December 1915)

Taft ceremonially retired the Fair's debt on September 3, when he dropped the mortgage into a bonfire. (Panama-Pacific International Exposition Photograph Album (SFP17), San Francisco History Center, San Francisco Public Library)

in Santa Rosa, then spent several days touring the Bay Area before traveling to San Diego and the Panama-California Exposition. While both Edison and Burbank had "special days" at the Fair, Ford politely but firmly declined the honor.

While Edison's year had gotten better, Ford's was about to get worse. Ford was a flawed and complex man whose anti-Semitic and anti-union beliefs are well documented. He was also a pacifist and in 1915 had become enamored with the idea that "continuous mediation" could put a quick end to the World War in Europe. He assembled a delegation, chartered a ship, and set sail across the Atlantic in December, despite word from Britain that the mission would be "irritating and unwelcome." His expedition seemed doomed. First it was delayed by storms, then Ford became ill and had to return to New York. Further, the mission was beset by acrimony and, ironically, infighting. Thus, while Edison's year had begun depressingly, it was Ford's that ended poorly.[12]

EMPIRES OF GOLD, SILVER, CHOCOLATE, AND SUGAR

Every night at the Exposition, crystal clinked musically across white tablecloths laden with heavy silver, fancy foodstuffs, and California vintages at banquets for those on the social register. For the "smart set" of San Francisco, the PPIE was the grandest of drawing rooms. Scions of the great California fortunes disported themselves within the walls they had helped build.

Prominent retail families who funded the Exposition included A. Schilling & Co. (coffee and extracts), M. J. Brandenstein & Co. (coffee), D. Ghirardelli Company (chocolate), M. A. Gunst & Co. (cigars), A. P. Hotaling & Co. (whiskey), Hale Brothers (department stores), M. H. de Young (newspaper), and Shreve & Co. (jewelry). Other contributors, descended from gold or silver mining riches, included William Randolph Hearst, Wendell P. Hammon, and James L. Flood. Many of these families were intertwined with banking, railroads, and manufacturing in California. Bankers Isaias W. Hellman, Herbert Fleishhacker, and Ogden Mills supported the PPIE. Also active in the management of the Fair were William H. and Charles T. Crocker, the son and grandson of Charles Crocker, who had been a founder of the Central Pacific Railroad before becoming a banker. Other California-grown businesses that lent funds and cachet were Levi Strauss & Co. (clothing), Adolph B. and Rudolph Spreckels (sugar and banking), Miller & Lux (ranching), Mark L. and William L. Gerstle (commercial ventures, real estate, and liquor), Pope & Talbot (lumber), and Matson Navigation Company (shipping). Magnates of the dry goods, hardware, lumber, milling, fishing, and oil industries threw the heft of their locally made fortunes behind the Fair effort.

Major General George Goethals (left), chief engineer of the Panama Canal, received a cased set of Novagems from PPIE president Charles C. Moore on September 7, Goethals Day at the Exposition. (Edward A. Rogers)

WHISTLEBLOWERS SHUT OUT

The main organizational development of the PPIE occurred in the wake of the corruption scandal that rocked San Francisco city government following the earthquake and fire. Curiously, being on the "righteous" side of the graft trials that began in 1907 consigned several powerful men to the wrong side of the Exposition. The scandal took down political boss Abe Ruef, Mayor Eugene Schmitz, and his board of supervisors after it was discovered that real estate, telephone, railroad, liquor, boxing, and power grid interests had paid bribes to Ruef, who passed them along to Schmitz's administration. The court cases wound down just as the management for the Exposition was selected.

While many of the powerful men implicated as bribe givers and called as witnesses were awarded prominent positions in the Exposition's hierarchy, those who had spearheaded the prosecution were excluded. The elite of the city had supported prosecution of politicians who had accepted "boodle," but that support abruptly ceased when the actions moved up the ladder to the men who had *paid* graft, many of whom were their business and society peers.

San Francisco Bulletin editor Fremont Older, Senator James D. Phelan, and Rudolph Spreckels, banker and scion of the Spreckels sugar fortune, were driving forces behind the graft prosecution, and while all promoted the PPIE, none was rewarded with any significant role in the Fair. *Overland Monthly* magazine said Spreckels "has warred against his class[;] in the eyes of many people he has become a social pariah."[13]

Meanwhile, the Ways and Means Committee of the PPIE, tasked with organizing and financing the proposed Exposition, was chock full of men who had testified, and of the Fair's twenty-nine directors, five had taken the stand: William H. Crocker, Homer S. King, Henry T. Scott, John A. Britton, and Thornwell Mullally. Mullally was actually indicted for his role, but charges against him were dismissed in 1911.

With summering in Europe inadvisable due to the war, many of the East Coast's wealthiest came instead to the Exposition. Floating soirées were held on yachts belonging to the Astor, Harriman, and Spreckels families in the Exposition harbor. Virginia Fair Vanderbilt, who owned the largest plot of Exposition land, was in the grandstand for the Vanderbilt Cup auto race, named in honor of her husband. The Tower of Jewels found a rival when James Buchanan "Diamond Jim" Brady arrived in San Francisco on Independence Day wearing one of his fifteen sets of jewels. The $75,000 "mixed sapphire set" he sported was encrusted with the azure gems and included shirt studs, cufflinks, tie and scarf pins, a watch fob, a belt buckle, a glasses case, and a gold pencil. Even his wallet was monogrammed in sapphires.

In New York, infamous millionaire Harry K. Thaw was so confident of acquittal in his 1915 retrial for the 1906 murder of architect Stanford White that as he listened to testimony he examined a map showing the route from the Big Apple to the Exposition. When freshly freed, Thaw drove over the Lincoln Highway to San Francisco, where a breeze of scandalized whispers followed him about the grounds of the Fair.

DIGNITARIES

Many international dignitaries and nobility attended the Fair, often as official representatives of their countries. These envoys and emissaries included Count Claes Bonde of Sweden, the Vicomte d'Alte of Portugal, Chevalier W. L. F. C. van Rappard of the Netherlands, and the Marquis and Marchioness of Aberdeen, Scotland.

Herr Granada and Mademoiselle Alma Fedora donned a two-person elephant suit and traipsed across a tightrope over the Zone in one of many hair-raising stunts performed by daredevils at the Fair. (Edward A. Rogers)

During visits just prior to Opening Day, Prince Kampengpetch of Siam (Thailand) called the PPIE "magnificent," and Admiral Baron Dewa Shigetō of Japan termed it a "Congress of International Peace."[14, 15]

Lord Richard Plantagenet Nevill, personal emissary of His Majesty George V of England, visited in July and presented a gold trophy cup for sloop racing on behalf of the king. Nevill's visit was considered especially important, as it was the first official recognition of the Exposition by the British government since it had declined participation early in 1914.

The directors and officials of the Jewel City responsible for greeting these august personages constituted their own form of royalty and were known affectionately as the "Silk Hat Brigade." Regular suits were worn for daily business, but for ceremonies they donned "afternoon attire" of long coats and top hats. With so many important visitors to be welcomed, these Exposition men had to be ready to host a reception at a moment's notice, so they took to keeping frock coats and

top hats in their offices should a ceremonial emergency occur.

The PPIE overflowed with generals, colonels, senators, congressmen, governors, mayors, and prominent citizens. An exhaustive list would fill a book, so for scale simply imagine that for every piece of sculpture at the Fair there was a politician or officer lurking about.

"Uncle Joe" Cannon, the pro–San Francisco speaker of the house who represented Illinois, had vowed to dance a Virginia reel at the PPIE should San Francisco defeat New Orleans in the congressional battle for the Fair. He made good on his promise to dance at the Exposition at a banquet on the grounds, though a bruised knee necessitated a sedate waltz in place of a "more strenuous hoedown."[16]

Naturally, many local politicians who'd fought for the right to hold a 1915 world's exposition in San Francisco were on hand to enjoy the fruition of their efforts. These included senator and former mayor James D. Phelan, and James Gillett, who was governor during the crusade.

THE HERO OF THE PANAMA CANAL

One San Franciscan was outraged that the chief engineer of the Isthmian Canal Commission, Major-General George Goethals, had been ignored in favor of daredevil celebrities. In May the *Chronicle* ran an irate anonymous letter from "Sunshine," who asked why "Goethals had been overlooked by the Exposition, while…Roy La Pearl, Art Smith and the tight-rope walker" were prominently featured. The writer continued, "[Goethals] should be worth a bronze plaque, anyway."[17]

"Sunshine" was unaware that Goethals would receive more than a bronze plaque. A day in his honor was already scheduled, during which he was recognized for his achievement with a grand prize. Goethals said on that occasion, "The Exposition was an inspiration to us in our work, for we were continually advised of the progress of its construction, and as the [land]slides increased at Panama we feared the celebration would begin before the thing it celebrated was ready; so we bent every effort to keep pace with

THE EXPOSITION GIRL

Perceptive visitors likely noticed similarities between many of the hundreds of murals and sculptures at the Exposition. They were not alike because of shared artists, styles, or mediums but because approximately 60 percent of the female figures were depictions of the *same woman*, Audrey Munson. Audrey's life had more ups and downs than the Safety Racer on the Zone, and more drama than any of the movies shown in Filmland.

Munson was "discovered" in 1906, when she was fifteen and living in New York. She quickly became a sought-after artists' model. By 1915 she was regarded as the "most perfectly formed woman in the world," and had nicknames including "The Girl with the Cameo Face," "The Exposition Girl," and "The Panama Girl," all of which suited her just fine. Of the PPIE, she said, "I feel a little glow of satisfaction in knowing that I have had ever so small a part in such beautiful work."[18]

She posed for many of the most admired sculptures at the PPIE, including *The Torch Bearer* by Sherry Edmundson Fry, *The Fountain of Ceres* by Evelyn Beatrice Longman, *Descending Night* by Adolph Weinman, and the *Star Maiden*s by Stirling Calder. Her fame was ascendant and her future success seemed assured, but within five years her fortunes had tumbled.

The American Film Company sought to capitalize on Munson's Exposition fame by casting her in three movies between 1915 and 1918: *Inspiration, Purity,* and *The Girl o' Dreams.* In each film the would-be actress played the role of a seldom-clad artists' model.

Before the Hays Code was implemented in 1930, filmic decency was governed in portions of the US by regional censorship boards, which frequently took exception to Audrey's lack of garments. Supporters characterized her films as "art pictures" and "of the highest type," yet slyly referred to them as "the most sensational screen production ever attempted," and "daring, but not offensive." Detractors asked, "Has she no soul?" In any case, her movies were successful. In its first New York run, *Purity* even outdrew *Birth of a Nation*.[19]

Likewise, the statuary at the PPIE came under fire from the founder and president of the Christian League for the Promotion of Purity. "San Francisco with her Barbary Coast is wicked enough," declared Elizabeth Grannis, "without strewing promiscuously through the Exposition grounds sculptured groups which beam with the same lack of wearing apparel that made Lady Godiva quite impossible."[20]

The model didn't see what all the fuss was about. "I have observed that the public is a good deal cleaner minded than most of the people who set themselves up to hand out morality," she asserted. Her notoriety seemed harmless, if titillating, until 1919, when she was embroiled in a lurid scandal involving the hammer murder of the wife of an older man, Dr. Walter Wilkins, from whom Audrey and her mother had rented a room.[21]

Multiple newspapers ran photos of Wilkins under the headline "He's Alleged Wife Murderer," along with a caption that included "[T]he beautiful Audrey Munson, who lived in a house belonging to the doctor's wife, is one of the principal witnesses in the case." While evidence suggests that any relationship with Audrey was in Wilkins' mind only, the damage to the model's reputation was done.[22]

Wilkins was found guilty, and although Audrey was cleared of any involvement, the scandal had dealt her career a fatal blow. The American Film Company cancelled her contract, she was unable to find modeling work, and she was left to share a shabby rented room with her mother. "I'll never count for anything again," she lamented. "The Wilkins case has ruined my career. From loving and admiring me, the public has turned to hating me."[23]

Audrey was determined to come back, but her efforts seemed increasingly desperate and more than passing strange. A series of articles under her name was syndicated nationally, describing her colorful escapades in glamorous artists' ateliers across the globe. She signed a contract to star in a film called *The Soul Within*, based on her own experiences, but she left the production after a few weeks, and most of the scenes were shot using another actress. The movie was eventually released under the title *Heedless Moths* and received scathing reviews. Where critics previously had called her performances "charming," "innocent," or "natural," now they said she was "atrociously bad" in a film only created to give her a chance to pose nude.

In a bizarre August 1921 proclamation, she announced to the newspapers that she would marry any man who met her exact specifications for physical perfection to equal her own beauty. These included a height of six feet, weight of 187 pounds, a forty-two-inch chest, eighteen-inch biceps, and nine-inch wrists. More than 250 men from across the nation responded to her challenge, and she settled on an aviator-turned-contractor named Joseph J. Stevenson of Ann Arbor, Michigan. Her critics reported no such man could be found in Ann Arbor or the vicinity.

Over the years her behavior became increasingly odd, and after a suicide attempt in 1922, Audrey largely disappeared from public view. For a few years, she and her mother lived in upstate New York, where the former model's behavior earned her the nickname "Crazy Audrey." A judge committed her to the state asylum at Ogdensburg, New York, on her fortieth birthday, in 1931. She remained institutionalized until her death in 1996, at the age of 104.

Journalist Clarence Locan predicted her legacy when he wrote in 1920, "Audrey Munson is 'done' as a popular favorite—by a turn of fate's wheel. But her memory will live in San Francisco in the memory of those wonderful white statues—symbols of purity and monument to the enterprise of the great city beside the Golden Gate. So no matter what she may have done or failed to do, Audrey Munson, when she goes out of this world, will leave something behind."[24]

Audrey Munson, the "Exposition Girl" who posed for more than half of the sculptures of women at the PPIE, led a life as melodramatic as any modern starlet's. (*Sunset*, July 1915) you." Goethals may have been exaggerating for his appreciative PPIE audience, as the canal opened on August 15, 1914, and the Fair opened a full six months later.[25]

THE GRANDEST PLAYGROUND IN THE WORLD

Writer William Saroyan was a six-year-old living in an Oakland orphanage when a kindly volunteer took him and seven other small boys to the Exposition. He recalled, "We saw shining, almost imaginary buildings, full of unbelievable works of sculpture, painting, weaving, basket-making, products of agriculture, and all kinds of magical inventions. It was too much of course for one day, but even when it was time to leave we did so with great reluctance, looking back as if we had been in a place that couldn't possibly be real."[26]

For children, the PPIE was a paradise almost beyond fantasy, and a visit to the Fair was indelibly impressed on the memory of any youngster who attended. For a quarter—sometimes even less—a kid could spend a day wandering the wide aisles of the palaces, fascinated by the working models, many of them illuminated and animated: gold mines, farms, factories, temples, castles, engines, ocean liners, submarines, airplanes, trains, all sorts of industrial machines, and even a house fly thirty-two times its usual size. His martial fires might be ignited by the crisp unison marching of the marine regiment stationed on the grounds. And naturally the siren's call of the Zone could not be denied. What child ever could resist the lure of cotton candy, a roller coaster, exotic sideshows, or the chance to win a souvenir? Children also marched in parades, gave concerts, competed in athletics, and danced at myriad celebrations.

Some youngsters had big roles to play. By the time she was five years old, angelic little Katherine Haglund had made a small career of "official mascotism." In 1912 the blonde-ringleted two-year-old Harbor View resident was crowned queen of the "San Francisco Beautiful" contest, and the

San Francisco's 1915 Mascot

Five-year-old Katherine Olivia Haglund was the Exposition's "Little Mascot." (Chuck Banneck)

next year she was "Balboa's Little Sweetheart" at the Portola Festival. In 1914, at age four, she drove her own automobile in a parade.

When Mayor Jim Rolph answered in the affirmative to her plea of "Mr. Mayor, make me 1915 mascot," Katherine became the Jewel City's official kiddie symbol. She was featured in a variety of costumes on postcards published by her father prior to the Exposition, but her real pinnacle came during the Fair. She raised the flag on the Cuban Pavilion, rode in an antique Wells Fargo stagecoach on Opening Day, and was pushed around the Fair in a wheeled wicker chair adorned with masses of flowers. Katherine seems to have retired from the mascot business after running for "fairy queen" at the 1916 Halloween festival in Golden Gate Park. Whether she was selected is not recorded.[27]

Haglund was not the only living talisman of the PPIE. Butler, an affectionate black and white mongrel dog, appeared at the grounds shortly after construction started and was adopted as a good luck charm. Soon the honorary menagerie included a female dog named Pannie, a three-legged cat who lived in the Palace of Food Products, and a carrier pigeon that nested in the abandoned Fulton Iron Works on the site. Mr. and Mrs. Joseph Ethen proudly announced on March 28, 1915, that their new son would be called "Paul Peter Ivan," which gave him the initials "P.P.I.E."

Several others who were youngsters during the PPIE went on to become acclaimed later in life. When high school senior Alexander "Sandy" Calder visited the sculpture workshop on the grounds, his eyes were drawn not to behemoth sea monsters, horses thrice a man's height, or the immense elephant from the *Nations of the East* but to the slender, animated iron arms of the Sculpto-point, used to enlarge small models into giant statues. In 1965 he explained why the device enthralled him: "The small sculpture and the framework for the large sculpture were placed on two turntables which turned together through sprockets and a bicycle chain. The sculptor would put a cross on the small plaster figure and drive a nail into the wood framework where the other needle came. I'd be particularly fascinated by the mechanics, the rotating motions and the parallel needles of the process." This inclination toward the mechanical presaged his future. After graduating from San Francisco's Lowell High School in 1915, Alexander Calder studied mechanical engineering at the Stevens Institute of Technology and became an innovative mobile-maker and sculptor.[28]

The Exposition was intended to be an educational forum—an extension of school— and for many special "city and county days," schools were closed so children could attend. In keeping with his vision of the Exposition as a university of the world, President Moore approved a plan in which groups of twenty or more students would pay only five cents admission each on weekdays if accompanied by a teacher. In many cases, a wealthy sponsor covered transportation, admission, meals, and treats for the children of his city.

For at least one child, the Exposition literally *was* his classroom. Ansel Adams, destined to become a famed photographer, celebrated his thirteenth birthday on Opening Day of the Exposition. His father bought him a season ticket book and said that if he kept up his home study of literature, language, and piano, the Exposition would be his school for the year. In

Virginia Stephens of Oakland was twelve years old when she suggested "The Jewel City" as the Fair's official nickname, winning a contest sponsored by the *San Francisco Call*. (*The Crisis*, November 1915)

his autobiography Adams wondered whether seeing the art of Bonnard, Cézanne, Gauguin, Monet, Pissarro, and Van Gogh at the Exposition might have influenced his own work.

He also characterized the Exposition as in some ways tawdry, calling it "a glorious and obviously temporary stage set, a symbolic fantasy, and a dream world of color and style." And as a youth unfettered by proper behavior or fences, he saw a side of the Fair many did not. He liked to cut through the alleyways behind the Zone as the most direct route to the streetcar that would take him home to the far side of the Presidio. One night, on his way through this land of "plywood, tar paper, trash[,]...drunks and assorted strange fragments of humanity," he was terrified when he encountered a man injecting himself with "a huge syringe." Adams was so frightened that he got on the wrong streetcar, but when he finally arrived home he was comforted by his father's words that a drug addict was to be pitied, not feared.[29]

The child who had the most profound effect on the Exposition was a twelve-year-old schoolgirl from Oakland. Virginia Stephens was the first person to suggest "Jewel City" when the *San Francisco Call* newspaper held a contest to give the Fair a nickname. Mayor Rolph's committee decided quickly and unanimously on her suggestion because it exemplified the "color, the magnificence and the distinction of the Fair."[30]

While San Francisco was more racially integrated than many parts of the nation, there was no escaping the fact that Virginia, who was African American, was growing up in a segregated country led by a pro-segregation president. Her father was wary of announcing her identity lest she be denied the honor of naming the Fair on account of her race. The NAACP magazine the *Crisis* noted that "when it was discovered that Miss Stephens had colored blood, there was a sudden silence on the part of the press and the only recognition ever given her was a season ticket to the grounds." Whether the lack of recognition was a racially based slight or a simple omission is open to debate, but her community, and especially pioneering journalist Delilah Beasley, were determined she should be recognized.[31]

Oakland's Bournemouth Circle club held the Jewel City Ball at which Virginia was presented with a gold cross necklace and a bouquet of roses. On a fair, breezy summer day, Virginia rode in state through the streets of San Francisco on a float emblazoned with a large banner identifying her as having named the Fair. The float bore about fifty African American children and was organized by the Alameda County Colored American Civic Center.

Virginia's early successes were predictive of her adult achievements. When she won the *Call* contest, she had just been promoted to eighth grade at the top of her class. Mary Church Terrell, a journalist and the founding president of the National Association of Colored Women, said of her, "One might travel a long distance before meeting a girl with brighter eyes, a more intelligent, pleasant countenance and a more prepossessing personality." Virginia attended the University of California at Berkeley, graduated from Boalt Law School, and in 1929 became the first African American woman admitted to the bar in California. She went on to a long career in the State Office of Legislative Counsel.[32]

Intrepid aeronauts filled their balloons with gas from the Exposition mains on June 9 in a contest to see which would cover the most distance. High winds ripped three of the balloons, and only one, the aptly named *Jewel City*, launched safely. (Edward A. Rogers)

THE DAREDEVILS

BALLOONS, BICYCLES, AND BALANCE

No world's fair would be complete without the pleasantly neck-tingling thrill of watching someone else risk his skin doing something patently unwise. The PPIE had more than its fair share of daredevil performers.

The windy evening of June 9 was a singularly bad time to start a long-distance balloon competition. Flags snapped atop the north wall of the Exposition and salty spray misted the thousands of spectators struggling to keep their hats in place. Four silken bags flapped wildly in the breeze as they were inflated with natural gas from the Exposition's pipes. Two of the balloons never made it aloft after gusts tore their fragile fabric. The *Venice* was almost filled when she, too, ripped. Her pilot, Leon Brooks, cried, "[T]urn her loose," and scrambled into the basket, which dragged and hopped across the lawn. Just as the *Venice* reached the water's edge, the wind died

and the balloon leapt into the air and out over the bay. The basket dropped into the water as gas escaped from the rent, and the folds of silk came down upon Brooks. As he struggled to get free of the entangling fabric, a tugboat shot out of the harbor and fished the damp aeronaut out of the bay.

The final balloon, fittingly called *Jewel City,* was the only craft to make it aloft without incident, but the wind had not finished its mischief. While coasting over the Central Valley, a 30 m.p.h. gale opened the bag's release valve and the *Jewel City* came down at Collegeville, near Stockton, about seventy-one miles from the Fair. Pilots George Harrison and Clarence Drake endured a bumpy ride across half a mile of tilled fields until they were able to escape the basket. Their flight lasted only two and a half hours—not quite the thirty- or forty-hour journey for which they were provisioned. The next day, one of the torn balloons, the *California,* was repaired, and it floated away from the Exposition bearing Edward Unger and Guy Slaughter, who made it

Dario Resta (holding trophy) drove a Peugot to victory in the two major auto races held at the PPIE: the Grand Prix on February 27 and the Vanderbilt Cup eight days later. (Donna Ewald Huggins)

to the town of Patterson, narrowly outdistancing Harrison and Drake and winning the contest in anticlimactic fashion.

But Unger's exploits were not complete. Next he piloted the *Jewel City* in her ascent from the Exposition on June 21. He was accompanied by Drake and another colleague, Thomas McClain, in pursuit of the balloon high-altitude record. They set an American mark at 28,900 feet but failed to match the 35,420-foot world's record. However, Drake set a new parachute mark when he jumped from the basket at 14,200 feet and splashed into the bay. His compatriot, who dropped sooner, slightly injured his arm when he landed on a pipe in the Southern Pacific yards. The doctor's write-up of McClain's case read, "Patient states he fell 8,500 feet and scratched his elbow."[33]

The Joy Zone was a natural home for stunts, including Oscar Babcock's Death Trap Loop, which was set up in the Zone's central plaza. Babcock plunged down a seventy-five-foot-tall ramp on a bicycle and whirled around a vertical loop that snapped open to receive him. Once escaping the loop, the rider shot across a twenty-five-foot gap onto a landing platform. On one souvenir photo of the contraption, Babcock scrawled an earnest thank-you to his chiropractor.

On other days, guests strolling through the Joy Zone, nibbling on Orange Blossom candy and wondering whether to pay a dime to ride the Bowls of Joy, were startled to see an elephant walking a tightrope seven stories above their heads, a balancing pole clutched in its trunk. A closer look revealed this to be a papier-mâché pachyderm atop four human legs.

THE AUTOMOBILE RACES

The effigies of Cortez and Pizarro watched impassively, rain dripping from the plaster noses of their steeds, as three dozen cars careened past, spattering mud upon their stony boots. The four-hundred-mile Grand Prix on February 27 was the first of the two major auto races at the Exposition. Eight days later, the tolerant horsemen were engulfed in clouds of dust when

A jaunty Silvio Pettirossi waves to the crowd as he takes off from the Marina Green during the Exposition. (Laura Ackley)

the three-hundred-mile Vanderbilt Cup was run.

The course for both races was hair-raising, starting from the plank-paved racetrack on the Presidio shoreline, running past the foreign pavilions, down the Avenue of Palms, and circling counterclockwise around the palaces, a route that included 90-degree intersections entering and leaving the Avenue of Progress. Some of the world's star drivers competed in the two contests, including Barney Oldfield, Eddie Rickenbacker, and the 1914 Grand Prix and Vanderbilt Cup victors, Eddie Pullen and Ralph DePalma.

Oldfield made a name for himself first racing bicycles, then automobiles, and in 1914 he and Lincoln Beachey staged a series of races pitting Oldfield's Fiat against Beachey's airplane. Rickenbacker was another successful automobile racer who drove Maxwell cars at the PPIE, but today he is better known for his exploits as a fighter pilot. By the end of World War I, he had twenty-six aerial victories against the Germans, and his nickname changed from "Fast Eddie" to the "Ace of Aces."

But it was a newly arrived Italian driver, Dario Resta, who swept across the finish first in both contests, victorious in both slippery and dry conditions. His Peugeot averaged 56.1 m.p.h. for the Grand Prix and 67.5 m.p.h. for the Vanderbilt Cup. The latter pace would have been faster if Resta had not stopped to offer

Aviator Lincoln Beachey's fatal March 14, 1915, fall was captured in this image, in which the broken wings of his Taube monoplane are clearly visible. (Donna Ewald Huggins)

assistance to "Wild Bob" Burman, who crashed spectacularly when he failed to negotiate the left-hand turn between the Palace of Machinery and the Marina Green. Burman's car flipped over the protective hay bale barrier and landed on top of the driver and his mechanic, Joe Cleary. The driver escaped serious injury, but Cleary sustained several broken bones. Like so many drivers of his era, Burman was not so lucky the following April, when he and another mechanic died in a crash at Corona, California.

THE AVIATORS

Lincoln Beachey, who flew his plane through the Palace of Machinery during its construction, was a hometown favorite. His flights were a major attraction of the pre-Exposition period and through the first few weeks of the Exposition. Tragically, he was killed at the Fair on March 14, 1915. Beachey was flying upside-down at insufficient altitude, requiring a tight loop to right his craft. According to accounts, the strain of the maneuver caused the wings of his new Taube monoplane to shear off, sending him into the bay, where he perished, apparently by drowning rather than from the impact. After brief debate, flights resumed at the Exposition the first week of April with pilot Art Smith.

Journalist R. L. Duffus captured the melancholy occasioned by Beachey's death in his 1960 book, *The Tower of Jewels*:

Beachey was replaced by Art Smith without delay. Flying was fun, it seemed, if you didn't get killed, and Art Smith didn't.... What if Beachey, spirit of the dawn, luminary in the night, died strapped in his plane? Art Smith took his place, and did not die.[34]

Wholesome-looking Indiana "Bird Boy" Art Smith was slight of build, with an engaging wide grin and a fondness for wearing his jaunty newsboy cap backward. He became the PPIE's favorite celebrity performer—posing with visiting dignitaries, driving a midget race car, and slipping into the barrel of a canon for a photo opportunity. Smith even had his own catchy tune, predictably titled "Flying."

The *Chronicle* described one night flight when 60,000 spectators watched Smith perform:

It was truly the night of nights in the career of the young airman.... Like a great comet the biplane rose from the center of the north gardens....Four times he soared around and around the great field like a flaming projectile suddenly hurled into the air....Then he started a series of loops and dips. Nine times the boy turned over and over, then dipped, flew upside down and finally dived into a low fog bank that lay over the waters of the bay....For a moment the blazing plane would be veiled in the mist of the fog, then with a roar as of a living thing protesting against the mad dash upward, would emerge and once more the series of spirals, dips and glides held the onlookers breathless.[35]

Smith left San Francisco in August to tour other parts of the country, and Charles Niles and Silvio Pettirossi took up the stunt flying duties. "Do Anything" Niles dropped bombs on a model fort as part of sham battles and even raced against a speedboat. On San Francisco Day, November 2, he "beat the motor boat 'Oregon Kid' in a 10-mile race through fog and cloud-rack, making nearly a mile a minute up and down the 2-1/2 mile course before the Marina."[36]

One day in September, Paraguayan Pettirossi narrowly escaped Beachey's fate when his engine malfunctioned and he, too, fell a thousand feet into the bay. Pettirossi coolly unfastened his harness before he hit the water, emerged uninjured, and stood atop the floating plane until a fisherman could retrieve him.

Among those also taking to the air was the Sun-Maid Raisin girl, Lorraine Collett, the model for the original image of a red-bonnetted brunette bearing a tray of grapes. She went up in a plane and tossed raisins to the fairgoers below.

Art Smith received a hero's welcome when he returned to the PPIE in November again to dazzle the crowds with his stunts, which included loops, death spirals, and night flights with phosphorus fireworks cascading from the fabric wings of his plane.

VESTIGES OF FRONTIER

Growing up in Indiana, Art Smith idolized frontiersman William Cody, whose Wild West show made him one of the most recognizable Americans in the world. So the young flyer was thrilled when one day his plane touched down on the grass of the Marina and "Buffalo Bill" was waiting to greet him. Cody took from his long frock coat a pin fashioned from a gold nugget he'd panned himself and worn for twenty-five years and presented it to Smith. Smith later said he was glad he was still strapped into the plane as Cody pinned it to his lapel, because "I couldn't have stood up while that pin was being hung on me."[37]

If Smith represented a new era, Cody was emblematic of one that was passing but was still close enough to see and touch. For many visitors to the Exposition, the romantic idea of the western frontier was still tantalizing, and exhibitors strove to indulge their fascination. Many of the signal events of the nineteenth century were within living memory, and their survivors attended the Fair. Buffalo Bill himself had been a Pony Express rider and US Army scout. Now he was in town with the Sells-Floto Circus after his own show had gone bankrupt.

Pilot Silvio Pettirossi's plane fell into the bay after an engine malfunction September 2, but he was able to unbuckle his harness and escape. Pettirossi (in hood) stood casually in a fishing boat after his rescue. (Chuck Banneck)

During a parade of the 101 Ranch troupe from the Joy Zone through the fairgrounds in June, young Seneca chief John American Big Tree reined in abruptly in front of James Earle Fraser's *End of the Trail* sculpture and leapt from the saddle. He touched the figure with joy, for he had posed for the heroic statue at Fraser's New York studio in 1913, not knowing the work's destination. Big Tree became a celebrity on the Zone and went on to a film career that spanned five decades. He also claimed his profile was one of three used by Fraser to create a composite portrait for the Buffalo nickel.

EDUCATORS AND ACTIVISTS

With an entire Exposition palace devoted to Education and Social Economy, teachers flocked to the Fair to learn about the latest ideas in their profession. Of all the speakers at the more than one hundred educational conferences held on the grounds, the most memorable were an Italian doctor and a blind and deaf activist and her teacher.

Dottoressa Maria Montessori, the first woman to earn a medical degree from the University of Rome and creator of the Montessori Method of education, came to speak and teach at the Fair. When she first arrived, she was feted at a luncheon in the California Building, where "her address, in Italian, was a plea for individuality." She returned later in the year to open a glass-walled model schoolroom in the Palace of Education and give a series of twenty lectures at the Exposition Auditorium and the Palace Hotel.[38]

The previous year she had met deaf and blind author and activist Helen Keller and her teacher, Anne Sullivan Macy, and marveled at how Sullivan Macy's approach to teaching paralleled her own. Sullivan Macy had never heard of Montessori when she confronted the difficulties of teaching Keller in 1887, but the techniques she developed were remarkably similar to those the Italian educator codified years later.

The teacher had discovered that Keller did not respond well to traditional discipline and therefore created free-form lessons around

When aviator Art Smith met his boyhood hero Buffalo Bill Cody, the famous westerner presented the flyer a pin fashioned from the first gold nugget the showman had found. (California History Room, California State Library, Sacramento, California)

Eighty-four-year-old Ezra Meeker displayed two taxidermied oxen, Dave and Dandy, in the Palace of Transportation. In his twenties he'd traveled the Oregon Trail in a covered wagon, and in old age he was dedicated to preserving the emigrant path, traversing it repeatedly, placing historical markers, and promoting its memory.

Winema "Toby" Riddle was hailed as the "Modoc War Heroine" during her November visit to the PPIE. A member of the Modoc tribe, she married a white settler and served as an interpreter and negotiator in the 1872–73 war on the California-Oregon border. The US government had attempted to relocate the Modoc to a reservation inhabited by the antagonistic Klamath tribe, and the Modocs resisted. Winema Riddle saved the life of Alfred Meacham, chairman of a peace commission, during a skirmish in the forbidding Lava Beds. She traveled from Oregon to see the PPIE, where she pronounced herself astounded by the buildings and exhibits.

the girl's interests. For instance, she saw it was pointless to teach Keller math when "she wanted to sail a boat." Instead Sullivan (her name at the time) substituted a lesson on navigation. "I changed the lesson as soon as Helen began to lose interest....Soon we were progressing so fast that it seemed almost too pleasant...." In 1904 Keller received her diploma from Radcliffe University, making her the first deaf and blind person to earn a Bachelor of Arts degree.[39]

The three women met again in mutual admiration on November 6, designated Helen Keller Day at the PPIE. Montessori declared Keller "the first pupil of the school of freedom" and said she considered "her teacher my teacher." Keller professed her deep interest in Montessori's work, saying, "I have learned the delight of doing things I love to learn and do, and through this free method I have been helped to build up my life in spite of many obstacles and discouragements."[40, 41]

In April Keller stopped by the women's suffrage booth and donated a portrait of herself.

Of her tour of the palaces and courts, Keller said she could "feel" the colors of the Exposition, and she especially appreciated the sculpture. "Oh, the exposition!" she exclaimed. "I felt that I was in Africa, Asia. I felt the wonderful California sunshine! I smelled the glorious flowers, and I saw the beautiful sculptures. They let me put my fingers over it, you see."[42]

She also took a ride on the Aeroscope on the Zone, made friends with "Captain, the Educated Horse," and became an unintentional escape artist. Her Festival Hall lecture with Sullivan Macy was so well-received that Keller had to climb out a window at the back of the building to evade her adoring fans.

Coincidentally, the most renowned escape artist in the world happened to be at the Fair on Helen Keller Day. Patrons had to choose between the ceremony honoring Keller and watching Harry Houdini, shackled and nailed into a crate weighted with five hundred pounds of pig iron, being dropped into the bay off the Exposition.

World's bucking-horse champion Dorothy Morrell, who performed at the 101 Ranch show on the Zone, also spoke at a women's suffrage conference at the Exposition in June. (Chuck Banneck)

Zintkala Nuni Allen played the role of Sacajawea in a suffrage pageant held in the Court of Ages. Like Lewis and Clark's famed guide, her short life was beset by tragedy. (*Sunset,* October 1915)

THE FEMININE FAIR

Several conferences promoting women's issues drew female celebrities to the Fair. Ishbel Hamilton-Gordon, Marchioness of Aberdeen and Temair, charmed local society when she presided over the International Congress of Women, which advocated human rights for women. In early July the Fair hosted the International Conference of Women Workers to Promote Permanent Peace. But no issue was discussed more than suffrage for women.

California had given women the vote in 1911, but national suffrage was still bitterly contested. The suffrage booth in the Palace of Education featured a registry for supporters, a display on the suffrage voting record of every congressman, and a large portrait of Susan B. Anthony. One of the Exposition guides even joked that the crowning female statue in the Court of Ages, Chester Beach's *Intelligence,* was actually "the highest product of civilization—a suffragette."[43]

The toughest suffragist may have been Dorothy Morrell, bronco-buster at the 101 Ranch. The petite young woman had large, dark eyes and a winsome smile framed by a cloud of brunette hair. She was also the reigning women's rough-riding champion of the world. During the second show on the afternoon of April 14, Dorothy's leg was broken when she was thrown and trampled by her horse in the 101 Ranch arena on the Zone. She was told she would never ride again.

Morrell used the downtime afforded by her injury to support the vote for women. Because she was not performing, Morrell was able to speak at the first of several suffrage conferences held at the PPIE, that of the Congressional Union for Woman Suffrage. On June 2 she told a crowd in the ballroom of the Inside Inn that while she might not ride a thrashing horse again, she "would always be able to handle the ballot." Eventually, she was able to do both, as by the next year she was literally back in the saddle and had years more rodeo success.[44]

Several nationally known suffrage workers spoke at the Exposition, including Alice Park, Alva Belmont, Esther Pohl Lovejoy, May Wright Sewall, Ida Husted Harper, Crystal Eastman

Benedict, Anita Charlotte Whitney, and Clara Bewick Colby.

Few knew that the tall, striking Native American woman performing in the Federal Suffrage Association pageant in July was Mrs. Colby's adopted daughter. Appearing on stage as Sacajawea, the stately Zintkala Nuni Allen presented an appealing picture of a young woman who had successfully integrated her Lakota heritage with modern American life. Newspapers described how she had been found in the frozen arms of her dead mother at the massacre of Wounded Knee in 1890 and was raised by Brigadier General Leonard Colby and his wife, Clara, a dedicated suffragist. *Sunset* magazine ran a full-page photo of Zintkala arrayed in an elaborate fringed costume, gazing solemnly past the reader. Her elegant appearance belied a life of tragedy during which she was never comfortable with or accepted by either of her cultures.

General Colby brought his National Guard regiments to Wounded Knee after the massacre and removed Zintkala Nuni, whose name means "Lost Bird," from the Lakota survivors' camp by duplicitous means, as a sort of human trophy. While the Colbys professed sympathy for the plight of Native Americans, they believed it would be best if Zintkala was removed from her tribe and educated in a Christian, Caucasian tradition.

Her adoptive father soon lost interest in the young girl, whom he termed "my relic of the Sioux War of 1891," and after an affair with the family nanny that produced a son, he dropped in and out of the lives of Zintkala, Clara, and another adopted child, Clarence. Clara finally divorced Colby in 1906.[45]

At sixteen, "Zintka" ran away from a school in Oregon and joined a Wild West show in South Dakota. In 1908 her absentee adopted father incarcerated her at a "reformatory home," where she gave birth to a stillborn boy. In 1909 she impulsively married and then divorced a man who gave her the incurable syphilis that gradually robbed her of sight. By 1914 she had married twice more and had two children, the younger of whom died in infancy. She struggled to survive as a Hollywood extra, in Wild West shows, and in vaudeville with her third husband, Ernest "Dick" Allen.

When her adoptive mother traveled to the San Francisco for the suffrage meeting, the nearly destitute Zintkala jumped at the chance to perform in Clara's pageant, which would depict the achievements of American women. Though also impoverished, Clara paid all of Zintka's expenses and gave her $10. This was the last time they would meet. Clara died of pneumonia in 1916.

The lovely "Lost Bird," who proudly represented her gender and her people in the flickering torchlight of the opulent Court of Ages, did not live to see thirty. Zintkala contracted Spanish influenza near the end of the 1918–20 pandemic and died February 14, 1920, six months before the Nineteenth Amendment was ratified and national women's suffrage—Clara Colby's lifelong dream—was granted.

TROUBADOURS

Harmonious voices rang across the courtyards nearly every day as singers in styles ranging from classical opera to vaudeville entertained. At times, the most sophisticated performers shared the stage with novelty stars. On Liberal Arts Day, soprano Inga Orner led the audience in the national anthem and sang arias from her days as a prima donna at Covent Garden and the Metropolitan Opera. Later that afternoon, stage and eventual movie icon Al Jolson borrowed bandleader Cassasa's baton and led the Official Band.

One lunchtime, the "thousands of people contentedly munching sandwiches and resting from the exertions of the morning, heard a deep mellow voice float out over the grounds, from an unseen source, in the jocund melody 'I'm on My Way to Dublin Bay.'" The voice was that of Roy La Pearl, who was standing on a parapet of the Tower of Jewels more than four hundred feet above his listeners. Also known as the "Singing Blacksmith" or the "Man with the Big Voice," La Pearl had made a career out of his vocal carrying power. He'd sung from a 110-foot-tall pavilion at Kennywood Park in Pennsylvania and the 750-foot Metropolitan Life Building and 790-

foot Woolworth Tower in New York. In 1920 La Pearl's "cannon baritone" defeated George Offerman's "steam calliope tenor" in a $1,000 singing contest on the roof of the 350-foot Masonic Temple on Chicago's downtown loop.[46]

Less impressive was presidential daughter Margaret Woodrow Wilson's sweet but rather thin rendition of "The Star-Spangled Banner," which was sold at the fair for $1 per record. The label read: "This record of my voice if sold by the Columbia Graphophone Company shall yield to the American Red Cross the sum of 25 cents covering my entire royalty."

THE SILVER SCREEN COMES TO SAN FRANCISCO

Tinseltown's luster dimmed temporarily in July when many of its most luminous stars visited the Exposition to attend a conference of the Motion Picture Exhibitors Association. The keynote speaker, producer/director D. W. Griffith, was then at the center of a roiling controversy involving racism and censorship.

The PPIE marked the first exposition featuring a fully fledged movie industry. At the convention,

Judge A. P. Tugwell of the International Motion Picture Association noted the first motion picture at a world's fair was shown in 1893 using a crude machine "in an obscure little corner of the grounds." The film was 120 feet in length, making the clip between five and eight seconds long. As the first nickelodeon had opened in 1904, the PPIE was the first world's fair at which the developing issues relating to production, distribution, and exhibition were argued.[47]

"It might be compared to the early days in gold mining in California, when plenty of free gold was found," said W. W. Hodkinson, president of Paramount Pictures. "After the free gold was exhausted, it was necessary that a property be developed. That is what we have to do today—develop our property."[48]

Griffith's controversial film *The Birth of a Nation* was raking in profits and raising hackles nationwide with its explicitly racist depiction of African Americans and glorification of the Ku Klux Klan. The film, however, was also a new acme in storytelling and technical filmmaking and was very profitable, though it incited protests and riots and was banned in some markets. The NAACP had tried, largely in vain, to have

Many movie stars, including Charlie Chaplin, Mabel Normand, and Roscoe "Fatty" Arbuckle, frolicked at the Fair. Normand and Arbuckle even shot a short film at the Exposition. (Chuck Banneck)

the racist scenes censored. For all its technical achievements, the film reinvigorated the Klan and gave fangs to the censorship movement.

At the Exposition, Griffith gave an address, "The Rise and Fall of Free Speech," arguing against the suppression of his film on the grounds that it was a morality play. Without freedom to depict characters in good and bad lights, "a play is of no educational value," he said. The filmmaker concluded dramatically, "The motion picture is a form of speech as beautiful and clean as that ever discovered by the mind of man...."[49]

The Supreme Court had just handed down a decision that movies were not protected speech under the First Amendment, and pro-censorship forces used *The Birth of a Nation* as a rallying point, a classic case of a bad action prompted by good intentions. The court's decision was not reversed until 1952.

Metro Day, July 15, honored the Metro Pictures Corporation. Its lantern-jawed leading man, Francis X. Bushman, was awarded a bronze medal, and the following evening a grand ball closed the convention. Movie fans were able to dance with their idols, including actors Geraldine Farrar, Lillian and Dorothy Gish, Raymond Hitchcock, Fred Mace, Mae Marsh, Beatriz Michelena, Owen Moore, Mabel Normand, House Peters, Blanche Sweet, and Marguerite Snow, and directors Mack Sennett and Cecil B. De Mille.

Charlie Chaplin, who spent the spring in Northern California filming *A Jitney Elopement,* took time off to explore the Fair. He whirled around the carousel on the back of a giraffe to the tune "Sister Susie's Sewing Shirts for Soldiers." The comedic actor took in Henry Ellsworth's Dayton Flood spectacle and rode the Aeroscope, but when Alligator Joe offered to let the actor handle his saurians, Chaplin politely declined.

Vivacious comedienne Mabel Normand frolicked through the Fair in April with her frequent onscreen partner, Roscoe "Fatty" Arbuckle, as they filmed *Fatty and Mabel Viewing the World's Fair at San Francisco*. On the steps of City Hall, under construction at the time, Mayor "Sunny Jim" Rolph presented the two with a card reading "Permitting Mr. Arbuckle

Gold rush–era stage actress and singer Lotta Crabtree made her final public appearance at the 1915 Fair. (Edward A. Rogers)

& Miss Normand to take pictures anywhere in San Francisco."

In the movie, Arbuckle meets opera star Madame Ernestine Schumann-Heink, who was in town following the special concert she had given just for children in the Festival Hall. As San Francisco winds try to lift the contralto's wide-brimmed feathered hat, Arbuckle gives her a sample of his own vocal abilities. Smiling impishly, Madame quickly covers his mouth with her gloved hand.

While Madame Schumann-Heink was the maternal figure among the Exposition's entertainers, Lotta Crabtree, though now a senior citizen, remained the much-adored kid sister. Crabtree was the most beloved performer to appear at the PPIE and was a living reminder of San Francisco's gold rush past. Lotta Crabtree Day was celebrated on November 9 at the Festival Hall, where the petite actress made her final public appearance.

Lotta, born in 1847, had been the darling of gold-rush era stages. As a child performer she had danced and sung ballads at mining camps, where enthusiastic forty-niners would toss gold nuggets onto the stage in appreciation. She became a national star during the latter decades of the 1800s before retiring from the stage in 1891 and eventually settling near Boston. In 1875 she had commissioned Lotta's Fountain at the corner of Market and Kearny in San Francisco, and after the 1906 quake, it became an impromptu meeting place where people would gather to learn news of their loved ones' whereabouts. To this day, citizens congregate at the fountain every April 18 at 5:12 a.m. to mark the anniversary of the disaster. Sirens ring out, followed by a moment of silence honoring the victims of the calamity.

For the first part of Lotta's 1915 homecoming festivities on November 6, thousands cheered as she rode down Kearny Street to her fountain in a barouche drawn by four white horses. When she reached the outdoor stage constructed for the occasion, adoring San Franciscans showered her with yellow chrysanthemums instead of gold nuggets. The still-gamine Lotta said, "My dear, old San Francisco. You were good to me in the old days, and you are good to me now." The next day she celebrated her sixty-eighth birthday at the St. Francis Hotel, where her room was filled with the California poppies she had said she longed to see.[50]

To San Francisco she represented the innocent side of its early boom, and on Lotta Day the Festival Hall was full to capacity, while 10,000 more crowded outside, hoping to see their idol of old. Silver-haired men and women who'd seen Lotta perform in their youth filled the first few rows. She received a bronze medal from Exposition president Charles C. Moore and a gold nugget from the town of Weaverville, and she watched as two little girls wearing replicas of her costumes danced in her style.

But the most poignant moment of the day occurred when Lotta arose to speak. After receiving her honors, Lotta's voice broke with emotion: "This is a very, very beautiful occasion….It doesn't seem possible that a little speck like me should be so honored. I thank you most sincerely. I—I just can't speak." So, instead, she reached over the footlights to shake the hands of her admirers.[51]

TALES OF THE FAIR

Wielders of the pen were plentiful at the Fair. Fiction writers, particularly those of kids' serials, had a field day using the Exposition as a setting for their tales. With so many characters running about, it's a wonder that Lieutenant Howard Payson's Boy Scouts didn't encounter Elizabeth Gordon's Twins as they explored the palaces. But certainly "Gullible," Mollie Slater Merrill's anthropomorphized seagull, must have conferred with "Billy Whiskers," Frances Trego Montgomery's anthropomorphized goat. There was also a cottage industry in writing about hayseeds at world's fairs around the turn of the century, and famous imaginary hicks Uncle Eb, Uncle Jeremiah, and Hiram Birdseed dispensed homespun wisdom and impressions of the PPIE in exaggerated yokel dialects.

Rose Wilder Lane was a journalist for the *Bulletin* in San Francisco in 1915 when her mother, Laura Ingalls Wilder, came to visit. Laura recorded her impressions of the PPIE in letters to her husband:

> One goes through beautiful archways in the buildings into the courts where fountains splash and lovely flowers and green things are growing….The foundation color of the buildings is a soft gray and as it rises it is changed to the soft yellows picked out in places by blue and red and green and the eye is carried up and up by the architecture…to the beautiful blue sky above.[52]

Rose Wilder Lane penned biographical sketches of Exposition personalities Art Smith, Charlie Chaplin, and Henry Ford for the *Bulletin*, as well as a fictionalized biography of Jack London, published in *Sunset* magazine shortly after his November 1916 death.

The raffish London and his wife, Charmian, made the trip south from their Glen Ellen ranch

Poet Edwin Markham, here in the South Gardens, was one of many popular writers who visited the PPIE. He said the Exposition illuminations would "give the world new standards of art and a joy in loveliness never before reached." (Seligman Family Foundation)

several times during the Exposition, including on Opening Day. They toured the exhibits, visited Toyland on the Zone, attended a wedding in the Maryland Building, and took home an award in the draft horse competition for their Shire stallion "Neuadd Hillside."

"The Hussy," the first of London's short stories published after his death, is set at the Fair. Three of the main characters sit beside the lagoon of the Palace of Fine Arts as one recounts a thrilling quest for gold in Ecuador. In the tale, the narrator's wife declares her Ecuadoran rival "heathenish," but London may also have been slyly alluding to criticisms of the PPIE's central feature:

> "Heathenish," said Mrs. Jones, and though her steady gaze was set upon the Tower of Jewels, I knew she was making no reference to its architecture.[53]

London represented a sort of nexus of the most notable authors who visited the PPIE. Among them was London's dear friend George Sterling, whose words were etched into the walls of the Exposition in the Court of Four Seasons. Sterling, the "poet of Carmel," had written the verse for a 1907 play at the grove of the Bohemian Club, of which both he and London were members.

> For lasting happiness we turn our eyes
>
> To one alone, and she surrounds you now—
>
> Great Nature, refuge of the weary heart,
>
> And only balm to breasts that have been bruised!
>
> She hath cool hands for every fevered brow,
>
> And gentlest silence for the troubled soul.[54]

Sterling also released a poem in book form to commemorate the Exposition. *The Evanescent City*, illustrated by Francis Bruguière, includes this stanza:

> And even thus our city of a year
>
> Must pass like those the shafted sunsets build,
>
> Fleeting as all fair things and, fleeting, dear—
>
> A rainbow fallen and an anthem stilled.[55]

Another of London's literary confederates, poet Edwin Markham, proclaimed the Exposition "an outpouring of the arts before the altar of humanity...."[56]

Markham lauded Ina Coolbrith, the woman Jack London called his "literary mother," when Coolbrith was invested as the first poet laureate of California before the Congress of Authors and Journalists at the Fair. The beauty of her youth was still evident as seventy-four-year-old Coolbrith, gowned in black brocade with a sash embroidered with golden poppies, faced the large audience. After tributes by Markham and Senator James D. Phelan, University of California president Benjamin Ide Wheeler placed a wreath of laurel leaves on her silver hair and said, "Upon thee, sole living representative of the golden age of California letters…I lay this poet's crown and name thee our California Poet-Laureate."[57]

The woman Bret Harte had termed "the sweetest note in California literature" accepted graciously, but made it clear she was not an ivory-tower poet able to write at leisure. "Mine has been a life of labor," she said, and indeed her life was not privileged. She had taught school and cared for members of her family and for poet Joaquin Miller's daughter. Coolbrith also wrote for Bret Harte's *Overland Monthly* magazine from its 1868 founding and served as a librarian for the Mechanics' Institute and the Oakland Public Library. It was at the latter location where she met Jack London, aged ten years, guided his reading choices, and encouraged his literary aspirations.[58, 59]

From the stage banked with roses, she noticed her longtime colleague Josephine

Clifford McCrackin in the throng and called her up. McCrackin's eyes glistened with tears as Coolbrith held her hand and said, "There is one woman here with whom I would share these flowers….For we are linked together, the last two living members of Bret Harte's staff of *Overland* writers." Later in 1915, Luther Burbank named a crimson hybrid poppy for Coolbrith, who had penned the poem "Copa de Oro" after the California state flower.[60]

Louis Stellman, who visited Jack London's ranch to interview the author just a few weeks before the author's death in 1916, also created a book celebrating the Fair. In it he wrote:

And yet—in our hearts is a memory

Of rapture that never can fade

Forever the spirit revisits

Bright garden and dim colonnade

To drink, like a fresh inspiration,

The Wine of a vanished repast;

To feast on the sweet recollection

Of splendors too vivid to last.[61]

The musicians of the Kumalae Quintet, seen here in the Palace of Liberal Arts, were among the stars popularized at the Exposition. (Donna Ewald Huggins)

Though Stellman wrote of the Exposition itself, he easily could have been describing the luminaries who walked within its walls during 1915.

The lifetimes of those who passed each other in the "bright gardens and dim colonnades" spanned years that saw a vast metamorphosis of culture. The Fair was attended by an older generation who had seen the end of American slavery, violent frontier conflicts, and the building of the transcontinental railroads. Those in their youth at the PPIE, like Virginia Stephens, William Saroyan, and Ansel Adams, would see the horse replaced by the automobile and the development from perilous hand-built aircraft to a man treading buoyantly on the moon. Fortunes based on natural resources like gold and silver

Pilots Silvio Pettirossi (left) and Charles Niles shared a collegial moment in front of one of their "aeroplanes." Like many early aviators, both men led short lives, each dying in 1916 crashes. (Laura Ackley)

were giving way to those based on technology, such as Henry Ford's cars and Thomas Edison's power distribution empire.

Acclaim and affluence also were evanescent. As films progressed from silents to "talkies," many of the movie stars who danced at the Motion Picture Ball did not negotiate the transition, though a few with staying power, including Lillian Gish, had long careers. The fortunes of many fairgoers, including Madame Ernestine Schumann-Heink, were wiped out in the Wall Street Crash of 1929.

Advocates of pacifism and preparedness used the Exposition as a stage from which to declaim their contradictory messages, but the ultimate goal of both groups was peace. The PPIE's creators saw the Jewel City as the embodiment of a new epoch of peace enabled by the same American genius that had completed the Panama Canal. The Exposition's own promotional literature touted that the canal, completed by the United

States after others had failed, would enable fulfillment of "man's loftiest dreams of world-commerce, world-friendship and world-peace."[62]

After the PPIE closed, a self-congratulatory volume entitled *The Legacy of the Exposition* returned again and again to the theme that the PPIE exemplified peace realized through American ideals. "The Panama-Pacific International Exposition was the great object lesson of peace set over against Europe ablaze as the result of war. Long may its memories and its lessons abide!" exclaimed Connecticut congressman John Q. Tilson.[63]

However, the nation that had brought the canal to completion would not retain the lasting peace it trumpeted as its bequest. Instead America plunged into the "Great War," followed by World War II and subsequent decades of military conflicts.

William Jennings Bryan's official political career was finished, but he was still a powerful man. He campaigned for Prohibition and led the prosecution team that attacked the teaching of evolution in the famous Scopes Monkey Trial of 1925. Young Franklin Delano Roosevelt's tenure in the White House was still ahead, but so too was the paralytic illness that in 1921 impaired his mobility.

Like the ephemeral Exposition, the lives of some of her celebrities were also too brief. Aviators Charles Niles and Silvio Pettirossi both died in 1916 plane crashes. Art Smith, who became a civilian test pilot and instructor during World War I, also perished when he crashed flying a US airmail route over Ohio in 1926.

Whatever their futures were to be, the nobles and notables who sojourned to the PPIE's glorious temporary citadel epitomized an era. When their paths crossed in the Jewel City, many were at the peak of fame or infamy, while some bright lives were in ascendance and some already had outlived their fame. Whether they were talented, powerful, beautiful, opinionated, sinful, audacious, brilliant, or scandalous, each represented an aspect of the ever-accelerating cultural change of the early twentieth century. ⋙

A PAGEANT OF ART

"It is admitted that the central attractiveness of almost every exposition lies in its art," declared a writer for the *Nation*, who continued, "...it is emphatically so at San Francisco." According to Frederick J. V. Skiff, director-in-chief of foreign and domestic participation, "Five times as many people will go into the Fine Arts Palace as into any other building of the same area."[1, 2]

Fine arts had long been a mainstay of world's fairs, and the PPIE was to be no different. Exhibits were staged in the pavilions of various participating nations and in the 148 galleries of the Palace of Fine Arts and its annex.

However, while the last century has confirmed Bernard Maybeck's Palace of Fine Arts as a cherished masterpiece, the show mounted within its walls has received less respect. During 1915 the art show was lauded, but modern critics usually have dismissed it as retrograde when compared to its contemporaries, and some have said the impact of its great art was diluted by thousands of less distinguished works. But making a cutting-edge artistic statement was never the goal of the fine arts department; what it aimed to do it accomplished admirably.

This was the first major international art show on the West Coast, and rather than offering a single, focused collection meant to illuminate a certain direction in art, it attempted to educate the audience as it exposed them to great works. And among the thousands of works in the show were subcollections aplenty to please the most finicky or forward-thinking observer.

ARRANGING THE ART

John E. D. Trask was selected as the director of fine arts for the PPIE in 1912. In February 1913 he resigned his post as manager of the Pennsylvania Academy of Fine Arts and set about creating the apparatus for selecting and procuring the artworks that would inhabit the Palace of Fine Arts, as well as the sculpture that would adorn her grounds. He aimed to be selective, and "to arrange an exhibition which will be in its various branches, thoroughly educational."[3]

He was especially excited about the concept behind the display of American works. Not only would current American art be shown, but several galleries would illustrate the *process* by which modern technique and style had been reached. A Historical Collection would present a survey of American art, and a Loan Collection would gather international paintings of various styles that had influenced the techniques and styles of current American artists.

Juries of artists convened in London, Paris, Boston, New York, Philadelphia, Cincinnati, Chicago, St. Louis, and San Francisco to select works for the Fair. The selection process was controversial. A coterie of rejected California artists and their supporters accused jurists Francis McComas, Arthur Mathews, and Eugen Neuhaus, abetted by William Wendt and Paul Gustin, of passing over superior works. The omitted artists further complained McComas, Mathews, and Neuhaus also overrepresented their own works in the Jewel City's galleries.

A local magazine, the *Wasp,* suggested the excluded artists mount their own show within the California Building. The idea had precedent. When Paul Gauguin was not invited by the Paris Exposition Universelle in 1889, he and his friends created a show in a café just outside the fair. But a 1915 version of this outsider statement never materialized.

Trask claimed the committees would be choosy. "Only about 20 per cent of those [pieces] submitted to juries were accepted," he announced. But ultimately the exhibit was vast, with 11,403 artworks.[4]

The advent of war complicated the retrieval of European art, but it also created some artistic windfalls for the PPIE. J. Nilsen Laurvik, the Fair's Norwegian-born fine arts representative, visited Rome, where artist Albert Besnard volunteered some of his recent paintings of India. In Venice, Laurvik persuaded Filippo Tommaso Marinetti, leader of the Italian "Futurists," to send fifty specimens of the new movement. There Laurvik also was able to secure for the Exposition fifty paintings by Finland's Akseli (Axel) Gallen-Kallela, as well as a large portion of the works assembled for the Venice Biennale, which had been cancelled because of the war. Then he went on to Austria, where he procured outstanding examples of graphic art and convinced Oskar Kokoschka, whom he regarded as "the greatest Austrian painter," to exhibit.[5]

A group of Hungarian artists campaigned against Laurvik's mission in Budapest, claiming that with a threatened Russian invasion, mounting an art show in America was inappropriate, not to mention that transporting artworks across the Atlantic could endanger them. But Laurvik was able to enlist Hungarian Count Julius Andrássy

Alma de Bretteville Spreckels lent six Rodin sculptures, including *The Thinker,* for display in the French Pavilion. Members of the French Commission posed with the famous artwork. (Donna Ewald Huggins)

A screen exquisitely embroidered with *Ocean Waves* in silk by Seizaburo Kajimoto was exhibited in the Japanese section of the Palace of Fine Arts. (Donna Ewald Huggins)

in the cause. The count not only lent works from his own famous collection but also, through the press, encouraged others to follow suit. His efforts, along with visits by Laurvik to more than one hundred people, turned the tide and secured an impressive Hungarian selection for the Jewel City.

When the 1914 International Urban Exposition at Lyon, France, ended, many of its works were stranded as a result of the war. Laurvik arranged for the entire Belgian display and some of the Austrian exhibits to be boxed up and loaded onto the US Navy collier *Jason,* the ship returning to America after delivering Christmas toys from American children to children in the warring European countries. In Pittsburgh, the annual Carnegie Museum exhibition had been abandoned, as organizers did not wish to compete with the PPIE, and among the art sent back across the Atlantic were forty German canvases. Once they reached

Europe, however, it was impossible to deliver them to their owners, so they were returned to the United States and became part of the Carnegie's foreign loan collection displayed in San Francisco.

THE SHOW

Twelve foreign nations sent collections curated by their own art commissions. These were Argentina, Cuba, China, France, Italy, Japan, the Netherlands, Norway, the Philippines, Portugal, Sweden, and Uruguay, and each was given one or more galleries in the Palace of Fine Arts or its annex. Denmark did not participate formally, simply placing eleven canvases in its home pavilion.

A variety of forms and media were displayed, including some peculiar to their originating nations. There were, of course, a multitude of oil paintings, but also watercolors, drawings, engravings, sculpture, carved gemstones, metal work, and ceramics. Illustration was becoming more recognized as a fine art and was exemplified within the galleries by works from Howard Pyle, Frank Schoonover, N. C. Wyeth, Frederick Remington, and Maynard Dixon. Prints and etchings by Americans Joseph Pennell, Ernest D. Roth, Gustave Baumann, and Dwight Sturges could be compared with those of Japanese masters Ando Hiroshige and Kitagawa Utamaro.

Japan's ten rooms contained not only the requisite modern paintings but also works in wood, bamboo, porcelain, cloisonné, and lacquerware, and masks for classical Noh theater. A four-part divided screen was embroidered by Seizaburo Kajimoto with sea waves so lifelike it seemed as though their spuming crests would cast foam into the gallery. While *Moving Clouds,* a painting on silk by Ranshyu Dan, excited much admiration, many considered the most charismatic the remarkable sculpted figures of a puppy and a devil, superbly wrought in hammered iron by Chozaburo Yamada.

Sweden mounted a well-balanced, comprehensive collection of nine galleries, second in number only to Japan. One of these rooms was filled with diverse works by Gustaf Fjæstad, who, according to the *American-Scandinavian Review,* demonstrated "an almost Japanese stylistic abstractness…coupled with a singular fidelity of observation…." Every object in the chamber was created by the polymath craftsman, including paintings, tapestries, furniture, and woodcuts.[6]

The French Pavilion was enriched by San Francisco society matron "Big Alma" Spreckels, who lent five bronzes by Rodin for display in the central hall. Her copy of *Le Penseur (The Thinker)* graced the forecourt, much as it is now placed in the courtyard of Lincoln Park's Palace of the Legion of Honor, itself a replica of France's pavilion at the PPIE.

The names of two men, Antonio Mancini and Ettore Tito, dominated articles about the Italian section. Mancini excelled at capturing the personalities of his subjects with an appealing impasto technique. In his *Art-Lover's Guide to the Exposition*, Sheldon Cheney said Tito's works

Harald Sohlberg's evocative landscape *Winter Night in the Mountains* drew admirers to the Norwegian galleries. (Public domain image; original held at the National Museum of Art, Architecture and Design, Oslo, Norway)

were "strong, and they are painted with a bigness and a sureness of touch that are compelling."[7]

Distant, icy blue peaks breathed a Norwegian chill from Harald Sohlberg's canvas *Winter Night in the Mountains*, in one of Norway's seven Fine Arts Annex galleries. Local newspaper critic Anna Cora Winchell said, "[T]he snap and glow of frost air are realistic, even in the face of the fact that the painter has made mountains, snow and everything else quite blue." Dancer La Loïe Fuller's opulently flowing silk draperies had been immortalized in bronze by Hans Stoltenberg Lerche, but at the Exposition his submissions took a more reverent turn in several portrait busts of Popes Pius X and Leo XIII.[8]

Entire volumes have been dedicated to the Palace of Fine Arts show, including its many international galleries. The focus of this overview will be on the exhibit's historical sweep, culminating in the Futurists and other modern schools. The concentration will be on paintings, though the prints, ceramics, wood- and metalwork, and sculpture of the PPIE could provide material enough for several dedicated books.

ARCHETYPAL ARTWORKS

The show was designed not only to present international artworks but also to showcase 4,500 works by American artists and to educate patrons on their evolution and influences, from colonial and revolutionary times to the present. Galleries containing the Historical Collection and the Loan Collection were integral to this effort.

The Historical Collection presented a chronological progression of strictly American art. Examples of colonial portraiture included *Portrait of Miss Peel,* painted by Benjamin West when he was but seventeen years old, and *Colonel Charles Pettit,* by Charles Willson Peale, best known for his dozens of paintings of George Washington. Early American history-makers also proved themselves a multitalented group. Included in the collection were paintings by telegraph inventor Samuel Morse, as well as prints by Paul Revere of "midnight ride" fame, who was described as "the first American engraver of note." A sentimental look at the Civil War was captured in *The Wounded Drummer Boy,* by Eastman Johnson. California scenes were showcased in more modern works by Thomas Hill, Thomas Moran, and William Keith.

The Loan Collection, or "retrospective collection," was a sampling of international art with effects that could be traced to modern American works. The earliest painting in the five Loan Collection galleries was a thirteenth-century Madonna by Guido de Siena, a master of the Italo-Byzantine style. There were Renaissance examples by Bassano, Luini, and Tintoretto, and a portrait by English painter and satirist William Hogarth. A painting by Diego Rodríguez de Silva y Velázquez represented the seventeenth-century Spanish "Golden Age." The Velázquez was lent to the Fair by jury member and artist Frank Duveneck, who was heavily influenced by the Spaniard. Duveneck's *Whistling Boy,* exhibited in his single-artist gallery at the PPIE, paid homage to the genre paintings of his idol.

The sequence continued with an early-eighteenth-century baroque work by Watteau, and portraits by Joshua Reynolds and Thomas Gainsborough. A Venetian scene by J. M. W. Turner and the *Portrait of Isidoro Maiquez* by Francisco José de Goya represented the Romantic movement. Barbizon school landscapes gave way to the realist style, which provided a bridge to Impressionism. A standout collection of

Impressionists was followed by some of the modes that had developed since the mid-1800s, including Post-Impressionism and Expressionism.

THE CRITICS DESCEND

Several factors contributed to the PPIE's sometimes poor critical evaluations. It was very difficult to absorb without fatigue the immense quantity of art presented. Art expert Dr. Christian Brinton described an encounter with an elderly lady in one of the overladen galleries: "Why do they paint so many pictures?" she asked timidly.[9]

In the years since, the Exposition show also has been criticized in comparison to more progressive shows presented contemporaneously. In the years immediately preceding the Fair, new artistic ideas were presented at several shows including the Vienna and Berliner Secession and the Venice Biennale shows. And the PPIE exhibition was especially unfortunate in following closely in the wake of the avant-garde 1913 International Exhibition of Modern Art in New York, better known as the Armory Show, which rocked the

Artist Frank Duveneck lent a portrait by Diego Rodríguez de Silva y Velázquez to the Loan Collection of the art galleries. His own 1902 *Whistling Boy* (above) revealed the influence of his Spanish predecessor. (Cincinnati Art Museum, gift of the artist, Bridgeman Images)

art world with its collection of Cubist, Futurist, and Fauvist works. This temporal proximity made the Jewel City's offering seem antiquated by comparison. With about 1,300 works, the Armory was a large show, but it was still modest when measured against the more than 11,000 works of art shown at the PPIE.

Others criticized the proportion of lesser works among the masterpieces at the Fair. Brinton found the masses of pictures hung together in "dual, sometimes even triple, alignment... stupefying rather than stimulating."[10]

James Ganz, currently a curator for the Fine Arts Museums of San Francisco, points out that the lavish profusion of works at the Fair

By the time Sargent's *Portrait of Madame Gautreau* (also known as *Madame X*) came to San Francisco, it was no longer considered scandalous but was regarded as a masterwork. (Cincinnati Art Museum, gift of the artist, Bridgeman Images)

was following tradition. "All the salons, all the international expositions were immense shows with thousands of works," he says. "Many of these are no longer considered important, but some endure."[11]

Critics who have since denigrated the importance of the PPIE art exhibit may be ignoring its planners' stated goals. It was never intended to be a purely cutting-edge demonstration of the latest artistic ideas. The show's primary raison d'être was to educate.

SHOWS WITHIN THE SHOW

Those who found the gallery spaces too eclectic, too broad, too inclusive, or overstuffed could discover more focused art experiences at the Exposition. Within the overabundance was the material of a curator's dreams; from this plenitude one could effectively extract dozens of exhibits elucidating specific styles, movements, or artists. Convincing collections of the Hudson River, Ashcan, and many other schools easily could be derived. Visitors who didn't want to make the effort to construct their own virtual shows could explore just a few galleries to concentrate on a desired style. For example, discriminating fairgoers could confine themselves to the dedicated artists' galleries or to those concentrated on Impressionism within the Palace and at the French Pavilion. Alternatively, they could limit their exploration to the Fine Arts Annex, a small building that opened after the start of the Fair and held more experimental art, including that of the Italian Futurists.

Further, fifteen distinguished American artists were honored with galleries dedicated to their works, effectively creating a number of one-man shows. These were William Merritt Chase, Frank Duveneck, John McClure Hamilton, Childe Hassam, William Keith, Arthur Mathews, Francis McComas, Gari Melchers, Joseph Pennell, Howard Pyle, Edward Redfield, John Singer Sargent, Edmund C. Tarbell, John H. Twachtman, and James McNeill Whistler. As Chase died in 1916, his gallery of thirty-two paintings constituted a true retrospective.

INFLUENTIAL IMPRESSIONISTS

"The atmosphere of the Luxembourg [Palace] has in brief been transported to San Francisco with the coming of these canvases which, in a sense, constitute the vanguard of modernism," said Brinton of the Impressionist paintings at the PPIE. Between the French section in the Palace of Fine Arts and the additional works shown in the French Pavilion, the Fair boasted an Impressionism collection that would put many of the world's richest museums to shame. Within the galleries, fairgoers could examine the paintings virtually alongside the later works they had influenced.[12]

Gallery 61 of the Palace of Fine Arts housed no fewer than seven Monets. The Palace also was home to three works by Pierre Auguste Renoir, three by Mary Cassatt, two by Camille Pissarro, and one each by Alfred Sisley, James Tissot, and Edgar Degas.

War-ravaged France had decided at the last possible instant to build a pavilion and used the opportunity to remove many major works from harm's way. In its national pavilion's "Impressionist Group" was another Monet, one of his luminous studies of the Cathedral of Rouen. Other paintings by Impressionists and their associates in the pavilion included works by Degas and one each by Manet, Cézanne, Raffaëlli, Sisley, Pissarro, and Renoir.

Although the movement had raised critics' hackles fifty or so years earlier, by 1915 many Impressionist paintings were established masterworks, and the PPIE provided an opportunity to trace their influence through the intervening decades. Works by European artists in the Palace and the French Pavilion, including Vincent Van Gogh, Henri de Toulouse-Lautrec, and Paul Signac, all demonstrated the impact of the Impressionists' pure hues. Paul Gauguin was represented with only two works, but his Tahitian fantasy *Faa Iheihe* is a striking example of his primitivist vision. This horizontal, panorama-like pastoral scene features natives in a verdant landscape soaked in rich golden hues. Pierre

Monet's 1891 painting *Haystacks at Sunset, Frosty Weather* (*Meule, Coucher de Soleil*) was one of many superb Impressionist paintings displayed in both the French Pavilion and the Palace of Fine Arts. (Private collection, Bridgeman Images)

Bonnard's *Dining Room in the Country* combined saturated zones of color with playful perspective manipulation of the room and adjacent garden. He and his comrades called themselves "Les Nabis" (the prophets), and indeed the *Dining Room* indicated the Post-Impressionist's foretelling of incipient abstract styles. Exemplifying how respected Impressionism had become, American Impressionist Frederick Carl Frieseke took top honors at the Fair, winning the Grand Prix for oil painting.

The many guidebooks to the Fair's art especially noted Impressionism's effect upon American painting as shown at the Exposition. "What a stimulating and beneficent tonic was this influence of the French impressionists upon American art may be seen in the work of such men as J. Alden Weir, Willard L. Metcalf, Childe Hassam, Ernest Lawson, John H. Twachtman, and Edward W. Redfield," read the *Catalogue de Luxe of the Department of Fine Arts*. "All of these men owe much...to their intelligent application of lessons taught by the Impressionists."[13]

William Glackens' five PPIE canvases—*Green Car, Family Group, Woman with Apple, Girls Bathing,* and *Chez Mouquin*—all manifest his admiration of Renoir's brushwork and soft, rich palette. However, Eugen Neuhaus, Exposition jurist and University of California professor, called *Woman with Apple* "absurd and vulgar beyond description."[14]

The Italian Futurists, whose gallery was in the Fine Arts Annex, sought to capture kinetic motion on canvas. They succeeded in eliciting impassioned responses, both positive and negative. (San Francisco History Center, San Francisco Public Library)

LOOKING FORWARD

Some said that the boxy layout of the Fine Arts Annex, which did not open until August 2, reflected its contents' composition. Its site, located in the western shadow of the main Palace of Fine Arts, was sequestered and distinctive, and its provocative contents almost dared patrons to come witness a new direction in art.

Those venturing inside partook of a feast of challenging new ideas. J. Nilsen Laurvik had secured works by Edvard Munch, Akseli Gallen-Kallela, and Oskar Kokoschka for the International Section, which comprised those countries that did not have dedicated arts commissions for the Fair. Munch, whose several versions of *The Scream* are among the best known paintings in the world, presented a roomful of etchings and nine paintings, including a moody self-portrait. Laurvik wrote that Munch had met with "opposition in his own country while being accepted abroad as one of the most forceful and original painters of modern times."[15]

One of the more memorable works sent by Symbolist artist Gallen-Kallela was *The Symposium,* also known as *The Problem.* In it, two seated men stare intently at a winged apparition, only a fraction of which is visible at the edge of the canvas. The men depicted are Finnish composers Jean Sibelius and Robert Kajanus. A third man is shown passed out on the white tablecloth littered with bottles and glasses. The fourth, standing character is the artist himself in mournful black.

FASCINATING FUTURISTS

"Hideous daubs." "Spasms." "Atrocities." "An unmistakable cross-breed between a lunatic and a dope fiend." These were among the epithets heaped upon the contents of the controversial Gallery 141 in the annex, home of the Italian Futurists.[16]

Futurists were experimenting with capturing the "persistence of vision" using multiple simultaneous viewpoints and moments expressed on canvas in fragmented segments of scenes. They even wrote a *Technical Manifesto of Futurist Painting* to explain their goal of capturing a "universal dynamism" in what they called "our whirling life of steel, of pride, of fever and of speed." The artists seized on this concept with gusto. Virtually all of the forty-eight paintings featured an active word in their titles, and the catalogue page for Gallery 141 is replete with "movement," "speed," "displacement," and "dynamic decompositions." Some, though, said the catalogue needn't have bothered printing the names of the paintings, as the titles had nothing to do with the compositions.[17]

Critic Michael Williams said one "corking good example" of Futurism was Gino Severini's painting *The Dynamic Decomposition of the Portrait of the Poet Marinetti*, a portrayal of Filippo Tommaso Marinetti, group leader and author of the 1909 *Manifeste du Futurisme*. Williams described the piece: "Out of a whirling medley of forms and colors that look like the edges of cups and saucers, mixed with bananas, the right eye of Signor Martinetti [*sic*] glares weirdly, while just below is one corner of his mouth surmounted by one-half of a mustache, which is represented by a tuft of real hair glued to the canvas, the other half, also of real hair, being stuck on six inches away, close to a

James McNeill Whistler's 1875 painting *Nocturne in Black and Gold—The Falling Rocket* interested fairgoers not only because of its virtuosity but also because it had been the subject of a feud between the artist and critic John Ruskin. (Detroit Institute of Arts, gift of Dexter M. Ferry, Jr., Bridgeman Images)

patch of printed paper torn from one of Martinetti's newspaper proclamations on Futurism. But there is nothing save the eye and the tufts of hair even remotely resembling humanity."[18]

San Franciscans alternately mocked, dismissed, and struggled to understand the works. Some allowed that innovations in art often were rejected initially by incumbent schools only to later find acceptance and admiration. Writer Ben Macomber said that while he respected the work of the Futurists, "I wouldn't have [a Futurist canvas] in my house."[19]

The Fair's official history describes the atmosphere in the gallery:

> How had people studied those blue and purple fields of slashed wallpaper, and how earnestly they strove to decipher cabalistic portents from such sculptural abstractions as "Muscles in Motion." They read books about the matter, and discussed it in paper-clubs, and were mentally aroused, excited, and rejuvenated....They might not care for "cubism" or "futurism," but at least it gave them a fresh topic of debate on the street car or the ferry boat.[20]

Though it's now evident that the work of the Futurists was prophetic of the development of twentieth-century modern art, the derision directed at PPIE Gallery 141 was extraordinary. The *Pan-Pacific Press Association* said, "In the Annex…were a number of daubs supposed to represent a new school of art. It is impossible by the wildest flight of imagination to ascribe any reason why an alleged artist should spoil good canvas and waste valuable paint unless these frightful, distorted apologies for human beings were painted for the purpose of curing a man of the drink habit. It is understood that these disgusting and distasteful objects were secured by J. Nilsen Laurvik, and in the opinion of a number the only excuse that can be offered is that square footage was desired."[21]

STORIED WORKS

Several paintings that arrived at the Jewel City were already famous, but for reasons unrelated to their accredited artistry.

One splash of sparks on billowing smoke touched off an incendiary battle between artist and critic. Whistler's 1875 *Nocturne in Black and Gold—The Falling Rocket* was the subject of a legal fight between the artist and John Ruskin. The painting showed an almost abstracted fireworks display over water on a misty night. The spectators were rendered translucently, as in a time-lapse photograph during which the subjects had moved. While evocative and oddly beautiful, the painting incensed Ruskin, who characterized it as "a paint-pot flung into the face of the public." Whistler sued, winning a libel settlement of one farthing, a coin he wore on his watch fob.[22]

John Singer Sargent exhibited two separate works with torrid histories. The first was a painting of Virginie Gautreau, better known as *Portrait of Madame X*, which had caused an uproar at the 1884 Paris Salon. There, Mme. Gautreau's deeply décolleté black gown, with one slender jeweled strap slipping off her ghostly pale shoulder, together with her haughty expression, were considered more erotically evocative than the commonplace nudes nearby. In the ensuing three decades, the picture had become acclaimed, and it was shown in San Francisco, albeit mislabeled as *Madame Gautrin* and with Sargent's amendment—he had repainted the offending strap securely on Madame's shoulder.

One May afternoon in the year before the Fair, the tranquility of a gallery at the Royal Academy in London was rent by the sound of shattering glass. An elderly member of a militant suffrage group called the Wild Women slashed through a portrait of novelist Henry James, also by Sargent, with a butcher's cleaver. Perpetrator Mary Wood declared the public would "not live in safety or peace until women have the vote. I have said it through destroying the picture." Sargent was able to repair the painting, and it was sent to the PPIE. Trask noted the painting had "attracted the more attention by reason of its being slashed by

In her *Self Portrait*, also known as *The Model*, painter Laura Knight daringly placed an image of herself between two female nudes. (© Reproduced with permission of The Estate of Dame Laura Knight DBE RA 2014. All Rights Reserved.)

suffragettes in London than it has had in tribute to its own splendid qualities."[23, 24]

Another sign of contemporary political turbulence was narrated in *The Assault,* also known as *La Charge,* by André Devambez, which hung in the French section of the Palace of Fine Arts. The moody nighttime Montmartre streetscape is viewed from above. A mob appears to flee from a line of uniformed men. Whether the rebels are anarchists, trade unionists, or nationalists is undiscernible, but the painting effectively encapsulates a turbulent era.

Some paintings supplemented superior technique and composition with the added interest of revealing personal connections within the artistic community. Oskar Kokoschka captured a fluid, incisive portrait of his friend and patron, architect Adolf Loos, while William Merritt Chase submitted a rendering of a dapper James McNeill Whistler. Thomas Eakins' painting of fellow artist Henry O. Tanner was interesting for several reasons: not only did the canvas depict an illustrious, successful African American, but Tanner also exhibited at the Exposition and served on its Fine Arts Advisory Committee for Europe.

Laura Knight broke with tradition in her *Self Portrait with Nude*, also known as *The Model*. The 1913 painting had shocked critics, as it portrayed the artist in the process of painting a nude figure from life. Knight's back is to the viewer and her face is seen in profile as she turns toward her subject. She is flanked on the right by the live model and on the left by her canvas of the woman. Thus the artist's own figure, garbed in a utilitarian red smock, is surrounded by naked female forms. The work was one of a limited number of British paintings shown in the International Section of the Fine Arts Annex and was part of the *Jason*'s cargo.

A PAGEANT OF ART

The art in the Palace of Fine Arts was regarded as the pinnacle of culture, the ultimate expression of achievement at the PPIE by organizers, visitors, and most critics, despite its vocal detractors. The sheer size of the Exposition's exhibit precluded it from having the sword-thrust impact of the Armory Show, but its goals were very different. In its magnitude and attempts to address not only modern movements but also historical influences, the show seemed muddled to many critics. Christian Brinton complained in the August 1915 *International Studio* magazine that without providing better explanations, the artworks' significance was lost on the average viewer.

Michael Williams came to the show's defense, writing in *Art and Progress*, "It is easy enough to point out flaws. By accumulating these flaws you could make a big bundle. Then by ignoring everything else and throwing the asphyxiating gas of negation into the trenches of public opinion, you could hide the tremendous merits of the exhibition....No general exhibition of works of art was ever exclusively a showing of masterpieces. Nor could it be, for its purpose is to display and illustrate the whole body of art...."[25]

Though the Jewel City's art collection was not as deliberately provocative as that of the Armory or some of the era's other shows, it still resonated. For example, yet another generation of artists would view Impressionist works and their lineal descendants at the PPIE, and incorporate their ideas in new ways. Author Nancy Boas says the "Society of Six," a group of well-regarded

California plein-air painters, found in the Impressionists at the Fair "sunny, descriptive subjects with no undercurrent of sermonizing or narrative. This was a genre to which the Six could relate...."[26]

And while the offerings in the Palace of Fine Arts may not have been revolutionary, they were nevertheless pivotal in exposing fairgoers to a great deal of high-quality art, something that no doubt shaped tastes, particularly on the West Coast, for decades.

Trask was proud of what his department had achieved. He said, "The Fine Arts exhibition... is the most intelligent representation of modern art ever shown in America...." He expected the PPIE show to take its rightful place in the annals of world's fair exhibitions, which he felt acted upon the development of art as "the influence of the sun upon the flowers," by engendering new art schools and fanning enthusiasm among the public, artists, collectors, and museums.[27, 28]

The show was tremendously popular. It was estimated that more than half of all Exposition attendees visited the galleries, many hiring guides for private tours. At club meetings all over the city, lectures analyzing the Fair's art were presented along with explanatory images projected through "magic lantern" slides. Docents became instructors for a school year lasting nine months, with many students attending "class" daily. During the final days of the Fair, the *Chronicle* said, "[T]he art wave that has been undulating through the women's club circles during the last year is reaching a crescendo movement in the last days of the exposition...."[29]

"Working exhibits" was the theme throughout the palaces of the Jewel City, and the theme also carried into the Palace of Fine Arts. In the Palace of Machinery, the immense Hoe Press demonstrated the latest in printing technology by cranking out color sections of the Sunday *San Francisco Examiner*. Analogously, the sequence of galleries in the Palace of Fine Arts manifested the production of art based on its antecedents, and suggested its possible future paths.

Like the color, vitality, and movement of an Exposition parade, the art show was not static: it was a pageant of the process and progress of art.

A STROLL ALONG THE JOY ZONE

mile of amusement. All good. All clean. All interesting." So claimed the concessions department about the Joy Zone, the great amusement street of the PPIE. It adjoined the main fairgrounds at its eastern end and from there extended like a peninsula all the way to Van Ness Avenue, taking a slight jog north at Laguna Street.[1]

Fantastically modeled façades lined the boulevard. A disembodied hand proffered a mammoth ice cream cone at the creamery, and shoppers purchased postcards inside a house-sized mailbox, or cigars beneath a patterned Moorish dome. Faux-Mesoamerican idols and cantilevered sculptures protruded from the stepped towers of the Tehuantepec Village. On one side of this Mexican concoction lay a medieval castle, on the other a jolly face with a pageboy haircut laughed down from a curving pediment. Immense sage-green elephant heads gazed imperturbably across the roadway at roly-poly clown figures in capacious urns. The clowns aimed long trumpets over the heads of passersby toward the pachyderms. Behind all these gay portals lay the pinnacles of contemporary diversions, some of which would be familiar to modern audiences, while many have passed into midway history.

Ten million dollars was spent to pack the seven-block thoroughfare with more than 250 attractions selected from more than 7,000 applicants. But the profligate investment celebrated in Exposition press releases led to sorrow both for concessionaires and for the Exposition. Surprisingly, some of the least expensively built attractions were the most profitable.

Since the name "Midway Plaisance" had been coined for the 1893 Columbian Exposition, a catchy nickname was considered requisite for every fair's entertainment street thereafter. The St. Louis 1904 Louisiana Purchase Exposition was the site of "The Pike." Smaller expositions in Portland, Jamestown, and Seattle in 1905, 1907, and 1909 featured "The

Trail," "The War Path," and "The Pay Streak." Early candidates for the PPIE's concession district name included "The Locks," "The Canal," "The Isthmus," and "The Ditch," but in May 1914, San Franciscan Mrs. J. Cortissoz suggested "The Joy Zone." It was chosen as the official name, and she was awarded a free Exposition season pass as her prize.

Monumental gates replicating the locks of the Panama Canal were proposed as a Zone entry, but this playful idea was supplanted by a pair of handsome buildings in an ornate French style by architect Clarence Tantau of Bakewell & Brown. Curved mansard domes adorned with bright pennants surmounted the glassed-in pavilions housing concessions by Ghirardelli Chocolate, a San Francisco favorite, and Welch's Grape Juice, fashionable among proponents of Prohibition.

These highbrow yet flamboyant twin oases marked the transition from the serene Beaux-Arts dreamland of the great palaces to the blast of color, movement, and noise that was the Joy Zone. As United Press correspondent Fred Ferguson put it, "Behind you are the works and ideals of America. Before you is America at play."[2]

"You're just in time, just in time! The show begins right away!" called barkers standing before the enticing entries. Flags fluttered in gay profusion. Lanterns flanking the path every seventy-five feet sported bright fabric banners and fishy finials. Between them slender wire arches spanned the way. Suspended from each arch were two dozen small flower-shaped lights hung with waving crimson ribbons. The aromas of freshly made candy and buttered popcorn filled the air, while rides, shows, games, and artfully arranged rows of souvenirs vied for fairgoers' attention.[3]

"Down the crooked street of the Zone we go," said the *Colorado Springs Gazette*. "On either side is a motley throng of revelers of all nations[,]…the turbaned sheik from the Streets of Cairo jostling elbows with the flower-clad Geisha girl from the Japanese village. Horns are blowing, tom-toms are beating, bells are ringing, cymbals are clashing, whistles are tooting, guitars and mandolins are strumming, and over and above all[,] the babble of human voices and laughter…."[4]

CHOOSING THE CONCESSIONS

"High class, clean, moral and educational attractions will mark the Panama-Pacific International Exposition," declared Frank Burt, director of the Division of Concessions and Admissions. Initially, the main complication of filling the Zone was selecting from an embarrassment of riches, as there were at least twenty-eight applicants for every available space. Attractions highlighting educational opportunities or innovative experiences were favored. In addition to the Zone, the Division of Concessions and Admissions supervised more than two hundred other concessions, including food and souvenir kiosks scattered about the Fair's grounds, and sales within the exhibit palaces and the state and national pavilions.[5]

Requirements for Zone concessionaires were stringent. Hopefuls completed a twelve-page, binding application that detailed the size, scope, and content of each attraction and listed references attesting to financial stability. Concessionaires often paid a one-time "bonus" and agreed to fork over a percentage of ticket revenue, plus a smaller percentage of any sales inside. Most concessions settled on 25 percent of "gate money" to the Exposition, though a few with high overhead received lower rates, and some with low operating expenses paid as much as 50 percent to the PPIE. The quota on inside sales was usually 15 percent, but some accepted higher and some negotiated lower rates.

Once the application was made, it was reviewed and evaluated against possible competitors. The concessions department had to decide "to what precise degree a ham sandwich interferes commercially with a Frankfurter sausage, or whether, in the affections of the public, a common ink pencil can ever supplant a Presidential Souvenir Penholder." Concessionaires were not allowed to be associated with any Fair directors, and if they claimed an association, they were disqualified. It was explicitly stated that "freak shows" were barred, as they were "out of harmony with

The Joy Zone's fantastical façades were almost as much fun as their attractions, and helped spur an emerging architectural trend. (Lynn Wilkinson)

modern ideas," though some attractions walked a fine line, particularly as the season progressed.[6]

At earlier world's fairs, midway operators had played fast and loose with the percentage they owed. Where concessions had handled their own receipts, it seemed that most days their business had been inexplicably bad. Cash registers were out of order with mysterious frequency, and shortfalls were common, as was the tardy submission of the exposition's percentage. Director Frank Burt had a plan to curb these abuses—one developed over his thirty years in the theater and amusement park industries. He suggested the Hundred Percent System, in which the Exposition would collect all receipts, then return what was owed the concessionaire, withholding the Fair's percentage and charges owed for utility bills, supplies, and cashiers' salaries.

All cashiers were hired and trained by the Exposition, but their salaries were paid by the concessions. Every morning, workers, mostly women, would exchange their numbered metal cashier's tags for cash boxes containing $45 in change before reporting to their assigned locations. To promote honesty, cashiers' stations were changed frequently so they would not get too chummy with the concessionaires.

ARCHITECTURAL FANTASYLAND

The Division of Concessions and Admissions directed concessionaires to create "fantastic" façades that would express what was offered inside. Ideally a person could identify the type of attraction without reading any signage. This resulted in a chaotic, quirky, and astounding mix of sculpted building fronts.

"It was a great amusement street," wrote official historian Frank Morton Todd, "and with its Golden Buddha, its tall suffragette and twin soldiers wonderful before Toyland, its Chinese pagoda, the giant holding back the waters of the Dayton flood,…its cliffs and crags of the Grand

Scenes from distant lands and eras were crammed together on the Zone. The towers seen here (l. to r.) are of the pagoda of the Chinese Village, the Evolution of the Dreadnaught, Alt Nürnberg, and the Tehuantepec Village. (San Francisco History Center, San Francisco Public Library)

Canyon, and of the Yellowstone, and particularly of the 'Submarines' with Neptune and his rearing sea horses, the square tower of Blarney Castle lifting above the 'Shamrock Isle,'...the whole scene had a grand and imposing aspect in spite of its necessary garishness."[7]

While novelty or "mimetic" buildings had been constructed before, improvements in stucco technology, developed especially for the PPIE, allowed incorporation of rich pigments and better plasticity. Earlier world's fairs had used this "programmatic" architecture to good effect, but the Zone façades at the PPIE made the prior midways' efforts seem clunky by comparison. Paul Denivelle, who developed the faux travertine for the Fair, devised seven different formulations of the finishing material to solve any architectural modeling challenge. The new technology, along with the stipulation that Zone façades be lavishly modeled, created a half-mile-long frontage filled on each side with three-dimensional creatures, objects, and landscapes that influenced commercial architecture for decades.

Concessionaires were allowed to retain their own architects as long as they cooperated with the Exposition's Department of Architecture. Some hired "starchitects" for their buildings. Ghirardelli and Welch's used Bakewell & Brown, and the M. A. Gunst & Co. smoke shop employed Ward & Blohme. However, a great deal of the work was assigned to the Exposition's in-house stable of designers. Edwin J. Symmes, who had worked previously with Bliss & Faville, coordinated with the external architects and personally designed the elaborate Tehuantepec Village and the Carousel building on the Zone, the Carnation Condensery and Muller-Luxus Café near the Palace of Fine Arts Lagoon, and the Desmond Supply Company's Garden and Festival Inns in the South Gardens.

The long-term architectural impact of the Zone might have been limited if not for Hollywood. When director D. W. Griffith needed to build a gargantuan replica of ancient Babylon for his 1916 movie *Intolerance*, he recalled the impressive plasterwork he had seen at the Fair and recruited Exposition craftsmen to create his scenery. His assistant director tracked down two PPIE sculptors and a painter and brought them to Tinseltown. Griffith proudly explained to *Moving Picture World* magazine that *Intolerance's* sets were of "the same material as that used at the San Francisco Exposition." Thus the Zone's programmatic DNA was spliced into Hollywood set design.[8]

Shortly thereafter, Southern California underwent a flourishing of midway-style commercial architecture. Concurrent with the popularization of the automobile, up sprang hot dog stands shaped like hot dogs, bakeries in the form of windmills, and diners housed in colossal coffee pots, all intended to catch the eyes of fast-traveling drivers. In his study of these whimsical vernacular structures, Jim Heimann draws a direct link from the Panama-Pacific Exposition "to Hollywood studio, and ultimately, to the California roadside."[9]

THE FAIR'S FARE

Delicious aromas wafting from the many Zone restaurants and snack booths were as diverse as the buildings from which they emanated, and eateries contributed their share to the bizarre appearance of the Zone. MJB Coffee's café featured a large cup and saucer hovering over the door, emblazoned with the company's nonsense slogan "WHY?" The Waffle Kitchen's parapet was decorated with a railing of jumbo-sized plates and forks.

Three buildings decorated with steer heads housed outlets of the Desmond Supply Company, which specialized in roasted meats. The half-timbered Primrose Inn, Bavarian-styled Frankfurter Inn, and wooden Sandwich Barn—complete with a simulated hayloft—all served chicken, beef, lamb, and pork, which patrons could watch roasting on spits behind plate-glass windows.

A club of Zone concessionaires, the "Cubs," celebrate on the dance floor of Young's Restaurant on the midway. Elizabeth Weiss, the "Living Doll," is standing near center in a light dress. (Edward A. Rogers)

The sweet tooth could be indulged at stands dishing out ice cream, fruits and nuts, chocolates, chewing gum, and "candy floss," now known as cotton candy. Savory snackers had their pick of peanuts, popcorn, and hot dogs. Regional delicacies included Southern, Mexican, and Irish food.

To prevent gouging, the Fair dictated prices for typical offerings, but purveyors had more leeway for unique menu items. The standard rate for soups was ten to fifteen cents, while sandwiches of various sorts cost between ten and twenty-five cents. A stein of buttermilk could be had for a nickel, while "sweet" milk, tea, coffee, or beer cost a dime. Entrees of fish and beef ranged between twenty and thirty-five cents, and you could finish your meal with pie or cake for ten to fifteen cents. Specialty dishes, however, could command $2 or more.

Virtually all large Zone restaurants featured dancing to live orchestras in the evenings. Young's Restaurant, the Shamrock Isle, the Marine and Vienna Cafés, and Alt Nürnberg all claimed they had the best musicians and dance floors.

Billed as "a German place of very good type," Alt Nürnberg seated diners around one of the Zone's most commodious floors. German-themed eating places had been a staple at American expositions since 1893, and Otto Muller's PPIE venue was one of the most popular restaurants on the grounds. Fare was served within a replica of the medieval village of Nuremberg, complete with a tower pierced by narrow lancet windows, a marketplace, and a copy of the municipal Rathaus. Comely maids in front-laced dirndls served Lobster Newburg or Russian caviar for seventy-five cents, while the most expensive item on the menu was a double porterhouse steak at $2.50. The extensive menu had four pages of wines, beers, and cocktails.

Not every restaurant was as successful. Those craving seafood entered the Marine Café beneath the protruding prow and bowsprit of a ship with boldly striped sails. While it had among the highest total receipts, it was expensive to build and run, and it closed about halfway through the Fair. Its desirable space, near the main entrance, later was used for selling rugs from the India exhibit and for a dog show. The simultaneous cat show was sagely placed in the likewise-defunct Vienna Café at the far end of the Zone.

THE SPECTACLES

The cyclorama and scenograph are no longer well-known entertainment forms, but at the PPIE these great scenic productions were among the largest and most expensive Zone attractions. Gigantic cylindrical paintings called cycloramas, predecessors of IMAX and Circle-Vision movies, became popular in the mid-nineteenth century, but by 1915 the cyclorama was past its prime and was being supplanted by more complex spectacles.

On the Joy Zone the lone cycloramic holdout was the Battle of Gettysburg. As patrons' eyes adjusted from the sunlight outside, they found themselves surrounded by the battle, amid the infantry charges, bayonet rushes, and hand-to-hand combat of the most pivotal fight of the Civil War. As if viewed from atop Cemetery Ridge, charging horses, exploding wagons, drifting smoke, and human carnage all appeared frozen mid-motion. Two former soldiers, Colonel E. C. Johnson from the Union side and Colonel M. R. Hughes from the Confederacy, narrated the story. The painting's realism was enhanced by special effects. Roads were bordered by real growing grain, and the air was scented with black powder smoke and rent by the crack of gunfire.

The Gettysburg cyclorama at the PPIE was widely advertised as one of four completed by French artist Paul Philippoteaux and his team in the 1880s. While its dimensions—four hundred feet long, fifty feet tall, and with 20,000 square feet of canvas and four tons of paint—are similar to the Philippoteaux paintings, Gettysburg Cyclorama expert Sue Boardman believes the painting shown at the Fair was a slightly later work executed by one of Philippoteaux's assistants. The concession, housed within a round, crenellated tower resembling a fortified keep, became a popular destination for actual Civil War veterans, who would "argue the battle over and over and then go inside to prove their points by the painted evidence," according to the *Riverside Daily Press*.[10]

The Joy Zone was also the site of naval battles, disasters, and no less than the creation of the cosmos, portrayed in "scenographs," some of the most expensive attractions on the midway. Scenographs were the latest in theatrical attractions, relying primarily on electro-mechanical illusions rather than actors to tell their stories. They featured moving scenery, lighting, and atmospheric effects like fog, water, and fire. One writer called scenographs "the logical evolution of the cyclorama, the diorama and the scenic theatre." Performances typically were accompanied by live music and narrators.[11]

A serenely topless three-story-tall angel with wings outlined in light beckoned from the façade of Creation. Viewers entered the theater beneath her arching pinions to watch an enactment of the biblical story of Genesis. The production began in darkness with a voice intoning, "Let there be light!" Then, jagged streaks of lighting crackled, thunder crashed through whirling mists, and torrential rain flooded the model world. One visitor said, "Great volcanoes appeared to rise up out of the sizzling water and poured forth streams of lava, and great reefs of earth appeared from mid-ocean." Gradually, a landscape of hills, valleys, rivers, trees, and flowers appeared, and birds began to sing. An actor—a rarity in scenographs—portrayed Adam awakening from deep slumber and searching for his Eve, who finally appeared, ensconced in an oversized eggshell. The spectacle was accompanied by narration, the silvery tones of a pipe organ, and live operatic singers performing four selections from Haydn's *Creation*. The scenograph was regarded as a "higher class of educational amusement" and enjoyed many repeat customers.[12, 13]

Monstrous gun-turrets of an ironclad battleship menaced the Zone just east of its central plaza. Inside the Evolution of the Dreadnaught, pocket-sized fleets, beginning with ancient galleys and finishing with modern battleships, fought noisy maritime battles with "real cannon." The centerpiece of the show was a depiction of the Civil War battle at Hampton Roads, and, after a simulated storm, sunrise illumined the Confederate *Merrimac* steaming stealthily into the harbor and ramming the Union's *Cumberland*, which sank into the miniature bay. As a finale, models of the current fleet of United States warships steamed through the Golden Gate and paraded past the Exposition, a scene that brought delighted "ahhs" from the crowd.

The Evolution of the Dreadnaught was not a moneymaker. Costing a whopping $150,000 to build (about $3.45 million in 2012), it took on water for a few months before capsizing and closing midsummer. Concessions director Frank Burt scolded that had this and other expensive attractions been financed and advertised properly at the start of the Fair, they might have been profitable. The Exposition's Finance Committee tried to bail out the Dreadnaught by infusing $3,000 to re-theme the attraction as the "World's Wars," which opened in September. When advertising characterized the German U-boat responsible for the sinking of the *Lusitania* as "The Assassin of the Sea," the German American

The scenographic spectacle Creation featured electro-mechanical effects replicating the biblical story of Genesis, including this scene of Adam meeting Eve. (Edward A. Rogers)

After the original attraction, Evolution of the Dreadnaught, closed midyear, the Exposition provided a cash infusion and re-themed the show, renaming the miniature warship battle the World's Wars, which opened in September. (Anne T. Kent California Room, Marin County Free Library)

community was outraged. German consul Franz Bopp protested vehemently and the offending language was deleted. Though the skirmish provided valuable publicity that boosted attendance near the end of the season, ultimately the concession was a financial failure.[14]

At earlier world's fairs, disastrous floods had been sure-fire draws, but the 1915 version, created by Henry Ellsworth to depict the 1913 Dayton Flood, was unsuccessful. Helen Eells, an eleven-year-old at the time, related her youthful indifference to the attraction: "The Dayton Flood was a great, big area, with a little, make-believe Main Street of houses....And then the man told you about how many people it killed and drowned. And all this tragedy was before you. And you sat there, with your mouth open.... But you wondered what all the excitement was about." The show closed in July.[15]

Ellsworth had built a career producing historical pageants, but 1915 was not his year. London to the South Pole, his other contribution to the PPIE, was also a financial failure. The spectacle illustrated the ill-fated quest of Robert Falcon Scott, whose party perished after becoming the second expedition to reach the pole. Scenes reproducing the trek were painted from actual photographs taken by Scott's party, and included was the dying explorer's final missive: "These rough notes and our dead bodies must tell the tale." While many admired the "heroic theme portrayed with wonderful exactness," London to the South Pole did not garner enough patrons and closed after just a few months. Other concessions moved into its space, leaving the ice-bound ship on its façade marooned above signs for "Toyland Midgets and Lilliputians," "Alice, That Strange Girl," "The Model's Dream," and a shop selling Chinese bags.[16, 17]

VIRTUAL TRAVEL

The Zone also offered "virtual travel" to scenic spots for fifty cents or less, and the model Panama Canal was the undisputed star. Visitors on a moving platform circled a 575-foot-long, 340-foot-wide recessed topographic map of the

Canal Zone while listening to a recorded lecture. It was praised publicly by high-profile personalities including Henry Ford, William Jennings Bryan, California governor Hiram Johnson, labor leader Samuel Gompers, and former House Speaker "Uncle Joe" Cannon. Even Major-General George Goethals, the engineer who successfully completed the real "Big Ditch," lauded the ride's realism and educational value. Despite earning more than $338,000, the attraction took a net loss because of its half-million-dollar cost.

One day the attraction's manager, Fred McClellan, was observing operations from one of the moving cars when he was chided by an elderly woman who had noticed he was not listening to the recording. "For heaven's sake put these things in your ears and listen to this lecture," she admonished. "It's something that you ought to know." McClellan obediently lifted the earpiece and completed the spin listening to the narrative he had authored.[18]

After passing between the high, steep walls of a simulated canyon, patrons entered the wide-open expanse of the Yellowstone Park

concession, built by the Union Pacific Railroad. Directly before them was a circular depression 250 feet across in which lay an enormous relief map of the park. Visitors could lean over a rock wall and peer down onto three-dimensional reproductions of mountains, hot springs, and lakes. Dotted around the basin were lampposts sculpted like gushing geysers.

The theme continued in the 1,000-seat Geyserland Spectatorium, hidden behind the rocky cliffs of the entrance. There a copy of Old Faithful ejected a great column of boiling water, steam, and spray every twenty minutes while colorful lights played across the dazzling plume. Nearby, 10,000 gallons of water per minute roared over an eighty-five-foot-high copy of Yellowstone Falls. Hardier fairgoers could hike a quarter-mile-long path, ascending a fern-lined mountain trail past marvelous "lava" formations to the high crags surmounting the park.

At the back of the concession, the rustic replica of the Old Faithful Inn provided dining in an immense, elegantly appointed room that could seat 2,000. Society folk often hosted

The tracks of roller coaster pioneer L. A. Thompson's Scenic Railway ran through the curled elephant trunks on the ride's whimsical façade. (*The Panama-Pacific International Exposition Illustrated in Color* (viewbook))

glittering banquets at the restaurant, where fifty-six cooks were kept busy. There, said one brochure, one could feast "on the best things in the world while seated in a veritable dreamland and listening to the choicest music." The railroad had underwritten the costs of twice-daily performances by the eighty-man Exposition Orchestra that took place when the ensemble was not playing in the Festival Hall or accompanying the famous visiting conductors, dancers, and vocalists.[19]

A long, low building resembling an adobe mission was the home of the "Grand Canyon of Arizona," built by the Atchison, Topeka & Santa Fe Railway. The entrance building held an office of the Daughters of the American Revolution and a gift shop run by the Fred Harvey Company, which displayed and sold "probably the largest and finest collection of Navajo blankets and Indian curios ever assembled at one place."[20]

Beyond the row of arches perforating the creamy, Spanish-style walls, passengers ascended a grand stairway onto a loading platform designed to look like El Tovar, the great hotel on the Grand Canyon's rim. Guests boarded one of eight full-scale, forty-passenger "observation parlor cars" for a virtual trip that simulated one hundred miles of the great chasm's landscape within the six-acre replica. A New York scenic painter used clever perspective to mimic the mile-deep gorge on 30,000 square feet of linen canvas.

The rail cars were built with one side open; riders sat facing outward as the electric-powered train traversed the canvas canyonscape for half an hour. As the train bumped gently along an elevated trestle, narrators described seven of the signature wonders along the route, including the Painted Desert and Bright Angel Trail, where mule trains descended toward the gushing river. To further the illusion, clouds floated between the walls of the canyon, and an electrical storm played brilliant flashes of lightning across the colorful rocks. While fanciful stone formations and gorgeous orange, gray, and purple geologic striations were the products of sculptors' tools and painters' brushes, the scent of sagebrush and dust in the air was real. The railroad had shipped

The Miller Brothers' 101 Ranch Wild West show staged mock battles between cowboys and Indians as well as sharpshooting, trick riding, and fancy roping, as demonstrated by this cowboy. (Edward A. Rogers)

twenty-six freight cars of desert material from the canyon to add to the verisimilitude of the attraction. The ride finished at a reproduction pueblo built of Arizona adobe, piñon pine, and red sandstone.

Though Yellowstone and the Grand Canyon were considered remarkable feats of scenic design, both operated at a loss. However, neither was required to make money, as they were essentially giant advertisements to draw passengers to the railroads serving the parks and were regarded as major successes in that light.

Wild West shows, replete with trick riding, sharpshooting, stagecoach robberies, and mock battles between cowboys and Native Americans, had been a staple of world's fairs since Buffalo Bill sent his troupe to Paris for the 1889 Exposition Universelle. The Joy Zone was home to two Wild West venues: the '49 Camp featured gold rush–themed shows and activities, and the 101 Ranch offered roping, riding, and Native American dances.

The 101 Ranch show had been staged for about a decade under the Miller Brothers, owners of the actual ranch by that name in Oklahoma. Confident in the success of the same show presented in London and at Madison Square Garden, the Exposition was willing to construct the sets and grandstands for the enormous arena needed for the show. In exchange, the large cast of the 101 Ranch supplemented its performances with a daily parade through the fairgrounds. In addition, bulldogging, dramatic gunfights, and cowboy music enlivened the bill. Indians herded bison around the muddy corral, and a sharpshooting cowgirl plugged targets with unerring accuracy, even as she was firing from horseback with the weapon balanced upside-down on her shoulder.

With so many human and animal mouths to feed, however, the Wild West circus was soon in trouble. In May it dropped its twenty-five-cent admission charge and became a free attraction, but it did not make enough from its restaurant and souvenir stands to survive and it was shut down in mid-June. Once the 101 Ranch moved out, the type of sideshows initially barred by the Exposition moved in, including Maxie, the Girl with Four Legs, and Lorita, the Armless Lady. Aside from an occasional barbecue, the

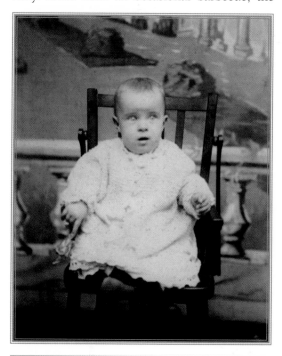

The author's paternal grandmother, ten-month-old Wilma, had her picture taken in one of the studios on the Joy Zone on the fifth day of the Fair. (Laura Ackley)

grandstands and paddock remained closed for the remainder of the Fair.

MIDWAY STAPLES

In addition to new attractions, scattered along the Zone were all the proven winners from earlier fairs, deemed requisite for any midway worth its salt. Inside each of five Postal Photo Studios, attendees could pose before a painted backdrop of an Exposition scene and have it made into a Real Photo postcard to treasure or send to envious loved ones. (The author's grandmother, then a ten-month-old infant, was thus immortalized on the fifth day of the Fair).

"Rajah Zaza" and other "genuine Egyptians" told fortunes in the Temple of Palmistry, which was topped by three inscrutable sculpted faces. Those of a mystical bent were advised on "All Affairs of Life," including love, marriage, business, and travel. Others who preferred to get their information more prosaically could pick up a newspaper or magazine at a newsstand. And those who simply needed a shave could patronize one of two Zone barbershops.

Competitive folk could partake of the usual ball-throwing, ring-toss, or weight-guessing challenges. The now-venerable Skee-Ball, invented in 1909, made its first world's fair appearance at the PPIE. Clacking prize wheels decided whether a child would receive a doll, a teddy bear, or a lesser premium. Two shooting galleries, each identifiable by a light-studded red-and-white target above the entrance, did a good business but found profits sadly diminished by the increase in ammunition prices due to World War I.

Elizabeth Weiss, the "Living Doll," represented a long heritage of little people at world's fairs. Always beautifully clad, the twenty-two-year-old Elizabeth stood thirty-two inches tall and weighed twenty-seven pounds. She was notable for her cultured manner, and the vibrant young woman played music, chatted with visitors, and occasionally inscribed postcards in one of the four languages in which she was fluent.

All manner of shows were performed in the many small theaters throughout the concessions district. Magicians, singers, vaudeville acts, and a variety of dancers, both traditional and erotic, were plentiful. "Pharaoh's Daughter" was billed as "the most beautiful of all illusions," but apparently ancient Egypt was not sufficiently titillating, so she became "Eve, or the Evolution of Woman," before finally transmogrifying into the "Devil's Daughter."

A voluptuous, naked plaster female was poised to dive from the shell-like apex of the Diving Girls' dedicated theater. On warm days, the real girls in modest thigh-length suits would sun themselves in front of the natatorium. Inside, spectators watched the women dive acrobatically from several stories above the water. The show concluded with King Neptune inviting the divers to become mermaids and enter his realm, whereupon the ladies plunged under water and disappeared, emerging out of the audience's sight. This concession raised the ire of the YWCA, which monitored the well-being of female Zone performers. On several occasions the women's organization protested that the water in the Diving Girls' tank was stagnant

and reported it to the Division of Works, which eventually instituted a regular cleaning program.

Coconuts, coffee mills, "electric flowers," and "Marconi's Revolving Balls of Fire" were among the musical instruments in Willard's Melodia. Charles D. Willard offered a show in which music was produced by all sorts of electrical contraptions, including whirling buzz saws from which women created sparks and melodies.

The Race for Life supplied entertainment of a more hair-raising sort. Viewers looked down over the rim into a sixty-foot-diameter circular pit lined with wooden planks forming a racetrack with steep sides. Automobiles speeding at 80 m.p.h. were held by centrifugal force to the 78-degree lower portion. Motorcycles traveling faster were able to race on a completely perpendicular band higher on the walls. Most death-defying were two speeding cyclists circling the Autodrome in opposite directions.

A show more sentimental than sensational was an exhibit of Incubator Babies. Live storks stalked elegantly through the garden in front

In the Race for Life, cars roared around the Autodrome track at an angle of 78 degrees from horizontal, while motorcycles were able to achieve a true, hair-raising perpendicular. (Chuck Banneck)

A colossal seated Buddha marked the entrance to Japan Beautiful, a warren of shows, shops, and games before a backdrop of Mount Fuji. In this view, taken from the Aeroscope, the '49 Camp and Grand Canyon are visible to the left and the grandstands of the 101 Ranch to the right. (Laura Ackley)

of a small building in which neatly uniformed nurses cared for several premature children. The infants lay in warm, white enamel chambers set with windows. According to one article, about thirty children were saved in the exhibit during the course of the Fair.

Dr. Martin Couney, whom many consider the father of neonatology, had already exhibited incubators at several previous Expositions, and at his PPIE concession he encountered a young woman, then attending Vassar College, who introduced herself as one of the incubator babies he had helped at the Omaha Exposition of 1897–8. Likewise, a sturdy young man shook Couney's hand and claimed, "I worked for you once…at the Buffalo Exposition, about fourteen years ago…." He, too, had been nurtured in an incubator.[21]

FAIR FAUNA

Shows on the Zone teemed with animals, both exotic and common. Japan Beautiful sponsored a monkey house, and simians joined in a show at the Dog and Monkey Hotel. For a more exotic experience, one could ride a camel in the Streets of Cairo or a donkey in Toyland. At the Cawston Ostrich Farm—its entrance guarded by a pair

of four-story-tall birds—riding was reserved for experts, but ostrich eggs and gorgeous plumes were available for purchase.

Other unusual souvenirs could be had within the realm of "Alligator Joe," who sold alligator teeth, eggs, and stuffed alligators. The Alligator Farm lay beyond a plaster gate decorated with painted bands of stiff-limbed Egyptian figures next to a saturnine seated pharaoh.

Like "Crocodile Hunter" Steve Irwin generations later, Alligator Joe, a.k.a. Warren Frazee, was a larger-than-life character, and descriptions of his concession were likewise exaggerated. Alligator Joe claimed he was bringing 4,500 animals to the Fair, including alligators, blue herons, pelicans, raccoons, a sea turtle, three manatees, and "man-eating" crocodiles. While this figure was a rank exaggeration, the actual total of several hundred creatures was still impressive. Joe gave daily demonstrations of his reptile-wrangling skills, lassoing, riding, and "hypnotizing" the great beasts for appreciative audiences. While he survived the saurians, Alligator Joe succumbed to pneumonia at the end of May.

In Selig's Animal Arena, "Princess Olga" presided over six trained leopards. During the act, elephants, lions, and tigers also gave "a marvelous performance of intelligence and understanding, and form an entertainment which always appeals to the children." When the Animal Arena folded, the new "Streets of Seville" staged "bloodless bullfights" in its amphitheater. To assure their non-sanguinary nature, the SPCA sent members to each show. While the animals remained healthy, the matadors visited the hospital on many occasions.[22]

The most famous animal on the Zone was Captain Sigsbee, "the Horse with the Human Brain." Patrons streamed into his dedicated theater under the pale abdomen of Captain's gigantic doppelgänger, which spanned the entrance. In the best tradition of "intelligent horse" attractions, Captain could add, subtract, and select the best-looking lady in the front row of seats. But the equine marvel's skills didn't end there. He also played several songs on a rack of chimes, including "Suwanee River," "Happy Days," and "Nearer My God to Thee."

Captain, however, became fatigued performing numerous daily shows, so in June a mind-reading act was added, alternating with Captain. Madame Ellis sat blindfolded upon the stage while her husband circulated among the

THE SIGSBEE-ELLIS COMBINATION

The mind-reading Ellises shared a theater with "Captain Sigsbee, the Educated Horse." Their alternating shows were among the most popular on the Zone. (Chuck Banneck)

crowd, collecting calling cards and small objects from the audience, which his wife then named with remarkable precision. Whether or not one believed in psychic powers, the success of the combined show was indisputable. After paying the Exposition its share, it pulled in more than $46,000 (about $1.1 million in 2012).

THE RIDES

The charmingly discordant tunes from a steam calliope floated out over the Zone's main entrance. The building housing "Looff's Carrouselle" was striped and sported a slim minaret on one end and a handsome dome on the other. Inside, the "finest Carrousel [sic]…ever built on this coast" was constructed to harmonize with the colors and themes of the Exposition. Riders on jeweled horses, camels, and goats enjoyed the tried-and-true pleasures of the merry-go-round, making it one of the few profitable concessions.[23]

Roller coaster pioneer L. A. Thompson built two exhilarating rides: the Safety Racer and the Scenic Railway, which was said to be the longest ever erected. Adventuresome fairgoers also enjoyed the Strauss Aeroscope, which lifted riders high in the air on the end of its long arm, balanced by a counterweight. One correspondent described the sensation: "You get the thrill of aviation, without the danger—a bird-like, gliding sensation."[24]

Boats drifted through dark tunnels in the Old Red Mill, a building that was a convincing replica of its namesake. There was a weathered-looking mill-house and a windmill with gently turning sails. In this classic "immersive" ride, passengers could "unattended float in boats through large subterranean caves and caverns, with here and there an appropriate scenic picture." This pastoral "dark ride" was a sort of aqueous lover's lane, the dim light and splendid scenery extra inducement to amorous couples.[25]

The Submarines were literally immersive. Up to fifty passengers at a time boarded a "submersible" that floated in the concession's tank. The boats didn't actually dip under water, and suspiciously dry-looking wonders of the deep appeared to move past the portholes. After

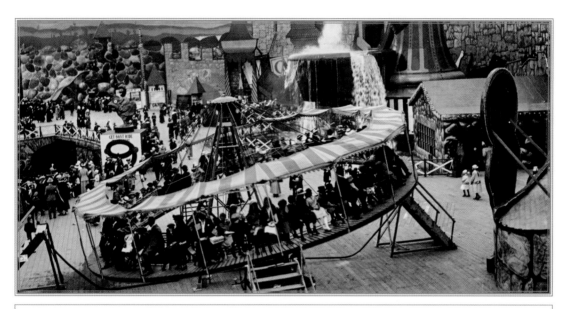

Toyland Grown Up was conceived as a magical playland where adults would feel small. In reality it was a pedestrian collection of rides, shows, and scenery. (Chuck Banneck)

coming ashore, passengers were guided on foot through Neptune's grottos before emerging from the gaping jaws of a papier-mâché whale.

BARKERS

With so many inviting attractions, it took a special kind of talent to pull customers away from competitors. As befitted an international exposition, the barkers who called to patrons on the Zone were masters of their craft. Also known as "spielers," they employed megaphones, props, animals and, of course, pretty girls to lure spectators.

The spieler for the Waffle Kitchen was dressed in floury white, while Fisher, barker at the Autodrome, shooed his customers in with a big sombrero. Rhodes, a one-legged ballyhoo, "talked" for several attractions during the PPIE and was known for his beautiful voice and descriptive language. Harry Le Breque was "everybody's friend," and the Callicott Brothers made it a family affair, but the reigning monarch was the suitably nicknamed King Karlo, of the Tehuantepec Village. He wore buckskin trousers, a colorful serape, and theatrical Mexican makeup, and had a low, musical voice and precise diction. Karlo became even more sympathetic when in August he was shot in the hand while trying

to break up a fight between rival suitors for a señorita within the village.

PERILS ON THE STREET OF JOY

King Karlo wasn't the only one to learn that working or playing among the concessions could be hazardous.

The Bowls of Joy was described as a "wicked ride," but inventor Horace A. Lockwood swore it was safe. Up to six riders boarded a car, which was propelled up a spiral track from the bottom of a cone-shaped "bowl." As the radius of the bowl increased, the speed of the car accelerated from about 3 m.p.h. in the first revolution to 30 m.p.h. at the top of the dish, from which the car would shoot across an elevated bridge into a second bowl. There, the car, impelled by gravity, descended in ever-shrinking loops and finished with a jolt as it completed the sharp final turn.

It was a matter of debate if the jerk entering the last turn was too severe. Early in March, a young woman was thrown forward and struck the seat in front of her, and another rider was ejected from the car. Rails and extra padding were added to the cars, measures the concessionaire claimed would prevent anyone from being thrown out.

After the "kick" was reduced again in April, some complained that management had taken "all the charm out of the ride, therefore spoiling it." But the Bowls of Joy still had kick to spare. Oscar Stewart, a gunner stationed at San Francisco's Fort Scott, was hurled from a car on April 14 and died the following day. Once again, corrections were made to reduce the lurch, but a second man, Ernest Pursel of Portland, was ejected and killed on June 2. With yet more precautions, the operators still could not run the ride safely, and it closed permanently in October.[26]

"Princess Torkia," a dancer in the Russian Ballet Theater, was murdered on the Zone. The "princess," really an Algerian named Zaehaeie Eddy, was on stage preparing for her March 18 performance on when gunfire cracked. Her brother Isack had burst into the theater and shot her with a revolver, killing her instantly. Later it was discovered that Zaehaeie's husband, Ameen Lufti, a ticket taker for the Streets of Cairo concession, was jealous over his wife's friendship with Zone restaurateur Joseph Sasso. Lufti had supplied the dancer's brother with the gun. Isack asserted, "Women in our country… obey men….The husband got right over the wife…; he can tell her; if she don't do, he can kill her. Honor is everything…."[27]

PRIVATION ON THE ZONE

Fair midways are complex, fragile ecosystems, and the Joy Zone of the PPIE suffered from constitutional weaknesses that caused many of its components to wither. The Exposition unwisely had allowed some large concessionaires to let subcontracts, which led to multiple failures and disputes between creditors, concessionaires, and Fair management.

Several aspects of the Zone's design proved liabilities. Its linear layout was a problem. Fairgoers who had just walked half a mile examining attractions on one side found themselves too tired to face the long walk back required to sample the attractions on the opposite side. When they reached a convenient exit, they tended to depart rather than retrace their steps along the midway. Likewise, the

hundred feet between building fronts had been intended as roomy but instead caused the Zone to seem deserted on all but the busiest days, and this ghost-town aura was bad for business.

The weather, too, seemed to conspire against the Zone. For the first time in twenty years, the rainy season extended into May, with nearly a month of soggy days over the nine-month run of the Fair. In his final report, the director of admissions lamented the weather. "Up to the middle of May there were eight consecutive wet Sundays," he wrote. As weekends naturally were the most-trafficked days at the Fair, this was a double whammy for attendance. The *Portland Oregonian* lauded San Francisco's optimism in the face of the wet weather: "If it rains—well, rain is good for the fair; the lighting is softened and beautified seen through a mist; well, this is perfectly true. No one could dispute it; and they say it with perfectly cheerful countenances."[28, 29]

All suffered, but some concessions could not withstand the deluge. The Joy Wheel, also known as "Human Roulette," was a contraption

The Dayton Flood concession used electro-mechanical scenic effects, plus "real fire and water," to depict the Ohio city's 1913 disaster. San Francisco residents found the drama ho-hum after their own city's earthquake and fire, and the attraction closed. (Glenn D. Koch)

The "London to the South Pole" spectacle chronicled explorer Robert Falcon Scott's doomed polar expedition with cleverly animated scenery, but it failed to pay its way. Its space was later filled by a hodgepodge of souvenir shops and sideshows. (Chuck Banneck)

in which passengers sat upon a revolving disc that spun faster and faster until the riders slid off onto the stationary perimeter. It was one of the first rides to go. Selig's Animal Arena succumbed to the elements and high overhead in May.

As the season progressed, the woes of the Zone compounded. Placards started to cover the original price signs on attractions; fifty cents was changed to twenty-five cents, then to ten cents. Some concessions that started out priced at a dime became a nickel, or even free, counting on the sale of souvenirs to carry them financially. Some classes of show that had succeeded at previous fairs failed at the PPIE. The Eden Musée, a wax museum featuring figures of celebrities, war heroes, and groups illustrating historical California events, gained little traction.

As with the animal show, attractions that were expensive to build or operate ran into trouble. The grand spectacles of Gettysburg, the Dayton Flood, the Evolution of the Dreadnaught, and London to the South Pole all flopped. Even Creation, well-loved by audiences for its "magnificent scenic sequences, gorgeous colorings and electrical effects," had to recoup an initial cost of a quarter of a million dollars. By the close of the year it had lost at least $120,000 (about $2.83 million in 2012).[30]

Peanut stands, each topped with a three-dimensional goober, were emblematic of the concessionaires who over-anticipated the popularity of their booths and paid too much for them. Amalgamated Concessions gave the Exposition a hefty bonus to secure the sales privilege for twenty-three small peanut and popcorn franchises dotted over the fairgrounds, but there were too many in total and far too many on the Zone. The peanut stands lost more than $9,400 (about $222,000 in 2012). The owner of the Postal Studio photography concession was similarly over-represented with five locations but escaped ruin by holding the contract to take the identification photographs for all the season ticket books and employee and exhibitor permits.

Other concessions overextended themselves with large casts and costs. The Somali, Maori, Samoan, and Tehuantepec villages and the 101 Ranch all had to support many performers. And while the human employees of the 101 Ranch might have been able to tighten their belts when austerity was required, the horses insisted on continuing to eat prodigious amounts of hay.

One of the largest Zone attractions proved the biggest failure of all. Five-story-tall toy soldiers with ticket booths peeping from the toes of their boots marked the entrance to the fourteen-acre "Toyland Grown Up." Frederic Thompson, impresario of the Luna Park amusement park on Coney Island and veteran of several expositions, had conceived a completely new type of attraction—one where adults would feel small next to immense versions of toys and fairy tale scenes.

With a wink to the many elaborate state and foreign pavilion groundbreaking events, Thompson held his own not-so-solemn ceremony for Toyland in October 1914. Children "planted" toys that would grow up to become the towering Toyland versions. The garden was fertilized with nuts, candy, and ice cream, then sprinkled with California champagne. A doll placed during the inauguration became a ninety-eight-foot-tall suffragette banging on a drum.

Twin soldiers guarding one of the entrances to showman Frederic Thompson's Toyland stood more than fifty feet tall and had ticket booths in the toes of their boots. (Laura Ackley)

Thompson had named her "Panama Pankhurst Imogene Equality," an obvious reference to suffrage icon Emmeline Pankhurst, but he was forced to change the moniker to "Little Eva" after the National American Woman's Suffrage Association complained.

Thompson was a talented illustrator, and his cartoony sketches for Toyland depicted all sorts of whimsical wonders, including a colossal town pump operated by an intricate pulley mechanism, a bandstand supported on mushroom columns, elephants pulling wagons, and a version of the "Trip to the Moon" attraction with which he had made his first fortune. In the drawings, the public frolicked in a thoroughly realized environment, but few of the complicated, expensive features were actually built, and those that were failed to match the lyrical renderings. Once visitors grew tired of looking at twenty-foot-tall boots, the opportunities for fun were limited. One of the few notable activities in Toyland was a mammoth horizontal spiderweb constructed of two-inch-thick ropes and suspended over a lake. Those who could traverse the web without falling into the safety net below would earn a prize.

Toyland was exceedingly expensive to build, opened after the Fair began, and was never completed. A financial failure, it closed in July. Thompson left town, after which his site was used for an assortment of sub-concessions and theaters.

AN EVER-CHANGING AVENUE

The Zone was capricious. Seemingly minor changes to some concessions transformed them from unprofitable to successful. Inside the Orange Blossom Candy Factory, employees were bathed in orange light streaming through the building's glass dome. The orange-uniformed confectioners operated machines that disgorged chocolates, toffees, and miniature orange-shaped bonbons. The original entrance was at the corner of the building, but when the proprietor found foot traffic strangely light, he cut a new door in the wall fronting the Zone promenade, and from then on buyers poured in and the concession sold more than $78,000 worth of sweets.

Patrons of the Orange Blossom Candy shop could watch young women mix, mold, pull, shape, cool, and wrap chocolates, bonbons, and toffees in the elegant marble-appointed factory under an orange-glass dome. (Edward A. Rogers)

After its conversion into the Streets of All Nations, the concession that had been the Shamrock Isle installed a "walk-over" at its entrance. The walk-over was a raised platform patrons had to cross before entering the concession, and apparently seeing others mounting the steps was an irresistible incentive to customers, especially since some concessions employed "shills" to cross the platform first.

Religiously themed attractions proliferated in the later months of the Fair. Among them was painter Henry Hammond Ahl's *In the Shadow of the Cross,* hyped as an "unfinished and unexplained miracle picture" of Christ. The artist claimed he had entered his dark studio one night in 1897 and noticed that the painting appeared to glow with its own light and a mysterious, shadowy cross appeared behind Jesus. Moved, Ahl left the work incomplete, and it had been touring ever since.

After the Dayton Flood spectacle closed, Lorenzo Blanchard's thirty-five-by-forty-five-foot painting of the Spanish palace-monastery El Escorial was installed in its place. The 1814 artwork was one of the treasures spirited out of Europe on the *Jason,* and between July 24 and Closing Day it drew approximately 200,000 visitors and made a tidy profit of about $21,000.

FICKLE FORTUNE

It was estimated that the Zone brought in about $7.2 million on the approximately $10 million invested. This amounted to a little more than thirty-eight cents per attendee, far below the wishful forecasts of concessionaires. Even if the initial cost was exaggerated in the grand tradition of showmen, there were more losers than winners along its extravagant length.

While the Zone didn't fare well overall, some concessions, including old standbys, prospered. The merry-go-round, L. A. Thompson's two roller coasters, and some of the stage shows and restaurants were well patronized. The Souvenir Watch Palace, above which Uncle Sam bowed stiffly from the waist and dangled a ten-foot-tall pocket watch over the thoroughfare, earned an impressive $94,885. The Aeroscope made $67,489. However, both of these had to offset heavy construction costs and ended barely in the black.

In many cases, the most successful shows were

those with small up-front or operating costs that caught the public's fancy. The one-two punch of Captain, the Educated Horse, and the Ellises' clairvoyance act kept their little theater crowded and profitable. The modest Infant Incubator building brought in more than $72,000.

"Have you seen Stella?" was the question on lips, banners, and even lapel buttons all over San Francisco. But who was Stella? She was not one of the lovely dancing girls on the Zone but rather a painting of a voluptuous nude, and one of the midway's most surprising successes. Norman Vaughan, *Stella*'s owner, had presented the painting to tepid audiences for years, but inexplicably she became a big hit on the Zone.

Her official copyright entry is humdrum: "*Stella*; by Napoleon Nani. [Figure of nude woman lying on couch with head resting on right arm and left arm resting on stomach.]" (The painting has also been attributed to Nani's pupil, Alver Regli, or to Gordon Coutts).[31]

Stella was, in truth, quite winsome. Her zaftig form reclined gracefully as she peeped coyly from under a slightly disheveled pile of curls. However charming, *Stella* was not high art. Some wondered aloud why anyone would

The query "Have you seen Stella?" led many men to pay their dimes to see an unexceptional painting of a nude woman that was the Zone's surprise hit. (Seligman Family Foundation)

pay ten cents to look at an average painting of a pretty girl while dozens of finer nudes could be enjoyed gratis in the Palace of Fine Arts. But others rhapsodized over her beauty. There was speculation that the deep frame and clever lighting concealed a bellows mechanism that moved the picture slightly to simulate breathing.

Vaughan invested only $4,000 to display *Stella*, and she brought in a staggering $58,996 (about $1.39 million in 2012) after deducting the Exposition's share.

THE BATTLE FOR RECEIPTS

Continuing travails on the Zone led to a pitched "battle for receipts" between the Exposition and its concessionaires, wherein the showmen tried to reduce the percentages they paid to the Fair, and the Fair struggled to retain as much of its contracted share as possible. This conflict was a time-honored tradition at world's fairs. Frank Burt's "Hundred Percent System," effectively stemmed the skimming of funds at the box office, but there was no inoculation against the pitiable pleas by concessionaires who said they could not survive the "exorbitant" percentages to which they had agreed.

An article in *Technical World* magazine described the techniques used by the artful showman in attempting to lighten his burden: "He goes and seeks the director of concessions, taking along a hard luck story....If he operates at a loss, he multiplies the deficit by five; if he is making a profit, he trebles his ostensible operating expenses. He begs, pleads, cries, threatens to close up, storms, rants, and prays."[32]

Even Norman Vaughan, who was making a mint from *Stella*, had the temerity to request a reduction on his less successful September Morn, a "girl show" with models enacting "living pictures of famous paintings." M. J. Brandenstein, vice chairman of the committee, was taken aback. He said of Vaughan, "He should take a little 'bitter' with the 'sweet'....He is the last one who should ask for any reduction."[33]

At the start of the Fair, the Exposition's publicity department proclaimed that at the 1893 Chicago Exposition, an attraction costing $100,000 was exorbitant, but at the PPIE, "the showman must be 'in' close to or quite up to a million dollars."[34]

As it transpired, most concessionaires would have been better served with cheaper initial investments. The two largest concessionaires provide cautionary examples: Combined Amusements owned the concessions for Joe's Alligator Farm, the Dayton Flood, the Submarines, and the Carousel. Only the last two were still open at the end of the Fair, and the company took a loss of $30,651. E. W. McConnell, known as the "Panorama King," spent about $1.25 million on nine different attractions: the Evolution of the Dreadnaught, the Battle of Gettysburg, Creation, the Pharaoh's Daughter, the Eden Musée, the Samoan Village, the Joy Wheel, the Narren Palast fun house, and Captain, the Educated Horse. Of these, only the Narren Palast and Captain made money.

Concessions director Frank Burt summed up the climate on the Zone: "The big, pretentious production that appealed to the thinking showman proved to be the least attractive to the multitudes...while the smaller and less dominant features proved to be the magnet and money-

getters." Burt added an "I told you so" to those who had doubted his judgment. "*Stella*, which the Director [Burt] presented to the Committee on four different occasions for their approval before [the] same was approved, made the strongest bid for public patronage, while other features that cost thousands of dollars to install and hundreds of dollars per day to operate did not seem to appeal to the public."[35]

Though the fates of the Joy Zone's attractions and performers ranged from the ecstatic to the tragic, the spirit of the PPIE's midway was captured by a limerick submitted to the *San Francisco Chronicle*:

If hungry for mental nutrition,

Come feast at the big exposition.

If joy is your diet,

The Zone will supply it,

In chunks, and without intermission.[36]

Throngs enjoying the Joy Zone strolled past the five-acre model Grand Canyon of Arizona (left). On the right side (near to far) were the Toyland suffragette, King Neptune and a lighthouse on the front of the Submarines ride, the toy soldiers at the far entrance to Toyland, and the Aeroscope in the distance. (Donna Ewald Huggins)

RACE AND RED LIGHTS ON THE MIDWAY

espite its merry name, the Joy Zone had darker aspects, including shameful depictions and treatment of minorities, and a continuing struggle against vice among the concessions.

The avenue was strewn with cultural land mines in the form of "ethnic villages," some claiming to be genuine portrayals of foreign cultures. But all the allegedly realistic villages failed financially, and most of their entertainment-focused counterparts caused headaches for PPIE management.

The Department of Concessions also battled drinking, gambling, bawdy shows, and prostitution on the Zone. Frank Burt, the concessions director, told newspapers in 1914 that "the chief aim of the exposition authorities is to maintain a strict censorship on the class of amusements permitted in the Zone. Our policy is to put nothing before women and children but clean amusement...." He also decried "objectionable dances" like the Bunny Hug, the Texas Tommy, and the Salome, saying they would not be permitted.[1, 2]

As the Exposition progressed and some concessions fell on hard times, many of the original "clean" shows were replaced with more prurient attractions. Crusades to close the offending offerings spurred ongoing conflict between the Exposition and its concessionaires.

THE ETHNIC VILLAGES

Since 1867 "native villages" had been popular at world's fairs. Representatives of various cultures were gathered into enclaves to demonstrate indigenous ways of life. As international expositions were uniformly held in industrialized, expansionist nations, the subtext of these attractions was the advancement of imperialism. At the Louisiana Purchase Exposition in 1904, several Filipino tribes were displayed side by side in "gradations of civilization," with the most "civilized" being those that most closely approached western lifestyles. Moral superiority was imputed to the colonizing nations.

By 1915, the drawing power of the "exotic" had declined compared to earlier fairs, though value judgments of the cultural villages were still implicit. The PPIE followed precedent in exhibiting cultures in a hierarchical manner that exalted the host country and the dominant white, male powers behind the Fair above the foreign, the non-white, and the female. Zone villages were promoted as illustrating "different phases of the human races."[3]

The San Francisco viewing public seemed less credulous. They realized the native villages on the Joy Zone were not entirely authentic and were offered with a wink and a nudge. Author Ben Macomber noted of the village performers, "All these people are genuine and live in primitive

style on the Zone, though, to tell the truth, they are quite likely to use college slang and know which fork to use first." Macomber's commentary shows that in 1915, audiences understood that such ethnic villages were deliberately nostalgic and, in some cases, completely fictional. Nonetheless, reaction to the Zone villages still signaled strong racial biases.[4]

ANTHROPOLOGICAL VERSUS SHOWCASE VILLAGES

Four Joy Zone villages purported to show the actual living habits of various cultures—Pueblo, Somali, Maori, and Samoan—while several other attractions were more like theme-park versions, packaged for entertainment. The Atchison, Topeka & Santa Fe railroad gathered a collection of peoples indigenous to the railway's route to augment its Grand Canyon concession with a "Pueblo Village," which did not have to make money to survive, as it was underwritten by the railroad. "Somaliland" and the Maori and Samoan

Denizens of the Somali Village on the Zone demonstrated spear throwing and dancing, but the concession was unprofitable and closed in May. (Chuck Banneck)

Samoans showcased dancing and diving, and made and sold native crafts. (Seligman Family Foundation)

Villages were populated by natives imported to demonstrate their traditional activities, but without corporate support they struggled from Opening Day.

The most sorrowful story was that of the more than sixty-person contingent from Somalia. The deep rumble of drums issued from the Somali Village near the eastern entrance to the Zone, where tall, slender inhabitants showcased tribal rites, knife throwing, spear fights, and flat-footed dances. Mothers tended their children before houses made of grasses and reeds. These proved insufficient allures, and the concession quickly fell behind financially. The Department of Concessions moved to eject the troupe, but its members protested, saying they could not afford to travel. However, the Exposition already had sold their space to the new Streets of Seville, and on May 14, Exposition guards ousted the villagers. A procession of solemn Africans, each carrying a bundle of possessions, boarded a Fadgl Auto Train bound for the Yacht Harbor. From there they were ferried to the Angel Island Immigration Station in the bay. In June, *Variety* reported that the Somalis had found work at Chicago's White City Amusement Park, but the official history of the Fair says they were deported.

Across from the African exhibit, Maori huts with heavy thatched roofs were installed behind the entrance to the "Australasian Village," over which was mounted a large relief map of Australia, incongruous with the performers inside, who actually hailed from the North Island of New Zealand. Different types of dwellings were on display, including several featuring beautifully carved door lintels known as *pare*. Maori women posed for photos in native garments, including opulent feathered cloaks, although sometimes they could be found in western dress. Both sexes sang, chanted, and danced while wearing *harakeke*-fiber "grass skirts" patterned with contrasting stripes. Men danced a *haka*, incorporating weapons called *patuki* or *hoeroa*. The Maori, too, failed to draw many customers, and their show ceased operation the last week of July.

The Samoan Village held out longest, but its inhabitants faced unique challenges. They, too, presented dances from the South Seas. Women danced a "Siva Samoa" using subtle, undulating arm movements, while men leaped through the athletic "Head-Knife" dance, twirling ceremonial weapons. The Samoans also executed graceful dives from an arched bridge over a miniature lagoon, maneuvered their canoes across its placid surface, and made and sold turtle shell earrings

RAILROADS AND NATIVE AMERICANS AT THE PPIE

How Native Americans came to promote railroads at the PPIE reveals the forces affecting tribes during the early 1900s. Railroads had facilitated settlement, cattle ranching, and mineral prospecting in the American West, all factors that harmed the traditional way of life of many Native American tribes. In the second half of the nineteenth century, railroad companies brought massive parties of bison hunters, and this large-scale hunting ravaged the livelihood of the indigenous peoples on the Great Plains.

By the twentieth century the railroads and the tourist industry recognized that native peoples could be an attractive lure for travelers. Some members of tribes that had been pushed off much of their territories gained a new source of income from posing for photos in ceremonial garb and making tourist versions of handicrafts to sell at railside shops.

On the Exposition Zone, the Atchison, Topeka & Santa Fe Railway built its faux pueblo atop the entry building of its "Grand Canyon of Arizona" concession. This village was populated with members of the Navajo, Zuni, Hopi, Supai, and Acoma tribes, groups that traditionally would not have lived together.

Patrons ascended to the roof on shallow red stairs paved with stone quarried in Arizona. Low rock walls described a path between stepped dwellings clad in real adobe. Unfinished tree trunks framed the doors, windows, and pergolas that extended from the tops and sides of the pueblo buildings. Wooden ladders leaning against the walls accessed the higher levels. Invisible beneath the uneven courses of pale, irregular adobe bricks was a framework of neatly laid, thoroughly untraditional lath.

Amid this scenery, tribe members practiced their traditional arts. According to one guidebook, "Navajo blanket weaving, pottery making, basket weaving, grinding corn by hand with stone pestle, and many other things of a similar character, are going on constantly." Hopi silversmiths hammered bracelets from silver dollars.[5]

Another group of Native Americans appeared on the Marina of the Exposition as representatives of the Great Northern Railway. In an attempt to stave off increasingly desperate conditions caused by the decimation of the bison population, in 1895 the Piikáni (or Piegan) Blackfeet sold the land that is now eastern Glacier National Park to the US government. The tribe retained access for religious use, hunting, and plant collecting on the then-public land, but when the area was converted to a national park in 1910, the government claimed that it was no longer "public," and the tribe's usage rights were cancelled. The Great Northern Railway, which served the park, recognized the potential of the Blackfeet for promotion, and employed them to greet trains and stage dances on the lawns of the grand hotels the railroad built within the park.

At the PPIE, the Piikáni contingent set up teepees next to the Great Northern building, which displayed native handicrafts inside. They raised a medicine lodge and demonstrated dances, competitions, and ceremonies. While the tribe members knew they were creating entertainment from their traditional activities, they strove to present the rituals in authentic form. Fair management was frankly puzzled when the Piikáni refused to have their medicine lodge ceremony interrupted by musical selections by the Official Exposition Band.

Honorary "adoptions" into the tribe were popular events. When Chief Many Tail Feathers dropped his cane, it was retrieved by ten-year-old Lowell "Tiger" Hardy and his seven-year-old sister, Rosemary. Several days later, the children's courtesy was rewarded when they were adopted in a ceremony on the Marina in which Blackfeet performers danced around them and gave them the monikers "Morning Star" and "Evening Star." Aviator Art Smith also received the honor and was renamed "Fly in the Sky." Ishi, made famous as the "last wild Indian in North America" by anthropologists Alfred and Theodora Kroeber, was also offered honorary membership when he attended the PPIE. While proud to be so recognized, he solemnly declined the invitation.

The media relished juxtaposing the Blackfeet delegation, always resplendent in their feathered headdresses and traditional costumes, with modern technologies and conveniences. Articles featured photographs of tribe members riding in automobiles, taking an airplane flight, and depositing their Fair salaries in the bank on the Exposition grounds. The Native American group also took part in a variety of Exposition parades and spectacles. Chief Bull Calf even allowed himself to be blessed by an actor in an astonishingly bad wig who portrayed Father Junípero Serra in a pageant honoring the padre.

The tenor of articles about the natives' participation in the PPIE ranged from appreciative to patronizing. "That the Blackfeet Indians made a spectacle of their ceremonial at all was an act of Indian graciousness to the white man's exposition," wrote journalist Helen Dare, who pointed out that what was entertainment for fairgoers was a reverent observance to the tribe.[6]

Though some coverage was respectful, other pieces regurgitated stereotypical ideas about Native American dialects and habits. "With many grunts and 'hows,' the visitors and their wives were welcomed [by the Blackfeet]," said one article.[7]

Hackneyed dialogue in service to whatever product was being touted in the story was often attributed to the Blackfeet. After Chief Eagle Calf rode in a Buick touring car, he was quoted as saying, "If the Great Spirit will only give me a machine like this when I reach the happy hunting ground, I will be satisfied."[8]

In a piece for *Overland Monthly* entitled "The Door of Yesterday," writer Anna Blake Mezquida admired Eagle Calf more than his fellows because the chief had assimilated into the dominant culture. He had a western education, owned land and businesses, and held traditionally "white" jobs. She praised him as a "figure who shares the aspirations of the white man...."[9]

Writers, no matter how appreciative, invariably framed the presence of Native Americans at the Fair as an elegiac coda to the music of a dying culture. Mezquida wrote that the Blackfeet's "moccasined feet are marking time in the land of shadow," while a sign on the Pueblo Village explicitly labeled its tribes "A Vanishing Race." Even Dare, one of the more sensitive auditors, wrote, "Americans are witnessing now, the passing of a great and extraordinary race." Though the changes affecting indigenous peoples in 1915 were profound, the publicized "demise" of the cultures may come as news to the millions of Native Americans still practicing traditional dances and rituals today.[10]

The Blackfeet, visiting the Fair from the Glacier Park area of Montana, performed a number of "adoptions" into their tribe. In addition to dignitaries and celebrities, they honored Lowell "Tiger" Hardy and his sister Rosemary after the children retrieved a cane dropped by Chief Many Tail Feathers. The children were dubbed "Morning Star" and "Evening Star." (Donna Ewald Huggins)

and necklaces of beads or sharks' teeth. The natives' brief costumes left them chilly during the early season, and Esther Dugan wrote in *Santa Fe Magazine*, "The Samoan village, with its scantily attired natives…will make you shiver—for it is cool in San Francisco, and you wonder how these poor creatures stand it."[11]

While they outlasted the bad weather, the Samoans did not make it to the end of the Exposition. In July they told the Exposition management that if the Fair's percentage was not waived, they would have to ship out on the next steamer. Even after the request was granted, the Samoan Village's revenue could not support its occupants, and they sailed for home on September 23.

Thus the last "authentic" village not supported by a corporation folded. Official historian Frank Morton Todd wrote that the Somali villagers "failed to commit any acts of cannibalism inside, so they lost their popularity and did no business of any great volume…." While jesting, Todd's words contain a kernel of truth: without the expected savage spectacles, the "primitive" cultures exhibited on the Zone foundered.[12]

THE INTERNATIONAL SHOWCASE VILLAGES

Several concessions were themed around foreign lands but were intended to entertain more than to educate. Much like Walt Disney World's EPCOT today, these attractions offered handicrafts, food, and entertainment that was theatrically packaged. These more fanciful re-creations included the Streets of Seville, Japan Beautiful, the Tehuantepec Village, the Chinese and Hawaiian Villages, the Streets of Cairo, and the Shamrock Isle. Several were respectable, but others caused international friction, and some became havens for drinking, gambling, and prostitution.

The Streets of Seville filled the void left by the defunct Somali Village and adjacent Animal Arena, vacated two months later. The Spanish fantasy was underfunded and beleaguered from the first, although its enticements were attractive enough. It offered a Plaza de Toros with "bloodless bullfights," and an evening café cabaret starring dancer La Estrellita, but its income could not meet expenses. Further, some of the bulls, apparently pacifists, tended to wait patiently next to the exit gate of the arena rather than put on a show. The Sevillan sidewalks rolled up after a scant two months.

At the north compass point of the Zone's round plaza, the serene, golden, 120-foot-tall Buddha of Japan Beautiful sat cross-legged atop an octagonal pedestal. Patrons entered through arches in the altar supporting the statue, and beyond this shadowy rotunda lay a warren of cobbled lanes filled with quaint souvenir shops, cookhouses, confectionaries, and carnival game booths. Sumo, ju-jitsu, and classical Japanese dance were performed inside, and there was a twenty-five-piece Japanese band.

One sightseer described a visit: "After patronizing the Monkey Show and the Mystic Cave we pause to let Baron Scotford execute our silhouettes. 'A Trip to Japan' gives us a good idea, by means of panoramic scenery, of the charms of that country. Then last, but not least, are the scores of ingenious games of chance which tempt us to part with our nickels and dimes."[13]

A large outdoor area in the back of the concession was fitted out as a tea garden, where customers were served under the teahouse's deep eaves by young ladies clad as geishas. The tableau was dressed with rustic bamboo fencing, stone lanterns, burbling streams, and a shrine-like gate. A multistory tin-clad backdrop completed the illusion that diners were eating in the shadow of Mount Fuji.

Japan Beautiful was one of the few sites on the Zone that was admission-free, but it did not need to make a profit or break even. Manager Yumeto Kushibiki was subsidized by $50,000 from the Japanese government, further illustrating Japan's comprehensive investment in the PPIE—from the foreign pavilions, through the exhibition halls, and onto the midway.

The façade of the Tehuantepec Village contradicted the offerings inside. The building's front consisted of three towering anthropomorphized step-pyramid gods, replete with sculptural encrustations. While this arrangement had little in common with genuine Mesoamerican architecture, Tehuantepec's

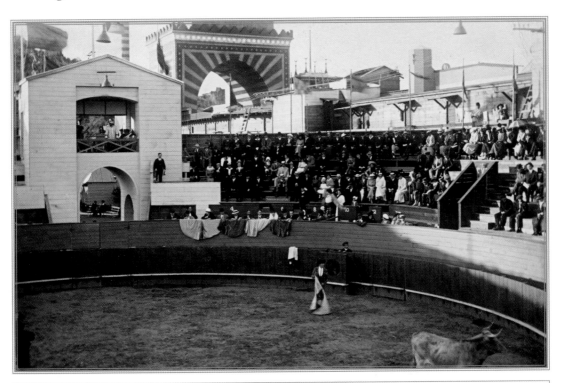

The Streets of Seville filled the vacant spaces left by the Somali Village and Selig's Animal Arena, offering a cabaret and a ring for "bloodless bullfights." (Chuck Banneck)

interior was undoubtedly the most true to its cultural roots of all the showcase villages.

American impresario Captain A. W. Lewis brought a selection of native artisans, dancers, and musicians from Mexico, which was no mean feat given the ongoing Mexican Revolution. According to the Tehuantepec Village's managers, the artifacts and performers were brought through the warring regions with cooperation from opposing factions, all of whom recognized that the village would serve in lieu of an official Mexican Pavilion.

While not a reproduction of any single region or culture, the Tehuantepec Village provided a composite display of the more charismatic and, most importantly, salable Mexican arts. Vendors from throughout Mexico plied their trades: Cuernavaca potters turned red clay vessels, Texcoco weavers loomed brilliant Saltillo serapes, Queretaro lapidaries polished luminous opals, and Tlaxcala woodworkers decorated canes. Guanajuato craftspeople created delicate silver filigree and lace goods, Veracruz sculptors carved clay figures, and Puebla onyx carvers worked the glossy black stone. Wax dolls, carved leatherwork, wooden baskets, and portraits of tropical birds assembled from bright feathers were sold from booths around the miniature marketplace.

Music from Torreblanca's "Orquesta Típica" issued from the small theater and harmonized with the soothing splash of a fountain in the courtyard. Cooks prepared fresh tortillas and frijoles underneath red-tile patio roofs. Vaqueros, resplendent in sombreros, serapes, waistcoats, and slim black pants embellished with long columns of silver conchos, twirled lariats or threw knives with great precision.

Consensus was that the Tehuantepec Village was one of the must-sees at the PPIE. "It is the old Aztec Land in all its dreamy loveliness," said one guide. But its cast was expensive to support, and profits were decreased under Lewis' atypical policy that the artisans could not solicit sales. Later in the season, some of the performers left to join the local vaudeville circuit, but even with the reduction in personnel the concession suffered. At the end of August, Lewis requested

After protests by the Chinese community, Sid Grauman, proprietor of Underground Chinatown, was forced to rename the attraction "Underground Slumming," although the concession was still filled with offensive stereotypes. Here a man offers an opium pipe to a mannequin among signs reading "Opium Den in Full Operation," "The White Slave Girl," and "The Dope Fiend's Dream." A tin on the table reads "morphine sulfate." (Edward A. Rogers)

an advance of $540 to transport the musicians back to their homes, but his plea was rejected by the Exposition.[14]

UNDERGROUND CHINATOWN

The seven fluted roofs of a Chinese pagoda proudly marked the bend in the Joy Zone, but hidden below was the one of the most reprehensible productions on the midway.

Originally, the Chinese Village and Pagoda had been planned by Chinese investors, but financial setbacks caused the group to withdraw during the planning stages, so Sid Grauman, who owned a string of theaters in California, took over. Several of the village's sub-concessions were unobjectionable. Its souvenir shops were loaded with silks, chopsticks, curios, toys, and idols, and its restaurants offered both American food and chop suey, a dish that even in 1915 chroniclers were careful to note was not Chinese but a Sino-Californian invention.

Several private clubs inhabited the upper floors. The Chinese Theater alleged its drama and dance were traditional, but as one reviewer said, they resembled "an American vaudeville producer's idea of what parts of Chinese drama would interest and hold American audiences."[15]

In the basement lurked the offensive attraction. "Underground Chinatown," a series of tableaux, simulated the worst real and imagined scenes from San Francisco's pre-earthquake Chinese quarter. In one room, wax figures puffed pipes in a squalid opium den. In another scene, enacted only when Chinese tourists were absent, actors portrayed a white woman being impressed into sexual slavery by a Chinese drug lord. Naturally, the local Chinese community and the Chinese government, who had invested heavily in its PPIE exhibits, were deeply offended.

Officials of San Francisco's Chinese Consolidated Benevolent Association called the attraction an "outrageous travesty of the Chinese people," and noted "the fact that the Chinese are humiliated and disgraced" was "immaterial to the white concessionaire." Chen Chi, China's commissioner to the PPIE, denounced Underground Chinatown as "degrading and revolting to the moral sense of all decent people."[16, 17]

Exposition president Charles C. Moore responded with placating letters. To the Chinese commissioner he wrote, "I assure you the Exposition will not permit anything that could in any way be considered as an insulting or degrading representation of the life of Chinese people." On the evening of March 26, a detail of Exposition guards shut down the concession.[18]

Grauman complained the Fair had "guaranteed him full protection" for his $12,000 investment in Underground Chinatown, and

Two outlets of the ball-throwing game "Soakum" (right) on the Zone illustrate that racist depictions were commonplace in 1915. (Glenn D. Koch)

said he hoped to reopen. In June "Underground Slumming," advertised as a morality play against the perils of drug addiction, opened in the space. Though the promoters advertised that the environments were "almost completely changed," descriptions of the revised attraction seemed nearly identical to its predecessor, albeit without overtly Asian characters. One viewer wrote, "So 'dopie' an appearance do the actors in…Underground Slumming possess that we wondered if indeed they might not be actual victims of the underworld…."[19, 20]

With all direct references to the Chinese removed, the local community could no longer complain, but it must have been galling to see Underground Slumming laden with allusions to Chinatown, including a large sign reading "Go slumming through Old San Francisco. A guide takes each party through opium dens—slave girls." Despite the offensive nature of his PPIE concession, Grauman was obviously inspired by Chinese design. A dozen years later, he opened his famous Chinese Theater in Hollywood.[21]

RACIAL CLIMATE

Mixed with the frivolity of the Zone were many additional examples of how racism was casually accepted in 1915. Three Zone façades were sculpted into offensive African American caricatures. Two outlets of "Soakum," a ball-throwing game, were shaped like exaggerated heads and upper torsos of African tribesmen with ear- and nose-rings. The game encouraged players to take out their aggression on a row of grotesque, hat-wearing target figures representing various nations that filed in through a swinging door, moved across the backdrop, and exited through another door. Each participant who successfully knocked off a hat received a cigar.

Dixie Land's front featured a quintet of leering, thick-lipped heads above a watermelon slice emblazoned with the name of the concession. Descriptions of the show glossed over the evils of slavery in favor of the fictitious "laughing, happy slave" stereotype. "Dixie Land tells of ante-bellum days in the south when the negro slaves were about the happiest and [most]

The Dixie Land façade was a veritable cornucopia of stereotypes, with leering caricatures and a watermelon slice. (Seligman Family Foundation)

carefree beings on earth," said one brochure. Dixie Land failed early, but a similar plantation show, "Creole Belles," took over the empty Maori Village space.[22]

The paternalistic attitude of the dominant white culture echoed frequently throughout the Palaces and the Zone. The Miller Brothers, proprietors of the 101 Ranch, boasted they had "fostered and cared for the whole redskin nation" who lived on the ranch founded by their father. "They have stood *in loco parentis* to a whole tribe and the tribe has thrived as have the Millers," said a press release issued by the Exposition.[23]

Some racism was more insidious and ingrained at the national level. In September, Exposition cafés with rights to sell liquor were scolded for selling alcohol to Native American women who worked as maids and servants for San Francisco families. Federal law considered these women wards of the United States government, and selling them alcoholic beverages was prohibited under an 1897 amendment to the Indian Appropriation Act.

THE BARBARY COAST COMES TO THE FAIR

In later years Helen Eells spoke laughingly about her parents shielding her eleven-year-old eyes from the salacious sights along the Zone. Her adult recollection was that her parents were overreacting, but the reality was that as the year wore on, a wave of vice swept over the Zone. Most of the programs starring dancers took a vulgar turn, and a plethora of new "girl shows" moved into spaces left vacant by failed attractions.

Drinking, gambling, striptease, and prostitution had been problems at all previous world's fairs, and despite promises and stringent efforts, the PPIE proved no exception. San Francisco had publicly committed to cleaning up its notorious Barbary Coast district in time for the Fair. Gambling was already illegal under state law, and the sale of liquor in San Francisco dance halls was outlawed by an order of the Police Commission on September 1, 1913. The Red Light Abatement Act, intended to suppress prostitution, went into effect on November 3, 1914. Mayor Rolph said local authorities were determined "to make San Francisco a clean, wholesome metropolis, worthy in every respect to be the world's exposition city."[24]

But by the time summer arrived, it seemed more like part of the Barbary Coast had simply moved onto the Zone, infiltrating its theaters and dance halls, especially the "showcase villages."

The Hawaiian Village started its life as a fairly benign traditional hula show, though slightly adulterated for mainland consumption. "Princess Kaela" gave the "Dance of Death," offering herself as a sacrifice to the crater of Mauna Loa. The production drew fire not only because it was inauthentic but also because of its increasingly unsavory character. After it had been shut down at least once, the village added an underground stage on which it offered a "dance so vulgar and so rotten that it had to be danced down in the cellar." Visiting islanders said the dances were not hulas nor the dancers Hawaiian. Instead, they were erotic dances by "white women…browned up for the occasion to simulate our Hawaiian

people." A. P. Taylor, acting director of the Hawaii Promotion Committee, asked President Moore to discontinue "this alleged Hawaiian Village…."[25]

After many grievances were filed, the concession disavowed any connection to Hawaii. The name was changed to "Hula-Hula Dancers" in late August, and later it became the even raunchier "Girl in Blue," before finally being closed by the Exposition in October.

THE STREETS OF SIN

The entrance to the Mysterious Orient was one of the most beautiful and evocative on the Zone, but when it came to its dancers, the concession took the term "thinly veiled" too literally. Parting the heavy curtains across its horseshoe-arch gateway revealed a twisting streetscape of bazaars filled with brass goods, jewelry, rugs, and pottery.

The pointed-arch gateway of the Streets of Cairo led into a Middle Eastern fantasy featuring bazaars, acrobats, fortune-tellers, and belly dancers. (Anne T. Kent California Room, Marin County Free Library)

Nimble acrobats tumbled and dashing swordsmen slashed. Inside were opportunities to ride a camel, have one's palm read, sample rich coffee, smoke an exotic cigarette, or try on embroidered Moorish slippers. Girls in diaphanous veils, ropes of beads, and fringed belts undulated gracefully on the theater's stage. According to historian Zeynep Çelik, belly dancers had catered to harem fantasies and "attracted great crowds and achieved major commercial success" at every world's fair since 1867.[26]

The Oriental opulence had been exceedingly expensive to construct, and the original concessionaire went bankrupt before the Fair opened. The Exposition stepped in and underwrote his costs, but this was not enough to save the Mysterious Orient. In May it was handed over to new management and dubbed "Streets of Cairo." The new management added a second theater wherein the wriggling became progressively racier, with "Princess Athena" dancing in a blouse of transparent black gauze, or no blouse at all.

The Exposition closed the Streets of Cairo in early August after receiving a slew of complaints, only to reopen it under yet another manager shortly thereafter. This time the wriggling lasted just eight weeks before the show was shut down for good.

The Shamrock Isle started its life innocently enough as an Irish village, much like those at previous world's fairs. Within its square-towered castle, colleens sang Irish tunes and danced jigs and reels. Visitors could examine Irish laces, kiss a replica Blarney Stone, and eat hearty Irish fare. As the season wore on, the village faltered. To revivify the attraction, Shamrock Isle was reimagined as the Streets of All Nations under the same concessionaire as the Streets of Cairo, and the crenellated castle façade was emblazoned with a sign advertising "Luna: Best Formed Woman in America."

CAIRO CAFÉ

In June a slice of vice landed smack dab in the middle of the thoroughfare, in a vacant space in front of the Submarines. Zarefa Maloof paid $700 for the right to sell Constantinople coffee, liquors, sweets, and cigarettes from her Cairo Café, but after a few weeks trouble began. The café was staying open until 2:00 a.m., well beyond the midnight closing hour stipulated by the Exposition. Waitresses were drinking with guests, and it was said that some were "making engagements with men patrons to meet them downtown."[27]

Even as the Exposition directorate was in the process of revoking Maloof's license, it received an anonymous letter from "a heart-broken mother," who claimed her son was "robbed and made drunk at a place on the Zone known as 'Cairo

While the winsome dancers from the Streets of Cairo were modestly dressed on the attraction's float, which took first prize in the May 27 Zone Day parade, they were scantily clad at best when appearing within the concession's theaters. (San Francisco History Center, San Francisco Public Library)

Entertainment inside the notorious '49 Camp included panning for gold, stagecoach robberies, a cowboy band, dancers, and even a live bear. The main attractions, however, were booze, women, and gambling. (Chuck Banneck)

Café' by a foreign woman who ownes [sic] the place." Maloof said she didn't know that some of her employees were habitués of the Barbary Coast and that the "heart-broken mother" was in reality an employee fired for just the sort of bad behavior the Exposition was trying to stamp out. The accusations, she said, were mere "jealousy and knocking," and other charges, made by the Woman's Board and the YWCA, were fictitious.[28, 29]

Fearing a lawsuit from Maloof, Exposition management allowed the Cairo Café to reopen as long as she signed and complied with a code of conduct, agreeing to close promptly at midnight and to make certain that female employees would not solicit business outside the café, smoke in public, drink, or converse with the clientele beyond taking orders.

But in October she stationed a girl out front with a megaphone to recruit customers and was caught keeping the business open late yet again. Another letter to the Department of Concessions alleged that services not on any menu were available "for the sum of $1–3 from different girls" working at the café. Finally, Maloof's operation was shut down.[30]

THE DAYS OF OLD, THE DAYS OF GOLD, THE DAYS OF '49

The '49 Camp was the "bad boy" of the Zone. Beyond a rectangular stockade gateway of rough-hewn logs lay a gold rush–themed playground, which *Current Opinion* called "an expurgated edition of a miners' camp of '49." In reality, the attraction was not particularly "expurgated," and it had more in common with the saloons of the notorious Barbary Coast than with a camp from California's boom days.[31]

Many of the camp's activities were inoffensive. Mine scenes included a reproduction of the California gold discovery site at Sutter's Mill and a tumbling mountain spring. A volcano spurted flames twenty feet above its peak, and a "miner's dream" tunnel simulated the treasures of a forty-niner's wildest imaginings. Fun-seekers could try panning for gold, although as one wag noted, "It is hardly possible to pan out enough gold here to amass a fortune. This, however, is exactly as it was in the days of 1849…."[32]

Gold rush–themed dramas were enacted around a dusty central plaza. Hardy argonauts toiled up the trails alongside their burros, dashing Pony Express riders delivered mail, and an especially unlucky stagecoach was held up a dozen times a day. Fairgoers practiced their aim at the shooting gallery and watched bronco-busting demonstrations, sharpshooting exhibitions, and the mock-hanging of horse thief Swede Sam. It was all in good fun, though sticklers for historical accuracy noted the cowboys ought to have been portrayed as Mexican vaqueros.

The savory smells of simmering beans, Chinese food, and spicy tamales and enchiladas wafted from booths ringing the camp, while a band of musicians from a Nevada tribe of Native Americans played sprightly airs like "It's a Long Way to Tipperary." In the Fandango Dance Hall, actors in red flannel shirts danced with fair señoritas. During each show, a fight would break out, a knife would flash, and one of the miners would slump to the floor. The dance hall manager would yell, "Roll the corpse out the back door and choose your partner for the next dance!"[33]

Many of these diversions echoed those of the '49 Mining Camp at the 1894 San Francisco Midwinter Fair. But the earlier production had been a staid affair compared to its descendant. The 1915 '49 Camp was wildly popular from the start, not because of its tame concessions but for its triple vices of loose women, drinking,

and gambling. Fastidious visitors took one peek inside the wild Jimtown Dance Hall, turned tail, and fled the camp.

Social Hygiene magazine proclaimed that known prostitutes frequented the camp's two dance halls and were "permitted by the management to…dance with the men and to persuade them to purchase alcoholic drinks which were at all times freely sold. They were not for the most part paid any salary, but made what they could out of the men."[34]

The Days of '49 Company, which owned the concession, had been told repeatedly since 1913 that a "stand-up bar," where drinks were served over the counter rather than by waiters, was not allowed. But when the Fair opened, liquor flowed liberally from behind the banned bar. Faro, roulette, and craps were played in the El Dorado Gaming Hall, despite a law against such games in California.

Within a week of opening, the camp was closed for "repair, remodeling or reform." It reopened in mid-March, ostensibly cleansed of features that might offend, but soon it became clear the concession's management was not committed to expunging vice. "It never was expected to be a Sunday school," said a '49 Camp employee.[35, 36]

After the Exposition first politely requested and then sternly ordered closure of its stand-up

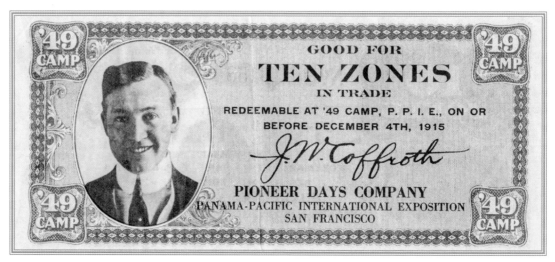

The '49 Camp reopened in September as "Pioneer Days," under the auspices of boxing promoter James Coffroth, who issued currency in denominations called "Zones," emblazoned with his own face. The illegal scrip was quashed in October, along with Coffroth's attraction. (Dr. William Lipsky)

bar, the lawyer for the '49 Camp whined that a sub-concessionaire had paid $10,000 for the bar privilege and the concession could not afford to lose the money. Next, the PPIE tried withholding the camp's percentage of revenues. In mid-April, Walker Smith, president of the Days of '49 Company, finally said he would close the bar, but days later it was discovered that bar service was still going strong.

Yet another problem occurred because the '49 Camp paid a smaller percentage to the Exposition on profits from its interior concessions than it did on admissions, so the concession attempted to bypass the gate fees whenever possible. On June 10, three Exposition guards were detailed to make sure all entrants to the '49 Camp paid for tickets. The manager of the camp countered by attempting to distribute free passes to all comers, but the guards refused to accept these. After three closures, this was the final straw, and in July the Exposition slammed the gates shut on the Days of '49 Company, revoking its privilege.

The Exposition scrambled to find a replacement to avoid a large abandoned space on the Zone. Eyebrows were raised when, at the end of August, James W. Coffroth, a boxing and show promoter who had been indicted for paying bribes during the graft trials, was chosen to manage the attraction. It was said that Coffroth's silent partner was notorious bookmaker Frank Daroux, though Coffroth denied it. He promised the Exposition his operation would be "letter-A perfect," so no doubt it seemed like a recurring nightmare when one of his first acts was to ask for a stand-up bar privilege.[37]

The camp was re-branded "Pioneer Days," and in addition to historical reenactments, it offered cafés and cabaret shows, a "beauty chorus of 25," and an occasional boxing match. But the main draw was gambling. Thousands flocked to the resort each night. Bejeweled society women flung dice alongside youths just out of their teens, roulette wheels clacked, and playing cards whispered. It was said that some Zone waitresses lost all their earnings at the tables. Coffroth tried to skirt California's gambling ban by using a system in which gamblers would wager with "scrip." Each of the notes, issued in

denominations called "Zones," was emblazoned with Jimmy Coffroth's smiling mug. Though the currency was fake, it was an open secret that the scrip was accepted at "well-advertised stores," some Zone concessions, and "certain restaurants, saloons and resorts of questionable character."[38]

Moral crusaders shook their heads. The situation should have been anticipated, they said, "when professional gamblers and prize fight promoters were permitted to become associated with the concession." But using scrip as currency was as illegal as the games themselves, and after Matt I. Sullivan, president of the State Exposition Commission, wrote a scathing letter about the camp, the Exposition shut down Pioneer Days in October.[39]

GIRL SHOWS

Skimpy or absent costumes were the hallmarks of the many titillating "girl shows" that went into storefronts vacated by failed concessions. The Diving Girls in their modest bathing suits looked downright dowdy when contrasted with the girls in "The Model's Dream" or "Luna." The star of "Living Venus" was draped in a meager three-inch-wide ribbon across her hips, and in "September Morn" and "Eve," the girls were completely naked.

In many cases, monitors of virtue did not object to the nudity so much as the vulgar outside barkers who drummed up business. The California Civic League, a women's suffrage organization, complained specifically about the spieler at the Streets of Cairo, who "persistently used language which is suggestively indecent. His appeals are skillfully calculated to arouse morbid sex curiosity." Many barkers would give their pitch accompanied by a girl wrapped in a heavy cloak who would throw open the garment and wiggle suggestively on cue.[40]

Some concessions offered a relatively tame show followed by a second show featuring dancers costumed only in "smiles and beads." "Now…we will have a second show," smirked one emcee, "where you will see the dancers as you like to see them—just a bit more pep and spice." Some of these girl shows did not

September Morn, one of many "girl shows," featured nude and semi-nude models posing in re-creations of famous paintings. At the end of their spiels out front, barkers often beckoned the audience closer, whereupon the women would throw open their cloaks and gyrate. (Donna Ewald Huggins)

stop at striptease but, according to one article, pantomimed "the act of sexual intercourse." Prostitution was nearly impossible to eliminate. After the 101 Ranch had closed up shop, the dance hall associated with it remained, and some of the women working there were known to be "regular girls" from the Barbary Coast.[41]

A number of concerned civic organizations protested. The YWCA and the PPIE's Woman's Board became the de facto defenders of morality on the Zone. When a concession overstepped someone's idea of decency, Fair management was sure to receive a complaint. These objections eventually were heard at the state level by the California Exposition Commission, which closed most of the girl shows during the first week of October.

But even though Burt, director of concessions, paid lip service to the Exposition's goal of a wholesome concessions district, his official report at the end of the Fair reflects his ambivalence about the profitable girl shows and his annoyance at the interference of the YWCA and the Woman's Board.

Other expositions permitted hoochy-hoochy dances and girl-shows that were indecent, and while these shows were permitted for a short time at this Exposition and were money getters, the pressure brought to bear upon the Directorate was of such nature that they were eliminated, to the financial detriment of the concessionaire and the exposition. While my experience in the show world has been entirely devoted to catering to ladies and children, I am free to confess that the average Exposition visitor wants something unusual...[;] he likes the pastimes and pleasures of the foreign countries, even in their crudest forms, as shown at other Expositions, and it is commendable that this was not permitted to any extent at the Panama-Pacific International Exposition, although the financial results were not as great as at other Expositions.[42]

He continued in a way that illustrates he did not think abolition of such shows as "commendable" as he claimed:

The reform wave which swept over the State Commission, aided by the Woman's Board, cost the Division many thousands of dollars...and left it prozy [sic]

indeed—what are the Streets of Cairo [without] its oriental dancing girls; what is left of a Hawaiian Village without the Hula Hula and their long grass skirts; what of the native villagers of the Southern Ocean Islands with their women bundled up like Esquimaux—but the wave of reform was supreme....[43]

The United Press reported wistfully in late October: "No longer do the 'Streets of Cairo' teem with handsome harem girls..., no more do the 'muscle dancers' shock the 'small town' folks in the 'Street of All Nations'; and likewise, the 'second shows' in the 'Model's Dream' and the 'Girl in Blue' have been deleted by the censor. The rattle of chips, the click of dice, and the whirring of roulette wheels in the '49 Camp are stilled.... [T]he Zone nowadays is fairly serene."[44]

Luna, the "Best Formed Woman in America," performed a "muscle dance" as part of the Streets of All Nations concession, which had replaced the Shamrock Isle. (Anne T. Kent California Room, Marin County Free Library)

FILLING THE PLAYBILL

George Stewart's adventures while pursuing international talent for the Fair read like a suspense novel. The PPIE director of music planned that every day of the Exposition would be packed with music, song, and dance, but acquiring the best artists was nearly stymied by the outbreak of World War I.

A compelling music program was considered essential to the financial success of the Fair. The Department of Music wanted to provide a robust array of offerings, particularly during the early season, when weather might be poor. As it happened, the first months of 1915 were unusually rainy. In June the directors reported, "The weather conditions have been extraordinarily severe." However, the music program encouraged attendance when Mother Nature did not. When the Vanderbilt Cup Auto Race was postponed due to rain on the fourth day of the Fair, crowds were kept entertained by multiple bands, as well as the great organ in the Festival Hall.[1]

Each day's lineup featured as many as a dozen outdoor band concerts, dancing by students or professionals, a noon organ recital in the Festival Hall, and two evening concerts by the Exposition Orchestra in the Old Faithful Inn on the Joy Zone. In addition to these daily attractions, the year was punctuated by appearances by such headliners as contralto Ernestine Schumann-Heink, composer Camille Saint-Saëns, violinist Fritz Kreisler, pianist Ignace Jan Paderewski, and the Boston Symphony Orchestra.

The Department of Music scheduled military-style bands, orchestras, choral groups, operatic and concert singers, dancers, instrumental soloists, chamber ensembles, and student groups—more than 2,200 events in 288 days. Because entertainment was viewed as an essential driver of attendance, the department's budget was $623,800. Once revenues were factored in, the total expenditure was $462,058, roughly equivalent to $10.9 million in 2012 dollars.

THE DEPARTMENT OF MUSIC

In 1913, PPIE president Charles C. Moore appointed J. B. Levison, then vice president of Fireman's Fund Insurance and an "amateur musician of unusual gifts," as a "Committee of One" for music. Levison promptly hired Dr. George W. Stewart as the director of music. Stewart had been a trombonist in the Boston Symphony Orchestra, the music manager of the 1904 Louisiana Purchase Exposition, and an organizer of successful large musical festivals for a quarter century. He was given authority to schedule all the performances for the huge PPIE Festival Hall.[2]

His St. Louis exposition experiences greatly influenced how the music department functioned in 1915. The musical program in 1904 was a blueprint for that of the PPIE, featuring "the liberal use of military bands playing in the open air," plus an orchestra, organ recitals, and choral performers. The only deviation from the earlier fair was that in 1915 there were no singing or music competitions under the auspices of the Exposition.[3]

THE ADVENTURES OF MUSIC DIRECTOR GEORGE STEWART

As negotiations for bands and orchestras commenced, the search was on for a top-notch symphony conductor. When Bay Area favorite Paul Steindorff called at the Fair's offices in September 1913 to offer his services as leader for the Exposition Orchestra, Stewart tactfully declined, citing the wish to employ a "great European conductor" to stimulate attendance.[4]

Stewart sailed to England in June 1914 to attempt to secure a first-class maestro and other premiere European musical attractions. For the next month he conducted meetings, visited musicians, and attended concerts with an eye toward booking the best European talent. After London, Stewart traveled to the Isle of Wight to visit organist Edwin Lemare, and then to Paris, where he met with legendary composer Camille Saint-Saëns and lunched with Gabriel Parés, former director of La Musique de la Garde Républicaine.

Stewart continued on to Montreux, Milan, Florence, Rome, and then Munich, where he picked up the music for the "Panama Hymn" from composer Amy Beach. He told her he was impressed with its "majestic beauty" and vowed to request that it be made the Official Hymn of the Exposition.[5]

The director was on his way to Vienna on July 26 when he found himself caught up in world-changing events. At the Salzburg train station he heard a group of people discussing the possibility of war between Austria and Serbia. That night, through the window of his

Intrepid Director of Music George W. Stewart traveled through the European war zone to secure top musical talent for the Fair. (*The Story of the Exposition*, vol. 2, Frank Morton Todd)

hotel in Vienna, he saw throngs demonstrating, cheering, and singing. After midnight, thousands of men marched through the streets singing the Austrian national anthem. Two days later the news came that the Austro-Hungarian Empire had declared war.

It was becoming clear that Stewart's designs for comprehensive European participation at the PPIE were impossible. Some of the venues there were completely dark. At one show a uniformed officer ascended the stage and said a few words, after which the musicians immediately took their instruments and abandoned the concert. They had been ordered to report for military duty the next day. Giving up his plans to visit Russia, Stewart decided to make just a few more stops, then retreat to America.

Travel was becoming increasingly difficult, and Stewart met with many obstacles on his way to Berlin. Upon reaching the city on August 3, he found that the steamship companies were "overwhelmed with Americans wishing to return," and that many of the US tourist agencies had closed.[6]

As the first battles of World War I began, he was not certain the Exposition would even take place. He was relieved when on August 25 the American embassy in Berlin sent him a dispatch from Secretary of State William Jennings Bryan. It read: "Department informed by Panama Pacific Exposition management that exposition will be held as originally planned. BRYAN."[7]

After trying for weeks to find passage, Stewart heard the steamer *New Amsterdam* might be leaving Rotterdam on September 12, so he pressed on to the Netherlands, securing a berth only on the morning of the steamer's departure. When he arrived in New York, Stewart wired Levison, suggesting that with such vast uncertainties abroad, the Department of Music should book talent only for the first few months of the Fair, "adding gradually afterward." Levison, relieved Stewart was safe, suggested he travel incognito to San Francisco so as not to alarm anyone about the perilous state of musical affairs.[8]

As he tried to shore up his program, Stewart lamented in January 1915, "On account of the European war, the extensive plans of

the Department of Music upon which I had labored industriously for nearly two years, were completely wrecked. It is quite impossible for us to secure such great musical attractions as shall give strong character to our musical features and attract the attention of the whole musical world."[9]

Alfred Holmes-Dallimore, who led a band of former British Grenadier Guards, sympathized: "Possibly this shocking war which has been forced upon us with such deliberate preparation has upset your calculations and will seriously affect any chance of your obtaining any Continental Bands...." It was true: the Grenadier Guards, the Roman Banda Communale, the Parisian Musique de la Garde Républicaine, Berlin's Philharmonisches Blas-Orchester, and all other major European bands and orchestras were now unobtainable.[10]

The PPIE was set to open in February, and Stewart still had no leader for its orchestra. His heart remained set on a "great European conductor," as American leaders were regarded as second tier. Composer and theatrical manager Rudolph Aronson, who was assisting Stewart, suggested that failing Europeans Josef Willem Mengelberg or Oskar Nedbal, perhaps Americans Victor Herbert or Max Bendix might be hired. As it was understood that no one man would handle the directing duties for every concert, the PPIE started talks with Bendix for at least a partial role.

Eventually, the Department of Music did secure a European conductor for its first ten weeks. Just eighteen days before the Fair opened, Auguste Bosc was anointed director of the Exposition Orchestra and given military leave by France to serve at the PPIE. Bendix was named associate conductor. Bosc was a graduate of the Paris Conservatoire, a fine composer, and a tactful soul. When asked why French popular music was superior to American popular music, Bosc responded, "I cannot attribute it to anything, because I do not believe it is a fact." After he conducted his final PPIE concert on May 12, the orchestra spontaneously broke into "Auld Lang Syne" as a tribute, and tears coursed down Bosc's cheeks.[11]

Max Bendix was a violinist who had risen to the rank of concertmaster at fourteen years old and had by 1915 conducted the Chicago Symphony Orchestra and the orchestras of the New York Metropolitan and Manhattan Operas. Bendix was a comparative unknown on the West Coast, but by the end of May, Alfred Metzger, editor of the *Pacific Coast Musical Review*, was a convert to his cult. He wrote, "Since the writer has been living in San Francisco there has never been an instance when orchestra and leader were of equal excellence, until Max Bendix began to direct the Exposition Orchestra."[12]

At last the PPIE had found its conductor. Bendix became the primary director for the remainder of the Fair, spelled by a number of other maestros, including Georges George of Paris; Richard Hageman, conductor of the Metropolitan Opera

orchestra; and Walter Damrosch, conductor of the New York Symphony Orchestra.

THE BOSTON SYMPHONY ORCHESTRA "LEAPS ACROSS THE CONTINENT"

As Stewart surveyed the ruins of his plans for great European musical ensembles, he desperately racked his brain for a domestic organization of equal allure. Finally he struck upon an audacious idea to bring the preeminent US orchestra, the Boston Symphony, to the Fair. He wrote, "The business of the entire world having been practically halted by the war, it is perfectly obvious that in order to make the Exposition the financial success necessary

The main auditorium of the Festival Hall, home to the 7,000-pipe, forty-ton Exposition Organ, was enlarged from about 3,200 to 4,000 seats in anticipation of the Boston Symphony Orchestra's thirteen-concert series in May. (The Bancroft Library, University of California, Berkeley)

for its very existence…the Boston Symphony Orchestra is the one organization in the world which would give such distinction to the music of the Exposition."[13]

The Boston Symphony had never traveled farther west than Kansas City, and bringing its 110 musicians to San Francisco would cost a staggering $60,000, almost 10 percent of the entire musical budget for the PPIE. It was a huge risk. Beyond this Stewart had to contend with serious union issues. The Boston Symphony Orchestra was not a union shop, and the PPIE had agreed to hire only union players for its major musical events. The San Francisco chapter of the American Federation of Musicians recognized the tremendous publicity value of the BSO visit and was inclined to be lenient, but the national organization was a different matter. It classed the symphony among its "unfair organizations." Frank Carothers, AFM president, was especially against the plan because union orchestras were available. On January 15, 1915, Stewart wrote again to Charles Ellis, the Boston Symphony manager, that the union had denied his requests and the orchestra's visit was off. Then, at the eleventh hour, a deal was struck, and on January 21 Chairman Levison accepted the celebrated orchestra's proposal.

The symphony was billed in the newspapers as "the World's Greatest Orchestra," and its engagement was seen as an opportunity to demonstrate symphonic excellence to San Francisco. The city's society buzzed with anticipation. Subscriptions for the series, priced from $7 to $25, poured in. When single seats went on sale, lines formed out the door of the Powell Street ticket office. As the orchestra gave no performances en route to the West Coast, some aficionados undertook long-distance excursions to San Francisco to hear it.

Interest was intense. The *Chronicle* said, "The Boston Symphony Orchestra, by a splendid stroke of genius on the part of Dr. George W. Stewart, is coming out to the exposition soon…. [The orchestra] leaps across the continent to play for us in Festival Hall for less money, per seat, than is paid by Boston music lovers." To prepare for the BSO, the Festival Hall was expanded and

its acoustics improved. The building was closed for eleven days, starting May 2, to add a balcony fronted by a horseshoe of boxes and to bring its total capacity from 3,200 to about 4,000. A new entrance was opened in the hedge fence opposite the Festival Hall especially for concertgoers.[14]

It was widely acknowledged that the Boston players, under conductor Karl Muck, had set a new standard for orchestral work. Prior to coming to America, the German-born Muck conducted Berlin's Kaiser Wilhelm Royal Opera and was considered an authority on Wagner. Sharp-eyed, hawk-nosed, and always excellently tailored, Muck was musically conservative. On his watch the BSO had not played works by more avant-garde composers, such as Stravinsky, Scriabin, and Schönberg.

At the Exposition, the Boston Symphony Orchestra played a collection described as "stiff programmes that will test the enthusiasm of the most musical public," but local audiences attended in ever-increasing numbers. Many of Muck's selections had a strong German accent—Beethoven, Strauss, Brahms, and Bach. One evening was dedicated to Wagner. Other concerts, however, were devoted to Italian, French, or Russian composers. Contemporary composers like Dvořák, Rimsky-Korsakov, Sibelius, and Americans George Wakefield Chadwick and Edward MacDowell were also on the slate.[15]

The series proved stunningly successful, drawing an aggregate audience of 46,000 for the thirteen concerts, an average of 3,538 per performance. Nearly 5,000 music lovers filled every available seat and crowded into every inch of standing room for the orchestra's final concert on May 26.

Writer Ben Macomber joked about the overabundance of musical stars playing the Jewel City during this period:

> John Philip Sousa has spent a long season at the Exposition. A blunder was somewhere made in dating the arrival of the March King and his splendid instrumentalists, who

came while yet the Boston Symphonists were playing in Festival Hall. As a result the finest of bands was placed in competition with the finest of orchestras. But nothing disastrous happened. Those who desired, to the number of 15,000, heard Sousa at his opening concert in the Court of the Universe; those who desired heard Dr. Muck's instrumentalists, to the seating capacity of Festival Hall.[16]

Stewart had transformed a terrifying dearth of musical acts just a few months before the Fair into a triumphant bounty.

THE EXPOSITION ORCHESTRA

The Exposition needed a house orchestra to support its panoply of star singers, instrumental soloists, organists, and conductors. To this end, eighty accomplished musicians, most of them Bay Area locals—and many regular members of the San Francisco Symphony—were assembled under Max Bendix's baton. The orchestra leader expressed his delight in the quality of the San Francisco players: "In all respects of artistry, experience and enthusiasm I find the local musicians equal to any to be found anywhere."[17]

Use of the Exposition Orchestra was similar to that of the 1904 World's Fair. The St. Louis exposition's management "sublet" the official orchestra to a large restaurant concessionaire on the midway called the Tyrolean Alps, which covered about half its cost. This approach was successful and profitable, so a similar plan was used at the PPIE.

On most nights, the PPIE's orchestra played two concerts at the 2,000-seat Old Faithful Inn, part of the Union Pacific Railroad's replica of Yellowstone Park. Union Pacific paid $77,500 for the privilege of hosting the Exposition Orchestra. Thus the expense was underwritten by a private entity, which benefitted by attracting paying dinner customers for two shows a night. This arrangement enabled the PPIE to produce weekly symphonic programs in the Festival Hall and to support visiting marquee acts. The Exposition Orchestra performed more than five hundred times during the ten months of the Fair.

While Bendix lauded his musicians, he was not quite so delighted with the busboys of the inn. In October they insisted the orchestra's five copper kettledrums were actual kettles and attempted to fill them with soup.

Paid Exposition musicians were required to be members of the American Federation of Musicians and received a negotiated union rate of $45 per week, the same salary as musicians at the 1904 fair. The first-chair musicians and librarian received more, and the bandleader got double the standard wage. This was a concession by the union: at St. Louis the salary had been for a six-day "week," while the PPIE rate was for a full seven days. Thus, the musicians at San Francisco received approximately 10 percent less, saving the music department on the order of $35,000.

Admission to most of the music, song, and dance at the PPIE was free, and the schedule was replete with outdoor recitals and concerts, plus music in the state and national pavilions. However, many programs in the main auditorium of the Festival Hall required an additional investment—typically twenty-five cents for the daily lunchtime programs on the new grand pipe organ (later reduced to a dime) and twenty-five or fifty cents for the gala evening events.

FESTIVAL HALL

For more formal programs, music-lovers streamed into the Festival Hall either to the big auditorium under the dome or upstairs to the smaller Recital Hall, used for more intimate concerts. At the start of the PPIE, the main auditorium was pronounced "acoustically perfect." No one was fooled for long, though, as listeners soon noticed that the dome created a "mausoleum-like echo," and the hard wall surfaces caused unpleasant acoustic reflections.[18]

When it was not supporting the marquee conductors and soloists in the Festival Hall, the eighty-piece Exposition Orchestra played nightly at the 2,000-seat Old Faithful Inn, within the Zone's Yellowstone concession. (Edward A. Rogers)

While the main hall was closed for eleven days for renovations in anticipation of the Boston Symphony Orchestra, the acoustic issues also were addressed. Heavy curtains were installed beneath the proscenium arch and before the lower portion of the pipe organ, and folds of felt were hung above the orchestra. These remedies did make the room less "live," but they also unfortunately dampened the higher frequencies of the strings and woodwinds.

THE ORGAN

The one beneficiary of the faulty acoustics may have been the massive pipe organ. Said the *San Francisco Chronicle*, "[W]e bathed in a sea of composite tone the like of which we had not heard before, and criticism in such a deluge of melody was properly submerged."[19]

The gleaming pipes in an arched niche behind the stage were arranged with the tallest—a forty-one-foot-long zinc pipe—at the center, with the shorter pipes in symmetrical ranks on either side. Beneath this giant musical reliquary, a four-manual console controlled the six-part instrument, consisting of great, swell, choir, solo, pedal, and echo organs.

While immense, the organ was never designed to be the largest in the world but rather the most advanced. The Austin Organ Company's $50,000, forty-ton machine was powered by two blowers, each run by a twenty-horsepower motor. It had more than 7,000 pipes and 114 speaking stops, and required about 100 miles of wiring. The organ was built of 30,000 board feet of lumber, including ebony, walnut, oak, birch, maple, whitewood, pine, and cherry. The drawstop heads and keys were solid ivory.

Dr. H. J. Stewart, head of the design committee for the instrument, declared the organ "the most legitimately perfect instrument...." Journalist Ben Macomber said of its lowest pitch, "Its vibrations are something like the roar of a railway train shooting across a trestle, still more like the deafening turmoil of Niagara, combined with the crash of breakers upon the beach."[20, 21]

When official organist Wallace Sabin, a local musician who also directed the Exposition

Chorus, was testing the unfinished organ, listening workmen "removed their hats as though they were in a church…." Indeed, despite pleas from music critics that the instrument transcended religious use, many, forgetting they were not in a house of worship, were startled when audiences applauded.[22]

Organ concerts were offered daily, usually at noon, for a twenty-five-cent admission. There also were evening performances, for a total of 368 organ recitals over the nine months of the Fair. In addition to Sabin, dozens of prominent organists played. Edwin Lemare, widely regarded the "world's greatest living organist," was slated to start performing in June and to give one hundred lunchtime shows, with no duplicates. Organist Clarence Eddy astonished audiences with his footwork: "He is surely as nimble with his feet as he is with his hands," said the *Pacific Coast Musical Review*.[23]

The instrument performed beautifully, save for one calamity just before composer Camille Saint-Saëns' closing concert on June 28. "The organ began hostilities by playing all by itself, unencouraged to utterance by any visible power," wrote Walter Anthony of the *Chronicle*. The pipes wailed and shrieked until the mechanical problem was solved, but Anthony joked that thereafter the experimental music of Arnold Schönberg, Igor Stravinsky, or Leo Ornstein would hold no terrors for him: "All three may play at once and they shall not confound my ears!"[24]

CAMILLE SAINT-SAËNS

Camille Saint-Saëns had become "a classic in his own lifetime" and was but a few months shy of his eightieth birthday when he arrived at the PPIE on May 21. That evening he stealthily attended a Boston Symphony Orchestra performance, the *Chronicle* noting that "the foremost French musician listened…to the foremost German conductor's interpretation of a programme provided by the foremost Italian symphonist." During the following night's French program, as the orchestra played Saint-Saëns' Symphony No. 3 in C Minor, whispers spread through the audience that the august composer was in the house. At

the piece's conclusion, the crowd waved their handkerchiefs and called his name until the stocky, white-bearded master stood and acknowledged their adulation with a modest bow.[25]

At Director of Music George Stewart's suggestion, Saint-Saëns had composed "Hail, California" in honor of the PPIE, a "fantasie [*sic*] in the form of a symphonic poem, a type in which the great master excels." He premiered the piece in the Festival Hall on June 19. It was performed by the eighty-member Exposition Orchestra, Sousa's band of sixty-five, the Exposition chorus of three hundred voices, plus piano, harp, and cello, with Wallace Sabin at the pipe organ. The composition's concluding march was a mélange of "The Marseillaise" and "The Star-Spangled Banner," during which the *Chronicle* reviewer claimed the organ, band, and orchestra "unlimbered all their noisy guns to fire this volley under the direction of the vivacious composer."[26, 27]

However, those were the only fireworks the composition engendered. Applause at the Fair was appreciative, but the lingering response

Organists played the six-part Exposition Organ using a four-manual console. The instrument comprised choir, echo, great, pedal, solo, and swell organs. (Edward A. Rogers)

WOMEN MUSICIANS

Though several applied, no all-female bands or orchestras were included in official Fair programming. A few women's ensembles played, but not through the auspices of the Department of Music. Vaudevillian Cora Youngblood Corson led her All-Girl Band at the state building shared by Arkansas and Oklahoma, where organizers had declared a special day in Corson's honor. Hand mirrors and buttons bearing her name and likeness were given away. The Girls' Ukulele Club of Oakland's Fremont High School gave a concert on the Music Concourse. As was typical of the era, no women were included in the Official Band or Orchestra of the Exposition. Only occasionally was there a female accompanist—a violinist here, a harpist there.

The exception to this underrepresentation was among pianists. Female pianists were featured in many of the most stupendous concerts of the year, sometimes as soloists. Laura Lundegard, Tina Lerner, Marie Sloss, Esther Hjelte, and Flora Mora all performed in the Festival Hall. Olga Steeb, who was said to have committed 10,000 pages of music to memory, "charmed her audience with the magic and poetry of her playing" at a program in Recital Hall, according to a *Chronicle* reviewer. Barcelonan prodigy Paquita Madriguera, just fourteen, made her American debut August 15 as a soloist with the Exposition Orchestra.[28]

The Exposition had stated early on that no California pianists would play because the overabundance of choices would make any selections "unfair," but this proscription was quickly overturned for Katherine Ruth Heyman, who was internationally esteemed. She was the featured pianist when Saint-Saëns directed his Concerto No. 2 in G minor on June 24.

One keyboard almost completely untouched by feminine hands was that of the great pipe organ in Festival Hall. After Annette Stoddard of Oregon played a recital on March 11, no other women are known to have played the instrument. When the Chicago Sunday Evening Club choir arrived for its June concert, it did so without its organist of six years, Katherine Howard Ward. The choir's conductor explained that understudy Edgar Nelson would play instead because the PPIE had forbidden women organists. Whether or not this prohibition was official, it applied in practice.

Pianist Olga Steeb gave her first San Francisco performance in the Recital Hall in March, then appeared again with the Exposition Orchestra on the main stage of Festival Hall in September. (Edward A. Rogers)

in musical circles was tepid. John Philip Sousa described the ephemeral nature of exposition compositions: "Strange to say, the official music for expositions and world fairs seems always to die an immediate death."[29]

Saint-Saëns' California visit did result in a more lasting legacy in music. While in San Francisco, he composed Elégie, Op. 143, in honor of local violinist and social lion Sir Henry Heyman, who hosted Saint-Saëns and other luminaries during the PPIE.

AMERICAN ARTISTRY

Although the war kept many European composers from attending the Fair, the conflict likely benefitted American composers by creating openings in the Festival Hall schedule for two domestic "composers' days." The first was American Composers' Day on August 1. For this event Stewart shrewdly capitalized on the recently concluded National Federation of Music Clubs' convention in Los Angeles, which had brought many nationally recognized musicians to the West Coast. Several of them journeyed north to perform in Festival Hall. Next came San Francisco Composers' Day, on November 14,

which featured two artists already quite familiar with the venue. Official organist Wallace Sabin presented his "Irish Jig," which he had written for the 1909 Bohemian Grove play, and Exposition Orchestra violinist Ulderico Marcelli conducted "Intermezzo Sinfonico," based on indigenous Ecuadorian music.

CONDUCTORS

To finish out the year, Stewart arranged to have three more outstanding conductors design and lead programs for the Exposition Orchestra. These were the noted Wagnerian interpreter Walter Damrosch; Comte Eugene D'Harcourt, master of the New York Symphony Orchestra; and the renowned Victor Herbert.

Herbert was smiling when he arrived on his first visit to San Francisco. Not only was he enchanted by the summerlike weather, but his tunes were being hummed and whistled all over town. The city was equally glad to see the genial conductor and composer, who at the PPIE drew large and appreciative audiences. Classically trained as a cellist, Herbert wrote across multiple genres, from grand opera to orchestral pieces to music for Broadway revues. The *Chronicle*'s

On American Composers' Day, artists conducted their own works. L. to r.: two unidentified men, then composers George W. Chadwick, William J. McCoy, Mabel W. Daniels, Amy Beach, Carl Busch, Horatio Parker, Ernest F. Kroger, and Director of Music George Stewart. (Donna Ewald Huggins)

Walter Anthony wrote, "If there is Celt in his heart there is Strauss in his spirit, Bach in his brain and Broadway in his blood."[30]

His seven-concert series in November was typically catholic, contrasting more sober pieces by Wagner and Liszt with suites, fantasies, and comic operas. The audience was particularly interested in his all–Victor Herbert evening, where they heard selections from his operetta *Babes in Toyland*, which had premiered in San Francisco nine years earlier. On opening night, April 16, 1906, famed tenor Enrico Caruso had applauded heartily from his box at the Columbia Theater. Two days later the Great Earthquake racked the city, the theater's walls collapsed, and it subsequently burned.

However, Herbert's tenure was not without some unexpected challenges. He usually looked to his wife to knot his dress tie, but she had been

called away. On the night of his first concert, a valet at his hotel tied it for him. The next night, he dressed in the Festival Hall, so he asked Otto Kegel, a trumpet player and the librarian of the Exposition Orchestra, for help, but Kegel could not do it right. Luckily, Mrs. Horace Britt, wife of a cellist, came to Herbert's assistance. On the third night, Kegel stepped up to Herbert and said, "Now, sir, your tie!" and the neckwear was tamed. When Herbert asked how he had learned the skill so quickly, Otto responded that he had ordered his dog to "sit," then practiced on his pet. "Now," Kegel said, "if he sees me with anything that looks like a tie, he sits up without me telling him to."[31]

On another night, Herbert's encore was interrupted three times by the "grewsome tones" of the Alcatraz foghorn. The clever Herbert switched to Dvorak's "Humoresque."[32]

ALFRED HERTZ

The PPIE was the site of a skirmish in a political conflict within San Francisco musical circles. In 1915 the city was attempting to form a permanent symphony orchestra. Henry Hadley had directed an existing ensemble for four years, however the excellent play of the Exposition Orchestra under Max Bendix—and especially that of the Boston Symphony Orchestra at the PPIE—highlighted the potential for improvement in San Francisco's symphonic scene. Those advocating a permanent symphony and a replacement for Hadley pointed out that the Boston orchestra comprised musicians whose careers were devoted to the symphony. They were paid a sufficient salary and were not permitted to play in cafés or restaurants between concerts.

Bendix's name was proposed for the San Francisco conducting position, but in July German-born Alfred Hertz of the Metropolitan Opera Orchestra in New York was selected. Unfortunately, Hertz committed a gaffe when he conducted a concert on August 6 at the Exposition Auditorium in conjunction with German Week festivities. Following the stirring final chords of Beethoven's Ninth Symphony, Hertz acknowledged the ovation and walked

Popular conductor and composer Victor Herbert led seven concerts in November, the most popular of which was a night dedicated to his own music. (Laura Ackley)

offstage, leaving the puzzled regular orchestra in place. Hertz did not realize he was expected to close the evening with an unannounced rendition of "The Star-Spangled Banner." After a pause, Concertmaster Adolph Rosenbecker assumed the baton and led the anthem.

The next night Hertz made another faux pas when he substituted the 1871 "Kaisermarch" by Wagner for the less-rehearsed "Les Preludes" by Liszt, on the very day that Kaiser Wilhelm's attack on Warsaw was anticipated. The *Bulletin* reported some audience members walked out in protest, while the *Chronicle's* music editor, a fan of Hertz, saw nothing amiss. He said the walkouts were typical at the end of a long evening program. Others cried Hertz's sympathies were "too German."

Despite this somewhat rocky beginning, Hertz went on to become a distinguished part of San Francisco musical history. He led the city's symphony for fifteen years and is generally acclaimed. A concert hall at the University of California at Berkeley bears his name.

In hindsight, Hertz was lucky to escape the "Star-Spangled" scandal so lightly. Only three years later Karl Muck, illustrious conductor of the Boston Symphony Orchestra, was interned in Georgia for the same omission. In 1918, America at war was less likely to forgive a perceived slight. After more than a year's internment, Muck was expelled from the US and never returned.

A VARIETY OF VOCALISTS

For choral music, the Fair depended heavily on local talent. The slate at the Fair included the Berkeley Lyric Trio, the Santa Rosa Choral Society, Oakland's Orpheus Club, the San Francisco Choral Society, the California Treble Clef, and the Berkeley Oratorio Society.

On Contra Costa County Day, a local 220-voice chorus intoned "It's a Short Way to Contra Costa" to the tune of "It's a Long Way to Tipperary." The Loring Club, a male chorus founded in 1876, was selected to sing when the

The Jewel City hosted several large choral gatherings, including the Pacific Coast Norwegian Singers' Association's Sangerfest, which concluded with Norway Day at the PPIE on June 3. (Laura Ackley)

Exposition Orchestra gave its final performance in Festival Hall.

Joseph F. Smith, president of the Church of Jesus Christ of Latter-day Saints and nephew of its founder, Joseph Smith, selected the Ogden Tabernacle Choir—over its rival Mormon Tabernacle Choir from Salt Lake City—to represent Utah at the Jewel City. The choir, directed by Joseph Ballantyne, had traveled only twice before. The people of Utah raised $20,000 to finance the trip.

Most nations represented among the pavilions were able to scrape together a community chorus to perform for their dedicatory exercises. Italian and Chinese schoolchildren sang, as did an Argentine chorus, and Northern European countries were particularly well-represented. As local Danish American singers began their celebration of Danish Week at the PPIE's castle-like Danish Pavilion, a cablegram arrived from Denmark. A great cheer went up from the celebrants as the wire announced King Christian X had signed a new constitution granting suffrage to women and citizens who did not own land.

Vikings invaded the Fair on June 3 for Norway Day, landing their long ship at the Yacht Harbor. They were greeted by a renowned concert band of theology students from Luther College of Decorah, Iowa, the "oldest Norwegian School outside of Norway." The ship was rowed by fifty armored men and filled with costumed Norwegian children. As it reached the shore, the band broke into Edvard Grieg's *Landkjending,* or *Land-Sighting,* and members of the Pacific Coast Norwegian Singers' Association took up the chorus.

The Luther College Band was joined by the singers from the Norwegian Synod Choral Union Church for concerts at the Festival Hall and other venues around San Francisco. At the dedication of the Swedish Pavilion on March 2, members of the Swedish Singing Society, the Svea Male Chorus, and the Songrens Vanner constituted the choir. A chorus of 175 men was gathered from numerous Swedish societies to perform June 18, when the United Swedish Singers of the Pacific Coast received a bronze medal. German Americans likewise were honored when they

At the Welsh Eisteddfod in July, prizes were offered for poetry, singing, and instrumental performances. (Laura Ackley)

brought their traditional "Sangerbund" to the Exposition as part of German American Week.

THE EISTEDDFOD

The greatest internationally based singing event was the Welsh Eisteddfod. Those taking a morning constitutional in the panhandle of Golden Gate Park on July 27 encountered an uncanny sight—a circle of a dozen men in druid robes, each standing atop an unhewn stone surrounding the "Maen Llog," or "Logan Stone," on which the Arch Druid stood. This was the Gorsedd, or "supreme seat," a reimagining of ancient Celtic ritual and the traditional opening of the Eisteddfodd, a venerable Welsh festival of music, literature, and performance that ran for four days.

While the San Francisco Exposition was profligate in distributing medals of merit to performers, there were no official musical competitions as there were at prior world's fairs. The only contests for music and song held in conjunction with the PPIE were sponsored by the International Society of the Welsh Eisteddfod. After the Gorsedd, the Eisteddfod moved to the new Exposition Auditorium for musical competitions and the awarding of literary prizes. Some $25,000 was given for singing, poetry, prose, translations, and music. Special prizes included a silver crown and a carved-oak bardic chair.

Each group played or sang the same selection or selections so they could be compared. Listeners generally agreed that among the top choruses the Haydn Choral Union of Chicago was better rehearsed and had superior phrasing, but Oakland's Eisteddfod Choir exhibited better tone. After the grand finale concert the next night, at which the aggregate choir of 1,200 performed *The Messiah*, the judges announced a split decision: the choirs from Chicago and Oakland would share the $10,000 prize.

After singing for an audience of children in the Festival Hall, revered contralto Ernestine Schumann-Heink gave a second performance, for orphans, in the theater of the Southern Pacific building on the fairgrounds. (Edward A. Rogers)

OPERA AND ORATORIO

From its very first day, those hungering for superb singing were served an auditory feast in the Jewel City. Even as the gates opened, 250 voices intoned "The Heavens Are Telling" in triumphant harmony. Although the Exposition did not stage full-scale operas, it did mount several oratorios, which are large-scale vocal works without costumes, sets, or dramatic action.

Oratorio culminated at the Autumn Music Festival with Mendelssohn's *Elijah* and Verdi's monumental *Requiem,* both led by Emil Mollenhauer, considered the "first choral conductor of America." Wallace Sabin presided at the organ. The Sunday matinee *Requiem* was so powerful that some in the audience knelt in reverence. The ability of the Bay Area to mount the elaborate composition, as it did twice in 1915, was regarded as a watershed moment in putting San Francisco among the major choral centers, along with New York and Boston.[33]

There also was a plethora of solo performances by stars who now have faded from the operatic firmament. For example, Ellen Beach Yaw, a coloratura soprano with a nearly four-octave range, earned the nicknames "Lark Ellen" and "The California Nightingale." During her stint at the PPIE, Lark Ellen often could be found on the Joy Zone, not onstage or enjoying the rides but visiting the midway's "educated horse," Captain, whose equine nerves were soothed by her singing.

But a name that remains a touchstone a century later is that of Madame Ernestine Schumann-Heink, whose rich and flexible contralto voice is still admired. When Mayor James Rolph and organist Clarence Eddy moved among the throng in the Festival Hall at her March 27 concert, they must have felt like giants, as they were among a handful of adults midst a crowd of children. On that day, Madame Schumann-Heink proffered a unique gift to the youth of San Francisco: more than 3,000 children packed Festival Hall, where "the grandest of singers sang for them alone."[34]

Madame, herself mother to a blended family of eight children and stepchildren, was distressed when she learned that although the Festival Hall admission was to be free, children would still be charged for admission to the Fair, although at a reduced rate of fifteen cents instead of the usual quarter. She said, "When I promised to come to San Francisco to sing for the children for nothing, I thought it was for nothing but love. Now I find that it is for fifteen cents. I shall sing, of course, but it is wrong to charge the children." Local newspapers encouraged citizens to pay a child's way into the grounds.[35]

DANCES OLD AND NEW

Dance, too, was on the daily program at the Exposition. Grand balls were held for PPIE boosters and visitors. New dances for the smart set were created especially for the Fair, among them the "PPIE One-Step," introduced at the Music Concourse by Ethyl Stewart and Addison Fowler in July. On many afternoons the soft green lawn of the Marina was splashed with the bright colors of picturesque costumes worn by capering children presenting charming folk dances. Come summer, La Loïe Fuller, the most influential dancer of her day, presented a sold-out series in the Festival Hall.

At the gala costume ball dedicating the new Exposition Auditorium in January 1915, there

La Loïe Fuller's company, in flowing costumes, performed a "dance spectacle" of Tennyson's "Elaine" for Fine Arts Preservation Day on October 16. (Edward A. Rogers)

were dances from Norway, Ireland, Germany, Switzerland, Russia, Spain, Italy, Japan, China, Mexico, and Hawaii. That night, soloist Anita Peters Wright also danced, her costume spangled with more than three hundred small versions of the Novagems from the Tower of Jewels.

Parisian danseuse Louise La Gai danced to the accompaniment of Victrolas at the Victor Talking Machine Company's neoclassical pavilion in the Palace of Liberal Arts. On fine days, she and the little girls from her San Francisco atelier danced on the lawns outside to music provided by a

NATIVE AMERICAN DANCES

Much of the Native American dance at the Exposition was authentic. Performers from the Glacier Park Blackfeet delegation and from the 101 Ranch concession gave several demonstrations of ceremonial tribal dances on the Marina Green and on the Zone, among them a Moon Dance by the Sioux of the 101 Ranch and a Potato Dance and "grass dances" by the Blackfeet. For the "Death of Custer" pageant in September, Blackfeet led war dances on a stage in the Court of the Universe, however, as they were accompanied by a group the *San Francisco Chronicle* termed "fifty imitation redskins," the authenticity of that particular performance is dubious.[36]

Among the Native American ceremonial dances the United States government had banned in its 1883 Rules for Indian Courts was the Sun Dance. When the Blackfeet group gave a July 15 feast at the Fair, the *San Francisco Chronicle* said the performance had "much the same significance as the proscribed Sun Dance," closely paralleling an 1883 description of the forbidden ceremony.[37]

The casual mention of native dances, especially war dances, in 1915 news media implies that the celebrations were no longer viewed as threatening but rather seen through the roseate lenses of nostalgia. Still, the laws suppressing dances were not repealed until 1934.

To advertise the Victor Talking Machine Company, Louise La Gai and her troupe danced on the lawn in front of the Palace of Liberal Arts to music played on a giant Victrola. (Edward A. Rogers)

gargantuan record player. Clog dancing was featured in the Irish village, and girls from the Zone's Japan Beautiful concession interpreted the "Cherry Blossom Dance" before former president Taft in the Festival Hall on the last day of September.

LA LOÏE FULLER

By far the most famous dancer at the PPIE was La Loïe Fuller. In one advertisement she even received billing above revered composer Camille Saint-Saëns. Fuller's place in the history of dance is assured, and she also influenced the physical fabric of San Francisco. La Loïe started life as plain Marie Louise Fuller from Illinois, but she became an important figure in dance and stage lighting, particularly after moving to Paris in the 1890s. She declared, "I was born in America, but I was made in France."[38]

Her first terpsichorean innovation was a voluminous garment of light silk, which she moved using long wands. Later she pioneered special stages where she would dance on a glass plate lit from below by multicolored light

arrangements she designed. Fuller's techniques were part of the new "aesthetic dance" movement, through which she tried to blend music and light kinesthetically. Her techniques influenced later artists, including her onetime protégée Isadora Duncan. She was sketched by Henri de Toulouse-Lautrec, and sculptor Auguste Rodin said of La Loïe, "Her creations will live forever." Her work with light was inspired by Impressionism, and she became an icon of Art Nouveau.[39]

By the time she reached the PPIE, La Loïe, then fifty-three years old, no longer danced, but she brought a troupe of Parisian students she called "Muses." The company pirouetted in several recitals in the Festival Hall, backed by the Exposition Orchestra, and its dancers cavorted in the rotunda of the Palace of Fine Arts to raise funds to preserve the building. After the PPIE closed, they gave a special performance of a new dance, "The Thinker," in honor of Rodin on December 20 in the Court of Abundance.

Diminutive, free-spirited La Loïe also teamed with six-foot-tall Junoesque society matron "Big Alma" Spreckels to change San Francisco. Alma de Bretteville first came into the public eye scandalously when, as a willowy twenty-one-year-old art student and model, she successfully sued a rich miner for breach of contract—or, as she later put it, "personal defloweration." According to her biography, Robert I. Aitken modeled the figure atop his 1903 Dewey Monument in Union Square after Alma. Five years later, she married Adolph Spreckels, one of the heirs to the Spreckels sugar fortune. As her social status and physique increased, she gained the "Big Alma" sobriquet.

Big Alma met La Loïe in Paris in 1914, and the dancer introduced her to Rodin and encouraged her to start collecting his work. Spreckels brought several Rodin sculptures to San Francisco, where they were exhibited at the PPIE in the French Pavilion, a replica of the Palais de la Légion d'Honneur in Paris. After the Fair, Spreckels, encouraged by La Loïe, was inspired to create a museum for arts in San Francisco, using money from fund-raisers and a

LOIE FULLER.

Not merely a dancer, La Loïe Fuller was also an innovator in theatrical lighting and stage design. (California History Room, California State Library, Sacramento, California)

large chunk of her husband's wealth. The Palace of the Legion of Honor opened in 1924, and she placed her Rodins there. On the outside it is an exact replica of the French Pavilion from the Fair, but on the inside it featured all the latest in museum technologies.

STEWART PERSEVERES

As the 288 days of the Fair wore on, Music Director Stewart's challenges multiplied as he dealt with hundreds of the world's greatest artistic temperaments. Bandmaster A. F. Thaviu had a bad habit of not submitting his programs in time for print. Organist Edwin Lemare whined that he was given insufficient rehearsal time. He told Stewart that if he was not allotted adequate quiet access to the Festival Hall instrument, he would be unable to present the one hundred unique programs he had promised. Several acts requested rescheduling of their dates, which the Department of Music resisted whenever possible. Just after Max Bendix's contract as Exposition Orchestra conductor was finalized in January, he casually wrote to Stewart, "Will you give me ten weeks leave of absence beginning middle of June? This…means three thousand to me every summer, so I feel sure that you will grant my request." Stewart was floored but eventually relented, and Bendix was able to leave midyear to direct the Chicago National Symphony.[40]

THE DISSONANCE OF WAR

As 1915 progressed, the effects of the war on the entertainment of the Exposition became obvious. Some of Europe's visiting stars added somber notes of war to the gay strains of the PPIE's music. With so many musicians of European birth or descent in the ranks of its players, the Department of Music wrote into the contract for the Exposition Orchestra: "_____ agrees that at no time during the period of this engagement, while upon the grounds of the Panama-Pacific International Exposition Company, will he engage in any argument with his colleagues relative to the European War."[41]

But the influence of World War I was still

evident on the PPIE's stages. Pianist Ignace Jan Paderewski's famed extravagant auburn locks were tinged with silver and his eyes were full of sadness as he took the stage of the Festival Hall on August 21 to describe the suffering of his Polish countrymen at the hands of "uninvited guests." After his lecture he played poignant and powerful works by another Pole, Frédéric Chopin, as well as his own "Minuet." Despite his melancholy, Paderewski's charisma was formidable; the auditorium was filled to capacity and hundreds were turned away, so a second show was added. Through these performances and a benefit garden party at the home of William Crocker, Paderewski raised $17,600 for the Polish Victims' Relief Fund.[42]

It took a Cossack lance to assure the PPIE appearance of Austrian violin virtuoso Fritz Kreisler, considered at that time the world's greatest violinist. Though he had resigned his military commission in 1912, when the war broke out he rejoined his regiment. He reached the eastern front near Lemberg in mid-August

1914. Kreisler recounted that for three weeks his company endured terrible privation and witnessed unexpected beauty and selflessness. Near midnight on September 6, Russian cavalry attacked Kreisler's platoon, and he was knocked down by an enemy horse, then stabbed in the thigh by a soldier. Kreisler was incorrectly reported slain but recovered and was discharged due to his injury.

In November 1914 he limped down the gangway of a Dutch steamer in New York to begin a series of concerts in Carnegie Hall. He was already popular in San Francisco when he was booked to play during the Autumn Music Festival at the Fair. Box office receipts from Kreisler's appearance as soloist in the 1913–14 season of the San Francisco Symphony were second only to those of Madame Schumann-Heink.

Many thought Kreisler's wartime experiences enriched his already impeccable and nuanced technique. After the Exposition Orchestra played Beethoven's overture "Leonore No. 3," Kreisler stepped through the curtains behind

Virtuoso pianist Ignace Jan Paderewski used his appearance at the PPIE to raise relief funds for his war-stricken home country, Poland. (Laura Ackley)

the stage and was greeted with a full minute of thunderous applause before he could commence playing Vivaldi's Concerto in C Major. Journalist W. W. B. Seymour summed up the city's affection: "[T]he suffering he has endured is manifest in a tone which, without having lost any of its sweetness, has gained in depth and vibrancy."[43]

While war enabled Kreisler's presence, it blocked another artist's performance. Top dramatic soprano Emmy Destinn of the Metropolitan Opera Company was widely advertised as the centerpiece of Verdi's *Requiem* at the Autumn Music Festival. However, the European departure date of the Prague-born singer kept slipping. Music Director Stewart showed foresight and a grasp of the tenuous European situation when he wrote on August 31 to Grace Bonner Williams, who was slated to perform earlier in the festival: "Emmy Destinn is engaged to sing the *Requiem* October 3rd. I should be very glad to have you prepare to sing the part in case she should fail." And Destinn did fail. She did not reach the United States until several weeks after her anticipated appearance at the PPIE.[44]

No musician was more anticipated at the PPIE than British virtuoso organist Edwin H. Lemare. "What Paderewski is to piano, Lemare is to organ," said one admirer. But his tenure at the Jewel City was also jeopardized by war. The previous time the celebrity musician had seen San Francisco, the city had been in flames after the 1906 earthquake, and his 1915 trip was scarcely less dramatic. To make it to San Francisco on time for his first scheduled program on June 7, he had purchased passage for himself, his expectant wife, Charlotte, and their son Edwin III on the Cunard ship *Lusitania*, leaving Liverpool on May 11.[45]

While on its way to Liverpool the great ocean liner was torpedoed May 7 by a German U-boat. The next day Lemare cabled George Stewart: SAILING DISORGANIZED OWING AWFUL DISASTER LUSITANIA SINCERELY HOPE POSTPONEMENT SEPTEMBER—LEMARE.[46]

Stewart granted him the postponement but asked the star to make his way to San Francisco as soon as he could. A new start date of August 25 was set. Lemare was concerned he would lose his

To reach the PPIE, organist Edwin Lemare planned to sail on the *Lusitania* from Liverpool on May 11, 1915. The ship was torpedoed and sunk on May 7, before it reached England. (Laura Ackley)

fee, so he sailed as soon as possible. "I shall have to leave Mrs. Lemare and my little boy here," he wrote to Stewart, "as the confinement will probably take place about the time of my departure."[47]

The RMS *Baltic* was harried by a German submarine on its way to Liverpool but arrived safely, and on its return trip to New York, it carried Edwin Lemare. On August 10 he wrote from on board, "I decided to start earlier on the only available White Star boat, and 'take my chance' of Submarines and everything rather than be a day late for my engagement with you....Please excuse this awful scrawl, as we are 'rolling some.'" His family, including his new daughter, followed him to San Francisco a few weeks later.[48]

Lemare gave his first recital without much fanfare. Likely the PPIE chose not to publicize the new start date lest a fresh calamity arise, but his concerts quickly gained immense popularity. "He weaves a magic spell over that great pipeorgan and makes it talk to you as sound never talked before—all for 10 cents," said the *Portland Oregonian*. At each concert the organist solicited ideas from the audience on which he would improvise. "[W]hether woven around a single note, a Maori chorus, a Negro lullaby or a Wagnerian theme, invariably [they] are the most appreciated numbers on the program....He has manifested a deep interest in the American Indian melodies, the Hawaiian folk songs and… the well-known rhythm of the South." His residence at the PPIE was to conclude after his hundredth performance on November 10, but audiences were so delighted that his run was extended until the end of the Fair.[49, 50]

Even then, San Francisco did not want to part with Lemare, so after Closing Day he was appointed municipal organist. In 1916 the great organ was moved into the Exposition Auditorium at the Civic Center, where he oversaw its rebuilding, revoicing, and tuning. Lemare continued to perform on the instrument from its re-debut in 1917 until 1921, when he accepted a similar post in Portland, Maine.

Still another performer directly affected by the war was "queen of song" Madame Schumann-Heink, who had sung for the children earlier in the year. In the final concert for German Week, she cried as the audience thundered its ovation for her performance. "Never before have we heard the Brahms 'Wiegenlied' sung with such motherly tenderness," wrote the *Pacific Coast Musical Review*. But perhaps Madame's tears were not only from gratitude but also for her eldest son, August Heink, in Germany. Just a few weeks earlier he had told his mother he was leaving the safety of the United States to join the German navy, as he held German citizenship. "The Kaiser needs me," he vowed. "It is my Fatherland, I want to go."[51, 52]

Later in the war, Madame's other sons, Ferdinand and George, and her stepson Walter became members of the United States armed forces, while several of her other relatives fought for Germany. Though her other sons survived, August died while serving on a German U-boat in 1918.

MEASURES OF SUCCESS

The relative success or failure of the musical program was open to interpretation. While the marquee events often were crowded, Festival Hall was rarely full for daily recitals or the Exposition Orchestra's symphonic programs. After the first three months, estimated symphony attendance was between 600 and 1,100 per night in an auditorium that held about 3,200. After seven months, Stewart reported that only one-sixteenth of 1 percent of fairgoers visited the Festival Hall. He said, "Unless something unusually sensational is offered them, they do not come." Nor was the smaller Recital Hall usually filled.[53]

There were many possible reasons for this less-than-stellar attendance. Stewart's vision for the music of the PPIE trended toward the serious. Popular music genres in 1915 included lighter fare, including minstrel songs, sentimental ballads, ragtime, show tunes, regional ballads, and music for social dances, such as the waltz, polka, and two-step. In the Jewel City, such "café music" could be found in the state and foreign pavilions and on the Zone, but it was largely absent from the Festival Hall.

Indeed, it was virtually impossible to concoct a slate of music that appealed to everyone. Some found the programs too sober, and even Stewart admitted that "people who visit a great Exposition are always in a holiday mood, and therefore do not always want classic music." Others found the musical diet too light, while some deplored the acoustics of Festival Hall, even after its renovations.[54]

A few patrons groused about the extra admission charged for the Festival Hall and the Old Faithful Inn in addition to the Fair's entrance fee. To add insult to injury, they contended, once one paid twenty-five cents to enter the Yellowstone concession in which the Inn was located, "one must naturally order something for the pleasure of sitting at a restaurant table when [the orchestra] performs." These malcontents were gently chided. It was pointed out that even adding Exposition admission to the cost, the concert tickets were still a wonderful value, and if they wanted free music, they had only to stroll the grounds to hear an array of leading bands "competent to return in harmony the worth of his ticket."[55]

With so many amazing things to see, some did not want to sit for a concert. The many competing events fragmented potential audiences. Walter Anthony of the *Chronicle* said, "It is exceedingly difficult after entrance to the grounds has been effected, to go indoors anywhere. The sight is so stunned by the beauty of Guérin's color, the majesty of the buildings, the symmetry of the statuary and the blossoming beauty of our parks." *Pacific Coast Musical Review* pointed out that "after fifty cents have been paid at the gate, the public wants to get as much entertainment as possible for these fifty cents, and evidently it does not desire to sit during an hour and one half listening to classic music."[56, 57]

While the Festival Hall was not always full, the orchestra was a major success. As early as April there were calls to simply name the entire Exposition Orchestra the permanent San Francisco symphonic body. While this did not come to pass, the city's reconstituted symphony announced in November that its next season's roster included twenty-two of the eighty musicians formerly on the Exposition Orchestra payroll.

The performances were a boon to the music community and to the PPIE as a whole. The lion's share of the Department of Music's $665,000 appropriation went to local musicians. And most of all, the program boosted Fair attendance. The PPIE director who presented Wallace Sabin with a gold medal for directing the Exposition Chorus asserted that 15 percent of the Fair's attendees came for the music. If true, the entertainment accounted for more than 2.8 million of the Fair's 18.9 million visitors. Assuming adult gate fees of fifty cents each for those seeking music, but omitting possible income from the Festival Hall or Old Faithful Inn, the money generated by the official music program totaled more than $1.4 million, pushing the Exposition from loss into profitability.

The *Portland Oregonian* described the Fair's music in a headline: "Highways and Byways of Music All Converge on San Francisco." With its program filled with military bands, symphonies, national music, great choirs, and luminaries like Paderewski, Kreisler, Saint-Saëns, Fuller, Lemare, Herbert, Schumann-Heink, and the Boston Symphony Orchestra, in 1915 the PPIE was indeed the focus of the world's "serious" music and dance.[58]

The Exposition Orchestra, seen here in the Old Faithful Inn, was very successful under its permanent leader, Max Bendix. Twenty-two of its musicians were recruited to the San Francisco Symphony. (Edward A. Rogers)

THE GRANDEST BANDS

here is music everywhere! At the Music Concourse, in the Court of the Universe, in Festival Hall, at the Philippino [sic] building, at the Marine Camp and on the Joy Zone there is music at all hours."[1]

The PPIE fell during a golden age of military-style brass bands. Bands played not only marches but also popular music, vaudeville tunes, and folk songs. At a time when many symphony orchestras were struggling, bands frequently introduced Americans to classical music. The works of both classical masters and relatively modern artists, such as Tchaikovsky and Wagner, were often debuted to the public by touring bands, many from the Chautauqua circuits. The Exposition took advantage of the popular personal-improvement movement by hiring bands proven as crowd-pleasers. Renowned bandleaders Patrick Conway, Frederick Innes, Giuseppe Creatore, A. F. Thaviu, and John Philip Sousa were all Chautauqua veterans.

As soon as Congress awarded the world's fair to San Francisco, thousands of applications poured in from all sorts of musical performers—bands, orchestras, ensembles, solo musicians, singers, dancers, and even novelty acts such as whistlers. Most were refused outright, some were referred to another part of the Fair, and a few applicants were asked to send proposals. The rarefied stars were actively pursued.

The PPIE planned to hire scores of bands, but hundreds applied. A typical appeal letter highlighted the band's accomplishments and plaudits. George Stewart, director of music, usually replied, gently in most cases, that the Exposition was considering "only the great military bands of Europe and America, bands ranging from 50 to 90 men."[2]

Some of the bands that had performed under Stewart's auspices at the 1904 Louisiana

Bands leading parades along the Avenue of Palms entertained visitors strolling that promenade. (Laura Ackley)

Purchase Exposition were hired for 1915, but even world's fair experience was not a guarantee. Several that had played in St. Louis were rejected. Impresario Francesco Fanciulli's outfit had performed at the 1904 fair and now he would not take no for an answer. Stewart lamented to Chairman of Music J. B. Levison, "It is true he brought a band to the St. Louis Exposition, but it was of very little importance and attracted very little attention and caused almost no enthusiasm."[3]

Occasionally, when the applying band seemed of particular interest or merit, Stewart would suggest that if the group wanted to visit the PPIE on its own nickel, it would be scheduled to play. He wrote to the director of the Luther College Band, "[N]o sum however small, shall be expended by the Department of Music for any bands visiting the Exposition, excepting professional bands of national or international

reputation." For situations in which a band was highly specialized, such as the Dixie Jubilee or La Tarantella Napolitaine, he recommended they contact Zone concessionaires or state and foreign pavilions for opportunities.[4]

Of course, exhibitors could sidestep the entire application process by endowing a large exhibit and having music played therein. Henry Ford did just that when he brought his Ford Motor Band, comprising fifty-five factory employees, from Detroit to play six concerts in the Palace of Transportation. The Motor Band was part of Ford's efforts to foster personal improvement and collegiality within the corporation. Although amateur and entirely volunteer, the organization was nevertheless respected. Every program either began or concluded with a march called "The Ford," a jaunty number Henry Ford had commissioned from Motor City composer Harry H. Zickel.

Some bandmasters were invited to send a proposal including the total fee to cover salaries, travel, and living expenses, but many well-known bands, such as Bohumir Kryl's Bohemian Band, ultimately were rejected.

Just two weeks after his appointment as musical director in 1913, Stewart sent a letter to John Philip Sousa requesting a bid for his musicians. Sousa's was among the exalted few

The largest bandstand, on the Music Concourse west of the Palace of Horticulture, could seat an audience of 11,000. (San Francisco History Center, San Francisco Public Library)

bands keenly sought by the Department of Music. Others included the French band headed by Gabriel Parés, Emil Mollenhauer's Boston Band, Frederick Innes' Denver Municipal Band, Giuseppe Creatore's Band, and the band of Patrick Conway, Sousa's friend.

Sousa's participation was regarded as practically essential, as the prolific director and composer had delighted audiences at the American world's fairs in 1893, 1901, and 1904, as well as at San Francisco's 1894 Midwinter Fair and the 1900 Paris Exposition Universelle. While the other bands cost from $2,000 to $3,700 per week, Sousa's initial quote was $7,000 per week for eight weeks. The Department of Music resisted initially but eventually agreed on a rate of $6,000 a week for nine weeks, with the additional concession that Sousa not play elsewhere in California in 1915.

AN ALL-STAR ROTATION

From the very first day of the PPIE, outdoor band concerts could be heard throughout the grounds. Even when a band was not in view, patrons enjoying the gorgeous courts could hear fragments of a martial air reflecting off the creamy travertine of the colonnades, or catch a glimpse of shiny uniform braid as a musician hurried to his assignment.

The bright notes of cornets and trombones, punctuated by the crashing of cymbals, emanated from four strategically placed bandstands. The most capacious venue was the Music Concourse, just west of the Palace of Horticulture. Its forty-one-foot-diameter pavilion accommodated 102 musicians and was surrounded by seating for 11,000 spectators. The Moorish-style domed bandstand in the northern arc of the Court of the Universe could shelter eighty-six performers, while the one north of the Service Building near the Fillmore Street entrance could hold ninety. The last platform, on the Zone, was the least desirable to bandleaders. Band director Walter H. Loving wrote that with noise "bursting forth from Camp 49, Japan Beautiful, and 101 Ranch, together with the reverberation of the characteristic war drum from the Samoan Village, we found ourselves

completely surrounded by a conglomeration of disharmonious sounds which made the rendition of a concert program impossible."[5]

THE PERMANENT BANDS

Only three bands were available for the entire run of the PPIE: the Official Exposition Band, the Philippine Constabulary Band, and the Marine Band from the neighboring Presidio. The last of these, consisting of active-duty servicemen, was used mainly for dedications of foreign and state pavilions, parades, and fetes for military and political dignitaries.

The Official Exposition Band of forty performers was led by husky, mustachioed Charles H. Cassasa. He was noted for exuberantly waving his arms, prompting a clarinetist to quip that if his boss would only smoke while conducting, he would "look like [pilot] Art Smith looping the loop!"[6]

On Closing Day, Charles Cassasa, leader of the Official Exposition Band, received the final medal of appreciation awarded by the PPIE, presented by PPIE director M. H. de Young (left). (*San Francisco Chronicle*, December 5, 1915)

THE PHILIPPINE CONSTABULARY BAND

The Philippine Constabulary Band, led from its inception by Captain Walter H. Loving, was detailed 75 percent at the discretion of the Exposition and 25 percent of the Philippine Commission. Loving, a talented cornetist, was born to former slaves just five years after the Civil War ended. After enlisting in the US Army in 1893, he served for nine years in the United States and the Philippines prior to joining the Philippine Constabulary, the civil government's police force.

He organized the Constabulary Band in 1902 at the behest of William Howard Taft, then governor-general of the archipelago. The band had visited the United States only twice prior to 1915, performing at the 1904 Louisiana Purchase Exposition and at Taft's presidential inauguration in 1909.

From a historical standpoint, Captain Loving and the Constabulary Band present a metaphorical double-edged sword. The band symbolized the alleged cultural superiority of the western colonialists over "primitive" subjects. Before the Constabulary Band's 1909 US visit, the *Nagasaki Press* suggested that the band was invited to the inauguration to "correct the impression reigning in many parts of the United States that the dog-eating Igorrot [*sic*] typifies the Filipino." Thus, what the newspaper called "little brown men" in their "natty uniforms" were perceived as exemplars of colonized peoples.[7, 8]

Yet Loving represented a major step up for African Americans in the US military. His unequivocal success as a bandleader raised the profile of African Americans among military conductors, paving the way for his successors, albeit typically within segregated regiments. President Theodore Roosevelt told his secretary of war, "I wish all the colored regiments supplied with colored bandmasters."[9]

By 1915 Loving's original thirty-piece group had grown into a well-drilled regiment of ninety musicians who prided themselves on sight-reading skill and on memorizing all their music. As at St. Louis, the Constabulary Band became a favorite, prompting one admirer to send a complimentary letter to the chief of the events department. It read, "Symphony concerts by symphony orchestras are all very well, but for punch and ginger and volume of sounds, and the glorious sweep of harmony, give us the Philippine Band."[10]

Walter H. Loving was one of few African American military bandleaders at the time. His Philippine Constabulary Band posed next to a colonnade of the Festival Hall. (Edward A. Rogers)

In addition to outdoor concerts and appearances in the Festival Hall, John Philip Sousa's band also played in the Old Faithful Inn within the Yellowstone concession on the Zone. (Edward A. Rogers)

As the "house band" of the fair, Cassasa's troupe was expected to play for dedications, commemorations, conventions, and parades, performing for as many as four hours a day, in addition to rehearsals. Historian Frank Morton Todd wrote of the demands on the Official Band, stating it "had to be in several places at once, and nearly succeeded, in attendance on almost every function that music could alleviate." A few weeks into the Fair it became clear that the Official Band had so many obligations that there was insufficient time to walk between gigs, and so its musicians were given permission to ride the Fadgl Auto Trains free of charge.[11]

On the last day of the Fair, M. H. de Young, PPIE vice president, presented Cassasa with the final bronze medal of appreciation issued at the Fair. When concerts in Golden Gate Park resumed, Cassasa received permission from the park commissioners to retain all the members of the Official Exposition Band.

Stewart moved the Official Band and the ninety-member Philippine Constabulary Band about the grounds like chess pieces, sometimes using them at the Old Faithful Inn when the Exposition Orchestra was playing at the Festival Hall.

THE GREAT VISITING BANDS

The trio of permanent bands was supplemented by visiting bands, billed as special attractions. Each visiting band performed for several weeks, and their terms usually overlapped.

Opening Day bandleaders A. F. Thaviu and Giuseppe Creatore were succeeded by Gabriel Parès and his French Band, which played for eleven weeks from March until mid-May. The flamboyant Italian Creatore was so popular that the citizens of San Francisco circulated a petition to have his band re-engaged for the fall, but the docket was already full and Exposition officials were unable to oblige. Parès' residency was more controversial, as the Frenchman's music selection was not entirely to San Francisco's taste. Levison, the music chairman, wrote to Stewart, imploring him to "say something to Mr. Parès in the matter."[12]

A few nights later, Levison attended a concert by the French Band in the Court of the Universe and said the "dainty French compositions" played were "not suitable to open air performances and…not 'catchy' in the American sense." Levison wanted to hear more marches, operatic selections, and popular music. Stewart discussed the matter with Parès and arranged for Cassasa and Thaviu to lend the French Band some sheet music from Italian operas. Stewart, however, was not entirely sanguine that the Department of Music's suggestions would stick. He said that "a very radical change can hardly be expected from these Frenchmen who do everything in their own way." Nonetheless, many listeners appreciated Parès' refined Gallic selections and the high quality of the musicians.[13, 14]

Patrick Conway and his Band of Famous Soloists came to town next, preceding his friend John Philip Sousa by a few days. In 1915 Conway was perhaps second in prestige only to Sousa among American bandleaders, although he was much more affordable at only $3,075 per week.

Sousa declared before he arrived at the PPIE, "I will be delighted to be among my many friends of the Golden West again." Owing either to Stewart's cleverness or a fortunate coincidence of scheduling, Sousa's sixty-five artists were able to support the most patriotic events of the Fair.[15]

The "March King" was a little grayer and a bit stouter than when San Francisco had last seen him, but he had lost none of his jauntiness as he conducted his new composition, "The Pathfinder of Panama," in front of a crowd of 15,000 in the Court of the Universe on May 22. The "Beau Brummel of Bandleaders" had written the march

Though several Native American bands applied, none was hired by the PPIE music department, so Indian musicians played only in the Zone's two Wild West concessions. (The Bancroft Library, University of California, Berkeley)

John Philip Sousa (left) struck up a friendship with composer Camille Saint-Saëns as they prepared for the inaugural performance of the Frenchman's "Hail, California," featuring Sousa's ensemble. (Glenn D. Koch)

in honor of the PPIE and inaugurated it on the first day of the band's nine-week tenancy, playing on the grounds, in the Festival Hall, and at the Old Faithful Inn. How hearts must have swelled with nationalistic fervor on July 17, when the actual Liberty Bell arrived amidst much pomp, after which Sousa played an outdoor concert in the Court of Abundance.

The sixty-five-piece Boston Band under Emil Mollenhauer arrived in July just before Sousa's outfit departed. Mollenhauer was not only a capable bandleader but also a noted orchestral and choral conductor in his role at the helm of the Handel and Haydn Society of Boston.

Another highlight was the forty-man Russian Band, with its bright lapels and red fezzes. Director Phillip Pelz cut a dash in his snow-white uniform draped with a sash adorned with medals presented him by Czar Nicholas II of Russia. When asked why he was no longer Imperial Court Conductor, Pelz recounted a possibly true yarn of being thrown in jail by the czar when

The PPIE was a boon for local music teachers, who showcased their pupils in concerts such as this one in the Eilers Recital Hall inside the Palace of Liberal Arts. (Edward A. Rogers)

his regimental band played the French anthem "La Marseillaise" after the 1906 signing of the Russian constitution. Pelz claimed he played the tune because its liveliness seemed appropriate, but the czar felt it smacked of revolution. Feeling the cold winds of Siberian exile blowing, Pelz promptly made for Germany, taking with him the jeweled testaments of Nicholas' former affection.

Frederick Innes and his popular fifty-piece Denver Municipal Band began their six-week term in mid-October. An outstanding trombonist, Innes was known for his orchestra-like instrumentation, adding harp, strings, and basses when playing indoors. For his swan song at the PPIE, Innes presented the premiere of his comic opera *The Ambassadors* in the Festival Hall.

The PPIE closed with a second engagement of A. F. Thaviu's Band, which distinguished itself by employing a cadre of opera singers. The singers enabled production of condensed or "tabloid" versions of famous operas including *Aida, Carmen, La Bohème,* and *Il Travatore.* Thaviu expressed pride that he was awarded a medal by Charles C. Moore and that his was the only band to play at both Opening and Closing Day festivities.

INDIAN BANDS AND INDIGENOUS MUSIC

When J. R. Wheelock wrote to George Stewart, director of music, regarding a position at the PPIE for his "Wheelock's Indian Band" of Native American musicians, he likely was surprised at the response. Stewart replied, "[I]t has practically been decided by the Department of Music that our department will not be able to invite any Indian Band to participate in the Exposition."[16]

This was a departure from the policies of previous expositions. Native American bands from US government schools had played at the previous two American international expositions. According to the *Evening Tribune* of Hornellsville, New York, forty-five "full blood Indians" played for a month at the Buffalo Pan-American Exposition in 1901. Haskell's Indian Band, with musicians from Indian schools in Kansas, had performed at St. Louis in 1904.[17]

Several other bands consisting of native peoples also applied to the PPIE and were refused. One band advertised that its musicians

Grand "massed band" concerts—such as this one in the Court of the Universe featuring Sousa's, Conway's, and Cassasa's ensembles—were popular patriotic spectacles. (Edward A. Rogers)

could be outfitted with "full Indian costume or military uniform, as desired." Eventually, the only Native American brass bands at the PPIE were those that performed at the 101 Ranch and '49 Camp concessions on the Zone. The troupe that played at the '49 Camp hailed from the Stewart Institute, an Indian school in Carson City, Nevada.[18]

In this era, however, there was an increasing interest in indigenous song, as reflected in opera, classical, and parlor music. *Pacific Coast Musical Review* commented that "the spirit of Indian folklore…has in recent years made such an impression on a large portion of the American music lovers." This fascination was evident at the PPIE, but most of the pieces were authored and arranged by musicians of European ancestry. As one might expect, the resultant compositions were fraught with preconceptions, nostalgia, stereotypes, and creative reimaginings.[19]

Still, the PPIE did ring with Native American–influenced music on many occasions. There were performances of MacDowell's "Indian Suite," Dvořák/Kreisler's "Indian Lament," Sousa's

"The Red Man," and an evening of principally Zuni-themed music and dance. Victor Herbert conducted selections from his grand opera *Natoma* and from Charles Cadman's "From the Land of the Sky-Blue Water," based upon an allegedly authentic Native American chant.

The Mormon church's Ogden Tabernacle Choir sang Cadman's "The Place of Breaking Light" and "From the Long Room of the Sea," which also incorporated actual Indian musical underpinnings. Others, like Carl Busch, who conducted his "Minnehaha's Vision," employed more stylized Indian themes.

While appreciative of the flavor of the music, many reviewers were in condescending agreement that the best native-inspired music was that which used the least genuinely indigenous material. "Mr. Busch very cleverly contents himself with just hinting at the Indian character of the music and introducing his poetic and emotional ideas connected with the story in good harmonies and solid theoretical treatment," wrote critic Alfred Metzger. Mrs. George Ketchum, first soprano of the Ladies'

Musical Club of Tacoma, which made a specialty of Native American–themed selections, offered a back-handed compliment in a newspaper feature entitled "Red Man's Songs to Mingle with Melody of Wales." She said, "Indian music is not crude as it is generally thought to be and neither is it so limited in its expressiveness as popular idea has it."[20, 21]

Many of the works played at the Exposition may have been influenced by actual indigenous music, but none was created in the actual traditions. However, listeners in 1915 may well have been aware of this and willing to play along with a fantasy. Michael Pisani argues in his *Imagining Native America in Music* that the Sousa and Herbert pieces were never meant to fool the public into believing them based on actual Native American melodies. Rather, they were "purely meant to be entertaining."[22]

MASSED BANDS

In the musical *The Music Man*, fictional professor Harold Hill proclaims, "[Y]ou'll feel something akin to the electric thrill I once enjoyed when Gilmore, Liberati, Pat Conway, the Great Creatore, W. C. Handy, and John Philip Sousa all came to town on the very same historic day!" Although this line is a joke (the careers of these bandleaders did not all overlap), composer Meredith Wilson, who actually played in Sousa's band in the 1920s, was likely inspired to create his mythical aggregation by "massed band" spectacles such as those at the PPIE.

One early plan by the Department of Music was to hold massed band concerts in the Festival Hall, which would be profitable occasions of much pomp and volume. First, however, they started with an outdoor "tune-up" on Zone Day, May 27, in which Sousa led his band, together with those of Cassasa and Conway, in a show on the Marina.

The next massed band concert was an elaborate program in the Court of the Universe celebrating Bunker Hill Day on June 17. The pageant depicted America's "history in music," again under Sousa's baton. The *San Francisco Chronicle* said, "In swelling crescendo, the melodic force of the three bands presented a tonal picture of the Nation's history since the days of '76, and achieved its climax in the 'Star-Spangled Banner.'" After a grand fanfare of trumpet and drums, the "shot heard round the world" was supplied by

Scores of community bands—including the Portland Police Band, seen here in front of the Oregon Building—were given the opportunity to play at the Exposition. (Edward A. Rogers)

a cannon on the USS *Oregon*, at anchor in the bay, and transmitted by wireless to the platform in the Court of the Universe. After the playing of a series of patriotic anthems, a young woman portraying the allegorical Columbia, drawn in a chariot by sailors from the *Oregon*, was escorted into the court by the Philippine Constabulary Band. This spectacle was so popular the bands repeated it later in the month.[23]

Thereafter it became clear that the increased gate receipts from these spectacles far eclipsed the possible revenue from 4,000 or so tickets that could be sold for the Festival Hall, so massed band performances became regular outdoor affairs.

The largest massed band of all, totaling three hundred musicians, was constituted when the American Federation of Musicians descended on the Exposition on September 27. Twelve thousand spectators watched the Exposition Band, the Boston Band, and eight ensembles

Many fine conservatory-trained musicians performed with Torreblanca's "Orquesta Típica" in the Tehuantepec Village on the Zone. (Laura Ackley)

representing various Musicians' Locals dramatize "The Death of Custer," assisted by Native Americans from Glacier Park.

A MUSICAL COMMUNITY

Scores of other community, student, and military bands played for shorter engagements, and fraternal societies also got into the act. If you were a Bay Area Moose, Elk, Knight, Native Son, or Odd Fellow, your chapter probably sent a band or a drum corps. Municipal bands from virtually every hamlet ringing the San Francisco Bay, from San Jose to Sonoma County, and even into the foothills of the Sierra Nevada, made the journey. These groups usually played at the Fair on the commemorative day for their community or at major celebrations like the ninth anniversary of the Great Quake, San Francisco Day, or Admission Day.

In the early twentieth century, musical education was undergoing a transition. Students once had learned to play instruments through participation in community bands, but more and more this skill came from the classroom. Stewart was eager to feature students at the PPIE. *Piano Magazine* said, "Orchestras, glee clubs, mandolin clubs and bands composed of school boys and girls will journey to the Exposition to show what modern education is doing to develop the children artistically as well as practically."[24]

Many Bay Area schools had well-developed music curricula and proudly showcased their pupils at concerts on the grounds, in Festival Hall, or at the Eilers Recital Hall in the Palace of Liberal Arts. The Fair was a boon to private music teachers, who booked the hall's upstairs rooms for recitals.

Cadet bands from the Oregon Agricultural College, the University of Wisconsin, and Salt Lake City high schools traveled to the Jewel City for a chance to perform. The University of California cadet band made a much shorter trip across the bay from Berkeley. (It later evolved into what is now known as the "Pride of California," the University of California Marching Band.) Cal's Glee Club also performed at the Fair, singing spirit songs that are still popular at

AFRICAN AMERICAN MUSICIANS

Conspicuously absent from the official musical program at the PPIE were African American artists, who during this era were driving exciting developments in music. Ragtime had peaked and jazz was nascent, but these styles were downplayed at the PPIE. Ragtime in particular was considered "lower class" and was included in programs at the PPIE in ways that were often stereotypical.

Sousa's "The Black Man," the ragtime-inflected third part of his *Dwellers in the Western World,* was played during Bunker Hill Day festivities. Sousa paired his piece with two verses of the poem "Banjo Song" by Paul Laurence Dunbar, himself an African American. The poem has not aged well, as it is written in exaggerated "plantation" dialect.

The single African American band at the Fair played in the short-lived Dixie Land concession on the Zone, where it was touted it as "southern darkies sing the songs of old plantation days."[25]

the university, including "Hail to California," "California Indian Song," "Big C," and "All Hail."

Military units lent panache to parades and ceremonials, and in addition to the Marine Band, detailed for the duration of the Fair, two other local regiments contributed liberally. The Third Artillery Band was but a few steps away at Fort Winfield Scott in the western part of the Presidio, but the First Cavalry Band had to march through 127 miles of mud and rain from Monterey to assist. Smartly accoutered bands from the Ninth Cavalry, Arizona First Infantry, and First Regiment of the Illinois National Guard also paraded along the avenues, filling the air with spirited melodies.

MUSIC ON THE ZONE

The Department of Music's official offerings were supplemented by hundreds of performances in the concessions on the Zone and in the various state and foreign pavilions. On the cacophonous Joy Zone, peanut hawkers and barkers competed with music floating from within the concessions. Many of the venues featured music in some form—provided by anything from a single Victrola to a pianist to full live bands in the numerous dance halls. Passing under the pointed arch of the Mysterious Orient attraction, the curious might see a sinuous dancer writhing to the tinkle of a tambourine and the wail of an oboe. Drums throbbed from the Maori and

Samoan Villages, and a brass band saluted the toy soldiers in Toyland. While enhancing the attractions, generally these musical offerings were usually just side dishes for the show inside and not meant as "auditory entrees."

One Zone ensemble, however, surpassed all others in its musical merit: the Mexican Orchestra in the Tehuantepec Village. Behind its elaborately sculpted, quasi-Aztec façade, visitors found themselves in a tropical setting featuring a miniature lake surrounded by fragrant blossoms, and a village where maidens from the Isthmus of Tehuantepec plied the arts of their native land. Nearby was a jewel-like theater wherein, said writer H. A. Eveleth, "[S]eñoritas gracefully whirl and dip to the accompaniment of Torreblanca's Orchestra. The selections given by this orchestra, many of the members of which are graduates of musical conservatories of Mexico City, have a charm which is best portrayed by the repeated encores from the delighted audience." Bandleader Juan Nepomuceno Torreblanca earned a gold medal for excellence from the Exposition for his Orquesta Típica and continued to tour successfully into the 1930s.[26]

AMERICAN MELODIES

Musical offerings within the state buildings were often standard classical or patriotic fare, including brass bands and popular organ concerts in the Illinois Building. Some state delegations,

ORIGINAL COMPOSITIONS FOR THE EXPOSITION

The most famous compositions created for the Exposition undoubtedly were Sousa's "Pathfinder of Panama," Saint-Saëns' "Hail, California," and Amy Beach's "Panama Hymn," which took its lyrics from a poem by federal justice Wendell Phillips Stafford.

Dozens of other original songs were created for and played at the Fair. Phillip Pelz dedicated his "March George" to Music Director George Stewart. The Hurtado Brothers Royal Marimba Band composed two new pieces, a waltz entitled "Wonderful California" and "March to PPIE," and Cassasa's Official Band featured "The Tower of Jewels March" by J. A. MacMeekin.

Though the record industry was ascendant, sheet music remained the predominant way most Americans experienced new music, and tunesmiths went wild for the PPIE. They wrote rags and drags, tangos, trots and two-steps, war-whoops, waltzes, one-steps and, most of all, marches.

First came the "booster songs," written while San Francisco was competing for the right to hold the Exposition. These celebrated San Francisco's recovery, fiscal solidity, and civic drive. The cover of "In San Francisco, the Fair Will Be the Best" featured the city still aflame. Inside, portions of the lyrics ran, "San Francisco's got the time, the place, she's got the money too / To fete the world's inhabitants when the Panama Canal is through" and "From the ashes of the past she raised a city bright and great / As a monument to all the world, and a pride to the Golden Gate."[27]

As the Exposition drew nigh, composers got to work writing songs to take advantage of national fascination with the Fair. Dedications were popular, with tunes inscribed in honor of the Exposition, the Woman's Board, the Zone concessionaires, the Portuguese Pavilion, and even Martha Dieterich, queen of the Los Angeles Fire Department, whose picture graced the cover of "At the 1915 Fair."

Regional ballads extolled the wonders of California, San Francisco, or the Fair itself. Travel songs recounted amusing tales of the journey to the Fair by train or through the Panama Canal. These songs had titles like "Shoot Me Back to California-Land," "Pack Your Duds for San Francisco," "Off for 'Frisco Town," and "They're on Their Way to the 'Frisco Fair." Fresh off the success of "Alexander's Ragtime Band," a twenty-five-year old Irving Berlin even penned a ditty called "San Francisco Bound."

Numbers published by East Coast songsters tended to present a stock set of images of the Golden State. According to these masterpieces, if you visited California in 1915, you'd find a land of not only milk and honey but also wine and poppies, where everyone was happy in the uniformly perfect weather. The more fanciful jingles depicted an entirely new San Francisco with gold-paved streets populated mostly by forty-niners and cowboys. Descriptions of the PPIE in these songs are sketchy at best, incorporating the kind information one could easily find in any feature story about the Exposition without ever visitng the Fair itself.

A few locals strove to search for deeper meaning in their lyrics or to invest their works with more Exposition specifics. In the ballad "The Meaning of P.P.I.E.," a father explains to his daughter the initials she sees painted on fences all over town. He explains that it not only stands for Panama-Pacific International Exposition but also "Pretty Prompt in Everything."

Don J. A. Gono, a Cuban American composer living in San Francisco, seems to have made a small career penning PPIE songs. After writing a travel song called "Meet Me at the San Francisco Fair," he managed to get at least three songs stamped with the "Official Exposition Songs" seal: "Flying," "My Big Night Off," and "The Zone," which he dedicated to Frank Burt, manager of concessions.

Dozens of original songs were published to promote the Fair and leverage its popularity. (Laura Ackley)

however, tried to impart a regional flavor with their programs. The "old-fashioned two-step," reels, and other Midwestern staples were featured at the dedication of the Iowa Building.

Performances in southern state buildings acknowledged reverberations of the Civil War, only one generation past. At one Missouri Building affair the well-known Dixie Trio played a medley of southern songs. At another, Lizzie Chambers Hull performed her own song, "Missouri," for which she'd won $1,000 in a contest sponsored by that state's governor. One verse ran, "She came, a compromise, for peace; Her prayer is still that strife may cease; She mourned her blue, wept o'er her gray, When, side by side, in death they lay—Missouri."[28]

The band at the West Virginia Building took a politic tack, first playing "Way Down South in Dixie," followed by "The Star-Spangled Banner," and finishing up with "America."

When the Music Teachers' Association of California met at the Exposition in July, it presented John Philip Sousa with a proposal that his "Stars and Stripes Forever" and traditional Southern song "Dixie" be proclaimed "dual official national marches." While the educators' idea fell by the wayside, "Stars and Stripes Forever" was indeed adopted—seventy-two years later in 1987.[29]

A MUSICAL FEAST

Today, fairs and festivals follow a time-honored tradition of booking marquee musical acts to bolster attendance. In 1915 the Official Band, the Marine Band, and the Philippine Constabulary Band anchored the entertainment of the PPIE, while a rotating slate of famous bands periodically injected fresh interest into the program. Acclaimed outfits under bona fide celebrity conductors suffused the grounds with high-quality music, and charismatic bandleaders—the rock stars of their era—were eagerly sought by the Fair's management, even as the Department of Music turned down hundreds of other professional applicants.

Most of the musicians at the Fair were "pale and male," although non-Caucasian and female performers were not entirely excluded. They were, however, usually relegated to performing in the state and national pavilions and on the Joy Zone. It was evident in the official musical offerings of the Jewel City that while many female musicians and musicians of color were virtuosos, their opportunities were limited by the era in which they lived. Even as John Philip Sousa played at what would be his last world's fair, African Americans were pioneering music that would one day develop into modern jazz, a unique American form. The absence of these progressive developments at the Exposition underscores the fact that international expositions were rarely venues for cutting-edge musical styles.

What the Fair did well, however, was give thousands of amateur musicians the opportunity to perform at this grandest of all venues. Members of community and student bands would always be proud to say, "I played at the World's Fair."

SEASONS
OF WONDER

In 100 AD, the Roman poet Juvenal described the eternal human impulse toward diversion as a longing for "bread and circuses." Eighteen centuries later, *Sunset* magazine writer Frances Groff concurred. She said humans would always "crave and demand thrills; and an exposition…must cater to this demand. There must be aeroplane flights, automobile races, electrical illuminations and fireworks, land pageantry, water carnivals, feats of horsemanship and marksmanship, sham battles and other military and naval features, outdoor concerts and dancing, horse racing, yachting, motor boat regattas, big athletic meets and a hundred other events…."[1]

Panama-Pacific International Exposition management also understood this and packed the Fair's calendar with parades, pageants, sporting events, drills, demonstrations, and "special days."

Every day merrymakers strolled about the grounds, whether under fog and drizzle or on sparkling summer afternoons, taking in all the wonders of the Fair. A visiting family may have stepped to one side of the Avenue of Palms to watch a regiment from the Presidio march by. They might have stopped in a palace to hear a lecture, or on the Esplanade to watch an aviator fly through air scented with sea salt and coal smoke from the miniature Overfair Railway. No day was without something extra—a speech, a parade, a competition, or a ceremony.

313

SPECIAL DAYS

Organizers wanted to maintain interest, especially among locals, by offering fresh experiences throughout the Fair. "Not only must there be 'something doing every minute,' but something doing in a hundred different places," said *Sunset* magazine. Each of the 288 days of the Fair was designated a "special day" in recognition of something—in fact, usually several somethings. To accommodate the requisite honors and activities, every day had to do double, triple, quadruple duty or more.[2]

A total of 828 special days, plus 966 special events, meant the average day was packed with about six extra events in addition to the regular lectures, movies, stunt flights, and musical entertainments. Added to that were whatever attractions individual exhibitors might offer. July 24 was exceptionally replete. It was a "special day" for Illinois, Utah, the

National Electrical Contractors, the National Society of the Sons of the Revolution, the Fraternal Brotherhood, Clan Irving, Victor Talking Machine Jobbers, Newspaper Men, the International Purity Congress, and the California Society of Commercial Secretaries. Also on the bill were track and field, swimming, army and navy sports, and baseball throwing competitions. That evening the Venetian Carnival was held on the placid waters of the Palace of Fine Arts Lagoon. While some days held more and some fewer events, a daily multiplicity extended over the whole season.

Most special days marked a gathering at the Fair. The participants might have hailed from the same place, industry, convention, club, fraternal group, society, or school. Typically these groups would form into a parade that would be greeted at the gates by PPIE officials and a military regiment from the Presidio and escorted into the grounds. If they did not bring their own band, they would

The March 23 parade for the "special day" honoring San Joaquin and Calaveras Counties stretched far down the Joy Zone. (Edward A. Rogers)

Groups celebrating special days usually posed for a panoramic photo in the Jewel City, as this immense throng did in the South Gardens on German American Day, August 5. (Glenn D. Koch)

receive an assist from the Exposition's Official Band or the Philippine Constabulary Band. The parade customarily was followed by an outdoor ceremony with requisite speeches, and then the entire group would line up in the South Gardens, the Court of the Universe, or the Court of Ages, where an official photographer would snap a panoramic photo using a "circuit camera."

The logistics of admitting a horde of individuals—some marching, some in automobiles—required a special system. Most participants already would have admission tokens, but those who did not would be met several blocks before reaching the Exposition by a gateman, from whom they would purchase tickets. When the parade arrived at the Jewel City, the cars drove through the automobile gates unhindered. The marchers could tramp four abreast through four turnstiles reserved for that purpose, resulting in a smooth, unbroken parade.

Some special days recognized particular causes, including those with conflicting goals. Tobacco Day was balanced by Anti-Cigarette League of America Day, and Wine Day by National Temperance Council Day. Butchers and bakers had their days, but it is unclear if candlestick makers were honored. Fruits were frequently commemorated, with special days for Oregon cherries, loganberries, and for grapes and their dehydrated siblings, raisins. There was a catchall tribute to miscellaneous fruits on American Pomological Society Day. Reigning over all were apples, with Wenatchee, Gravenstein, Douglas County, and Montana varieties recognized on four separate days.

REGIONAL REVELS

Every California city and county, each state, and all the nations exhibiting at the Fair were accorded their own celebratory days, and each had special features. Often, fair maidens were used to advertise the locales. Girls handed out daffodils for Santa Cruz's dedication day, apples for Sonoma, strawberries for Monterey, lemons for Santa Barbara, and roses for Oregon. Foreign pavilion dedications called for appropriate national costumes, but some outfits were more creative. Ladies from Shasta County dressed as daisies, while those from Solano County, home of the Mare Island Naval Yard, marched as "middies." On Patriots' Day, Anna Bell Logan appeared in Minuteman costume, complete with flintlock rifle. But perhaps the most fetching were the piscatorially arrayed Salmon Girls from Washington State, whose dresses featured spangled scales and fringed tails as they gave

The honorary queen and her court rode on an imaginative float symbolizing "United Slavonia" on Slavonic Day, September 20. (Edward A. Rogers)

away 5,000 tins of canned salmon.

Pageantry was a PPIE specialty. All the usual holidays—St. Patrick's Day, Orange Day, May Day, and California Admission Day—were observed with special programs. But there were also dozens of events for occasions like the San Francisco favorite Portola Day, and Queen Victoria's birthday, dubbed British Empire Day.

Father Junípero Serra was kept busy at the Exposition, despite having been dead for 130 years. Several crowd-pleasing "mission pageants" with hundreds of players featured the "good padre." Performed on the beautiful verge of the Palace of Fine Arts Lagoon and in the Court of the Universe were a variety of historical reenactments, which also included Christopher Columbus, Vikings, characters from Arthurian legend, and riders for the Pony Express.

San Francisco in 1915 also seemed to have an appetite for spectacular destruction. A stage set representing Babylon was constructed on the Marina for the October 2 salute to Joy Zone concessionaires. After a cast of five hundred "beautiful girls, women, men and children clad in flowing robes" portrayed life in the ancient city, the structure was set on fire. On Zone Day the "Good Ship Zone"—the hull of the old ferryboat *Amador* disguised by canvas to look like a battleship—was detonated in the bay, creating a terrific fountain of water and debris. Ostensibly, its destruction was a vivid depiction of submarine mines, but mostly San Franciscans just liked to blow up stuff. Aviator Charles Niles destroyed miniature forts from the air as part of several elaborate "sham battles" enacted by thousands of troops in the racetrack stadium.[3]

The detonation of an old ferryboat hull disguised as a battleship on Zone Day, May 27, was one of many gratuitous explosions staged to entertain Exposition patrons. (Seligman Family Foundation)

The Souvenir Watch Palace's float for the Zone Day parade included a Tower of Jewels hung with pocket watches in place of Novagems. The bride and groom in the foreground were married on the Aeroscope that day. (Edward A. Rogers)

NINE YEARS AFTER

Major-General George Goethals was accorded due reverence for his role in completing the canal after which the Exposition was named. However, he was feted on only one day. In contrast, the "Nine Years After" gaieties—commemorating San Francisco's recovery from the April 18, 1906, great earthquake and fire—spanned six days. The Fair was just as surely a declaration of recovery as it was a recognition of the "Big Ditch."

For the Nine Years After celebration, the Jewel City went positively pyromaniacal. Imitation "earthquake shacks" were burned on the Marina Green. Two days later, the Tower of Jewels appeared to burst into flames, an illusion created by colored spotlights thrown onto swirls of smoke coming from pots concealed on its parapets. Just as the simulated inferno died down, a ship in the bay next to the Fair actually *did* burst into flames. Again the sacrificial vessel was a repurposed old barge, and one of San Francisco's trusty fireboats put out the fire, but not before the "onlookers experienced all the thrills of watching a ship burning to its waterline."[4]

The jubilation kicked off on April 17 with a parade of 20,000 that started at the Ferry Building and made its way to the Fair. Police, PPIE dignitaries, military squadrons, firefighters, cadets, city employees, insurance professionals, and Joy Zone performers passed before a reviewing stand at the Tower of Jewels. The next day was Sunday, and an interfaith thanksgiving service was held in the Court of the Universe. Episcopalian, Catholic, and Jewish leaders spoke, as did Benjamin Ide Wheeler, president of the University of California, and David Starr Jordan, chancellor of Stanford University. At the conclusion of the observances, the audience joined the four-hundred-person Exposition Chorus in singing "Now Thank We All Our God"

and "O Praise Ye the Lord."

A "Wild Carnival of Joy" highlighted Monday's program, with the motto "Let the world slide, let the world go, a fig for care, a fig for woe." The Press Club produced a pageant featuring two hundred costumed riders re-creating famous mounted characters, including Don Quixote, Falstaff, Joan of Arc, and Lady Godiva. This was followed by dancing on the Joy Zone.[5]

Patriots' Day and a day honoring fire underwriters were next. The Nine Years After merrymaking concluded on the sixth day with yet another massive parade. More than one hundred decorated floats and thousands of fraternal society members participated.

ZONE DAY

Though the Joy Zone had suffered through the soggy early months, it frolicked in grand style

The Exposition mounted a variety of equestrian events at the race track, including show jumping, polo, and racing. (Seligman Family Foundation)

on Zone Day, May 27. It took more than two hours for a long train of concessionaire floats and briskly marching bands and military units to circumambulate the walled palaces and reach the middle of the Zone. To encourage construction of elaborate moving displays, the PPIE sweetened the pot by offering prizes for the best floats. A double-deck concoction resembling the façade of the Tehuantepec Village supported the Mexican attraction's band. The contingent from Japan Beautiful was pulled along in a boat designed to look like a blue-breasted pheasant. The oversized crockery on the Bowls of Joy float also was dramatic, but it was the lovelies under the canopy of the Streets of Cairo's entry who took home first prize.

INDEPENDENCE DAY

On Independence Day weekend, the Jewel City was at its most patriotically beautiful. Vessels in the warship flotilla off its northern margin were decorated stem to stern with signal flags and illumined by spotlights at night. Saturday, July 3, kicked off with a Universal Pageant parade of Joy Zone attractions and cavalry. Cutter crews

from the military ships raced in the bay while games were held on the lawn of the Marina. These featured a race between Exposition cashiers, greased pole climbs, and a tug-o-war between PPIE firefighters and sailors from the USS *Oregon*. The firemen were victorious after ninety seconds.

The ultimate patriotic experience was on Independence Day itself, when 10,000 packed the great Court of the Universe to hear the massed band concert featuring the Exposition Band, Patrick Conway's Band of Soloists, and John Philip Sousa's band playing in unison. "Dolphin sports" took place in the Yacht Harbor, including swimming, canoe, and tub races, as well as "fancy diving" and boat jousting. Over on the Band Concourse, the little dance pupils of Miss Ida Wyatt formed patriotic tableaux including "The Spirit of '76." Fraternal groups drilled in competition on the plaza in front of the Fountain of Energy while daylight fireworks crackled over the Marina.

The festivities culminated on Monday with the arrival of William Jennings Bryan, who, recently resigned as secretary of state, preached his pacifist message under the Tower of Jewels

On Cadillac Day, the new Model Eight was revealed, Charlie Chaplin imitators entertained, and a beauty contest was held. The winner received a string of pearls. (Donna Ewald Huggins)

The Liberty Bell's visit to the PPIE was the last time the relic left Philadelphia, and a few visitors were allowed to get very close to the national emblem. (Edward A. Rogers)

from a stand draped with Old Glory. This was preceded by another grand parade, this one around the Embarcadero from downtown to the Fair. Bryan was followed by poet Edwin Markham reading his new "Ode to Freedom." A drum corps contest and soccer game were held on the Marina Green, a wood-chopping competition on the Zone, and horse and harness racing at the racetrack. All this, of course, was supplemented by the usual program of band and organ music. The afternoon continued with the almost obligatory destruction of a fake torpedo boat in the harbor, to the delight of the crowd. The long weekend of entertainment and sentiment concluded with an illuminated night flight by Art Smith.

LIBERTY BELL DAY

The nation's most precious revolutionary relic went on its last and longest road trip when it paid a call to San Francisco and the Fair. In 1912, Pennsylvania governor John Tener suggested California children circulate a petition to bring the Liberty Bell to the Jewel City. This was a tried-and-true stratagem, as it had been used to bring the bell to the 1904 St. Louis fair. By late autumn of 1912, half a million schoolchildren had signed a scroll of paper two miles long, which was rolled onto a huge reel. The petition was paraded down Market Street on Thanksgiving Day before it was

sent off to the Keystone State.

Prior to the PPIE, the Liberty Bell had been downright peripatetic. The bell had visited New Orleans in 1885, Chicago in 1893, Atlanta in 1895, Charleston in 1902, and Boston in 1903. When it was requested for the 1909 Alaska Yukon-Pacific Exposition in Seattle, it was found that a second crack was developing, extending up from the famous early repair. The bell stayed home, and a new, padded support was designed to relieve the pressure of its own weight.

As 1915 approached, many Philadelphians vigorously protested the Liberty Bell's removal because of its fragility. "Should it again be sent on a railroad journey across the continent, it is by no means unlikely that it would arrive there in two pieces," pronounced expert metallurgist Alexander Outerbridge after examining the bell in early 1915. However, the opponents were overruled after sustained lobbying by former President Taft, Secretary of the Interior Franklin K. Lane, publisher William Randolph Hearst, San Francisco banker Herbert Fleishhacker, Philadelphia mayor Rudolph Blankenburg, and others. On April 15, the Select and Common Councils in Philadelphia voted to send the bell to the Exposition. To prepare for the trip, its clapper was removed and a steel skeleton installed inside the bell.[6]

After a reverent sendoff from Philadelphia on July 5, the bell began a whistle-stop tour across the country on an open gondola car cushioned by special shock absorbers and enclosed by an iron railing. At night, the brightly illuminated bell was visible from a mile away as it moved at a sedate pace through the darkened countryside. In daylight, veterans of the Civil War donned their military caps and stood at the doors of their homes waving flags at the passing train.

The bell made more than seventy stops along its 3,000-mile route to San Francisco and, rain or shine, it was greeted by patriotic crowds. In some cities, special platforms were constructed so that children could walk across a ramp, file past the bell, and touch or kiss it. The train bearing the bell finally chugged into San Francisco's Townsend Street Station after midnight on July 17. A boisterous throng had stayed awake to cheer its arrival.

A few hours later, the Liberty Bell had been mounted on a flatbed truck massed with roses for its trip across the city to the PPIE. An American flag was formed in blooms beneath the relic. At 10:00 a.m. a military escort formed and the procession started from the station. Hundreds of thousands lined the sidewalks to watch the bell pass, and some spectators cast golden poppies before the cortège. Inside the Fair, forty-eight little girls, representing the states, were attired in red, white, and blue costumes and bonnets. Each placed a wreath below the national symbol, after which a diminutive Columbia and Uncle Sam raised the American flag. House Speaker Champ Clark told the assembled multitude that from the Liberty Bell's "brazen throat rang forth the startling message for all nations...that here in this western world a handful of brave and self-supporting people, weary of tyranny from across the sea, were establishing a new government and free...."[7]

Finally the Liberty Bell was wheeled to the state section, gently plucked from its car by a crane, and transferred onto a solid, wheeled cart at the Pennsylvania Building. For four months it spent each day on view under the central loggia, but every evening it was rolled into a vault. Finally, on November 11, the bell was prepared for travel once more. It left the Exposition accompanied by cheers and church bells, and by tearful smiles of farewell.

SAN FRANCISCO DAY

"Everyone was there except the sick, and some of *them* came" is how the Fair's official history described San Francisco Day, November 2, the anniversary of Don Gaspar de Portolá's discovery of San Francisco Bay. Governor Hiram Johnson proclaimed a statewide holiday, businesses closed, and children were released from school. The upper crust was entreated to give servants the day off.[8]

Attendees were encouraged to pay separate admission rather than use their season tickets, and the San Francisco Day ticket had a decorative stub reading "I Paid," designed to be worn on the lapel to proclaim civic pride and support. Businesses donated more than 30,000 drawing prizes for that day, including trinkets, phonographs, pianos, automobiles, and even a plot of land.

Chronicle publisher M. H. de Young hectored readers: "You who are careless, you who are indifferent, you who are willing to let somebody else do what you should do yourself, wake up for once in your life and do for yourself by going to the exposition tomorrow."[9]

Japanese girls were featured on many of the floats in the Japan Day parade, but it was the cherry dancers on Japan Beautiful's offering who took first place. (Chuck Banneck)

Architect Bernard Maybeck playfully reinterpreted the classical colonnade of his nearby Palace of Fine Arts into a rustic form on the whimsical House of Hoo-Hoo that he designed for a lumbermen's society. (Edward A. Rogers)

348,472 times, far surpassing any previous day's attendance. While not as great in number as Chicago Day in 1893 (716,881 visitors) or St. Louis Day in 1904 (404,450), the Jewel City's managers were nevertheless elated. They had drawn far more in terms of relative percentage. St. Louis had gleaned 57 percent of its city's population, and Chicago 51 percent. San Francisco had captured fully 70 percent of its resident population.

FRATERNAL ORGANIZATIONS

The lyrics of "1915 Rag," a ditty penned in commemoration of the Fair, went, "You'll meet the Elks, the Eagles and the Shriners too / and when they get together, Oh! The things they'll do!" And so it was that many brotherhoods, sisterhoods, and societies held their annual meetings at the PPIE. One could see a variety of Knights—of Columbus, Templar, and Pythias— as well as Native Sons and Daughters. The daily programs were positively littered with the Greek letters of fraternities and sororities. Several thousand Freemasons celebrated at the Festival Hall in June, and a red-fezzed horde descended on the Jewel City in July when the Shriners came to town.

Perhaps the most whimsical fraternal ceremony started at nine minutes past the ninth hour of the ninth day of the ninth month, when the black-robed Snark of the Universe intoned, "By the tail of the great black cat, Hoo-Hoo!" The fun-loving society of lumbermen, whose mascot was the inky feline, held its conclave in an equally whimsical building, the House of Hoo-Hoo, created by master architect Bernard Maybeck. It was the only order to construct its own pavilion at the Fair, and the edifice had three purposes: promoting the use of Pacific coast lumber, providing hospitality to visiting lumbermen, and encouraging sociability among local members.[10]

The House of Hoo-Hoo was tucked just south of the Palace of Horticulture. Two forty-foot-tall pylons simulating redwood trunks, each covered in bark, flanked the entry to the forestry

Whatever the inducement, San Franciscans responded in droves. Early comers flooded into the Fair to witness the colorful Pageant of Nations, produced by the states and countries participating in the PPIE. Highlights of the gala parade included a Hawaiian quintet playing from atop the territory's float, a Viking ship presented by Norway, and California's entry, with portrayals of Spanish padres, gold miners, and the California grizzly. Oregon's entry was a big hit because of ten marchers in redwood tree costumes scampering about like animated logs.

Harness, airplane, and boat races, football, and the presentation of the Pacific Coast Baseball League pennant on the Marina satisfied sports fans. A spectacular sham battle in the stadium included yet another exploding model fort, with an exploding faux-torpedo boat in the bay thrown in. After the fireworks, the Civil War battle of the *Monitor* and *Merrimac* was enacted in the bay, providing yet more naval carnage.

Crowds were so thick that it was a struggle to see these many wonders or to find room on one of the many dance floors. When the turnstiles were locked for the night, they had turned compound. Just beyond, the courtyard was enclosed by two arcing colonnades supported on unfinished logs, a clever reference to the much grander colonnades of the nearby Palace of Fine Arts, also designed by Maybeck. The façade was embellished with four sets of columns, two deep and four across. The pillars were formed from the "eight commercial trees of the coast" and were labeled redwood, sugar pine, white pine, Douglas fir, western hemlock, western spruce, red cedar, and Port Orford cedar. The wood products motif continued in the men's reading room, paneled in Douglas fir; the ladies' restroom, done in redwood; and the committee room, finished in white pine.[11]

MARCHING ORDERS

Plans for an international military tournament collapsed shortly after the first shots of World War I were fired in Europe, but San Francisco was still full of marines and soldiers from the Presidio and sailors from ships anchored in the bay. At any time, as many as 1,550 men from visiting units were housed at a barracks near the Zone, and the USS *Oregon* was anchored in the bay for much of the Fair. Military escorts were used as honor guards for important visitors. Servicemen in uniform were admitted free.

One notable use of Presidio lands was the Model Marine Camp, located west of the Texas Building. It is described by Exposition historian Frank Morton Todd: "The Marines' Camp was one of the main attractions of the west end of the grounds....All day, people wandered through the neat, orderly little streets of the city of khaki tents, admiring the spotless accouterments and the slim, upstanding sentries with their business-like rifles and trig uniforms...."[12]

Thrilling water rescues were an exciting attraction at the edge of the Marina near the Palace of Transportation. Crews of sailors from the US Life-Saving Service, stationed at nearby Fort Point, put on a great show rescuing and resuscitating hapless ersatz victims and demonstrating "self-righting, self-bailing" lifeboats.

Working in a team of seven, the men practiced flipping boats over by standing in them while pulling on ropes attached on the opposite side. Once upside down, the men used their body weight to continue the roll, right the craft, and clamber back inside, never losing their jaunty white caps despite their dousing. That year the service was merged with the US Revenue Cutter Service and was renamed the Coast Guard.

PHYSICAL CULTURE

Some PPIE events spanned the entire season, including livestock competitions, the ever-changing horticultural displays, and athletics.

The men of the US Life-Saving Service, soon to be renamed the Coast Guard, demonstrated a variety of rescue drills in boats and on ropes strung above the bay. (Anne T. Kent California Room, Marin County Free Library)

Sumo wrestling was just one of many sports contested at the Fair, including all the Amateur Athletic Union's 1915 championships. (The Banneck)

When he arrived at the Jewel City, bronzed, lithe twenty-four-year-old Duke Kahanamoku was better known as an Olympic swimming champion than for his surfing, though today he is credited with popularizing the latter sport. Kahanamoku visited the Fair to compete in the Exposition Swimming Championships, part of an ambitious sports program planned by James E. Sullivan, legendary exponent of amateur athletics.

Tragically, Sullivan died on September 16, 1914, following emergency surgery. That same week, the World War began in earnest, dragging many of the globe's finest athletes into the trenches and impairing Sullivan's plans for 1915. The PPIE tried to pick up the pieces, first under J. J. McGovern, Sullivan's secretary. In May the responsibility finally settled upon William Humphrey and John Elliott of the Olympic Club and E. G. McConnell of the Amateur Athletic Union.

Some of the most ambitious plans for championships were scuttled, but scores of sporting events still were contested in conjunction with the Fair. The Amateur Athletic Union brought all its 1915 championships to the Exposition, including basketball, gymnastics, swimming, and track and field.

The Jewel City's specially designed cinder running track with its 440-yard straightaway was touted as the fastest ever built, and at least a dozen track and field competitions were held there. These ranged from children's meets to high school, collegiate, and club-level contests.

To win the Exposition's "modified marathon," held July 5 as part of the Independence Day festivities, C. J. Lippert had to thread his way through crowds of merrymakers starting at the Van Ness end of the Zone, trot down to the South Gardens, circle the palace block three times, then retrace his first steps to finish at the plaza at the center of the Zone, a total distance of seven miles. The half- and Olympic-length marathons held later in the season started and finished on the Fair's track. Auto races and equestrian competitions also were held in the stadium, and the polo tournament split its games between that site and other local fields.

Though they were official Exposition events, competitions that required special facilities, such as swimming, had to be held at venues scattered across the Bay Area. When Kahanamoku broke the world record for the 100-yard swim at the PPIE swimming championships on July 18, with a time of 54.4 seconds, it was not on the fairgrounds but in the saltwater pool at the Sutro Baths on San Francisco's rocky western shore. Other swimming contests were held in the Fair's Yacht Harbor, and a few in the pool in front of the Press Building in the South Gardens.

The venerable Olympic Club hosted the fencing, basketball, and handball championships, and boxing and wrestling were held in the new Exposition Civic Auditorium downtown. Gymnasts tumbled at the San Francisco YMCA, tennis players volleyed on the lawns of the California Tennis Club at Bush and Scott Streets, water polo players splashed in the Post Street Tank, and trapshooters took aim on the Easton Shooting Grounds in San Mateo. Yacht and motorboat racing had an outstanding facility in the bay itself, on the veritable doorstep of the Jewel City, and the adjacent wide swath of grass of the Marina Green made an excellent field for soccer, football, rugby and, oddly, camel races.

Fresh off the 1914 US Open, the first of his eleven major championship victories, future Hall of Famer Walter Hagen won the PPIE golf championships in dominant fashion on the San Francisco Golf and Country Club's Ingleside Links, which also hosted the women's golf event, won by Edith Chesebrough.

Some sporting events were staged purely for entertainment. Coast League baseball stars dropped balls three hundred feet from a balcony of the Tower of Jewels to players below. The first ball missed the roped-off target area and went into the crowd. No one was injured, and San Francisco Seals pitcher Charles "Spider" Baum quickly corrected his aim, successfully tossing balls to several players.

Typical national sports were often arranged for the "special day" of that country. Irish hurling and Gaelic football were played on St. Patrick's Day, and cricket was a feature of British Empire Day. Filipino athletes demonstrated ring-tilting, in which contestants on bicycles tried to spear rings, and there was kite fighting on Philippine Islands Day. Japanese sumo wrestling was a common attraction in Japan Beautiful on the Zone, and a German "Turn Fest" included track and field competitions, dancing, calisthenics, and gymnastics. On Closing Day the final sporting event ended when a soccer team made up of alumni from rivals UC Berkeley and Stanford defeated a team of local club players on the Marina field.

SPORTS OF SORTS

Perhaps the most popular PPIE "sport" was a daily melee during which ribs were squeezed, voices were raised, and fingers dripped with butter. "Sconing" (pronounced "scahn-ing") was the name given the scrimmage in the Palace of Food Products whenever fresh, hot scones were available. Crowds thronged the scone counters, elbowing, pushing, and jockeying for position. The humble pastries were baked by Fisher Flouring Mills, Quaker Oats Company, and a few other purveyors. After the crusty triangles were removed from the oven, they were slathered in butter and raspberry jam and dispensed for a nickel each in paper envelopes, held aloft in triumph by the victors. These "Scotch scones" were the certifiable food craze of the Exposition, making sconing the Fair's unofficial sport.

Chronicle reporter Helen Dare said sconing required "courage, coolness, presence of mind and endurance—especially endurance." The skilled sconer could be identified by crumbs about the mouth and telltale jam stains. One magazine writer sheepishly admitted, "I spent so much time in the Palace of the Nibbling Arts partaking of the Scotch scones with raspberry jam, that I was forced to leave without visiting the majority of the Foreign Buildings...."[13, 14]

An estimated 800,000 of the delectable pastries were sold, and sconing devotees were bereft when their sport ended along with the Fair. Dare lamented, "Our daily 'sconing'.... How we will miss the tang and zip of that! How flabby and enervated we will grow, for want of it."[15]

For those who preferred "cheesecake," there were dozens of beauty contests. Lovely maidens from the Exposition were touted in viewbooks, magazines, and newspapers. Ada Whitton was the Queen of Ripe Olive Day, Viola Willett was the Queen of Portola Day, and Maidie Roberts of Japan Beautiful was elected Queen of the Zone. Female employees even named A. J. Goldsmith the handsomest PPIE guard.

LIVING EXHIBITS

Even as World War I caused cancellation or scaling back of a number of events, a different kind of war seriously curtailed the Fair's livestock program. Early plans included livestock exhibits and contests on a grand scale. At previous world's fairs the livestock shows had been brief events, but departmental chief D. O. Lively announced that the PPIE's livestock arena would present continuous exhibits across all 288 days.

Such an elaborate show required a great deal of planning and space. Thirty acres were dedicated to the livestock facilities, for which architect Bernard Maybeck designed an elegant complex of offices and stables. Silos were constructed, and appropriate types of feed ordered for all the different breeds.

Then, in 1914, the dreaded, highly contagious foot-and-mouth disease, which affects cloven-hooved animals such as cattle, pigs, and sheep, broke out in the eastern parts of the US. Dr. Charles Keane, California State Veterinarian, forbade shipping to California animal breeds susceptible to foot-and-mouth from the infected areas and those adjoining them. The ban was to be enforced until the Department of Agriculture declared the affected areas clean. This quarantine included all states east of the Mississippi, along with Minnesota, Iowa, Kansas, Missouri, and Montana. Cattlemen, particularly from the Midwest, called the quarantine a "trick" by "politicians and cattlemen who desire to win by unfair means the big prizes offered at the Panama Exposition."[16]

As it transpired, caution was justified. The outbreak was the largest ever in the United States. Eventually 170,000 cattle, sheep, pigs, and goats were destroyed to prevent its spread, at a cost to producers of $4.5 million (about $106 million in 2012). However, prohibition on animals was applied unequally, and some herds that had been exhibited alongside herds from the banned states were allowed at the PPIE. The *Pan-Pacific Press Association* concluded that had it been "a strictly California exhibit, less unfavorable comment would have been caused."[17]

Despite the dearth of eastern hoofstock, there were plenty of animals to see. Immense Percheron horses and petite Shetland ponies,

Exotic long-tailed Japanese fowl were part of the Jewel City's extensive livestock program. (Glenn D. Koch)

angora and milk goats, and a vast collection of sheep and poultry all were displayed. The Persian government sent a flock of Karakul and other fat-tailed sheep. Japan contributed valuable specimens of Yokohama or Phoenix fowls, whose roosters had tails as long as twenty-three feet. Nearly half a million dollars in prizes and a reported three miles of silk ribbons were awarded in contests for such domesticated animals as horses, cattle, sheep and swine, poultry, pigeons and pets.

Farmers could investigate new milking machines and hog feeding contraptions or attend the massive milk and cream show. "View herds" of Berkshire pigs and Holstein cattle were maintained for the run of the Fair, and collections of Shire, Belgian, and Hungarian horses and Guernsey and Shorthorn cattle appeared for shorter periods. The 125 Holsteins provided milk for the Carnation Milk Condensery near the Palace of Fine Arts.

Nineteen-year-old Lily Ramatici, who styled herself a "Petaluma Chicken," won the milking competition in the livestock arena. (Edward A. Rogers)

Lily Ramatici, nineteen years old, traveled the thirty-five miles south from Petaluma to the Fair on October 23. She took a train, then boarded a ferry across to the Exposition, where, in an homage to her region's primary industry, she entered the cow-milking competition as "a Petaluma Chicken." Lily won by coaxing more than seventeen pounds of milk from her bovine.[18]

There were also a variety of other animal-centric competitions. Horse and harness races were held on the PPIE's track, and show jumping, polo, and utility dog trials were contended inside its oval. Animal judging took place in its own capacious arena. "Dogs of All Nations" were shown by W. E. Mason in a building near the stock stadium, and an egg-laying contest spanned the entire Exposition period. On the Zone, the season closed out with the Children's Pet Show of dogs, cats, guinea pigs, canaries, mice, and assorted birds.

GLEAMING GARDENS

Between the glistening, iridescent bubble of the horticultural dome and the hedge fence on the city side of the Fair flourished a living exhibit—the demonstration gardens. Nine acres of plantings created a gorgeous display that changed with every visit. In addition to its beauty, the garden was to illustrate "the improvement of variety through seed selection, the creation of new varieties through plant hybridization, and the origination of new species through the Mendelian theory of segregation," according to George A. Dennison, director of horticulture.[19]

Open to the winds from the bay, the site was regarded as "about as unpromising for general flowers as anything that could be found on the peninsula," but nonetheless eleven nations and twenty-three states exhibited there. When the plots bloomed profusely, head gardener Carl Purdy averred, "I knew what could be done in California, even in a spot like this." Special events sponsored by the Department of Horticulture included the spring apple and flower exhibitions, and the summer sweet pea and autumn dahlia shows.[20]

As a leading agricultural state, California was very concerned that horticultural exhibits might introduce pests and plant diseases. The Exposition guarded against this "entomological aftermath" by establishing a quarantine facility,

A nine-acre plot near the Palace of Horticulture was planted with lavish demonstration gardens representing twenty-three states and eleven nations. (Panama-Pacific International Exposition Photograph Album (SFP17), San Francisco History Center, San Francisco Public Library)

with an inspection shed and a fumigating room. Every plant arriving from states with California quarantine orders had to be certified as examined and determined pest-free within thirty days of shipment. All plant products received from outside of California were inspected before release to the relevant PPIE department, and a system of "regular continuous inspection" was instituted for living plants in the Palace of Horticulture and demonstration gardens.[21]

"Nearly everything in California begins with a plant," claimed the admittedly biased *Pacific Rural Press*. Given the importance of agriculture to the state, the Exposition was proud to showcase a local celebrity, plant scientist Luther Burbank, who lived about fifty miles north of the Fair in Santa Rosa. A special display of Burbank's latest developments was featured in the Sonoma County section of the California Building. Here were his rainbow corn, beardless barley, spineless cactus and cactus fruit, improved deciduous trees, a new grain known as "thread wheat," thornless blackberries, a giant sweet pepper, and the Standard prune and the Santa Rosa plum. Among Burbank's floral creations were show roses, zinnias, amaryllises, and Shasta daisies with their abundant rings of snowy petals.[22]

Burbank was honored on June 5 with Burbank Day. He was awarded a bronze medal for his "services to mankind," the ceremony taking place fittingly in the South Gardens. The crowd

followed the "wizard" to a reception in the Palace of Horticulture, and once inside the great glass dome, attendees were presented with envelopes of seeds developed by Burbank.[23]

MEMORIES FOR A LIFETIME

The Jewel City's myriad special events kept the PPIE lively from beginning to end. Newspaper headlines reflected the kaleidoscopic calendar with headlines including "Much Crowded into Day at Exposition," "Amusement Is Diversified," "Variety to Spice Exposition," and "Big Exposition Week Begins Tomorrow." The Fair commemorated holidays, places, cultures, organizations, vocations, and individuals, usually with official awards.

Journalist William Benedict wrote, "[E]very day was a gala day. They came from the world over to celebrate—every kind and manner of men, organizations and creeds. These were made to feel that they were welcome. They were not only told so, but they were given plaques and medals and jewels, that they might remember the fact in years to come."[24]

On June 5, "plant wizard" Luther Burbank was honored with a medal. Those attending received commemorative packets of seeds. (Seligman Family Foundation)

IMPERIUM IN IMPERIO

he moniker "Jewel City" was not just a nickname. The Exposition was in many ways a metropolis. In April 1913 the San Francisco Board of Supervisors granted the PPIE "Imperium in imperio"—"city within a city"—status.[1]

The Exposition was given authority to establish police, fire, health and sanitation, and building regulations within the grounds. Along with these rights, the PPIE also acquired many of the social, commercial, and fiscal challenges of a real town.

METROPOLITAN COMFORTS

Once construction of the Fair was under way, numerous "municipal" amenities blossomed. The Anglo-California Trust Company, of which PPIE president Charles C. Moore was a director, opened a branch bank just inside the Fillmore Street Exposition gate. Concessionaires deposited their receipts and employees their paychecks there. Telegraph and express services were available, and the principal railroads and steamship lines maintained onsite offices to facilitate travel to and from San Francisco. Army and navy enlisted men could play billiards in their private clubhouse on a lot west of the Palace of Fine Arts.

As in any great cosmopolis, the PPIE offered a range of international dining options. "You may eat in any language at the Exposition!" enthused a booklet distributed by Owl Drug Stores. Supplementing the restaurants on the Zone and around the main palace block, an international menu was available at cafés among the nation and state pavilions. On the loggia around the upper story of the Norwegian Pavilion, young women dressed

Aviator Art Smith posed with adoring fans near the Official Photographers concession and Anglo California Bank in the South Gardens. These were two of the many city-like amenities at the Exposition. (Seligman Family Foundation)

as peasants served lunches of fish pudding and other traditional dishes. To accompany fragrant Japanese tea served in the teahouse of the Japan Central Tea Association, one also could feast somewhat incongruously on chicken salad and strawberry shortcake. There was always the irreverently nicknamed "Palace of Nibbling Arts," more formally known as the Palace of Food Products, where one could dine to satiation on food samples. As Julia Davis Chandler wrote in *American Cookery*, one's stomach might be a bit "mixy" after sampling "tuna salad and clam chowder, cheese crackers and noodles, oat meal, pineapple, angel cake, gelatin, griddle cakes, pickles, sardines, Hindo chupattis [sic], and Japanese cakes…not to mention sweet indulgence in 'Candy Cotton' at five cents per bag."[2, 3]

LOOKING AFTER THE POPULACE

The Fair provided a number of helpful social services to both visitors and employees. The Exposition Emergency Hospital, headquartered in the Service Building, treated more than 14,000 patients between February 1914, when it opened, and the last day of the Fair. Patients were treated mainly for construction injuries or for exhaustion caused by "trying to 'do' the Exposition in its entirety." The hospital, maintained by the US Department of Health, was staffed by two physicians and six nurses. Its two ambulances, sterilizing room, x-ray facility, library, operating chairs, laboratory, and pharmacy were donated by manufacturers. The hospital served double-duty as an exhibit representing a "model emergency hospital."[4]

"Hello, operator. Has anyone been looking for James of Kokomo today?" was a sample inquiry received by the Human Lost and Found Bureau. This service exploited the network of telephone lines that ran from the far end of the Zone at Van Ness Avenue to the racetrack on the western edge of the Fair. A simple phone call to the central switchboard usually could reunite separated loved ones. When a child was discovered wandering alone, a guard would bring him to the Service Building, where matrons were on duty. During the Fair 2,575 lost children, and more than a few lost adults, were found through this system.[5]

The nonsectarian Travelers' Aid Society maintained a twenty-four-hour office in the Ferry Building, at the foot of Market Street, as well as bureaus in the California Building, the Service Building, and the Palace of Education. Representatives wearing gold star Travelers' Aid badges were deployed to meet trains and ferries and were available at the Fair daily from 9:00 a.m. until closing. Their charter was to assist

and protect all travelers, especially women and children from "unscrupulous persons, who by offers of apparent friendship and assistance, or by appealing for sympathy and help, prey upon and lure away the unsuspecting."[6]

Travelers' Aid worked in conjunction with the Woman's Board of the Fair, which absorbed more than half of the $28,000 cost of operation in an effort to ensure visitors could travel to and from the PPIE safely. In all, it directed 21,551 travelers to safe lodging places during the Fair.

In April 1915, the *Idaho Statesman* printed a warning to young women from the General Federation of Women's Clubs advising against trying to seek employment at the Fair. The article said the Woman's Board was battling a movement to give over a section of the fairgrounds to prostitution. The Woman's Board was outraged, stating it never had to fight such an issue "because it never existed." The Woman's Board also acted as an official subcommittee of the Exposition and was responsible for hosting visiting dignitaries.[7]

"Don't stay home on account of the baby—

The caryatid-columned YWCA building provided a very popular cafeteria, an information bureau, reading and writing rooms, and a "baby-checking" service. (Edward A. Rogers)

check him!" read an ad for the childcare services offered at the YWCA Building in the South Gardens. After a child was examined and found healthy, a parent could check the tyke into the day nursery featuring twenty beds, snacks, and a playground with sandbox, slides, and swings. It cost twenty-five cents for a full day, or fifteen cents for half a day. On San Francisco Day, which was second in attendance only to Closing Day, 159 boys and girls were squeezed into the space.[8]

"Baby checking" was just one of many services provided by the Young Women's Christian Association at the Fair. Inside the building, with attractive interior spaces designed by architect Julia Morgan, was an information bureau, a reading room with hometown newspapers, a writing room, and a ladies "rest room," where women could lie down and receive treatment from a nurse. The YWCA cafeteria was rated "the best place on the grounds to get a square meal at a reasonable price." About 5,000 people visited the building on an average day, 3,000 of them eating in the restaurant. On Sunday afternoons, patrons were drawn to the front porch by the

harmonies of local choral societies singing an open-air vesper service.[9]

Perhaps more importantly, the "Y" also ministered to the needs of the estimated 3,000 female Fair employees, many of whom were new to the city, lonely, and unprotected. The YWCA helped women find "reliable boarding places," provided legal advice and minor medical treatment, and "made calls" to check on the welfare of the employees. In emergencies the organization would provide financial assistance, perhaps helping a girl make her rent or redeem her luggage.

The association warned against the perils to an attractive female who might be hungry and susceptible to "some stranger waiting to escort her home at night or invite her out to dinner." It hosted weekly social gatherings to foster wholesome camaraderie among the workers. At one party a roll call by state introduced to each other nine young ladies from Massachusetts. All worked in different Fair buildings.[10]

The welfare of the three hundred to four hundred female Joy Zone performers, many of

The Girls' Clubhouse, constructed under the tracks of the Scenic Railway, was a comfortable retreat for the hundreds of women who worked in difficult conditions on the Joy Zone. (Seligman Family Foundation)

whom slept in cramped rooms behind or above their concessions, was a particular concern. The *Pan-Pacific Press Association* described their plight: "The circus girls lived with the show in little tent dressing rooms where their sleep was broken by the champ and stamp of ponies. The Russian ballet girls slept in their tiny, third floor rooms. The Maoris shivered in imitation huts and the Navajo Indians thickened their war-paint to keep out the brisk breezes of San Francisco Bay....To look upon each of these as a human girl, no matter what her costume or her 'stunt' on the stage—this was the real accomplishment of the Young Women's Christian Association."[11]

About midyear, the concessionaires financed construction of a Girls' Clubhouse, built beneath the tracks of the Scenic Railway roller coaster and likely also designed by Julia Morgan. Here a young woman could get a good meal for twelve cents, cheap even by Exposition standards. She might write letters, socialize, read, sew, or just rest. Best of all, there was plenty of hot water for a bath or for soaking one's feet. The little wooden building featured a piano and homey touches from around the Fair—Japanese paper lanterns, a Maori weaving, and a print of Fraser's *End of the Trail.* Girls from twenty-seven nations called the little club home.

Toward the end of the Fair, the YWCA's goals changed from making workers at the Exposition more comfortable to preparing the women for life after the Fair. The association offered evening job training classes in stenography, typewriting, and "store salesmanship." Whether or not YWCA services safeguarded women "who did not know there was peril, and turned away from danger some who were attracted to it," as an article in the *Colorado Springs Gazette* said, it assuredly made life easier and more comfortable for many women who worked in the Jewel City.[12]

PROTECTING AND SERVING

The city-in-miniature had its own law enforcement personnel—its gatemen and guards.

Applicants for gateman jobs were assessed on neatness, accuracy, sobriety, honesty, and courtesy. Those hired trained for weeks before Opening Day, each purchasing his own uniform of blue trousers, a jacket trimmed with loops of white braid on the sleeves, and a neat billed cap. At the start of the Fair each man was able to admit about 1,200 patrons per hour through the turnstiles, but as their proficiency increased, they were able to process as many as 1,700. During Opening Week, things looked rosy for the gatemen. In the first four days of the Fair, 472,000 attendees passed through the turnstiles, yet only one bad coin was used. And of the tens of thousands of ticket books issued, only eighteen patrons tried to use someone else's book illegally.

With improved efficiency, however, many gatemen worked themselves out of their jobs. E. C. Conroy, director of the admissions department, started the season with 280 employees, but he was able to reduce the force as performance improved. Conroy said he managed the department on a "strickly business" [*sic*] line, so there were layoffs. He explained, "Towards the close of the Exposition, when its business was at its zenith, the Department of Admissions handled its work with a little less than half the number it had on opening day."[13]

Early on, admissions rules were vague. "Free permits" were too easily granted and there were far too many types of coupons, so new regulations were implemented. Tightening the rules reduced "free" admissions from 34.6 percent to about 23.2 percent, significantly improving the bottom line.

GUARDS

Exposition guards were chosen from among former US soldiers, sailors, and marines and also included a few former police officers. Only those with excellent discharge ratings were accepted. Guards had to be taller than five foot eight, between the ages of twenty-five and forty-five, and pass a physical by the Exposition surgeon. PPIE guards were granted "special policeman" status by the city, and they were trained using a manual developed especially for the Exposition. There were two to four companies, each divided into three platoons. Each platoon was on duty for eight hours, ensuring the grounds were patrolled twenty-four hours a day.

The guards were kept jumping, as among the PPIE's nearly nineteen million attendees were a fair share of folks who had light fingers or eager fists, or who had imbibed too much "joy" on the Joy Zone. The mounds of treasures deployed in the palaces were an irresistible temptation to petty thieves, and those who rented "Electriquettes" to motor about the Jewel City seemed to have a distressing tendency to run into people.

Gate jumpers became a constant hassle. Admissions director Conroy's end-of-Fair report described them as "a nuisance" and said his department "suffered great embarrassment and annoyance because of its inability…to prevent people from gaining access to the grounds by crawling under and scaling over fences and by landing at unprotected parts of the waterfront of the exposition."[14]

Conroy suggested that a few arrests would have cleared up the problem easily, but reports indicated the guards were often outnumbered. The manager of the Grand Canyon concession described a horde of up to twenty young men climbing the fence into the attraction one night. "Some of our employees discovered them and chased them out, endeavoring to scare them by firing revolvers into the ground." They captured three and ejected them, but the Exposition guard on duty said he was powerless against the rest of the hooligans, who "threw clubs and stones at him."[15]

There were a few arrests, but most miscreants simply were ejected from the premises. At the beginning of the Fair, the guards numbered around 600, but retrenchments saw the force reduced to 300 men. This corps was tiny compared to the world's fairs at Chicago in 1893 and St. Louis in 1904, where law enforcement contingents had averaged about 1,700 and 1,000, respectively, over the runs of those fairs.

Yet even with the scant guard force, the PPIE was remarkably peaceable, a fact credited to the onsite detectives of the Pinkerton National Detective Agency. A year before the Fair, the Pinkertons amassed a dossier of "celebrated criminals" and traced their movements in an attempt to keep the lawless away from the Jewel City. During the Fair, a group of undercover male and female operatives patrolled the grounds, apprehending those who would pick pockets or attempt to pass counterfeit money.

"I have attended every exposition since 1876 and I think I know the game," said detective chief William A. Pinkerton, son of the agency's founder. "This time we are not going to give the crooks a chance." His words were borne out. Eight people were arrested as pickpockets, and no successful attempts were reported.[16]

A VISIBLE RECORD

The Jewel City also spawned a dedicated industry—its souvenir trade. Rare was the fairgoer who came home without a memento. Tourists were allowed to take their own photographs, but they were required to purchase a camera permit and were prohibited from using large-format film. Experimental color film technology existed, but it was unavailable to the consumer, so the best way to remember the incredible architecture and fascinating exhibits was to buy a viewbook. Dozens of different books were published, some in sepia or black and white, but many included color plates of widely varying quality.

Viewbooks came in sizes ranging from softcover examples a few inches wide and a few pages long to the hardcover *Blue Book,* published by Robert A. Reid, which weighed more than five pounds and featured more than three hundred pages of large-format images. The tiniest viewbook was *The Exposition in a Nutshell,* a series of minuscule scenes on accordion-pleated paper folded inside a walnut shell. Grandest of all was *The Splendors of the Panama-Pacific International Exposition,* a twenty-inch-wide tome bound in red silk and leather, with gilt embellishments. Inside, thirty-two individual color prints were attached to the ivory-hued pages and protected by sheets of translucent vellum. The volume, printed in limited edition and presented to Exposition directors and luminaries, was also available for purchase. For those unable to afford *The Splendors'* $37 price tag (about $872 in 2012), a humble book of postcards was a satisfactory alternative.

BLANCHE PAYSON

The most visible PPIE "guard" was statuesque special policewoman Blanche Payson, who patrolled the Zone as a mobile attraction and helped protect women from "mashers." Impresario Fred Thompson hired Blanche not only because William Pinkerton recommended her but also because she promoted Toyland's purpose, which was to make adults feel diminutive. She was six feet, four inches tall and weighed more than two hundred pounds. After her swearing in by six-foot-two Chief of Police David White, she remarked, "Such a nice little man!"[17]

Later in 1915, she was retained by the Palace Hotel as a traffic officer, with the unintended consequence that she literally stopped traffic. The spectacle of Blanche, mounted atop a horse and wearing a blue serge skirted police coat with gold buttons and braid, halted streetcars, jitney buses, and a crowd of admiring men. After less than ten minutes, management realized their "copette" impeded rather than aided the flow of traffic and bought out her contract.

Blanche was featured in *Collier's* magazine saying she hoped to become a regular member of the San Francisco police force, but this was not to be. Film director Mack Sennett hired her as "official chaperon" to guard the virtue of the bathing beauties under contract with his Keystone Studios, but as the beauties did not especially want their virtue protected, her chaperon duties did not last. Sennett and his directors, however, quickly realized Blanche Payson's potential as a character actress, and she went on to appear in more than one hundred films.

Payson was often paired with petite co-stars for effect. One such colleague was Diana Serra Cary, better known by her stage name "Baby Peggy," who was about three years old when she first worked with Blanche Payson. Cary says Payson was "a great favorite of mine. Though her roles were always very stern, she was a very cheerful, good-natured person."[18]

Through the 1920s Payson was well known as the "tallest woman in movies," and in a career that continued through the mid-1940s, she performed with many of the best-known actors of the age, including Laurel and Hardy, Buster Keaton, the Three Stooges, Lillian Gish, Bela Lugosi, ZaSu Pitts, Shirley Temple, and the kids from Our Gang.

Six-foot-four-inch-tall Blanche Payson, who patrolled the Zone as a policewoman, was an attraction in her own right. (Branson DeCou Digital Archive, University of California, Santa Cruz, Special Collections)

Postcards were in their heyday, providing speedy communication between private individuals for just a penny stamp. According to postcard expert Ed Herny, sending a postcard in 1915 was akin to sending a text message a century later. "Postals" were not reserved for gloating from a vacation destination but also were used daily for short communications and greetings. Herny says, "An Oakland resident might take the ferry over to San Francisco and send 30 postcards back across the Bay in one day." In addition, they made inexpensive, colorful souvenirs.[19]

For those wishing a more thorough documentation of their visits, a number of full-length books described the architecture, art, murals, sculpture, landscape gardening, metaphysical meaning, and legacy of the Fair. Even cooks could preserve memories of the PPIE with *The Pan-Pacific Cookbook: Savory Bits from the World's Fare*.

NUMISMATICS AND PHILATELY

Some types of collectibles offered at the PPIE—among them coins and stamps—remain popular today. Tourists on limited budgets could have a penny flattened and embossed with an image of the Tower of Jewels. State and foreign delegations minted "so-called dollars" to raise funds for their exhibits or as tokens for special visitors. The pockets of many a child were weighed down by heavy, oversized "lucky pennies" as much as three inches across.

A souvenir medal, designed by Robert Ingersoll Aitken and struck at the US Treasury exhibit in the Palace of Mines and Metallurgy, depicted a pair of female figures representing the two hemispheres on one side and the god Mercury on the other, along with the motto "On! Sail On!" a reference to Joaquin Miller's poem *Columbus*. The bronze version cost only twenty-five cents, but the wing-footed god's full-frontal nudity, "looking ready for his bath," affronted more sensitive individuals and sales were lower than expected.[20]

The most expensive PPIE coins were the official US currency struck at the San Francisco Mint in denominations of fifty cents, $1, $2.50, and $50 in round and octagonal versions. Any coins unsold by November 1, 1916, were destroyed, and since only 1,129 of the two types of $50 coin survived, they are especially rare and can sell today for thousands of dollars.

The US government also issued promotional postage stamps for the PPIE. Perhaps more interesting were the "poster stamps," also called "Cinderellas," produced by commercial firms. These colorful stamp-sized advertising labels with no postal value were popular collectibles just before World War I, and dozens of companies printed special versions commemorating the PPIE.

UTILITARIAN MEMORABILIA

One could set an entire dinner table with PPIE souvenirs. Decorative commemorative spoons were sought after in 1915, and hundreds of variants were available with Exposition themes, along with the rarer forks, knives, and serving pieces. The Danish Pavilion sold limited-edition plates from the Royal Porcelain Factory (today Royal Copenhagen). The Rowland & Marsellus and Wheelock companies each offered plates with cobalt-and-white renderings of Exposition scenes, while countless cottage-industry china painters created one-of-a-kind plates and teacups with scenes from the Fair. Ruby flash glass souvenirware had been fashionable since the late 1800s, and in 1915 one could have small cups and pitchers painted with the buyer's name alongside "P.P.I.E." Food could be presented on myriad trays, either cast in high relief or etched with scenes of the Exposition. For those who wanted their drinkables "to go," chrome Thermoses in several sizes, artfully inscribed with an image of the Tower of Jewels, could be used to pour liquid into a collapsible cup with a picture of the Palace of Horticulture on its lid.

Similarly, a businessman might equip his desk with PPIE pens, pencils, paperweights, letter openers, and rulers. Other useful mementos included walking sticks, handbags, and ashtrays. Handsome leather coin purses featured the

Exposition seal embossed on their shiny metal frames. Handkerchiefs were embroidered with the Palace of Horticulture, and jacquard tapestries were woven with an image of the Tower of Jewels.

INSIDE AND OUTSIDE THE GATES

Because licensing was in its infancy, anyone could make Fair-related items, and many PPIE souvenirs were sold outside the Exposition's grounds—perhaps even more than were available inside. Most of the state and national displays also had wares for sale, and many of these were typical regional goods rather than expressly Exposition-related. These items often were not marked, making it impossible to ascertain whether the keepsake was purchased within the Fair or without. Some things, however, were labeled, such as clay teapots and soapstone carvings from the Chinese Pavilion, tiny wooden shoes from the Netherlands, fans from the Japanese teahouse, and paintings on silk from the Swedish Pavilion, *of* the Swedish Pavilion.

Many souvenirs were aimed at children, including balloons, felt pennants, stuffed animals,

Peggy Newall was one of several artists who cut custom silhouette portraits, popular souvenirs for fairgoers. (Edward A. Rogers)

and dolls. Rose O'Neill's Kewpies—whimsical winged infant characters—had burgeoned in popularity since their 1909 introduction, and bisque Kewpie figurines were sold from a booth on the Zone. Another Zone shop was alarmingly emblazoned "Electric Eyed Zono Bears." These were not terrifying ursine cyborgs but rather part of a fad for teddy bears with glowing lightbulb eyes.

Fairgoers also could purchase items commemorating the history of the Fair or the achievement it celebrated—the Panama Canal. The very first concession approved was for Souvenir Spades, replicas of the Shreve & Co. shovel used to turn the first earth at the PPIE's 1911 groundbreaking. It also was possible to treat oneself to a replica of the pen President Taft used to sign the Exposition bill into law.

Inside the Panama Canal Model concession, souvenirs with actual material from the "Big Ditch" were for sale, including chunks of railroad tie from the line laid across the isthmus in 1852. Small glass vials containing soil and gravel from the bottom of the Culebra Cut were offered, as well as trophies designed as bronze eagle claws clutching stones from the same source.

SPARKLING SOUVENIRS

Many merrymakers' watch fobs, cuff links, and scarf pins were adorned with miniature frying pans. At first this decorative cookware might have been puzzling, until one realized the pun. At the 1901 Pan-American Exposition, small skillets with scenes stamped into the bowl had been introduced as a play on "PAN-American," and these were brought back for the "PAN-Pacific." Buyers could collect an entire set of twelve pans featuring the Official Seal of the Fair and eleven Exposition buildings.

Celluloid pinbacks for special days at the Fair embellished many lapels, as well as the more expensive and elaborate enamel PPIE brooches, which often featured symbols of the state of California, such as bears, poppies, and oranges. Other jewelry that referenced the Golden State included pieces made of iridescent abalone shell and "flower beads," infused with the fragrance of California blooms.

This exquisite silver miniature Tower of Jewels, which held either lipstick or perfume, was a special gift from the San Francisco Islam Temple. (Donna Ewald Huggins)

The pocket watch was the order of the day, and the PPIE offered a staggering selection of watch fobs. If you wished to match a PPIE timepiece to your fob, an official souvenir watch was sold at the Watch Palace on the Zone, its case modeled after the Exposition seal. A few of the new "wristwatch" styles also were produced. Jewel City jewels needed storage, so pin trays and jewelry boxes depicting Exposition buildings were on sale.

For today's collectors, the ultimate PPIE memento is a Novagem, one of the jewels that gave the Tower of Jewels its moniker. One could purchase a full-sized "official souvenir" version about two inches across, and miniature versions of the Novagems were mounted in letter openers, lavalieres, bar pins, hat pins, gentlemen's stick pins, brooches, watch fobs, lapel chains, cuff links, and rings. These items were priced from fifty cents to $3. Visitors also could buy actual, mounted Novagems in several sizes for between $1 and $2.75.

At the end of the Fair, jewels that actually had hung on the tower were sold for $1 each as the structure was dismantled. These are generally distinguishable by a commemorative tag along with chips in the glass caused by 288 days' buffeting by San Francisco Bay winds. Buyers who purchased five or more Novagems also received one of the smaller jewels that had adorned the crowns of the *Star Maiden* figures in the Court of the Universe. This concession, owned by Chief of Illumination Walter D'Arcy Ryan, was not especially lucrative. The Novagems did not sell out, and after the Fair, Ryan purchased the remaining stock of tens of thousands of gems for less than ten cents each, a fraction of what it had cost to manufacture them. In 2015 Novagems sell for between $150 and $650, depending on color and condition.

Jay Stevens, the leading expert on Novagems, explains why they are so desirable: "Novagems inspired the name 'Jewel City,' and no other artifact so perfectly captures the glittering, ephemeral nature of the PPIE."[21]

A PRECARIOUS BUSINESS

When PPIE president Moore addressed a meeting of stockholders during Opening Week, he was confident in the Exposition's financial health. He declared, "Today we would not have one cent indebtedness if the money so confidently expected by us from Alameda County were at our command."[22]

The support of which he spoke was $1 million promised by the county east across the bay from San Francisco, which included the substantial cities of Oakland, Berkeley, Emeryville, and Alameda. The money had been pledged during the 1911 congressional fight to secure the Exposition for San Francisco, and a bond measure to fund it was on Alameda County's March 1915 ballot. When the votes were tallied, the measure had earned a majority of the votes, but not the two-thirds needed for passage. Alameda County had "slipped in under the tent" of the PPIE, according to the *Reno Evening Gazette*.[23]

Without the Alameda million and with the Joy Zone faring poorly, the Exposition directorate grew concerned. The problem was compounded by the unusually relentless rainy season. Worse still, much of the rain fell on weekends, when attendance otherwise would be concentrated. The Fair was expensive to run, whether patrons came or not: thousands of salaries were paid, utilities were consumed, daily cleaning and maintenance of the palaces was required, costly fireworks were detonated, and the canvas-lined pools and racetrack were constantly under repair.

Despite its large administrative size, the PPIE pivoted nimbly. Just before the Alameda County bond failed, the Exposition instituted a "retrenchment" program to reduce costs. Hundreds of jobs were cut, reducing the payroll by nearly 20 percent. Some departments were consolidated, and operational responsibilities were adjusted.

Some changes were painful. Fifty-eight young men, many of them college students, had been trained as guides, and while these nattily attired docents were informative and helpful, they were not largely patronized. The entire service was disbanded around the beginning of April. Deep cuts also were made to the gatemen and guards corps.

The Exposition Company took over several failing concessions to keep them afloat but laid off hundreds of Joy Zone workers in June. Some of the eight hundred young women trained as cashiers were let go after only two weeks, each having paid $3 for a uniform and $1 each for her badge and official photograph. The prices of these items was deemed exorbitant. *The Wasp* said, "If the Exposition only cleared $2 cash off of each girl, the total would be over $1,600."[24]

Like a leviathan ocean liner making a turn, the Fair started to come about. Late in May, fine summer weather arrived to stay and the grounds began to fill. Eastern vacationers poured into San Francisco to enjoy the long, balmy days. The PPIE closed its New York office, and with

The variety of PPIE souvenirs included Novagems, Panama Canal mementos, servingware, glassware, books, jewelry and jewelry boxes, paperweights, spoons, pennants, watches, fans, coin purses, desk accessories, and goods from the exhibits and state and international pavilions. (Donna Ewald Huggins and Laura Ackley)

Cashiers would exchange numbered metal tags for cash boxes each morning before reporting to their stations. Unfortunately, when cost-cutting measures were implemented, many of the cashiers were laid off after just a few weeks on the job. (Donna Ewald Huggins)

further cutbacks in May and June, total operating expenses were slashed by 25 percent. The Exposition was now running in the black, and its debt began to erode swiftly. The Fair turned a profit by September 3, an occasion marked by the dramatic nighttime mortgage-burning at which former president Taft consigned the now-superfluous document to the pyre.

A PROUD RECORD

Many a true city would be proud to call the Jewel City's municipal achievements its own. Its populace of employees and fairgoers was provided with an array of amenities. These ran the gamut from services designed for comfort and enjoyment—such as travel offices, telephones, and delicious international foods—to those that tended to the welfare of the participants. The day nursery and Human Lost and Found Bureau allowed visitors to enjoy the pleasures of the Fair without worry, while the Travelers' Aid Society and Young Women's Christian Association protected the most vulnerable visitors and employees, especially young women.

Kiosks dotted around the palace perimeter, fanciful shops studding the Zone, and even stores in greater San Francisco did a brisk business selling PPIE-themed souvenirs, many of which have been handed down through the generations along with recollections of the Fair.

Likewise enviable was the Exposition's final balance sheet. When faced with a sudden million-dollar deficit, and with war, weather, and the economy conspiring to jeopardize the Fair's finances, the directorate and department chiefs implemented a series of retrenchments that tipped the ledger to the positive. Many of these measures were onerous, such as the elimination of the guides and the major reductions of the guard and cashier contingents. Others required adjustment. When overzealous cutting of the guard corps resulted in frightening understaffing, some men were rehired to stabilize the protective force.

For its last three months, the Jewel City operated at a profit, which was, according to its managers, a feat never before attained by a world's fair. And the world took heed of its success. Just after the PPIE closed, a writer for the *Buffalo Express* said, "San Francisco is to be congratulated. She has not only conducted a successful exposition, but also a profitable exposition. Moreover, this has been done after the country had seen so many expositions that all the wise heads said it would be impossible ever to make a success of another one."[25]

BILLY HOOPER, THE OFFICIAL HERALD

Perhaps the most ingenious employee of the entire Exposition was Billy Hooper, whose self-invented job guaranteed his invitation to most of the great parties before and during the PPIE.

The story started in 1911, when Hooper, smart but down on his luck, returned to San Francisco from living in Hawaii. In the midst of all the pre-Exposition excitement, he couldn't find a suitable job, so he took his quest east. In Philadelphia he found and bought a six-foot-long trumpet. Then he hit upon a brilliant plan and hied himself back to San Francisco.

His story was documented by the *Highway Magazine*, provided by the Pennsylvania Metal Culvert Company:

> *Arriving at the City of the Golden Gate, he secured lodgings and began his preparations....[He] went straight to a good tailor with an order for a uniform. White it was to be—white and gold from head to foot; cap, gloves and shoes were snow white, and buttons and epaulettes of flashing gold. A banner of white silk, the length of the trumpet, was lettered in gold, Panama-Pacific Universal Exposition, San Francisco, 1915; and Billy saw a magnificent spectacle in the cracked mirror of the lodging house bureau.*

> *One fine morning there marched down Pine Street a one-man procession. A crowd of urchins followed behind....Billy walked straight up the street, made a right wheel at the door of the Exposition Building and marched into the office where the Grand High Officers were holding a consultation."* [26]

Apparently Mayor Rolph told Hooper the directors would give him a chance to prove he could promote the Exposition—without pay, of course. The musician took his horn, banner, and uniform and headed up to Oregon. Hooper, an African American, later told his story to the NAACP's *Crisis* magazine: "I took my stand in the center of the main street of Portland and began making all the noise I could on my brass trumpet...." The chief of police was not amused and ordered Hooper to cease and desist, but the incident made headlines. Hooper's point was made, he was hired, and the next time he visited Oregon it was as an official member of the booster mission to Astoria in August 1911. [27]

The *Highway Magazine* concluded:

> *Since that time Billy has been the Official Herald of the Exposition. His trumpet calls the forces into action in the morning and dismisses them when the day's work is done. No jollification, commemoration or dedication is complete without Billy on the job....The reveille and the requiem of Nineteen Fifteen will be sounded on that glittering clarion, and the Official Herald will be remembered when the great San Francisco Fair has passed into memory.* [28]

Billy Hooper's self-invented job as the Exposition's Official Herald guaranteed him a front-row seat at all the most important events. (*The Highway Magazine*, November 1912)

DEATH AND LIFE OF A FAIR

A PERFECT DAY

The PPIE opened with rain, and it seemed as though it would close with rain. Downpours had drenched San Francisco on December 3, and the forecast was for more showers the next day. But Closing Day dawned with a benediction instead of a baptism—summerlike blue skies and balmy temperatures. A mass of humanity, 459,022 guests, many wearing special Closing Day badges, clicked through the turnstiles to partake of the Fair's glories one last time.

A booming twenty-one-gun salute from the warships in the bay welcomed the 150,000-person throng packed into the ten-acre Court of the Universe for midday commemorations. Arthur Arlett, one of the state's official Exposition commissioners, read George Sterling's poem *The Builders*, which includes the line, "And though the columns and the temples pass, let none regret; let no man cry 'Alas!'"[1]

PPIE president Charles C. Moore, flanked by Exposition directors, representatives from the foreign pavilions, and military men, gave the official toast sent by US president Woodrow Wilson, which was read simultaneously by officials in New York, Buenos Aires, Stockholm, Paris, Tokyo, and Melbourne. After a brief allegorical pageant, the Philippine Constabulary Band played "The Star-Spangled Banner," a flag and wreath descended on a wire over the crowd, and a flock of doves was released. In the afternoon, a town crier in Colonial garb preceded President Moore as he made the rounds of all the exhibit palaces. At each, he met the department chief and ceremoniously lowered the Exposition flag.

As the lights dimmed at midnight on the final day of the Fair, the crowd hushed and a single spotlight beam focused on Adolph Weinman's figure *Descending Night*. (Panama-Pacific International Exposition Photograph Album (SFP17), San Francisco History Center, San Francisco Public Library)

A carnival atmosphere pervaded, as though participants were trying to condense the entire Exposition into a single day. Children danced on the music concourse, Edwin Lemare gave a triumphant concluding organ concert in the Festival Hall, the Philippine Constabulary Band played again in the Court of the Universe, and the Official Orchestra performed in the Old Faithful Inn. "California Nightingale" Ellen Beach Yaw sang her original composition, which began "San Francisco! Wondrous Fair!" Inside the palaces, exhibitors declaimed their spiels with extra gusto and tried to give away their remaining stock of pamphlets, while muddy football and soccer games were played on the Marina.[2]

The ships' cannons fired once again at sunset, officially closing the palaces and touching off a final frenzy of events. A parade of illuminated floats circled the palaces from 8:30 to 10:00

p.m., after which the "greatest display of fireworks ever seen in the West" began. The colored beams of Walter D'Arcy Ryan's Great Scintillator splayed across the heavens for the final time, and thousands of sparkling rockets shot into the sky. The waters of the bay reflected back a 1,000-foot-long "curtain of fire" formed by a multitude of golden fountains of sparks.[3]

As midnight drew nigh, the temperature stayed mild and the air still. Crowds again filled the Court of the Universe, this time to dance to Thaviu's Band in anticipation of the final ceremonial. The Exposition Chorus sang *Hallelujah,* then a hush, remarkable in so large a gathering, fell as President Moore took the stage for his final proclamation. "Friends!" he began, "This is the end of a perfect day, and the beginning of an unforgettable memory." At precisely midnight he touched a button dimming the illuminations. As the lights slowly faded, a single beam remained focused on Adolph Weinman's graceful statue *Descending Night*, standing with semi-furled wings atop her column. From the darkened Tower of Jewels, the notes of a bugle playing "Taps" floated down upon the crowd. Suddenly, the word "Finis" appeared across the lower gallery in lights, and the lone beam winked out. Aviator Art Smith looped again and again, trailing fire from his aeroplane, and a volley of six hundred mortars discharged the final grand salvo of fireworks over the bay. After the spectacle was complete, the revelers remained for hours, dancing in the dim glow of the patrol lights before finally filing, exhausted, out of the Fair.[4]

EPILOGUE TO A DREAM

Once Closing Day was over, there was little time for mourning. Many of the leases for land under the Joy Zone expired June 1, 1916, and others

the following December 31. The land had to be returned to its owners in cleared and restored condition. Restoration required not only the removal of the Exposition buildings but also of gas, power, and water lines, and replacement of sidewalks and fences. Power transmission equipment leased from Pacific Gas and Electric was salvaged, depreciated for any damage, and returned to the company. Though a vast amount of land had been filled, still more fill was needed on some lots to achieve the grades promised in the leases.

Weeks before the end of the Fair, exhibitors and concessionaires had started selling exhibit goods and fixtures. As early as October, the Exposition itself began taking purchase orders for plants and decorative elements such as urns, benches, and lamp standards. For many participants, it was more expensive to ship back display wares than to sell them. A banner hanging across the façade of Japan Beautiful on the Zone announced "Closing Out Sale. None Sent Back."

The closing festivities concluded with spectacular illuminations, a salvo of hundreds of fireworks, and pilot Art Smith trailing loops of flame across the sky over the Jewel City. (Donna Ewald Huggins)

Local newspapers were littered with ads from auction houses disposing of exhibits. Gorgeous rugs from the Turkish Pavilion were sold at the Palace Hotel, while those from India could be purchased at the previously vacant Marine Café on the Joy Zone. The Balkan states' silver and copper wares, as well as jewels, were offered by an auction house on Sutter Street, while shoppers on Post Street could select treasures from the Japanese and Chinese exhibits. Many of the state buildings simply sold their furniture, decorations, and draperies directly from the pavilions.

The buildings themselves also were sold, either for material salvage or as whole structures. The architects had planned the buildings with easy demolition and salvage in mind, and bargain hunters could buy a piece or all of a building. State pavilions were particular steals. The $45,000 Washington State pavilion was purchased for a measly $800. All of the booth structures within the Palaces of Agriculture, Horticulture, and Food Products together sold for $200. The Palace of Horticulture, which cost about $400,000 to build, sold for $5,000, and the $420,000 Tower of Jewels for just $9,000.

Ultimately, it is impossible to trace the destinations of each bit of building, each souvenir, each item exhibited at the PPIE. They were distributed as the seeds of a dandelion borne on the wind. Architectural salvage allowed those who either loved the Fair or simply wanted a home improvement bargain to enrich their dwellings with a transom window here or a column there. Others chose a palm tree,

Many Exposition structures, including the thousand-ton Ohio Building, were moved by water to various new sites around the Bay Area. (San Francisco History Center, San Francisco Public Library)

bougainvillea, or rose bush.

Dissolution of the Fair began just three days after it closed. Roadways and lawns that had covered the Exposition Railway lines into the palaces were stripped away so trains could retrieve what they had delivered. Grilled surrounds framing the palace portals were knocked out, leaving large apertures through which trucks and freight cars could enter. Once participants had settled any debts, typically for utilities or the Exposition's percentage of sales, they were free to remove their goods.

Demolition proper began April 15, 1916, when the Exposition made a spectacle of pulling down the first of the four Italian Towers. Its underpinnings were cut, and it was yanked down, its full two-hundred-foot height crashing across the Court of Palms. The Palace of Machinery followed shortly. After its faux-travertine skin was removed, the palace's high trusses were destroyed, thundering more than a hundred feet to the earth. Meanwhile, a crew lifted the decorative armillary sphere "cake topper" from the summit of the Tower of Jewels, preparatory to dismantling its steel skeleton. All steel recovered from the tower and other buildings was sold at $16.25 a ton to the Pacific Coast Steel Company. Where one arcing colonnade in the Court of the Universe had stood solid and true, now the columns leaned drunkenly. One end of the entablature had been demolished, leaving the cornice dangling cockeyed and unsupported.

By April 24, sales of salvage material had netted the Exposition $247,000. After the cost of the work was subtracted, it netted approximately $10.1 million in 2012 values. By June the Joy Zone was nearly completely clear, Lobos Square was being restored as a park, and Exposition warehouses had been sold to the government and removed. The Palace of Nibbling Arts was but a memory, and the Palace of Education three-quarters demolished.

PERIPATETIC PAVILIONS

A team of horses was hitched up to the 1,000-ton neoclassical Ohio Building in August 1916, and the entire pavilion was dragged across

The massive trusses of the Palace of Machinery were dynamited. Almost all of the private land on which the PPIE stood had to be returned to its owners within mere months after the Fair's closure, so demolition and salvage of most structures began nearly immediately. (Donald G. Larson Collection on International Expositions and Fairs, California State University, Fresno)

rollers onto a barge tethered just off the Marina. Ferryboat passengers did a double take as the columned pavilion, pulled by two tugboats and still flying an American flag, floated past on the way to its new site, twenty-three miles south in San Carlos. It was to be used as the Peninsula Country Club, but this scheme fell through when the speculator was unable to locate a suitable water supply. According to local lore, the building was eventually used as a Prohibition speakeasy and then a machine shop before being declared unsafe and razed in 1956.

Several other buildings made similar voyages. The Central Tea Association's teahouse was purchased by E. D. Swift, who barged it down the peninsula to Belmont to be used as a residence for his daughters. It was dragged into the local hills in 1921 by a team of horses and mules. Later it served as a saloon, and it is now home to The Van's Restaurant.

Several buildings found their way north to San Rafael in Marin County. The Home of Redwood became a country house. The Indiana and Virginia state pavilions were barged to the new Santa Venetia neighborhood, where developer Mabry McMahan planned to create a nouveau "Venice by the Bay." After the project foundered, both buildings were eventually lost. The elegant, copper-domed Victor Talking Machine Company "temple" inside the Palace

of Liberal Arts also found a home in San Rafael, where it has survived to this day at the corner of 5th Avenue and H Street.

Sausalito was beautified when architect William Faville, who designed the eight central palaces, chose three items from the PPIE to bring to his hometown. He selected two sculpted elephant flagpole bases by McKim, Mead & White that had been stationed in the Court of the Universe, and a cast concrete fountain of his own design from beneath the half-dome of the Palace of Education. In April 1916 they were barged over the water and installed in the small Plaza Viña del Mar, designed by Faville. On June 14 a festive dedication was held in which students from nearby Tamalpais High School portrayed "The Spirit of the Fountain." The fountain still sprays, and the elephants, recast in 1936 and each mounted with a cluster of illuminated globes, still guard the entrance to the plaza.

Other buildings went east. The quaint half-timbered cottage erected in the Palace of Agriculture to house the office of the Holt Manufacturing Company traveled to Berkeley, where it was hauled into the hills by two Holt tractors and incorporated into the home of UC professor Arthur Pope. A selection of hardwood panels from the Japanese, Philippine, and Argentine Pavilions was put on display in UC Berkeley's Mulford Hall, then home of the

Many of the Fair's large-scale architectural sculptures, including James Earle Fraser's famed *End of the Trail*, were left by the bay to deteriorate for several years. (Laura Ackley)

forestry department. The rigorously pruned London plane trees on the university's Campanile Esplanade are also PPIE survivors.

The Hagiwara family, proprietors of Golden Gate Park's Japanese Tea Garden, itself a survivor of the 1894 Midwinter Fair, purchased several elements of the Japan Pavilion, including the five-story pagoda, a gateway, paving stones, and stone lanterns.

A number of other PPIE relics also enhanced Golden Gate Park. Exotic totara trees from New Zealand's pavilion were planted in the arboretum. Charles Grafly's statue *Pioneer Mother* stayed near the Palace of Fine Arts for many years. Then, after an appearance at the 1939 Golden Gate International Exposition on the bay's Treasure Island, she found her permanent home in the park.

When the official Exposition corporation was dissolved in the 1920s, the Board of Trustees of the War Memorial of San Francisco was named as the successor organization. Most of the surviving Exposition murals were transferred to its care. Frank Brangwyn's eight paintings of the four elements remain on display in San Francisco's Herbst Theater, and others survive in storage. The official Fair records were transferred to the Bancroft Library at the University of California, Berkeley, in the 1930s.

Objects that undertook longer journeys included the fountain that had graced the courtyard of the Italian pavilion, which now resides in Lithia Park in Ashland, Oregon, where it is called the Butler-Perozzi Fountain, after its donors.

Countless museums and private collections received works displayed at the PPIE. Cyrus Dallin's ten-foot-tall bronze *Scout* stands in Kansas City's Penn Valley Park. Many copies were made of James Earle Fraser's *End of the Trail* sculpture, but the large faux-travertine version was left at the bayside in ignominy for several years before residents of Tulare County brought the sculpture to Mooney Grove Park near Visalia, California. In 1968 it was acquired by the National Cowboy Museum and now resides in Oklahoma City.

More than $100,000 in artworks from the Palace of Fine Arts was sold to museums and private collectors. Robert Harshe, assistant director of the Department of Fine Arts, arranged for the Oakland Museum to receive numerous works from the Chinese and Japanese displays, as well as some seven hundred baskets created by California Indians, and A. A. Ackerman, proprietor of the Pig 'n Whistle restaurants, scored twenty-two paintings from the Palace of Fine Arts to adorn one of his eateries. John Singer Sargent's *Portrait of Madame Gautreau* came to rest in the Metropolitan Museum in New York City.

PRESERVATION EFFORTS

Just a few weeks after Opening Day, discussion began about which parts of the Jewel City could be preserved after the Exposition ended. It was clear from the outset that saving the Palace of Fine Arts was at the top of the list. An official committee was formed to explore options, headed by publisher and Exposition director M. H. de Young. He had campaigned for the Golden Gate Park site for the Fair, but he threw himself into the preservation efforts with gusto, though he was not above taking a dig at those who had chosen Harbor View as the PPIE's location. "Of course," he wrote in the *Chronicle*, "if the exposition had been located in Golden Gate and Lincoln Parks, we would not be confronted by this difficult problem."[5]

De Young proposed saving the Palace of Fine Arts, the Marina, the California Building, and the Column of Progress. He also suggested reconstructing the Palace of Horticulture in Golden Gate Park as a mammoth new plant conservatory, and widening Bay Street to three

Saving the Palace of Fine Arts was the top priority for those who wanted to preserve parts of the Jewel City, as demonstrated by this editorial cartoon of August 28, 1915. (*San Francisco Call and Post,* August 28, 1915)

hundred feet to preserve the Avenue of Palms as a stately thoroughfare akin to the Champs-Élysées in Paris. Some members of the preservation committee cautioned that many of the ideas were impractical because of private ownership of the land and the complexity and expense of implementing the plan. But others joined in, suggesting an extensive laundry list of additional artifacts they hoped could be saved, including many of the large architectural sculptures.

After the dust of demolition settled, only a few structures remained. In addition to the Palace of Fine Arts, the preservation of which is described in this book's chapter "An Architectural Tour of the Palaces and Courts," the only structures left standing on the otherwise barren plain were the California Building, the Oregon, Chinese, and Siamese pavilions, and the Column of Progress. The California Building was to be the new site for the San Francisco Normal School, but during years of political and financial wrangling, the building deteriorated and finally was demolished in March 1920. The log Parthenon built by Oregon, which stood on Presidio land, was retained as a venue for military celebrations until "it swayed dangerously every time a crowd entered it" and was finally taken down in August 1921. Although the Chinese and Siamese buildings were offered to the city, they, too, were dismantled.[6]

The Column of Progress stood lonely by the bay, chunks of faux travertine falling off its substructure, until, as San Francisco supervisor Warren Shannon said in 1922, it looked "like a relic of ancient Pompeii." It was sacrificed in 1924 when it became a traffic impediment on the new Marina Boulevard, as well as a hazard to planes landing at Crissy Field, located on the former site of the Exposition racetrack.[7]

Exposition stockholders did, however, band together one last time to save the wide bayside lawn known as the Marina Green. About 60 percent of the Exposition stock was assigned in 1916 to purchase the privately held waterfront lots, as well as the speculative underwater lots just north of the shoreline. The greensward remains a popular recreation space today.

DEATH AND LIFE OF
A WORLD'S FAIR

On Closing Day, one celebrant declared, "[A]ll San Francisco, with a smile on its face and a sob in its throat, surged and jostled, feasted the eye, bathed the soul in undying impressions and universally regretted it had not visited the Exposition oftener."[8]

Yet locals and visitors alike *had* visited with gratifying frequency. Total attendance was calculated to be 18,876,438, far exceeding the most optimistic predictions of twelve million. More than 500,000 visitors had traveled from east of the Rockies. It was estimated that more than $45 million had been injected into California's economy from outside the state (about $2.1 billion in 2012). Approximately $12 million of this (about $565 million in 2012) was spent inside the Exposition on the Zone, in cafés, and toward purchases from Exposition exhibitors.

The Fair had cost about $50 million to build, about $17.5 million of this coming from city and state coffers, and the rest from exhibitors and concessionaires. The benefits to the region and state were immeasurable and long-lasting. Some had criticized the very idea of holding the Exposition, believing San Francisco would be better served devoting all its energies to recovery while many were still suffering privations after the 1906 earthquake and fire. However, the audacity of the Jewel City's promoters succeeded in presenting to the world a largely revived metropolis, attracting tourist and investor dollars, as well as new residents. After the cost of the Exposition Auditorium was deducted, the Fair's profits totaled $1.31 million, about $62.7 million in 2012.

It may seem as though nothing as ambitious as the Jewel City could be built today. Yet international expositions continue to be celebrated worldwide about every five years. And even as we smile at the naiveté and quaintness of many aspects of the PPIE, we can also marvel at the ingenuity of many of its exhibits.

Examination of the Panama-Pacific International Exposition reveals many parallels to the current era. The Fair showcased an explosion of evolving technologies destined to profoundly influence world cultures over the ensuing decades, including breakthroughs in illumination, film, food safety, machinery, electricity, automobiles, aviation, manufacturing, and communications. Similarly, in the decades bracketing the year 2000, Internet and mobile technologies spawned extraordinary cultural changes. Some advances viewed in 1915 as huge leaps forward, such as the use of radium, were later found to have darker implications. Likewise, the early twenty-first century embraced the advantages of a technologically connected world only to encounter unforeseen erosions of personal privacy.

Race, gender, and war were all contentious topics, albeit in slightly different form than the analogous arguments today. At the Fair, strides in racial and gender equity were visible in an increasing sensitivity to discrimination and the move toward national women's suffrage. Also evident, however, were the constraints of these strides at a celebration where opportunities for minorities and women were limited, casual racism was tolerated, and "race betterment" was seen as a panacea for societal ills.

The opposing addresses delivered by William Jennings Bryan and Teddy Roosevelt at the Exposition illustrate the schisms between political viewpoints of the time. Each was certain, as disputants are today, that he was correct. The PPIE supposedly portended advances in civilization that have yet to be realized. At the Nine Years After celebration in 1915, Episcopal rector Frederick W. Clampett said, "While the old world is plunged in the horrors of a senseless war, working misery and death and every form of human suffering, the new world has been graciously privileged to engage in the glorious pursuits of peace." Yet two years later the United States was drawn into the very war to which the "new world" had hoped to be immune.[9]

The overwhelming message of the PPIE, mounted a veritable instant after the tragedy of the 1906 earthquake and fire, is one of an optimistic, audacious San Francisco, not unlike the city of today. University of California president Benjamin Ide Wheeler said in a speech at the Fair, "The opening of the Panama Canal gives [San Francisco] the place in the modern world which Byzantium held in the old....The world has faced about; the ancient gate of the West was at Byzantium and the Golden Horn; to-day it is at San Francisco and the Golden Gate."[10]

For most, the Jewel City was remembered for the life that had existed within its gates, rather than the images of the Fair after its death: of toppled towers, piles of salvaged wood, and an empty marsh punctuated by the solitary Column of Progress. Season ticket holders who had spent many a day tramping the long verge of the bay, losing themselves among the myriad exhibits in the miles of palatial aisles, exploring the decadent crannies of the Joy Zone, or picnicking on the lawns of the South Gardens, probably preferred to remember the Panama-Pacific International Exposition in its heyday. Perhaps the beautiful Hawaiian Night on the Palace of Fine Arts Lagoon was the favored recollection, or the first meeting with a sweetheart who would one day become a spouse. Noted PPIE historian Donna Ewald Huggins credits her very existence to the Fair, as her grandparents courted among its majestic colonnades.

Fairgoers recalled the scents of exotic flowers and fresh baked scones, the fabulous parties and banquets, lively parades, and bustling exhibit halls rumbling with the sounds of music, hawkers, and machinery. And many especially treasured the memory of the last, mild night, when the Court of the Universe was packed with a jovial mass of celebrants who together watched Art Smith trail fire across the sky from the wings of his plane, inscribing "Farewell PPIE" upon the firmament.

San Francisco's Jewel City was the realization of the common dream of many individuals, a goal achieved. Author Juliet James described its legacy:

> And the pastel city by the sea will not leave us, for as the years go on, whatever be our mission, the vision of this dream-city will float before us, leading us to finer, higher works, strengthening our ideals, and causing us to give only of our finest fibre.[11]

The glamour of the Jewel City was captured in this poetic photo, taken by Louis J. Stellmann and hand-tinted by Edith Kinney Stellmann. (*That Was a Dream Worth Building*, by Louis Stellmann)

Note: For this work I have drawn from thousands of sources, most of them contemporary to the Exposition. To streamline the citations and prevent repetition, quoted sources appear here while other major sources are collected in the Explanation of Sources section.

Authoritative documentation was gleaned from the official business records of the PPIE, which are held at the Bancroft Library, located on the campus of the University of California, Berkeley. The collection's official designation is:

BANC MSS C-A 190, Panama Pacific International
Exposition Records, 1893–1929, bulk 1911–1916.

In the notes below, sources from this collection are cited by carton number, folder number, and page number as, for example, "Bancroft 56:35, 1." Where bound volumes from the collection are referenced, the citation will read "Bancroft vol. (volume number)."

CHAPTER 1

1. "1900: Let the Next Great World's Fair Be Held in San Francisco," *San Francisco Examiner,* December 25, 1891, 4.

2. Frank Morton Todd, *The Story of the Exposition,* vol. 1 (New York: G. P. Putnam's Sons, 1921), 26–27.

3. Louis Levy, *Chronological History of the Panama-Pacific International Exposition,* vol. 1 (San Francisco: Panama Pacific International Exposition Co., 1915), 2.

4. Ibid., 2–3.

5. Todd, *Story of the Exposition,* vol. 1, 42 (see ch. 1, n. 2).

6. Ibid., 43.

7. "San Francisco's Exposition in 1915 Indorsed by President Taft," *San Francisco Call,* December 29, 1909, 1.

8. John Smith Kendall, *History of New Orleans,* vol. 2 (Chicago: The Lewis Publishing Company, 1922), 562.

9. "Will Thrash Out Rival Fair Claims," *San Francisco Call,* March 20, 1910, 48.

10. "San Diegans Say Call Is Framed by San Francisco," *Los Angeles Herald,* March 13, 1910, 11.

11. "Conference Effects a Compact," *San Francisco Call,* May 7, 1910.

12. "Conquering Committee Returns from Panama Exposition Campaign at Washington," *New Orleans Times-Picayune,* March 18, 1910, 1; and "Exposition Boom Launched at Capital," *New Orleans Times-Picayune,* March 15, 1910, 1.

13. *Hearings on the Panama Exposition* (Washington, DC: Government Printing Office, 1910), 2.

14. "The Dominion of the Valley," *Logical Point* (November 1910): 2.

15. "Cities Urge Claims for Panama Fair," *New York Times,* January 16, 1911, 4.

16. *San Francisco: The Exposition City 1915* (pamphlet), 1910, 2–3.

17. "The Dominion of the Valley," 2 (see ch. 1, n. 14).

18. *Tale of Two Cities: San Francisco: The Exposition City* (pamphlet), 1910, 7.

19. "Voice of United West Heard in Washington," *San Francisco Chronicle,* January 24, 1911, 1.

20. Todd, *Story of the Exhibition,* vol. 1, 96 (see ch. 1, n. 2).

21. "The San Francisco Crowd Using Trickery," *New Orleans Times-Picayune,* January 24, 1911, 1.

22. "Exposition Winners Praise Kahn's Leadership," *San Francisco Chronicle,* March 14, 1911, 18.

23. "Joy Greets News from the Senate," *San Francisco Chronicle,* February 9, 1911, 3.

24. "Californians at Banquet Board in New York," *San Francisco Chronicle,* February 4, 1911, 1.

25. "Mullally Returns from Washington," *San Francisco Chronicle,* February 14, 1911, 1.

26. Todd, *Story of the Exposition,* vol. 1, 130 (see ch. 1, n. 2).

27. Ibid., 124.

28. Daniel Burnham, Daniel Chester French, F. D. Millet, Charles C. Moore, and Cass Gilbert, "Letter to William H. Crocker," April 25, 1911, Bancroft 32:24.

29. Marsden Manson, *Report on Harbor View* (San Francisco: 1911). "Seven Places Advocated for Many Reasons," *San Francisco Call,* February 2, 1911, 2.

30. *Success of Exposition Depends on Location* (San Francisco: Harbor View Improvement Association, 1911).

31. Ibid.

32. Todd, *Story of the Exposition,* vol. 1, 129–130 (see ch. 1, n. 2).

33. "Meeting of the Architectural Commission and Site Committee," September 20, 1911, Bancroft 140:7.

34. "Minutes, Buildings and Grounds Committee," December 5, 1911, Bancroft v. 119.

35. "Vanderbilt Telegram," December 28, 1911, Bancroft 61:36

CHAPTER 2

1. Jessie Lynch Williams, "The Color Scheme at the Panama-Pacific Exposition," *Scribner's Magazine* (September 1914): 277.

2. Clarence P. Kane, "Jules Guérin Talks on Color," *Pacific Coast Architect* (May 1915): 196.

3. Ben Macomber, *The Jewel City* (San Francisco: John H. Williams, 1915), 41.

4. "First World's Fair to Have Careful Color Scheme," *New York Times,* June 1, 1913.

5. "The City of Color," *Popular Electricity Magazine* (July 1913): 307.

6. Guy L. Bayley, "Engineering Features of the Panama-Pacific International Exposition," *Journal of the American Society of Mechanical Engineers* (October 1915): 571.

7. Charles J. O'Connor, et al., *San Francisco Relief Survey: The Organization and Methods of Relief Used After the Earthquake and Fire of April 18, 1906* (San Francisco: Russell Sage Foundation, 1913), 85.

8. Anna Pratt Simpson, "From Green Refugee Shacks to Cozy Homes of Their Own," *San Francisco Call,* May 2, 1909, magazine section.

9. San Francisco Department of Public Health, *Annual Report for the Fiscal Year July 1, 1911, to June 30, 1912* (San Francisco: 1912), 11.

10. "Sees Great Future for Chamber of Commerce," *San Francisco Chronicle,* January 22, 1913, 11.

11. T. G. Howe, "Letter to Fred Hansen," July 11, 1912, Bancroft 61:34.

12. "Owners of Refugee Cottages Go to Court," *San Francisco Call,* January 31, 1912, 5.

13. R. G. Brodrick, "Letter to Harris Connick," September 27, 1912, Bancroft 61:34.

14. Todd, *Story of the Exposition,* vol. 1, 162 (see ch. 1, n. 2).

15. "New Plan of Mrs. Hearst: She Would Lay Out San Francisco Along New Lines," *San Francisco Chronicle,* December 4, 1898, 32.

16. Robert Cherny, "City Commercial, City Beautiful, City Practical: The San Francisco Visions of William C. Ralston, James D. Phelan, and Michael M. O'Shaughnessy, *California History* 73, no. 4 (winter 1994/95), p. 302.

17. Charles Moore, *Daniel Burnham: Architect, Planner of Cities,* vol. 2 (Boston and New York: Houghton Mifflin Co., 1921), 3.

18. "Exposition Architecture," *Transactions of the Commonwealth Club,* (August 1915): 352.

19. Richard Longstreth, telephone interview with the author, September 24, 2012.

20. "Mr. Clarence R. Ward Discusses Architects and Architecture," *Architect and Engineer of California* (June 1917): 69.

21. "Minutes, Buildings and Grounds Committee," September 11, 1911, Bancroft 23:11.

22. Ibid., September 8, 1911.

23. "Pacific Service Day at the Exposition," *Pacific Service Magazine* (April 1915): 370.

24. William Faville, "A Brief Resume of the Organization Under Which the Architecture of the PPIE Has Been Developed," *Pacific Coast Architect* (May 1915): 174.

25. "The World's Fair Site, Civic Center, and Architectural Commission," *Architect and Engineer of California* (January 1912): 35.

26. Vernon Armand DeMars, "A Life in Architecture: Indian Dancing, Migrant Housing, Telesis, Design for Urban Living, Theater, Teaching," an oral history conducted by Suzanne B. Reiss (Berkeley: The Bancroft Library Regional Oral History Office, 1992), xvi.

27. Eugen Neuhaus, *The Art of the Exposition* (San Francisco: Paul Elder and Company, 1915), 4–5.

28. "Exposition Architecture," 353 (see ch. 2, n. 18).

29. "Minutes, Buildings and Grounds Committee," June 11, 1912, Bancroft 23:13.

30. Walter Steilberg, "The Julia Morgan Architectural History Project," *Reminiscences of the Department of Architecture, University of California, Berkeley, 1904 to 1954*, vol. 1, an oral history conducted by Suzanne B. Reiss (Berkeley: The Bancroft Library Regional Oral History Office, 1976), 144–145.

31. Charles Peterson, "A Visit with Bernard Maybeck," *Journal of the Society of Architectural Historians* (October 1952): 31.

32. "Letter to Wm. H. Crocker from Moore," September 10, 1912, Bancroft 17:1.

33. Ibid., September 24, 1912.

34. Ibid., September 10, 1912.

35. Ibid., September 24, 1912.

36. "Minutes, Buildings and Grounds Committee," September 17, 1912, Bancroft 23:15.

37. "Letter from Maybeck to Polk," March 6, 1915, Willis Polk Papers, College of Environmental Design Archives, University of California, Berkeley.

38. "Willis Polk Tells of Exposition's Rise," *Santa Barbara Morning Press*, April 1914.

39. "Minutes, Buildings and Grounds Committee," March 2, 1915, Bancroft, vol. 120:553.

40. "Willis Polk Suggests a Plan for Partial Preservation of Exposition Buildings," *Architect and Engineer of California* (August 1915): 101.

41. "Meeting of the Architectural Commission," August 14, 1912, Bancroft 17:1, 8.

42. "President's Daily Letter," October 15, 1912, Bancroft 17:24.

43. William Woollett, "Color in Architecture at the Panama-Pacific Exposition," *Architectural Record* (May 1915): 437.

44. Williams, "Color Scheme," 289 (see ch. 2, n. 1).

45. Clarence P. Kane, "Jules Guérin Talks on Color," *Pacific Coast Architect* (May 1915): 196.

46. "Minutes, Meeting of Mural Painters," April 4, 1913, Bancroft 62:19, 5.

47. Williams, "Color Scheme," 289 (see ch. 2, n. 1).

48. Untitled, *The Wasp* (March 20, 1915): 4.

49. A. H. Markwart, "Wall Surfaces : 36.

50. Paul E. Denivelle, "Texture and Color at the Panama-Pacific Exposition," *Architectural Record* (November 1915): 563.

51. Markwart, "Wall Surfaces," 36 (see ch. 2, n. 49).

52. "Meeting of the Architectural Commission," August 14, 1912, Bancroft 17:1.

53. Ibid.

54. Juliet James, *Palace and Courts of the Exposition* (San Francisco: H. S. Crocker Company, 1915), 18.

55. "The Exposition That Will Be Ready," *Sunset* (October 1914): 738.

56. *Thirty Days at the Panama-Pacific Exposition* (San Francisco: Owl Drug, 1915), 35.

57. "Minutes, Meeting of Mural Painters," April 2, 1913, Bancroft 62:19, 2.

58. Hamilton Wright, "Mural Decorations at the Panama-Pacific International Exposition," *California's Magazine* 2 (1916): 313.

59. "Minutes, Meeting of Mural Painters," 6 (see ch. 2, n. 57).

60. "Minutes, Meeting of Mural Painters," July 12, 1913, Bancroft 62:19, 2.

61. "Letter to Kelham from Guérin," November 10, 1913, Bancroft 62:17, 1.

62. Todd, *Story of the Exposition,* vol. 1, 351 (see ch. 1, n. 2).

63. Williams, "Color Scheme," 278 (see ch. 2, n. 1).

64. Porter Garnett, "Report and Recommendations Regarding the Inscriptions for the Buildings and Monuments of the Panama-Pacific International Exposition," Bancroft 56:41, 3.

65. Frederick J. V. Skiff, "Letter to Connick Regarding Inscriptions," March 16, 1914, Bancroft 56:41, 2.

66. Porter Garnett, *The Inscriptions at the Panama-Pacific International Exposition* (San Francisco: Taylor, Nash and Taylor, 1915), 33.

67. Garnett, "Report and Recommendations," 2–4, 11 (see ch. 2, n. 64).

68. "The Landscape Gardener of the Panama-Pacific International Exposition, 1915," *Sunset* (December 1913): 1215.

69. John McLaren, "California's Opportunities in Artistic Landscaping," *California's Magazine* 2 (1916): 139.

70. Alice McGowan, "Exposition's Pastel City a Dream of Soft Color," *New York Tribune*, February 14, 1915, 3.

71. Todd, *Story of the Exposition,* vol. 1, (see ch. 1, n. 2).

CHAPTER 3

1. "Letter from Artificial Floral and Decorating," March 30, 1912, Bancroft 66:14.

2. Todd, *Story of the Exposition,* vol. 1, 163 (see ch. 1, n. 2).

3. E. C. Eaton, "Source and Purification of Water Supply for Panama-Pacific International Exposition," *Pacific Municipalities* (November 1915): 590.

4. Grant Ute, "Fair Please: Streetcars to the 1915 Panama-Pacific Exposition," *Inside Track* (Winter 2005): 10.

5. Helen Eells Vandevere, "Recording by Helen Eells Vandevere of Her Life Story," unpublished audio cassette, Vandevere Family Collection, 1979.

6. "Thousands Cheer for Exposition," *San Francisco Call,* January 2, 1913, 2.

7. "First Shovelful of Earth Turned at The Exposition: Actual Work Commenced on Mammoth Machinery Palace," *San Francisco Chronicle,* January 2, 1913, 11.

8. A. H. Markwart, "Engineering Features of the Panama-Pacific International Exposition," *Engineering Record* (June 6, 1914): 654.

9. Todd, *Story of the Exposition,* vol. 2, 10 (see ch. 1, n. 2).

10. Guy L. Bayley, "Engineering Features of the Panama-Pacific International Exposition," *Journal of the American Society of Mechanical Engineers* (October 1915): 574.

11. Todd, *Story of the Exposition,* vol. 2, 11 (see ch. 1, n. 2).

12. Ibid., 15.

13. "Accident Report: W. C. Wilson," February 12, 1914, Bancroft 154:48.

14. "Panama-Pacific International Exposition Notes," *San Francisco Municipal Record,* February 4, 1915, 35.

15. Daniel Chester French, "Letter to Alexander S. Calder, Esq.," February 5, 1915, Chesterwood Archives Microfilm, Chapin Library, Williams College, Williamstown, MA.

16. Margaret French Cresson, *Journey into Fame: Daniel Chester French* (Boston: Harvard University Press, 1947), 229.

17. H. D. Dewell, "Memo Regarding Mohamet's Mountain," January 6, 1914, Bancroft 63:16.

18. W. M. Johnson, "Memo Regarding Mohamet's Mountain," January 9, 1914, Bancroft 63:16.

19. "Begins 1915 Work in a Bower of Flowers," *San Francisco Chronicle,* July 8, 1914, 11.

20. Thomas Hastings, "Letter to H. D. Connick," February 2, 1915, Bancroft 56:35.

CHAPTER 4

1. Ralph Emmett Avery, *The Greatest Engineering Feat in the World at Panama* (New York: Leslie-Judge Company, 1915), 315.

2. "Dynamite Blast Removes Final Panama Canal Barrier," *San Francisco Chronicle,* October 11, 1913, 17.

3. "The Last Barrier Broken," *San Francisco Chronicle,* October 11, 1913, 20.

4. Todd, *Story of the Exposition,* vol. 1, 206 (see ch. 1, n. 2).

5. Ibid., 243.

6. "Rules and Regulations of the Division of Exhibits," VF Guides for Exhibitors, August 1913, p. 7, Daniel E. Koshland San Francisco History Center, San Francisco Public Library.

7. Asher C. Baker, "Division of Exhibits: Official Report," PPIE Exhibits: Director's Report, p. 4, Daniel E. Koshland San Francisco History Center, San Francisco Public Library.

8. James Gillett, *Hearing on Panama Exposition*, United States House Committee on Foreign Affairs (Washington, DC, 1912), 10.

9. Frank Van Nuys, "A Progressive Confronts the Race Question: Chester Rowell, the California Alien Land Act of 1913, and the Contradictions of Early Twentieth-Century Racial Thought," *California Historical Quarterly* (Spring 1994): 5.

10. Franklin Hichborn, *The Story of the Session of the California Legislature of 1913* (San Francisco: James H. Barry Company, 1913), 231.

11. "Exposition Chiefs Oppose Hostile Legislation," *San Francisco Chronicle*, April 3, 1913, 1.

12. "To Confer on Alien Land Bill," *San Francisco Chronicle*, April 9, 1913, 4.

13. Mauricio Tenorio-Trillo, *Mexico at the World's Fairs: Crafting a Modern Nation* (Berkeley: University of California Press, 1996), 197.

14. Reuben Brooks Hale, "Report of the Commission Extraordinary to Europe," August 28, 1912, Bancroft 7:27, 4.

15. William Sesnon, "Letter to Charles C. Moore," June 8, 1912, Bancroft 7:27, 5.

16. "Panama-Pacific Exposition Commission in Berlin," May 9, 1912, Bancroft 7:32, 1.

17. "England and the Exposition," *Sunset* (October 1913): 759.

18. "Rules, Regulations and Rates Governing Transportation and Delivery of Exhibits and Merchandise at the Panama-Pacific International Exposition," booklet (San Francisco: PPIE Traffic Department, June 20, 1914), 9. Laura A. Ackley Collection.

19. George Hough Perry, "Report of the Director of Exploitation to the President, Board of Directors and the Committee on Exploitation of the Panama-Pacific International Exposition," PPIE Exploitation: Director's Report, p. 5, Daniel E. Koshland San Francisco History Center, San Francisco Public Library.

20. Larry Harris, "Interviewing an International Exposition: The Pod of Exploitation and Its Four P's," *San Francisco Call*, December 27, 1913, 12.

21. "Exposition Progress," *San Francisco Chronicle*, December 13, 1913, 2.

22. "P.P.I.E. Division of Exploitation," *Journal of Electricity, Power and Gas* (June 5, 1915): 490.

23. "Bill Board Advertising," PPIE Exploitation: Director's Report, p. 1, Daniel E. Koshland San Francisco History Center, San Francisco Public Library.

24. Perry, "Report of the Director of Exploitation," 12 (see ch. 4, n. 19).

25. Harris, "Interviewing an International Exposition," 12 (see ch. 4, n. 20).

26. Perry, "Report of the Director of Exploitation," 2 (see ch. 4, n. 19).

27. Todd, *Story of the Exposition*, vol. 2, 221 (see ch. 1, n. 2).

28. Perry, "Report of the Director of Exploitation," 7 (see ch. 4, n. 19).

29. "Hotels Not to Put Up Rates for Fair," *Portland Oregonian*, January 3, 1915, 4.

30. *Official Exposition Hotel Guide* (PPIE Division of Exploitation, April 1915), 2.

31. E. C. Conroy, "Report of Chief of Admissions," PPIE Concessions and Admissions, December 5, 1915, p. 1, Daniel E. Koshland San Francisco History Center, San Francisco Public Library.

32. "The Tattler," *The Wasp* (January 23, 1915): 11.

CHAPTER 5

1. Todd, *Story of the Exposition*, vol. 2, 134 (see ch. 1, n. 2).

2. "Exposition Will Not Be Delayed," *San Francisco Chronicle*, September 10, 1914, 5.

3. Todd, *Story of the Exposition*, vol. 2, 245 (see ch. 1, n. 2).

4. "Southern Pacific Advertisement," *The Argonaut*, January 2, 1915, 16.

5. William Jennings Bryan, "The Exposition Will Not Be Postponed," *Sunset* (November 1914): 951.

6. "The European War and the Panama-Pacific Exposition—A Monumental Contrast," *Current Opinion* (May 1915): 318.

7. Ibid.

8. Ibid., 320.

9. Ibid., 316.

10. "Exposition Will Not Be Delayed," 5 (see ch. 5, n. 2).

11. Todd, *Story of the Exposition*, vol. 3, 21 (see ch. 1, n. 2).

12. John J. Breen, "Daring Aviators to Encircle Globe," *Idaho Statesman*, March 1, 1914, 11.

13. "All Aboard for Aero Express[,] Across Ocean Round the World," *Rockford [Illinois] Daily Register-Gazette*, April 6, 1914, 12.

14. "Collecting Art Exhibits in War-Ridden Europe," *Review of Reviews* (April 1915): 462.

15. Ibid., 462–463.

16. "The San Francisco Exposition," *Travel* (February 1915): 40.

17. "Jason's Cargo Is a Puzzle to US Customs Officials," *San Francisco Chronicle*, April 15, 1915, 5.

18. "Collecting Art Exhibits," 464 (see ch. 5, n. 14).

19. "Captain Tells of His Voyage," *San Francisco Chronicle*, April 12, 1915, 1.

20. Ibid.

21. "French Exhibit Inspired by Sympathy," *San Francisco Chronicle*, January 6, 1915, 9.

22. "Strong Friendship for America from Across the Seas," *San Francisco Chronicle*, April 10, 1915, 4.

23. Emile Verhaeren, *Belgium Catalogue* (San Francisco: Belgian Commission to the Panama-Pacific International Exposition, 1915), 3–4.

24. Todd, *Story of the Exposition*, vol. 2, 248 (see ch. 1, n. 2).

25. "Fair Wonderful Now But Not Yet Complete," *Idaho Statesman*, April 27, 1915, 7.

26. "The European War," 315 (see ch. 5, n. 6).

27. "Peace Pageants in Every Town," *New York Times*, June 27, 1915.

CHAPTER 6

1. Emily Post, *By Motor to the Golden Gate* (New York: D. Appleton and Company, 1916), 4, 229.

2. "Tramp Houses of San Francisco," *San Francisco Chronicle*, November 17, 1901, A2.

3. Post, *By Motor*, 230 (see ch. 6, n. 1).

4. Christian Brinton, "The San Diego and San Francisco Expositions Part II: San Francisco," *International Studio Magazine* (July 1915): 56.

5. Todd, *Story of the Exposition*, vol. 1, 288 (see ch. 2, n. 1).

6. Willis Polk, "The Panama-Pacific Plan," *Sunset* (April 1912): 487.

7. Louis C. Mullgardt, "The Panama-Pacific Exposition at San Francisco," *Architectural Record* (March 1915): 194.

8. Frederick Jennings, "Some Architectural Features of Alameda's New Amusement Park," *Architect and Engineer of California* (December 1915): 91.

9. Octavius Morgan, "The Fair—Octavius Morgan's Impressions of It," *Architect and Engineer of California* (June 1915): 85.

10. George Wharton James, *California, Romantic and Beautiful* (Boston: Page Company, 1914), 171.

11. "Exterior Walls of Main Group of Buildings," August 14, 1912, Bancroft 17:1.

12. Gray Brechin, "Destruction of the Fair," on FoundSF.org's Shaping San Francisco's Digital Archive, accessed February 6, 2013, http://foundsf. org/index.php?title=Destruction_of_the_Fair. Excerpted from Gray Brechin, "Sailing to Byzantium: The Architecture of the Fair," in *The Anthropology of World's Fairs: San Francisco's Panama Pacific International Exposition of 1915*, edited by Burton Benedict (London and Berkeley: Lowie Museum of Anthropology in association with Scolar Press, 1983), 108.

13. "Exposition Architecture," 364 (see ch. 2, n. 18).

14. Ibid.

15. Ibid., 372.

16. Ibid., 381.

17. Stella G. S. Perry, *The Sculpture and Mural Decorations of the Exposition* (San Francisco: Paul Elder and Company, 1915), 87.

18. Hamilton Wright, "The Exposition at San Francisco," *Travel* (December 1914): 51.

19. Perry, *Sculpture and Mural Decorations*, 58 (see ch. 6, n. 17).

20. "Exposition Architecture," 384 (see ch. 2, n. 18).

21. Macomber, *Jewel City*, 78 (see ch. 2, n. 3).

22. Ibid., 81.

23. Ibid., 78.

24. Henry Bacon, "West Court," August 14, 1912, Bancroft 17:1.

25. Sheldon Cheney, *An Art-Lover's Guide to the Exposition* (Berkeley: Sunset Publishing, 1915), 25.

26. "Exposition Architecture," 380 (see ch. 2, n. 18).

27. B. J. S. Cahill, "The Exposition—Impressions and Expressions," *Pacific Coast Architect* (April 1915): 177.

28. John D. Barry, *The City of Domes* (San Francisco: John J. Newbegin, 1915), 108.

29. Thomas Hastings, "Architecture at the Panama-Pacific Exposition, 1915," *Architectural Record* (February 1914): 171.

30. Post, *By Motor*, 229–230 (see ch. 6, n. 1).

31. "Says Tower of Jewels Might Be Made of Ice Cream," *Architect and Engineer of California* (June 1915): 87.

32. Ibid.

33. Irving F. Morrow, "Recent Work of Louis Christian Mullgardt," *Architect and Engineer of California* (December 1917): 40.

34. Louis C. Mullgardt, "Architecture of the Panama-Pacific International Exposition," *California's Magazine* 2 (1916): 157–158.

35. "Some Recent California Architecture: The Work of Louis Christian Mullgardt, Architect," *Architectural Forum* (August 1920): 51.

36. Cahill, "The Exposition," 178 (see ch. 6, n. 27).

37. Ben Macomber, "Glamor of Romance Invests Court of Ages," *San Francisco Chronicle*, March 28, 1915, 26.

38. "Exposition Architecture," 359 (see ch. 2, n. 18).

39. Beatrice Wright, "Eventide," from *The Court of Ages*, found on *Books about California*, accessed May 7, 2014, http://www.books-about-california.com/Pages/The_Court_of_Ages/The_Court_of_Ages_Eventide.html. Excerpted from *The Court of Ages* (San Francisco: Ricardo J. Orozco, 1916).

40. Cahill, "The Exposition," 178 (see ch. 6, n. 27).

41. Macomber, *Jewel City*, 65 (see ch. 2, n. 3).

42. Barry, *City of Domes*, 87 (see ch. 6, n. 28).

43. Bernard R. Maybeck, *Palace of Fine Arts and Lagoon* (San Francisco: Paul Elder and Company, 1915), 7–8.

44. Ibid., 10.

45. Ibid., 10, 12.

46. Barry, *City of Domes*, 63 (see ch. 6, n. 28).

47. Bernard R. Maybeck, "Architecture of the Palace of Fine Arts at the Panama-Pacific International Exposition," *California's Magazine* 2 (1916): 163.

48. Post, *By Motor*, 234 (see ch. 6, n. 1).

49. Ibid., 232.

50. Cahill, "The Exposition," 178 (see ch. 6, n. 27).

51. "Beauties That Pass," *Morning Oregonian*, November 27, 1915, 8.

52. Charles G. Odd, "A Southern California Architect's Visit to the Fair," *Architect and Engineer of California* (November 1915): 48.

53. William Winthrop Kent, "The New San Francisco," *Architectural Review* (May 1919): 127.

54. Almus Pratt Evans, "Exposition Architecture: 1893 versus 1933," *Parnassus* (May 1933): 20.

CHAPTER 7

1. Willis Polk, "Introduction to the Guest of the Evening," speech at a meeting of the Downtown Association of San Francisco, January 11, 1916, 1–2.

2. General Electric Company, "G-E Historical File, Publicity Department, Illumination of the Panama-Pacific International Exposition," Schenectady Museum, 1035.

3. A. F. Dickerson, in ibid., 1033.

4. Katharine "Virginia" Ryan Durrant, personal interview with the author, April 2003.

5. Walter D'Arcy Ryan, "Illumination of the Panama-Pacific International Exposition," booklet, p. 418, from a presentation given for the Schenectady Section of the American Institute of Electrical Engineers, Schenectady, New York, May 4, 1916.

6. Walter D'Arcy Ryan, "The Illumination of the Exposition Buildings," *Western Architect and Engineer* (December 1914): 83–85.

7. "Edwin Markham on the Exposition," *New York Times*, February 17, 1915, 10.

8. General Electric Company, "G-E Historical File," 1035 (see ch. 7, n. 2).

9. James A. Buchanan, ed., *History of the Panama-Pacific International Exposition* (San Francisco: Pan-Pacific Press Association, Ltd., 1916), 457.

10. F. F. Barbour, "The Ryan Electric Color Scintillator at the Exposition," *Pacific Service Magazine* (June 1915): 6–7.

11. General Electric Company, "G-E Historical File," 1049 (see ch. 7, n. 2).

12. Walter D'Arcy Ryan, "Illumination, Panama-Pacific International Exposition," n.d., Bancroft 85:28, 6.

13. Ryan, "Illumination," 424 (see ch. 7, n. 5).

14. Howard Payson, *The Boy Scouts at the Panama-Pacific Exposition* (New York: Hurst and Company, 1915), 115.

15. Barry, *City of Domes*, 105 (see ch. 6, n. 28).

16. John Winthrop Hammond, *Men and Volts: The Story of General Electric* (Philadelphia: Lippincott Company, 1941), 366.

17. "Says Tower of Jewels Might Be Made of Ice Cream," *Architect and Engineer of California* (June 1915): 87.

18. Macomber, *Jewel City*, 139 (see ch. 2, n. 3).

19. Barry, *City of Domes*, 104 (see ch. 6, n. 28).

20. Walter D'Arcy Ryan, "Building Exterior, Exposition and Pageant Lighting," *Illuminating Engineering Practice: Lectures on Illuminating Engineering Delivered at the University of Pennsylvania*, compiled by the Illuminating Engineering Society (New York: McGraw-Hill, 1916), 554.

21. Ibid., 551.

22. Ibid.

23. C. B. Babcock, "The Part Gas Plays in Lighting the Panama-Pacific Exposition," *Pacific Service Magazine* (June 1915): 51.

24. Larry Harris, "Interviewing an International Exposition: The Department of Illumination, W. D'A. Ryan, Illuminating Engineer," *San Francisco Call*, December 13, 1913, 14.

25. Walter D'Arcy Ryan, "Illumination of the Exposition," *California's Magazine* (July 1915): 317.

26. Walter D'Arcy Ryan, "Illumination of the Panama-Pacific Exposition," *General Electric Review* (June 1915): 579–593.

27. Barry, *City of Domes*, 137 (see ch. 6, n. 28).

28. General Electric Company, "G-E Historical File," 1036 (see ch. 7, n. 2).

CHAPTER 8

1. French Strother, "The Panama-Pacific International Exposition," *World's Work* (July 1915): 337.

2. Todd, *Story of the Exposition*, vol. 2, 381 (see ch. 1, n. 2).

3. Strother, "Panama-Pacific International Exposition," 355 (see ch. 8, n. 1).

4. Arthur Wallace Dunn, "Dr. Wiley and Pure Food," *World's Work* 22 (September 1911): 14961.

5. Ben Macomber, *Jewel City*, 153 (see ch. 2, n. 3).

6. "Exposition Interests the Ladies," *Pacific Rural Press*, May 15, 1915, 596.

7. Ben Macomber, "Palace of Food Products Is a Temple of the Tin Can," *San Francisco Chronicle*, July 11, 1915, 26.

8. "The Best Exhibit," *Pacific Rural Press*, October 23, 1915, 411.

9. Todd, *Story of the Exposition*, vol. 4, 270–271 (see ch. 1, n. 2).

10. *Official Guide of the Panama-Pacific International Exposition, 1915* (San Francisco: The Wahlgreen Company, 1915), 60.

11. W. D. Egilbert, "The Panama-Pacific International Exposition," *California Blue Book or State Roster 1913–1915*, compiled by Frank C. Jordan (Sacramento: California State Printing Office, 1915), 535.

12. Don Cameron Shafer, "The Home Electrical at the Panama-Pacific International Exposition," *General Electric Review* (June 1915): 572.

13. Ibid., 575.

14. Todd, *Story of the Exposition*, vol. 4, 124 (see ch. 1, n. 2).

15. Ibid., 134.

16. "Exposition Interests the Ladies," 596 (see ch. 8, n. 6).

17. "A Day with Dr. Maria Montessori and Her Youthful Charges Is an Eye Opener for the Average Parent," *San Francisco Chronicle,* September 12, 1915, 6.

18. "Victor Temple Scene of Entertainment," *Pacific Coast Musical Review* (May 8, 1915): 4.

19. Strother, "Panama-Pacific International Exposition," 354 (see ch. 8, n. 1).

20. "Ceremonies at Opening of Transcontinental Telephone Line, San Francisco," *Pacific Telephone Magazine* (February 1915): 5.

21. Strother, "Panama-Pacific International Exposition," 354 (see ch. 8, n. 1).

22. Hamilton Wright, "The Panama-Pacific Exposition in Its Glorious Prime," *Overland Monthly* (October 1915): 291–292.

23. Todd, *Story of the Exposition,* vol. 4, 246 (see ch. 1, n. 2).

24. James A. Buchanan, ed., *History of the Panama-Pacific International Exposition* (see ch. 7, n. 9).

25. "Edison and Ford Delighted After Strenuous Trip at Exposition," *San Francisco Chronicle,* October 20, 1915, 11.

26. Strother, "Panama-Pacific International Exposition," 359 (see ch. 8, n. 1).

27. "Panama-Pacific Exposition Notes," *World's Advance* (May 1915): 666.

28. Todd, *Story of the Exposition,* vol. 4, 199 (see ch. 1, n. 2).

29. Geddes Smith, "A Shop-Window of Civilization," *Independent* (June 28, 1915): 534.

30. G. W. Danforth, "Introduction, Department of Machinery," *Official Catalogue of Exhibits, Panama-Pacific International Exposition* (San Francisco: The Wahlgreen Company, 1915).

31. Todd, *Story of the Exposition,* vol. 4., 188 (see ch. 1, n. 2).

32. Ibid., 186.

33. H. A. Eveleth, "Panama-Pacific Exposition Notes," *World's Advance* (September 1915): 340.

34. "Safety Racer Is a Mile Long," *San Francisco Chronicle,* February 20, 1915, 4.

35. Todd, *Story of the Exposition,* vol. 2, 149 (see ch. 1, n. 2).

36. Ibid., 357.

37. Eveleth, "Panama-Pacific Exposition Notes," 339 (see ch. 8, n. 33).

38. Smith, "Shop-Window of Civilization," 534 (see ch. 8, n. 29).

39. Macomber, *Jewel City,* 146 (see ch. 2, n. 3).

40. Strother, "Panama-Pacific International Exposition," 354 (see ch. 8, n. 1).

41. Laura Ingalls Wilder, *West from Home: Letters of Laura Ingalls Wilder to Almanzo,* edited by R. L. MacBride (New York: Harper, 1974), 37.

CHAPTER 9

1. Jessica B. Peixotto, "San Francisco: What the Panama-Pacific Exposition Promises to a Social Worker," *The Survey* 34, no. 14 (July 3, 1915): 308.

2. Baker, "Division of Exhibits: Official Report," 2 (see ch. 4, n. 7).

3. John L. Heaton, "As the Stranger Sees It," *San Francisco Chronicle,* February 17, 1915, 6.

4. James A. Barr, "An Announcement: Congresses, Conferences, Conventions," booklet (San Francisco: Panama-Pacific International Exposition, 1915), 6.

5. Teachers of San Francisco and the Office of the Superintendent of Schools, "Course of Study at the Panama-Pacific International Exposition for the Elementary Grades of the San Francisco School Department," May 1915, 23.

6. *The Exhibits of the Smithsonian Institution at the Panama-Pacific International Exposition* (San Francisco: H. S. Crocker Co., 1915), 12.

7. "Call Your 1915 Meeting for San Francisco," n.d. SF EPH Administrative: Congresses, Conferences and Conventions, California Historical Soceity.

8. "Religion at the Panama-Pacific," *Literary Digest* (January 23, 1915): 154.

9. Todd, *Story of the Exposition*, vol. 4, 32 (see ch. 1, n. 2).

10. Rube Goldberg, "Boobs at the Fair," *Anaconda [Montana] Standard,* August 25, 1915, 11.

11. Alvin E. Pope, "Introduction: Department of Education," *Official Catalogue of Exhibitors: Panama-Pacific International Exposition San Francisco 1915* (San Francisco: The Wahlgreen Company, 1915), Department B, p. 12.

12. "Child Labor Exhibit for Panama-Pacific International Exposition," *Trenton [New Jersey] Evening Times,* January 24, 1915, 15.

13. "Dr. Aked Disapproves of Sunday," *San Francisco Chronicle,* August 5, 1915, 1.

14. Russel Lawrence Barsh, "An American Heart of Darkness: The 1913 Expedition for American Indian Citizenship," *Great Plains Quarterly* (Spring 1993): 100.

15. "Newthot World Congress," *Official Program, Panama-Pacific International Exposition,* September 1, 1915, 23.

16. "Dr. Newo Newi New, Newthot Founder, Receives a Medal," *San Francisco Chronicle,* September 12, 1915, 35.

17. Chloe S. Burke and Christopher J. Castaneda, "The Public and Private History of Eugenics: An Introduction," *Public Historian* 29 (Summer 2007): 5–17.

18. "Perfect Babes After Six Generations," *San Francisco Chronicle,* August 3, 1915, 5.

19. "Here Are Many Bits of Practical Wisdom," *San Francisco Chronicle,* August 4, 1915, 3.

20. "Eugenic Mating May Go Too Far," *San Francisco Chronicle,* August 7, 1915, 5.

21. "The Perfect Woman," *San Francisco Chronicle,* August 8, 1915, 28.

22. Teachers of San Francisco, "Course of Study," 16 (see ch. 9, n. 5).

23. "The Burbankism of It," *Pacific Rural Press,* August 14, 1915, 146–147.

24. Burke and Castaneda, "Public and Private History of Eugenics," 7 (ch. 9, n. 17).

25. Smith, "Shop-Window of Civilization," 534 (see ch. 8, n. 29).

26. Todd, *Story of the Exposition,* vol. 1, 244 (see ch. 1, n. 2).

27. Charles H. Green, "Introduction: Department of Manufactures," *Official Catalogue of Exhibitors: Panama-Pacific International Exposition San Francisco 1915* (San Francisco: The Wahlgreen Company, 1915) Department E, p. 8.

28. Francis T. Simmons, "Splendid Exposition Accomplishments at San Francisco and San Diego," *Chicago Commerce* (April 30, 1915): 16.

29. Jiro Harada, "Japan at the Exposition," *California's Magazine* 2 (1916): 334.

30. Smith, "Shop-Window of Civilization," 535 (see ch. 8, n. 29).

31. "The World's Progress for a Decade in All Lines Mirrored at the Panama-Pacific International Exposition," *Gas Institute News* (June 1915): 257.

32. Rube Goldberg, "Boobs at the Fair," *Anaconda [Montana] Standard,* August 31, 1915, 11.

33. "California's Building at the Fair," *California Fruit News* (June 26, 1915): 3.

34. Smith, "Shop-Window of Civilization," 535 (see ch. 8, n. 29).

35. "The Largest Spherical Relief Map in the World," *Scientific American* (June 12, 1915): 589.

36. "Mining and Metallurgy at the Exposition," *Mining and Scientific Press* (September 11, 1915): 408.

37. Egilbert, "The Panama-Pacific International Exposition," 548–549 (see ch. 8, n. 11).

38. Herman Whitaker, "A Great University—The Exposition," *Rotarian* (June 1915): 29.

39. "Panama-Pacific International Exposition News Condensed," *Sausalito News,* April 10, 1915.

40. "Gold Nuggets Given Away," *Official Program, Panama-Pacific International Exposition,* August 13, 1915, 15.

41. "Rules and Regulations, Elusive Miss Maud Contest," *Official Program, Panama-Pacific International Exposition,* May 28, 1915, 22.

42. Strother, "Panama-Pacific International Exposition," 335 (see ch. 8, n. 1).

43. Todd, *Story of the Exposition,* vol. 1, 244 (see ch. 1, n. 2).

44. Baker, "Division of Exhibits: Official Report," 2 (see ch. 4, n. 7).

45. Hamilton Wright, "The Panama-Pacific Exposition: A World Epitome," *National Magazine* (March 1915): 1089.

46. Edith K. Stellmann, "With the Crowd at the P.P.I.E.," *Overland Monthly* (June 1915): 515.

CHAPTER 10

1. Gilbert K. Harrison, "The 1915 Panorama of the World," *Spectator* (June 10, 1915): 5.

2. Eugene Rimmel, *Recollections of the Paris Exhibition of 1867* (Philadelphia: J. B. Lippincott and Co., 1868), 1.

3. "Noting Progress of the World's Fair," *Pacific Service Magazine* (January 1913): 288.

4. William Woollett, "Color in Architecture at the Panama-Pacific Exposition," *Architectural Record* (May 1915): 444.

5. "Exposition Progress," *San Francisco Chronicle,* November 17, 1913, 8.

6. Rube Goldberg, "Boobs at the Fair," *Anaconda [Montana] Standard,* August 27, 1915, 11.

7. Todd, *Story of the Exposition,* vol. 4, 97 (see ch. 1, n. 2).

8. "Hawaiian Music Is Hit of Exposition," *Duluth News-Tribune,* October 17, 1915.

9. *The Blue Book: A Comprehensive Official Souvenir View Book of the Panama-Pacific International Exposition* (San Francisco: Robert A. Reid, 1915), 200.

10. Catherine Hurtado Wood, telephone interview with the author, November 26, 2013.

11. Egilbert, "The Panama-Pacific International Exposition," 545 (see ch. 8, n. 11).

12. "Home of Redwood Dedicated," *The Timberman* (June 1915): 49.

13. "The Facts of the Brick House," *Brick and Clay Record* (September 7, 1915): 350.

14. *California Redwood Homes* (San Francisco: California Redwood Association, 1919), 15.

15. Sacramento County Exposition Commission, *Report of the Sacramento County Exposition Commissioners on Sacramento County's Participation* (Sacramento: News Publishing Co., 1916), 27–34.

16. Carrie Williams, "Diary of a Trip to the Pan Pacific Exposition," California History Room, California State Library, 5.

17. James A. Buchanan, ed. *History of the Panama-Pacific International Exposition,* 333 (see ch. 7, n. 9).

18. "The European War and the Panama-Pacific Exposition—A Monumental Contrast," *Current Opinion* (May 1915): 320.

19. Ibid., 318.

20. "Occident Meets Orient at the Fair," *Portland Oregonian,* March 15, 1915.

21. European War," 315 (see ch. 10, n. 18).

22. "Dynamite Blast Removes Final Panama Canal Barrier," *San Francisco Chronicle,* October 11, 1913, 17.

CHAPTER 11

1. "Secretary Lane Visits Joy Zone," *San Francisco Chronicle,* February 20, 1915, 9.

2. "Vice-President Thomas R. Marshall Reviews the Fleet," *San Francisco Chronicle,* March 23, 1915, 9.

3. "Bryan as Secretary of State," on U.S. Department of State website, accessed March 29, 2013, http://future.state.gov/when/timeline/1914_timeline/bryan_as_sec.html.

4. Todd, *Story of the Exposition,* vol. 3, 80 (see ch. 1, n. 2).

5. Ibid., 80.

6. Theodore Roosevelt, "Letter to Henry L. Sprague," Albany, New York, January 26, 1900, Manuscript Division, Library of Congress.

7. "Roosevelt Delighted as Crowd Cheers," *San Francisco Chronicle,* July 21, 1915, 1.

8. "Right to Vote Carries an Obligation to Bear Arms, Says Roosevelt," *San Francisco Chronicle,* July 22, 1915, 1.

9. "Liberty Bell Reaches Fair," *Springfield [Massachusetts] Republican,* July 22, 1915, 12.

10. "Full Text of Former President Taft's Speech Urges Heavy Increase in Size of the Navy," *San Francisco Chronicle,* September 3, 1915, 9.

11. Todd, *Story of the Exposition,* vol. 3, 151 (see ch. 1, n. 2).

12. "British Laugh at Ford Peace Plan," *San Francisco Chronicle,* December 7, 1915, 2.

13. Arno Dosch, "Rudolph Spreckels—the Genius of the San Francisco Graft Prosecution," *Overland Monthly* (November 1907): 481.

14. "Exposition Makes Impression on Kampengpetch," *San Francisco Chronicle,* January 8, 1915, 9.

15. "Japanese Admiral Finds New Name for Exposition," *San Francisco Chronicle,* January 3, 1915, 9.

16. "Uncle Joe Keeps Pledge; Waltzes at Exposition," *Albuquerque Journal,* April 27, 1915, 5.

17. "We Shall See and Honor Him Later," *San Francisco Chronicle,* May 24, 1915, 16.

18. Nina Carter Marbourg, "The Panama Girl: Miss Audrey Munson," *Tampa Morning Tribune,* March 7, 1915.

19. "Censor Passed a Kiss Film," *Kansas City Star,* October 22, 1916.

20. "Shocking! She Calls Exposition Figures," *Philadelphia Inquirer,* April 18, 1915.

21. "Celebrated Model Raps Prudes Who Attack Art Poses," *Salt Lake Telegram,* September 8, 1916.

22. "He's Alleged Wife Murderer," *Saginaw [Michigan] News,* June 13, 1919, 16.

23. "Audrey Munson, Ex-Film Idol, Seeks Waitress' Job," *Baltimore Sun,* October 18, 1920, 1.

24. Clarence A. Locan, "Beautiful Exposition Girl, Idol of Artists and Once Celebrated Movie Star Now in Shadow of Starvation," *San Francisco Chronicle,* November 7, 1920, 6.

25. Todd, *Story of the Exposition,* vol. 3, 131 (see ch. 1, n. 2).

26. William Saroyan, *Places Where I've Done Time* (New York: Praeger Publishers, 1972), 143.

27. "Mr. Mayor, Make Me 1915 Mascot," *San Francisco Call,* January 21, 1913, 8.

28. Alexander Calder, *Calder: An Autobiography with Pictures* (New York: Pantheon Books, 1966), 36.

29. Ansel Adams, with Mary Street Alinder, *Ansel Adams: An Autobiography* (Boston: Little, Brown and Company, 1996), 16.

30. "'Jewel City,' says Field. Gives Reasons for Name," *San Francisco Call,* January 27, 1915, 1.

31. "Branches and Locals: Northern California," *The Crisis* (November 1915): 35.

32. Ibid.

33. Waldemar Young, "Bits of Color," *San Francisco Chronicle,* June 25, 1915, 20.

34. R. L. Duffus, *The Tower of Jewels: San Francisco Memories* (New York: W. W. Norton and Company, Inc., 1960), 125.

35. "Smith's Biplane Like Flaming Comet," *San Francisco Chronicle,* April 25, 1915, 27.

36. Todd, *Story of the Exposition,* vol. 3, 160 (see ch. 1, n. 2).

37. Rose Wilder Lane, ed. *Art Smith's Story* (San Francisco: The Bulletin, 1915), 85.

38. Todd, *Story of the Exposition,* vol. 3, 51 (see ch. 1, n. 2).

39. "How She Taught Helen Keller," *Boston Herald,* November 13, 1915, 3.

40. "Helen Keller Day at Big Exposition," *Boston American,* November 7, 1915.

41. "Now Conducting School in Washington, D.C., Is Pioneer of Work in United States," *Daily Illinois State Register,* September 10, 1915, 8.

42. "Helen Keller Tells of Jilting a Mormon," *Boston Journal,* June 3, 1914, 14.

43. Waldemar Young, "Bits of Color," *San Francisco Chronicle,* March 28, 1915, 22.

44. "Women Gaining from Iceland to China," *San Francisco Chronicle,* June 3, 1915, 4.

45. Renée Sansom Flood, *Lost Bird of Wounded Knee: Spirit of the Lakota* (New York: Scribner, 1995), 83.

46. Todd, *Story of the Exposition*, vol. 3, 47 (see ch. 1, n. 2).

47. "San Francisco Convention," *The Moving Picture World* (July 31, 1915): 790.

48. Ibid., 791.

49. Ibid., 794–819.

50. "San Francisco Welcomes Lotta," *Salt Lake Telegram*, November 7, 1915.

51. "'Lotta' Weeps with Happiness as Big Crowd Demonstrates Affection," *San Francisco Chronicle*, November 10, 1915, 11.

52. Laura Ingalls Wilder, *West from Home: Letters of Laura Ingalls Wilder to Almanzo Wilder, San Francisco, 1915*, edited by Roger Lea MacBride (New York: Harper and Row, 1974), 36.

53. Jack London, "The Hussy," *Cosmopolitan* (December 1916): 18.

54. Porter Garnett, *The Inscriptions at the Panama-Pacific International Exposition* (San Francisco: San Francisco News Company, 1915), 31.

55. George Sterling, *The Evanescent City* (San Francisco: A. M. Robertson, 1915), 12.

56. Maud Wotring Raymond, *The Architecture and Landscape Gardening of the Exposition*, introduction by Louis Christian Mullgardt (San Francisco: Paul Elder and Company, 1915), 50.

57. Marian Taylor, "Congress of Authors and Journalists at the Panama-Pacific Exposition," *Overland Monthly* (November 1915): 440.

58. Josephine Clifford McCrackin, "Ina Coolbrith Invested with Poets' Crown," *Overland Monthly* (November 1915): 450.

59. Ella Sterling Mighels, "Crowned Poet Laureate," *The Grizzly Bear* (August 1915): 4.

60. McCrackin, 450 (see ch. 11, n. 58).

61. Louis J. Stellman, *That Was a Dream Worth Building: A Tribute and Retrospect* (San Francisco: H. S. Crocker Company, 1916), viii.

62. "Panama-Pacific International Exposition: Popular Information," San Francisco, 1913, 3.

63. James A. Barr, *The Legacy of the Exposition: Interpretation of the Intellectual and Moral Heritage Left to Mankind by the World Celebration at San Francisco in 1915* (San Francisco: John H. Nash, 1916), 162.

CHAPTER 12

1. "Art Lessons of the Exposition," *The Nation* (July 15, 1915): 86.

2. Todd, *Story of the Exposition*, vol. 1, 205 (see ch. 1, n. 2).

3. "Panama-Pacific Exposition Notes of General Interest," *San Francisco Municipal Record*, March 20, 1913, 94.

4. John E. D. Trask, "The Department of Fine Arts at the Panama-Pacific International Exposition," *California's Magazine* 2 (1916): 81.

5. "Collecting Art Exhibits in War-Ridden Europe," *Review of Reviews* (April 1915): 462–463.

6. Christian Brinton, "Scandinavian Art at the Panama-Pacific Exposition," *American-Scandinavian Review* (November–December 1915): 351.

7. Sheldon Cheney, *Art-Lover's Guide to the Exposition* (Berkeley: At the Sign of the Berkeley Oak, 1915), 93.

8. Anna Cora Winchell, "The Fine Arts Annex," *San Francisco Chronicle*, August 15, 1915, 22.

9. "An Exhibition Defeating Itself," *Literary Digest*, (August 28, 1915): 405.

10. Christian Brinton, "American Painting at the Panama-Pacific Exposition," *International Studio* (August 1915): 28.

11. James Ganz, telephone interview with the author, January 16, 2014.

12. Christian Brinton, "Foreign Painting at the Panama-Pacific Exposition," *International Studio* (October 1915): 89.

13. John E. D. Trask and J. Nilsen Laurvik, eds., *Catalogue de Luxe of the Department of Fine Arts* (San Francisco: Paul Elder and Company, 1915), 20.

14. Eugen Neuhaus, *The Galleries of the Exposition* (San Francisco: Paul Elder and Company, 1915), 78.

15. J. Nilsen Laurvik, "Notes on the Foreign Paintings," *Art and Progress* (August 1915): 359.

16. "Art for Fun's Sake," *The Wasp* (September 11, 1915): 9.

17. Umberto Boccioni et al., "Technical Manifesto of Futurist Painting," in *Futurist Manifestos*, edited by Umbro Apollonio (New York: Viking Press, 1973).

18. Michael Williams, "'Crazy' Is Usual Verdict on Futurists," *Portland Oregonian*, October 28, 1915, 6.

19. Ben Macomber, "Weird Pictures at PPIE Art Gallery Reveal Artistic Brainstorms," *San Francisco Chronicle Sunday Magazine*, August 8, 1915, 1.

20. Todd, *Story of the Exposition*, vol. 4, 24–25 (see ch. 1, n. 2).

21. James A. Buchanan, ed. *History of the Panama-Pacific International Exposition*, 364 (see ch. 7, n. 9).

22. J. Nilsen Laurvik, "Evolution of American Painting," *Century Magazine* (September 1915): 782.

23. "Sargent Painting Cut to Pieces by Militant," *Charlotte [North Carolina] Observer*, May 5, 1914, 3.

24. John E. D. Trask, "The Department of Fine Arts at the Panama-Pacific International Exposition," *Art in California* (San Francisco: R. L. Bernier, 1916), 84.

25. Michael Williams, "A Pageant of American Art," *Art and Progress* (August 1915): 338.

26. Nancy Boas, *The Society of Six: California Colorists* (San Francisco: Bedford Arts, 1988), 71.

27. John P. Young, *Journalism in California: Pacific Coast and Exposition Biographies* (San Francisco: Chronicle Publishing Co., 1915), 328.

28. John E. D. Trask, "The Influence of World's Fairs on the Development of Art," *Art and Progress* (February 1915): 116.

29. Annie Wilde, "Final Instructions Being Absorbed by Students," *San Francisco Chronicle*, November 28, 1915, 20.

CHAPTER 13

1. Elizabeth Platt Dietrick, *Best Bits of the Panama-Pacific International Exposition and San Francisco* (San Francisco: Galen Publishing Co., 1915), 27.

2. Fred Ferguson, "Interesting Sights at Great Exposition," *Springfield [Massachusetts] Daily News*, July 16, 1915, 24.

3. Fremont Wood, "The 'Zone' with Its Sixty-five Acres of Fun," *American Building Association News* (June 1915): 272.

4. George Randolph Chester and Lillian Chester, "The Fun of the Thing," *Colorado Springs Gazette*, February 28, 1915, 7.

5. "Frank Burt[,] Boss of Concessions," *San Francisco Chronicle*, October 17, 1912, 2.

6. Todd, *Story of the Exposition*, vol. 3, 173–175, 370 (see ch. 1, n. 2).

7. Todd, *Story of the Exposition*, vol. 2, 155 (see ch. 1, n. 2).

8. Edward Weitzel, "The Making of a Masterpiece," *The Moving Picture World* (September 30, 1916): 2084.

9. Jim Heimann, *California Crazy and Beyond: Roadside Vernacular Architecture* (San Francisco: Chronicle Books, 2001), 24.

10. "Gettysburg, Best of All War Pictures," *Riverside [California] Daily Press*, September 6, 1915, 8.

11. Richard H. Barry, *Snapshots on the Midway: Pan-American Exposition* (Buffalo: Robert Allan Reid, 1901), 44.

12. J. B. Eldridge, "Striking Impressions of San Francisco Exposition," *Idaho Statesman*, October 1, 1915, 3.

13. Panama-Pacific International Exposition Editorial Bureau, "Exposition 'Zone' Is Palace of Infinite Jest: Joy Lane at San Francisco Fair Is a World Wonder," California History Room, California State Library, 2.

14. "Germans Protest on Zone Feature," *Riverside [California] Daily Press*, September 9, 1915, 1.

15. Helen Eells Vandevere, "Recording by Helen Eells Vandevere of Her Life Story," unpublished audiocassette, Vandevere Family Collection, 1979.

16. "The Funfest of the Fair," *Kansas City Star*, March 8, 1915, 16.

17. *Peoples Easy Guide of the Panama Pacific International Exposition* (International Exhibition Bureau, Ltd., 1915), 13.

18. Waldemar Young, "Bits of Color," *San Francisco Chronicle*, July 19, 1915, 14.

19. "Guide to the Joy Zone," Donald G. Larson World's Fair Collection, Henry Madden Library, California State University, Fresno, 2.

20. *San Francisco Blue Book* (San Francisco: Smith-Hoag, 1915), xxxi.

21. Helen Dare, "While on the Subject of Subnormal Babies," *San Francisco Chronicle*, November 20, 1915, 5.

22. *Peoples Easy Guide of the Panama Pacific International Exposition*, 21 (see ch. 13, n. 17).

23. *San Francisco Blue Book*, xxviii (see ch. 13, n. 20).

24. Wood, "The 'Zone' with Its Sixty-five Acres of Fun," 273 (see ch. 13, n. 3).

25. *Peoples Easy Guide of the Panama Pacific International Exposition*, 14 (see ch. 13, n. 17).

26. "Letter to Wm. Waters Re: 'Kick' Bowls of Joy," April 5, 1915, Bancroft 63:48, 1.

27. Helen Dare, "To Be Too Modern for Her Menfolks—Zaehaeie's Fate," *San Francisco Chronicle*, March 23, 1915, 7.

28. E. C. Conroy, "Final Report on Admissions," December 5, 1915, Daniel E. Koshland San Francisco History Center, San Francisco Public Library, 15.

29. "Busy Days Seen Before Fair Opens," *Portland Oregonian*, February 22, 1915, 8.

30. Panama-Pacific International Exposition Editorial Bureau, "Exposition 'Zone' Is Palace of Infinite Jest," 2 (see ch. 13, n. 13).

31. United States, Government Printing Office, *Catalogue of Copyright Entries, Part 4: New Series, Volume 11* (Washington, DC: Library of Congress, 1916).

32. Walter V. Woelke, "The Battle for the Gate Receipts," *Technical World* (August 1915): 715.

33. "Letter from Brandenstein to Frank Burt," November 5, 1915, Bancroft 80:13, 1.

34. Panama-Pacific International Exposition Editorial Bureau. "Exposition 'Zone' Is Palace of Infinite Jest," 2 (see ch. 13, n. 13).

35. Frank Burt, "Report of the Director of the Division of Concessions and Admissions," December 28, 1915, Daniel E. Koshland San Francisco History Center, San Francisco Public Library, 1.

36. F. Howard Seely, "Zone Limerick," *San Francisco Chronicle*, March 14, 1915, 28.

CHAPTER 14

1. "The Music of Laughter," *Philadelphia Inquirer*, September 30, 1914, 11.

2. "Frank Burt[,] Boss of Concessions" (see ch. 13, n. 5).

3. "Joy Zone Ready to Do Its Part," *San Francisco Chronicle*, February 20, 1915, 4.

4. Macomber, *Jewel City*, 193 (see ch. 2, n. 3).

5. *San Francisco Blue Book*, xxxi (see ch. 13, n. 20).

6. Helen Dare, "Blackfeet Medicine Lodge Spectacle and Ceremonial," *San Francisco Chronicle*, June 17, 1915, 7.

7. "Red Men Here to Hold Big Pow-Wow," *San Francisco Chronicle*, June 14, 1915, 7.

8. "Blackfoot Tribesmen Favor 'Iron Horse,'" *San Francisco Chronicle*, March 28, 1915, 52.

9. Anna Blake Mezquida, "The Door of Yesterday," *Overland Monthly* (July 1915): 8.

10. Dare, "Blackfeet Medicine Lodge," 7 (see ch. 14, n. 6).

11. Esther L. Mugan, "Doing the Zone at San Francisco," *Santa Fe Magazine* (August 1915): 37.

12. Todd, *Story of the Exposition*, vol. 2, 375 (see ch. 1, n. 2).

13. Eveleth, "Panama-Pacific Exposition Notes," 341 (see ch. 8, n. 33).

14. "Guide to the Joy Zone," Donald G. Larson World's Fair Collection, Henry Madden Library, California State University, Fresno, 5.

15. "Dramatic Art and the Exposition," *California Outlook* (March 6, 1915): 8.

16. Chinese Consolidated Benevolent Association, "Letter to C. C. Moore," March 19, 1915, Bancroft 64:32, 2.

17. Chen Chi, "Letter to C. C. Moore," March 19, 1915, Bancroft 64:32, 2–3.

18. Charles C. Moore, "Letter to Ch'en Ch'i," March 21, 1915, Bancroft 64:32, 1.

19. "Grauman Hopes to Reopen," *San Francisco Chronicle*, March 28, 1915, 40.

20. Mugan, "Doing the Zone," 39 (see ch. 14, n. 11).

21. PPIE Photo Album, Anne T. Kent California Room, Marin County Free Library, A1919.003.072.

22. "Guide to the Joy Zone," 12 (see ch. 14, n. 14).

23. Panama-Pacific International Exposition Editorial Bureau, "Exposition 'Zone' Is Palace of Infinite Jest," 6 (see ch. 13, n. 13).

24. Bascom Johnson, "Moral Conditions in San Francisco and at the Panama-Pacific Exposition," *Social Hygiene* (September 1915): 590.

25. A. P. Taylor, "Letters to Moore," August 5, 1915, and August 13, 1915, Bancroft 64:18.

26. Zeynep Çelik, *Displaying the Orient: Architecture of Islam at Nineteenth-Century World's Fairs* (Berkeley: University of California Press, 1992), 24.

27. F. S. Brittain, "Letter to Frank Burt re: Cairo Café," August 19, 1915, Bancroft 64:6, 1.

28. "Letter from 'A Heart-Broken Mother,'" August 15, 1915, Bancroft 80:27, 1.

29. Zarefa Maloof, "Letter to Exposition Board," August 18, 1915, Bancroft 80:27, 1.

30. [Anonymous businessman,] "Letter to O'Neil," October 8, 1915, Bancroft 80:27, 3.

31. "The European War and the Panama-Pacific Exposition—A Monumental Contrast," *Current Opinion* (May 1915): 318.

32. "The Fun of the Thing," *Colorado Springs Gazette*, February 28, 1915, 7.

33. "Famous Forty-Nine Camp of Midwinter Fair Is Reproduced in All Its Picturesqueness for Panama-Pacific Exposition," *San Francisco Chronicle*, January 16, 1915, 20.

34. "Moral Conditions in San Francisco," *Social Hygiene* (September 1915): 598.

35. "Where Are the '49ers?" *The Wasp* (March 6, 1915): 9.

36. "Oh Joy! '49 Camp Opens Again; Naughty Features Eliminated," *Oakland Tribune*, March 13, 1915, 18.

37. James W. Coffroth, "Letter to H. D. H. Connick," September 1, 1915, Bancroft 63:18, 1.

38. Matt Sullivan, "Letter to Board of Directors of the Panama-Pacific International Exposition," September 21, 1915, Bancroft 33:47, 1.

39. "Taming the Animals," *Oakland Tribune*, September 22, 1915, 8.

40. Julia George, "Letter to Charles C. Moore," July 16, 1915, Bancroft 64:6, 1.

41. "Lid Clamped Down on Frisco Exposition," *Springfield [Massachusetts] Daily News*, October 29, 1915, 12.

42. Frank Burt, "Report of the Director of the Division of Concessions and Admissions," 10 (see ch. 13, n. 35).

43. Ibid., 11–12.

44. "Zip Extracted from the Zone at the Exposition," *Ann Arbor News*, October 27, 1915, 5.

CHAPTER 15

1. "Exposition's Finances Are in Good Condition," *San Francisco Chronicle*, June 2, 1915, 2.

2. "Comprehensive Music Plans for 1915 Exposition," *Piano Magazine* (February 1914): 77.

3. David Rowland Francis, *The Universal Exposition of 1904* (St. Louis: Louisiana Purchase Exposition Company, 1913), 192.

4. Louis Levy, *Chronological History of the Panama-Pacific International Exposition*, vol. 3 (San Francisco: Panama Pacific International Exposition Co., 1915), 33.

5. Ibid., 155.

6. Ibid., 165–169.

7. Ibid., August 25, 1915, 171.

8. Ibid., September 1915, 177.

9. Ibid., January 5, 1915, 339.

10. A. Holmes-Dallimore, "Letter to Stewart," September 11, 1915, Bancroft 80:42.

11. Walter Anthony, "Paris Sends Her Gayest Composer," *San Francisco Chronicle*, March 2, 1915, 4.

12. Alfred Metzger, "Boston Symphony Orchestra Reveals Essence of Symphonic Art," *Pacific Coast Musical Review* (May 22, 1915): 1.

13. Levy, *Chronological History*, 339 (see ch. 15, n. 4).

14. Walter Anthony, "Great Music in Festival Hall," *San Francisco Chronicle*, March 7, 1915, 14.

15. "Boston Symphony Orchestra's Triumph," Bancroft 82:6, 1.

16. Macomber, *Jewel City*, 143 (see ch. 2, n. 3).

17. "Expert Praises Local Musicians," *San Francisco Chronicle*, March 14, 1915, 16.

18. "Music Thrills Great Audience," *San Francisco Chronicle*, March 16, 1915, 18.

19. Ibid.

20. James Crawford, "Musical Program of the Panama-Pacific International Exposition," *Pacific Coast Musical Review* (February 20, 1915): 1.

21. Ben Macomber, "Stories of the Exposition," *San Francisco Chronicle*, February 21, 1915, 28.

22. "Great Organ to Sing Hallelujah," *San Francisco Chronicle*, February 14, 1915, 16.

23. "Clarence Eddy, a Great Organist," *Pacific Coast Musical Review* (March 6, 1915): 1.

24. "Mishap Mars Melody at Concert," *San Francisco Chronicle*, June 28, 1915, 33.

25. Walter Anthony, "Italian Music Is Interpreted by Orchestra," *San Francisco Chronicle*, May 22, 1915, 6.

26. "Saint-Saens to Visit Exposition," *Pacific Coast Musical Review* (March 20, 1915): 8.

27. "'Hail, California' Is History in Music,'" *San Francisco Chronicle*, June 20, 1915, 73.

28. "Steeb Bewitches Exposition Piano," *San Francisco Chronicle*, March 10, 1915, 4.

29. John Philip Sousa, *Marching Along* (Boston: Hale, Cushman and Flint, 1928), 304.

30. "Victor Herbert a Baton Wizard," *San Francisco Chronicle*, November 2, 1915, 8.

31. Waldemar Young, "Bits of Color," *San Francisco Chronicle*, November 14, 1915, 22.

32. "Wails of Alcatraz Foghorn Vanquish Conductor Herbert," *San Francisco Chronicle*, November 5, 1915, 1.

33. George Stewart, "Letter to the Sub-Committee," August 3, 1915, Bancroft 84:21, 2.

34. Macomber, *Jewel City*, 143 (see ch. 2, n. 3).

35. "'Let the Children Come in Free, Says Great Diva,'" *San Francisco Chronicle*, March 26, 1915, 7.

36. "Musicians in Massed Band at Exposition," *San Francisco Chronicle*, September 28, 1915, 3.

37. "Red Men Here to Hold Big Pow-Wow," 7 (see ch. 14, n. 7).

38. Marie-Françoise Christout and Barbara Palfy, "Review: Loïe Fuller, The Dancing Muse of the Belle Époque," *Dance Chronicle* 19, no. 2 (1995): 216.

39. "Display Ad: La Loïe Fuller and Her Marvelous Company," *San Francisco Chronicle*, May 30, 1915, 19.

40. Levy, *Chronological History*, January 11, 1915, 271 (see ch. 15, n. 4).

41. "Exposition Orchestra Contract," 1915, Bancroft 82:23, 1.

42. "Paderewski Arouses Monster Audience to Enthusiasm," *Pacific Coast Musical Review* (August 28, 1915): 1.

43. W. W. B. Seymour, "Kreisler's Violin Sings Sorrow of War," *San Diego Union*, October 4, 1915, 5.

44. "Letter to Grace Bonner Williams," August 31, 1915, Bancroft 84:21, 1.

45. "Press Release on Edwin Lemare," May 4, 1915, Bancroft 83:23.

46. "Cablegram from Edwin Lemare to Stewart," May 8, 1915, Bancroft 83:23, 1.

47. "Letter from Edwin Lemare to Stewart," June 14, 1915, Bancroft 83:23, 1.

48. "Shipboard Letter from Edwin Lemare to Stewart," August 10, 1915, Bancroft 83:23, Lemare, Edwin.

49. "Music Is Thrilling," *Portland Oregonian*, November 11, 1915, 5.

50. "Press Release on Edwin Lemare," 2 (see ch. 15, n. 45).

51. "Beethoven Festival of Music Proves Unqualified Success," *Pacific Coast Musical Review* (August 14, 1915): 8.

52. Mary Lawton, *Schumann-Heink: The Last of the Titans* (New York: The Macmillan Company, 1928), 269.

53. Alfred Metzger, "Music at the Exposition," *Pacific Coast Musical Review* (September 25, 1915): 5.

54. Ibid.

55. Anthony, "Great Music in Festival Hall," 14 (see ch. 15, n. 14).

56. Ibid.

57. Alfred Metzger, "Exposition Orchestra Proves Artistic Success in Third Month," *Pacific Coast Musical Review* (May 8, 1915): 1.

58. "Highways and Byways of Music All Converge on San Francisco," *Portland Oregonian*, August 8, 1915, 4.

CHAPTER 16

1. "Australia Today Dedicates Her Palace," *San Francisco Chronicle*, March 10, 1915, 2.

2. "Letter to E. B. Burchett from George Stewart," April 18, 1914, Bancroft 80:47, 1.

3. "Letter from Stewart to Levison Regarding Fanciulli," December 15, 1914, Bancroft 81:1, 1.

4. "Letter from Stewart to Anderson," December 30, 1913, Bancroft 80:46, 1.

5. "Letter from Walter H. Loving to Stewart," April 28, 1915, Bancroft 81:12, 1.

6. Waldemar Young, "Bits of Color," *San Francisco Chronicle*, August 31, 1915, 14.

7. Roger D. Cunningham, "The Loving Touch: Walter H. Loving's Five Decades of Military Music," *Army History* (Summer 2007): 15

8. "Came Here to Honor Taft," *Colorado Springs Gazette*, August 29, 1909, 20.

9. Elting E. Morison, ed., *The Letters of Theodore Roosevelt*, vol. 6 (Cambridge: Harvard University Press, 1952), 1365.

10. "Letter to Chief of Department of Events," April 18, 1915, Bancroft 81:12, 1.

11. Todd, *Story of the Exposition*, vol. 2, 407 (see ch. 1, n. 2).

12. "Letter from Levison to Stewart re: French Band," April 16, 1915, Bancroft 81:39, 1.

13. Ibid., April 22, 1915.

14. Ibid., April 23, 1915.

15. "Letter from John Philip Sousa," April 19, 1915, Bancroft, 81:15, 1.

16. "Letter to J. R. Wheelock," January 5, 1914, Bancroft 81:17, 1.

17. "Great Week at Pan-Am," *Hornellsville [New York] Evening Tribune*, July 29, 1901, 1.

18. "Letter to Stewart from C. E. Lindall," February 26, 1914, Bancroft 81:7, 1.

19. Alfred Metzger, "American Composers' Day Proves Artistic Triumph at Exposition," *Pacific Coast Musical Review* (August 7, 1915): 8.

20. Ibid., n.p.

21. "Red Man's Songs to Mingle with Melody of Wales," *San Francisco Chronicle*, July 11, 1915, 24.

22. Michael Pisani, *Imagining Native America in Music* (New Haven: Yale University Press, 2005), 212.

23. "Massed Bands Tell History of Country in Tonal Pictures," *San Francisco Chronicle*, June 18, 1915, 3.

24. "World of Children to Sing at the Panama Pacific International Exposition," *Piano Magazine* (May 1914): 229.

25. "Dixie Land on the Amusement Zone," *Weekly Press* (Beaver City, Utah), May 28, 1915, 5.

26. Eveleth, "Panama-Pacific Exposition Notes," 342 (see ch. 8, n. 33).

27. A. J. Bloom and Sam Harrison, *In San Francisco, the Fair Will Be the Best*, sheet music (Oakland: Southwest Music Publishing Co., 1910).

28. "Missouri Will Dedicate Today," *San Francisco Chronicle*, March 13, 1915, 11.

29. "Official Marches for United States Proposed to Sousa," *San Francisco Chronicle*, July 22, 1915, 1.

CHAPTER 17

1. Frances A. Groff, "Sugar on the Candy," *Sunset* (October 1915): 749.

2. Ibid., 750.

3. "Fall of Babylon Tonight," *Ann Arbor News*, October 2, 1915, 2.

4. "Tower of Jewels Wreathed in Flames," *San Francisco Chronicle,* April 20, 1915, 4.

5. "Nine Years After Program," April 1915, Bancroft 84:19, 3.

6. "The Illness of the Liberty Bell," *Literary Digest* (March 13, 1915): 543.

7. "Great Crowd Swayed by Orator," *San Francisco Chronicle,* July 18, 1915, 32.

8. Todd, *Story of the Exposition,* vol. 3, 159 (see ch. 1, n. 2).

9. "San Francisco Day at the Exposition," *San Francisco Chronicle,* November 1, 1915, 14.

10. "Supreme Bojum Greets Hoo-Hoos," *San Francisco Chronicle,* September 10, 1915, 9.

11. "Lumberman's Building," *Western Architect* (September 1915): 25.

12. Todd, *Story of the Exposition,* vol. 2, 387 (see ch. 1, n. 2).

13. Helen Dare, "Now Sconing, with the Exposition, Also Ends," *San Francisco Chronicle,* December 5, 1915, 19.

14. "Philately at the Fair," *Mekeel's Weekly Stamp News* (December 4, 1915): 420.

15. Dare, "Now Sconing" (see ch. 17, n. 13).

16. "Call Quarantine a Trick," *Kansas City Star,* October 5, 1915, 3.

17. James A. Buchanan, ed. *History of the Panama-Pacific International Exposition,* 384 (see ch. 7, n. 9).

18. "Milkmaids Are Floored by Cows," *San Francisco Chronicle,* October 24, 1915, 35.

19. *Official Catalogue of Exhibitors: Panama-Pacific International Exposition* (San Francisco: The Wahlgreen Company, 1915), 248.

20. Ben Macomber, "Garden Exhibits Intended to Educate Public Taste," *San Francisco Chronicle,* June 25, 1915, 28.

21. "Excellent Work of Quarantine Service at Exposition," *California Fruit News* (November 6, 1915): 4.

22. "Notable Exhibits at the Exposition," *Pacific Rural Press,* April 24, 1915, 499.

23. "Medal Is Presented to Luther Burbank," *San Francisco Chronicle,* June 6, 1915, 36.

24. William F. Benedict, "Nineteen-fifteen[:] A Year of Contrasts," *San Francisco Chronicle,* January 12, 1916, 2.

CHAPTER 18

1. "Full Authority for Exposition," *San Francisco Chronicle,* April 16, 1914, 20.

2. *Thirty Days at the Panama-Pacific Exposition* (San Francisco: The Owl Drug Co., 1915), 45.

3. Julia Davis Chandler, "The Panama-Pacific Exposition," *American Cookery* (June–July 1915): 21.

4. "Exposition Hospital Treats 112 Cases," *San Francisco Chronicle,* December 5, 1915, 29.

5. "1915 Human Lost Bureau Planned," *San Francisco Chronicle,* May 19, 1914, 5.

6. "International Exhibit: Traveler's Aid," pamphlet (Panama-Pacific International Exposition San Francisco, 1915), 2.

7. "San Francisco Woman's Board Is Indignant," *Idaho Statesman,* June 5, 1915, 5.

8. *Thirty Days at the Panama-Pacific Exposition,* 39 (see ch. 18, n. 2).

9. "YWCA at Exposition," *Riverside [California] Daily Press,* June 12, 1915, 8.

10. "YWCA at the Fair," *The Key* (February 1916):15.

11. James A. Buchanan, ed. *History of the Panama-Pacific International Exposition,* 456 (see ch. 7, n. 9).

12. "YWCA Subscription Reaches Total of $2,718," *Colorado Springs Gazette,* November 7, 1915, 7.

13. E. C. Conroy, "Final Report on Admissions," December 5, 1915, Daniel E. Koshland San Francisco History Center, San Francisco Public Library, 15.

14. Ibid.

15. W. F. Sesser, "Letter to Frank Burt," April 24, 1915, Bancroft 63:31, 1.

16. "Pinkerton Here to Curb Crooks," *San Francisco Chronicle,* February 8, 1915, 12.

17. "Amazon Is to Arrest 'Mashers'; Will Protect Women at the Fair," *Riverside [California] Daily Press,* February 20, 1915, 3.

18. Diana Serra Cary, telephone interview with the author, March 21, 2012.

19. Ed Herny, telephone interview with the author, January 12, 2014.

20. Todd, *Story of the Exposition,* vol. 4, 119 (see ch. 1, n. 2).

21. Jay Stevens, telephone interview with the author, December 20, 2013.

22. "Reception Is Tendered Fair's Stockholders," *San Jose Mercury News,* February 24, 1915, 1.

23. "East Bay Cities Slip Under Tent," *Reno Evening Gazette,* March 20, 1915, 1.

24. Ella Costillo Bennett, "Knocks from the Iconoclast," *The Wasp* (April 3, 1915): 3.

25. "San Francisco's Achievement Lauded," *San Francisco Chronicle,* December 13, 1915, 4.

26. "The Official Herald," *Highway Magazine* (November 1913).

27. "Along the Color Line," *The Crisis* (December 1915): 61.

28. "The Official Herald" (see ch. 18, n. 26).

CHAPTER 19

1. Frank Morton Todd, *The Lights Go Out: An Account of the Closing Exercises of the Panama-Pacific International Exposition* (San Francisco: Blair-Murdock Company, December 1915), 2.

2. "Programme at Exposition To Be Duplicated," *San Francisco Chronicle,* December 1, 1915, 11.

3. *Closing Day Program,* December 4, 1915 (San Francisco: The Wahlgreen Company), 25.

4. Fremont Wood, "'The End of a Perfect Day'—Passing of San Francisco's Big Fair," *American Building Association News* (December 1915): 553.

5. M. H. de Young, "What Can We Save Out of the Exposition?" *San Francisco Chronicle,* August 21, 1915, 16.

6. "Fair Buildings Tottering on Oblivion's Brink," *Idaho Statesman,* August 20, 1923, 2.

7. "Repair Column or Remove It, Is Ultimatum," *San Francisco Chronicle,* November 14, 1922, 7.

8. Wood, "'The End of a Perfect Day,'" 551 (see ch. 19, n. 4).

9. F. Robertson Jones, ed., *History and Proceedings of the World's Insurance Congress* (San Francisco: Central Committee of the National Insurance Council, 1915), 546.

10. Ibid., 550–551.

11. Juliet James, *The Pastel City by the Sea* (San Francisco: Ricardo J. Orozco Press, January 1915), 8.

EXPLANATION OF SOURCES

For this work I have drawn from thousands of sources, most of them contemporary to the Exposition. To streamline the citations and prevent repetition, quoted sources appear in the endnotes while other major sources are collected here.

ESSENTIAL SOURCES

PANAMA-PACIFIC INTERNATIONAL EXPOSITION RECORDS, BANCROFT LIBRARY

Authoritative documentation was gleaned from the official business records of the PPIE, which are held at the Bancroft Library, located on the campus of the University of California, Berkeley. The collection is officially designated:

BANC MSS C-A 190, Panama Pacific International Exposition Records, 1893–1929, bulk 1911–1916.

Sources from cartons in this collection are cited below by carton number, folder number, and page—for example: "Bancroft 56:35, 1." Where bound volumes from the collection are referenced, the citation will read "Bancroft vol. (volume number)."

KEY TEXTS

A number of sources that are used in the majority of this book's chapters deserve special mention. These are:

Barry, John D. *The City of Domes: A Walk with an Architect about the Courts and Palaces of the Panama-Pacific International Exposition*. San Francisco: John J. Newbegin, 1915.

Bayley, Guy L. "Engineering Features of the Panama-Pacific International Exposition." *Journal of the American Society of Mechanical Engineers* (October 1915): 571–591.

Bernier, R. L., ed. *California's Magazine: Edition De Luxe*. 2 vols. San Francisco: California's Magazine Company, 1916.

Buchanan, James A., ed. *History of the Panama-Pacific International Exposition*. San Francisco: Pan-Pacific Press Association, Ltd., 1916.

James, Juliet. *Palaces and Courts of the Exposition*. San Francisco: H. S. Crocker Company, 1915.

Jordan, Frank C., comp. *California Blue Book or State Roster, 1913–1915*. Sacramento: California State Printing Office, 1915.

Levy, Louis. *Chronological History of the Panama-Pacific International Exposition*. 3 vols. San Francisco: Panama Pacific International Exposition Co., 1915.

Macomber, Ben. *The Jewel City: Its Planning and Achievement; Its Architecture, Sculpture, Symbolism, and Music; Its Gardens, Palaces, and Exhibits*. San Francisco: John H. Williams, 1915.

Neuhaus, Eugen. *The Art of the Exposition*. San Francisco: Paul Elder and Company, 1915.

Perry, Stella G. S. *Sculpture and Murals of the Panama-Pacific International Exposition*. San Francisco: The Wahlgreen Company, 1915.

Perry, Stella G. S. *The Sculpture and Mural Decorations of the Exposition*. Introduction by A. Stirling Calder. San Francisco: Paul Elder and Company, 1915.

Raymond, Maud Wotring. *The Architecture and Landscape Gardening of the Exposition*. Introduction by Louis Christian Mullgardt. San Francisco: Paul Elder and Company, 1915.

Strother, French. "The Panama-Pacific International Exposition." *World's Work* (July 1915): 337.

Todd, Frank Morton. *The Story of the Exposition*. 5 vols. New York: G. P. Putnam's Sons, 1921.

Wickson, E. J., ed. *California's Magazine*. Vol. 1. San Francisco: California Publishers Co-operative Association, 1915.

PRINCIPAL PERIODICALS

Several magazines covered development of and events at the Fair extensively between 1909 and 1915. Details mentioned in the book were found in hundreds of articles from the *San Francisco Municipal Record, Sunset, Overland Monthly, Review of Reviews, World's Work, Scientific American,* and *Scribner's*. Local newspapers provided invaluable, if sometimes highly politicized accounts; among them are San Francisco's *Chronicle, Examiner,* and *Call* and other Bay Area newspapers including the *Oakland Tribune, Sausalito News,* and *San Jose Mercury-News*

MONETARY VALUES

Unless otherwise noted, all post-Fair financial results were found in Frank Darrell, *Panama-Pacific International Exposition Company Final Financial Report* (San Francisco: Lester Herrick and Herrick, General Auditors, 1920).

All modern comparative valuations were determined using the relevant calculator (real price, real value, or labor value) at www.measuringworth.com/uscompare/.

SELECTED CHAPTER SOURCES

In addition to the sources above, each chapter draws from specialized sources relevant to its content. These are as follows:

CHAPTER 1: FAIR FIGHT: THE BATTLE FOR THE 1915 EXPOSITION

Along with the Northern California periodicals listed under "Principal Periodicals" above, this chapter draws extensively from newspapers and magazines nationwide that covered San Francisco's recovery from the 1906 disaster and the contest to host the 1915 world's fair. These include the *Los Angeles Herald, New Orleans Times-Picayune,* and *New York Times*. Other key sources include:

Hall, William Hammond. "The Panama-Pacific International Exposition Site: A Review of the Proposition to Use a Part of Golden Gate Park." April 25, 1911. Bancroft 32:24, 9–14.

Kendall, John Smith. *History of New Orleans*, vol. 2, p. 561. Chicago and New York: The Lewis Publishing Company, 1922.

"List of Costs for Sites." 1911. Bancroft 32:11.

Manson, Marsden. *Report on Harbor View*. San Francisco: 1911.

Manson, Marsden (Assumed), City Engineer. "Report on Golden Gate Park." San Francisco: 1911.

McCullough, David. *The Path between the Seas: The Creation of the Panama Canal, 1870–1914*, pp. 394, 402. New York: Simon and Schuster, 1981.

"Minutes, Buildings and Grounds Committee." Bancroft vol. 119.

Moore, Charles C. "Telegram to James McNab." January 4, 1912. Bancroft 61:36.

Salfield, C. D. "Letter in Response to William Hammond Hall." 1911. Bancroft 32:13.

"Seven Places Advocated for Many Reasons." *San Francisco Call,* February 2, 1911, 2.

United States. Thirteenth Census of the United States. Washington, DC: Government Printing Office, 1910.

Winchester, Simon. *A Crack in the Edge of the World: America and the Great California Earthquake of 1906,* pp. 301–302. New York: Harper Perennial, 2006.

CHAPTER 2: ENVISIONING THE EPHEMERAL CITY

Bancroft cartons 16 and 17 include correspondence concerning the architectural organization and development of the fair. Cartons 23 and 24 and volumes 115 to 121 contain minutes of the Buildings and Grounds Committee, which provide insight into the land acquisition, preparation, and planning. Other key sources include:

"Art and Nature Personified." *Pacific Coast Architect* (February 1915): 51.

Burnham, Daniel H., and Edward H. Bennett. *Report on a Plan for San Francisco.* San Francisco: City of San Francisco, 1905.

Connick, Harris. "Letter Regarding Porter Garnett." August 14, 1914. Bancroft 56:41.

Croy, Homer. "Making Statues for a Great Exposition." *Leslie's Magazine* (April 30, 1914).

De Bille, Waldemar. "Panama-Pacific Exposition Buildings." *Building Age* (August 1914): 58.

DeMars, Vernon. *A Life in Architecture: Indian Dancing, Migrant Housing, Telesis, Design for Urban Living, Theater, Teaching,* p. xvi. Oral history conducted in 1988–1989 by Suzanne B. Riess, Regional Oral History Office, Bancroft Library, University of California, Berkeley, 1992.

Francis, David Rowland. *The Universal Exposition of 1904.* St. Louis: Louisiana Purchase Exposition Company, 1913.

Hastings, Thomas. "Architecture at the Panama-Pacific Exposition, 1915." *Architectural Record* (February 1914): 171.

"The Important Part Played by Pacific Service in Furnishing Gas and Electricity to the Panama-Pacific Exposition." *Pacific Service Magazine* (January 1916): 260.

"Karl Bitter." *The Outlook* (New York, NY), April 21, 1915, 904.

"Karl Bitter Felled by Auto." *New York Times,* April 10, 1915.

Leurey, L. F. "Soft-Ground Foundations, Panama-Pacific International Exposition." *Engineering News* (July 30, 1914): 254.

McAdie, Alexander. "Letter to Architectural Board." February 20, 1912. Bancroft 64:51.

McHenry, Katherine V. "Color Scheme at the Pan-American." *Brush and Pencil* (June 1901): 151.

McLaren, Donald. "Gardening Features of the Panama-Pacific International Exposition." *Pacific Service Magazine* (July 1914).

McLaren, Donald. "Landscape Gardening at the Exposition." *Pacific Coast Architect* (July 1915): 13.

"The New San Francisco: Fire Hastens the 'Dream City.'" *Springfield [Massachusetts] Republican,* April 29, 1906, 13.

"Noting Progress of the World's Fair." *Pacific Gas & Electric Magazine* (July 1912): 68.

"Panama-Pacific Exposition: Some of the Horticultural Features." *American Florist* 45 (August 14, 1915): 149.

Peterson, Charles. "A Visit with Bernard Maybeck." *Journal of the Society of Architectural Historians* (October 1952): 31.

"Plaster Statuary Is Being Placed." *Engineering News* (August 27, 1914): 458.

Schevill, Ferdinand. *Karl Bitter: A Biography,* p. 56. Chicago: University of Chicago Press, 1917.

Schnaittacher, Silvain. "San Francisco Chapter Fails to Indorse World's Fair Commission." *Architect and Engineer of California* (October 1911): 100.

"Tramps Start Fire." *San Francisco Call,* February 2, 1913, 21.

Wright, Hamilton. "Mural Decorations at the Panama-Pacific International Exposition." *California's Magazine* 2 (1916): 313.

CHAPTER 3: BUILDING THE DREAM

The *San Francisco Municipal Record* followed the Fair's construction in its dedicated "Panama-Pacific Exposition Notes" column between 1913 and 1915. Bancroft carton 62 illuminates the development of the mural decorations and problems with the toilets concession. Carton 159 includes details on creating many of the Joy Zone concessions. *Pacific Service Magazine,* the corporate periodical of Pacific Gas & Electric, covers many of the technical aspects of the Exposition in its 1913–1916 editions. Other key sources include:

Arnold, Bion J. "Development of Transit System Part 1: Transportation Facilities for Panama-Pacific Exposition at Harbor View." City of San Francisco, Board of Supervisors, 1912.

Cashin, T. A. "Improvements in Transit Lines to Handle Exposition Traffic." *Electric Railway Journal* (September 11, 1915): 518.

"The Cobwell Garbage Reduction Process." *Engineering News* (December 24, 1914): 1249.

Dewell, H. D. "Tests of Some Joints Used in Heavy Timber Framing." *Engineering News* (March 19, 1914): 593.

Evermann, Barton W. "Steinhart Aquarium, California." *American Angler* (May 1920): 19.

"Exploiting Childhood." *Collier's Weekly* (November 15, 1913): 13.

"Fake Alleged in Childhood Temple." *New Orleans Item,* December 4, 1913.

"The Fire at the Exposition." *World's Columbian Exposition Illustrated* (August 1893): 160.

French, Daniel Chester. "Letter to Alexander S. Calder, Esq." February 5, 1915. Chesterwood Archives Microfilm, Chapin Library, Williams College, Williamstown, MA.

Hanvey, Howard G. "Safeguarding a Fifty-Million Dollar Exposition from Fire." *The Spectator* (June 10, 1915): 39.

Harris, Frank. "Design and Construction of the 435-ft. Steel Framed Tower of Jewels at the Panama-Pacific International Exposition." *Engineering and Contracting* (January 20, 1915): 54.

"Hope to Have Separate Building for Autos at Panama Exposition." *The Club Journal* (April 26, 1913): 39.

Markwart, Arthur H. "The Organization and Description of the Panama-Pacific International Exposition." July 30, 1913. Bancroft 16:28, 94.

Markwart, Arthur H. "Engineering Problems of the Panama-Pacific Exposition." *Engineering News* (February 18, 1915).

McBirney, Alexander. "Telephone System of the Panama-Pacific Exposition." *Telephony* (January 2, 1915): 30.

McLaren, John. "California's Opportunities in Artistic Landscaping." *California's Magazine* 2 (1916): 142.

"Municipal Street Railways." *Engineering News* (February 18, 1915): 320.

Official Handbook (Pre-Exposition Period) of the Panama-Pacific International Exposition—1915, p. 25. San Francisco: The Wahlgreen Company, 1914.

"Orange Blossoms Bloom." *The International Confectioner* (June 1914): 49.

"Photograph Plan Has Opposition." *Harrisburg [Pennsylvania] Patriot,* November 11, 1913, 5.

Polk, Willis. "The Panama-Pacific Plan." *Sunset* (April 1912): 489.

"San Francisco's First Municipal Tunnel." *Western Architect and Engineer* (April 1915): 118.

Spalding, A. W. "The Construction and Architecture of the Panama-Pacific International Exposition." *Technology Monthly* (May 1914).

"Two-Car Trains on 25 Per Cent Grade." *Electric Railway Journal* (May 22, 1914): 977.

Wright, Hamilton. "Miracle Workers of the Exposition." *California's Magazine* 1, (1916): 6.

CHAPTER 4: A GLOBAL COURTSHIP

The Daniel E. Koshland San Francisco History Center at the San Francisco Public Library holds several of the directors' final reports for the PPIE that yield excellent assessments of the Exhibits, Admissions, and Exploitation departments. Bancroft carton 7 contains detailed reports of the Commission Extraordinary to Europe, and carton 63 has information about the debate over the Inside Inn. Other key sources include:

"10,000 Athletes for San Francisco." *New York Times,* March 24, 1914.

"Advertising the Great Fair." *Chicago Commerce* (July 24, 1914): 41.

City and County of San Francisco. *Municipal Record,* p. 87. March 13, 1913.

Daniels, Roger. *The Politics of Prejudice: The Anti-Japanese Movement in California and the Struggle for Japanese Exclusion.* Berkeley: University of California Press, 1977.

"A Diesel Engine the First Exhibit in Machinery Palace at San Francisco Fair." *Industrial World* (June 8, 1914): 669.

"England May Reconsider Action and Send Exhibit." *Idaho Statesman,* December 1, 1913, 1.

"England Warned of Blunder in Regard to Canal." *Idaho Statesman,* December 31, 1913, 1.

Faville, William. "A Brief Resume of the Organization under which the Architecture of the PPIE Has Been Developed." *Pacific Coast Architect* (May 1915): 176.

Hichborn, Franklin. *The Story of the Session of the California Legislature of 1913,* p. 219. San Francisco: James H. Barry Company, 1913.

"Hotels Fall Into Line." *Portland Oregonian,* December 6, 1913, 2.

"Panama Exposition Exhibits." *Iron Age* (February 5, 1914): 369.

"Phelan Optimistic." *Columbus [Georgia] Ledger,* October 30, 1913, 7.

"Rules and Regulations of the Division of Exhibits." VF Guides for Exhibitors, August 1913, p. 7, Daniel E. Koshland San Francisco History Center, San Francisco Public Library.

"San Francisco for San Franciscans." *The Wasp* (February 27, 1915): 3.

"Social Economy: How to Prepare Exhibits." VF Guides for Exhibitors, p. 4, California History Room, California State Library, Sacramento.

"Tiny Electric Trucks Handle Heavy Exposition Freight." *World's Advance* (July 1915): 2.

Van Nuys, Frank. "A Progressive Confronts the Race Question: Chester Rowell, the California Alien Land Act of 1913, and the Contradictions of Early Twentieth-Century Racial Thought." *California Historical Quarterly* (Spring 1994), 3.

"Water Is Turned into Culebra Cut." *New York Times,* October 2, 1913.

"Western Train Triumphant Success." *Idaho Statesman,* December 16, 1911, 1.

Whitaker, Herman. "A Great University—The Exposition." *The Rotarian* (June 1915): 26.

"Winning Germany for Panama Fair." *Trenton [New Jersey] Evening Times,* October 26, 1913, 27.

Wright, Hamilton. "Panama-Pacific Exposition: The Mecca of the Nation." *Overland Monthly* (September 1915): 254.

CHAPTER 5: THE EXPOSITION WILL NOT BE POSTPONED

The most detailed accounts of the *Jason's* adventures and cargo were found in the *San Francisco Chronicle*. Other key sources include:

"Aero Club Cheers News that Prize Money Is in Bank." *Philadelphia Inquirer,* March 20, 1914, 1.

"Aeronauts of Fifteen Nations to Enter Airship Race around the World." *Riverside [California] Independent Enterprise,* July 9, 1914, 10.

"All American Battlers Can Pass Canal in Day." *Tampa Tribune,* September 4, 1915, 9.

"Arnold Kruckman." *Cleburne [Texas] Morning Review,* July 15, 1914, 8.

"Capt. Baldwin First Entrant." *Springfield [Massachusetts] Daily News,* February 2, 1914, 1.

"Christmas Ship Sails." *Chicago Commerce* (November 20, 1914): 9.

Holanda, Ray. *A History of Aviation Safety: Featuring the U.S. Airline System.* Bloomington, IN: AuthorHouse, 2009.

"The Human Telephone." *Telephony* (June 13, 1914): 33.

"Joint Exhibit by Cincinnati Manufacturers at San Francisco." *Industrial World* (October 26, 1914): 1313.

"New Features at Panama Exposition." *Tulsa World,* April 5, 1914, 14.

Perry, George Hough. "Report of the Director of Exploitation to the President, Board of Directors and the Committee on Exploitation of the Panama-Pacific International Exposition." PPIE Exploitation: Director's Report, pp. 10–11. Daniel E. Koshland San Francisco History Center, San Francisco Public Library.

"Prizes of $300,000 Offered by Panama-Pacific Exposition to Aviators Who Girdle World." *Salt Lake Telegram,* February 2, 1914, 4.

"Programme: Preliminary Estimate of Size of Various Buildings." Bancroft 66:33, 1.

"The San Francisco Exposition." *Travel* (February 1915): 40.

"Summary of the News." *The Nation* (November 26, 1914): 617.

"Uncle Sam's Treasure Ship." *The [New York] Independent* (March 1, 1915): 206.

"War Will Not Halt Panama-Pacific Exposition." *San Jose Mercury News,* September 25, 1914, pp. 6 and 9.

"Warships Can Use Canal in Ten Days." *Evening Star* (Washington, DC), August 5, 1914, 4.

"Works of Fifty German Artists and Paintings from Nine Belligerent Countries on Way to Exposition." *Arts and Decoration* (February 1915).

CHAPTER 6: AN ARCHITECTURAL TOUR OF THE PALACES AND COURTS

The August 1915 *Transactions of the Commonwealth Club* features "Exposition Architecture," an article with revealing quotes by various PPIE architects. Bancroft carton 16 contains an important document by Arthur Markwart titled "The Organization and Description of the Panama-Pacific International Exposition." Other key sources include:

"Exposition's Architectural Beauty a New World Wonder." *San Francisco Examiner*, February 20, 1915.

Farnum, Royal B. "The 1915 Expositions." *Industrial Arts Magazine* (November 1915): 184.

Harris, Larry. "Interviewing an Exposition: Machinery Hall and Clarence R. Ward." *San Francisco Call*, November 29, 1913, 16.

"Heritage Returns to City Hall for Soiree 2000." *Heritage News* (January/February 2000): 6.

Information for the Instruction of the Exposition Guards and Guides, p. 11. San Francisco: Panama-Pacific International Exposition, 1915.

"Jean Louis Bourgeois." *Architect and Engineer of California* (March 1915): 108.

Kennedy, Thomas H. *The Devil at the Fair*, p. 9. San Francisco: Thomas Kennedy, 1915.

Knaufft, Ernest. "The Architecture of the Panama-Pacific International Exposition." *Review of Reviews* (February 1915): 170.

Macomber, Ben. "My Flesh Longest for Thee in a Dry and Thirsty Land." *San Francisco Chronicle*, April 25, 1915, 26.

Macomber, Ben. "South Gardens Form Lovely Foreground for Exposition." *San Francisco Chronicle*, May 9, 1915, 26.

Mead, William. "Letter to Willis Polk." June 11, 1912. Bancroft 66:27.

"Minutes, Buildings and Grounds Committee." October 31, 1911. Bancroft 23:1.

Press Reference Library (Western Edition). *Notables of the West*, p. 99. New York: International News Service, 1915.

"Thirtieth Annual Exhibition Architectural League of New York." *American Architect* (March 3, 1915): 150.

CHAPTER 7: A MASTERPIECE OF ILLUMINATION

Insight into the illumination program can be gleaned from the source "G-E Historical File, Publicity Department, Illumination of the Panama-Pacific International Exposition," held by the Schenectady Museum. The most authoritative source is Walter D'Arcy Ryan's paper "Illumination of the Panama-Pacific International Exposition," delivered to the Schenectady Section of the American Institute of Electrical Engineers, on May 4, 1916, in Schenectady, New York. Other key sources include:

Babcock, C. B. "The Part Gas Plays in Lighting the Panama-Pacific Exposition." *Pacific Service Magazine* (June 1915): 51.

Bayley, Guy L. "Illumination of the Panama-Pacific Exposition." *Electrical World* (February 13, 1915).

Bayley, Guy L. "Lighting the Panama-Pacific Exposition." *Pacific Service Magazine* (September 1913).

Bowers, Brian. *Lengthening the Day: A History of Lighting Technology*. Oxford: Oxford University, 1998.

"Electrical Equipment of Panama-Pacific International Exposition." *Electrical World* (December 26, 1914).

Halvorson, C. A. B., Jr., and R. B. Hussey. "Evolution of Light Projection." *Transactions of the Illuminating Engineering Society* (August 30, 1917).

"Illumination of Ohio State Capitol Building." *Electrical Review and Western Electrician* (May 15, 1915).

"Panama-Pacific Illumination." *Edison Monthly* (June 1915): 9.

Panama-Pacific International Exposition Company. *Information for the Instruction of the Exposition Guards and Guides of the Panama-Pacific International Exposition*. San Francisco: Panama-Pacific International Exposition Company, 1915.

"P.P.I.E. Engineering Constructional Features." *Journal of Electricity, Power and Gas* (October 3, 1914).

Ryan, Walter D'Arcy. "Illumination of the Panama-Pacific Exposition." *General Electric Review* (June 1915).

"Searchlights for Exposition Are Tested." *World's Advance* (January 1915): 49.

Willoughby, Arthur A. "Illumination Features of the Panama-Pacific International Exposition." *Electrical Review and Western Electrician* (June 5, 1915): 1032.

CHAPTER 8: STATE OF THE ART: 1915

In 1915, several periodicals featured extensive coverage of new technologies presented at the PPIE. These included the *Pacific Rural Press*, *World's Work*, and *World's Advance*; specific articles are cited in the notes for this chapter. In April, *Printer's Ink* ran an informative piece entitled "High Spots in the Exhibits at San Francisco Exposition." Other key sources include:

Apgar, Charles. "How I Cornered Sayville." *Wireless World* (November 1915): 518–520.

Bayley, Guy L. "The Thordarson One-Million-Volt Transformer." *Pacific Service Magazine* (April 1916).

Boyne, Walter J. *Beyond the Horizons: The Lockheed Story*. New York: St. Martin's Press, 1998.

"Current Events and Editorial Comment." *Photographic Times* (May 1915): 214.

Demonstration Mine, Panama-Pacific International Exposition. United States Bureau of Mines. New York: Read Printing Co., 1915.

Hall, George Weed. "The General Electric Company's Exhibits at the Panama-Pacific International Exposition." *General Electric Review* (June 1915).

Hardee, Theodore. "Liberal Arts." *California's Magazine*, p. 331. Edited by E. J. Wickson. San Francisco: California's Publishers Co-operative Association, 1915.

Lee, Bart. "America's Wireless Spies." Self-published, 1990.

"A Marvel of Mechanical Construction." *Typewriter Topics* (March 1915): 143.

Mudgett, F. G. "Progress of Our South Yuba–Bear River Power Developments." *Pacific Service Magazine* (July 1913): 39.

"Notes and Comment." *The Photo-Miniature* (September 1915): 452.

Nye, D. E. *Electrifying America: Social Meanings of a New Technology, 1880–1940*. Cambridge: MIT Press, 1990.

The Panama Canal at San Francisco. Booklet. San Francisco: Panama Canal Exhibition Company, 1915.

Panama Canal, Panama-Pacific International and Panama-California Expositions. Chicago: International Harvester Companies, 1915.

"The Pelton Water Wheel Exhibit at the Panama-Pacific International Exposition." *Pacific Service Magazine* (August 1915): 86.

Roberts, Russell, and Rich Youmans. *Down the Jersey Shore*. New Brunswick, NJ: Rutgers University Press, 1993.

Waterhouse, E. W. A. *Strauss Aeroscope Souvenir Booklet*. San Francisco: Johnston and Fulton, 1915.

"Zone Concessionaires Big Losers." *The Wasp* (November 20, 1915): 9.

CHAPTER 9: THE UNIVERSITY OF THE WORLD AND SHOP-WINDOW OF CIVILIZATION

Overland Monthly, Pacific Rural Press, and *World's Work* all covered the Fair's exhibits in detail throughout the year. Other key sources include:

American Gas Light Journal (April 26, 1915): 270.
American Machinist (April 8, 1915): 622.
Barr, James A. "Address of Welcome." *Journal of Education* (September 9, 1915): 212.
"California's Exposition." *Marietta [Georgia] Daily Journal,* April 16, 1915, 4.
"'Ceresit' at Frisco Fair." *American Carpenter and Builder* (June 1915): 136.
"China's Exhibit at the Panama-Pacific International Exposition." *Popular Educator* (June 1915): 586.
Conwell, Paul S. "Bleeding Kansas." *The Fra* (May 1916).
"Forty-one Educational Conventions in Two Weeks." *Western Journal of Education* (March 1915): 5.
"The Growth of Safeguarding Machinery." *American Machinist* (April 22, 1915): 687.
Honig, Louis. "High Spots in the Exhibits at San Francisco Exposition." *Printer's Ink* (April 15, 1915).
Kavanagh, D. J. *The Zi-ka-wei Orphanage,* p. 3. San Francisco: James H. Barry Company, 1915.
Laughlin, Harry Hamilton. *Eugenical Sterilization in the United States.* Chicago: Psychopathic Laboratory of the Municipal Court of Chicago, 1922.
Official Proceedings of the Second National Conference on Race Betterment. Battle Creek, MI: Race Betterment Foundation, 1915.
"Palace of Horticulture Has Many Interesting Exhibits." *California Fruit News* (June 5, 1915): 8.
"Panama-Pacific International Exposition." *Brooklyn Daily Eagle Almanac* (1916), 384.
"A Pygmy Locomotive." *Santa Fe Magazine* (February 1915): 65.
"Railway Exhibits at the Panama-Pacific Exposition." *Scientific American Supplement* (July 24, 1915): 61.
Sacramento County Exposition Commission. *Report of the Sacramento County Exposition Commissioners on Sacramento County's Participation.* Sacramento: News Publishing Co., 1916.
"Westinghouse Electric and Mfg. Company Exhibit at Panama-Pacific Exposition." *Electric Journal* (June 1915): 19.

CHAPTER 10: A WORLD TOUR WITHIN THE GOLDEN GATE

Superb analysis of the history of the ukulele can be found in Jim Tranquada and John King's *The 'Ukulele: A History* (Honolulu: University of Hawai'i Press, 2012). Information about the Hurtado Brothers can be found in David P. Eyler, "Hurtado Brothers Royal Marimba Band of Guatemala," *Percussive Notes* (February 1993). The PPIE's editor-in-chief of the exploitation department, Hamilton Wright, penned several articles mentioning the international aspects of the Fair for *National Magazine* in 1915. Other key sources include:

"American Republics at the San Francisco Exposition." *Bulletin of the Pan-American Union* (August 1915): 185.
Clark, Robert Judson. "Louis Christian Mullgardt and the Court of the Ages." *Journal of the Society of Architectural Historians* (December 1962): 173.
"Facts from Many Lands." *New York Times,* April 16, 1916.
"Guatemala Day at Exposition." *Philadelphia Inquirer,* November 21, 1915, 7.
"The 'Home of Redwood.'" *Chicago Lumberman* (January 25, 1917): 48.
Ito, B. "The Japanese Garden at the Panama-Pacific Exposition." *Architect and Engineer* (December 1914): 87.
King, John, and Jim Tranquada. "A New History of the Origins and Development of the 'Ukulele, 1838–1915." *Hawaiian Journal of History* 37 (2003): 1–34.
"A Nation in Perspective." *Scientific American Supplement* (July 10, 1915): 25.
"National Pavilions at the Panama-Pacific Exposition." *Dun's Review* (June 1915): 82.
"The Nations of the World in Friendly Rivalry." *Dun's Review* (September 1915): 53 and 54.
"The North at the Golden Gate." *American-Scandinavian Review* (July–August 1915): 220.
"Portable Houses at the Exposition." *Lumber World Review* (November 10, 1915): 50.
"Size of 1925 Fair." *Oregon Voter* (December 3, 1921): 11.
Soulas, Marie. *The French Pavilion and Its Contents,* p. 33. San Francisco: Pernau Publishing Co., 1915.
United States 63rd Congress, 2nd Session. *House Reports (Public), Report 1161: Government Exhibit, Panama-Pacific International Exposition,* p. 1. Washington, DC: Government Printing Office, September 19, 1914.
United States Treasury Department. *Digest of Appropriations for the Support of the Government of the United States,* p. 313. Washington, DC: Government Printing Office, 1915.
Virgin, P. S. "PPIE Trip Diary." July 15, 1915. Collection of Laura A. Ackley.
Wood, Dallas E. "Resources and Activities of San Joaquin Valley Displayed at the Great Exposition." *San Joaquin Light and Power Magazine* (March 1915): 128–129.

CHAPTER 11: FAMOUS AND INFAMOUS VISITORS

For more information on Audrey Munson, see Diane Rozas and Anita Bourne Gottehrer, *American Venus: The Extraordinary Life of Audrey Munson, Model and Muse* (Los Angeles: Balcony Press, 1999). For a biography of Zintkala Nuni Allen, see Renée Sansom Flood, *Lost Bird of Wounded Knee: Spirit of the Lakota* (New York: Scribner, 1995), 115. Other key sources include:

"Balloonists at Fair." *Idaho Statesman,* June 22, 1915, 6.
"Baritone Roy La Pearl to Sing at Kennywood." *The Gazette Times* (Pittsburgh, PA), August 27, 1911.
Bean, Walton. *Boss Ruef's San Francisco: The Story of the Union Labor Party, Big Business and the Graft Prosecution.* Berkeley: University of California Press, 1952, 303.
Beasley, Delilah L. *The Negro Trail Blazers of California.* Los Angeles: Delilah Beasley, 1919, 302.
Bland, T. A. *Life of Alfred B. Meacham, Together with His Lecture Tragedy of the Lava Beds,* p. 43. Washington, DC: T. A. and M. C. Bland, 1883.
"Bob Burman Is Killed in Race." *Charlotte [North Carolina] Observer,* April 9, 1916, 1.
Buckenmeyer, Robert G. *The California Lectures of Maria Montessori, 1915.* Santa Barbara: Clio Press, 1997.

"Burn Exposition Mortgage." *Springfield [Massachusetts] Republican,* September 9, 1915, 16.

"Comedienne of Early Days Honored at Fair." *Oregonian,* December 12, 1915, 9.

"Fail to Locate Munson's Perfect Man in This Town." *Ann Arbor News,* April 8, 1922.

"Ford Delegates Wage 'Bloody' Battle Aboard." *Cleveland Plain Dealer,* January 8, 1916, 1.

Geyer, Andrea. "A Text Upon a Text Upon a Text." 2004. Accessed April 2, 2012. http://www.andreageyer.info/projects/audrey_munson/munson_book/MunsonPages/PDF/AndreaGeyer.pdf.

"Harry Thaw Planning Visit to Fair When He Is Released in N.Y." *San Jose Evening News,* July 13, 1915, 5.

Hichborn, Franklin. "The Day at San Francisco." *California Outlook* (May 13, 1911): 2.

Jowett, Garth S. "'A Capacity for Evil': The 1915 Supreme Court Mutual Decision." *Historical Journal of Film, Radio and Television* 9:1 (1989): 59–78.

Laurie, Annie. "Helen Keller's Visit to the Panama Fair." *Boston American,* April 7, 1915.

"Light Up Night in Honor of Mr. Edison at San Francisco During the 'Edison Day' Celebrations." *Edison Sales Builder* (December 1915).

McCarthy, Nancy. "Annie Coker: A Pioneer California Lawyer." *California Bar Journal.* Accessed April 16, 2013. http://archive.calbar.ca.gov/Archive.aspx?articleId=90453&categoryId=90541&month=2&year=2008.

"No Excuse for Showing Audrey Munson's Latest Failure in Film." *Cleveland Plain Dealer,* June 12, 1921, 7.

"Oakland Jottings." *Western Outlook* (January 9, 1915): 3.

O'Day, Edward. "The Laureate of California." *The Lantern* (November 1917): 230.

"Suffrage Exhibit Well Patronized." *Seattle Daily Times,* May 13, 1915, 7.

"Thomas A. Edison's Visit to California." *Pacific Service Magazine* (November 1915): 202.

"Those 1915 'Stove Pipes.'" *The Wasp* (May 8, 1915): 9.

CHAPTER 12: A PAGEANT OF ART

Dozens of detailed articles on the Exposition's art offerings can be found in 1915 periodicals. These included the *Century Magazine, Fine Arts Journal, American Magazine of Art, National Magazine,* and especially *Art and Progress* and *International Studio.* Additionally, the exhibits spawned numerous guidebooks and catalogues, listed below with other key sources:

"André Devambez: *The Charge.*" Musée d'Orsay. Accessed January 17, 2014. http://www.musee-orsay.fr.

Barry, John D. *The Palace of Fine Arts and the French and Italian Pavilions.* San Francisco: H. S. Crocker Co., 1915.

Brinton, Christian. "American Painting at the Panama-Pacific Exposition." *International Studio* (August 1915): 28.

Brinton, Christian. *Impressions of the Art at the Panama-Pacific Exposition.* New York: John Lane Company, 1916.

Catalogue de Luxe of the Department of Fine Arts, Panama-Pacific International Exposition. San Francisco: Paul Elder and Company, 1915.

Cheney, Sheldon. *Art-Lover's Guide to the Exposition.* Berkeley: At the Sign of the Berkeley Oak, 1915.

"Collecting Art Exhibits in War-Ridden Europe." *Review of Reviews* (April 1915): 462–463.

Laurvik, J. Nilsen. *Is It Art? Post-Impressionism, Futurism, Cubism.* New York: The International Press, 1913.

Neuhaus, Eugen. *The Galleries of the Exposition.* San Francisco: Paul Elder and Company, 1915.

Official Catalogue (Illustrated) of the Department of Fine Arts, Panama-Pacific International Exposition. San Francisco: The Wahlgreen Company, 1915.

Official Catalogue of the Department of Fine Arts, Panama-Pacific International Exposition. San Francisco: The Wahlgreen Company, 1915.

Panama-Pacific International Exposition, San Francisco, 1915, Fine Arts: French Section Catalogue. Paris: Librairie Centrale des Beaux-Arts, 1915.

"The Self-Elected Great." *The Wasp* (January 30, 1915): 1.

Trask, John E. D. "The Department of Fine Arts at the Panama-Pacific International Exposition." *California's Magazine* 2 (1916): 81.

Williams, Michael. *A Brief Guide to the Department of Fine Arts, Panama-Pacific International Exposition.* San Francisco: The Wahlgreen Company, 1915.

"Works of Fifty German Artists and Paintings from Nine Belligerent Countries on Way to Exposition." *Arts and Decoration* (February 1915): 155.

CHAPTER 13: A STROLL ALONG THE JOY ZONE

Several informative press releases from the PPIE Editorial Bureau are collected in the California History Room at the California State Library in Sacramento, including one describing the Joy Zone in detail, entitled "Exposition 'Zone' Is Palace of Infinite Jest: Joy Lane at San Francisco Fair Is a World Wonder." Information on specific concessions can be found in Bancroft cartons 62 to 64. A remarkable "Guide to the Joy Zone" is held in the Donald G. Larson World's Fair Collection at the Henry Madden Library, California State University, Fresno. The 1915 *San Francisco Blue Book*, published by Smith-Hoag, also contains excellent attraction descriptions. Other key sources include:

"Candy at the Exposition." *International Confectioner* (April 1915): 42.

Denivelle, Paul E. "Texture and Color at the Panama-Pacific Exposition." *Architectural Record* (November 1915): 564–570.

"The Fun of the Thing." *Colorado Springs Gazette,* February 28, 1915, 7.

"Gettysburg Warmed Over," p. 2. Daniel E. Koshland San Francisco History Center, San Francisco Public Library.

Harris, Larry. "Interviewing an International Exposition: The Combined Amusement Company." *San Francisco Call,* December 20, 1913, 11.

Joseph Henabery. Quoted on p. 53 of Kevin Brownlow. *The Parade's Gone By.* Berkeley: University of California Press, 1968.

"Letter to Mr. Connick re: Bowls of Joy." March 8, 1915. Bancroft 63:48, 1.

"List of Zone Concessions and Managers." 1915. Bancroft 80:29.

"Mexicans Duel Over a Pretty Senorita." *Rockford Republic* (August 27, 1915): 5.

"Model Shows Panama Canal in Operation." *Popular Mechanics* (September 1915): 389.

Mugan, Esther L. "Doing the Zone at San Francisco." *Santa Fe Magazine* (August 1915): 35–36.

"Panama-Pacific Exposition Notes of General Interest." *San Francisco Municipal Record,* June 12, 1913, 191.

Panama-Pacific International Exposition. *Santa Fe Railroad Booklet.* San Francisco, 1915, 13.

Panama-Pacific International Exposition Company. *Information for the Instruction of the Exposition Guards and Guides of the Panama-Pacific International Exposition.* San Francisco: Panama-Pacific International Exposition Company, 1915.

Rubin, Barbara. "Aesthetic Ideology and Urban Design." *Annals of the Association of American Geographers* 69:3 (September 1979): 350–351.

Schooley, Eula. "Letter to Connick re: Diving Girls." July 24, 1915. Bancroft 63:17, 1.

"She Is 98 Feet Tall; Her Name Is 'Little Eva.'" *San Francisco Chronicle,* March 17, 1915, 5.

"Taking an Imaginary Submarine Trip at the Panama-Pacific Exposition." *Popular Science Monthly and World's Advance* (October 1915): 468.

"Union Pacific System at San Francisco." *International Railway Journal* (April 1915): 7.

"Zone Attractions Had Varied Luck." *Seattle Daily Times*, December 10, 1915, 9.

"Zone Concessionaires Big Losers." *The Wasp* (November 20, 1915): 9.

"'Zone' Shows Closed." *Variety* (July 30, 1915): 5.

CHAPTER 14: RACE AND RED LIGHTS ON THE MIDWAY

The minutes of the Committee on Concessions and Admissions, in Bancroft cartons 24 and 80, give a good sense of the challenges facing the department in its quest to suppress vice. Information on specific concessions, including the '49 Camp, the Mysterious Orient/Streets of Cairo, Underground Chinatown, and the Samoan, Maori, and Hawaiian Villages, can be found in cartons 62 to 64. Other key sources include:

"'49 Camp Causes Trouble Again." *Oakland Tribune*, September 21, 1915, 16.

"The '49 Camp—Gambling on the Joy Zone." *The Survey* (October 23, 1915): 79.

"Aged Chief to Repay Kindness." *San Francisco Chronicle*, March 28, 1915, 33.

"An Anachronism and a Base Misapprehension." *San Diego Union*, March 25, 1915, 8.

"Aviator Initiated into Indian Tribe." *San Francisco Chronicle*, June 16, 1915, 5.

Burke, Emma Maxwell. "A Milliner at the Fair." *The Illustrated Milliner* (May 1915): 145.

Davidson, Marie Hicks. "Reminiscent of the Work of the Woman's Board, P. P. I. E." *California's Magazine* 2, (1916): 16.

"Facts about Vice at San Francisco." *The Survey* (September 4, 1915): 498.

"'Girl' Concessions on the Zone Are to Be Closed by Commission." *San Jose Evening News*, October 7, 1915, 5.

"Japan Beautiful." *California's Magazine* 2, (1916): 345.

Johnson, Bascom, "Moral Conditions in San Francisco and at the Panama-Pacific Exposition." *Social Hygiene* (September 1915): 589–609.

People's Easy Guide of the Panama Pacific International Exposition, p. 22. San Francisco: International Exhibition Bureau, Ltd., 1915.

Sackman, Douglas Cazaux. *Wild Men: Ishi and Kroeber in the Wilderness of Modern America*, p. 256. New York: Oxford University Press, 2009.

"Somaliland Natives Ousted from Zone." *San Francisco Chronicle*, May 15, 1915, 4.

Spence, Mark David. "Crown of the Continent, Backbone of the World: The American Wilderness Ideal and Blackfeet Exclusion from Glacier National Park." *Environmental History* (July 1996): 30–36.

"'Tehuantepec' Mexican Village." SF EPH Exhibits International, pp. 1–4, California Historical Society North Baker Library, San Francisco.

"Variety's San Francisco Office." *Variety* (June 4, 1915): 19.

Wood, Fremont. "The 'Zone' with Its Sixty-five Acres of Fun." *American Building Association News* (June 1915): 271.

CHAPTER 15: FILLING THE PLAYBILL

The third volume of PPIE publicity man Louis Levy's *Chronological History of the Panama-Pacific International Exposition* covers the music department's efforts exclusively. Bancroft cartons 80 to 84 contain entertainment correspondence and contracts. The Bay Area music periodical *Pacific Coast Musical Review* covered the Exposition entertainment program in detail, as did the *San Francisco Chronicle, Call,* and *Examiner.* Other key sources include:

"9,000 Hear Fine Free Fair Concert." *San Francisco Examiner*, November 29, 1915, 8.

"Among Musicians." *San Diego Union*, September 5, 1915.

Barden, Nelson. "Edwin H. Lemare." November 7, 2001. Accessed July 12, 2012. http://www.orgel.com/music/ehl/ehl-4.html.

First Pacifikkystens Norske Sangerforbund. *Souvenir Program of the Tenth Sangerfest*. San Francisco: Pacific Coast Norwegian Singers' Association, 1915.

Francis, David Rowland. *The Universal Exposition of 1904*, p. 193. St. Louis: Louisiana Purchase Exposition Company, 1913.

"Fritz Kreisler Is Reported Killed." *Trenton [New Jersey] Evening Times*, September 12, 1914, 1.

Irwin, Lee. "Freedom, Law, and Prophecy: A Brief History of Native American Religious Resistance." Academia.edu, University of Nebraska Press, 2000. Accessed July 2, 2012. http://www.academia.edu/1329720/Freedom_law_and_prophecy_A_brief_history_of_Native_American_religious_resistance.

James, George Wharton. *The Story of Captain*, p. 25. Pasadena: The Radiant Life Press, 1917.

"Kreisler, Wounded, Tells of War as He Saw It." *New York Times*, November 29, 1914.

"Native Composers' Day." *Springfield [Massachusetts] Republican*, August 15, 1915, 11.

Parker, H. T. "Surveying Symphony Standards." *Boston Transcript*, May 2, 1914, 36.

Scharlach, Bernice. *Big Alma: San Francisco's Alma Spreckels*, pp. 51–77, 144. San Francisco: Scottwall Associates, 1997.

Seymour, W. W. B. "Among Musicians." *San Diego Union*, October 10, 1915, 19.

CHAPTER 16: THE GRANDEST BANDS

As noted above, the *Chronological History of the Panama-Pacific International Exposition*, vol. 3, and Bancroft cartons 80 to 84 are filled with information on the creation of the entertainment program for the Fair. Other key sources include:

Cunningham, Roger D. "The Loving Touch: Walter H. Loving's Five Decades of Military Music." *Army History* (Summer 2007): 4–20.

"Ford Motor Band Programs." August 1915. Bancroft 81:1, 1.

"Grand Concert—Massed Bands." May 17, 1915. Bancroft 81:16, 1.

"Guatemalans Give a Special Concert." *San Francisco Chronicle*, November 22, 1915, 7.

"Last Medal Ceremony Honors Cassasa, Band Leader of Exposition." *San Francisco Chronicle*, December 5, 1915, 55.

Lewis, David. *The Public Image of Henry Ford: An American Folk Hero and His Company*, p. 52. Detroit: Wayne State University Press, 1987.

"Motor Band on Way to This City." *San Francisco Chronicle*, June 25, 1915, 47.

"Patrick Conway's Band." *The Canadian National Herald*, August 1, 1913, 4.

"Phillip Pelz Program." August 14, 1915. Bancroft 81:12, 1.

"Program of the University of California Glee Club." May 1, 1915. Bancroft 84:19, 1.

"Programme for Next Symphony Is Contributed by Allies." *San Francisco Chronicle*, December 26, 1915, 24.

CHAPTER 17: SEASONS OF WONDER

The special events at the PPIE were covered extensively in the newspapers listed earlier under "Principal Periodicals." Other key sources include:

"200,000 Persons See Liberty Bell, Breaking All Records." *Denver Post,* July 10, 1915, 4.

"Beauty Contest Picks Guard as Most Beautiful." *San Francisco Chronicle,* January 29, 1915, 1.

"Bell Gives New Message of Freedom." *San Francisco Chronicle,* November 18, 1915, 29.

"Catch Balls as They Drop from the Tower of Jewels." *San Francisco Chronicle,* June 27, 1915, 9.

Conroy, E. C. "Final Report on Admissions." December 5, 1915. Daniel E. Koshland San Francisco History Center, San Francisco Public Library.

"How We Got the Liberty Bell." *San Francisco Chronicle,* April 23, 1915, 18.

"Kern and Tulare and State of Washington Celebrate." *San Francisco Chronicle,* March 13, 1915.

"Liberty Bell." *Information Annual 1915,* p. 360. New York: R. R. Bowker Company, 1916.

"Liberty Bell Is Speeded on Its Way." *San Francisco Chronicle,* November 12, 1915, 9.

"Live Stock at the Exposition." *The Field Illustrated* (March 1915): 155.

Smith, Tim. "Everything You Wanted to Know about Foot and Mouth Disease But Were Afraid to Ask." Iowa Department of Agriculture. Accessed January 14, 2014. http://homelandsecurity.iowa.gov/.

"Three Day Carnival of Fun Starts Joyously at Exposition." *San Francisco Chronicle,* July 4, 1915, 33.

"Two-Mile Petition for Bell." *Boston Evening Transcript,* November 29, 1912, 1.

CHAPTER 18: IMPERIUM IN IMPERIO

The directors' reports held in the Daniel E. Koshland San Francisco History Center at the San Francisco Public Library provide insight into many challenges involved in running the Fair. The *History of the Panama-Pacific International Exposition* by the Pan-Pacific Press Association is also full of excellent details. The *San Francisco Municipal Record* for 1914 and 1915 reports on various aspects of the Exposition. Other key sources include:

"Copette Lasts on Street Job Just 8 Minutes." *San Francisco Chronicle,* August 3, 1915, 1.

"The Emergency Hospital, Panama-Pacific International Exposition." *Annual Report of the Surgeon General of the Public Health.* Washington, DC: Service Treasury Department, October 1, 1916, 289.

"Exposition's Finances Are in Good Condition." *San Francisco Chronicle,* June 23, 1915, 3.

Hodgen, Margaret T. "Workers at Frisco Fair Cared for by Young Women's Christian Association." *Augusta [Georgia] Chronicle,* August 8, 1915, 21.

"Mark Exposition Visitors about 100 in Honesty." *San Francisco Chronicle,* February 5, 1915, 4.

Markwart, Arthur. "Letter to Special Committee on Retrenchment." March 30, 1915. Bancroft 66:17.

"Novagems: The Wonder of the Century." Advertising pamphlet. San Francisco: Novagem Jewel Company, 1915.

"Panama-Pacific International Exposition." *Brooklyn Daily Eagle Almanac* (1916), 384.

"Sculptor Pleased with Design of Great Medal." *San Francisco Chronicle,* February 21, 1915, 66.

"Secrets of the Movies." *Fort Worth Star-Telegram,* April 10, 1922, 9.

"Standing Room Only on Baby Beds at Y.W.C.A. Checking Booth." *San Francisco Chronicle,* November 3, 1915, 4.

"Woman Cop Causes Traffic Blockade in San Francisco Street." *San Diego Union,* August 3, 1915, 3.

"Women Warned to Beware of Frisco Lures." *Idaho Statesman,* April 19, 1915, 6.

"Y.W.C.A. a Factor at the Exposition." *Tampa Tribune,* May 9, 1915, 16.

"The Y.W.C.A. at Work in the Joy Zone." *The Survey* (July 31, 1915): 389.

"Y.W.C.A. Subscription Reaches Total of $2,718." *Colorado Springs Gazette,* November 7, 1915, 7.

CHAPTER 19: DEATH AND LIFE OF A FAIR

The Blair-Murdock Company published an account of the closing exercises written by Frank Morton Todd, the Fair's official historian: *The Lights Go Out: An Account of the Closing Exercises of the Panama-Pacific International Exposition* (San Francisco: Blair-Murdock Company, December 1915). The minutes of the Buildings and Grounds Committee, in Bancroft cartons 23 and 24, contain detailed information on the salvage and restoration process. Other key sources include:

"$45,000,000 Brought Here by Exposition." *San Francisco Chronicle,* November 21, 1915, 29.

"Buildings Moved by Water." *Literary Digest* (October 14, 1916): 948.

Connick, Harris. "Letter to Charles C. Moore re: Salvage Income." April 24, 1916. Bancroft 56:34, 1.

Haller, Stephen A. *The Last Word in Airfields: A Special History Study of Crissy Field.* San Francisco: National Park Service, 1994.

Horner, Jim. Campus Landscape Architect, UC Berkeley. Telephone interview with the author, October 22, 2009.

"Letter to Connick re: Demolition." June 8, 1916. Bancroft 56:34, 1.

"Sales of Objects of Art at the Panama-Pacific Exposition." *American Architect* (October 20, 1915): 302.

"San Francisco's Notable Engineering Works." *Engineering Record* (February 20, 1915): 230–231.

Seares, Mabel Urmy. "Exposition Aftermath." *American Magazine of Art* (December 1916): 63–65.

Turner, Frank I. "City Planning a Part of San Francisco." *Architect and Engineer of California* (June 1918): 74.

"Visitors at the Exposition Now Closed Spent over Twelve Millions of Dollars." *San Jose Evening News,* December 6, 1915, 5.

"Yes, It Was the Ohio Building." *San Francisco Chronicle,* April 18, 1941, 18.

IMAGE CREDITS

Captions and credits appear alongside all images except for those used at the starts of chapters.

CHAPTER 1

Evelyn Beatrice Longman's *Fountain of Ceres* dances in the richly colored beams of the Great Scintillator. (Donna Ewald Huggins)

CHAPTER 2

The Arch of the Rising Sun supported the monumental sculptural group *The Nations of the East*. (Lynn Wilkinson)

CHAPTER 3

The Festival Hall, by Robert Farquhar, located in the South Gardens. (Donna Ewald Huggins)

CHAPTER 4

The Japanese Pavilion was one of twenty-one international offerings located on the western portion of the fairgrounds. (Donna Ewald Huggins)

CHAPTER 5

The Fountain of Energy, by Stirling Calder. (Panama-Pacific International Exposition Photograph Album (SFP17), San Francisco History Center, San Francisco Public Library)

CHAPTER 6

The Tower of Jewels as seen in a reflecting pool in the South Gardens. (Donna Ewald Huggins)

CHAPTER 7

Night in Louis Christian Mullgardt's Court of Ages. (Laura Ackley)

CHAPTER 8

More than 250,000 guests packed the Fair on Opening Day, eager to see the marvelous advances displayed within the palaces. (Laura Ackley)

CHAPTER 9

One of two *Mermaid* fountains by Arthur Putnam, this one in front of the translucent dome of the Palace of Horticulture. (Laura Ackley)

CHAPTER 10

A courtyard and arcade in the Italian Pavilion. (Seligman Family Foundation)

CHAPTER 11

Illumination of the Tower of Jewels. (Lynn Wilkinson)

CHAPTER 12

The colonnades of the Palace of Fine Arts served as outdoor sculpture galleries. (Lynn Wilkinson)

CHAPTER 13

A view looking west along the Joy Zone midway. (Laura Ackley)

CHAPTER 14

The Column of Progress stands guard over the PPIE Yacht Harbor. (Donna Ewald Huggins)

CHAPTER 15

The Court of Flowers by George Kelham featured opulent, spiral-twist lampposts. (Lynn Wilkinson)

CHAPTER 16

The illuminated half-dome of the Court of the Four Seasons, by Henry Bacon. (Laura Ackley)

CHAPTER 17

Military units parading down the Avenue of Palms were a common sight. (Branson DeCou Digital Archive, University of California, Santa Cruz, Special Collections)

CHAPTER 18

The Palace of Fine Arts colonnade and the half-dome of the western wall of the Faville palaces. (Lynn Wilkinson)

CHAPTER 19

Fireworks as seen from behind the Stirling Calder's *Star Maiden* figures atop the colonnade of the Court of the Universe. (Donna Ewald Huggins)

ABOUT THE AUTHOR

(Miguel Farias)

Architectural historian Laura A. Ackley holds graduate degrees from Harvard University's Graduate School of Design and from the College of Environmental Design at the University of California, Berkeley. Her master of science thesis at Berkeley was titled "Innovations in Illumination at the Panama-Pacific International Exposition of 1915."

Ms. Ackley's interest in the 1915 world's fair began in an undergraduate "cultural landscapes" course at UC Berkeley. Much of the research for this book was completed at the Berkeley campus' Bancroft Library, where she helped catalogue the Exposition's original records.

Previously, the author worked for Lucasfilm, Bechtel Corporation, and Autodesk. She has published articles about the San Francisco Bay Area special effects and animation industries and has taught 3D computer modeling and animation at Harvard and UC Berkeley, where she received an Outstanding Instructor Award. She also has produced digital visualizations of historic buildings and for archeological projects.

A recognized authority on the PPIE, she has developed a series of popular lectures on various aspects of the Fair, and frequently delivers her commentaries before historical, arts, and civic organizations.

A Bay Area native, Ms. Ackley lives in Marin County with her husband, Sander Temme, a computer security specialist.

HEYDAY

into California

ABOUT HEYDAY

Heyday is an independent, nonprofit publisher and unique cultural institution. We promote widespread awareness and celebration of California's many cultures, landscapes, and boundary-breaking ideas. Through our well-crafted books, public events, and innovative outreach programs we are building a vibrant community of readers, writers, and thinkers.

THANK YOU

It takes the collective effort of many to create a thriving literary culture. We are thankful to all the thoughtful people we have the privilege to engage with. Cheers to our writers, artists, editors, storytellers, designers, printers, bookstores, critics, cultural organizations, readers, and book lovers everywhere!

We are especially grateful for the generous funding we've received for our publications and programs during the past year from foundations and hundreds of individual donors. Major supporters include:

Anonymous (6); Alliance for California Traditional Arts; Arkay Foundation; Judith and Phillip Auth; Judy Avery; Paul Bancroft III; Richard and Rickie Ann Baum; BayTree Fund; S. D. Bechtel, Jr. Foundation; Jean and Fred Berensmeier; Berkeley Civic Arts Program and Civic Arts Commission; Joan Berman; Nancy Bertelsen; Beatrice Bowles, in memory of Susan S. Lake; John Briscoe; Lewis and Sheana Butler; Cahill Contractors, Inc.; California Civil Liberties Public Education Program; Cal Humanities; California Indian Heritage Center Foundation; California State Parks Foundation; Joanne Campbell; Keith Campbell Foundation; John and Nancy Cassidy Family Foundation, through Silicon Valley Community Foundation; Graham Chisholm; The Christensen Fund; Jon Christensen; Community Futures Collective; Compton Foundation; Creative Work Fund; Lawrence Crooks; Nik Dehejia; Chris Desser and Kirk Marckwald; Frances Dinkelspiel and Gary Wayne; Doune Fund; The Durfee Foundation; Megan Fletcher and J.K. Dineen; Flow Fund Circle; Fulfillco; Furthur Foundation; The Wallace Alexander Gerbode Foundation; Nicola W. Gordon; Wanda Lee Graves and Stephen Duscha; The Walter and Elise Haas Fund; Coke and James Hallowell; Steve Hearst; Historic Resources Group; Sandra and Charles Hobson; Nettie Hoge; Donna Ewald Huggins; JiJi Foundation; Claudia Jurmain; Kalliopeia Foundation; Marty and Pamela Krasney; Robert and Karen Kustel; Guy Lampard and Suzanne Badenhoop; Christine Leefeldt, in celebration of Ernest Callenbach and Malcolm Margolin's friendship; Thomas Lockard and Alix Marduel; Thomas J. Long Foundation; Sam and Alfreda Maloof Foundation for Arts & Crafts; Michael McCone; Giles W. and Elise G. Mead Foundation; Moore Family Foundation; Michael J. Moratto, in memory of Berta Cassel; Karen and Thomas Mulvaney; The MSB Charitable Fund; Richard Nagler; National Wildlife Federation; Humboldt Area Foundation, Native Cultures Fund; The Nature Conservancy; Nightingale Family Foundation; Northern California Water Association; Ohlone-Costanoan Esselen Nation; Panta Rhea Foundation; David Plant; Spreck and Isabella Rosekrans; Alan Rosenus; The San Francisco Foundation; Greg Sarris; Sierra College; Stephen Silberstein Foundation; William Somerville; Martha Stanley; Radha Stern, in honor of Malcolm Margolin and Diane Lee; Roselyne Chroman Swig; Tides Foundation; Sedge Thomson and Sylvia Brownrigg; Sonia Torres; Michael and Shirley Traynor; The Roger J. and Madeleine Traynor Foundation; Lisa Van Cleef and Mark Gunson; Patricia Wakida; John Wiley & Sons, Inc.; Peter Booth Wiley and Valerie Barth; Bobby Winston; Dean Witter Foundation; and Yocha Dehe Wintun Nation.

BOARD OF DIRECTORS

GETTING INVOLVED

To learn more about our publications, events, membership club, and other ways you can participate, please visit www.heydaybooks.com.

CALIFORNIA
HISTORICAL
SOCIETY since 1871

ABOUT THE CALIFORNIA HISTORICAL SOCIETY

Founded in 1871, the California Historical Society (CHS) is a nonprofit organization with a mission to inspire and empower people to make California's richly diverse past a meaningful part of their contemporary lives. We hold one of the state's top historical collections, revealing California's social, cultural, economic, and political history and development through books and pamphlets, manuscripts, newspapers and periodicals, photographs, fine arts, costumes, prints and drawings, maps and ephemera—including some of the most cherished and valuable documents and images of California's past.

PUBLIC ENGAGEMENT

Through high-quality exhibitions, public programs, publications, research, and preservation, CHS keeps history alive through extensive public engagement. In opening the very heart of the organization—our vast and diverse collection—to ever wider audiences, we invite meaning, encourage exchange, and enrich understanding.

PUBLICATIONS

From our first book publication in 1874, to our 90-year history as publisher of the *California History* journal, to the establishment of the annual California Historical Society Book Award in 2013, CHS publications examine the ongoing dialogue between the past and the present. Our print and digital publications reach beyond purely historical narrative to connect Californians to their state, region, nation, and the world in innovative and thought-provoking ways.

SUPPORT

Institutional support is provided by: S. D. Bechtel, Jr. Foundation, Bernard Osher Foundation, Barkley Fund, Cal Humanities, Hearst Foundation, Hewlett-Packard, James Irvine Foundation, Koret Foundation, San Francisco Grants for the Arts, United Healthcare, and Wells Fargo.

For more information, visit www.californiahistoricalsociety.org

THE CENTENNIAL OF THE PANAMA-PACIFIC INTERNATIONAL EXPOSITION

In 2015, the California Historical Society led a unique citywide community celebration of the 100th anniversary of the Panama-Pacific International Exposition (PPIE). The Centennial Celebration brought together more than fifty Bay Area cultural organizations, presenting a variety of exhibitions, performances, lectures, and symposia throughout the year. Through this effort, and in partnership with the City and County of San Francisco, CHS told the important definitive history of the PPIE and explained its role in establishing San Francisco as a modern global city in 1915, while showcasing the spirit of ingenuity and innovation that continues to characterize the Bay Area today. An exhibition at CHS headquarters in San Francisco illustrated aspects of this publication.

For more information, visit www.ppie100.org

An historic moment in the history of technology took place on January 25, 1915, just prior to the opening of San Francisco's Panama-Pacific International Exposition. The American Telephone and Telegraph Company (now AT&T) conducted the first transcontinental telephone call between New York City, San Francisco, Jekyll Island, Georgia and Washington, DC. Alexander Graham Bell, inventor of the telephone and co-founder of AT&T, initiated the historic call with a group of dignitaries in New York. His one-time assistant Thomas Watson received the call in San Francisco, AT&T President Theodore Vail participated from Jekyll Island, and U.S. President Woodrow Wilson spoke from the White House.

In recognition of the 100th anniversary of this transformational moment in telecommunication history, AT&T was a major sponsor of the 2015 Centennial Celebration of the Panama-Pacific International Exposition.

The first transcontinental telephone call from New York to San Francisco, January 25, 1915. Dr. Alexander Graham Bell (center) with the Honorable J. P. Mitchel, Mayor of New York City and other dignitaries. (Courtesy of AT&T Archives and History Center)

NEW YORK

SAN FRANCISCO

The first transcontinental telephone call received in San Francisco by Thomas A. Watson, assistant to Alexander Graham Bell, with Charles C. Moore, President of the Panama-Pacific International Exposition; James Rolph, Jr., Mayor of San Francisco; and other dignitaries. (Courtesy of AT&T Archives and History Center)

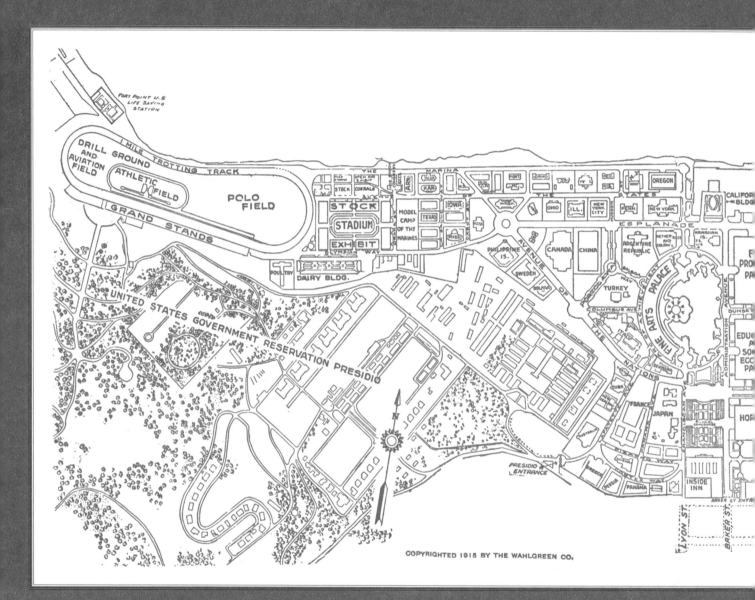

COPYRIGHTED 1915 BY THE WAHLGREEN CO.

SAN FRANCISCO'S
JEWEL CITY